CAMBRIDGE SOUTH ASIAN STUDIES

SEPARATISM AMONG
INDIAN MUSLIMS

CAMBRIDGE SOUTH ASIAN STUDIES

These monographs are published by the Syndics of Cambridge University Press in association with the Cambridge University Centre for South Asian Studies. The following books have been published in this series:

SEPARATISM
AMONG INDIAN MUSLIMS

THE POLITICS OF THE
UNITED PROVINCES' MUSLIMS, 1860–1923

FRANCIS ROBINSON

Lecturer in History, Royal Holloway College
University of London

CAMBRIDGE UNIVERSITY PRESS

CAMBRIDGE UNIVERSITY PRESS
Cambridge, New York, Melbourne, Madrid, Cape Town, Singapore, São Paulo

Cambridge University Press
The Edinburgh Building, Cambridge CB2 8RU, UK

Published in the United States of America by Cambridge University Press, New York

www.cambridge.org
Information on this title: www.cambridge.org/9780521204323

First published 1974
This digitally printed version 2008

A catalogue record for this publication is available from the British Library

Library of Congress Catalogue Card Number: 73-93393

ISBN 978-0-521-20432-3 hardback
ISBN 978-0-521-04826-2 paperback

CONTENTS

v

PLATES

Between pp. 256 and 257

MAPS AND TABLES

TO MY PARENTS

PREFACE

This book has suffered several incarnations. It first took shape as a fellowship dissertation written in 1969, then as a doctoral thesis submitted in 1970, and gained its present form during the last three years. The whole process has taken some seven years and I have been helped by many.

I would like to thank the Department of Education and Science for a Hayter Research Studentship which enabled me to work in India during 1967 and 1968. Since then I have been indebted to the Master and Fellows of Trinity College who have provided me with generous financial assistance and, by electing me to a research fellowship in 1969, have enabled me to continue my work over the past four years.

I am grateful to the librarians and staff of the National Archives of India, the Nehru Memorial Museum and Library, the Uttar Pradesh Secretariat Archives, the Lucknow Commissioner's Archives, the Aligarh University Library, the Jamia Millia Islamia Library, the India Office Library and Records, the British Museum, the National Library of Scotland, the Wren Library, the Seeley Historical Library, the Cambridge Centre of South Asian Studies and the Cambridge University Library for their kind and courteous help.

I am much obliged to the Government of India, the Government of Uttar Pradesh, Shri B.D. Sanwal (late Commissioner of Lucknow), Maharajkumar Mohammad Amir Hyder Khan of Mahmudabad, Mufti Reza Ansari of Firangi Mahal, Shri Salahuddin Usman (Secretary of the Lucknow Jalsa-i-Tahzib) and Shri B. Mehta (Manager of the *Leader* Press) for permission to consult records, newspapers and private papers in their possession.

In India many people generously devoted their time and energy to my problems. I am particularly grateful for the kindness and assistance of Shri Ram Advani, Professor Mohibbul Hasan, Shri V. C. Joshi, Miss D. G. Keswani, Miss Raj Rallia Ram, Shri Sourin Roy, Shri Satyapal Sakhuja and Colonel R. S. Seth. Many

Preface

too have helped with Urdu translation; my debt of gratitude to Dr Gail Minault and Miss Salma Ajmeri is especially great.

In its various forms this work has benefited greatly from the help and criticism of colleagues and friends in Trinity, in Cambridge and elsewhere. In particular, I would like to thank Christopher Bayly, Judith Brown, Jack Gallagher, Richard Gordon, Peter Hardy, Gordon Johnson, Ralph Leigh, Peter Musgrave, Eric Stokes, Brenda Stones and David Washbrook. To Pat I owe much for her forbearance, but my greatest debt is to Anil Seal who from the time I began to work on the subject of this book has acted both as goad and guide.

FRANCIS ROBINSON

Royal Holloway College
University of London
1974

ABBREVIATIONS

AICCP	All-India Congress Committee Papers.
As	Annas.
B&O	Bihar and Orissa.
CP	Central Provinces.
CUL	Cambridge University Library.
CWG	The collected works of M. K. Gandhi.
D.	Deposit.
DC	Decentralisation Commission.
DG	District Gazetteer of the United Provinces.
DIG	Deputy Inspector-general.
D-O	Demi-Official.
ECNWP&O	Education Commission, evidence taken in the North-West Provinces and Oudh.
Educ	Education.
FM	Firangi Mahal, Lucknow.
FR	Fortnightly Report.
GAD	General Administration Department.
ICS	Indian Civil Service.
IMS	Indian Medical Service.
IOL	India Office Library.
IOR	India Office Records.
JMI	Jamia Millia Islamia, New Delhi.
LCA	Archives of the Commissioner of Lucknow.
M.A.-O.	Muhammadan Anglo-Oriental College, Aligarh.
Mss.	Manuscripts.
NAI	National Archives of India.
NLS	National Library of Scotland, Edinburgh.
NMM	Nehru Memorial Museum, New Delhi.
NWP	North-West Provinces.
NWP&O	North-West Provinces and Oudh.
NWP&OMAR	North-West Provinces and Oudh Municipal Administration Report.
Poll.	Political.
P.P.	Parliamentary Paper.
Ps.	Pice.
PSC	Public Service Commission.
RDPI	Report of the Director of Public Instruction.
Rs.	Rupees.
SR	Settlement Report.
UP	United Provinces of Agra and Oudh.

Abbreviations

UPCC	United Provinces' Congress Committee.
UPLC	Proceedings of the United Provinces' Legislative Council.
UPMAR	United Provinces' Municipal Administration Report.
UPNNR	Native Newspaper Report of the North-West Provinces or the North-West Provinces and Oudh or the United Provinces.
UPS	Uttar Pradesh Secretariat Archives.
WRDCI	Weekly Report of the Director of Central Intelligence.

A NOTE ON SPELLING

A consistency in the spelling of Indian names which would not be false or deceptive is difficult to achieve. For instance, over the last hundred years the accepted spellings of most place names have changed, e.g. Cawnpore has become Cawnpur and then Kanpur, while at any one time proper names have been spelled in several different ways, e.g. Mahomed, Mohamed, Mohammad, Mohammed, Muhammad etc.... To impose a comprehensive system on the names used would undoubtedly bring greater phonetic and linguistic precision but it would be at the cost, first of making some names almost unrecognisable to the reader, and second of eliminating differences in the English spellings of proper names which Indians were themselves concerned to perpetuate, e.g. one man would spell his name Ahmad or Husain, another Ahmed or Hussain, and such differences have become an accepted part of Indian life – there are for instance twenty-four different spellings of the name Choudhri in the most recent edition of the Delhi telephone directory. The plan which has been adopted in this book, therefore, has been to spell place names according to the *District Gazetteers of the United Provinces of Agra and Oudh* of 1903–11, and proper names as they were most commonly spelled during the period.

Introduction

The British united the peoples of India under one government, but left them under two. As the empire drew its subjects together, and they organised to face the challenges of imperialism, some of the divisive tendencies of Indian society were broken down, but others were exacerbated. The most notable was the tendency of some Muslims to claim that the Indian Muslims were a distinct and separate group. By the end of the nineteenth century, they had begun to express this view in politics. In 1906, they secured public recognition from government of their special status, and of their particular need for a reserved share of the power which was being devolved upon Indians. In 1916, they gained acceptance of this same point from the leading organisation of nationalist politics, the Congress. Moreover, from 1909, this principle of Muslim separateness was implemented in every constitutional change. In the last years of British rule, Muslim demands for a separate Muslim state were so strong that neither the government nor the Congress could deny them. So the British were forced to leave India divided, a result which has contributed to two wars, twenty-five years of preparation for war, and immense expense in life, money and lost opportunities for development. Clearly the existence of Muslim separatism under British rule is a fact of the first importance in the recent history of the Indian subcontinent.

Various explanations of Muslim separatism already exist. Some, after a long and vigorous life, are beginning to be discredited; others still persist. The first derives from the theory put forward by W. W. Hunter in 1870 that the Muslims had been discriminated against by the British, had been slow in taking advantage of western education, and as a result had fallen behind in the competition for jobs and economic advancement.[1] This theory of Muslim backwardness was loudly repeated by Muslim leaders at the time. Since

[1] W. W. Hunter, *The Indian Musalmans*, reprinted from the 3rd edn, London, 1876 (Delhi, 1969).

Introduction

then it has found favour with Marxist and Muslim historians in showing why Muslims organised as a community.[1] A second proposition is that the British deliberately created division in Indian society for their own imperial purpose. An important pillar of this view is the statement attributed to Elphinstone: '"Divide et impera" was the old Roman motto, and it should be ours.'[2] On occasion it is thought to be proof enough of British iniquity. When further explanation is resorted to the British are usually seen as throwing their weight first behind one community and then behind the other to keep them divided. Indian nationalist historians found the argument particularly attractive and accuse their imperial rulers of having broken an evolving synthesis of Hindu–Muslim culture.[3] A third, less common but still important, theory suggests that Indian nationalists would do well to look at their own record. Muslim communalism, it is argued, was due to the failure of nationalism to develop a truly non-communal ethos. Nationalism was associated with a frequently aggressive Hindu revivalism, and its symbols, its idiom and its inspiration were all Hindu.[4] Most Pakistani historians readily admit such arguments concerning the Hindu face of Indian nationalism; they provide ammunition for their own explanation that there was not one nation in India but two. They emphasise, of course, that Muslim separatism was no Pavlovian reaction to Hindu organisation, but the natural expression of the realisation that Indian Muslims were a separate community. This fact, they claim, had been evident right

[1] For approaches influenced by Marxist thinking see W. C. Smith, *Modern Islam in India* (London, 1946), and A. R. Desai, *Social Background of Indian Nationalism* (Bombay, 1948). For Muslim historians influenced by the Muslim backwardness theory, see Abdul Hamid, *Muslim Separatism in India: A brief Survey 1858–1947* (Oxford, 1967), and Rafiq Zakaria, *Rise of Muslims in Indian Politics* (Bombay, 1970).

[2] Desai, *Indian Nationalism*, p. 354. For variations on the same theme see R. P. Dutt, *India Today*, revised Indian edn (Bombay, 1949), p. 428.

[3] The best formulation of the divide and rule thesis is in A. Mehta and A. Patwardhan, *The Communal Triangle in India* (Allahabad, 1942). The most prominent of the more recent subscribers to this view is Ram Gopal, *Indian Muslims: A Political History (1858–1947)* (Bombay, 1959). For the arguments concerning the smashing of a Hindu–Muslim cultural synthesis, see J. Nehru, *An Autobiography* (London, 1936), and *The Discovery of India*, 4th edn (London, 1956), and K. B. Krishna, *The Problem of Minorities or Communal Representation in India*, cited in Gopal Krishna, 'Religion in Politics', *The Indian Economic and Social History Review*, VIII, No. 4 (December 1971), p. 374.

[4] See recent papers by I. Ahmad and P. Gupta cited by Gopal Krishna, *ibid.*, p. 377.

from the eighth-century invasion of Muhammad Bin Qasim, was manifest in the way Muslims lived in India and was acknowledged, as it should have been, by the creation of Pakistan.[1] These are the four main lines of explanation. They have many variants and refinements. Most explanations, moreover, are not confined exclusively to one approach but present a blend of several in which one ingredient is predominant. Many, it should be noted, assume that the Indian Muslims were a group whose situation, outlook and interests were generally the same.

This book will consider the problems raised by these various theories of Muslim separatism. Its aim, however, is not to produce a critique of other men's ideas but to ask and answer two basic questions. Unashamedly it asks again: why did Muslim separatist politics develop on the Indian subcontinent under British rule? It couples this with a second question: which Muslims promoted and organised these politics? The time is ripe to reopen the case. Much fresh research material has recently become available. In 1966, the reduction of the fifty-year rule to thirty released at one stroke a large quantity of government records and private papers housed at the India Office Library in London. The activity of the new Nehru Memorial Museum, in addition to that of the National Archives of India, has led to the accumulation in Delhi over the last few years of a considerable collection of material on modern Indian history, in particular the files of Indian newspapers. Elsewhere, the private papers of several men closely connected with Muslim politics have come to light, among them those of Mahomed Ali and Maulana Abdul Bari.

The origins of Muslim separatism will be investigated not so much in the context of the subcontinent as in that of one region, the United Provinces.[2] This may appear strange; the UP Muslims

---

[1] The classic formulation of this argument is in I. H. Qureshi, *The Muslim Community of the Indo-Pakistan Subcontinent (610–1947)* (The Hague, 1962). It is followed quite faithfully by more recent works, for instance the introduction to a recent collection of Muslim League documents, Syed Sharifuddin Pirzada (ed.), *Foundations of Pakistan: All-India Muslim League Documents: 1906–1947* (Karachi, 1970), Vol. II, pp. xi–xxxv.

[2] Throughout this work the area known variously between 1860 and 1923 as the North-West Provinces and Oudh, and the United Provinces of Agra and Oudh, will be referred to in the text as the UP. The term 'UP Muslim', however, has a slightly broader application. It does not refer merely to those Muslims born and brought up in the province, but also to those who made it the centre of their political activities. I refer particularly to men such as Raja Ghulam Husain, Syud Hussain and Hakim Ajmal Khan.

I-2

were a mere fourteen per cent of the population of the area and a smaller proportion of the Muslim population of India. Why not choose Bengal or the Punjab, where the Muslim population was large? The answer is very simple: for much of the period of British rule Muslims from both these provinces contributed little to specifically Muslim politics, their politicians preferring to use other platforms. UP Muslims, on the other hand, were at the heart of Muslim separatism. They mainly founded and, with the exception of the Bombay-based Jinnah, mainly led the organisations which represented the Muslim interest in Indian politics. Syed Ahmed Khan founded in 1875 the Muhammadan Anglo-Oriental College at Aligarh, which directed much early Muslim political activity and nurtured many Muslim League politicians. He followed this with the establishment of the All-India Muslim Educational Conference in 1886, which helped him impress his political will on Indian Muslims. In 1906, large numbers of Muslims from the UP flocked to Dacca to found the All-India Muslim League. In this organisation the secretaryship was the most powerful position; and between 1906 and 1910 it was held by UP Muslims in Aligarh, and between 1910 and 1926 by UP Muslims in Lucknow. After World War One, Muslims from the same province set up an association of Indian ulama and made the Central Khilafat Committee an organisation of all-India importance.

Men with such a big part to play in the organisations of Muslim separatist politics played no smaller part in the formulation of their policies. Syed Ahmed Khan taught Muslims that government was the best protector of their interests and shepherded many of them away from the Congress and from political agitation of any kind. When in 1906 this policy was weakened both by the apparent withdrawal of government favour and by the threatened broadening of elective government, his political heir, Mohsin-ul-Mulk, strengthened it. He organised the Muslim deputation to the Viceroy which gained government's recognition of the Muslim claim to separate representation on elected bodies in which the proportion of seats was to be worked out on the contentious basis of the community's 'political importance'. When a few years later government seemed to be even less well disposed towards Muslim interests than it had been in 1906, it was Wazir Hasan of Lucknow who, as secretary of the All-India Muslim League, managed the

UP Muslim campaign to ensure that Muslim claims were not ignored. His endeavours culminated in the Lucknow Pact of 1916 in which the Congress agreed to the same privileges for Muslims in future constitutional reforms as the government had agreed to in 1906. Then, when Muslim political and religious interests appeared to be endangered after World War One, it was these same Muslims who, with Gandhi, virtually captured the Congress for the Muslim cause and helped to launch it into a policy of non-co-operation with government. Using the mass religious fervour, which only the unfurling of the green flag of Islam could unleash, they pressed this policy home throughout the subcontinent and helped to transform the politics of the Congress from those of the 'discreet dialogue' of the few in council and durbar into the clamour of the many in the towns and villages of India.

In the 1920s and 1930s, many UP Muslims deserted the organisations of Muslim separatist politics. Muslim landlords went into landlord politics, professional men joined the Congress, and many left politics altogether. Muslim political organisations shrank; some disappeared. Muslim separatism was no longer the powerful force it had been. Nor was it till UP Muslims rejoined the Muslim League in large numbers after the 1937 elections that Muslim separatism revived. In the League's years of glory from 1940 to partition, UP Muslims were at the heart of the organisation; they held the two most important posts after that of the president, and dominated its committees.[1] Throughout the development of Muslim separatism in British India, whenever the politics of All-India Muslim organisations were vigorous they were more the politics of UP Muslims than those of any other group of Indian Muslims.

This book examines what might be termed the first period of Muslim separatism under the British raj. It stretches from the beginnings of communal politics during the break-up of the Urdu-speaking elite in the second half of the nineteenth century to their decline and the breakdown of the organisations of all-India Muslim politics in the early 1920s. No magic should be attached to the date 1860; it is merely a point at which to begin. There is, however, something special about 1923; this was the year in which Muslims lost the power to dictate Congress policy, and the Muslim front in Indian politics fell to pieces.

---

[1] Khalid B. Sayeed, *Pakistan: The Formative Phase 1857–1948*, 2nd edn (London, 1968), p. 192.

Introduction

The first four chapters of the book are concerned primarily with the problem of how by 1909 an All-India Muslim League had been founded and separate representation had been granted. The situation of Muslims in mid-nineteenth-century UP society is analysed with a view to discovering how far they were organised as a community and how strong the connections of different Muslim groups were with other communities. The impact of political, bureaucratic and economic change on these various elements of UP society, and their reaction to it, is examined. We need to know how uneven this impact was, how different the reactions of various groups were, and how their relationships with each other were altered. Throughout, close attention will be paid to the needs and attitudes of government and the part they played in influencing the various reactions to change. This should reveal why some Muslims organised for politics on a communal basis and why government was willing to recognise the Muslims as an important group in Indian politics. It should also tell us, to some extent, how UP Muslims were able to assume leadership of all Indian Muslims. It will not, however, reveal anything about the more overt forms of communalism, such as the insensate violence which erupted periodically in the bazars and mohullas of Indian towns. The emphasis of the analysis will be on the various elite groups concerned in making politics, and it is interested in other manifestations of communalism only in so far as they might affect these politics.

The last five chapters are mainly devoted to discovering the objectives of Muslim communal politics between 1909 and 1923. To do this they seek to discover who supported Muslim separatism, when they did so, and why. The different groups in Muslim politics are identified, the relationships between them are examined, and their impact on politics as a whole is assessed. With the aid of over 130 biographies of leading Muslim politicians, three major groupings in the politics of UP Muslims have been uncovered, the 'Old Party', the 'Young Party' and the 'Ulama'. The labels are crude and are employed largely for convenience, although they are descriptions which were often used at the time. The groupings were not parties in any narrow sense; they had no formal organisation, and the differences within them are as illuminating as those between them. Nevertheless, they do represent three major interests among Muslims in the UP. The result of this study should show why the Muslim League became hostile to the government and why it allied with the Congress. It should illustrate how UP Muslims maintained the leadership of Indian Muslim politics and how they came to be of great influence in the Congress between 1920 and 1923. Moreover, it should explain why the Khilafat agitation grew so great and why the organisations of specifically Muslim politics declined in the 1920s and 1930s.

India under British rule had its fair share of selfless men and selfish men, of heroes and cowards, of great men and ordinary men. There were many who went to gaol for the cause; there were some who betrayed it. This study illustrates the role of those who were fired by religious beliefs or spurred by nationalist ideals; it also illustrates the many calculations of advantage and political interest which every politician must make. A man may have both ideals and political skills, indeed he must temper the former with the latter if he is to survive in politics. Only in myth does Shiva drive a straight path through the opposition with his trident. In human affairs great national leaders must bow before the political process; they must make accommodations with their fellow men. This is not to deny their greatness but to emphasise another dimension of it – their mastery of politics. Myth is an important part of the fabric of national life, but so also is a proper understanding of what happened in the past. With the aim not of reducing the reputations of historical figures but of enlarging our knowledge of them it is hoped that this book will shed light not only on the causes and nature of Muslim separatism but also on the workings of imperialism, nationalism and Islamic responses to the west in modern times.

Map 1. The United Provinces: geographical features.

Map 2. The United Provinces: districts and divisions, 1911.

CHAPTER 1

The Muslims in the United Provinces

The UP lay at the heart of the Indian subcontinent midway between the Hindu Kush, over which Muslim invaders had poured in search of land and loot, and the shores of Bengal, where British traders had first beached their boats in search of commerce and profit. To the north, the province was shut off from Tibet by the great Himalayan barrier; to the south, it was divided from the Deccan by the Vindhyan mountain range.[1]

The province was an artifact. It had been formed gradually by conquest and annexation. In 1775, the British first acquired formal sovereignty in the region when Benares was ceded. In 1801, Wellesley acquired the lower Doab (the Doab was the land between the rivers Jumna and Ganges), Rohilkhand, and Gorakhpur. In 1803, the Anglo-Maratha War led to the annexation of the upper Doab and Bundelkhand (the districts of Jalaun, Hamirpur and Jhansi). In 1815, after the Anglo-Nepalese War, most of Kumaon was added. Other small enclaves were absorbed and finally, in 1856, the last major territorial acquisition was made with the annexation of Oudh. This mosaic, put together by the victories of British arms and the failures of British policy, was administered by a lieutenant-governor who controlled officers in nine revenue divisions which were divided again into forty-nine districts.[2]

As was to be expected from such a piecemeal construction, the result was not homogeneous. The province fell into roughly three major geographical areas – the northern mountains, the southern hills and the central plains. The northern region, Kumaon, forms the central part of the Himalayan range. The southern hill and plateau districts, including Mirzapur, Jhansi, Jalaun, Hamirpur and Banda, lie on the fringe of the Vindhyan range of hills. The central plains, where nine out of ten of the people live in just over two-thirds of the area of the province, form part of the Gangetic basin. The central plains themselves can be divided into two distinct

[1] Map 1.   [2] Map 2.

geographic regions – the Upper Ganges Plain, comprising all the western and central plains, and the Middle Ganges Plain in the east. The line of division runs roughly from the confluence of the Jumna and Ganges at Allahabad to the point where the Gogra issues from the Himalayas.[1]

The UP, with the city of Delhi on its western border, was the traditional centre of Muslim rule and civilisation in India. Here were cities redolent with the past glories of Muslim power: Jaunpur, capital of the Sharqi Kings; Fatehpur Sikri, city of Akbar; Agra, city of Shah Jahan; Bareilly, centre of the Rohilla Kingdom; Fyzabad and Lucknow, in turn the seats of the Kings of Oudh; and 'seven-citied' Delhi, witness of the glory and the destruction of Muslim empires. In their time, these cities all harboured courts under whose generous and discerning patronage architects, painters, and above all poets flourished. Here the distinctive character of Indian Muslim civilisation was formed. But here also had Hindu civilisation been forged. Here were the holiest places of Hinduism, like Ajodhia, the birthplace of Rama, and a string of towns along the Ganges: Hardwar, where the mighty river emerges from its Himalayan fastness; Muttra, where Krishna dallied with the milkmaids; Prayag (Allahabad), the holy point where the confluence of the sacred stream with its huge tributary the Jumna takes place; and Kashi (Benares), the ecclesiastical centre of Hinduism. In this heartland of Aryavarta, for eight centuries before the British conquest, the Muslims had been the dominant group. Now they were just another subject people mocked by the relics of their former glory and by the equal status of their former subjects.

More people lived in the UP than in any other province of India except Bengal. In 1881, its population numbered 44,107,869 or over one-fifth of the total living on British territory. Thirty-eight million were Hindus, nearly six million, or over thirteen per cent, were Muslims.[2] The distribution of Muslims throughout the province was uneven, ranging from thirty-seven per cent in Moradabad to under one per cent in Almora (see Map 3).

---

[1] O. H. K. Spate and A. T. A. Learmouth, *India and Pakistan: A General and Regional Geography*, 3rd edn (London, 1967), pp. 545–6.

[2] Throughout the period the population was growing, and the Muslim population was growing more rapidly than the Hindu. By 1931, Muslims were nearly fifteen per cent of the province's population. *1931 Census, UP*, Part I, p. 495.

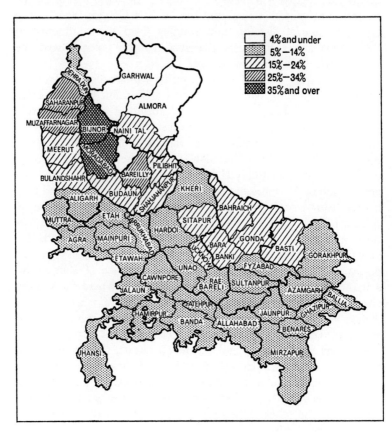

Map 3. The United Provinces: distribution of Muslims by district.

Muslims in the United Provinces

The size of the Muslim population in different areas varied with the extent of their influence in the past. As a rule they were far more numerous in the west and north of the province than in the east and south. They were most numerous in the two western divisions: Meerut, the 'Home Counties' of the Mughal Empire, and Rohilkhand, the centre of Rohilla power. In some Rohilkhand districts more than one-third of the population was Muslim whereas in the province as a whole less than half this proportion was Muslim. Muslims were less numerous in Bundelkhand, where the intractable Bundelas, aided by the unattractive nature of the country, kept Muslim power at bay till the Banda Nawabs established themselves in the eighteenth century. They were weak in the strip of land from Rae Bareli to Muttra where strong and united Rajput clans, proudest and purest of their race, presented a firm front. In the Himalayas, where Muslim power had never penetrated, they did not settle.

The Muslims were essentially town-dwellers. Though only just over one-eighth of the provincial population, they were almost two-fifths of the urban population. The unevenness of their distribution in the towns followed a similar pattern to that of the districts. More lived in towns north of the Ganges than in those of the Doab and Benares division. They were particularly numerous in the towns of the two north-western divisions, and in Rohilkhand accounted for more than half the urban population. As a rule Muslims were to be found in strength in the old capitals of Muslim empires, in the former headquarters of Mughal Subahs and in the centres of British government.

The Muslims, therefore, were a minority in both town and country. This is important because the religious differences which separated them from the Hindus were fundamental. The Hindus worshipped idols, the Muslims abhorred them. The Hindus had many gods, the Muslims had one. The Hindus revered the cow, the Muslims ate it. Such differences created a basic antipathy between Hindus and Muslims which helped to set them apart as modern politics and self-governing institutions developed in town, district and province. The Muslims feared that the Hindu majority would not only interfere with their religious practices such as cow-sacrifice, but also, out of religious hatred, would discriminate against them in a wider range of secular fields upon which their progress depended such as education and employment. In a word, the fact that Muslims were a minority in the UP was likely to colour many of their political attitudes.

Almost to the end of the nineteenth century, however, that Muslims were a minority did not matter: there were no elections that counted. Power in society was divided between three groups: landlords who controlled the fortunes of thousands of tenants and had influence with government; traders and money-lenders who had the funds to bribe officials and to manipulate their debtors; and above all government servants who apportioned patronage, made decisions and put them into effect. So a more real estimate of Muslim influence in the UP at the beginning of our period will be concerned less with counting heads than with showing where Muslims stood in land, commerce and government service.

Most traders, whether local shopkeepers or Cawnpore magnates, lent money, but fewer money-lenders traded. Nevertheless these categories overlap so much that it is difficult to distinguish between them. In the earlier part of the century, traders and money-lenders tended to be most influential in the towns. In the countryside, they had little chance of rivalling the prestige of the landlord who was usually ritually superior. However, in the second half of the nineteenth century their influence increased significantly, in part through the action of British land revenue policy which helped to bring land under the hammer, and in part as a result of the spread of railways and roads which encouraged the growth of commercial agriculture. Although it would be too much to suggest that his change represented any serious threat to the authority of landlords in the rural areas, by 1891 commercial men had extended their networks of influence enough for government to have 'no hesitation in believing that the trader is in the provinces yearly advancing in wealth and importance, that whilst the Thakur may be falling into the background the Baniya steadily increases his wealth and importance'.[1]

Twenty-two per cent of those earning a living from commerce were Muslims.[2] That so many did so is a little surprising. Muslim leaders represented the community as one which avoided trade, and government itself explained the community's poor showing in

---

[1] *1891 Census, UP*, Part I, p. 333.
[2] *1911 Census, UP*, Part II, Table XV, Part C, pp. 550–61. Of those returned as living off trade in 1911 – the 1911 Census provides the first analysis of employment by community – seven per cent were returned as doing so mainly from banking and money-lending, and of these, seven per cent were Muslims. *Ibid.*

14

the income returns, declaring that 'Muslims as a rule do not trade'.[1] Yet in numbers Muslims dominated the trades in clothing, transport, hides, perfumes and luxury articles, and played a large part in the food trade and others, though in spite of this they do not appear to have made much money. Apart from one or two trading and money-lending communities such as the Pathans of Shahjahanpur and the Syeds of Jansath, nearly all the middling and all the big trading and banking concerns in the province were Hindu-owned. Muslims were mainly pedlars, stall-holders and shopkeepers – a minor section of the commercial community. Such men had little share in the wealth which was pouring into the towns from the opening up of the countryside, and this weakness was to be important in the early development of Muslim politics. In 1907, for example, twenty-two per cent of those sitting on municipal boards in the UP were Hindu businessmen, but only two per cent were Muslim.[2]

The landlords were rather more powerful than the men of commerce. The land provided the greater part of the government's revenue, most people gained their living from it and in their doings the landlords had a major say. The power of the landlord depended on how he held his land. There were three major types of land tenure: pattidari, zamindari and taluqdari. In Agra province and about one-third of Oudh most land was held in pattidari or zamindari tenure; in pattidari tenure, government made land revenue settlements with a co-parcenary group, which was often a cohesive community belonging to a single caste, sept or family, and in zamindari tenure government dealt with an individual landholder. There were few large estates. The effect of early settlement policy had been, according to one nineteenth-century commentator, to 'flatten the whole surface of society as eventually to leave little of distinguishable eminence between the ruling power and the cultivators of the soil'.[3] This effect was so increased by the growth in

[1] *Report on the Administration of the Income Tax Act under Act II of 1886 in the North-Western Provinces and Oudh for the Financial Year ending 31st March, 1889* (Allahabad, 1889), p. 10.
[2] Calculated from 'Statement showing the occupations of members of Municipal Boards' (Incomplete; returns for Benares, Lucknow, Gonda, Balrampur, Nanpara, Sultanpur, Nagina and Najibabad missing), Municipal 1908, 594 D, UPS.
[3] Comment by Robertson, lieutenant-governor of the North-West Provinces 1840–2, on the land settlements of the province, quoted in E. T. Stokes, *The English Utilitarians and India* (Oxford, 1959), p. 115.

population,[1] and by the workings of Hindu and Muslim inheritance laws, that most of the land was held by small landholders whose members were rapidly increasing.[2] Much of the province was owned by pattidars. Their influence was small. Their estates were usually the results of minute subdivision; they were litigious and often heavily in debt. Frequently pattidars had to seek employment in order to eke out their slender means. Many zamindars were in little better condition, although a few did have large estates. They were not powerful as a group as were the Oudh taluqdars; in the second half of the nineteenth century they had a few district associations but were not organised as a provincial force, and even when they attempted to do so they soon found themselves divided between the Muzaffarnagar Zamindars' Association, founded in 1896, and the Agra Zamindars' Association, founded in 1914. But large zamindars could be quite powerful as individuals. Their wealth, rivalled by only a few of the native banking houses, gave them patronage, the position they sometimes held as lineage heads gave them great social power, while their authority was augmented by the willingness of government to view and to represent them as the 'natural leaders' of the people.

More influential, both as individuals and as a group, were the taluqdars of Oudh who held two-thirds of Lucknow and Fyzabad divisions. After the Mutiny, 272 taluqdars had been granted sanads conveying rights of ownership and revenue collection. Some of these were quite small, paying no more than a few hundred rupees land revenue, but some were very large paying well over a lakh of rupees.[3] Many were given minor jurisdiction over criminal, civil

---

[1] The population of the province was 44,107,869 in 1881: by 1911, it had risen to 47,182,044, and by 1971 it was over eighty-eight million. It is probable, however, that the growth of numbers among landholding groups was significantly greater in contrast with the population as a whole, since they were comparatively immune from famine.

[2] Table entitled 'Number of landholders in the U.P. by Divisions, 1881–1945'. P. D. Reeves, 'The Landlords' Response to Political Change in the United Provinces of Agra and Oudh, India, 1921–37'. (Unpublished PhD thesis, Australian National University, 1963), p. 63.

[3] The largest taluqdars were: Balrampur 1153 villages and shares in another 411, Ajodhia 635 and Kapurthala 544. The next two in size, Nanpara 439, and Mahmudabad 363, were the largest Muslim landowners in British India. As a body the taluqdars paid a crore of rupees land revenue or about one-sixth of the total revenue of the whole province. Minute by Harcourt Butler, 1 December 1918, GAD, 1918, 423, UPS.

and revenue suits. Their strength as landlords was sustained by the introduction of primogeniture, which protected them against the divisive effect of the Hindu and Muslim laws of inheritance, and by the Oudh Encumbered Estates Act, which helped to preserve them from the results of their own extravagance.[1] Their power as a group was increased by the sharing of a common organisation, the British Indian Association (founded in 1861), a common culture, the Urdu–Muslim culture of northern India, and a common centre, Lucknow. The taluqdars were by far the most powerful group of landlords in the province. They were powerful because they were intrinsically strong, and because government, having learned to respect their strength, had turned it into a fundamental aspect of policy.[2]

Table I shows that the Muslims held approximately one-fifth of the land in the province. They tended to hold particularly large amounts around former centres of Muslim power such as Jaunpur, Allahabad and Fatehpur, Bareilly and Moradabad, Lucknow and Bara Banki; and since Allahabad and Lucknow were also centres of British power this helped to add to their influence in government and politics. Overall, the Muslims were well placed in Oudh and were dominant in Rohilkhand. With Hindu Rajputs, Brahmins, Banias and Kayasths, they were a major landholding group.

In Agra province, just as there were few large landlords, there were few large Muslim landlords. Taking the payment of Rs. 5000 land revenue as the mark of a landlord of substance, in the divisions of Allahabad, Benares and Gorakhpur, only in Allahabad district were there more than ten Muslim landlords paying Rs. 5000, while there was only one landlord of any great eminence, Nawab Abdul Majid of the Maulvi estate of Jaunpur, whose estate paid Rs. 70,000

---

[1] Primogeniture was introduced by the Oudh Estates Act of 1869, and the Court of Wards by the Encumbered Estates Act of 1870.

[2] For example, Lyall, lieutenant-governor of the province from 1882 to 1887, warned the government of India, when it was preparing Oudh land legislation to be very wary in dealing with the taluqdars. 'No general orders,' he urged, 'be issued that might alarm or estrange the Taluqdars as a body...If...they are threatened with drastic measures they are quite capable of making a very good fight both here and in England.' Lyall to Primrose, Private Secretary to the Viceroy, 8 July 1882, Lyall Papers, 63 D, IOL. Lyall would not consider UP representation on the Viceroy's Imperial Council if the first seat did not go to a taluqdar. Lyall to Primrose, 29 February 1884, Lyall Papers, 43, IOL. This policy gained its strongest expression in Harcourt Butler's tract, *Oudh Policy: The Policy of Sympathy* (Lucknow, 1906).

Separatism among Indian Muslims

TABLE I. *Holdings per cent of major landowning groups in the UP by district at the beginning of the twentieth century*

District	Muslim	Rajput	Brahmin	Kayasth	Bania	Other castes
Meerut division						
Dehra Dun	3.2	32.8	14.5	N.A.	10.9	—
Saharanpur	10.7	16.4	3.1	N.A.	22.3	Gujar 20.7
Muzaffarnagar	29.6	5.5	3.0	N.A.	24.0	—
Meerut	18.0	7.5	3.8	N.A.	9.8	Jat 26.4
Bulandshahr	28.4	13.6	6.7	5.6	10.4	—
Aligarh	20.6	24.3	14.4	3.4	9.3	—
Agra division						
Muttra	4.9	13.2	18.8	3.2	9.3	Jat 26.2
Agra	5.2	24.5	26.1	5.6	12.5	Jat 7.5
Farrukhabad	17.0	38.0	19.0	8.0	4.0	—
Mainpuri	2.7	45.7	20.4	5.4	5.2	Ahir 10.1
Etawah	2.3	34.0	43.0	8.3	6.6	—
Etah	15.9	39.0	13.2	12.5	7.7	—
Rohilkhand division						
Bareilly	33.1	16.0	12.5	11.6	11.3	—
Bijnor	19.4	24.5	2.7	—	11.3	Jat 16.3 Ahir 10.1
Budaun	29.5	27.5	6.6	5.2	12.5	Ahir 11.2
Moradabad	42.0	9.5	4.8	3.6	15.8	Jat 6.6
Shahjahanpur	23.6	42.4	9.7	4.1	8.0	—
Pilibhit	25.1	16.3	6.1	4.2	10.4	Banjara 20.4
Allahabad division						
Cawnpore	6.8	30.3	33.2	4.5	—	Kurmi 8.6
Fatehpur	23.9	28.7	20.9	6.8	4.8	—
Banda	9.4	26.0	36.0	7.1	8.0	—
Hamirpur	5.6	28.1	24.1	4.7	7.5	Marwari 7.6 Lodhi 18.3
Allahabad	35.4	18.2	17.0	6.2	11.9	—
Jalaun	2.6	30.2	28.0	4.0	3.0	—
Jhansi	1.1	38.6	19.5	2.6	6.0	Lodhi 8.1 Ahir 9.1
Benares division						
Benares	7.0	23.7	19.0	3.7	7.0	Buinhar 27.5
Jaunpur	25.4	44.1	16.1	4.2	3.5	—
Ghazipur	17.0	31.4	10.9	5.5	3.8	Buinhar 23.2
Ballia	8.4	58.6	10.0	3.3	2.6	Buinhar 11.4
Mirzapur	N.A.	—	—	—	—	
Gorakhpur division						
Gorakhpur	6.5	22.3	25.4	6.0	6.7	Buinhar 10.3

Muslims in the United Provinces

District	Muslim	Rajput	Brahmin	Kayasth	Bania	Other castes	
Basti	8.6	30.8	34.8	7.0	3.4	—	
Azamgarh	23.4	34.7	11.3	4.2	4.0	Buinhar	14.5
Lucknow division							
Lucknow	34.6	35.2	12.4	4.5	2.7	—	
Unao	14.1	44.8	18.9	3.4	1.3	—	
Rae Bareli	12.9	67.6	5.4	3.5	0.6	—	
Sitapur	N.A.	—	—	—	—	—	
Hardoi	19.6	64.9	7.2	6.5	0.6	—	
Kheri	21.1	56.4	7.5	6.3	3.1	—	
Fyzabad division							
Fyzabad	23.1	47.3	21.5	2.3	0.9	—	
Sultanpur	16.6	76.2	4.5	1.7	0.8	—	
Bahraich	26.5	57.6	0.5	1.4	—	—	
Gonda	7.8	58.2	24.6	2.9	0.1	—	
Partabgarh	5.1	90.6	2.6	0.7	0.2	—	
Bara Banki	45.6	37.5	3.4	4.5	0.8	—	

SOURCE: *SR Dehra Dun, 1907*, p. 4; *SR Saharanpur, 1891*, p. 53; *SR Muzaffarnagar, 1921*, p. 35; *SR Meerut, 1940*, p. 13; *SR Bulandshahr, 1919*, p. 33; *SR Aligarh, 1886*, p. 30; *DG Muttra*, VII, 33; *DG Agra*, VIII, 86; *SR Farrukhabad, 1903*, p. 13; *DG Mainpuri*, X, 104; *SR Etawah, 1915*, p. 36; *DG Etah*, XII, 80; *DG Bareilly*, XIII, 100–1; *DG Bijnor*, XIV, 108; *DG Budaun*, XV, 84; *DG Moradabad*, XVI, 88; *DG Shahjahanpur*, XVII, 87; *DG Pilibhit*, XVIII, 101–2; *DG Cawnpore*, XIX, 129–30; *DG Fatehpur*, XX, 101; *SR Banda, 1909*, p. 11; *SR Hamirpur, 1908*, p. 29; *DG Allahabad*, XXIII, 104; *DG Jhansi*, XIV, 105–6; *DG Jalaun*, XXV, 69–70; *DG Benares*, XXVI, 114; *DG Jaunpur*, XXVIII, 94–5; *DG Ghazipur*, XXIX, 96; *SR Ballia, 1886*, p. 23; *SR Gorakhpur 1891*, p. 40; *DG Azamgarh*, XXXIII, 106; *SR Lucknow, 1930*, p. 46; *SR Unao, 1931*, p. 39; *SR Rae Bareli, 1898*, 28A–29A; *SR Hardoi, 1932*, p. 53; *SR Kheri, 1902*, p. 8; *SR Bara Banki, 1930*, p. 33; *SR Partabgarh, 1896*, p. 22; *SR Sultanpur, 1898*, p. 9; *SR Bahraich, 1939*, p. 46; *SR Gonda, 1944*, p. 17; *SR Fyzabad, 1942*, p. 25.

land revenue.[1] Further west, where Muslims were more numerous and Muslim influence had been greater, their situation was better. In one area, the districts of Aligarh and Bulandshahr, where the

[1] The following were the districts of the province with more than ten Muslim landlords paying more than Rs. 5000 land revenue: Bara Banki (28), Aligarh (22), Bulandshahr (16), Moradabad (15), Allahabad (14), Lucknow (13), Muzaffarnagar (12), Budaun and Farrukhabad (11), Meerut (10). Calculated from the Muslim Electoral Roll of the UP legislative council, *United Provinces Gazette*, 1909, Part VIII, pp. 106–59.

estates of the Lalkhani Rajputs and the Sherwani Pathans were situated, there was a very powerful concentration of Muslim landlords.[1] Their presence encouraged Sir Syed Ahmed Khan to found his Muhammadan Anglo-Oriental College at Aligarh, and through the College and their own influence as powerful landlords they had a considerable impact on the politics of the province. But the Muslims were strongest on the land where the landlords were strongest – in Oudh. Seventy-six taluqdars were Muslims and they held many of the largest estates. The Rajas of Mahmudabad were Presidents of the British Indian Association and represented it on the Imperial Legislative Council: one became the first Home Member of the province.[2] But the best indication of Muslim influence is that, although they numbered only thirteen per cent of Oudh's population, and although they held only twenty per cent of the land, they were able to elect about forty per cent of the members of the district boards.[3] The influence of Muslim landlords, particularly in Oudh, was considerable.

The most powerful group in nineteenth-century India were the government servants. Of the 54,000 who helped to govern the province in 1880, a mere 200 belonged to the ruling race; the great body of administration was transacted, as in other provinces, by Indians. The powers of government servants were great. They estimated the peasant's land revenue, they assessed the trader's income tax. They decided who was right in squabbles over irrigation and religious customs. They even chose who should succeed

[1] The chief Lalkhani estates were those of Pindrawal, Sadabad, Danpur, Dharampur, Pahasu and Chhatari. The main Sherwani estates were those of Haji Muhammad Ismail Khan, Muhammad Yaqub Khan, Muhammad Yusuf Khan, Muhammad Yunus Khan and Haji Muhammad Musa Khan. Also worthy of mention are the Bhikampur Pathans: Habibur-Rahman Khan, Ahmad Said Khan and Muzammilullah Khan. Of these Pahasu, Chhatari, Haji Muhammad Ismail Khan, Haji Muhammad Musa Khan and Muzammilullah Khan took a leading part in Aligarh, Muslim League, landlord and provincial politics. Almost all these landlords and the numerous progeny they supported played some part in Muslim and Congress politics.
[2] Raja Amir Hasan Khan of Mahmudabad was President of the British Indian Association from 1882 to 1892; in the 1880s, he also represented the province in the Imperial Council. His son Raja (later Maharaja) Muhammad Ali Muhammad was President of the British Indian Association from 1917 to 1921 and 1930 to 1931. He also represented the landlords of Oudh in the Imperial Council and was Home Member of the province from 1920 to 1925.
[3] Calculated from 'Distribution by religion of electorate and elected members of district boards in the U.P. as on 1. 4. 1911', Home Educ, Municipal A, April 1914, 22–31, NAI.

them in these functions. These may not seem odd powers for government servants to wield, but in a society in which family and clan loyalties were strong, in which communal antagonism was endemic, in which, in fact, impartiality was practically impossible and thought to be so, they were less the reasonable powers of government than a licence to confer favour, to withhold rights and to harass.[1]

The most powerful native officers were those in the covenanted civil service (later the provincial civil service), the subordinate judges, munsifs, deputy collectors and tahsildars who worked directly under their British rulers. Not much less powerful were the sheristadars who managed the various offices controlling both the flow of information upwards and the wide range of minor appointments beneath them. These men interpreted society to government and government policy to society; they were the bearings on which the smooth running of the Raj depended. Government had no illusions about its dependence on them. 'These officers', it declared in 1882, 'already carry on a very large proportion of the judicial and executive work in the North-Western Provinces and upon their zeal, ability, and experience, upon their knowledge of the ways and wants of the people, the proper working of local government must in a very great measure depend.'[2] In the various areas of India, different positions seem to have been the most important. In south India it was the sheristadar who called the tune,[3] but in the UP it seems to have been the tahsildar who was particularly influential.[4] So great an influence did the tahsildar have on the 'well-being of the community' that the 1886 Public Service Commission declared that 'it is impossible that such an officer can be too well selected'.[5]

[1] Even today some writers stress that the power of government servants, which is rather difficult for those unacquainted with the agrarian economies of the east to comprehend, cannot be overemphasised. See for instance, Chaudhri Muhammad Ali, *The Emergence of Pakistan* (New York and London, 1967), p. 10.

[2] Resolution No. 1711 of 1882, 17 May 1882, NWP&O GAD, June, 1883 IOR.

[3] R. E. Frykenberg, *Gunter District 1788–1848* (Oxford, 1965).

[4] 'The Tahsildars controlled the Sharistadars and other record keepers...' A Jaunpur judge quoted in Bernard S. Cohn, 'Structural Change in Indian Rural Society 1596–1885', R. E. Frykenberg (ed.), *Land Control and Social Structure in Indian History* (Wisconsin, 1969), p. 70. See also, Bernard S. Cohn, 'The Initial British Impact on India: A Case Study of the Benares Region', *The Journal of Asian Studies*, XIX, No. 4 (August 1960), p. 425.

[5] *PSC 1886–7*, Report, *P.P.* 1888, XLVIII, p. 89.

TABLE II. *Hindus and Muslims serving the government of the North-West Provinces and Oudh in 1882*

	Total Muslims	Total Hindus	Percentage of Muslims to total employed
Offices under commissioners and deputy commissioners	5,605	7,776	42
Police	9,257	16,061	37
Public instruction	2,097	5,596	27
Post office	219	2,095	9
Other government departments	2,310	3,193	42
Judicial Commissioner, Oudh	293	504	37
High Court, North-West Provinces	47	37	56
Total	18,828	35,302	35

Calculated from 'Abstract of returns submitted by heads of departments and officers consulted', NWP&O GAD, June 1883, IOR, and *Correspondence on the subject of the Education of the Muhammadan Community in British India and their Employment in the Public Service Generally* (Calcutta, 1886), p. 287.

If any of these officers took it into his head to be more than usually partial, it could go hard with his victim. He might appeal to the courts and expose himself to the feebleness of the subordinate judiciary or to the harassment of the police. Finding no satisfaction here, he could resort to traditional methods and petition the huzur, but then few petitions reached the collector without first passing through the native registrar. If the victim finally succeeded in seeing the collector, he was little better off as all the information on his case would be drawn up by the sheristadar. All would exact their toll which might be more than the poor sufferer could afford. All might, in fact, be working in concert – a common occurrence before 1850 and not impossible in 1880 – in which case his chances of retribution were slim. Much real power over peasant, trader and landlord lay with native government servants. Government knew this. It also knew how little it could control them. In the nineteenth century the major aim of government's reforms in the bureaucracy was to enable it to control its native officials more effectively. But,

Muslims in the United Provinces

TABLE III. *Posts held by Hindus and Muslims in the Uncovenanted Civil Service in the North-West Provinces and Oudh, 1886–1887*

	Hindus	Muslims	Sikhs
Executive service			
Deputy collectors	90	51	1
Tahsildars	101	122	1
Total	191	173	2
Judicial Service			
Subordinate judges	20	15	
Munsifs	51	47	
Total	71	62	
Total of both	262	235	2

SOURCE: *PSC 1886–7*, Report, *P.P.* 1888, XLVIII, p. 55.

in 1880, Couper, the lieutenant-governor, was so sceptical of the success of these reforms that he would not agree to a reduction of the British cadre in the administration.[1]

In 1882, Muslims held nearly thirty-five per cent of all government posts (see Table II). But their share of the influential posts was greater. Table III shows that in the uncovenanted service they had forty-five per cent of all posts and, though stronger overall in the subordinate judicial service, were best placed in the powerful tahsildarships of which they had fifty-five per cent. It is not remarkable that so many Muslims held government posts. Government service was the traditional occupation of many Muslims; they had dominated the province for a long period; and the reforms in the bureaucracy, begun by the Permanent Settlement, reinforced by abolition of Persian and redoubled after the Mutiny, although they had swept Muslims from the administration in Bengal, had hardly been applied in the UP. In the second half of the nineteenth century, therefore, the strength of the Muslims in government service, particularly in the higher echelons, made their influence not much less than that of the Hindus.

So far the Muslims have been treated as a monolithic bloc. This

[1] Secretary to Government NWP&O, to Secretary to Government of India, Home, Revenue and Agriculture, 5 July 1880, NWP&O GAD, April 1882, IOR.

23

has been a matter of convenience. It was not a matter of fact. In most things Muslims were far from united. First, they were divided into two major ethnic groups: those who claimed to be the descendants of Muslim immigrants, Syeds, Sheikhs, Mughals and Pathans, often known collectively as the ashraf, and those of indigenous origin whose ancestors had been converted to Islam. The latter may be subdivided into three distinct groups: converts from Hindu high castes such as Muslim Rajputs, converts from clean occupational castes such as Julahas and Qassabs, and converts from unclean occupational castes such as Bhangis and Chamars.[1] Among the occupational groups the Julahas or weavers were the most numerous and most important. Most of the high-caste Hindu converts were members of Rajput septs whose service of and close association with Muslim rulers had resulted in a convenient change of faith; the most prominent of these were the Lalkhanis and Bhale Sultans centred in Bulandshahr and the Khanzadas of Oudh. But by far the most important group were the Ashraf Muslims. They numbered over two and a half million representing just under half of the Muslim population of the province. Their four sections were not divisions sanctified by ritual but merely those of blood and birth. They could and did intermarry.[2] If they preferred not to do so, it was on social grounds.[3] Marriages also occurred with groups outside the Ashraf category, wives, for instance, being taken from high status Muslim Rajputs.[4] Thus within the Ashraf category, and to a certain extent this included Muslim Rajputs, differences were not so marked as to make for strong divisions. Between the Ashraf and the converted occupational groups a wide social gulf existed. But even this, at least

[1] The most important clean occupational castes were: Julaha (weaver), Darzi (tailor), Qassab (butcher), Nai (barber), Kabariya (greengrocer), Mirasi (musician), Kumhar (potter), Manihar (bracelet-maker), Dhuniya (cotton-carder), Faqir (beggar), Teli (oil-presser), Dhobi (washerman), Gaddi (grazier). The Bhangis (sweepers) and the Chamars (tanners) were the most important unclean occupational castes. Some of these castes, such as the Julahas and Qassabs, had been converted in their entirety from Hinduism; others, such as the Kumhars, Telis and Chamars had opposite numbers within the Hindu caste structure. Ghaus Ansari, *Muslim Caste in Uttar Pradesh* (Lucknow, 1960), pp. 35, 41–8.
[2] J. C. Nesfield, *A Brief View of the Caste System of the North-Western Provinces and Oudh* (Allahabad, 1885), p. 123.
[3] There is a good instance of such grounds being given against intermarriage in Ahmed Ali, *Twilight in Delhi*, 2nd edn (Oxford, 1966), p. 60.
[4] Ghaus Ansari, *Muslim Caste*, p. 40.

theoretically, had its limitations. When Muslims came to pray in the mosque, they all stood in a line, not one an inch in front of the other. Potentially the equality of all believers united Muslim society more than the inequalities of descent divided it.

If religion was an important factor in unifying Muslims, it also divided them. First, there were important differences among the Sunnis. They were divided according to the various schools their ulama followed, and they were bitterly divided over doctrine – on any one issue there were usually many conflicting religious views.[1] Second, there were fundamental differences between the Sunnis and the Shias, the two major sects. The Sunnis were theocrats, who believed that church and state should be one, while the Shias wanted to separate them.[2] The Sunnis were prepared to accept a Sultan of Turkey or ruler of the Hedjaz as the supreme sovereign of the Islamic world, the Shias could only accept the descendants of Ali.[3] The Shias were a small community, a mere three per cent of the Muslims of the province. They were found largely in districts which had been important Muslim centres, that is Lucknow, Fyzabad, Jaunpur, Moradabad, Allahabad and Farrukhabad. Many lived in Meerut division, once the commuter belt for Mughal civil servants working in Delhi. Most notable of these were the Jansath Syeds of Muzaffarnagar. The Shias were influential out of all proportion to their numbers. Several rulers in the province had been Shias, for example the Kings of Oudh and the Sharqi Kings of Jaunpur, and the community had benefited. Many large land-lords were Shias, among them some of the largest, Mahmudabad, Pirpur, Qizilbash and Bilehra, and several leading politicians, for example Syed Wazir Hasan and Syed Riza Ali. Whatever the relations between Hindu and Muslim, wherever Shias were power-ful, they tended to clash with Sunnis.

Muslims were further divided by conflict between their different interests in government service, land and religion. Many Muslims depended on employment in government service. It was to serve, usually in the army, at the wealthy courts of the Muslim rulers of India that most of the Ashraf had come from their barren home-lands in Arabia, Persia and Central Asia. The ancestors of the

---

[1] For the various schools of ulama in the UP, and the conflicts between and within them, see Chapter 7.

[2] H. A. R. Gibb and J. H. Kramers, *Shorter Encyclopaedia of Islam* (London, 1961), p. 534.

[3] *Ibid.* pp. 165–6.

Mahmudabads had come from Arabia in the thirteenth century to seek their fortune at the Delhi Court; those of the great Sherwani clan were invited by Bahlol Lodi to come and share in the plunder of northern India, while, as late as the end of the eighteenth century, the grandfather of the poet Ghalib came from Persia to serve Shah Alam.[1] If successful, after reaching the position of a captain of 1000 or 5000, a vizier or a minister, these adventurers retired to the lands they had carefully accumulated during their service. If their descendants were fortunate, these lands survived the vicissitudes of several centuries to become the nucleus of a great estate and they were absorbed into the landed interest. More often than not, however, these lands suffered much subdivision through Muslim laws of inheritance, and the family would again look to government service to release it from poverty. Some were able to find employment in native states such as Hyderabad and Bhopal, but the majority looked to the service of the British. If unsuccessful in their aim, they would turn to the professions, mainly the law; anything else was beneath their dignity. Muslims such as these were clearly likely to be sensitive to changes in qualifications for service or changes in the direction of government patronage. If they failed to get a job, because as a rule they had nothing to lose, they protested vigorously. It was in this group that political consciousness grew most quickly, and it was from it that most Muslim political leadership came.

Muslims usually gained land through service. Those who had done so most recently were the tahsildars, sheristadars and other native officials who had purchased their estates from fortunes made in service under the Company,[2] and those who received land in return for their loyalty in the Mutiny. The representatives of the Muslim landed interest were the large landowners, men who paid more than Rs. 5000 land revenue and depended mainly on the land for a living. Like all large landlords, whether Hindu or Muslim,

---

[1] The fortunes of Ghalib's forebears are typical of those of his class. His grandfather took service under Shah Alam with the command of fifty horse and a jagir to support them. On his death this estate was lost and his father entered the service of first, the Nawab Asaf ud Daula of Oudh, then of the Nizam of Hyderabad, and finally of the Raja of Alwar under whom he was killed in battle. Ghalib's uncle, who then cared for him, was a Governor of Agra under the Marathas and then a commander of 400 cavalry under Lord Lake. Ralph Russell and Khurshidul Islam, *Ghalib* (London, 1969), p. 23.

[2] Bernard S. Cohn, 'Structural Change in Indian Rural Society 1596–1885', R. E. Frykenberg (ed.), *Land Control*, pp. 78–9.

government was concerned to have them on its side because they were powerful. For their part, they were just as eager to be on the government's side. The Mutiny settlement had taught them to respect their ruler's power to make and break men of broad acres. Moreover, although the growth of government power steadily eroded their influence over their tenants, they still remained loyal. They did not risk their position to preserve their own interests, and they certainly would not do so to protect those of professional men or ulama. In many ways they had more in common with the large Hindu landlords than anyone else, and their backwardness in supporting 'Muslim' interests brought them into conflict with other Muslims.

The ulama represented the traditional Indo–Islamic society which had flourished before the modernising impulses of British rule had begun to take effect. In this society, Muslims learned enough Arabic at mosque schools to repeat the suras (prescribed chapters from the Koran), they prayed five times a day, attended the mosque on Friday, and the ulama played their part by teaching the Islamic sciences and by interpreting the holy law. The ulama were the only interest which in no way relied on government patronage. They were supported mainly by the endowments and votive offerings of the faithful. Their real influence and their real importance lay in their ability to move the Muslim masses. They had a particular hold over the Muslim artisans of the towns, notably the Julahas who were renowned for their bigotry. Some idea of the extent of this influence can be gained from the fact that in the 1880s thirty-eight per cent of Muslim schoolchildren attended private schools most of which were run by ulama,[1] while their power over the minds of the illiterate – about ninety-seven per cent of the community – especially the women, was particularly strong.

This traditional Indo–Islamic society, however, was slowly being undermined by British rule. British law was increasingly encroaching on Islamic law. British courts were making it harder for the faithful to create waqfs to support the holy.[2] Legislation introducing local self-government was raising men of all kinds, Muslims of secular education and ideals, and even Hindus, into positions

---

[1] Calculated from *RDPI (NWP&O) 1883–4*, Table III, pp. 42A–43A. Almost forty years later, thirty per cent of the Muslims at school were still at private schools run by ulama.

[2] This right in Muslim personal law was seriously affected by judicial decisions of 1887, 1890 and 1894.

of authority over the lives of the faithful. Moreover, the growth of British might in the world at large had led directly to the decline of the great Muslim powers. The ulama had many reasons for opposing the government, but not all of them were anti-British. Many were content to accept things as they were and government was, of course, careful to woo the influential among them, such as Wilayat Husain, the head of the Allahabad Diara Shah Hajatullah, and Shibli, the leading force in the Lucknow Nadwat-ul-ulama. Indeed for every alim who declared India dar-ul-harb there would be one who would declare it dar-ul-islam. But those ulama who examined their position rigorously could not fail to come to the conclusion that it was at odds with British rule. Conflict, however, with government was bound to involve them in conflict with other Muslims. Muslim landlords, although they might support the individual alim in order to ensure their place with Allah, could not support ulama who agitated vigorously against the government and declared that it was opposed to Islam. The Muslim service classes might support the ulama in such agitation, but eventually they were bound to fall out with them. The service classes wished to gain power in the new secular state being created by the British; the ulama wished to bring back the middle ages and the rule of the priests.

These were the basic divisions among the Muslims. Nevertheless, when they are set against the developing political scene, the distinctions between them will be rapidly blurred by a new range of interests which cut across them, founded on faction and personality. The Muslims were more a multiplicity of interests than a community.

Hindus were no less divided than Muslims. They had conflicting centres of interest in land, trade and government service. They were also divided by their common system of social discipline, caste, which created much more rigid divisions than those among Muslims. The most important castes in the UP were: the Rajputs, the warrior and landed elite; the Brahmins, the priests and teachers; the Kayasths, the traditional clerisy of northern India; and the Khattris and Banias, the traders and money-lenders. Castes were divided into sub-castes, the major units of organisation. The Rajputs of the province, for example, had fourteen exogamous septs and the Brahmins twenty-one major sub-castes. These sub-castes were further divided into sections. The Srivastava Kayasth sub-caste, for example, contained two sections entitled the Khara the 'right' or 'excellent', and the Dusra or the 'rest'. The Agarwal

Bania sub-caste not only divided into seventeen and a half gotras itself but these were also split into endogamous sub-sections, Dasa and Bisa, clean and unclean.[1] These segments of Hindu society could well be divided again by factional strife, or by differences of opinion, reflected in the formation of supra-caste organisations such as the Arya Samaj and the Sanatan Dharm, as to how Hindus should respond to the intellectual and spiritual challenges of the West.

The connections, past or present, of Hindus with government dictated the closeness of their relationships with Muslims. Those whose interests centred on trade, banking and religious instruction, mainly Banias, Khattris and Brahmins, and whose connections with the Muslim and British governments of Hindustan had been slight, tended to have little in common with Muslims. There were, of course, exceptions. There were Bania families, such as the Qanungoyan of Meerut and the Seths of Muttra, which had lent money to Muslim governments and which had assimilated the Nawabi (extravagant) life-style of the Muslim aristocracy; indeed so extravagant was the style of the Muttra Seths, and so close were their connections with the Rampur court, that they were only saved from ruin by the timely intervention of the Nawab himself.[2] Descendants of such families came to contribute to the essentially Muslim culture of northern India: Raja Siva Prasad, descended from the Jagat Seths of Murshidabad, wrote Urdu poetry under the takhullus 'Wahbi', while the man whose word was law on Persian poetry was a Khattri, Dilwali Singh.[3] On the whole, however, men from these castes had little in common with Muslims and little contact with them. With the Brahmins, they were the major protagonists of the Hindi language and the Hindu religion.[4]

Those whose interests centred on land and service had more in common with Muslims. The Rajputs, for instance, had a historical

---

[1] W. Crooke, *Tribes and Castes of the North-Western Provinces and Oudh* (Calcutta, 1896), Vols I, pp. 16–17; II, pp. 8–9; III, p. 188.

[2] The provincial government also helped. *Jain Gazette* (Muttra), 1 January 1899, UPNNR 1899.

[3] Dilwali Singh, takhullus 'Qatil', came from Faridabad near Delhi. He was converted to Islam and moved to Lucknow where he built up a considerable reputation as a Persian and Urdu poet. He had many followers, and Ghalib quarrelled bitterly with them. Russell and Islam, *Ghalib*, pp. 47–8: A. S. I. Tirmizi, *Persian Letters of Ghalib* (Ghalib Academy, New Delhi, 1969), pp. xxix–xxxi.

[4] Crooke, *Tribes and Castes*, Vol. III, p. 265; Fox notes in his recent study of 'Tezibazar' in Jaunpur district that 'the most anti-Muslim of status categories

connection. The leading members of the community had, as a warrior and landed elite, been important collaborators with their Muslim overlords, sometimes giving their daughters in marriage to Muslim ruling families. Under the British their fighting days were done, but on the land the connection was still maintained. Rajputs and Muslims were the two most influential groups in the associations of large landlords and usually worked together to promote landlords' interests. The service interests, Kayasths and Kashmiri Brahmins,[1] also had a historical connection with Muslims; they had worked as the civil servants of Muslim empires and still worked in the service of Muslim states.[2] Outside the native states Muslims could no longer employ them in government, but Muslim landlords still employed them on their estates. For instance, the Mahmudabad Raj gave jobs to large numbers of Kayasths in its offices[3] and the Raja himself hired a Kashmiri Brahmin and a

are the Baniyas and the Brahmins. In fact, most of the Jana Sangh following in Tezibazar and, for that matter, the whole district derives from these two groupings. Local people say that Baniyas and Brahmins are especially anti-Muslim because these castes most retain the spirit of Hinduism in social habits and ideals and are therefore most inimical to Islam.' Richard G. Fox, *From Zamindar to Ballot Box* (Cornell, 1969), p. 113.

[1] The Kashmiris are a small but extremely influential Brahmin sub-caste – in 1891 they numbered a mere 791 members in the UP – which came originally from Kashmir. Ritually their status is the very highest and physically they are renowned for their good looks.

[2] The antecedents of leading UP Kashmiri Brahmin families, such as the Nehrus, Chaks, Kunzrus and Saprus, had all served at the Delhi Court in the eighteenth and early nineteenth centuries. Take, for example, the Nehru family. The earliest known ancestor, Raj Kaul, had come to the Delhi court in the early eighteenth century and he and his descendants continued in service there until 1861 when Motilal Nehru's father, Pandit Ganga Dhar Nehru, who had been Kotwal of Delhi in the Mutiny, died, and the family moved to Agra to seek service under the British. The Kayasths had served the Mughal empire in the same way. Members of the community had accompanied.Muslim military expansion to south India and helped to rule Bhopal, Hyderabad and the Carnatic. The administration of Muslim Hyderabad in the late nineteenth century was peopled by both Hyderabad Kayasth families of long-standing and Kayasths from north India who had sought service there in the same way as the UP Muslims. Karen B. Leonard, 'The Kayasths of Hyderabad City: their internal history, and their role in politics and society from 1850 to 1900' (Unpublished PhD thesis, University of Wisconsin, 1969), in particular, chapters IX and X.

[3] For instance, in offices attached to the estate and household, the Mahmudabad Raj employed twenty-two senior officers; judging by the names, nine were Muslims and at least seven of thirteen Hindus were Kayasths. Such a large proportion of Hindus, however, was not typical of the administration of the Raj as a whole. *Thacker's Indian Directory* (Calcutta, 1909), Mofussil Directory, p. 467.

Rajput to run his newspapers. Kayasths and Kashmiri Brahmins returned the compliment. Ram Garib, the Kayasth banker of Gorakhpur, employed a Muslim to manage his bank, and the great Kashmiri Brahmin lawyer, Pandit Ajudhia Nath, appeared in cases with Nawab Abdul Majid and Syed Abdur Rauf.[1] Men from both castes vigorously defended Urdu against attempts to reduce its status,[2] and with Muslims and Rajputs filled a large majority of the important posts in the public service.[3]

In the second half of the nineteenth century, Kashmiris, Kayasths, Rajputs, Muslims, Banias and Khattris, whose ancestors had served, or who were now serving, the governments of northern India, were in the main the men with power. They may be defined as a group, almost a class, by their adherence to a government-bred culture, the culture of those whose lives revolved around government service and the towns. Its external forms were Muslim: the sherwani, Muslim food, mushairas, nautch parties and conspicuous extravagance. Its strongest expression was literary, and membership of this class is best defined by the use of the changing languages of government. Persian was the language of government up to 1837, and not only Muslims but Kayasths and Kashmiri Brahmins contributed much to its literature. The Kashmiri Brahmin, Tej Bahadur Sapru, was renowned for his fine Persian; the leading Persian poet of nineteenth-century Lucknow was a Kayasth, Dwarka Prasad (takhullus Ufuq); while Ghalib's chief disciple was Munshi Hargopal, a Kayasth of Sikandrabad. After Urdu replaced Persian as the language of government, it also replaced Persian as the main vehicle of literary expression. Towards the end of the nineteenth century, most leading men in the

[1] It is probable that these men were working as Ajudhia Nath's juniors. C. A. Bayly, 'The Development of Political Organization in the Allahabad Locality, 1880–1925' (Unpublished DPhil thesis, Oxford, 1970), p. 257.
[2] For instance, in 1880, Pandit Ajudhia Nath vigorously opposed the government's proposal to suspend the Urdu law classes at Muir Central College, Allahabad. NWP&O GAD, August 1880, IOR. Kayasths joined the Muslims in their bitter protests against the Nagri resolution of April 1900. Minute by A. P. Macdonnell, October 1901, p. 40. Macdonnell Papers, Bodleian Library, Oxford.
[3] In 1886–7, Muslims, Kayasths and Rajputs held seventy-six per cent of the posts in the Uncovenanted Civil Service – unfortunately it is not possible to ascertain the number of Kashmiri Brahmins. The numbers by community were: Muslims 235, Kayasths 107, Brahmins 89, Kshatriyas (Rajputs) 37, Banias 25, Shudras 1 and others 3. *PSC 1886–7*, Report, *P.P.* 1888, XLVIII, pp. 55–9.

major towns of the province spoke and wrote Urdu. It was the language in which most books were written,[1] most newspapers were published,[2] and most prominent associations recorded their affairs. The centres of this Urdu-speaking culture were the cities, notably Agra, Allahabad, Meerut, Moradabad, Bareilly and Lucknow, because here there were many Muslims, and here there were centres of government. Lucknow was the cultural capital. Before the Mutiny it had shared the position with Delhi, but after the Mutiny it was able to assert itself over the fallen city of the Mughals. The reason is not far to seek. Government made Lucknow the social and political centre of the taluqdars of Oudh[3] who had vast patronage to dispose of among poets and writers. More important, Lucknow remained an important centre of government, first of Oudh and later of the United Provinces of Agra and Oudh.

This dominant class, mainly of landlords and government servants who were drawn together by common connections, past or present, with government, will be termed the Urdu-speaking elite. It should be clear that Muslim government servants and landlords were just a part, though a large part, of this elite, and that their connections with Hindus who belonged to the elite were far stronger than their connections with Muslims who did not, such as the butchers of the towns or the bigoted weavers of the villages. Members of this elite of Hindus and Muslims led the responses of UP society to the modernising processes of British rule. They founded the associations which discussed the problems which British rule set for Indians; they also discovered the solutions to these problems, such as colleges for community education and political associations.

[1] In the decade 1881–91, 4380 books were published in Urdu, 2793 in Hindi, 1022 in Persian, 531 in English, 462 in Sanskrit and 414 in Arabic, *1911 Census, UP*, Part I, Subsidiary Table X, p. 277.
[2] In 1886, sixty-four vernacular newspapers were published in Urdu, five in Hindi and Urdu, two in English and Urdu, twelve in Hindi, one in Hindi and English, two in English and one in Hindi and Bengali. The circulation of papers in Urdu alone was 12,110 and in Hindi alone 4824. Calculated from 'Statement of Vernacular Newspapers Published in the North-Western Provinces & Oudh', Home Public B, March 1886, 122–4, NAI.
[3] Here the organisation of the taluqdars, the British Indian Association, was established and here also was their town residence in the old Nawabi palace of the Kaiserbagh which had been given to them by the government after the Mutiny.

CHAPTER 2

Threats to the Urdu-speaking elite in the late nineteenth century

A key question in the history of the UP and in that of modern India is why political alignments based on religion should have developed at all. Muslims had little in common with each other apart from their religion; Hindus were fundamentally divided even by their faith. Many Muslims and Hindus had more in common with each other than with their co-religionists, and in late-nineteenth-century UP the political connections which really mattered were based on the common outlook and interests of Hindu and Muslim landlords and government servants. Why did these connections fall apart and why did some Hindus and Muslims of the Urdu-speaking elite begin to find it easier to develop political constituencies among men of their own faith rather than among men of other faiths? Part of the answer can be found in the pressures of change to which the elite was exposed, part in its response to these pressures, and part in its reactions to government policy. This chapter tackles the first part, the next examines the second and third.

Towards the end of the nineteenth century, the dominance of the Urdu-speaking elite was gradually undermined by several factors, most of them arising from the effects of British rule. For political reasons government was concerned to build up landlord power. Nevertheless, once the bureaucracy began to assume control over matters such as local posts, roads and police, which used to be in the hands of local magnates, it steadily cut down the very landlord power it was concerned to support. At the same time there was another challenge to the magnates' position. Commercial men were growing richer as communications developed, as cash cropping increased, as trade expanded and as the law was enforced more rigorously. In some areas they not only rivalled the influence of the landlords but also began to buy up their land. This general pressure on the influence of landlords forms the background to changes which levelled quite specific threats at the position of the Urdu-speaking elite, in particular its Muslim

33

members. Government's attempts to develop education, to introduce western learning and to encourage the vernacular languages threatened the elite's religious beliefs, social customs and political position. Reforms in the bureaucracy reduced its power in government offices. The introduction of the elective principle in local government undermined its influence, particularly in the towns. Moreover, these changes were taking place side by side with the development of a Hindu revivalist movement which threatened the heart of the elite's political and cultural supremacy.

1. EDUCATION POLICY

Up to the middle of the nineteenth century, British educational policy had a very limited effect on the North-West Provinces. Almost from the beginning Macaulay's policy of downward filtration was a dead letter.[1] By 1844, when the Government of India handed over the control of education to the provincial government, only three colleges, Agra, Benares and Delhi, and six Anglo-vernacular schools had been established; and they taught a mere 1739 boys. So limited was their appeal that by 1850 their number of pupils had decreased by one-third. Few wanted to learn the oriental classics in government institutions; they could do so in their own schools without running the gauntlet of missionaries and other threats to their religion. Few wanted to learn English; there was no need. In northern India, unlike the maritime provinces, there were few Europeans. There was no wealthy body of merchants doing business in English, there was no court administering justice in English, there were few jobs in public service that required a knowledge of English and most Europeans spoke the vernacular. Few needed and few wished to come forward to act as Macaulay's 'interpreters'[2] between the British and the millions they ruled. The vast majority, nearly 70,000, of those who went

[1] Macaulay's education policy, dominant from the mid 1830s, was to give a good education, i.e. in western learning through the medium of English, to a few who would then educate the masses themselves. For Macaulay's brilliant exposition of his policy see his 1835 minute on education reproduced in full in G. O. Trevelyan, *The Competition Wallah* (London, 1864), pp. 410–24.

[2] Much of the stimulus for Macaulay's policy came from the British experience in Bengal. The reasons for its failure in northern India were given pithily by a French observer: 'L'enseignement européen a assez bien réussi au Bengale, mais le Bengale n'est pas l'Inde.' J. H. Garcin de Tassy, *La Langue et la Littérature Hindoustanies en 1871* (Paris, 1872), p. 39.

to school went to indigenous schools where, for the most part, they were taught as their fathers had been before them the classical learning and languages of Islam and Hinduism. Among them were members of the Urdu-speaking elite who continued to be educated in Arabic and Persian. They needed no more to get the jobs they wanted in government.[1]

From the middle of the century, however, the local government under James Thomason abandoned downward filtration and made massive attempts to extend government-sponsored education. So successful were his endeavours that Wood's despatch of 1854 pointed to them as 'the model by which the efforts of other presidencies for the same object should be guided'.[2] An education department was set up with machinery for school inspection. At the headquarters of each tahsil, a government village school, teaching in the medium of the vernacular languages, was established to act as a model for schools in the area. At a central point in each cluster of four or five villages, a school with slightly lower standards was fixed. Known as the Halkabandi school this was maintained by local landlords who voluntarily paid an education cess of one per cent of their land revenue. Self-improvement was encouraged. Boys who did well were given prizes, so were teachers, while standards were maintained through examination and inspection.[3] As government schools were established, private schools declined and one Director of Public Instruction could barely conceal his pleasure at the fact that they 'were being closed one after the other'.[4] The result was such a rapid growth in attendance at government primary and secondary schools that by 1860–1 there were over 83,000 boys in government schools and only 65,000 in private schools. By 1880–1 these figures were 224,000 and 68,000 respectively, and at the turn of the century 350,000 and 80,000. The growth in higher education was not so marked. In 1860–1, there were 1066 students in colleges, but forty years later there was only just over double the number.

[1] *Report by the North-Western Provinces and Oudh Provincial Committee: with evidence taken before the committee and memorials addressed to the Education Commission* [henceforth *ECNWP&O*] (Calcutta, 1884), pp. 1–9.
[2] Syed Nurullah and J. P. Naik, *A History of Education in India* (Bombay, 1951), p. 131.
[3] See *ECNWP&O*, pp. 10–19; Nurullah and Naik, *History of Education*, pp. 126–31; Sir Richard Temple, *James Thomason* (Oxford, 1893), pp. 170–4.
[4] *ECNWP&O*, p. 88.

2-2

Separatism among Indian Muslims

With this expansion in education there came several changes of emphasis in the curriculum. In colleges greater stress was put on western learning and on English as the medium of instruction. The evidence of the Mutiny, it was believed, showed that Britain's Indian subjects were loyal in proportion to the extent of their English education.[1] Consequently, oriental learning in Persian, Arabic and Sanskrit was almost wiped out of the system. The oriental departments in Agra, Bareilly and Delhi colleges were abolished – some of their professors had, as the Director of Public Instruction never tired of pointing out, been involved in the Mutiny – and only the Sanskrit department at Benares was retained. In the 1870s, when government tried to encourage Muslims to come to its schools, this drive against oriental learning was partially relaxed, but with reluctance.

More important, however, than the emphasis on English at the higher levels of education was the stress on the vernaculars at the lower levels. From the 1840s, it was seen that the Persian, Arabic and Sanskrit languages used in many of the better indigenous schools attracted a limited clientele and that 'the vernacular will be the best medium, if...we wish to produce any perceptible impression on the general mind of the people in this part of the country'.[2] But there were no vernacular text books and there was little vernacular literature. Government had to make the former and to create the latter. Text books were written by members of the education department; by 1868, one member alone, Siva Prasad, had produced nineteen works.[3] Native translation societies in Bareilly and Aligarh received government grants to help them translate into Hindi and Urdu works of European scholarship. To encourage the growth of vernacular literature nearly half of the circulation of the native newspapers published in the province was bought by the education department and distributed to its schools.[4] Rewards were given to authors who produced good work,

[1] T. R. Metcalf, *The Aftermath of Revolt: India, 1857–1870* (Princeton, 1965), pp. 124–6.
[2] *ECNWP&O*, p. 8.
[3] Of these eleven were in Hindi, seven in Urdu and one in Hindi and Urdu. For a list see enclosure in M. Kempson, Director of Public Instruction NWP, to Government NWP, 16 October 1868, NWP GAD, December 1868, IOR.
[4] In fact, the education department must have kept many newspapers in business. This patronage of the press was begun by A. O. Hume in the early 1860s. By 1868, 3118 copies out of a total circulation of 7220 were purchased by the department. Report on the Native Press for 1866, enclosed in M. Kempson

36

and from 1868 the government gave away up to Rs. 5000 a year in prizes for original literary compositions in the vernaculars. The scheme stimulated a remarkable activity in the vernaculars. By 1874, 1164 works had been submitted of which 125 received prizes totalling over Rs. 25,000. Four-fifths of the prize-winning works were in Urdu.[1] Among them were some of the finest pieces of nineteenth-century Urdu writing: Nazir Ahmad's *The Bride's Mirror, The Daughters of the Bier* and the *Repentance of Nasuh*.[2] Nearly half of the authors, including Nazir Ahmad, belonged to the education department. Indeed, much of the early stimulus behind the creation of literature in Urdu and Hindi was given by the education policy of the government of the North-West Provinces.

The effects of this education policy were felt differently by different sections of the Urdu-speaking elite. For the supple Hindu service groups it presented little problem; they took to English and western learning just as their ancestors had taken to Persian and later Urdu. Equally, this policy did not affect Hindu and Muslim landed magnates. Their wealth sheltered them from the need to seek employment. Government schools could not teach them to manage their estates, while if they wanted a little cultural gloss they could always afford to pay for a private tutor. There was no question of their entering a government institution: 'A well-born Rajput or Muhammadan', declared the 1882 Education Com-

Director of Public Instruction NWP to Secretary to Government NWP, 23 March 1867, NWP GAD, June 1867, IOR. Under Muir, every newspaper published was patronized. This policy was maintained until 1875 when the growing militancy of some papers made them unsuitable for distribution to schools and demands for economy forced government to cut back its patronage to those papers of particular educational interest, such as *Kashi Patrika*, and those to which its patronage was of political importance such as the *Aligarh Institute Gazette*.

[1] Most of the competitors came from the NWP, but some came from Oudh and the Punjab the two main cities of which, Lucknow and Delhi, were the homes of the best Urdu speakers. Hindi works came almost exclusively from the NWP. Of the writers, sixty-eight were Muslims, fifty-three Hindu and four European. The following subjects were covered: Female Education (25 entries), Morals (23), Science (17), History (11), Fiction (11), Poetry and Drama (9) and Language (8). Memorandum by M. Kempson on the working of Notification No. 791A of 20 August 1868 enclosed in M. Kempson, Director of Public Instruction NWP, to Secretary to Government NWP, 23 September 1874, NWP Educ, October 1874, IOR.

[2] For Nazir Ahmad, see Appendix IV. The three novels are described in Ralph Russell, 'The Modern Novel in Urdu', in T. W. Clark (ed.), *The Novel in India: Its Birth and Development* (London, 1970), pp. 117–22.

mission, 'abhors the notion of his son's associating with the sons of men far below him in social rank, the class to which the vast majority of students in Government schools and colleges belong.'[1] The Muslim service families, however, could not afford to cock a snook at government schools. Their fortunes depended on employment in government, and towards the end of the century jobs in government offices became increasingly hard to get for those who had not been to government schools. Nevertheless, they were slow to go to them. Syed Ahmed Khan traced this aloofness to four sources: 'to their political traditions, social customs, religious beliefs, and poverty'. Their poverty, he said, spoke for itself. Their social and political traditions made it difficult for them to associate in government schools with those whom they regarded with contempt. Their religious duties compelled them to make their boys learn the Koran before they learned anything else, and by the time they had done this it was usually too late to learn much more; their religious beliefs told them that western learning was incompatible with Islam. 'Their antipathy was carried so far indeed', he declared, 'that they began to look upon the study of English by a Musalman as little less than the embracing of Christianity...'[2] As a result, Syed Ahmed Khan claimed that UP Muslims were backward in going to government educational institutions.[3] He was quite right. Table IV records a steady growth in the number of Muslims in government colleges and schools. But it was not until the late 1860s that the proportion of Muslim students in government primary and secondary schools was as large as their proportion of the population, and it was not until the 1890s that they achieved this in higher education. Since most Muslims lived in the towns and were, as a community, traditionally well educated, these figures point to the reluctance of Muslims to enter government schools. Syed Ahmed's claim, however, is really substantiated

---

[1] *ECNWP&O*, p. 75.
[2] Evidence of Syed Ahmed Khan before the 1882 Education Commission, *ibid.*, p. 77.
[3] See, for instance, the evidence of Sir Syed Ahmed Khan before the Indian Education Commission quoted in *Report of the Indian Education Commission* (Calcutta, 1883), p. 298. Syed Ahmed Khan wrote to a friend: 'If the Muslims do not take to the system of education introduced by the British, they will not only remain a backward community, but will sink lower and lower until there will be no hope of recovery left to them...' Syed Ahmed Khan to Maulvi Tassaduq Husain, quoted in W. T. de Bary (ed.), *Sources of Indian Tradition* (New York, 1958), pp, 744–5.

TABLE IV. *Hindus and Muslims attending schools
and colleges in the UP, 1860/61–1920/21*

1860–1		1870–1		1880–1		1900–1		1920–1	
Hin-du	Mus-lim	Hin-du	Mus-lim	Hin-du	Mus-lim	Hin-du	Mus-lim	Hin-du	Mus-lim
Pupils in government colleges, per cent									
85.7	8.4	92	7.3	75.2	12.6	78	16.2	79.2	18.1
Pupils in government secondary, primary and special schools, per cent									
90	10	84.1	15.9	81	16.6	81.7	15.4	82.1	16.4
Pupils in private schools as a percentage of all pupils going to school									
—	—	—	—	17.7	43.7	13.2	39.7	3.8	16.5
Proportion of the provincial population, per cent									
—	—	—	—	86.3	13.4	85.5	14.1	85	14.3

N.B. The figures for 1860–1 and 1870–1 are for the North-West Provinces only.
Calculated from:
RDPI (NWP), 1860–1, Tables I, III and IIIA.
RDPI (NWP) 1870–1, Part II, Tables I, III, IIIA and IIIB.
RDPI (NWP&O), 1880–1, Subsidiary forms, 1, 2, 4 and 5.
RDPI (NWP&O), 1900–1, General Table IIIA.
RDPI(UP), 1920–1, General Table IIIA.

by the statistics of private education. In 1900 almost forty per cent of the Muslims who went to school still went to private schools which taught the traditional Islamic syllabus. Clearly Muslims found the process of adjustment to western education particularly hard.

2. BUREAUCRATIC REFORM

The reforms that were carried out in the administration of the UP in the nineteenth century have been described as a process in which government by contract gave way to government by bureaucracy.[1] When the Company assumed control of the various

---

[1] For an elaboration of this argument see C. A. Bayly, 'The Development of Political Organization in the Allahabad Locality, 1880–1925' (Unpublished DPhil thesis, Oxford, 1970), pp. 88–99.

provinces of the UP it merely took over the role of its predecessors as the supreme revenue-collecting agency, handing over the tasks of government to local men who were in a position to discharge them. So revenue collection was farmed out to zamindars who knew the capacity of the land and the tenancy. Zamindars themselves subcontracted their functions: they gave the job of keeping accounts to groups such as the Kayasths, the traditional patwaris or village accountants, and that of keeping order to groups such as the criminal tribe of Pasis, the traditional village watchmen. Government finance was managed by native banks while the general control of administration was given mainly to Muslims, Kayasths and Kashmiri Brahmins who had a monopoly of expertise in the law, in the complicated system of estate management and in Persian, the language of the bureaucracy. The system was inefficient. Government was kept ignorant of its subjects, was rarely able to interfere with its contractors and could not benefit from any increase in revenue. Connection and corruption rather than competence were the key to promotion in the service. Appointments were carefully guarded: 'it is difficult to conceive', wrote the Principal of Bareilly College, 'of a closer species of patronage...'[1] A man entered a government office as an unpaid apprentice to his father or to a family friend; promotion depended on the favour of the sheristadar and later the tahsildar and collector.[2] Men with examination certificates from government schools but without connections found that there was no ladder of success in the service of the Raj. They generally resigned. Official careers tended to be monopolised by particular families rather than open to talents.[3]

[1] Report from M. Kempson, principal of Bareilly College, 12 August 1861, enclosed in H. S. Reid, Director of Public Instruction, to Secretary, Government NWP, 24 August 1861, NWP GAD, August 1868, IOR. The object of the report was to point out that the existence of amla cliques prevented educated men from getting into government service and that this discouraged people from sending their sons to school.

[2] How a man might climb to power in a government office is well demonstrated by the career of Paunchkouree Khan in a contemporary exposé of mofussil abuses. Paunchkouree Khan, *The Revelations of an Orderly* (Benares, 1848).

[3] Frykenberg has shown how, between 1788 and 1848, in the Guntur district of Madras, Indian district officers, notably Maratha Brahmins under the leadership of the sheristadar, captured real control of district administration. R. E. Frykenberg, *Guntur District 1788–1848* (Oxford, 1965). No similar analysis exists for a district in the UP. Nevertheless, there can be no doubt that such cliques did exist. An investigation into the connections of native officials in 1864 revealed that such cliques were operating in Gorakhpur and

This system became increasingly unworkable during the nineteenth century. Finance was one problem. Faced with rising prices and imperial debts, government needed to raise more revenue to pay for defence, railways, irrigation and the administration of justice. Security was a second problem. Government, particularly after the Mutiny, wanted to keep a much closer watch on its subjects than its servants' *imperium in imperio* allowed. The employment of the educated was a third problem. The increasing number of boys who were passing through government schools had to be found jobs in government service. Opening the public services to the educated would both encourage more boys to attend government schools and make government more efficient. Hardinge saw this as early as 1844,[1] Wood's education despatch of 1854 made the same point,[2] and it was the constant refrain of the NWP director of public instruction.[3] Government, therefore, set about trying to transform the bureaucracy by introducing regular supervision, competitive recruitment and more rigid educational standards.

Government began to refashion the bureaucracy by replacing

Rohilkhand. 'The cliquedom in this district is great,' wrote the Collector of Gorakhpur. 'Goruckpore has long been a happy home for the amlah; they have acquired land in the most marvellous way, and every man has one or more relatives. The ties of connectioning ramify through all departments. How mohurrirs on Rs. 10 and 15 a month have honestly acquired so many acres of land...[one Brijlall Singh (on Rs. 25) had bought 1900 acres and Luchmun Pershad (on Rs. 10) 1300 acres] is difficult to understand.' C. R. Lindsay, Offg. Commissioner, Gorakhpur, to Secretary, Government NWP, 1 May 1865, NWP GAD, August 1868, IOR. Moreover, their existence is implicit in the picture painted by Paunchkouree Khan, Paunchkouree Khan, *Revelations, supra*, in the works and deeds of the more perceptive European officers, see John Rosselli, 'Theory and Practice in North India', *The Indian Economic and Social History Review*, VIII, No. 2 (June 1971), pp. 148–9, and in the difficulties that some landlords had in controlling their estates, see P. J. Musgrave, 'Landlords and Lords of the Land: Estate management and social control in Uttar Pradesh 1860–1920', *Modern Asian Studies*, VI, 3 (1972), especially pp. 268–70.

[1] Nurullah and Naik, *History of Education*, pp. 95–6.
[2] *Ibid.*, p. 212.
[3] In the early 1860s, the reports of the director of public instruction were full of quotations from inspectors' reports and passages written by the director saying that the best way to improve both the quality of the bureaucracy and attendance at government schools was to give pupils from these schools jobs in government service. See, for instance, *RDPI (NWP) 1861–2*, pp. 20, 32–3; *RDPI (NWP) 1862–3*, pp. 17–18, 23; *RDPI (NWP) 1863–4*, pp. 55–7. From 1863–4, the reports had a special section devoted to analysing the employment of students in the service of government.

41

Persian with Urdu in 1837; and from 1855 it started to keep 'records of connections' to prevent 'the formation in districts of cliques of relatives in public service'.[1] There were, however, two main ways in which reform was implemented. The first was by the introduction of caste or communal proportions in recruitment, the reasoning behind which is summed up by a government statement of 1869 that 'there can be no doubt that where any single element prevails [in a department of government] to the exclusion of all others it may be both necessary and advisable to introduce an admixture of other castes'.[2] In the 1860s, this principle was applied to the police establishment, and in 1873 to the subordinate revenue and judicial service. The second way was by the introduction of educational qualifications. From the 1860s, police officers had to pass a literacy test. From 1874, examinations were made compulsory for tahsildars; from 1882, every munsif had to pass the lower standard examination and could not expect promotion until he had passed the higher standard. From 1877, a pass in the middle class vernacular examination was made 'an absolute preliminary condition' of appointment to any office of Rs. 10 and above;[3] and from the 1890s all who wished to become tahsildars or naib tahsildars had to pass the University Entrance examination. All these changes attacked long-standing monopolies in the public service.

In the late 1890s, bureaucratic reform was given a new impetus by Sir Anthony Macdonnell.[4] Unlike most lieutenant-governors of the UP, Macdonnell did not spend the early part of his career in the province.[5] He served in Bengal which he found compared very

---

[1] Circular issued by the Board of Revenue with reference to district establishments. NWP&O GAD, April 1882, IOR.

[2] *NWP Police Administration Report, 1869–70*, p. 53B, quoted in Bayly, 'Political Organization in the Allahabad Locality', p. 57.

[3] E. White, Offg. Director of Public Instruction, NWP&O, to Chief Secretary, Government of NWP&O, 9 January 1885, NWP&O GAD, January 1885, IOR.

[4] See Appendix IV.

[5] Between 1880 and 1920, Lyall, Auckland Colvin, Crosthwaite, La Touche, Hewett, Meston and Butler all began and spent the majority of their ICS careers in the UP. Macdonnell, however, began and spent most of his service life in Bengal. This is important. Quite naturally, men were influenced by those places in which they gained their early impressions of India; Butler was a man of Oudh, Meston of Agra, La Touche had a soft spot for Aligarh and its M.A.-O. College. Macdonnell, however, brought from Bengal prejudices and policies which were very different from those of the UP men.

favourably with the UP: 'My impression is', he told the Viceroy, 'that the North-Western Provinces are in many respects behind Bengal. The Judicial and Revenue (Native) officials I have seen are distinctly inferior in education and class, while the Police are, I fear, even more corrupt.'[1] The province was a mess. He smelled corruption everywhere because many traditional administrative practices went unchecked. 'The truth is', he wrote to the Viceroy a little later, 'that as long as we employ natives bred up in the old ways, and advanced from a petty clerkship to responsible office, so long will the corrupt practices of the *Sherista* (office) cling to them.'[2] Wherever there were Muslims, in addition to corruption he scented disloyalty. Unlike his predecessors, who had treated Muslim landlords and government servants as pillars of British rule, Macdonnell developed a remarkable prejudice against them. He invariably described them as 'fanatical' and in time of Muslim agitation was sure that Muslim officers did not pull their weight.[3] Muslims were a danger to security and their strong position in government service had to be reduced as far as was politically expedient.[4]

To achieve this end Macdonnell used the methods that had been employed before. He applied the principle of fixing communal quotas for employment in government service to Muslims: they were appointed in the ratio of three to five Hindus – an arrangement which he thought very liberal. Then the Nagri resolution of 1900 imposed a new educational qualification. The script employed in government offices, the script in which all petitions had to be written and in which all proclamations were made, was Persian. This was not understood by the vast majority of the Hindu population which used the Nagri script. The resolution declared that petitions to government could now be presented in either script and that all government summonses and proclamations in the vernacular would be in both scripts. Macdonnell defended the

---

[1] Macdonnell to Elgin, 2 January 1896, Elgin Papers (68), IOL.
[2] Macdonnell to Elgin, 27 June 1896, Elgin Papers (68), IOL. For a description of the corrupt and unregenerate condition of government offices at the end of the century see Major-General Fendall Currie, *Below the Surface* (London, 1900), pp. 251–61. The author, however, admits that matters were better than they had been a generation before.
[3] Macdonnell to Curzon, 18 May 1900, Curzon Papers (201), IOL.
[4] It is possible that Macdonnell was strongly prejudiced against the Muslims as a result of his early service experience, much of which took place in Bihar at the height of the Wahabi crisis in the late 1860s and early 1870s.

43

measure on the grounds that it was no more than natural justice that the bulk of the people should be able to approach government in the script they knew.[1] However, the unadvertised but no less important purpose of the resolution was revealed in its third and last clause which announced the changes in the qualifications for office which its first two clauses had made necessary. It declared that 'no person shall be appointed, except in a purely English office, to any ministerial [clerical] appointment henceforward unless he can read and write both the Nagri and Persian characters fluently'.[2] No more effective method could have been devised of purging government offices of 'natives bred up in the old ways' and in preventing their future appointment. Moreover, because Muslims did not come across the Nagri script in the normal course of their education, and would not read it for pleasure, the resolution threatened them more than any other vested interest in government service.

The impact of such reforms on the bureaucracy was not always immediate. First, their effectiveness was limited by opposition

[1] Macdonnell to Curzon, 18 May 1900, Curzon Papers (201), IOL, and Minute by A. P. Macdonnell, October 1901, p. 40. MacDonnell Papers, Bodleian Library, Oxford.

[2] Clause (3) of paragraph four of Resolution No. 585/III-343C-68 of the NWP&O government dated 18 April 1900, NWP&O GAD, October 1900, IOR. The fate of clause (3) is interesting. On receiving it the Government of India decided that the rule was 'too strict, and that it may act with unnecessary harshness on certain classes of applicants for Government employment', and suggested the following amendment:

'No one shall be appointed, except in a purely English office, to any ministerial appointment after one year from the date of this Resolution unless he knows both Hindi and Urdu; and any one appointed in the interval who knows one of these languages, but not the other, shall be required to qualify in the language which he does not know within one year of his appointment.'

J. P. Hewett, Secretary to the Government of India, Home Department (Judicial), to the Chief Secretary to Government, NWP&O, 14 June 1900, published in the *Indian Daily Telegraph* of 1 July 1900 from the NWP&O Gazette of 30 June 1900, quoted in Hamid Ali Khan, *The Vernacular Controversy: An account and criticism of the Equalisation of Nagri and Urdu, as the character for the Court of the North-West Provinces and Oudh, under the Resolution No. 585/III-343C-68 of Sir A. P. MacDonnell, the Lieutenant-Governor, N.-W.P., and Chief Commissioner, Oudh, Dated 18th April 1900* (Lucknow, 1900), pp. 17–18. The UP government accepted the change and, on 26 June 1900, the Government of India's suggestion replaced the original clause (3). It is not clear, however, that this change made matters any easier for the Muslims. Indeed, the change in the requirement from Nagri and Persian script to Hindi and Urdu language could well have made matters more difficult for them.

from British officers. One lieutenant-governor felt that making educational qualifications necessary for public office was 'playing the game of the educated and forward classes among the natives...'.[1] The Board of Revenue constantly attacked such qualifications because they enabled the wrong kind of man to get into the service.[2] District officers tended to agree and anyway they often preferred to oblige a useful subordinate by appointing his son or relative rather than to appoint some unknown quantity from a government school.[3] In fact, only the education department really wanted educational qualifications to be the passport to office.[4] Secondly, attempts to break down caste and communal monopolies could be thwarted by a small number of applicants from the new groups government wished to encourage. For instance, in the last forty years of the nineteenth century, government tried to reduce the number of Muslims in the police, but because most of the qualified candidates continued to be Muslims, their share of posts in the force actually increased during the period from just over thirty-five per cent to nearly forty-four per cent.[5] But although there were factors militating against reform in the bureaucracy, in the long run, government did succeed in changing the caste and communal composition

[1] Sir A. C. Lyall to Sir Henry Maine, 19 December 1886, Lyall Papers (48), IOL.

[2] For instance, when, in 1880, the Board of Revenue was asked to put forward a specimen tahsildari examination, it first objected strongly to examinations as a means of selection, J. S. Mackintosh, Secretary to the Board of Revenue, NWP&O, to Secretary, Government of NWP&O, 27 January 1880; NWP&O GAD, March 1880, IOR. Then, when its objections were overruled, it recommended that 50 per cent should be allowed to the *viva voce* part of the exam (50 per cent was needed to qualify), that is that it should retain discretion. NWP&O GAD, June 1880, IOR.

[3] *RDPI (NWP) 1862–3*, p. 17.

[4] There was little doubt about the unwillingness of most government officers to appoint educated men. In 1885, the director of public instruction noticed that of 211 men recently appointed to posts in government, only 31 had the educational qualifications deemed necessary for the post. E. White, Offg. Director of Public Instruction, NWP&O, to Chief Secretary, Government of NWP&O, 9 January 1885, NWP&O GAD, January 1885, IOR.

[5] In 1865, out of a police force of 25,990, 9210 were Muslims, and in 1905, out of a force of 28,548, 11,416 were Muslims. The first figures are for NWP alone, the second include those for Oudh; the amalgamation of the NWP with Oudh in 1877 made little difference to the Muslim proportion. *NWP Police Administration Report, 1865*, pp. 78–9 and *UP Police Administration Report, 1905*, p. 23A. It should be noted that the police department was the only one in which Muslims did increase their number of appointments during the period.

TABLE V. *The position of communal and caste groupings in the subordinate judicial and executive services in the UP* 1857–1913*

	1857	%	1886–7	%	1913	%
TOTAL	316	100	521	100	378	100
MUSLIMS	202	63.9	235	45.1	131	34.7
HINDUS	76	24.1	262	50.3	227	60
Brahmins	—	—	89	17.1	80	21.2
Rajputs	—	—	37	7.2	19	5
Kayasths	—	—	107	20.6	73	19.3
Banias	—	—	25	4.8	38	10
Sudras	—	—	1	0.2	—	—
Other Hindus	—	—	3	0.4	17	4.5
SIKHS	—	—	2	0.4	—	—
OTHERS	38	12	22	4.2	20	5.3

Calculated from the *Agra Civil List, 1 January 1857* (Agra, 1857), pp. 52–8; *PSC 1886–7*, Report, *P.P.* 1888, XLVIII, pp. 55 and 59; and *PSC 1913*, Report, Appendix VIII, *P.P.* 1916, VII, p. 604.
* The figures for 1857 are for the North-West Provinces alone.

of its services. Table V looks at the highest ranks of the bureaucracy to which Indians could normally aspire and those that carried the greatest patronage. It shows that, between 1886–7 and 1913, the position of Muslims, and to a lesser extent Kayasths and Rajputs, deteriorated, while that of Brahmins, Banias and other Hindus improved. It also shows that from the Mutiny to 1913 Muslims lost their dominant position and Hindus gained a much larger share of appointments. What the table cannot show is the number of new families within these caste and communal categories which had entered government service. But it does suggest that by and large reforms in the bureaucracy were putting pressure on the traditional government service groups, a pressure which under Macdonnell was concentrated almost entirely on the Muslims.

3. ELECTIVE GOVERNMENT

Recurring financial crises were the main cause of the growth of local responsibility in government, particularly elective government. In the last forty years of the nineteenth century, government was under persistent and heavy financial pressure.[1] It was committed to large capital expenditure on public works both to develop the resources of the country and to increase financial and military security. But it had also to meet obligations outside India; the revenues of the subcontinent supported the India Office, civil service pensions, and a large British contingent in the Indian Army. The cost of these items, known as the 'home charges', became crippling when the rate of exchange, tied to the price of silver, began to work strongly against India.[2] So serious had this problem become by 1885 that the Finance Member of the Viceroy's Council urged him 'never for a moment let yourself lose sight of the exchange question. It is our incubus, and succubus, and every other form of unholy drain. In season and out of season urge on Her Majesty's Government that this is a danger to us *far greater* than the Cossack...'[3] Moreover, till the end of the century, this problem was exacerbated by frequent wars. Military costs rose during the period by fifty per cent.[4]

Since government could not rely on land revenue to raise more funds, it resorted to direct taxation. This form of taxation was not popular. 'The natives' language regarding direct taxation...', wrote a district officer, 'uses up all his abuse for his own and his wife's female relatives, and isn't fit for publication even in

---

[1] For the overall growth of government expenditure see C. N. Vakil, *Financial Developments in Modern India, 1860–1924* (Bombay, 1924), pp. 110–336, and for a general analysis of the financial problems which confronted government in the last forty years of the nineteenth century and the measures, particularly measures of decentralisation, which were undertaken to deal with them, see P. J. Thomas, *The Growth of Federal Finance in India: Being a Survey of India's Public Finances from 1833 to 1939* (Oxford, 1939), pp. 73–283.

[2] Before 1873, the price of silver and gold was kept stable at the legal ratio of 15½ to 1. But when the Latin Union in 1874 suspended the free coinage of silver and gave up the legal ratio, the link between the two metals was broken and silver began to slump rapidly. This had an immediate effect on the Indian government's finances. Its dues in England had to be paid in gold, but revenue was received in silver rupees and therefore when the exchange rate fell more rupees had to be paid. In 1873, the exchange value of the rupee was about 2s., by 1885, it had fallen to 1s. 6¼d. *Ibid.*, p. 211.

[3] Auckland Colvin, Finance Member, Government of India to Dufferin, 23 February 1885, Dufferin Papers (Reel 528), IOL.

[4] Fifty per cent represents the rise in expenditure of defence and foreign affairs (foreign affairs taking no more than five per cent of the total) between the average of the two years 1883/4, 1884/5, and 1895/6. Over the previous twenty-three years, costs under the same heads had risen by only fifteen per cent. 'Final Report of the Royal Commission on the Administration of the Expenditure of India', *P.P.* 1900, XXIX, pp. 598–9.

expurgated form'.[1] Income tax was the form principally favoured. Introduced for a brief spell after the Mutiny, it was brought back by Mayo but caused such discontent in the UP (the lieutenant-governor told him that 'frequently I am almost mobbed by the press of petitioners, I have never seen such discontent before'[2]) that his successor, the cautious Northbrook, withdrew it. By 1886, however, government was in such dire straits that it had to resuscitate the tax to pay for its frontier wars.

For financial salvation, government placed greater reliance on the development of local responsibility in province, district and town. In 1872 certain categories of expenditure were transferred from the central to the provincial government. In the quinquennial financial settlements which followed further categories of expenditure were transferred and the powers of the provincial government steadily grew. If the provincial government wished to spend more, it was empowered to raise local taxes. But this could be done only by the development of local self-government; more taxation needed more representation. 'Our ultimate economies', urged Auckland Colvin,[3] Finance Member of the Government of India in 1885, 'must be found in popularising our administrative system',[4] and three years later as lieutenant-governor of the UP he explained that 'our object...in popularising the machinery of Government is to consult native opinion'.[5] The aim of 'bringing forward our leading native gentlemen' and consulting them lay behind the previous lieutenant-governor's[6] demand in 1885 that the UP should be given a provincial council, and the same purpose inspired the reforms of 1892 which introduced something like an elective element to provincial councils generally.[7]

[1] Fendall Currie, *Below the Surface*, p. 91.
[2] Muir to Mayo, 24 January 1871, Mayo Papers (56), CUL.
[3] See Appendix IV.
[4] Auckland Colvin to Mackenzie Wallace, Private Secretary to the Viceroy, 22 December 1885, Dufferin Papers (Reel 529), IOL.
[5] Note by Auckland Colvin, 11 June 1889, Home Public A, August 1892, 237–52, NAI.
[6] Sir Alfred Comyn Lyall, see Appendix IV.
[7] In urging the UP's case to the Viceroy, Lyall made no bones about the administrative reasons for increasing the democratic element in government. He urged Dufferin that 'As a matter of policy, to give this Government a legislative Council would be, in my opinion, advantageous. What is wanted in these provinces is to bring forward out leading native gentlemen, and to encourage them to undertake some responsible share in the higher administration...Any step toward drawing out these classes and enlisting their aid in

Threats to Urdu-speaking elite

Because the provincial council was designed primarily as a sounding board for government policy, its powers were limited. It could discuss the budget and raise administrative questions but not vote on them. Because government designed the council as a stabilising force, it drew local magnates, particularly landlords, into the processes of government. Generally, it bolstered rather than undermined the influence of the Urdu-speaking elite, members of which occupied most of the elected and nominated seats between 1893 and 1909.[1]

The introduction of local representation and elections into the districts also had little immediate effect on the position of the Urdu-speaking elite. District committees grew up in the 1840s. They were set up to manage the local cesses, or additional percentage taxes on the land revenue, which government levied after it took over the landlords' duties to maintain local posts and roads. In 1871, these committees acquired a formal structure, and election was introduced in Ripon's reforms of 1883 by which district boards were set up with authority over such matters as education, public works and health. The powers of these boards were broader than those of their predecessors; nevertheless decisions continued to be made by the district officers. They were 'at best little more than petty departments of the district administration'[2] employed

support of local administration, will, to my mind, be a measure of Conservative policy, and I am also convinced that the establishment of a local council will be very popular generally...My own view is that the institution of a Council would soon prove itself to be very useful and would operate to strengthen, and to enlarge the basis of the local Government, which is at present somewhat too entirely official and personal.' Lyall to Dufferin, 12 July 1885, Lyall Papers (46), IOL. Soon after receiving this letter Dufferin took up the matter of Council reform more generally and made his case to the Secretary of State along similar lines. Anil Seal, *The Emergence of Indian Nationalism* (Cambridge, 1968), pp. 184–5.

[1] Of the seven Indians nominated to the council between 1893 and 1909, six (the Maharaja of Ajodhia, the Rajas of Jehangirabad and Mahmudabad, the Nawab of Pahasu, Nawab Yusuf Ali Khan and Syed Mahmud) were members of the Urdu-speaking elite. Of the twelve Indians elected to the council, at least nine (the Rajas of Kalakankar, Partabgarh and Awa, Seth Lacchman Das, Sundar Lal, Nihal Chand, Babu Sri Ram, Munshi Madho Lal and Pandit Bishambhar Nath) were members of the Urdu-speaking elite. It should, however, be noted that the council while reflecting the strength of the Urdu-speaking elite also reflected the divisions within it. For instance, at least three Urdu-speaking elite councillors, Sundar Lal, Nihal Chand and Kalakankar, were strong protagonists of Hindu revivalist causes.

[2] Hugh Tinker, *The Foundation of Local Self-Government in India, Pakistan and Burma* (London, 1968), p. 54.

to give acts of government the seal of public approval.¹ Moreover elections barely touched the authority of the landlords in the districts. The electorate was chosen by the district officer from local notables and his intention was that it should reflect the status quo. In addition the boards usually contained one or two large proprietors 'who', Auckland Colvin wrote, 'everywhere exercise great influence in them'.² In fact, elections to the district boards did not disturb the structure of power in the districts.

The effect of the introduction of elections into the towns on the position of the Urdu-speaking elite was very different, in part because the powers which non-official Indians had on municipal boards were much greater than on other elected bodies, and in part because the elective principal was much more of a reality. As urban administration grew in scope in the nineteenth century, and became concerned increasingly with making local improvements, government found that it made sense to involve local leaders more and more closely with its activities. From 1814, ward committees of non-officials were set up to manage the police rate. From 1837, savings from this rate were set aside for making improvements on the advice of local leaders. Acts of 1842 and 1850 made it possible to create municipal committees with power to levy octroi (a tax on commodities) and, with government sanction, to make regulations regarding public nuisances. Members of these municipal committees were nominated, but during the last forty years of the century they came mainly to be elected. The financial pressures of the period meant that more money for local improvements had to be raised locally. This, it was felt, could only be done safely if elected representatives had a hand in raising these larger sums of money and spending them. Nowhere was the introduction of elective government more closely associated with the financial crisis than in the towns. The abolition of the temporary income tax in 1865 was followed by the North-Western Provinces Municipalities Act of 1868, in which the elective principle was introduced as a more efficient method of 'drawing forth local resources and in ministering to local requirements'.³ Lord Mayo's ambitious plans

¹ For the development of district boards in the UP see *ibid.*, pp. 33, 52–4, 60.
² Note by Auckland Colvin, 11 June 1889, Home Public A, August 1892, 237–52, NAI.
³ *Report on the Administration of the N.-W. Provinces for the year 1868–69* [hereafter *NWP Administration Report*] (Allahabad, 1870), p. 50. Tinker suggests that the most important motive behind the Government of India

Map 4. The United Provinces: municipalities, 1911.

for public works and social services were hampered by another fiscal crisis. As a result, in 1873, the elective principle was developed further.[1] Lord Ripon, faced with the problem of revising these settlements, combined necessity with principle, and in 1883 municipal boards with elected majorities were established in one hundred towns of the North-West Provinces and Oudh with powers to tax, to make bye-laws and to spend money on a wide range of civic amenities.[2] Such changes in the urban political system severely threatened the position of established leaders. To understand the extent of the threat, it is necessary to examine the nature of the powers municipal boards had and to discover how far the elective system put them into the hands of new groups.

It has too often been assumed that non-official members of municipal boards had little real power.[3] Admittedly, government took care to curb the freedom of municipal boards, and the influence of their non-official members. 'The principle of self-government',

Resolution of August 1864, which led to the North-Western Provinces Municipalities Act of 1868, and the establishment of municipal institutions throughout British India, was imperial financial difficulties. Tinker, *Local Self-Government*, p. 36.

[1] The stimulus for this bout of financial decentralisation came first from the Public Works Department which was concerned about the financing of the construction and maintenance of roads. But the eventual result was the transfer from imperial to provincial management of the departments of jails, registration, police, education, printing, medical services and civil buildings, in addition to that of roads. *NWP Administration Report 1870–71*, pp. 13–19. Tinker adds that decentralisation was given an extra push by charges incurred in the Orissa famine of 1866. Tinker, *Local Self-Government*, p. 37.

[2] The origin of the 1883 Act lay in the plans of the Finance Department of the Government of India to deal with the problem of revising the provincial settlements. To extend financial devolution and to simplify the task of taxing at the local level, the Finance Member, Evelyn Baring, suggested that the elective principle should be put to work by letting municipalities and rural districts administer local receipts and charges. 'The credit is yours', Ripon told Baring, 'I feel convinced that you have laid the foundation of a system of municipal self-government which will confer increasing benefits upon India as time goes on.' Ripon to Baring, 7 October 1881, quoted in Seal, *Indian Nationalism*, p. 153.

[3] Indian politicians, thirsting for more power, were keen to give the impression that there was little power worth having in the towns. See, for instance, the evidence of Madan Mohan Malaviya and Sundar Lal before the Decentralisation Commission, *Royal Commission upon Decentralisation in India* [hereafter *DC*], *P.P.* 1908, XIV, pp. 749 and 754. Some historians have been of the same opinion. See, for instance, Tinker, *Local Self-Government* and John Lowell Hill, 'Congress and Representative Institutions in the United Provinces, 1886–1901' (Duke University doctoral thesis, 1966). Neither provides much evidence to support the view that local power was not valued.

it declared, 'is to be kept steadily in view, so far as may be compatible with public safety and happiness.'[1] The elected majority of non-officials could only block official suggestions[2] and if it wished to take the initiative, it was forced to win official approval for its proposals. The chairman was the main restricting factor. In six important municipalities he was appointed by the provincial government.[3] Other boards had the right to elect a non-official. But in practice they tended to choose an ex officio member, usually the district magistrate, either because they knew government preferred it, or because they felt that an official chairman was a guarantee of impartiality, or because it was difficult, particularly in small towns, to find suitable non-officials to take on a time-consuming task. So official chairmen became the rule. Since these men had much business besides running the boards, they tended to use them as rubber stamps. Nevertheless, non-officials did have some indirect influence. In theory, the municipal board, meeting in ordinary or special session, made policy. But, as municipal work grew and meetings became impossibly numerous, some of the business came to be left to subcommittees or individuals who thus had an important say in local affairs.[4] Admittedly the municipal commissioner's influence over policy was slight, but it was compensated for by the control he could exercise over the administration. This depended largely on the patronage he commanded in the municipal establishment. 'The social status conferred by a seat on the board' was, according to the District Magistrate of Ghazipur, 'as nothing to the power of patronage',[5] and the best job in the influential commissioner's gift was the post of secretary. The secretary himself had many jobs under his control, and he was the board's agent in everyday administration. His importance is

[1] *NWP Administration Report 1869–70*, p. 70.
[2] The UP municipal boards had the highest percentage of elected members in India. Tinker, *Local Self-Government*, p. 48, Table 3. In 1904–5, out of 1249 municipal commissioners, 155 were nominated by government and 155 were members ex officio, usually the local district magistrate or joint magistrate, a deputy Collector and a tahsildar. The rest were elected.
[3] The municipalities of Lucknow, Benares, Allahabad, Agra, Bareilly and Moradabad.
[4] Note on the 'Agency for the exercise of the executive powers of a municipal board', n.d. Municipal 1910, 1 E, UPS.
[5] H. R. Nevil, District Magistrate Ghazipur, to Commissioner Benares Division, 20 June 1911, and see also J. C. Fergusson, District Magistrate Saharanpur, to Commissioner Meerut Division, 29/30 August 1911, Home Education Municipal A, April 1914, 22–31, NAI.

Separatism among Indian Muslims

well illustrated by events in Fyzabad. As soon as the Kayasth, Balak Ram, leader of one faction, captured the chairmanship of the board from another faction, he replaced the secretary, Jehangir Shaw, with his own nominee, a Kayasth, Dwarka Prasad, and used the municipal servants as his private force.[1] At election time, his opponents were harassed by delays in the preparation of ward rolls,[2] and had to contend with 'the whole host of the municipal army' deployed against them by Balak Ram.[3] In Agra the secretary was said to ensure that 'old contractors enjoy as it were a hereditary right';[4] in Moradabad, administration was brought to a halt by clashes between old municipal employees and the placemen of a new secretary.[5] It was worth getting control of the municipal establishment with its opportunities for manipulation; and these the Municipalities' Acts of 1900 and 1916 tried, without complete success, to eliminate.[6]

Towards the end of the nineteenth century, the scope of urban administration grew rapidly. The few municipal amenities which had once been donated by rich patricians[7] were now, with many new ones, provided by the municipality. Since municipal em-

---

[1] Soon after Balak Ram gained the upper hand in Fyzabad, the municipal servants spent over a week decorating the city in honour of the maktab ceremony of his grandson for which they were rewarded with a holiday on the great day. *Leader* (Allahabad), 5 April 1911.

[2] *Leader* (Allahabad), 20 June 1913.

[3] *Leader* (Allahabad), 1 April 1915. In 1912, a *Leader* mofussil correspondent wrote of the Fyzabad municipal employees who had gone canvassing with Balak Ram; 'The subordinates generally think their loyalty consists only in their proving useful in elections and upon this their future prospects entirely depend.' *Leader* (Allahabad), 6 April 1912.

[4] *Nasim-i-Agra* (Agra), 7 December 1887, UPNNR 1887.

[5] *Jam-i-Jamshed* (Moradabad), 3 January 1892 and 27 March 1892, UPNNR 1892.

[6] *Report of Municipal Administration and Finances in the North-Western Provinces and Oudh 1900–01* [hereafter for reports up to 1900/1 *NWP&OMAR* and for reports from 1901/2 *UPMAR*] (Allahabad, 1902), p. 1; the report for 1914–15 declared that one of the aims of the imminent municipalities bill was to ensure that the municipal staff were 'secure in the tenure of their posts under varying party majorities'. *UPMAR*, 1914–15, p. 8.

[7] For instance many of the glories of Muttra were supplied by its great family of Seths: the temple of Dwarkadhis, the Jamuna Bagh Chhattris and the good repair of the property in the civil lines. F. S. Growse, *Mathura: A District Memoir* (North-Western Provinces' Government Press, 1874), Part I, pp. 91, 99, 103. The role of the large landowner in creating a market centre and adorning it is well illustrated in Fox's description of the activities of Rai Udai Baks Singh, Raja of Bilampur, in building up the Sahibganj area of 'Tezibazar'. Fox, *Zamindar to Ballot Box*, pp. 75–7.

ployees could be influenced, commissioners were able to affect many aspects of this expanding urban government. One of these was taxation. The amount of taxation levied in the towns was not small; already by 1895 it was as much as one-eighth of the provincial budget.[1] Until 1912, this revenue was mainly raised by indirect taxation, in particular by the octroi,[2] and as a committee of enquiry realised in 1909, the schedule of taxes could easily be arranged so as to benefit particular interests.[3] The octroi could, for instance, be used by one group of traders to attack another; or it could be used by other interests to bring pressure on traders during elections.[4] In large municipalities, the management of octroi encouraged a 'tendency to the development of hostility between the municipal bureau and the traders generally'.[5]

Influence on the municipal board could mean patronage in contracts. The large number of ambitious public works undertaken by the municipal board meant that it was usually the largest source of business in the town. In principle, members were not allowed to tender for contracts for works within their municipality, but this did not mean that their friends could not benefit: 'it is no uncommon thing', revealed one district officer, 'for members of the Finance and Works' Committees to apply for contracts under fictitious names, sanction these applications, obtain the contracts, sub-let them at a higher rate, and sit as a board of inspection on the skimped work of the sub-contractors, and pass them as satisfactory!'[6] Worse could happen. In 1911, a local correspondent

---

[1] In 1895–6, the provincial income was Rs. 324,87,000 and the total municipal income Rs. 52,92,780. *NWP Administration Report, 1895–6*, pp. 67 and 148.

[2] The octroi was the traditional trading impost of Hindustan. In 1884–5, it was levied in seventy-seven towns and raised sixteen and a third lakh rupees out of a total municipal taxation of nineteen and a half lakh rupees. In 1914–15, octroi, although levied in only thirty-seven towns still provided twenty-seven and a half lakhs out of a total of eighty-eight and two-thirds lakh rupees. *NWP&OMAR 1884–85*, Form 1 and *UPMAR 1914–15*, Abstract of Statement No. 11.

[3] *Enquiry into the subject of municipal taxation with special reference to the limitation of the octroi tax* (Allahabad, 1909), p. 16, Municipal 1908, 700 D, UPS.

[4] 'Octroi officials brought undue pressure to bear on the traders', the *Hindustani* complained when Babu Sri Ram beat Bishen Narain Dhar in the Lucknow municipal elections of 1892. *Hindustani* (Lucknow), 9 March 1892, UPNNR 1892.

[5] *Municipal taxation enquiry*, p. 16.

[6] Fendall Currie, *Below the Surface*, p. 100. Currie has two remarkable chapters entitled 'The Lokil Sluff Microbe' in which he attempts to reveal what really happened in municipal government.

reported that, in Fyzabad, where municipal affairs verged habitually on the picaresque:

Party spirit is active, of late certain municipal contracts of Porass, markets, sites etc.... were given by public auction by responsible members of the board to particular persons, their bid being the highest. In other instances the contracts were re-sold without any rhyme or reason in a very un-businesslike manner.[1]

In 1907, at least sixty contractors thought it worth their while to get onto the municipal boards of the province.

Naturally, municipal government affected most aspects of local life. One aspect was particularly affected: religion. The new-found influence of municipal commissioners over an increasing number of regulations, particularly concerning sanitation, bore increasingly on religious susceptibilities in the towns. Before the institution of the municipal board, control over such regulations had been in the hands of the Kotwal,[2] an autocrat whose word was law. Now they were in the hands of the chairman of the municipal board whose task, in principle, was to give effect to the wishes of the majority party. So, under the guise of the hygienic management of slaughter houses and kebab shops, Hindus could defend the cow and impose their standards on Muslims, while, for Muslims, the maintenance of their right to slaughter cows and eat them could become a symbol of their ability to protect their religion and culture.

Apart from power within the towns, a municipal commissionership could also be the route to added prestige, the honours list of the Raj, and what were potentially even greater powers beyond the municipality. It could help to make the unknown vakil known, get a man an honorary magistracy or higher honours such as a Rai or Khan Bahadurship, while from 1892 it was the first step to a seat in the provincial council.[3] Naturally, the power, the status and the training it offered in executive government were highly

---

[1] *Leader* (Allahabad), 5 April 1911.
[2] Very often the Kotwal was a Muslim. Under the Mughals he was firmly abjured to avoid all points of religious tension. Abu Fazl Allami, *Ain i Akbari*, trans. Colonel H. S. Jarrett, Vol. II (Calcutta 1891), Ain IV 'The Kotwal', pp. 41–3.
[3] Under the 1892 Councils Act, the possession of a municipal commissionership was one of the qualifications for prospective candidates. The more important municipalities of the UP were divided into two constituencies which each recommended a representative from their commissioners to the provincial council.

TABLE VI. *Guidelines for drawing up electoral qualifications laid down for individual towns under the Municipalities Act of 1883*

Municipalities		Municipalities with income p.a. (Rs.)	Those could vote who had		
			Income p.a.	House rating p.a.	Municipal tax p.a.
Class I	over	1,00,000	500	60	5
Class II	over	50,000	300	36	3
Class III	over	12,000	200	24	2
Class IV	under	12,000	120	12	1 8 annas

SOURCE: *NWP&OMAR 1884–5*, p. xvii.

valued.[1] The position was powerful because it combined deliberative and executive functions. This combination, together with the right to make and administer regulations, created wide openings for patronage, peculation and prejudice which meant that a seat on a municipal board brought both status and power worth having. For the commercial and professional men brought forward by British rule, as well as for some of the less fastidious established notables of urban society, a municipal commissionership was, in the late nineteenth century, the means by which they consolidated their local influence.

In the competition for places on the municipal board, wealth had the advantage. The 1883 Municipalities Act gave the vote to men of substance with incomes ranging from Rs. 120 to Rs. 500 or houses rated from Rs. 12 to Rs. 60. The qualifications for candidates were three times as high. Auckland Colvin, as lieutenant-governor, complained that the result of these regulations was that:

The class which was formerly regarded, if not as being altogether without value, at least as beneath contempt, has assumed a position corresponding

[1] When government set about circumscribing the executive functions of the municipal commissioner in preparing for the 1915/16 municipalities legislation, local politicians protested vigorously. Under the provisions of the draft legislation, commissioners were to deliberate and municipal servants, with greater security of tenure and under the control of a civil servant, were to administer. A committee on which they were represented warned that 'boards would strongly resent total exclusion from executive functions and control...' Typed draft of the Lucknow committee recommendations, 8 April 1914, Municipal 1915, 230 E, UPS.

to the policy of the present masters of the country, who give to education and commerce increasing consideration, and to mere social position or military skill less attention.

There could be no better proof, he continued, of the 'formidable weapon which the elective system in Municipalities has put into the hands of new men, than the hatred and fear with which the system is almost universally regarded by Muhammadans, and by the majority of Hindus of the conservative class...At present it serves only as another illustration of the levelling, and what seems to them revolutionary element, introduced into their society by British rule...'[1]

Colvin's assessment was rather too simple. First, there were 'new men', and men to various degrees established, to be found in most sections of society. There were 'new men' in the landed interest, Muslims and Hindus who had, through success in the law or government service in the early nineteenth century, been able to buy themselves landed estates.[2] On the other hand, there were some commercial men who had been landowners and men of influence in their localities for centuries,[3] and others whose local dominance had been marked before the Mutiny, had been reinforced by their loyalty at that time and had been strengthened further by the development of municipal self-government.[4] Nevertheless, by and large, those connected with the land were the Muslims and the Hindus of the 'conservative classes', or the Urdu-speaking elite, and the 'new men' were mainly Hindu money-lenders and traders to whom the municipal franchise gave a marked advantage. Second, the levelling effect which Colvin

[1] Note by Auckland Colvin, 11 June 1889, Home Public A, August 1892, 237–52, NAI.
[2] See Bernard S. Cohn, 'Structural Change in Indian Rural Society 1596–1885', in Frykenberg (ed.), *Land Control*, pp. 78–80.
[3] Members of the great Qanungo family of Meerut had 'from time immemorial ...been bankers and zamindars'. The family was founded by one Jograj in the reign of Aurangzeb. At the turn of the twentieth century, three Qanungoyan, Lala Murari Lal, Lala Banarsi, Das and Lala Jainti Parshad, sat on the Meerut municipal board. *DG Meerut*, IV, 93.
[4] The fortunes of Lala Nihal Chand's family are a good example. The joint estates of his father and uncle were increased in return for lending British officers money during the Mutiny. By the beginning of the twentieth century, they contained forty-one villages. Under Nihal Chand and his son, Lala Sukhbir Sinha, the family dominated the Muzaffarnagar municipal board where it provided vice-chairmen (up to 1910 the highest position that a non-official could normally expect to reach) and the district where it ran the Muzaffarnagar Zamindars' Association. *DG Muzaffarnagar*, III, 113.

lamented was not the same in all parts of the UP. The traditional influence of the commercial and landed groups varied from area to area of the province and so did the impact of economic changes. So to discover where pressure on the urban influence of the Urdu-speaking elite was most severe it is necessary to examine more closely who commanded wealth in the different municipalities of the province. Two indicators will be used. First the distribution of trade; this will indicate where traders were doing well. Second, the direction in which land was being transferred; this will provide an idea of the relative strength of landed and commercial wealth. After applying these criteria, two areas of the UP with certain distinctive characteristics emerge. The first, east UP and Oudh, contains the divisions of Benares, Gorakhpur, Lucknow and Fyzabad; the second, west UP and Doab, contains the divisions of Meerut, Agra, Rohilkhand and Allahabad.[1]

In east UP and Oudh, the coming of the railway[2] destroyed the wealth of the riverine trade marts. The massive commerce of Benares, once the entrepôt of Upper India, became largely local,[3] and the merchants of the city switched their capital from trade to banking.[4] Money-lending firms deserted Mirzapur, commercial capital of Bundelkhand, and Fyzabad, Ghazipur and Jaunpur were all in decline.[5] The railways, however, did develop two new trade centres: Gorakhpur, serving the area north of the Goghra river, and Lucknow, at the hub of a road and rail network serving Oudh. Everywhere else in east UP and Oudh, trade was not a major source of wealth. This area had more than half the province's

---

[1] The division is made along administrative boundaries. At first this might seem an unsophisticated method of delineating economic regions in the vast Gangetic plain where one area shades imperceptibly into the next. But land policy played an important part in determining concentrations of wealth. So initially the dividing line falls between those areas under Agra rent law and those under Oudh rent law and Permanent Settlement. But some of Benares division and all of Gorakhpur divison was under Agra rent law. These have also been included in east UP and Oudh largely because, rent legislation apart, they had more in common with it than with west UP and Doab.

[2] The broad-gauge reached Cawnpore in 1859, Saharanpur in 1869. During the 1870s and 1880s, the broad and medium gauge traversed every district and, by 1900, even the most remote areas of the province were connected with Calcutta, Delhi, the Punjab, Bombay and western India.

[3] *DG Benares*, XXVI, 58.

[4] *Ibid.*, 53–5, 120–2.

[5] *DG Mirzapur*, XXVII, 100; *DG Ghazipur*, XXIX, 65–9; *DG Jaunpur*, XXVIII, 67; *DG Fyzabad*, XLIII, 44.

population but a quarter of the trade.[1] Only twenty-five towns were big enough to earn municipal status and only nine per cent of the population lived in them. In some, population was declining,[2] in others, there was not enough trade to make the levying of octroi worthwhile.[3]

In west UP and Doab the picture was very different. The railway brought wealth to towns from Cawnpore to Saharanpur, from Chandpur to Shahjahanpur. Between 1873 and 1907, the rail-borne traffic in wheat, sugar and cotton of Chandausi, one of the great Rohilkhand wheat marts, grew eight times.[4] Between 1881 and 1901, Agra's rail-borne traffic rose by over forty-four per cent,[5] and between 1847 and 1907, Cawnpore's imports grew twenty times.[6] The west UP and Doab had less than half the province's population but nearly three-quarters of its trade.[7] Fifty-eight towns were municipalities and nearly fourteen per cent of the area's population lived in them. Cawnpore became the great entrepôt of northern India and the largest manufacturing centre in India outside the Presidency capitals. Hathras was the commercial centre of west UP. Agra and Khurja became important manufacturing centres, and most of the large towns developed native and joint-stock banking concerns.[8]

There was, however, a connection between regional variations in the growth of trade and the transfer of land. Many traders were

[1] See Table entitled 'The Distribution of Railway-borne Trade by Division in 1000s of maunds for the quinquennium 1911–16, and the percentage increase since the quinquennium, 1884–89', in Francis Robinson, 'Municipal Government and Muslim Separatism in the United Provinces, 1883 to 1916', *Modern Asian Studies*, VII, 3 (1973), p. 398.

[2] For instance, Khairabad, *DG Sitapur*, XL, 240 and Hardoi, *DG Hardoi*, XLI, 267.

[3] For instance, Unao, *DG Unao*, XXXVIII, 108; Lakhimpur, *DG Kheri*, XLII, 128; Hardoi, Sandila, *DG Hardoi*, XLI, 121; Balrampur, *DG Gonda*, XLIV, 132; Tanda, *DG Fyzabad*, XLIII, 133.

[4] *DG Moradabad*, XVI, 55–6.   [5] *DG Agra*, VIII, 52.

[6] Cawnpore's imports grew from 648,580 maunds in 1847 to 13,733,725 maunds in 1907. *DG Cawnpore*, XIX, 75.

[7] See Table entitled 'The Distribution of Railway-borne Trade...' in Francis Robinson, 'Muslim Separatism in the United Provinces', *Modern Asian Studies*, VII, 3 (1973), p. 398.

[8] Native banking firms, in particular, sprang up in all the large towns of this prosperous area: Cawnpore, Meerut, Agra, Bareilly, Moradabad, Muttra, Hathras and Allahabad. In east UP and Oudh only Benares and Lucknow had many banking institutions; Fyzabad and Gorakhpur were the only other towns in the east with native banks, but these were few in number and small in capital.

also money-lenders. After the Mutiny, money-lenders pursued property with vigour. The reduction in the revenue demand, the growth of irrigation, the development of communications, the expansion of trade, the rise in prices[1] and the more efficient enforcement of law all helped to make land worth having.[2] 'The money-lenders...are anxious to buy land, simply because they cannot find a better investment for their capital',[3] wrote one commentator. However, the money-lender whose capital came from trade was not the only man in the land market. He competed with the large landlords, and with the richer co-parceners who bought up the pattis of their poorer fellows. Some landowners were also money-lenders; Raja Rampal Singh of Kurri Sidhauli, head of the Naihasta Bais Rajputs, made nearly five lakhs a year out of money-lending.[4]

In east UP and Oudh, money-lenders added little to their holdings except in the vicinity of the large cities.[5] Around Lucknow

[1] Taking 1873 as 100, the index of retail prices of food-grains in India rose from 102 for the quinquennium 1870/75 to 188 for the quinquennium 1910/15. Calculated from Summary Table III, *Index Numbers of Indian Prices 1861–1931* (Department of Commercial Intelligence and Statistics India, Delhi, 1933).

[2] The author of the Mainpuri district gazetteer described the process. 'After the Mutiny, however, a totally new condition of things came into being. Hitherto the speculating classes had only looked upon land as a form of security and had no ambition to become landed proprietors themselves. The money-lender who intruded into a Thakur or Ahir village to oust the original owners of the land would have needed more than a common degree of courage, and the adventure was not generally considered to be worth the risk. But the reign of law and order which has prevailed since 1859, together with the great security of landed property and the high profits to be derived from it, have brought about a new era. The banking classes who before the Mutiny lent out their capital grudgingly and showed no desire to drive landlords to extremity, now compete with one another to accommodate the zamindar and encourage his extravagant habits, and by foreclosures and auctions in execution of decrees are steadily and persistently increasing their hold upon the land.' *DG Mainpuri*, x, 111.

[3] Reply of the editor of the *Hindustani* to the Raja of Bhinga's article in *Nineteenth Century* entitled 'Old Nobility of India'. The editor attempted to show that just because money-lenders were buying up landed estates it did not mean that they were hostile to the landed classes. *Hindustani* (Lucknow), 8 June 1892, UPNNR 1892.

[4] Booklet on Lucknow Division, Revenue and Agriculture 1918, 578, UPS. Another prominent taluqdari money-lender was Nawab Mirza Baqar Ali Khan of Shish Mahal. He was thought to be so miserly that he 'mentally never recovered having to give Rs. 500 to the Medical College'. *Ibid.*

[5] See Table entitled 'Landholding and gains in land of castes associated with trading and money-lending in the UP by District at the beginning of the twentieth century', in Francis Robinson, 'Muslim Separatism in the United Provinces', *Modern Asian Studies*, VII, 3 (1973), pp. 403–4.

and Benares traders were prominent in the land market. They did best in Unao which was between Lucknow and Cawnpore.[1] Outside these areas, they were, if anything, being dispossessed by landed magnates. In Oudh, taluqdars, well-protected by the law of primogeniture and by the Court of Wards, were successful in retaining their property and in buying zamindari and pattidari estates coming under the hammer.[2] In the permanently settled districts of Benares division, the landed communities were now holding their own.[3] In 1909, an observer in Ghazipur remarked that of 'late years the old families have managed to retain their ground with more success than in the first half of the nineteenth century, and the recent acquisitions on the part of the money-lenders have been relatively unimportant'. He stressed that 'probably the only class that has failed to improve has been that of the traders'.[4] In the remainder of Benares division and Gorakhpur, wealthy landowners such as Nawab Abdul Majid of Jaunpur did better than the money-lenders,[5] in others, the pattidari communities fought them off.[6] Therefore, land tended to circulate within the landed community rather than being transferred from Rajputs and Muslims to Banias and Khattris. In the land market of east UP and Oudh, the money-lender was no match for the landlord.

In west UP and Doab, the contrast is marked. Commercial men were doing well in land. Their holdings ranged from three per cent in Jalaun to twenty-five per cent in Saharanpur and forty-one per cent in Cawnpore. Where there were several large landed estates, for instance Agra division where the Sherwani family and the Rajas of Awa and Tirwa held large quantities of land, com-

---

[1] Cawnpore, although in the Doab, had considerable influence over the trans-Ganges district of Unao; many wealthy Cawnporis owned land there and it was an area favoured by political agitators from the city.

[2] *DG Kheri*, XLII, 72; *DG Bahraich*, XLV, 71; *DG Lucknow*, XXXVII, 88; *DG Unao*, XXXVIII, 83; *DG Rae Bareli*, XXXIX, 68 and *SR Sultanpur*, 1898, p. 10.

[3] This was in contrast to the first half of the nineteenth century in which the landed communities had had a hard time, large quantities of their property entering the hands of government servants, merchants and bankers. B. S. Cohn, 'The Initial British Impact on India: A Case Study of the Benares Region', *Journal of Asian Studies*, XIX, No. 4 (August 1960), pp. 418–31.

[4] *DG Ghazipur*, XXIX, 118–19.

[5] *DG Jaunpur*, XXVIII, 91, and for purchases made by Nawab Abdul Majid see the booklet on Benares division in Revenue and Agriculture 1918, 578, UPS.

[6] *DG Basti*, XXXII, 88; *DG Azamgarh*, XXXIII, 106, and in Gorakhpur and Mirzapur the money-lending groups had not done well enough to be regarded as proprietors, *DG Gorakhpur*, XXXI, 109; *DG Mirzapur*, XXVII, 129.

mercial men did less well: their holdings ranged from four per cent in Farrukhabad to nearly fourteen per cent in Agra.[1] The purchasers were mainly Banias, Khattris, Kalwars and Brahmins. 'Among castes Vaishyas now occupy the first place holding nearly a quarter of the district', wrote the settlement officer of Muzaffarnagar; 'the avidity with which these shrewd men of business have seized every opportunity of extending their possessions, is speaking testimony of the value of land as an investment.'[2] The dispossessed were mainly Muslims and Rajputs.[3] A commentator on Cawnpore noted that 'nothing is more striking in the general history of the district than the disappearance of the old estates, especially those of the Rajputs...'[4] While the settlement officer of Bulandshahr remarked that 'the money-lending class (Vaishyas, Khattris and Bohras) hold a large area, about 11 per cent of the whole district, and have gained distinctly since the last settlement. The principal losers, however, seem to have been Pathans, Saiyids and Kayasths, who have lost no doubt through debt and extravagance.'[5] In west UP and Doab, commercial men appear to have monopolised the property market.

In east UP and Oudh, just as the landed interest sustained its economic position against the trading and money-lending castes,

[1] See Table entitled 'Landholding and gains in land of castes associated with trading and money-lending...', in Francis Robinson 'Muslim Separatism in the United Provinces', *Modern Asian Studies*, VII, 3 (1973). pp. 403–4.

[2] *SR Muzaffarnagar*, 1921, p. 6. The landlord who was gaining land through money-lending was rare enough for the settlement officer of Muzaffarnagar to suggest that 'a notable exception is the influential family of Jansath town [an important Muslim family, the Jansath Syeds] of which the members are steadily increasing their wealth by money-lending'. *Ibid.*, p. 7.

[3] Kayasths too lost land in many districts and also groups restricted to particular areas such as the Gujars, but, in nearly every district, Rajputs and Muslims lost land. *DG Saharanpur*, II, 116 (Rajputs only); *DG Muzaffarnagar*, III, 117; *DG Meerut*, IV, 83–5; *DG Bulandshahr*, V, 92, 106; *DG Aligarh*, VI, 91–2; *DG Muttra*, VII, 121 (Muslims only); *DG Etawah*, XI (Rajputs only); *DG Mainpuri*, X, 104 (Rajputs only); *DG Agra*, VIII, 87 (Rajputs only); *DG Farrukhabad*, IX, 80 (Rajputs only); *DG Bijnor*, XIV, 108; *DG Budaun*, XV, 84; *DG Moradabad*, XVI, 88; *DG Pilibhit*, XVIII, 101; *DG Cawnpore*, XIX, 129–30; *DG Allahabad*, XXIII, 102; *DG Fatehpur*, XX, 101 (here Muslims lost and Rajputs gained); *DG Hamirpur*, XXII, 84 (Rajputs only); *DG Jalaun*, XXV, 70 (Rajputs only); *DG Jhansi*, XXIV, 116 (Rajputs only). Muslim holdings appear to remain stationary in Agra and Shahjahanpur, *DG Agra*, VIII, 87 and *DG Shahjahanpur*, XVII, 87. Muslims actually gained land overall in Saharanpur, Farrukhabad and Mainpuri, *DG Saharanpur*, II, 116; *DG Farrukhabad*, IX, 80 and *DG Mainpuri*, X, 104.

[4] *DG Cawnpore*, XIX, 130.

[5] *SR Bulandshahr*, 1919, p. 4.

so it succeeded in holding its political position. In 1907, landlords and zamindars held over thirty-nine per cent of municipal seats, men in the professions, landlord and government service held nearly forty-two per cent, and commercial men no more than seventeen per cent.[1] The landed interest was stronger than its percentage would suggest. Landlords had influence over those who worked on their estates as revenue agents or managers, while legal business concerning land supplied lawyers with the bulk of their work. This hidden strength is well illustrated by the way in which the Kayasth leader was hoisted into the chairmanship of the Fyzabad municipal board by the Rajas of Jehangirabad and Partabgarh.[2] It was a typical alliance within the Urdu-speaking elite with which most of the landed, service and professional men were connected. The links between the Kayasths, who occupied one quarter, and the Muslims, who held two-fifths of municipal board seats, appear to have been particularly strong.[3] Of course, they did not mean that these groups allied invariably; they had far too many conflicting interests and internal divisions for this. But, in practice, they often did work together in municipal politics. The campaign to make Balak Ram the Fyzabad chairman is one example. So also are the operations of the Kayasth Ram Garib, manager of the Gorakhpur Kayasth Trading and Banking Corporation, who employed a leading Muslim, Qazi Ferasat Husain, and, even when relations between Hindus and Muslims were deteriorating, backed him for the Gorakhpur board against the leader of the Agarwal community, Jugul Kishore.[4] In east UP and Oudh, links of caste, community, culture, and common interest tended to unite men around a landed interest in such a way that members of the Urdu-speaking elite managed to hold their own in the new conditions.

In west UP and Doab they did not. Traders and money-lenders

---

[1] Calculated from statements showing the occupation of members of Municipal Boards (incomplete; returns for Benares, Lucknow, Balrampur, Gonda, Nanpara and Sultanpur missing), Municipal 1908, 594 D, UPS.

[2] 'Muslim Separatism in the United Provinces', Francis Robinson, *Modern Asian Studies*, VII, 3 (1973), pp. 423–6; Harold A. Gould, 'Local Government Roots of Contemporary Indian Politics', *The Economic and Political Weekly*, 13 February 1971.

[3] Kayasths had 24.5 per cent and Muslims 38.4 per cent of seats on east UP and Oudh municipal boards. Calculated from 'Statement showing caste of members of Municipal Boards', Municipal 1908, 594 D, UPS.

[4] *Leader* (Allahabad), 25 March 1910. Qazi Ferasat Husain won and his victory was celebrated by Muslims and Kayasths with a party given by Ram Garib at which the Muslims' praises were sung by a Kayasth pleader in a qasida. *Ibid.*

were doing better than the landed classes both economically and
politically. Prima facie it might not seem so. Landlords held
thirty-eight per cent of the seats, men in service and the professions
twenty-eight per cent and men connected with commerce only
thirty-two per cent.[1] But, as in the case of landlords in the east, the
percentage disguised the extent of commercial influence. Ten per
cent of those described as landlords or zamindars were Banias
many of whom had acquired their property recently with the
proceeds of commerce and retained their connection with it. In
addition trading interests were often represented by the professions. In Allahabad, there was a close connection in municipal
politics between the Khattri banker Ram Charan Das and the
Brahmin lawyer Madan Mohan Malaviya.[2] In other towns lawyers
sometimes acted for caste organisations of low status. A district
magistrate of Meerut remarked that:

In nearly all big towns there are large and often powerful trade castes or
communities which though they have strong caste organisations and
frequently take concerted action over caste matters have no direct say in
municipal affairs as a section or caste. They may, and often do, control
elections in certain wards, but are hardly ever represented by members of
their own community and their social status would in some cases make
them unwelcome on the board.[3]

In east UP and Oudh, men in service and the professions usually
owed their living to landowners; in west UP and Doab, where the
dominant political alignment was based not on land but on commerce, which the Hindus largely monopolised, these professional
men were often in the pay of traders and money-lenders. Moreover,
this common interest was not confined to municipal politics. It was
often bolstered by a joint adherence to Hindu revivalism which
vigorously assailed the Urdu culture which landlords and professional men usually shared in the east. Commercial men were

[1] Calculated from statements showing the occupation of members of municipal
boards (incomplete; returns for Nagina, Najibabad, Fatehpur, Jhansi,
Lalitpur and Mau Ranipur missing), Municipal, 1908, 594 D, UPS.
[2] This was just the most striking example of a more general connection between
the Khattris and Malavi Brahmins of Allahabad's South Kotwali ward. For a
description of its workings see C. A. Bayly, 'Patrons and Politics in Northern
India', *Modern Asian Studies*, VII, 3 (1973), pp. 370–6.
[3] J. R. Pearson, District Magistrate, Meerut, to Commissioner, Meerut
Division, 16 August 1911, Home Education Municipal A, April 1914, 22–31,
NAI.

frequently behind revivalist activity: 'The Banias', observed a Commissioner of Meerut, 'have always been the caste from which new sects such as the Arya Samaj have been chiefly recruited...'[1] And they often worked together with their professional contacts to achieve revivalist ends.[2] In the towns of west UP and Doab, the power of the commercial connection compared very favourably with that of the landlords and Muslims, groups which supplied the bulk of the Urdu-speaking elite.

4. HINDU REVIVALISM

The first three threats to the position of the Urdu-speaking elite in northern India stemmed from government. The fourth threat, however, was derived from the reactions of Indian society to the problems created for it by British rule. From the early nineteenth century, Hindus in different parts of India had been attempting to re-interpret and reform their religion and reinforce and reform their society in the light of the new world of learning and the spirit with which they came into contact through the state education system and the activities of Christian missionaries. The movements inspired by these Hindus, and the reactions they stimulated among orthodox Hindus, were the basis of Hindu revivalism.

Major organisations representing various solutions to the intellectual and spiritual problems set by British rule developed in different places. They also developed at different times, a new organisation often being stimulated by contact with reforming influences from another part of India. The first was the Brahmo Samaj founded in Calcutta in 1828. It worked for social reform compounded with a theistic form of belief that in doctrine and practice owed much to Christianity. Its message was disseminated as the Brahmos, mainly Bengali government servants, spread from Calcutta into Bengal and upper India. In 1867, the sermons of the Samaj's leader, Keshub Chandra Sen, had a hand in inspiring the formation of Bombay city's Pratharna Samaj which pressed eagerly for social reform but, unlike its Bengal counterpart, was not pre-

---

[1] Extract from a fortnightly D-O report from H. C. A. Conybeare, Commissioner Meerut, 20 May 1907, Home Poll. D, August 1907, 4, NAI.

[2] In Allahabad, for example, Khattris and Malavi Brahmins, traders and lawyers, joined together in setting up the Bharti Bhawan library for propagating Hindi and Sanskrit literature, in founding a Hindu Samaj and in agitating for a Hindu Boarding House.

pared to move outside Hinduism. Both these societies contributed much to the formation of a third organisation, which had its greatest impact in the Punjab, the Arya Samaj. Founded by Dayananda Saraswati in 1875, it aimed at purging Hinduism of its degenerate forms by establishing virtually a new religion which was based on a reasoned interpretation of the Vedas and supported all those social reforms urged by western-educated Hindu society. Saraswati's teaching so impressed the leaders of the Theosophical Society founded in New York in 1875 that, with the aim of amalgamating their movement with the Arya Samaj, they came to India. The connection with the Samaj was brief and ended in tears. Nevertheless, the Theosophical Society's spirited defence of the glories of Hinduism and its work for the raising of the depressed caste received much support in south India where it made its base.[1]

The aims of these organisations and many minor ones, led by some of the most talented men of the time, were similar. All were concerned to come to terms with Christianity, though they differed as to how they should do so. All wished to pursue social reforms, but though they tended to agree about the abolition of sati, thagi, female infanticide and child marriage, they quarrelled over the abolition of caste.[2] All, however, were agreed that western education in English and the vernaculars should be provided for boys and girls, and many were interested in fostering the vernaculars as a means of reaching a much larger audience. The vigorous attack that these organisations directed against orthodox Hinduism did not go unanswered. From the beginning it called forth a vigorous response. The founding of the Brahmo Samaj was immediately countered by the foundation of a Dharma Sabha. The spread of the Arya Samaj and Theosophy inspired a variety of orthodox reactions which culminated in the formation of an all-India

---

[1] This paragraph is based on the accounts in J. N. Farquhar, *Modern Religious Movements in India* 1st Indian edn (Delhi, 1967) and C. N. Heimsath, *Indian Nationalism and Hindu Social Reform* (Princeton, 1964).

[2] Brahmo Samajists eschewed caste altogether. The Pratharna Samajists decided they could best reform Hinduism from within. The Arya Samajists, however, were bitterly divided over caste. Dayananda's vision was of a casteless society. But little was done to implement this by the Samaj. Indeed, had it attempted to do so it would have been divided. And, as the Samaj drew towards orthodox Hindu movements in the second and third decades of the twentieth century, the matter was dropped. J. Reid Graham, 'The Arya Samaj as a Reformation in Hinduism with special reference to caste' (Yale PhD dissertation, 1942).

orthodox defence association in 1902, the Bharat Dharma Mahamandal.[1] Caste Sabhas became the arenas of innumerable battles
over reform. At the beginning of the twentieth century the orthodox reaction gradually gathered way and its effectiveness is best
illustrated by the Hindu University movement which, in 1915,
brought Hindu revivalism one of its great achievements in the
foundation of Benares Hindu University.[2]

Clearly, Hindus in the nineteenth century were divided over
how they should react to the new influences from the west. The
organisations of Hindu revivalism had a wide variety of often
conflicting approaches to this problem. But all, whether concerned
with the reform or with the defence of orthodox Hinduism, contributed to a new and greater sense of Hindu identity. There was
in this new Hindu consciousness implicit opposition to western
influences and alien rule. Also implicit was opposition to those
elements of Islamic culture which had been absorbed from India's
Muslim invaders; and this was extended by the Arya Samaj in
particular to explicit opposition to the Muslims themselves. In
the first years of the Samaj this feelng was muted; in fact, Dayananda went so far as to invite Syedi Ahmed Khan together with
Keshub Chandra Sen, Babu Kanhya Lal, Munshi Indraman, Babu
Haris Chandra and Babu Navin Chandra Roy to a colloquium
in 1877 to discuss measures for joint action on behalf of social and
religious reform.[3] But this was as far as conciliation went, and in
the 1880s and 1890s Arya Samajists attacked the Muslims with
increasing intensity. The leader of the crusade, Pandit Lekh Ram,
condemned all forms of Islam, particularly the 'naturalist Muham-
medis' that is Syed Ahmed Khan's Aligarh movement, and
demanded that the Muslims should be either expelled from India
or converted to Aryanism.[4] The crusade lost vigour only after

---

[1] Farquhar, *Modern Religious Movements*, pp. 186–352 and Heimsath, *Indian Nationalism and Hindu Social Reform*, pp. 317–21.

[2] For the Hindu University Movement, see S. L. Dar and S. Somaskandan, *History of the Banaras Hindu University* (Banaras, 1966), especially pp. 1–315.

[3] This remarkable meeting took place at the Delhi Durbar of 1877. Graham, 'The Arya Samaj', p. 182.

[4] In 1892, Lekh Ram published his views in *Jehad or the Basis of Mohammedi Religion*. He was out to antagonise the Muslims. He appealed to them to become Aryas and listed Muslim atrocities from the invasions of Mahmud of Ghazni. He gave all forms of Islam short shrift. Eventually, one Muslim was provoked enough to kill him. K. W. Jones, 'The Arya Samaj in the Punjab: A Study of Social Reform and Religious Revivalism 1877–1902' (Berkeley PhD thesis, 1966), pp. 163–4.

Lekh Ram's assassination in 1897. Such antagonism towards the Muslims and Muslim culture resulted, almost inevitably, from the growth of a new sense of Hindu identity. It had important political implications.

The UP's part in this great nineteenth-century reassessment of Hindu culture and values was small. As befitted the heartland of Aryavarta, it was the home of the orthodox reaction. This did not mean that the province did not feel the effects of the reform movements; in the nineteenth century it was particularly influenced by the Brahmo and Arya Samajs.[1] The former was brought up-country by Bengali government servants and had great influence on the intellectual life of the cities of the east, especially Benares. The latter was effective in the west, an area in which the conditions were very similar to those in its homeland of the Punjab just over the border. These influences stimulated in particular development of the Hindi language and the demand for the introduction of the Nagri script in the courts and government offices, and in general an increased awareness of the need to protect Hindu interests. These developments were crucial. They strained the links which held together the Urdu-speaking elite. They must be examined more closely.

In the later nineteenth century, the campaigns to develop the Hindi language[2] and to establish the Nagri script as the court and

[1] For the influence of the Brahmo and Arya Samajs in the UP see Jurgen Lutt, *Hindu-Nationalismus in Uttar Prades 1867–1900* (Stuttgart, 1970), pp. 99–123.
[2] Because the campaign to develop the Hindi language and to establish the Nagri script in government had great influence on the politics of late-nineteenth-century UP, it is important that the precise differences between Hindi and Urdu should be made clear. In the UP there were three main languages: Bihari (spoken by twenty-one per cent), Eastern Hindi (spoken by thirty-one per cent), the principal dialects of which were Awadhi and Bagheli, and Western Hindi (spoken by forty-five per cent), the principal dialects of which were Bundeli, Kanauji, Braj and Urdu (Hindustani). The origins of Urdu are well described by Hoernle: 'It originated during the twelfth century in the country around Delhi, the centre of the Muhammadan power. In that spot the Braj dialect comes into contact with the Marwari and the Punjabi, and there, among the great camps (Urdu) of the Muhammadan soldiery in their intercourse with the surrounding population, a mixed language grew up, which as regards grammar is in the main Braj, though intermixed with Punjabi and Marwari forms, while, as regards vocabulary, it is partly indigenous and partly foreign (Persian and Arabic).' Dr Hoernle, *Introduction to the Grammar of Eastern Hindi* (London, 1880), quoted in *1881 Census, NWP&O*, p. 89. Thus, this dialect grew to become the vernacular of the Delhi region, the lingua franca of India's Muslim overlords, and later it came to challenge Persian as the language of literature. High Hindi did not evolve; it was

government character were the most vigorous aspects of Hindu revivalism.[1] For the Hindus and Muslims the question of language and script had a more than ordinary significance. For the Hindus, Hindi was a language purged of all the Arabic and Persian accretions which served to remind them of the Muslim supremacy while the Nagri script had a religious significance as the character which Brahmins used and in which Sanskrit was written. For the Muslims on the other hand, Hindi was gandi (dirty) and they thought it 'most degrading to learn it...'[2] Muslims did not particularly like Urdu, that is Hindi with Arabic and Persian accretions, but in the second half of the nineteenth century Urdu and the Persian script in which it was written became a symbol of Muslim power and influence, and they came to bestow upon it an almost religious significance. It was the dominant language. In 1837, it had been given a great fillip when it replaced Persian as the language of government. Indeed, so rapid was its growth that, by 1863, out of

deliberately invented. At the beginning of the nineteenth century, Lallu Ji Lal, under the direction of Dr Gilchrist of Fort William College, took a version in Braj of the tenth book of the Bhagwat Purana and rewrote it in the dialect of Urdu using no words of foreign origin. This is generally regarded as the beginning of High Hindi. Hence, Urdu and High Hindi are really the same language, or the same dialect of one language; they have an identical grammar and differ merely in the vocabulary, the former using as many foreign words, the latter as few as possible. Urdu was usually written in the Persian script, Hindi in Nagri, the script of the holy Sanskrit literature. *1881 Census NWP&O*, I, pp. 88–9; *1901 Census, NWP&O*, I, pp. 174–94; G. A. Grierson, *Linguistic Survey of India*, Vol. I. 1 (Calcutta, 1927), pp. 158–68; Vol. VI (Calcutta, 1904); Vol. IX, Part I (Calcutta, 1916), pp. 1–605; Aziz Ahmad, *Islamic Culture*, pp. 239–59; J. H. Garcin de Tassy, *Histoire de la Littérature Hindouie et Hindoustanie*, 2nd edn (New York, 1870), reprinted, Burt Franklin: Research and Source Works Series 326, Preface pp. ii–iv.

[1] For the development of the Hindi–Urdu conflict and the campaign for Hindi and the establishment of Nagri in government as an aspect of Hindu revivalism, see Jurgen Lutt, *Hindu-Nationalismus*, especially pp. 37–52; Kerrin Dittmer, 'Muslims in the United Provinces' and Jurgen Lutt, 'The Hindi-movement and the origin of a cultural nationalism in Uttar Pradesh', both unpublished papers given before the Second European Conference on Modern South Asian Studies, Copenhagen, July 1970; R. S. McGregor, 'Bengal and the Development of Hindi, 1850–1880', *South Asian Review*, v, 2 (1972); Aziz Ahmad, *Islamic Culture*, pp. 259–62; Ram Gopal, *Indian Muslims: A Political History (1858–1947)* (Bombay, 1959), pp. 30–43; Anil Seal, *Indian Nationalism*, pp. 325–6; Garcin de Tassy, *La Langue et la Littérature Hindoustanies de 1850 à 1869: Discours d'Ouverture du Cours d'Hindoustani*, 2nd edn (Paris, 1874), pp. 271–3, 322–8, 379–80, 421–6, 453–64, and for the years after 1870 much can be found in Garcin de Tassy's annual review, *La Langue et la Littérature Hindoustanies*.

[2] Evidence of Babu Siva Prasad before the Education Commission, *ECNWP&O*, p. 314.

twenty-three newspapers published in the province, seventeen were in Urdu and only four in Hindi,[1] and a Hindu revivalist school inspector was compelled to admit that 'Urdu is now becoming our mother tongue...'[2]

Many Hindus did not approve of this. By the 1860s, they were beginning to find that the strong position of the Persian script, and the boost it gave to Urdu, interfered with their interests. It held back the growth of primary education. Primary school teachers tended to teach the vernacular of the majority, and as most of the rural population spoke some dialect of Hindi they learnt to read and write in Nagri. Inevitably villagers found that what they learned at school was of little use in dealing with the courts. So witness after witness before the 1882 Education Commission echoed the point made by a Benares Professor of Mathematics that:

The adoption of the Persian character in court documents and orders hinders...the spread of primary education among the people. They see that practically Hindi is of little use to them, and that Urdu is so hard to acquire that they generally do not attempt it.[3]

The Persian script also gave Muslims the advantage in entering government service and enriching themselves. Government service was the goal of many who went to school and much of the drive for attacks on Persian came from Hindus who wished to break down the closely-guarded patronage in government jobs of the Urdu-speaking elite. The attitude of such civil service hopefuls was made quite clear by the militant pro-Hindi paper, the *Kavi Vachan Sudha*: 'The Muslims', it said, 'it is true might suffer by the change [from Persian to Nagri script] but they are only a small portion of the community and the interests of the few must always yield to the many.'[4] Generally, the supremacy of the Persian script was felt to threaten the very existence of Hindi, and Hindus were not slow to equate the fate of the Hindi language with that of Hindu nationality. 'It is not...too much to conjecture', a Hindu wrote in 1868, 'that with the

[1] *NWP Administration Report 1862–3*, p. 91.
[2] This was written by Babu Siva Prasad in his Preface to his *Ittihas Tirmirnasakh* (A History of India in Hindi) published on 1 January 1864 and quoted in *RDPI (NWP) 1863–4*, p. 7, footnote.
[3] Evidence of Umesh Chandra Sanyal, Professor of Mathematics, Benares College, before the Education Commission, *ECNWP&O*, p. 354.
[4] *Kavi Vachan Sudha* (Benares), 8 August 1873, UPNNR, 1873.

extinction of Hindi, the death-knell of Hindu nationality will
begin to ring.'[1]

The development of Hindi owed its real impetus to the emphasis laid on teaching in the vernacular by the NWP education
department. In the 1840s and 1850s, opinion was divided in the
department over whether the language should be encouraged as
well as, or even in place of, Urdu.[2] But, as a result of two events,
matters took a turn in favour of Hindi. The first was the appointment of Siva Prasad[3] as joint inspector of the Benares Circle in
1854. Siva Prasad's aim was to encourage people to write a de-
persianised Urdu in the Nagri script. This was not because he
necessarily preferred the language in this form – he liked Urdu well
enough to write poetry in it – but because it was the best means
of spreading education. Until his retirement in 1878, he diligently
promoted his cause within the education department. Outside it
he endeavoured to create a favourable climate of opinion towards
Hindi through the columns of his newspaper, the *Benares Akhbar*.
The second event was the appointment in 1862 of Kempson[4]

[1] 'Vernacular Education in India – No. 2', paper by Deena Nauth Gungooly
of Etawah dated 2 February 1868 (it was written to set out the danger presented to Hindi in the NWP British Indian Association's suggestion in 1867
that a Vernacular University using Urdu should be established in northern
India), enclosed in M. Kempson, Director of Public Instruction NWP, to
Secretary to Government NWP, 24 July 1868, NWP GAD, December 1868,
IOR.
[2] For instance, in 1845, the superintendent of vernacular schools wrote saying
what a desirable effect the abolition of Urdu in government would have on
teaching in vernacular schools. C. Fink, Superintendent Vernacular Schools,
to J. Middleton, Secretary Local Committee of Public Instruction, Agra,
30 April 1845, *RDPI (NWP) 1844–5*, Appendix I, p. lxii. Ten years later, the
first Director of Public Instruction recommended that in colleges every
English student should learn just Urdu and that the study of Hindi should be
abolished everywhere in the NWP except Benares. *RDPI (NWP) 1854–5*,
p. 21.   [3] See Appendix IV.
[4] M. Kempson entered the Education Department in 1858 when he was
appointed principal of Bareilly College; 1861, Inspector of the Agra Circle;
1862–78, Director of Public Instruction. His career spans the period in which
primary and secondary education was successfully established on a large scale
in the NWP. He was opposed to Urdu as a medium of instruction and to all
vestiges of orientalism. The tone of all his writing suggests that he had a poor
opinion of the Muslims, and of Muslim learning he said 'apart from theology,
it is a thing of the past'. A memorandum on Muslim education enclosed in
M. Kempson, Director of Public Instruction NWP, to Secretary to Government NWP, 18 August 1873, NWP Educ, November 1873, IOR. He translated Siva Prasad's History of India into English; the translated book caused
such resentment among the Muslims that eventually it had to be withdrawn
from government schools.

as director of public instruction, a post which he held till his retirement in 1878. Kempson saw eye to eye with Siva Prasad, and made much of him. Frequently he quoted his views in his reports and correspondence with government, lauding him as a man 'whose fitness and ability to speak on national topics are so well recognised that, supposing a Parliament existed, he would undoubtedly represent his native city'.[1] Kempson also believed that Hindi was the vernacular to be encouraged and did his best to promote it. Urdu and its literature, he said, 'are undoubtedly Mahomedan creations'. Most Hindus 'will generally avoid it on principle and to the rest it will be...unlikely to be either popular or intelligible'.[2] The encouragement such men gave to Hindi found support outside the education department. In the early 1860s, Lakshmi Singh, a tahsildar of Etawah, began to make translations from English and Persian into a de-persianised Urdu in the Nagri script, and Babu Navin Chandra Roy, a Brahmo Samaj missionary, used a similar form to get his message across in the Punjab.

At the same time, the problem of which vernacular should be favoured by government began to be discussed in the works of philologists[3] and in the debating clubs of the educated.[4] In the late 1860s, the matter was quickly brought to a head by the proposal of the British Indian Association of the NWP, of which Syed Ahmed Khan was the secretary, that a 'Vernacular University' using Urdu should be founded in Upper India, and that series of works for university courses, which the Aligarh Scientific Society might translate into Urdu, should be recommended by government. The government rejected the university proposal but asked several institutions and people for their views on the subject of translation, and for the first time many UP men were forced to think hard about their vernacular languages. Syed Ahmed had set a cat among his pigeons. Once Hindus began to think about it, many decided

---

[1] M. Kempson, Director of Public Instruction NWP, to Secretary to Government NWP, 24 July 1868, NWP GAD, December 1868, IOR. [2] *Ibid.*

[3] Muttra Prasad discussed the question in the preface to his *Trilingual Dictionary* published in 1865, scholars such as M. J. Beames and W. N. Lees engaged in almost continual debate on the subject, while Garcin de Tassy's works amount to one long defence of Urdu. Growing European interest in Sanskrit acted as a stimulus to the debate in India.

[4] See, for instance, the lecture given by Pandit Badri Lal in the Educational Section of the Benares Institute on 'The system of teaching Hindi in the Government College and the advantages to be derived from the study of the same' in *The Transactions of the Benares Institute, for the session 1864–65* (Benares, 1865).

that Hindi rather than Urdu was their real vernacular. The Allah-abad Institute began to keep its proceedings in Nagri instead of Persian. The Maharaja of Benares asked the government if he could make a similar change in the offices of his estate.[1] Raja Jai Kishen Das, the acting secretary of the Aligarh Scientific Society, and one of Syed Ahmed Khan's closest friends, began to urge the cause of Hindi and the Nagri script in every possible way: he pressed for the abolition of Urdu in government offices; he placed a pandit at the service of the Aligarh High School; and he campaigned for the establishment of a Sanskrit University.[2] Eventually he resigned from the Aligarh Scientific Society on the grounds that he was about to be stationed at Allahabad, but this did not prevent him from becoming secretary of the Indian Sanskrit Association at Hathras, a few miles from Aligarh. When the Hindi–Nagri standard was raised, many of the Urdu-speaking elite fell in behind it.

The controversy culminated in a memorial to the government asking for the introduction of Nagri as a court script. The government was not moved and the agitation died down. It did not die away. Hopes that government's intransigence would weaken were sustained when, in 1873 in the CP and in 1881 in Bihar, government replaced the Persian script with Nagri. In fact, throughout the period up to 1900, there was a continuous undercurrent of concern that occasionally rose to the surface in protests to the government. Benares was the main source. Here the Maharaja encouraged and supported the propagation of Hindi.[3] Here lived Siva Prasad, and here from the 1870s, mainly through the efforts of Haris Chandra[4]

---

[1] Statement of native newspapers, 12 February 1870, NWP GAD, April 1870, IOR.

[2] *Aligarh Institute Gazette* (Aligarh), 23 April 1869, 30 April 1869; *Muir Gazette* (Meerut), 7 May 1869, UPNNR 1869; *Oudh Akhbar* (Lucknow), 19 December 1873, UPNNR 1873.

[3] The Maharaja was closely involved in work in support of Hindi and Sanskrit. In 1868, he had much to do with the Benares memorandum to government on the future of the Sanskrit College; in 1869, he put forward a plan for the translation of vernacular books; in 1871, he was involved in the preparation of a Nagri petition to the lieutenant-governor. It appears that there may have been some close connection between him and Siva Prasad dating from the latter's office as Mir Munshi of the Benares Agency.

[4] Haris Chandra (1850–85). Born in a wealthy Agarwal family and educated at Queen's College, Benares, his cultural range was broad including Persian, Urdu, Sanskrit and Bengali. For more details on the life of Haris Chandra and an assessment of his importance, see Jurgen Lutt, *Hindu-Nationalismus*, pp. 65–88.

and his circle, Hindi began to acquire a body of literature and standard form as a language. Much of this activity involved Hindi translations of Bengali works, and in it Haris Chandra and his followers were supported by the Bengalis themselves.[1] A second source of activity, which began to make an impression towards the end of the century, was the Arya Samaj. The Arya Samaj, a vigorous proselytising movement, wanted to make contact with the masses. It found that it could do so only by using the Hindi language and the Nagri script. Much of the spread of Hindi in west UP was owing to the work of the Samaj.[2] Sustained by these two sources, there was a string of newspapers, Haris Chandra's *Kavi Vachan Sudha*, Balkrishna Bhatta's *Hindi Pradip*, and *Bharat Jiwan, Bharat Bandhu, Hindustan*, and many others which, by constantly sniping at government and at Urdu, sedulously maintained popular interest in the script and language issues.

As the movement developed, it became concerned less with the introduction of Nagri than with the more general advancement of Hindi and Hindu interests. In the 1880s, Siva Prasad protested at this change:

It was in 1868 that I wrote a memorandum on court characters in the Upper Provinces... My object was to speak only about characters. I would have won the battle, though I had all the Muhammadan official world arrayed against me; but I have now to cry out 'Save me from my friends![']
My friends, my countrymen, the foolish Hindus, made a question of Hindi and Urdu language, and left the question of characters quite aside. They proclaimed a crusade against all the Persian words which have now become our household words and which are now used by all our women, children, and the rustic population, as well as the urban.[3]

He was hopeful if he imagined that the Nagri question could be kept distinct from Hindi. Nevertheless, he touched upon what was to be an increasingly important development in the 1880s and 1890s: the tendency of the Hindi movement to become a communal crusade against the Urdu language and Muslims in government service. 'If Urdu cease to be the court language,' Haris Chandra prophesied, 'the Mussalmans will not easily secure the numerous offices of Government, such as peshkarships, sarishtadarships, muharrirships, etc., of which at present they have a

---

[1] R. S. McGregor, 'Bengal and the Development of Hindi, 1850–1880', *South Asian Review*, V, 2 (1972), pp. 137–46.
[2] *Ibid.*, pp. 144–5.
[3] Evidence of Siva Prasad before the Education Commission, *ECNWP&O*, p. 327.

sort of monopoly.'[1] Such was the attitude of many. This development was important. The more the matter was made one of
community, the more the links that connected Hindu and Muslim
members of the Urdu-speaking elite were weakened, and the
Muslims began to stand apart as the defenders of Urdu and the
Persian script. Evidence given before the Education Commission
illustrates this. The Muslims supported Urdu, the Hindus, Hindi.
Even men such as the Raja of Bhinga, very much a representative
of the Urdu-speaking elite, stressed that Hindi was the real
vernacular and urged that Nagri should become the Court script.[2]
And Hindus and Muslims divided increasingly in this way, a
process that was further stimulated by the Nagri petition to
Macdonnell in 1898 followed by the promulgation of the Nagri
resolution in 1900. Thus the language and script questions made
their contribution to the growth of communal politics.

There is another important point to note. With increasing
government support for Hindi and the Nagri script, and the
toppling of Urdu and the Persian script from their supreme position in the government machine, there also came the end of the
dominance of Urdu culture in Hindustan. Throughout the nineteenth century, Persian and Urdu had remained the favoured forms
of cultural expression, but by the 1880s the work of the education
department both in pushing education into the largely Hindu
countryside and in fostering the development of a Hindi literature,
combined with the efforts of the Hindu revivalists, had created
a Hindi literature and culture which competed with the Urdu
culture of the towns. Tables VII and VIII show that, by 1910, it
was beginning to overwhelm its rival. By 1915, there was a large
enough Hindi reading public for north India's leading novelist,
the Kayasth, Prem Chand, to feel it worth his while to change
from writing in Urdu to writing in Hindi.[3] The declining position
of Urdu was indicative of the declining position of the non-Hindu
revivalist elements of the Urdu-speaking elite, particularly the
Muslims, in the UP as a whole.

---

[1] Statement of Babu Haris Chandra for the Education Commission,
ECNWP&O, p. 100.
[2] Evidence of the Raja of Bhinga before the Education Commission,
ECNWP&O, p. 347.
[3] Madan Gopal, *Munshi Premchand: A Literary Biography* (London, 1964),
pp. 99–113. By the early 1920s, Prem Chand found it difficult even to find
publishers for his Urdu books. *Ibid.*, pp. 232–4.

TABLE VII. *Number of books published in the UP in the major languages, 1881–1910*

Total of decade 1881–90	Total of decade 1891–1900	1901	1902	1903	1904	1905	1906	1907	1908	1909	1910	Total of decade 1901–10
					English							
531	722	87	85	70	95	82	145	89	89	188	188	923
					Urdu							
4380	4218	488	434	484	451	386	417	248	303	318	435	3547
					Hindi							
2793	3186	429	405	412	567	517	640	552	565	811	807	5063
					Sanskrit							
462	517	63	83	75	88	88	109	81	76	97	79	730
					Arabic							
414	—	23	19	19	21	27	24	11	21	11	20	196
					Persian							
1022	615	63	38	44	36	32	23	8	15	25	20	281

SOURCE: *1911 Census, UP*, Part I, Subsidiary Table X, p. 277.

The campaign for Hindi and the Nagri script was merely the most prominent aspect of a growing awareness of the need to protect and promote Hindu interests. At the same time, a number of other actions were being taken to advance more specifically religious interests. This was evident in the Hindu reaction to the massive increase in government activity that accompanied the growth of local government. For instance, when, in 1890, the Hindu-dominated municipal board of Benares attempted to demolish an ancient Hindu temple in order to erect a waterworks pumping station, there was a riot.[1] But such vigorous assertion of Hindu interests was much more evident in dealings with the Muslims. In the countryside this took the form of the cow-protection movement. Hindus had always objected to Muslims sacrificing cows on their annual festival of the Baqr Id.[2] In the

[1] NWP&O GAD, September 1891, IOR.
[2] The festival of Baqr Id commemorates Abraham's sacrifice. It is called among other names, Baqr Id, the Bull Id, Baqarah Id, the cow festival which is often corrupted to Baqri Id or goat festival. H. Yule and A. C. Burnell, *Hobson-Jobson*, new edn, W. Crooke ed. (London, 1903), p. 36. At this festival, it is

77

TABLE VIII. *Number and circulation of newspapers in the UP by language, 1891–1911*

Language	1891		1901		1911	
	No.	Circ.	No.	Circ.	No.	Circ.
English	—	—	34	19,558	56	57,482
Hindi	24	8,002	34	17,419	86	77,731
Urdu	68	16,256	69	23,757	116	76,608
Others	7	3,491	5	1,850	20	13,925
Total	101	28,759	142	62,584	278	225,746

SOURCE: *1911 Census, UP*, Part I, Subsidiary Table IX, pp. 275–6.

1880s, on the initiative of Arya Samajists, these objections began to take positive form. In 1882, Swami Dayananda formed the Gaurakshini Sabha or cow-protection association, and published *Gokarunanidhi*, a book which aimed to rouse the Hindus against the beef-eating Christians and Muslims and to encourage them to petition government to stop cow-killing.[1] In 1886, the agitation spread to the UP, when the High Court declared that a cow was not an 'object' within the meaning of section 295 of the Penal Code, and ruled that Muslims who slaughtered them could not be held to have violated the legal provisions against incitement to religious violence. In Allahabad alone, three cow-protection organisations were set up, and from them lecturers fanned out through east UP and west Bihar setting up an extensive rural organisation. The movement reached its climax in 1893 when vicious rioting broke out in these areas in which Muslim villagers were massacred by lawless bands of Hindus.

But it was in the towns that this drive to protect Hindu interests

obligatory for every free Muslim who can afford it to buy a sacrificial victim, a sheep for one person, cattle or a camel for one to seven persons. H. A. R. Gibb and J. H. Kramers, *Shorter Encyclopaedia of Islam* (London, 1961), p. 156. Under the Nawabi, the Baqr Id was a time when the King bestowed honours and received homage. For his subjects it was a time of rejoicing and for the giving and receiving of presents. In the 1820s, the Lucknow Id celebrations were said to be the most magnificent in India. For an excellent description of them, see Mrs Meer Hassan Ali, *Observations on the Mussulmauns of India*, 2nd edn, W. Crooke ed. (Oxford, 1917), pp. 140–52.

[1] Farquhar, *Modern Religious Movements*, p. 111.

from Muslim interference had its biggest impact. Nearly two-fifths of the urban population was Muslim. In the towns Muslim influence was greatest. But here also were concentrated supporters of militantly anti-Muslim revivalist groups. Onto this communal tinder the municipal legislation of the 1880s showered sparks by placing wide powers in the hands of Indians. Almost all of these powers could be turned to communal advantage; and some – for instance, those to make regulations concerning kebab stalls, butchers' shops and slaughter houses – could hardly fail to affect religious sensibilities. Nevertheless, Hindu concern to use these new powers to protect religious interests differed markedly in towns in the two areas of the province which have already been delineated, east UP and Oudh, and west UP and Doab.

In east UP and Oudh, the dominant factor in the politics of the towns tended to be an Urdu-speaking elite connection based on landed interest. Of so little importance were communal matters in Lucknow politics that, in the 1893 and 1895 Legislative Council elections, local Hindu Congressmen felt it quite safe to put forward a Muslim barrister, Hamid Ali Khan, as their candidate for the northern municipal board seat against the Kayasth taluqdar and representative of the landed interest, Babu Sri Ram. In 1893, there were, it is true, cow-protection riots in Gorakhpur division, but the towns on the whole were not affected by them.[1] Urban politicians in the east made sure that cows were kept in their byres and not allowed to foul the paths of politics.

In west UP and Doab, the cross-communal alliances of the east seem, from the outset, to have been less common. Dominant alignments in urban politics tended to be based on commerce, largely a Hindu affair, and Hindu businessmen were among the foremost supporters of Hindu revivalism. So it is not surprising that in some towns Hindus were to be found eagerly pressing forward their religious interests. In Agra, for example, as soon as the 1883 Municipalities Act was passed, greatly increasing the powers of the Hindu majority on the municipal board, Hindus began to refurbish and celebrate with vigour festivals that clashed

---

[1] In 1893, east UP and Oudh saw the most severe communal outbreaks of the century. But the disturbances in Gorakhpur and Azamgarh districts, as in the case of 1913 and 1914 in Fyzabad, were rural not urban affairs. J. M. Rizvi, 'Muslim Politics and Government Policy: Studies in the development of Muslim organisation and its social background in North India and Bengal, 1885-1917' (Cambridge PhD thesis, 1969), pp. 102–3.

with Mohurram.[1] 'Hindus here as elsewhere', wrote the divisional commissioner, 'have begun to assert themselves, and will not now willingly acquiesce, as they appear formerly to have done, in the superiority of the Muhammadans.'[2] The Agra case was not unique. In the 1870s, Hindu traders and professional men of Allahabad launched a campaign to transfer the control of the Magh Mela,[3] a great religious festival and also a great source of patronage, from the Muslim Kotwal to a Hindu subcommittee of the municipal board. In 1886, they succeeded. In other towns, however, where the Muslims were strong in terms of population, culture and a tradition of influence, they were able to give themselves political protection. For instance, in Moradabad, where the community was particularly strong,[4] and politicians were renowned for their communalism,[5] Muslims manipulated the electoral machinery to their advantage. Under the rules laid down in 1884, more Hindus than Muslims in Moradabad had the vote. But the secretary of the municipality was a Muslim. He drew the ward boundaries so that many Hindu voters, who lived in the centre of the town, were jammed in one ward, leaving the Muslims with the advantage in the remaining five wards.[6] As a result, the Muslims always had a majority. In 1898, Babu Brijnandan Prasad, vice-chairman of the board, complained to the government that:

[1] In India, Mohurram is the period of fasting and mourning during the first month of the Muslim year which commemorates the death of Hassan and his brother Hussain. On important days of mourning during the month anything from the blowing of a temple conch to the celebration of some joyful Hindu festival such as the Ram Lila was likely to cause conflict. For an excellent description of Mohurram celebrations see Mrs Meer Hassan Ali, *Observations*, pp. 6–54.
[2] A. Cadell, Offg. Commissioner Agra Division, to Chief Secretary, Government of NWP&O, NWP&O GAD, June 1890, IOR.
[3] An annual fair at the *sangam* at Allahabad, which is thought to be the point of confluence of the mythical holy river, Saraswati, with the Ganges and Jumna, it ranks with those at Hardwar and Benares among the most important of Hindu bathing festivals. With millions of pilgrims, the management of this festival provided considerable patronage in the grant of monopolies to pan, incense, flower sellers etc. For detailed evidence on the management of the fair see NWP&O GAD, October 1882, IOR.
[4] In the city, Muslims represented nearly sixty per cent of the population. In the district, they held forty-two per cent of the land. Muslims were more powerful in Moradabad than in any other district of the province.
[5] An illustration of the city's reputation lies in the Hindu saying that 'In Moradabad there are nothing but mukkhiam, macchar aur musalman [flies, mosquitoes and Muslims]'.
[6] *NWP Administration Report, 1871–2*, pp. 4, 10–12.

Threats to Urdu-speaking elite

Ever since the introduction of the principle of local self-government, the Hindus in Moradabad have had no share in Municipal administration, and are really worse off than they would have been if local self-government had never been granted to Moradabad.[1]

The result of this vigorous assertion of religious interests was a tendency for the parties of municipal politics to become increasingly religious parties. As soon as cross-communal alliances broke down, and Muslims began to operate as Muslims in municipal politics, they found that they were a minority. In 1884, of fifty-eight[2] west UP and Doab municipalities, the Muslims had a majority of the population in eighteen, but a majority of municipal commissioners in only eleven. This poor electoral showing was largely due to poverty.[3] But not only did the Muslims have fewer seats than they might have expected in relation to their numbers, they were also losing them. They did so because Muslim voters and candidates tended to be rent receivers, government servants, or impoverished artisans, groups that suffered more severely than the commercially based Hindus from the sharp rise in prices which occurred between 1880 and 1910.[4] They also lost in the redrawing of ward boundaries that followed the 1900 Municipalities Act. In Moradabad, for instance, the Muslim majority was destroyed.[5] Nor were the Muslims helped by their own electoral incompetence. In Bareilly, Muslims numbered fifty per cent of the population and Hindus forty-nine per cent. In 1901, each community had nine seats. But, one electioneering slip by a Muslim followed by manipulation of the electoral rolls by a Hindu changed the position

[1] Minute by Babu Brijnandan Prasad, vice-chairman, Moradabad municipal board, 28 February 1898, Municipal A, October 1898, 92f, UPS, cited in Hill, 'Congress and Representative Institutions', pp. 130–1. Hill also stresses the prevalence of communal politics in west UP, *ibid.*, p. 130.

[2] In 1884, there were more municipalities in existence in west UP and Doab. Fifty-eight is the number which remained in existence up to the Municipalities Act of 1916.

[3] The only figures that appear to be available for UP municipal electorates are for 1911. An indication of Muslim poverty, which would of course be revealed by municipal electorates based on wealth, is that, in 1911, although the Muslims had a majority of the population in eighteen west UP and Doab municipalities, they had a majority of voters in only six.

[4] This price rise reached peaks in the years 1897 and 1908. *Index Numbers of Indian Prices.* Summary Table III.

[5] In 1897, the Muslims had a nine to eight majority on the board, but, by 1907, they were in a four to eight minority. The Muslim press claimed that the Hindus had influenced the redrawing of the ward boundaries. *Naiyar-i-Azam* (Moradabad), 26 April 1910, UPNNR 1910.

to eleven to seven in favour of the Hindus.[1] Then the very fact that the Muslims were usually in a minority did not help them; the majority and stronger community in a municipality was better placed to capture Tammany Hall. In the Allahabad elections of 1891, hired ruffians saw that only the supporters of Badri Prasad reached the polling booth.[2] At Cawnpore, in the same year, Muslims declared that such was the danger of incurring the displeasure of a candidate by not voting for him 'that it would be well if memberships were sold by public auction'.[3] So between 1884 and 1908 Muslims lost seats steadily in important cities such as Meerut, Agra and Cawnpore, and in the first decade of the twentieth century the same trend was apparent in Rohilkhand towns such as Moradabad, Budaun and Chandpur.[4]

Such losses of seats mattered. If power actually changed hands, the victorious community often used the opportunity to settle religious scores. For instance, after the Hindus gained the upper hand in Moradabad, they compelled Muslim butchers to dry their hides outside the city:[5] in Chandpur, they ended cow-slaughter.[6] In Bijnor, where Hindus dominated the board, the Hindu Kotwal thrashed Muslim butchers for offering beef for sale in a market place.[7] When the Muslims had a chance they replied in kind. Cows were openly killed in Najibabad after the Muslims

---

[1] In 1900, out of twenty-seven elected members of the Bareilly municipal board there were fourteen Muslims and thirteen Hindus. In 1901, after the redrawing of the ward boundaries, the communities held nine seats each out of a total of eighteen members. But, through manipulation of the ward rolls of ward six and a Muslim error, this parity was lost. Between 1901 and 1904, the communal proportions in the electorate of ward six were as follows: 1901, Hindu 203, Muslim 550; 1902, 208 and 531; 1903, 215 and 610; 1904, 208 and 577, but in 1905, one of the Muslim members was ousted because he failed to get his nomination paper in on time. His place was taken by a Hindu, who, the following year, prepared the electoral roll, which then had 351 Hindus and 139 Muslims. As a result, a second Muslim was displaced. Note for the Collector of Bareilly by Munshi Asghar Ali Khan, 1911, Home Education Municipal A, April 1914, 22–31, NAI.

[2] *Prayag Samachar* (Allahabad), 19 March 1891, UPNNR 1891.

[3] *Amir-ul-Akhbar* (Cawnpore), 13 March 1891, UPNNR 1891.

[4] For the performances of Muslims in municipal elections in the towns of west UP and Doab between 1884/5 and 1907/8 see table entitled 'Hindu and Muslim performance in municipal board elections, 1884/5–1907/8' in Francis Robinson, 'Muslim Separatism in the United Provinces', *Modern Asian Studies*, VII, 3 (1973), p. 412.

[5] *Rohilkhand Gazette* (Bareilly), 24 February 1903, UPNNR 1903.

[6] *Sahifa* (Bijnor), 12 June 1904, UPNNR 1904.

[7] *Ibid.*, 5 August 1903, UPNNR 1903.

gained power.[1] In religious fanaticism there was little to choose
between the two communities, but Muslims, who found themselves
cast increasingly as a religious minority in the politics of west UP
and Doab towns, were in a poor position to protect themselves
against assaults of militant Hindus.

Clearly, towards the end of the nineteenth century, the Hindu
and Muslim landlords and government servants who comprised
an important part of the Urdu-speaking elite found themselves
under increasing pressure. In general, their position was being
weakened by the development of communications and the growth
of trade; in particular, it was threatened by the subversive effects
of government's educational policy, by government's attempts to
gain a better hold of the lower levels of the bureaucracy and by its
willingness to open up power in the towns to competition from
the wealthy. But this was not the full extent of pressure. It was
increased and given particular emphasis by developments within
Hindu society. The growth of an awareness of the need to protect
and promote Hindu interests came at a time when Indians were
gaining greater opportunities for advancing their own interests in
the towns. So, in some towns of the west UP and Doab, where
Hindu revivalists were strong, the advent of municipal self-
government created the conditions in which religious grievances
could be satisfied and the Muslims come to feel the full weight of
the Hindu majority. In addition, the Hindu revivalists' vigorous
assertion that Hindi was the provincial vernacular, accompanied by
their strident demand that Nagri should become the Court character, came at the same time as government's drive to clean up the
administration. This campaign for Nagri, moreover, was brought
to a successful conclusion in the midst of Macdonnell's attempts to
cut down Muslim influence in the bureaucracy. Hindu revivalism,
however, not only pressed the Urdu-speaking elite hard but also
weakened, and in many places broke, the links that held its Hindu
and Muslim components together. Hindus such as Siva Prasad,
Jai Kishen Das and the Raja of Bhinga found it difficult to resist
the claims of the new and burgeoning sense of Hindu nationality.
Indeed, because of Hindu revivalism, Muslims, particularly professional men living in the towns, were more sensitive to the
changes made by government in the late nineteenth century than
any other part of the Urdu-speaking elite.

[1] *Gohar-i-Hind* (Najibabad), 5 February 1902, UPNNR 1902.

CHAPTER 3

Separatism grows among Muslims
1860-1900

Muslim government servants and landlords felt the pressures of change in the late nineteenth century rather more than any other group; their power was most obviously reduced, their culture was most openly held of small account, and their religion was most strongly attacked. Muslims had been most prominent in the old order which the British wished to reform; it was only natural that they should be most prominent in the Urdu-speaking elite's reaction to change. The problem with which we are confronted is why, between 1858 and 1900, does this reaction shift from being a movement of Hindu and Muslim landlords and government servants led by Muslims to being a movement composed almost entirely of Muslim government servants and landlords?

Part of the answer has been hinted at already. An elite of Muslims and Hindus, born of service to the successive governments of Hindustan and drawn together by Urdu culture, could not withstand the erosive effects of Hindu revivalism. Part will become evident below in the reactions of the Muslims of this elite to the reform policies of their rulers. Their aim in the beginning was to preserve the power of the Urdu-speaking elite and the Urdu culture which went with it. But as Hindus, some from the Urdu-speaking elite itself, began to press forward the interests specifically of Hindus, and to rediscover their own Hindu culture and traditions, the elite divided: Hindus found the claims of Hindu revivalism hard to resist and Muslims found that they were working increasingly just for themselves. When Hindus began to attack the Urdu language and the Islamic faith, the division hardened. Then, in time, the measures which Muslims had taken purely to defend the interests of the Urdu-speaking elite came to have the offensive purpose of reviving the fortunes of Muslims more generally.

The growth of Hindu and Muslim revivalism, however, does not explain everything. No consideration of political change in India is complete without an assessment of the role of government. In the late nineteenth century, those who wished to improve their position or to protect it against the effects of change were rarely rich or powerful enough to do so by their own efforts: they could achieve their ends only with the approval and assistance of government. But if their efforts to gain government's aid and imprimatur were to succeed, it was important that they should represent interests which government believed existed, which it imagined needed help, and which, for political or other reasons, it wished to help. There was a tendency, therefore, for politicians to mould themselves into the shapes which they thought their rulers wished to see. This chapter will trace the growth of a Muslim alignment in politics out of those of the Urdu-speaking elite and attempt to assess the part which Muslim revivalism and government policy played in the process.

On the morrow of the Mutiny, the first problem which confronted the Urdu-speaking elite was the need to come to terms with the rapidly increasing pressure exerted upon them by British rule. Throughout the province, societies were formed to discuss its implications. In 1861 the Benares Institute was founded, in 1864 Ghazipur Scientific Society. In 1867 the Allahabad Institute was set up, and in 1868 the British Indian Association of Moradabad. In the same year, the Lucknow Jalsa-i-Tahzib or Reform Club was established, forming the model for a rash of similar institutions which sprang up throughout the districts of Oudh. By 1870, over twenty associations existed which were devoted in various ways to discussing and dealing with the problems thrust on UP society by British rule.

Most of these societies were organised by Hindu and Muslim landlords and government servants of the Urdu-speaking elite. The Lucknow Jalsa was run by Kayasths, Kashmiris and members of the city's Muslim nobility.[1] The Sitapur Jalsa was founded by an extra assistant commissioner, Munshi Brij Lal, and boasted the Muslim Raja of Mahmudabad as patron;[2] the Gonda Jalsa, on the other hand, was founded by two Muslim government servants with the assistance of the Hindu Maharaja of Balrampur.[3] Local Hindu and Muslim notables of Bareilly sat on the committee of the Rohilkhand Literary Society.[4] But not every society was over-

[1] *RDPI (Oudh), 1870–1*, pp. 177–8.   [2] *RDPI (Oudh), 1869–70*, p. 132.
[3] *Ibid.*   [4] Garcin de Tassy, *La Langue et la Littérature de 1850 à 1869*, p. 294.

whelmingly an affair of the Urdu-speaking elite; this was particularly so in the case of the Benares Institute where there was a large Bengali element and in 1865, out of a membership of 124, only five Muslims.[1] Most, however, were organisations of the Urdu-speaking elite, especially in Oudh where Muslim rule had ended only just before the Mutiny. Moreover, all these societies received support, in the form of membership, money and advice from Europeans, both government servants and missionaries.[2]

These societies usually met in the house of a leading member, or when they became established in a building of their own. At meetings, as a rule, one member read a paper which was then discussed by those present. Reports of the occasion, sometimes with the paper published in full, often appeared in the vernacular press. Such events might seem tame but their talk was not without effect. After a paper on social reform was read before the Sitapur Jalsa, the local Kayasth community immediately set about improving its ways.[3] Moreover, when subjects of topical importance were hit upon, as in Dina Nath Ganguli's two papers on the vernaculars read before the Etawah Reading and Debating Society,[4] such activities could stimulate more general discussion and influence government action. The range of subjects covered was wide; the Benares Institute was divided into Educational, Sociological, Medical and Sanitary Improvement, Philosophy and Literature, and Science and Art sections. The interests of other societies stretched from the encouragement of social reform to the improvement of agriculture. Most organisations published their proceedings, some their own newspapers. Many provided library facilities: seven years after its foundation the Lucknow Jalsa subscribed to

---

[1] See the list of members in *The Transactions of the Benares Institute, for the session 1864-65* (Benares, 1865).

[2] For instance, in 1865 the presidents of the five sections of the Benares Institute were: H. B. Henderson, Judge of Benares City; G. P. Money, Offg. Commissioner of the Benares division; Dr J. Dunbar, Deputy Inspector General of Hospitals; H. Kern, Professor of Queen's College, Benares; and the Reverend M. A. Sherring of the London Missionary Society. In 1864, there were twelve Europeans and five Indians on the Directing Council of the Ghazipur Scientific Society.   [3] *RDPI (Oudh)*, 1869-70, p. 132.

[4] When asked to state what the education department was doing to encourage the development of the vernaculars, the Director of Public Instruction found Ganguli's two papers on the vernaculars of great use in making out a case for the encouragement of Hindi in preference to Urdu. M. Kempson, Director of Public Instruction NWP, to Secretary to Government NWP, 24 July 1868, NWP GAD, December 1868, IOR.

seven English and forty-eight vernacular newspapers and had a library of 4018 books.[1]

Many of the attitudes and activities of these societies were inspired by those of one, the Aligarh Scientific Society. Indeed, this society, broadcasting news of its affairs through its newspaper, the *Aligarh Institute Gazette*, dominated the Urdu-speaking elite's response to British rule in the 1860s.[2] The Scientific Society was, in turn, dominated by one man, its life Honorary Secretary, Syed Ahmed Khan. Much of the growth of a more communal approach to affairs among the Urdu-speaking elite between 1858 and 1869 can be understood in the development of the ideas and of the political and educational initiatives of this individual.

Syed Ahmed Khan was a big man in every sense. In 1885, a close friend, Colonel Graham, described him as being 'of middle height and of massive build': he weighed nineteen stone. He was a 'born

[1] *RDPI (Oudh), 1874–5*, p. 82.

[2] No list appears to exist of native societies and their circumstances in Oudh at this time, but the table below should illustrate the strong position of the Aligarh Scientific Society among the societies of the NWP in 1870.

Society	Income from govt (Rs. p.a.)	Total income (Rs. p.a.)	Members or visitors	Date of foundation
Scientific Society, Aligarh	960	10397	241	1864
Rohilkhand Literary Society		1404	19	1865
Fatehpur Literary Society		18	3	1864
Reading and Debating Club, Etawah		200	30	1865
British Indian Association, Moradabad	600	1959	92	1868
Suttya Sobha, Agra		460	58	1864
Shajahanpur Literary Institute		962	120	1861
Benares Institute		360	183	1861
Gorakhpur Reading Room				1867
Debating Society, Meerut			124	1868
Allahabad Institute		1312	107	1867
Naini Tal Institute		1040	83	1869
Social Improvement Society, Agra		239	87	1869
Social Improvement Society, Cawnpore				1869
Indian Reform League, Aligarh		688	36	1868
Native Literary Society, Mogulserai		97	318	1868
Debating Club, Almora		40	80	1870

RDPI (NWP), 1870–1, Vol. II, Appendix E, Part C.

orator', independent of mind and argued 'with a freedom of tone and language which Natives seldom use...'[1] He possessed 'untiring energy', great breadth of view and an uncommon eye for detail. There was little in which he was not interested and about which he had no opinion; his table talk moved easily from religion and metaphysics to politics and Persian poets. Few who met him, European or Indian, failed to fall beneath his spell.[2]

Syed Ahmed's background marks him out as an excellent representative of the Urdu-speaking elite. He was born in Delhi in 1817, and both his paternal and maternal ancestors were public servants of note under the Mughal empire. His greatgrandfather came to India from Herat. His grandfather, in the reign of Alamgir II, was a commander of 1000 foot and 500 horsemen. His father, a recluse and a man of deep religious feeling, was 'the most intimate of the Emperor's [Akbar II] friends...'[3] His maternal grandfather was Khwaja Fariduddin Ahmed, a mathematician, politician and man of affairs, who served both the East India Company and the Emperor. From 1797 to 1803, he was superintendent of the Calcutta Madrassa. He followed this with postings as company agent at the Persian and the Burmese courts, and then he brought a career, conspicuous both for its ability and its loyalty to the British, to its close as Prime Minister of the Mughal Empire from 1815 to 1819.

Syed Ahmed, then, scion of one of the Mughal Empire's great service families, was brought up in the pathetic survival of the court of Akbar. In 1836, he was invested, by the last emperor, Bahadur Shah, with his grandfather's magniloquent but meaningless titles. But almost as soon as he had accepted the honours of the old Empire, he took service in the new one. In 1837, much against his family's wishes, he entered British service as a sheristadar in the Delhi Sadr Amin's office. In 1839, he was transferred to Agra as naib munshi, or deputy reader, in the Divisional Commissioner's office. In 1841, he became a munsif or sub-judge in Fatehpur Sikri, and in 1846 he was transferred to Delhi. In Agra and Fatehpur Sikri, Syed Ahmed was a lively member of the set of

---

[1] Report of an interview between Kempson and Syed Ahmed Khan in 1867 in M. Kempson, Director of Public Instruction NWP, to Secretary to Government NWP, 8 March 1867, NWP GAD, March 1867, IOR.
[2] Based on a personal description of Syed Ahmed in G. F. I. Graham, *The Life and Work of Sir Syed Ahmed Khan, K.C.S.I.* new and revised edn (London, 1909), pp. 265–8.   [3] *Ibid.*, pp. 3–4.

Separatism grows among Muslims

Muslim vakils which revolved around the Sadr Diwani Adalat. In Delhi, he was a close friend of Ghalib, whom he called 'uncle', and was intimate with the poet's circle, many of whom were Wahabis. Thus Syed Ahmed spent his early life amongst the most accomplished men of his day and amidst the relics of Mughal splendour. Of these relics he was most conscious, and one of his earliest publications was a description of the architectural remains of Delhi entitled 'Traces of the Great'.[1] The outbreak of the Mutiny found him as a munsif in Bijnor. Here he rescued the entire British population of the district, and for a time ruled it for his stricken masters with the aid of loyal Hindu landlords. These deeds, which required considerable courage and initiative, gave him a very special place in the eyes of government.[2]

With such a background it is not surprising that Syed Ahmed was always first and foremost a Muslim. 'Before the Mutiny', according to his biographer, Hali, 'his piety was terrifying',[3] and, like many Muslims, he wrote on religious subjects, producing a biography of the prophet, a defence of the Sunnis against the Shias, a discussion of Wahabism, and other tracts. The works were anxiously orthodox and 'could have been written by a third-rate Moulvi...'[4] After the Mutiny, the emphasis of Syed Ahmed's religious writing shifted. On the one hand, he was concerned to

[1] *Asar-i-Sanadid* or 'Traces of the Great' is a work of considerable importance in architectural history as it is the best description of many of the remains of Muslim Delhi which were destroyed during the Mutiny or decayed afterwards. On its publication in 1847, it made little impact and it was not until it was translated into French by Garcin de Tassy in 1861 that its value began to be appreciated. As a result, Syed Ahmed was made a fellow of the Royal Asiatic Society in 1864. The composition of *Asar-i-Sanadid* is reported to have made a great impression on Syed Ahmed. Mohsin-ul-Mulk said that it 'brought home to him the fact that the Muslims were now plunging into an abyss of wretchedness...' Muhsin-ul-Mulk, *Majmu'a Lectures wa Speeches*, part I, p. 315, quoted in Rahmani Begum Mohammad Ruknuddin Hassan, 'The Educational Movement of Sir Syed Ahmed Khan 1858–1898' (PhD London, 1960), p. 66.

[2] The basic work on the life of Syed Ahmed is Altaf Husain Hali's *Hayat-i-Jawid* in Urdu. The description above of Syed Ahmed's background and early life is based on the following works, several of which draw heavily on Hali: Graham, *Syed Ahmed Khan*, pp. 1–23; Hassan, 'Educational Movement', pp. 55–69; Shan Muhammad, *Sir Syed Ahmad Khan: A Political Biography* (Meerut, 1969), pp. 41–8; S. M. Ikram, *Modern Muslim India and the Birth of Pakistan (1858–1951)*, revised edn (Lahore, 1965), pp. 19–32.

[3] Hali, *Hayat-i-Jawid*, quoted in Hassan, 'Educational Movement', p. 69.

[4] An assessment made by Mr Justice Shah Din in 1904 and quoted in J. M. S. Baljon Jr., *The Reforms and Religious Ideas of Sir Sayyid Ahmad Khan* (Leiden, 1949), p. 48.

create greater understanding between his co-religionists and their Christian rulers; and he began a commentary on the Bible, much less orthodox than his earlier writing, which was designed to explain the book of the Christians to the followers of Islam.[1] On the other hand, he attempted to rehabilitate the Muslims, whose reputation had been blasted by their share in the Mutiny, in the eyes of their rulers. In a series of pamphlets begun in 1860, and entitled *An Account of the Loyal Mahomedans of India*, he set out to prove that jihad was not permissible in India, and listed the loyal services performed by Muslims during the uprising. The pamphlets stopped after number three; the uncharitable said he had run out of material.[2]

Syed Ahmed's concern for the reputation of the Muslims should not be allowed to conceal his major interests in the years following the Mutiny. There is a temptation, to which many have succumbed, to view his whole life from the aspect of its last twenty-eight years, and to see all his efforts as directed towards the good of his community alone. This is misleading because it is the very changes in and development of his ideas which shed most light on him and his times. After the Mutiny, he was concerned about relations between government and Muslims, but he was much more concerned about the way in which government's policies were affecting the interests of the Urdu-speaking elite of which Muslims were only a part.

In 1858, Syed Ahmed set down what he thought was wrong with government's policy in his pamphlet, *The Causes of the Indian Revolt*.[3] He listed the causes under five heads:

1. Ignorance on the part of the people; by which I mean misapprehension of the intentions of Government.
2. The passing of such laws and regulations and forms of procedure as jarred with the established customs and practice of Hindustan, and the introduction of such as were in themselves objectionable.
3. Ignorance on the part of the Government of the condition of the people, of their modes of thought and of life, and of the grievances through which their hearts were becoming estranged.

---

[1] The first parts of Syed Ahmed's commentary, *Tabyin al-kalam*, appeared in 1862. Contemporaries found his theological flexibility astonishing. Garcin de Tassy, *La Langue et la Littérature de 1850 à 1869*, p. 197.
[2] For a summary of the contents of the pamphlets see M. S. Jain, *The Aligarh Movement: Its Origin and Development, 1858–1906* (Agra, 1965), pp. 13–15.
[3] The pamphlet was translated into English in 1873 by G. F. I. Graham and Auckland Colvin, who was later to be lieutenant-governor of the province.

4. The neglect on the part of our rulers of such points as were essential to the good government of Hindustan.

5. The bad management and disaffection of the army...[1]

He spoke of interference with religion, of the growth of secular education, of the difficulties of getting into public service without a certificate from a government school, and of the resumption of revenue-free lands. To remove the misconceptions of government concerning native society, he recommended that Indians should be admitted to the Legislative Council. Without them, 'Government', he said, 'could never know the inadvisability of the laws and regulations which it passed. It could never hear as it ought to have heard the voice of the people...'[2] To remove the misconceptions of the people concerning government, he advocated education; his motto, Graham said, was '"Educate, educate, educate." "All the socio-political diseases of India may...be cured by this treatment."'[3]

Although Syed Ahmed was convinced that education was the answer to India's problems, he was not sure of what kind it should be. He was strongly opposed to government's educational policy which he thought Macaulay had made insensitive to the people's concern for their religion. 'The study of Arabic', he wrote in *The Causes of the Indian Revolt*, 'is little thought of. The "Fickah" and "Hadees" were suddenly dropped. Persian is almost entirely neglected. Books and methods of teaching have been changed. But the study of Urdu and of English has greatly increased. All this has tended to strengthen the idea that Government wished to wipe out the religions which it found in Hindustan.'[4] He was particularly opposed to the local government's encouragement of the vernacular. In a statement on the vernaculars, most probably written in 1859, he argued that these languages, especially Urdu, were not a fit medium for higher learning and recommended that government should concentrate on using English.[5] In the same year, Syed Ahmed put these views into practice at Moradabad where he established a Persian school in the traditional style with new elements grafted on to it, such as an attendance register, a fixed curriculum and examinations. The most important innovation was the introduction of the study of modern history; Syed Ahmed

[1] Graham, *Syed Ahmed Khan*, p. 28.   [2] *Ibid.*, p. 27.
[3] *Ibid.*, p. 48.   [4] *Ibid.*, p. 32.
[5] The 'Statement' is quoted in Hali's *Hayat-i-Jawid*, see Hassan, 'Educational Movement', pp. 88–9.

believed that, if Indians had known more recent history, the Mutiny might have been avoided.[1] The school was founded with the aid of a committee of local notables, both Hindus and Muslims.[2]

In 1862, Syed Ahmed was transferred to Ghazipur. By 1863, it was clear that he had begun to revise his opinion concerning the suitability of the vernaculars as a medium of instruction. In September, he gave an address at Nawab Abdul Latif's house in Calcutta urging that in order to advance Indian society needed western learning, and that because most of this learning either was in or could be translated into the language of their rulers, English was the language they must learn.[3] But this was a long process, and so he recommended the formation of a society 'composed of as many Hindus as Muslims, without discriminating between caste, belief or area, from which a committee would be drawn responsible for publishing translations in Hindustani (Hindi and Urdu) and also, if it seemed fitting, in the learned Indian languages, of useful European works that were of interest at the time to Hindus and Muslims, taking care to avoid those which dealt with religious matters.'[4] Syed Ahmed's address, according to Garcin de Tassy, led to the foundation of the Muhammadan Literary and Scientific Society of Calcutta.[5] This is uncertain, but there can be no doubt that it was followed, in 1864, by the foundation of the Ghazipur Scientific Society.[6]

[1] This theme was developed by Syed Ahmed in a speech he made at the inauguration of the Ghazipur Scientific Society, 9 January 1864. Graham, *Syed Ahmed Khan*, p. 53.

[2] For a detailed description of the Moradabad school see Hassan, 'Educational Movement', pp. 81–7

[3] Graham, *Syed Ahmed Khan*, pp. 50–1.

[4] Translation of Syed Ahmed's Calcutta address as summarised by Garcin de Tassy, *La Langue et la Littérature de 1850 à 1869*, p. 256.

[5] *Ibid.*, p. 255.

[6] The Scientific Society was not the only organization to be founded as a result of Syed Ahmed's activities in Ghazipur and, in 1864, some of the local notables decided to found an independent school run by a local committee. There had been a missionary school in Ghazipur since 1853, but many avoided it for religious reasons. Syed Ahmed was asked to draw up the curriculum and regulations of the new institution and, though unwilling, he finally assented. He decreed that the languages taught in the school should be Urdu (Hindi was not mentioned), Arabic, Persian, Sanskrit and above all English, and that it should be open to boys of all classes and creeds. Raja Deonarain Singh was elected patron and, on account of their liberality in giving Rs. 2000 and Rs. 1000 respectively to the Institution, Lalla Hurbense Lall was made Life-Honorary Member of, and Lalla Sheo Baluk Singh Life-Honorary Secretary to, the Committee of Management. Two months after the founda-

Separatism grows among Muslims

Section two of the Scientific Society's Bye-Laws declared that '...until the Society be thoroughly set agoing, it shall be wherever Principal Sudder Ameen Syud Ahmud Khan be stationed'.[1] The Society, in fact, was almost totally dependent on his vigour. So when, in April 1864, he was transferred to Aligarh, it moved with him and here it subsequently settled. The aims of the Society were mainly those set out by Syed Ahmed in his Calcutta address and expanded in his foundation speech. The Society was to concentrate on translating into the vernacular works of political economy and history, particularly the latter. The first work chosen was Rollin's *History of Greece* on the grounds that it showed how the Greeks, by their own efforts, had lifted themselves from a state of barbarism to one of civilisation.[2] By 1875, twenty-seven works had been translated. All were in Urdu; Hindi was ignored.[3] The Society was also particularly concerned about problems of agricultural improvement. It translated an agricultural treatise, set up a model farm, experimented with seeds, with agricultural machinery and displayed the results to local landowners.[4] From time to time, lectures on important topics were given. In 1866, a building was erected, known as the Aligarh Institute, which became the focal point of the Society's operations. In the same year, its journal, the *Aligarh Institute Gazette*, was founded. With articles in English and Urdu, mainly on social and educational questions and many written by Syed Ahmed himself, this weekly newspaper quickly became the foremost of its kind in the province.[5] From the beginning the

tion of the Ghazipur Scientific Society, the four corner-stones of the school were laid by B. Sapte, the district judge, Raja Deonarain Singh, Moulvee Mahomed Faseeh and Thakoor Dutt Pundit. See the description of the laying of the foundation of the new Ghazipur College and particularly Syed Ahmed's speech on the occasion in *RDPI (NWP), 1863–4*, Appendix B, and Hassan, 'Educational Movement', pp. 108–12.

[1] 'Bye-Laws of the Scientific Society' in Yusuf Husain (ed.), *Selected Documents from the Aligarh Archives* (London, 1967), Part I, No. 10, p. 16. This bye-law also stated that the Society should eventually find its fixed abode at Allahabad. Had this happened and the Society been set up in this strong Hindu centre the history of north India might have been different. As it was, Syed Ahmed's posting to Aligarh led to the establishment of the Society in one of the strongest Muslim centres in the province.
[2] Graham, *Syed Ahmed Khan*, pp. 52–4.
[3] Hassan, 'Educational Movement', pp. 117–18.
[4] 'Memo. about the Govt. Garden prepared by Syed Ahmad Khan', 24 May 1877, Husain, *Documents*, No. 80, pp 120–4.
[5] J. H. Garcin de Tassy, *La Langue et la Littérature Hindoustanies en 1871* (Paris, 1872), p. 34.

93

Society had much assistance, both official and unofficial from the British. Government gave money to assist the Society's projects and displayed public approval of its efforts. Officials, such as the young Auckland Colvin[1] and the police officer Graham, privately contributed money and time. At the outset, the Society was also, like all Syed Ahmed's early organisations, an example of Hindu–Muslim co-operation; in 1864, there were four Muslims and three Hindus on its executive council,[2] and in 1873 there were thirty-five Muslim and fifty-two Hindu members.[3]

The network of connections built up by Syed Ahmed through the Aligarh Scientific Society provided him with the platform from which, in the ensuing years, he launched many of his social, educational and political initiatives. The first came in 1866 with the foundation of the British Indian Association of the North-West Provinces – not to be confused with the Oudh taluqdars' organisation of the same name – an association mainly of Aligarh landlords and government servants, both Hindu and Muslim, the membership of which was almost the same as that of the Scientific Society. The members of the Scientific Society gathered under this new banner so that the Society's purely educational ends would not be harmed. The British Indian Association's ends were more political: 'The leading aim and object of this Association shall be', its Bye-Laws declared, 'to improve the efficiency of the British Indian Government and to promote its best interests, by every legitimate means in the power of the Association...To this end, the Association shall from time to time draw the attention of the Government to redress and amend such already existing measures as appear likely to prove injurious to the interests of the country, or to adopt such other measures as may be calculated to promote those interests...'[4] So the Association petitioned government to improve railway arrangements for native passen-

[1] Colvin gave advice, attempted to spread the word about the Society in his district and donated Rs. 100. See Auckland Colvin to Syed Ahmad Khan, 11 October 1863 and 7 December 1863, in Husain, *Documents*, Part I, Nos. 2 and 4, pp. 2–3, 5.
[2] 'Proceedings of the first meeting of the Scientific Society', 9 January 1864, *ibid.*, No. 6, p. 13.
[3] List of members of the Aligarh Scientific Society who paid their subscriptions in 1873 in the *Aligarh Institute Gazette*, 21 July 1876, quoted in Hassan, 'Educational Movement', Appendix IV, p. 460.
[4] *A Speech by Syud Ahmed Khan on the Institution of the British Indian Association, N.W. Provinces, with the Bye-Laws of the Association* (Allygurh, 1867).

gers,[1] to reduce the rate on book postage,[2] and to help it set up a department for encouraging travel to Europe.[3]

Trivial petitions such as these were not the real purpose of the British Indian Association. Syed Ahmed, the honorary secretary, aimed that it should launch his most full and sustained attack on the government's education policy. In an article entitled 'Public Education of India', published as a British Indian Association pamphlet, he declared that 'although the question might have been decided in favour of English education, it by no means follows its arguments out-weigh those that may be brought forward for Oriental education, or indeed that it has any solid argument at all'.[4] Indeed, the defects of a system of government education 'raised on as light and unsubstantial basis as a paper minute by Macaulay'[5] were grave: first, since government schools attracted few people and these were mainly of the 'lower classes' 'with all their instruction in European science, the country remains as un-affected and untouched as ever'.[6] Secondly, education 'through a difficult language like the English' was unjust because it limited European learning to the few,[7] and thirdly, education in the English language left no more than a veneer on the native mind.[8] Instead of the present system, 'we want an educational system or policy that will avoid these defects... This can only be done by the Ver-naculars – the languages of the people themselves.'[9] But, this talk of vernaculars did not mean that there was any room for Hindi.

[1] *A Petition to the British Government praying for certain reforms in the Railway arrangements for the convenience of Native Passengers, with the Governments Circular received in reply thereto* (Allygurh, 1869).

[2] *A Memorial to the British Government soliciting a reduction of the Book Postage with the Governments reply thereto* (Allygurh, 1869).

[3] *Supplement to Bye-Laws of the British Indian Association, N.W.P.: Relative to the Department for encouraging travel to Europe: together with the correspondence of the Association with the Government North Western Provinces on the same subject* (Allygurh, 1869). With the Associations' educational activities, these appear to have been the total of its approaches to government apart from a petition of 1877 to raise the age limit for application to the I.C.S. to twenty-two instead of lowering it to nineteen.

[4] *Article on the Public Education of India and correspondence with the British Government concerning the education of the Natives of India through the Ver-naculars* (Allygurh, 1869), p. 1.

[5] *Ibid.*, p. 4. Ironically, when, in 1866, Syed Ahmed was invested with a gold medal by the Viceroy in acknowledgement of his educational work, he was presented with a complete set of Macaulay's works. H. V. Hampton, *Bio-graphical Studies in Modern Indian Education* (Oxford, 1947), p. 222.

[6] *Article on the Public Education of India*, p. 6.

[7] *Ibid.*, p. 7.   [8] *Ibid.*, p. 8.   [9] *Ibid.*, pp. 10–11.

'The question of which vernacular for which province', he declared, 'is a very trivial and unimportant one, as there can be no doubt as to the boundaries of Bengalee or Ordoo or Gujeratee.'[1] What a change this was from the man of 1858! Then Urdu was unfit to be a medium of instruction and English was the ideal, now English was the bane of Indian education and Urdu its panacea.

Syed Ahmed began to try to put his ideas into effect by arranging a petition which demanded, in effect, that in each district the education department should surrender the control over primary and secondary education which it had acquired since the 1850s to a committee consisting of 'local education officers, landholders and gentlemen' presided over by the Collector.[2] Understandably, the Director of Public Instruction would have none of this, and did his best to torpedo the idea by blasting the reputation of all involved and demonstrating that the petition was a ramp for one of Syed Ahmed's intrigues.[3] Government, however, was prepared to institute local educational committees in Aligarh and elsewhere, but they were shorn, of course, of the control of local educational affairs sought by Syed Ahmed and his friends.

After his sally against government schools, Syed Ahmed completed his assault on the educational system by conducting a protest against the predominance of English in the Calcutta University system. In August 1867, four Hindus and six Muslims[4] presented a petition to the Viceroy on behalf of the British Indian Association

[1] *Article on the Public Education of India*, p. 11.
[2] Syed Ahmed's attack was dressed up as a petition from the 'Landholders of the Allygurh district soliciting of the Government certain improvements on the existing system of public education', 16 May 1866. The petitioners suggested that, as government education was partly paid for by a one per cent cess on the land revenue of the landholders in the district, it was only reasonable that these landholders should have a say in how the cess was spent. They went on to ask that the proposed committee should be given complete control over the type of education and school that existed in the district. *RDPI* (*NWP*), *1866–7*, Appendix B, pp. 27a–29a. The committee proposed for the Aligarh district consisted of fifteen Hindus and nine Muslims. Raja Teekum Singh was President, Mahomed Inayutullah Khan of Bhikampore, Vice-President, and Syed Ahmed, Secretary. Syed Ahmed, Secretary of the Scientific Society, to the Collector, Aligarh, 24 November 1866, NWP GAD, March 1867, IOR.
[3] M. Kempson, Director of Public Instruction NWP, to Secretary to Government NWP, 28 January 1867 and 8 March 1867, NWP GAD, March 1867, IOR.
[4] They were: Issur Chunder Mookerjee, Budree Pershad, Munnoo Lall, Raja Jykishen Dass Buhadur and Syud Ahmud, Mahomed Yoosiff, Muddud Hoosain, Mahomed Inayetoolla Khan, Mahomed Abdoosshakore Khan, Hafeezooddeen Ahmud.

of the NWP which repeated, in more judicious language, the arguments set out by Syed Ahmed in his pamphlet on Public Education in India. The petitioners requested that it should be made possible for a university student to acquire a degree in any subject working entirely in the vernacular and that, towards this end, either a vernacular department should be attached to the Calcutta University or an independent vernacular university should be created for the North West Provinces.[1] The Government of India replied saying that such aspirations were wholly in keeping with the policy laid down in the 1854 Education Despatch, but they could not be realised because there were not enough works translated into the vernaculars to make it possible to teach and learn in them.[2] Government offered help for practical suggestions, and the British Indian Association asked it to recommend two series of books for every class of university examinations which the Scientific Society might translate.[3] Soon afterwards, the local government asked the societies of the province for their views on the possibility of promoting the use of the vernacular in education. The result was that people asked which vernacular, Urdu or Hindi? Then, which script, Persian or Nagri? Because it seemed that one or the other might receive government's exclusive imprimatur, claims on either side were put forward with passion and prejudice. Thus the seeds of dissension were sown amongst the Urdu-speaking elite.

Hindus associated with the Urdu-speaking elite, though they might contribute to and prefer Urdu culture, found it difficult to defend the language and script connected with Islam against the language and script connected with their own religion. Many of the supra-communal associations founded in the 1860s divided. Hindus and Muslims became less interested in working for the good of the people of Hindustan than in furthering that of their respective communities. The number of specifically communal associations increased. Syed Ahmed's organisations were not immune to

[1] 'The humble petition of the British Indian Association, North-Western Provinces', 1 August 1867, in J. P. Naik (ed.), *Selections from the Educational Records of the Government of India* (Delhi, 1963), Vol. II, No. 6, pp, 21–8.
[2] E. C. Bayley, Secretary to the Government of India, to the President and Members of the British Indian Association, North-Western Provinces, 5 September 1867, *ibid.*, No. 7, pp. 29–32.
[3] Raja Jai Kishen Dass, Secretary to the British Indian Association NWP, to E. C. Bayley, Secretary to the Government of India, 12 November 1867, NWP GAD, December 1868, IOR.

the communal miasma. Hindu members of the Aligarh Scientific Society began to demand that its proceedings and its translations should be in Nagri. Muslims, of course, opposed them. The two leading lights of the British Indian Association, Syed Ahmed and Raja Jai Kishen Das found themselves in opposite camps.[1] The Association collapsed: an organisation which anticipated some of the approach and several of the ideas of the Congress had come to an ignominious end; and Syed Ahmed's faith in the efficacy of further supracommunal action was completely shattered. In an interview with the commissioner of Benares just before he left for England in 1869, he talked for the first time of purely Muslim progress, and from this moment devoted himself to work entirely on behalf of the Muslims.[2]

At the very point when Syed Ahmed realised that his educational and political work could only be carried forward on behalf of the Muslims, government turned its especial attention towards them. But, whereas Syed Ahmed had only just begun to treat his co-religionists as a political and cultural entity – remembering, of course, that those who were not 'respectable' did not count – government always had regarded and always was to regard them as such. Why was this so? The Muslims, as we have seen, were very divided, split by sect, status and occupation. They had no communal associations of the modern sort: they did not present themselves as a political category. The politics of the 1860s had little truck with communalism and every district officer knew that a man like Syed Ahmed had much more in common with his great

[1] See Ch. 2, pp. 73–4.
[2] Hali described the incident thus:
 'In 1868 some prominent Hindus in Benares decided to try to replace Urdu written in the Persian script with [Hindi] *bhasha* in Devanagri characters as the language of the law courts.
 'Sir Syed said this was the first time that he became convinced that the fusion of Hindus and Muslims into one people or their co-operation in mutually beneficial efforts would be an uphill task. "One day," he declared, "when the issue was gathering momentum in Benares, I was talking to Mr. Shakespeare, the Commissioner of Benares, about the education of Muslims. He listened to my conversation wide-eyed. At last he said that this day was the first time he had heard me talking about the advancement of Muslims in particular. Previously, I had always spoken of the betterment of all Indians. I said I was certain now that the two communities would not be able to participate in any work with a sincere heart."' Translated from the Urdu, Altaf Husain Hali, *Hayat-i-Jawid* (Lahore, 1965), p. 142.

political antagonist Siva Prasad than he ever had with a humble Muslim weaver. Yet the British insisted on discussing Indian politics and society in terms of Muslims and Hindus.

They had done so from the beginning of their contact with Indian society. Travellers from Europe naturally drew a distinction between the Muslim rulers and the Hindu subjects. Christians naturally picked out the followers of Islam as people with whom they had an affinity[1] and from whom they expected hostility. Religious differences were the most apparent and the most easily understood so they were the most readily employed by those who wished to describe the society and its politics. British historians of Muslim India from Dow to Elphinstone assumed automatically that Hindus and Muslims were distinct groups[2] and Indian history was divided into Hindu, Muslim and British periods. After the British became the paramount power, they tended to see the Muslims as the displaced rulers whom they expected, as a group, to resent the loss of their former power and to be strongest in resisting foreign rule and western civilisation. From this anticipation there sprang the most important source of British awareness of the Muslims: the threat they presented to the security of the Raj. This threat did not diminish in the nineteenth century. Muslims had a large proportion of government posts. One sect, the Wahabis, was felt to be fanatically opposed to everything that British rule represented and had been discovered preparing rebellion.[3] Although

[1] A. J. Greenberger, *The British Image of India: A Study in the Literature of Imperialism 1880–1960* (London, 1969), p. 45. This sense of affinity was particularly strong among the British who saw the Muslims as sharing the same values and as having been in the same position, as conquerors. *Ibid.*, pp. 45–7.

[2] J. S. Grewal, *Muslim Rule in India: The Assessments of British Historians* (Oxford, 1970), p. 168.

[3] The Wahabis were a Muslim sect that followed the doctrines of Abdul Wahab, an eighteenth-century Arab reformer. They were puritanical, rejecting all accretions to and movements away from 'pure' Islam as they imagined it had been practised in the Prophet's Arabia. Their chief objective was to establish an independent Muslim state in which the true Islam could be practised and to achieve this jihad was necessary. The Wahabis established themselves in two areas of the subcontinent. The first was the hills of the Afghan frontier where they set up a miniature theocracy. It was aimed primarily at the Sikhs and, only after the downfall of the Sikh kingdom, at the British. When the frontier Wahabis got involved in the Mutiny and were found to have connections throughout northern India, government launched expeditions against their frontier headquarters and hunted them throughout India. The great Wahabi hue and cry came to an end with the trials of the Patna Wahabi leaders in 1870. The second area was Bengal where, in the first part of the

there was plenty of evidence to the contrary, many thought that the Mutiny was the product of a Muslim conspiracy,[1] and 'almost universally' the Muslims 'were regarded as the fomentors of the revolt and its chief beneficiaries'.[2] Moreover, they had connections with other Islamic countries and some looked to these countries for a revival of their fortunes, making government particularly sensitive to the possibility of invasion from without and insurrection from within. No wonder the Muslims were regarded as the most important group in India,[3] and Mayo told Muir in 1870 that being constantly on the look out for disturbances within this group 'is one of the most important duties of every officer Civil and Military in India'.[4] The parts of this group in their occupations as landlords, liquor-distillers and so on, were relatively harmless but the whole, as the Muslim community, was regarded as potentially the most dangerous threat to British rule in India. So it was to these parts, lumped together as Muslims, that government directed its policy. This is one of the most important facts of British Indian history; it was a potent force in encouraging the growth of political groups or parties on the basis of religious community. For, if the government wished to woo 'the Muslims', 'Muslims', whether true believers or not, would most assuredly step forward to take whatever was going.

Nevertheless, for all the concern about the danger which Muslims were thought to represent, British policy towards them after the Mutiny contained some inherent contradictions. On the one hand, there was a general policy of conciliation framed by the govern-

nineteenth century, the Farazi movement flourished. The Farazis claimed that all land belonged to God and that therefore there was no need for cultivators to pay taxes to landlords and to the government. Religious courts were organised for Muslims and, for some time, there was almost a parallel government in existence. The movement was similar, though not at first related to, that of the frontier Wahabis. Qeyamuddin Ahmad, *The Wahabi Movement in India* (Calcutta, 1966); W. W. Hunter, *The Indian Musalmans*, reprinted from the 3rd edn (Delhi, 1969), pp. 1–137; Ahmad, *Islamic Culture*, pp. 209–17.

[1] For the conspiracy theory see E. C. T. Chew, 'Sir Alfred Comyn Lyall: A Study of the Anglo-Indian Official Mind' (Cambridge PhD thesis, 1969), pp. 16, 18; Sir Richard Temple, Bart., *Men and Events of My Time in India* (London, 1882), p. 113; P. Hardy, *The Muslims of British India* (Cambridge, 1972), pp. 62–70.

[2] T. R. Metcalf, *The Aftermath of Revolt: India 1857–1870* (Princeton, 1965), p. 298.

[3] Sir Alfred C. Lyall, *Asiatic Studies: Religious and Social* (London, 1899), p. 290.

[4] Mayo to Muir, 11 July 1870, Mayo Papers (40), CUL.

ment of India and endorsed by the government of the NPW.[1] In 1859, the taluqdars of Oudh, both Hindu and Muslim, received back their estates and were given minor jurisdiction over criminal, civil and revenue suits. When this policy was seen to be a success, it was extended to the North-West Provinces and, in January 1861, local officers were instructed to 'initiate a more generous policy'. Their chief aim, they were told, should be 'to raise the chiefs and the principal gentlemen in their own estimation, as well as in the eyes of the native community; to form a bond of union between them and the Executive Officers of the Government; and at the same time to secure the exercise of their influence on the side of the government, by admitting them to active and responsible partici-pation in the work of the administration'.[2] These orders were implemented without regard for religion, and of course Syed Ahmed's projects benefited greatly from them.

On the other hand, government's immediate reaction to the supposed Muslim instigation of the Mutiny was ferocious. Take, for instance, the fate of Mughal Delhi. The Great Mosque was confiscated. The larger part of the Fatehpuri Mosque was auctioned off. The Daryaganj Mosque became a bakery and the great Mughal palace a barrack.[3] The massive area between the Red Fort and the Great Mosque was cleared to provide a field of fire for British cannon. House after house was razed to make way for the canals, roads and railways which ploughed their way into the city. In the longer term this policy was extended to the relics of Mughal administration. Oriental departments were abolished at govern-ment colleges; Persian schools were taken over by the education department; the court of Sadr Diwani Adalat was set aside; the functions of the Hindu and Muslim law officers came to an end, and in 1868 the centre of government in the NWP was moved from Agra, scene of great Mughal glories, to Allahabad, holy city of the Hindus. Moreover, government departments, particularly those involved in reforming old ways and breaking down the influence of established groups in the bureaucracy, appeared to carry this

[1] Hardy, *Muslims of British India*, pp. 71–3.
[2] Summary of a Circular issued to Commissioners of Divisions in the NWP in *NWP Administration Report, 1860–1*, p. 35.
[3] For the post-Mutiny treatment of Mughal Delhi see Percival Spear, *Twilight of the Mughuls: Studies in Late Mughul Delhi* (Cambridge, 1951), pp. 220–2; Narayani Gupta, 'Military Security and Urban Development', *Modern Asian Studies*, V, Part 1 (January 1971), pp. 62–4.

animus against the Muslims into their work.[1] The numbers of Muslims in the police[2] and judicial[3] departments, it was announced, were too large. The education department severely criticised the fact that they still had a strong position in the bureaucracy generally. 'It is a well-known fact that there is no nation on earth more opposed to education or enlightenment than the bigoted Muhammadans', wrote a school-inspector in 1864, 'and yet the Government seem disposed to allow them a monopoly of the best employments...let not educated men be taunted by these Bahadurs...'[4]

Some of the contradictions that existed between government's political and administrative policies were resolved by Mayo. In the late 1860s, the Government of India faced increasing dissatisfaction among the Muslims. There was a recrudescence of Wahabism, particularly in Bengal and Bihar. In 1868, a military expedition had to be despatched to deal with a Wahabi centre on the North-West Frontier. Mayo was convinced that men and money were being sent to it from the Wahabi base in Patna. Wahabi agents were arrested, and in mid-1870 their trials began. Simultaneously, there was some stir among the Muslims at Allahabad and Bareilly, and signs that the British population feared another Mutiny. Again the Muslims became one of the government's foremost preoccupations, and as the Wahabi trials dragged on through the following year – the Wahabis were brilliantly defended by an English lawyer – they were to remain so.

During this time, Mayo was also concerned with education in

---

[1] The following gives some idea of the spirit in which some government officers conducted the post-Mutiny changes: 'They [the Muslims] deliberately planned and tried to carry out a war of extermination', Lyall told his father in 1858, 'and retaliation in such a case is sanctioned by every human law. If the Mussulman *could* by any means be entirely exterminated, it could be the greatest possible step towards civilizing and Christianizing Hindostan.' A. C. Lyall to his father, 14 May 1858, quoted in Chew, 'Lyall', p. 18.

[2] *NWP Police Administration Report, 1866*, p. 3.

[3] Memorandum by M. Kempson, Director of Public Instruction, 5 June 1862, quoted in Hassan, 'Educational Movement', p. 177.

[4] The inspector was Siva Prasad. *RDPI (NWP), 1863–4*, p. 57. The provincial education reports of the early 1860s are full of such attacks on the strong position of the Muslims in the public services, see, for instance, *RDPI (NWP), 1861–2*, p. 33 and *RDPI (NWP), 1862–3*, p. 7. The contradictions in British policy to the Muslims that these attacks imply were but a part of a broader conflict in Indian government in the 1860s between paternalism and the ideal of bureaucratic efficiency. Muir was the voice of the former, Kempson that of the latter. For an assessment of the part that these ideas played in government in the 1860s, see Eric Stokes, *The English Utilitarians and India* (Oxford, 1959), pp. 268–9.

Separatism grows among Muslims

Bengal. He found that, while over 110,000 Hindus attended government schools, only 14,000 Muslims did so and declared:

> There is no doubt that, as regards the Mahomedan population, our present system of education is, to a great extent, a failure.
> We have not only failed to attract or attach the sympathies and confidence of a large and important section of the community, but we may even fear that we have caused positive disaffection as is suggested by Mr. O'Kinealy and others.[1]

He made an obvious connection; the failure of Muslims to go to government schools in Bengal was at the root of Wahabism in the area. Having drawn his conclusions from Bengal, Mayo then set out to form policy for the Muslims of all India. In a Resolution of August 1871 he suggested ways in which they might be encouraged to go to government schools and colleges, and asked local governments for their opinion as to how they might be implemented 'without infringing the fundamental principles of our educational system'.[2] Thus the need to woo the Muslims began to soften the harsh impact of post-Mutiny administrative policy.

The new emphasis which Mayo gave to Muslim policy received considerable impetus from the publicist's pen and the assassin's dagger. The Honorary Principal of the Calcutta Madrassa, W. N. Lees, who had for many years criticised the government education policy on the grounds that it set Muslims at odds with British rule, opened a fresh front in 1871 with three strong letters to the London *Times*.[3] At the same time, a Bengal civil servant, W. W. Hunter, laid up in bed after being tipped out of a gharry, was passing his convalescence in writing articles on Wahabism for the Calcutta *Englishman*. These caught Mayo's eye, and he asked Hunter to write a book on the question of the day: 'Are Indian Musalmans bound by their religion to rebel against the Queen?'[4] Hunter wrote the book in three weeks. He showed that Muslims did not need to

---

[1] Note by Mayo, 26 June 1871, Mayo Papers (12), CUL. O'Kinealy was the officer in charge of the Wahabi prosecutions. One of the 'others' was E. C. Bayley, the Secretary to the Government of India and a man of Muslim sympathies. Both men had analysed the Muslim problem for Mayo and suggested lines of action. Hunter, *Indian Musalmans*, pp. 141–3.

[2] Extract enclosed in Secretary to Government of India, Home Department, to Offg. Secretary to Government NWP, 7 August 1871, NWP GAD, October 1871, IOR.

[3] The dates of the letters were: 14 October, 20 October and 2 November 1871. They were reprinted in W. Nassau Lees, *Indian Musalmans* (London, 1871).

[4] F. H. Skrine, *Life of Sir William Wilson Hunter* (London, 1901), p. 199.

rebel providing that the ruling power was sympathetic. Yet Muslims had rebelled; there was a Wahabi camp on the Frontier and a Wahabi conspiracy throughout northern India. Clearly British rule was unsympathetic to Muslim needs. He examined this conclusion in the light of evidence from Bengal and found that the administrative policies of the British had dried up the sources of Muslim wealth: the Permanent Settlement had seriously reduced their income from land; the army under the British was taboo for Muslims of rank and no longer a source of gain; opportunities in government service and the professions, which Muslims had monopolised one hundred years before, had come almost completely to an end. The reason for this was, wrote Hunter, 'that our system of public instruction, which has awakened the Hindus from the sleep of centuries, and quickened their inert masses with some of the noble impulses of a nation, is opposed to the traditions, unsuited to the requirements, and hateful to the religion, of the Musalmans.'[1] They did not want to be taught in Bengali or by Hindus 'whom the whole Muhammadan community hates'. They wanted to learn Persian and Arabic and have some provision made for their religious education. The Muslims were dissatisfied because British rule had engineered their downfall and 'we shall find', he warned, 'that our unsympathetic system of Public Instruction lies at the root of the matter'.[2] In conclusion, he suggested making recommendations along the lines of Mayo's Resolution of 7 August 1871, that government should temper its educational system to Muslim requirements. The effect of the book was considerable, not because it was particularly well-argued or well-written, but because five weeks after its publication the acting Chief Justice of Bengal was assassinated by a Muslim on the steps of the High Court, and five months afterwards Mayo himself was stabbed to death by a Muslim convict.[3] As a result, all attention was focused on the need to do something about the Muslims. Thus, Mayo's education measures and Hunter's arguments about Muslim backwardness attained an all-India importance that they did not deserve and they might not otherwise have had.

In the NWP, the Government of India's demand for special measures for Muslim education was vigorously attacked by the

[1] Hunter, *Indian Musalmans*, pp. 168–9.
[2] *Ibid.*, p. 189.
[3] It is sometimes claimed that one or both the assassins were Wahabis. There is no evidence for this in either case.

Director of Public Instruction. Any departure from the education policy laid down in Macaulay's minute of 1835 and Wood's despatch of 1854 would be, he said, 'a grave political error'.[1] The arguments of Hunter he declared to be erroneous, and 'the question of Mahomedan education in India' to have been 'unnecessarily and unfortunately hampered by political considerations'.[2] Grudgingly, he made some suggestions along the lines of Mayo's Resolution.[3] His recommendations were accepted; his views were ignored. He was informed by the secretary to the local government that

The decadence of Mahomedan scholarship in India, and the disinclination of the Mahomedans, as a body, to fall in with our University system, and the appropriate remedy for these evils, are matters of the highest importance, both socially and politically. Socially, because it is a duty incumbent on the British Government so to shape its educational measures as to make them agreeable to this large section of the people, who at present, by their predilections, or it may be prejudices, are shut out from the influence of our educational system. Politically, because the enlightenment of the Mussulmans, and the gaining of them over to co-operate with ourselves in the education of their youth, would prove one of the surest means of attaching them to our rule. But for this purpose, it is essential that the teaching of modern science be combined with that of their own literature, and thus made acceptable, and we may trust in the end even popular, amongst them.[4]

As far as the Muslims were concerned, politics now came first and administrative policy second. This was to have far-reaching consequences.

Once Syed Ahmed had decided to devote his energies to the welfare of his co-religionists, his one overriding aim was to enable them to exert in the future the power in Indian affairs that they had wielded in the past. In the 1860s, this had been his objective for the Urdu-speaking elite as a whole; it was now his aim for its Muslim members alone. Education had been his means to maintain

[1] Memorandum by M. Kempson, Director of Public Instruction, August 1872. NWP Educ, June 1873, IOR.
[2] Memorandum by M. Kempson, Director of Public Instruction, enclosed in Director of Public Instruction to Secretary to Government NWP, 18 August 1873, NWP Educ, November 1873, IOR.
[3] Director of Public Instruction to Secretary to Government NWP, 18 August 1873, NWP Educ, November 1873, IOR.
[4] Secretary to Government NWP, to Director of Public Instruction, 14 November 1873, NWP Educ, November 1873, IOR.

the power of the Urdu-speaking elite; educated men would be reconciled to British rule and able to take a leading part in it. Education was no less the answer to the problem of maintaining, and perhaps increasing, the influence of Muslims. The methods he advocated to realise this new end were derived directly from those he had proposed for his old one. Syed Ahmed, therefore, set out to eradicate the factors which prevented Muslims from going to government schools: the Macaulayesque aspects of the educational system and the Muslims' ignorance, bigotry and suspicion of it.

In 1869 and 1870, Syed Ahmed visited England.[1] He was impressed by the ruling country's power, by its civilisation[2] and particularly by the extent of and interest in education. Every impression went to strengthen his convictions, and his plans for Muslim education began to ripen. Soon after he arrived, he published his *Strictures upon the present educational system in India*, a pamphlet which attacked the Indian educational system as 'nothing but a delusion' because it had 'wholly failed to diffuse the light of instruction among the masses'.[3] The reason for this was the government's failure to use the vernacular at all levels of education. 'The cause of England's civilisation', he told the editor of the *Aligarh Institute Gazette*, 'is that all the arts and sciences are in the language of the country.'[4] He continued. 'Let this advice of mine to the future generation be printed on the top of the Himalayas in the largest characters. If all the arts and sciences are not taught in this language only, it will never be the good fortune of Hindoostan to make fitting advancement. This is true! – this is

[1] The idea that Syed Ahmed should visit England seems to have been suggested by his friend, Colonel Graham. Syed Ahmed was accompanied by his two sons, Syed Hamed, later a District Superintendent of Police in the NWP, and Syed Mahmud. The latter was going to Cambridge as the first holder from the NWP of a government scholarship enabling Indians to complete their education in England, which in 1866 Syed Ahmed had recommended the Viceroy to institute.
[2] Syed Ahmed kept the public informed of his impressions in a series of letters to the *Aligarh Institute Gazette*. His praise for English civilisation was rather too fulsome: 'We are in comparison with the breeding and affability of the English', he told the editor, 'as dirty, unclean, wild beasts in the presence of beautiful and worthy men.' *Aligarh Institute Gazette*, 19 November 1869, UPNNR 1869.
[3] Syed Ahmed's *Strictures* quoted in Sivaprasad, *Strictures upon the Strictures of Sayyad Ahmad Khan Bahadur, C.S.I.* (Benares, 1870), p. 6.
[4] Letter from Syed Ahmed to the Editor of the *Aligarh Institute Gazette*, 19 November 1869, quoted in Graham, *Syed Ahmed Khan*, p. 132.

true!! – this is true!!!'[1] But despite his apparent concern for the masses, Syed Ahmed's remedy was for the few. He decided to found a college, an institution which could only benefit Muslims of the Urdu-speaking elite. 'No night passes', he wrote to Mohsin-ul-Mulk from England, 'but we talk about and plan for the establishment of such a College.'[2] Nevertheless, if this college was to provide the kind of education that would appeal to the Muslims, it had to be independent of the government. The achievement of private enterprise in England made him confident that it could be. 'Looking at this', he told Mohsin-ul-Mulk, 'one can realise that in India, if a good number of individuals pay attention to and strive for learning and civilisation they can achieve much without the help of government.'[3]

On 26 December 1871, two months after his return from England, Syed Ahmed set up in Benares a 'Committee for the better Diffusion and Advancement of Learning among the Muhammadans of India'. The committee announced that it would give prizes of Rs. 500, Rs. 300 and Rs. 150 for the best essays answering the questions: Why was the proportion of Muslims at government schools and colleges less than that of the Hindus? What were the causes of the decline of oriental learning? Why had the study of modern sciences not been introduced among the Muslims? By September 1871, thirty-two essays had been received. On the basis of these, Syed Ahmed produced a report on Muslim education in India. Most of the essayists had attacked the Muslims for their prejudices against government education, Syed Ahmed's report attacked the educational system itself. Government, he said, had committed a 'grave political error' in undertaking the management of public instruction: the system it imposed upon the natives of India was defective and barren of

[1] Letter from Syed Ahmed to the Editor, *Aligarh Institute Gazette*, 19 November 1869, UPNNR 1869.
[2] Syed Ahmed to Mohsin-ul-Mulk, 29 April 1870, quoted in Hassan, 'Educational Movement', p. 201.
[3] While in England, several times Syed Ahmed met the Secretary of State for India, the Duke of Argyll, the retired Viceroy, Lord Lawrence, and many retired civil servants and persons interested in India. It is possible that the idea of founding a Muslim college could have been suggested to him here but, according to Graham (*Syed Ahmed Khan*, p. 63), he went to England with this idea already in his mind and, though there seems to be no evidence for this, all that his powerful English acquaintances could have done was to confirm him in an idea that he already had. When Mayo raised the alarm about Muslim education, Syed Ahmed was already back in India.

results.[1] Concluding, he urged the Muslims to set up an independent college at Aligarh. This college, known as the Muhammadan Anglo-Oriental College, was the outcome of years of passionate opposition to official education policy, a fact often obscured by Syed Ahmed's close political connections with government in later life.

The circular issued by the College Fund Committee set out the institution's origins and aims: 'Ever since the fall of the Mogul Empire...the Musalmans have steadily been losing ground...Of late...the English language having become an indispensable requirement for any office under the English Government, the Musalmans have most remarkably fallen off the list of the Government appointments.' Nothing but education could 'remedy the evils from which they are now suffering'. But because the government's educational system was 'not suited to the domestic and social requirements of the Musalman community', few Muslims went to government schools. Consequently, some leading Muslims had decided to found a 'College after the system of Oxford and Cambridge'; it would they hoped 'attract the higher classes of the Muhammedans'. The curriculum represented a compromise between the Muslims' 'national education' and the need to learn more English; the College was to teach European sciences through the medium of Urdu, English literature, classical and oriental languages. The committee concluded:

There is no doubt that, if the present attempt to regenerate the Musalmans meets with success, the political and social relations between England and India will become firmer and more intimate. The English nation being the successors of the Mahammedans in the supremacy over India, are apt to be regarded more as rivals than as friendly rulers. The leading and most intelligent Musalmans, however, are fully convinced of the great advantages which the enlightened rule of England confers upon India, and, with a view to raise their co-religionists from their present state of ignorance and degradation, have begun to organize a system for imparting genuine and sound education calculated to make the future generations of Mahammedans better citizens and better British subjects.[2]

[1] Summary of the argument of the Benares Committee Report in a memorandum by M. Kempson, Director of Public Instruction, August 1872, enclosed in Director of Public Instruction to Secretary to Government NWP, 28 August 1872, NWP Educ, June 1873, IOR.
[2] *Circular from The Mahammedan Anglo-Oriental College Fund Committee*, signed by Syed Ahmed Khan, Life Honorary Secretary, Mahammedan Anglo-Oriental College Fund Committee and undated but most probably published in 1872.

Separatism grows among Muslims

If Syed Ahmed's College was to be a success, he had to break down Muslim prejudices against the new sciences from the west. The sciences that Muslims traditionally learnt had over many centuries acquired the authority of religion. Syed Ahmed had to show that western learning was compatible with Islam. To do this, he founded in December 1870 a monthly magazine, the *Tahzib-ul-Akhlaq* or 'Muslim Social Reformer'. Through its columns, he attempted to substitute reason for authority in the interpretation of the Koran. 'Reason alone', he said, 'is a sufficient guide.'[1] His aim was to create an Islam thoroughly compatible with progress.

Such unorthodoxy amounted to heresy. The ulama and the orthodox of northern India threw up a massive barrage of opposition to Syed Ahmed's new approach to Islam. Indeed, for the indigent alim assaults upon him became a profitable industry.[2] The leading alim of Firangi Mahal, Maulvi Abdul Hai, denounced him as a follower of Satan,[3] while 'in every town and village fatwas were issued by the Maulawis which declared him to be a Kafir'.[4] As always in time of Islamic controversy, the newspaper business boomed. Special newspapers were founded to rebut Syed Ahmed's dangerous heterodoxy. In Cawnpore the *Nur ul Afaq* and the *Nur ul-Anwar*, in Moradabad the *Lauh i Mahfuz*, and in Agra the *Terhawin*. Threats against Syed Ahmed's life were frequent; one man told him that 'Shere Ali, who assassinated Lord Mayo, was an idiot for doing so, as he could have assured Paradise for himself by killing Syed Ahmad.'[5] Inevitably, much of this opposition was transferred to the College project. One opponent travelled to Mecca and received the following verdict from the local ulama:

It is not allowed to support this College – may God damn its founder! – and if this College has been finished, it must be demolished and its supporters severely punished, and everyone who defends Islam must oppose this College as much as he can.[6]

In the early 1870s, there were not many Muslims who recognised the need for Syed Ahmed's College, and there were few who were willing to risk damnation in order to support it.

[1] Hampton, *Biographical Studies*, p. 226.
[2] Baljon, *Sir Sayyid Ahmad Khan*, p. 68.
[3] Hali's *Hayat-i-Jawid* quoted in Hassan, 'Educational Movement', p. 271; Firangi Mahal was at this time the most important school of ulama in northern India, see Ch. 7, p. 266, n. 1.
[4] Hali's *Hayat-i-Jawid* quoted in Baljon, *Sir Sayyid Ahmad Khan*, p. 70.
[5] Graham, *Syed Ahmed Khan*, p. 140.
[6] Hali's *Hayat-i-Jawid* quoted in Baljon, *Sir Sayyid Ahmad Khan*, p. 70.

So great was the opposition that the birth of the College was protracted. In 1873, it was begun as a primary school by Samiullah Khan.[1] In 1875, this school was officially opened. In 1877, the College's foundation stone was laid, and not until 1881 were degree courses taught. Overall, numbers at the school and college grew steadily. By 1895, there were 565 students and, in the five-year period 1898–1902, the College educated over three-fifths of the Muslim graduates in the UP and nearly one-quarter of those in India.[2] But, though called the Muhammadan Anglo-Oriental College, it was not a purely Muslim affair; the contacts of the Urdu-speaking elite were not broken quite so easily. The Maharajas of Patiala, Benares, Vizianagram and others all gave generous support,[3] and up to the end of the century between one-fifth and one-sixth of the students were Hindus.[4]

Syed Ahmed scored a great victory over the opposition to Western learning, but ironically it was only consolidated by making further concessions not to the opposition but to the government scheme of education. Indeed, within a few years of its foundation, the College, which had been born out of opposition to Macaulay's education policy, had become a tribute to its principles. The College began with three departments: English, Urdu and Persian/Arabic. By the early 1880s, only the English department remained; students were not prepared to learn in languages which were unlikely to help them get jobs. Syed Ahmed now referred to Macaulay as the man who had 'breathed the breath of life into our nostrils';[5] institutions concentrating on oriental subjects, such as Benares Sanskrit and Lahore University College, were dismissed as producing a 'few beggars more'.[6] Those who went to Aligarh, however, had more than an education in English; they had an English education. The students, unlike those at other Indian colleges,

---

[1] See Appendix IV.
[2] T. S. Morison, *The History of the M.A-O. College, Aligarh* (Allahabad, 1903), Appendix D.
[3] Not all Hindu support, however, was well-intentioned. Siva Prasad offered the College Fund Rs. 1000 with the impossible condition that it should be founded at Allahabad. Siva Prasad to Syed Ahmed Khan, 29 July 1872, Husain, *Documents*, Part II, No. 21, p. 167.
[4] S. K. Bhatnagar, *History of the M.A.O. College Aligarh* (Aligarh, 1969), p. 134.
[5] *Aligarh Institute Gazette*, 27 November 1880, cited in Jain, *Aligarh Movement*, p. 58.
[6] *Aligarh Institute Gazette*, 15 January 1888, quoted in *ibid.*

lived on the premises in rooms arranged around Courts. Their chief teachers were Englishmen of ability: among them Theodore Morison, Thomas Arnold and Walter Raleigh, all of whom were later knighted. Their recreations consisted of cricket, debating and tea-parties. The abler were groomed to go on to English universities and to sit the civil service examination. All were encouraged to see themselves as the leaders of the future. Many were to play a big part in restoring Muslim power in India.

A college was not enough to fight the political battles of the Muslims of the Urdu-speaking elite. For a start, it was unlikely to succeed without government favour. Syed Ahmed knew that the Muslims were still the source of many British fears; these he laboured to dispel. One fear, almost an *idée fixe*, was that Muslims were fanatical, narrow-minded and believed that the sword was the inevitable penalty for the denial of Islam. This view gained further currency with the publication of a *Life of Mahomet* by William Muir, the lieutenant-governor. So, in 1870, Syed Ahmed published in London *A Series of Essays on the life of Mohammed, and Subjects Subsidiary thereto* the aim of which was to emphasise the Koranic verse 'Let there be no forcing in religion; the right way has been made clearly distinguishable from the wrong one'.[1] Another fear was that Muslims were, as a matter of faith, bound to perform jihad against the British – the question Mayo asked Hunter and a source of anxiety which the Wahabis, the assassinations of 1871–72, and Hunter's book tended to confirm. Reviewing Hunter's book, Syed Ahmed dismissed concern on this point: 'as long', he wrote, 'as Mussulmans can preach the unity of God in perfect peace, no Mussulman can, according to his religion, wage war against the rulers of that country, of whatever creed they be'.[2] A third fear, and one that gained force from the pan-Islamist propaganda of Jamal al-din al-Afghani[3] and the obvious interest of some

---

[1] Chapter X, 98 of the Koran quoted by Syed Ahmed in his *Series of Essays on the Life of Mohammed.* Graham, *Syed Ahmed Khan*, p. 71.

[2] Syed Ahmed's review of W. W. Hunter's *Indian Musalmans* quoted in *ibid.*, p. 153.

[3] Jamal al-din al-Afghani (1838–97), an Afghan not an Indian Muslim, was with Syed Ahmed the leading influence on Indian Muslim political thought in the late nineteenth century. Moreover, his were some of the basic ideas which were developed later by the leaders of the Khilafat movement. He regarded it the religious duty of Muslims to reconquer any territory taken from them by others and, if this was not possible, to migrate to some other land that was still part of the Dar-ul-Islam. Resistance to infidel aggression and reconquest was

111

Muslims in the fate of their co-religionists elsewhere, was that
Muslims were more loyal to other Islamic countries than to the
British Raj. Consequently, when, during the Russo-Turkish war
of 1877–8, the Sultan of Turkey claimed to be Khalifa of all
Muslims and the priests of Mecca appealed for the assistance of
all Muslims in fighting the Christians, Syed Ahmed had to act.
The Sultan of Turkey, he wrote in the *Aligarh Institute Gazette*,
had no right to be Khalifa, and he was sure that there was not
a single Indian Muslim who considered him as such.[1] Political
rights, he said, were more important than religious traditions, and
so long as the Muslims lived freely under British rule they would
remain good subjects.[2] During the Afghan War of 1878–80 and
the bombardment of Alexandria of 1882, Syed Ahmed took the
same reassuring line.[3]

Government also had to be convinced that the Muslims were
loyal in their secular as well as in their religious politics. So Syed
Ahmed hailed Lytton's repressive and discriminatory Vernacular
Press Act as a very liberal measure.[4] Though the government itself
supported the Ilbert bill, he advised his co-religionists not to
agitate for it as it was being opposed by the Anglo-Indian com-
munity.[5] When Muslims became disturbed, as in 1897 over the
Plague Prevention Rules and Turkey, he warned government.[6]
When he became involved in agitation, as in the Surendranath
Bannerjee contempt case of 1883, he wrote to the government

the duty not merely of the Muslims of the particular region involved, but of
all Muslims. The cause of the decline of Islam was that the Dar-ul-Islam was
no longer politically integrated. Afghani's solution was that the ulama should
build up regional centres in the various parts of the Dar-ul-Islam and that
these regional centres should be affiliated to a universal centre based at one
of the holy places where regional representatives would meet to try to create
a unified approach. Aziz Ahmad, *Islamic Culture in the Indian Environment*
(London, 1964), pp. 61–2. Afghani was Syed Ahmed's major ideological
opponent. He opposed Syed Ahmed's extreme rationalism as heresy. He
regarded Syed Ahmed's religious views and educational programme as part of
loyalty to the rule of the British to whom he was bitterly opposed. For obvious
reasons, he was particularly opposed to Syed Ahmed's attempts to isolate the
Indian Muslims from the rest of the Dar-ul-Islam and to run down the concept of a universal Muslim Khilafat. *Ibid.*, pp. 55–6.

[1] *Aligarh Institute Gazette*, 10 July 1880 and 31 July 1880, cited in Jain, *Aligarh Movement*, p. 131.
[2] *Aligarh Institute Gazette*, 1 October 1878, cited in *ibid.*, p. 133.
[3] *Aligarh Institute Gazette*, 15 July 1882, cited in *ibid.*, p. 135.
[4] *Aligarh Institute Gazette*, 23 March 1878, cited in *ibid.*, p. 137.
[5] *Aligarh Institute Gazette*, 13 March 1883, cited in *ibid.*, p. 137.
[6] Macdonnell to Elgin, 9 May 1897, Elgin Papers (68), IOL.

explaining his actions.[1] Moreover, the rules of each one of his associations based on Aligarh declared support for British rule.[2]

Towards the end of the nineteenth century, however, government's distrust of Muslims in general was not the only threat to the Muslims of the Urdu-speaking elite. There were also the effects of government's reforms in the bureaucracy and its development of representative institutions in town, district and province. More important, there were political organisations springing up which were concerned to take aspects of these government policies much further in a direction which could only damage the interests of this particular group of Muslims.

The danger came from outside the UP. From the 1850s, there had been associations, such as the British Indian Association of Calcutta and the Bombay Association, eager to press their interests on the government. But their efforts were tame and they were overtaken in the 1870s by others such as the Calcutta Indian Association and the Poona Sarvajanik Sabha. Those new associations not only made more radical demands but did so more radically. They attempted to raise agitations outside their own provinces and to co-ordinate their activities. Their endeavours culminated in the meetings of the National Conference and the National Congress in 1885 which merged as the Indian National Congress in 1886. The National Congress, as its title suggests, claimed to represent all Indians, though its support was drawn almost completely from the Hindus of the maritime provinces. Its demands were those which the Presidency associations had been making for years; the right to volunteer, the right to possess arms, the reduction of military expenditure, the raising of the minimum income liable to income tax, reforms in the legal system, the police administration, the separation of judicial and executive functions.[3] But these were mere

---

[1] 'Syed Ahmed sent me a long letter, explaining that his action had been very cautious and colourless.' Lyall to Primrose, Private Secretary to the Viceroy, 30 May 1883, Lyall Papers (43), IOL.

[2] 'To have implicit faith in the British rule and to make the Muslims loyal to the British' was among the objects of the Muhammadan Political Association founded at Aligarh in 1883. *Aligarh Institute Gazette*, 7 April 1883, Jain, *Aligarh Movement*, p. 126, fn. 1. See also clause 2(c) of the objects of the United Indian Patriotic Association founded in 1888 and clause 2(iii) of the objects of the Muhammadan Anglo-Oriental Defence Association of Upper India founded in 1893, Zafar-ul-Islam, 'Documents on Indo-Muslim Politics (1857–1947): The Aligarh Political Activities (1888–93)', *Journal of the Pakistan Historical Society*, XII, Part I (January 1964), pp. 14, 23.

[3] Seal, *Indian Nationalism*, p. 280.

padding behind the two basic demands: simultaneous examinations in England and India for the Indian Civil Service, and more representation for Indians on the legislative councils. Achieve these, declared a leading Bombay Congressman, 'and India will have nothing or little to complain [of]'.[1]

The reaction of UP men to bursts of political effervescence from the maritime provinces was guarded. Surendranath Bannerjee's tours of the late 1870s met with little sympathy; just one branch of the Calcutta Indian Association was founded in Allahabad. Agitation incited from Calcutta over the Ilbert Bill met with greater response. But 'in these Provinces', Lyall declared concerning the Saligram Idol case which led, in 1883, to Bannerjee's conviction for contempt of court, 'the people at large take no interest in the matter; and it has excited no religious feeling at all among the Hindus'.[2] Nor does there seem to have been much greater enthusiasm for the protests which followed in 1884 and 1885 over municipal reform and the refusal of local government to recommend a native volunteer force. Only two UP men attended the first Congress. The politicians of northern India had little interest in the issues that fascinated those of the presidencies. Moreover, they were staunchly opposed to the major plank in the Congress platform: the demand for simultaneous examinations. In 1886, Pandit Ajudhia Nath, the leading pleader of the Allahabad High Court and spokesman of Hindu educated opinion in the UP, told the Public Services Commission that the services ought not to be recruited by competitive examination unless this was done on a strictly provincial basis. The 'difference...in the education of the different Provinces' made this necessary, particularly since opinion in upper India held strongly that 'it is better to be ruled by gentlemen who belong to the same Province'.[3] UP men, backward in English education when compared with those in the presidencies, felt that they would stand little chance in competition for Indian Civil Service places if thrown in with candidates from the maritime provinces, particularly Bengal. Moreover, few from the aristocratic service families of north India fancied working under the despised Babu. In the UP, the major political objective

[1] Seal, *Indian Nationalism*, p. 280.
[2] Lyall to Primrose, Private Secretary to the Viceroy, 30 May 1883, Lyall Papers (43), IOL.
[3] *Proceedings of the Public Services Commission*. Vol. II, *Proceedings Relating to the North-Western Provinces and Oudh* (Calcutta, 1887), section 2, p. 18.

concerning the bureaucracy was not getting a few places amongst the heaven-born but controlling the great mass of provincial civil service patronage that was still held by the Urdu-speaking elite.

The initial lack of enthusiasm for Congress on the part of most UP politicians was quickly dispelled. When the Public Service Commission's recommendations were published, few found them adequate. As Congress policy took shape, most were attracted by its demands for legislative council reform while many, particularly those concerned with the cow or with court characters, seem to have discovered local advantages in association with the Congress as a leader of all-India agitations. Government measures and events beyond government's control encouraged the change in opinion by creating suitable conditions for agitation. In 1886 income tax was reimposed, and professional men, many of whom rarely dabbled in politics, quickly found common cause with the mercantile classes, who were already groaning under a licence tax. Moreover, after 1885, there was a massive rise in the price of those two products essential to Indian life, food-grains and cloth. For three years, prices remained at a level that had been reached only in the famine years of 1869 and 1879. Government was blamed and the Congress grew strong in the UP. Pandit Ajudhia Nath came forward as the leading Congressman of upper India, and in 1888 and 1892 Congress sessions were held at Allahabad.[1]

The outbreak of Congress activity in the UP between 1888 and 1892 was not, as has been supposed, just the work of western-educated literati. A brief glance at the 1888 Congress delegate list will show that a wide range of interests was involved. From the Lucknow Congress Circle there came most of the Urdu-speaking elite of the Nawabi city and the chief towns of Oudh, elected by public meetings and associations such as the Rifah-i-Am and the Jalsa-i-Tahzib. From the Allahabad Circle came professional men, but also representatives of merchants, priests, pragwals, the Khatri caste, the Kayasth caste and depressed Eurasian railway workers. From the Benares Circle came myriads of Bengalis and several princes of the deposed Mughal imperial family. Nearly one quarter of the 583 UP delegates were Muslims; several wasikdars (pensioned members of the former Oudh Royal House), who were no

---

[1] For an analysis of the economic and political background of the outbreak of Congress activity in the UP between 1888 and 1892 see Bayly, 'Allahabad', pp. 261–8.

doubt feeling the effects of price inflation; a whole group of Shia zamindars from the depressed Dariabad area of Allahabad district; several Muslim newspaper editors; and some Muslim lawyers, among them Hafiz Abdur Rahim, who was for the next twenty-five years to be the centre of Congress activity in Aligarh city, and Hamid Ali Khan, who was to be put up twice in the 1890s as the Congress candidate for the northern municipal board seat in the legislative council.[1] Admittedly, there were no Muslims of any great importance, but there were enough to give the lie to the Aligarh claim to represent Muslim interests. Paradoxically, what was much more marked than the large number of Muslims present was the Hindu revivalist character of the Congress organisation and support. Many secular organisations in the UP took a Hindu approach to affairs. For instance, the Benares Institute played a leading part in the Hindi agitation of the late 1860s, and in 1886 the Allahabad People's Association petitioned the municipality to put an end to the Bakr Id cow slaughter. Moreover, the 1888 Congress had several specifically Hindu revivalist electorates, for instance the Arya Samaj, and the Madhya Hindu Samaj, an Allahabad organisation devoted to promoting Nagri and cow-protection. The newspapers which supported the Congress were mainly those which supported Hindu revivalist causes.[2] The actual organisers of the Congress in Allahabad, Madan Mohan Malaviya, Charu Chandra Mitter and their circle, were closely involved with Hindu politics; while in 1888 and 1889 agents of cow-protection leagues toured the east of the province, campaigning not only for the end of cow-slaughter but also for Congress and for Council reform. In the UP, the Congress was not just the cat's paw of Bengalis demanding reforms in the bureaucracy and the legislatures, it was also closely associated with the protagonists of Hindu revivalism who, Tyabji's resolution notwithstanding,[3]

---

[1] *Report of the fourth Indian National Congress held at Allahabad on the 26th, 27th, 28th and 29th of December 1888* (Calcutta, 1889), pp. 117–41.

[2] The following are newspapers that supported both Hindu revivalist and Congress aims: the *Bharat Jiwan* and *Kavi Vachan Sudha* of Benares, the *Hindustan*, *Prayag Samachar* and *Hindi Pradip* of Allahabad, the *Bharat Bandhu* of Aligarh, the *Arya Darpan* of Shahjahanpur and the *Hindustani* of Lucknow.

[3] At the Allahabad Congress of 1888, the Bombay Muslim leader, Badruddin Tyabji, introduced a Resolution (No. XIII) with the aim of reconciling Muslims to the Congress. It read, 'Resolved – That no subject shall be passed for discussion by the Subject Committee, or allowed to be discussed at any

Separatism grows among Muslims

aimed to rub out every vestige of Mughal rule and Muslim power.[1]

Syed Ahmed's immediate reaction to the growth of Congress activity in Upper India was to oppose it. This surprised many, both then and later. Indeed, he has been accused of executing a complete volte-face. It is deposed that in his *Causes of the Indian Revolt* he had demanded that Indians should be allowed to serve on the legislative council; that during his British Indian Association days he had laboured to enable the sons of the Urdu-speaking elite to go to England to prepare for the civil service examination; and that in his Punjab tour of 1884 he had made much of Hindu–Muslim unity. Yet as soon as the Congress gained a hold in the UP, he turned against many of the aims for which he had once fought.[2] Some claim that he fell under the influence of the callow young Aligarh Principal, Theodore Beck.[3] Others less charitable, suggest that he was seduced by the favours rained upon him by the government.[4] But a close examination of the writings and activities of Syed Ahmed and his circle reveals no such sudden change.

Admittedly, Syed Ahmed did suggest that Indians should sit on the legislative council and did help Indians go to England to compete in the civil service examination. But there was the world of difference between this and the demands of Congress. When, in 1858, Syed Ahmed brought up the question of the legislative council, he said nothing of election, and in the mid-1870s the *Aligarh Institute Gazette* attacked elections and representative government as totally unsuited to India.[5] Syed Ahmed made his

Congress...to the introduction of which the Hindu or Mahomedan Delegates as a body object...provided that this rule shall refer only to subjects in regard to which the Congress has not already definitely pronounced an opinion.' Seal, *Indian Nationalism*, pp. 332–3 and 333 fn. 3.

[1] For an analysis and as assessment of the Hindu revivalist background of the Congress in the UP in the 1880s see Bayly, 'Allahabad', pp. 206–71.

[2] See, for instance, *Open Letters to Sir Syed Ahmad Khan, K.C.S.I.*, 'By the Son of an Old Follower of His', reprinted from the *Tribune* (Lahore, 1888).

[3] The source of this accusation appears to Tufail Ahmad whose family was closely connected with Aligarh College circles. Tufail Ahmad, *Musalmanon ka roshan mustaqbil* (Budayun, 1938), pp. 299–300, cited in Jain, *Aligarh Movement*, p. 123. The suggestion is often repeated, see for instance, A. Mehta and A. Patwardhan, *The Communal Triangle in India* (Allahabad, 1942), pp. 23–4; B. N. Pandey, *The Break-up of British India* (London, 1969), p. 60.

[4] *Ram Gopal, Indian Muslims: A Political History (1858–1947)* (Bombay, 1959), pp. 74–5.

[5] *Aligarh Institute Gazette*, 4 September 1874, 11 December 1874 and 16 July 1875, cited in Jain, *Aligarh Movement*, p. 112.

position quite clear when, in 1883, the legislative council was debating a local self-government bill for the CP, where the Muslims were in a small minority. He told the Council:

The system of representation by election means the representation of the views and interests of the majority of the population...in a country like India, where caste distinctions still flourish, where there is no fusion of the various races, where religious distinctions are still violent, where education in its modern sense has not made an equal or proportionate progress among all the sections of the population, I am convinced that the introduction of the principle of election, pure and simple, for representation of various interests on the Local Boards and Districts Councils would be attended with evils of greater significance than purely economic considerations. So long as differences of race and creed, and the distinctions of caste form an important element in the socio-political life of India, and influence her inhabitants in matters connected with the administration and welfare of the country at large, the system of election pure and simple cannot safely be adopted. The larger community would totally override the interests of the smaller community, and the ignorant public would hold Government responsible for introducing measures which might make the differences of race and creed more violent than ever.[1]

Equally, the fact that he helped Indians compete for the civil service did not mean that he, at any time, approved of the principle of competition. In fact, he detested it for the competition it brought the Urdu-speaking elite. When in December 1886 Beck told the Public Service Commission that competitive examinations would, by flooding the service with men from the Lower Provinces, dispossess 'Mahomedans and the upper classes in general, such as the Rajput aristocracy', and that this would have 'a very bad political effect',[2] he was merely echoing the attitudes in which Syed Ahmed and his followers were soaked. These attitudes were well formed before Beck came to Aligarh in November 1883 and before Syed Ahmed received the greatest marks of government recognition in the late 1880s. Syed Ahmed was working to maintain the influence of the Muslims of the Urdu-speaking elite in Indian society. The main demands of the Congress and its associates in the UP cut right across this ambition. His opposition to the Congress, therefore, was consistent and predictable.

Syed Ahmed opened his political campaign against the Congress

---

[1] *Proceedings of the Indian Legislative Council*, Vol. 22 (1883), pp. 19–20 quoted in Seal, *Indian Nationalism*, p. 320. Almost the same excerpt is quoted in C. H. Phillips (ed.), *The Evolution of India and Pakistan 1858–1947: Select Documents* (London, 1962), p. 185.
[2] *Public Service Commission* (*NWP and O*), II, section 2, pp. 37–8.

in December 1887. His first assault came with a speech in the Kaiserbagh Baradari during the Muslim Educational Congress at Lucknow. By raising the spectre of Bengali superiority in any form of competition, he attempted to rouse Hindus as well as Muslims of the Urdu-speaking elite. 'Now, I ask you', he said on the subject of competitive examinations, 'have Mahomedans attained to such a position as regards higher English education, which is necessary for higher appointments, as to put them on a level with Hindus or not? Most certainly not. Now, I take Mahomedans and the Hindus of our Province together, and ask whether they are able to compete with the Bengalis or not? Most certainly not. When this is the case, how can competitive examination be introduced into our country. (Cheers). Think for a moment what would be the result if all appointments were given by competitive examination. Over all races, not only over Mahomedans but over Rajas of high position and the brave Rajputs who have not forgotten the swords of their ancestors, would be placed as ruler a Bengali who at sight of a table knife would crawl under his chair. (Uproarious cheers and laughter)...In the normal case', he continued on the subject of election to the Imperial Legislative Council, 'no single Mahomedan will secure a seat in the Viceroy's Council. The whole Council will consist of Babu So-and-so Mitter, Babu So-and-so Ghose, and Babu So-and-so Chuckerbutty. (Laughter). Again, what will be the result for the Hindus of our Province, though their condition be better than that of the Mahomedans? What will be the result for those Rajputs the swords of whose ancestors are still wet with blood?...Everybody knows well that the agitation of the Bengalis is not the agitation of the whole of India...'[1] In reply to criticisms of his speech, he asked, 'Can any Bengali honestly say that the schemes which they have advocated in the Congress would benefit anybody except themselves, and next to them the Mahrattas and Brahmans?...The Congress', he concluded, 'is in reality a civil war without arms. The object of civil war is to determine in whose hands the rule of the country shall rest. The object of the promoters of the National Congress is that the Government of India should be English in name only, and that the internal rule of the country should be entirely in their own hands.'[2]

[1] Speech at Lucknow, 28 December 1887, Syed Ahmed Khan, *On the Present State of Indian Politics* (Allahabad, 1888), pp. 10–15.
[2] 'Reply of Sir Syed Ahmed to some criticisms' of his Lucknow speech, *ibid.*, pp. 26–7.

Separatism among Indian Muslims

Syed Ahmed's stand, followed up, of course, by a vigorous campaign in the *Aligarh Institute Gazette*, caused a great stir. Men were forced to take sides. The Congress machine got rapidly into gear, and by midsummer, the Congress agent, Mahomed Ali Bhimji, was organising meetings and Pandit Ajudhia Nath was stumping the province to address them. Syed Ahmed's followers were not far behind. In March, the Muslims of Allahabad declared against the Congress;[1] in April, so did the Taluqdars of Oudh.[2] In July, the Hindus and Muslims of Jaunpur sent Bhimji packing[3] and, soon after, the Maharaja of Benares joined the anti-Congress bandwagon.[4] Syed Ahmed had succeeded in creating a front consisting of Hindus as well as Muslims of the Urdu-speaking elite.

In August 1888, this front was consolidated with the foundation of the United Indian Patriotic Association.[5] Several of the leading Hindus who joined had opposed Syed Ahmed on the Hindi question, for instance the Raja of Bhinga, the Maharaja of Benares and Raja Siva Prasad, though he defected eventually. The basis of support, however, came from Muslims, but not just from local Muslims. Of the fifty-four Muslim anjumans affiliated to the Patriotic Association, the majority came from Bengal, Punjab, Madras and the CP. This is important; it was the first time that Muslims from the UP succeeded in dragging Muslims from other provinces, even if many of them only in name, into their political agitation.[6] The chief aim of the Association was to persuade the British that Congress demands were unrepresentative.[7] For this

[1] *Aligarh Institute Gazette*, 3 March 1888, UPNNR 1888.
[2] In an address to the retiring Viceroy, Dufferin, the Taluqdars declared that Syed Ahmed had converted them to his views. *Hindustan* (Kalakankar), 12 April 1888, *ibid.*
[3] *Alam-i-Taswir* (Cawnpore), 27 July 1888, *ibid.*
[4] *Aligarh Institute Gazette*, 11 August 1888, *ibid.* The native newspaper reports of the last five months of 1888 are packed with details of pro- and anti-Congress meetings.
[5] The Association began as the Indian Patriotic Association and only acquired the extra 'United' in its title later in order to emphasise its supra-communal nature.
[6] Zafar-ul-Islam, 'Documents on Indo-Muslim Politics (1857–1947): The Aligarh Political Activities (1888–1893)', *Journal of the Pakistan Historical Society*, XII, Part I (January 1964), pp. 17–18.
[7] This is well illustrated by the first two objects of the Association: '(a) To publish and circulate pamphlets and other papers for information of members of Parliament, English journals, and the people of Great Britain, in which those misstatements will be pointed out by which the supporters of the Indian National Congress have wrongfully attempted to convince that all the nations

purpose, there was a branch in London which, in 1889, presented a petition to the House of Commons against Bradlaugh's Indian Councils Bill.[1]

The Patriotic Association, however, did not last long. *Oudh Punch* lampooned the Hindu–Muslim alliance with a cartoon of a donkey entitled 'Opposition to the National Congress' on which Syed Ahmed, in a Turkish hat, was finding it difficult to sit with a Hindu.[2] The mockery was not misplaced. In the early 1890s as Nagri campaigners sniped with renewed vigour and the cow-protection agitation moved towards its violent climax, Muslims and Hindus, however great their hostility to the Congress, found it increasingly difficult to work together. Moreover, once Council reform had been granted in 1892, the Association lost much of its *raison d'être*. There was no longer any point in making the anti-election case to the British Parliament: the damage was done. What was needed now was first, measures not so much to oppose the Congress as to protect Urdu-speaking elite interests in the Councils, about which of course it would be harder to agree, and second, measures to curb the young educated Muslims who, disturbed at their elders' inability to protect the community's interests, were threatening to take the burden on their own more vigorous shoulders.[3]

So the United Indian Patriotic Association was abandoned, and at the Muslim Educational Conference in December 1893, the Muhammadan Anglo-Oriental Defence Association of Upper India was founded. Its objects were those of its predecessor rewritten in Muslim form, but with one difference: it aimed 'to discourage popular political agitation among Mahomedans'.[4] No public

of India and the Indian Chiefs and Rulers agree with the aims and objects of the National Congress.

(b) To inform members of Parliament and the newspapers of Great Britain and its people by the same means of the opinions of Muhammadans in general, of the Islamic Anjumans, and of those Hindus and their societies which are opposed to the objects of the National Congress.' *Ibid.*, p. 14.

[1] For the Muslim Petition see *ibid.*, pp. 19–22. In 1889, Bradlaugh introduced an Indian Councils Bill into the House of Commons on behalf of the Congress. The scheme of reforms it proposed were the same, except for elections to the central council, as that put forward by the Viceroy, Lansdowne. Gopal, *British Policy*, p. 187.

[2] *Oudh Punch*, 25 October 1888, UPNNR 1888.

[3] *Aligarh Institute Gazette*, 30 January 1894, Jain, *Aligarh Movement*, p. 126.

[4] Rules of the Defence Association, Rule No. 2(ii), enclosed in T. Beck to H. S. Fowler, Secretary of State for India, 2 January 1895, L/P&J/6/110, 1895, IOR.

meetings were to be held and no Islamic associations were to be affiliated. The young men had to be muzzled. Beck appears to have been the chief organiser; Syed Ahmed, now nearly eighty, had little to do with it. But this is not to say that it was Beck's affair. Business was controlled by a Council which usually met during Muslim Educational Conference sessions.[1] Much more important, the Association's policies were derived directly from Syed Ahmed's programmes and Muslim political experience of the 1870s and 1880s. The Association demanded the abolition of competitive examinations for Punjab provincial civil service posts,[2] and congratulated the Secretary of State for rejecting the Congress demand for simultaneous examinations.[3] Regarding representation, it followed solutions suggested by the experience of west UP and Doab municipalities.[4] In Muzaffarnagar municipality, for instance, where fifty-eight per cent of the population were Hindu and forty-one per cent Muslim, and there was only one Muslim out of twelve elected members, Muslims demanded separate representation.[5] In Allahabad, where Muslims with thirty per cent of the population found difficulty in electing a single representative, the Anjuman-i-Rifah-i-Islam insisted that Muslim interests could only be safeguarded properly by giving equal representation on the municipal board to the two communities.[6] Thus when in 1896 the Defence

---

[1] The following were the Council of the Defence Association: K. B. Barkat Ali Khan, Khwaja Yusuf Shah, Niaz Mahomed Khan, Shah Din, Abdur Rahman Khan, Abdul Hakim Khan, Sir Syed Ahmed Khan, Hon. Ismail Khan, Nawab Mohsin-ul-Mulk, T. Beck, Hon. Syed Mahmud and Mahomed Mir. *Ibid.*

[2] *MAO College Magazine*, February 1895, Jain, *Aligarh Movement*, p. 128.

[3] Resolution of the Defence Association, dated 27 December 1894, enclosed in Beck to Fowler, 2 January 1895, L/P&J/6/110, 1895, IOR.

[4] For this argument in greater detail see F. C. R. Robinson, 'Municipal Government and Muslim Separatism in the United Provinces, 1883–1916', *Modern Asian Studies*, VII, 3 (1973). As early as 1889, Muslims used their experience in the municipalities to make a more general point about the effect that elections had upon their ability to protect their interests. The Muslim petition to the House of Commons declared 'That inasmuch as the Indian Mahomedans are not confined, like the nationalities of Europe, to any special locality, but are dispersed throughout India among the multitude of other races and castes inhabiting the continent, they are in most parts of India in a considerable minority; and that therefore in any system of election they must of necessity be outvoted. Overwhelming proof of this is furnished by the existing municipalities.' Zafar-ul-Islam, 'Documents on Indo-Muslim Politics (1857–1947): The Aligarh Political Activities (1888–1893)', *Journal of the Pakistan Historical Society*, XII, Part I (January 1964), pp. 19–20.

[5] *Kashshaf* (Muzaffarnagar), 21 January 1896, UPNNR 1896.

[6] Municipal, January 1890, 36 B, UPS, cited in Hill, 'Congress and Representative Institutions', p. 129.

Association produced a memorial regarding the means for securing 'proper' representation of the community in elected bodies, it demanded separate communal electorates, with Muslims voting only for Muslims, equal representation for the Muslims on the UP legislative council 'on account of their past historical role', and weightage in representation on municipal and district boards.[1] All these demands were to be repeated, in some form, in the Muslim memorial of 1906. The 1896 memorial was submitted to Auckland Colvin and Sir John Strachey for approval; but it went no further.[2] In the late 1890s, the Aligarh circle became less concerned with protecting the interests of the Muslims of the Urdu-speaking elite than with preserving the College itself. In 1895, the institution was shaken by the discovery of massive embezzlement.[3] Syed Ahmed died in 1898 and Beck in the following year. Succession struggles broke out among those that remained and the College appeared to lose government favour. Consequently, Syed Ahmed's successors had little time for political initiatives. Nevertheless, a blueprint of the future Aligarh Muslim political programme had been made.

In his efforts to further the interests of the Muslims of the Urdu-speaking elite. Syed Ahmed created a centre of Muslim political activity in India. First, in the business of publishing the *Aligarh Institute Gazette* and the *Tahzib-ul-Akhlaq*, and in the problems of running an independent college which existed largely on voluntary subscriptions, he drew together leading Muslims from the Urdu-speaking elite. They were all members of service families, several like Syed Ahmed from the old Delhi Court, and all were successful servants of either the UP or the Hyderabad government. Among them were: Syed Mahmud,[4] Syed Ahmed's son, the first native judge of the Allahabad High Court, who was brilliant,

---

[1] The principles of weightage were as follows:
  (a) In towns where the Muslims form 15% of the population, at least one Muhammadan member must be allowed to sit on the council.
  (b) In towns where the Muslim population was between 15 and 25 per cent half the members should be, as far as possible, Muslims.
  (c) In towns where the Muslim population was above 25%, half the members must be Muhammadans.
  MAO College Magazine, December 1896, quoted in Jain, *Aligarh Movement*, pp. 128–9.
[2] *Ibid.*, p. 129.
[3] Between 1885 and 1895, the head clerk in the College secretariat, Shyam Behari Lal, embezzled over a lakh of rupees. Lal committed suicide in prison and none of the money was recovered. Bhatnagar, *M.A.O. College*, pp. 125–8.
[4] See Appendix IV.

erratic and often drunk;[1] another relation, Samiullah Khan,[2] a subordinate judge, who shouldered much of the early burden of getting Aligarh off the ground while Syed Ahmed was stationed in Benares; two members of the education department, Nazir Ahmad[3] the novelist and Zakaullah[4] the mathematician; Chiragh Ali,[5] who was one of Syed Ahmed's strongest supporters on religious questions, Shibli[6] the poet and historian, who eulogised the Aligarh movement in verse, and Hali[7] poet and biographer, whose *Musaddas*, or epic poem on the Rise and Fall of Islam, written at Syed Ahmed's behest, awakened generations of Indian Muslims to the decline of their political influence.[8] The most important were two top-ranking Hyderabad civil servants, Mohsin-ul-Mulk,[9] an early collaborator of Syed Ahmed's who not only gained the massive patronage of the Nizam for the College but also saved it from disaster after its leader's death, and Viqar-ul-Mulk,[10] who also helped the College greatly with money and influence; these were the two men of affairs who directed Aligarh politics into the second decade of the twentieth century. Few of this talented circle agreed with Syed Ahmed all the time, indeed Samiullah Khan, after a quarrel over administrative policy in 1889, moved to Allahabad where he founded a Muslim hostel and, in 1893, Mohsin-ul-Mulk became so disgusted with Syed Ahmed's management techniques that he moved to Bombay. Almost all disagreed with Syed Ahmed over religious matters.[11] Nevertheless most were prepared to work together for Syed Ahmed's educational objectives and thus they formed a nucleus of Muslim leadership.

Second, by founding the Muhammadan Educational Conference

---

[1] Crosthwaite to Lansdowne, 17 January 1894, Lansdowne Papers (25), IOL.
[2] See Appendix IV.   [3] *Ibid.*
[4] *Ibid.*   [5] *Ibid.*
[6] See Appendix III.   [7] See Appendix IV.
[8] The success of Hali's *Musaddas* made political themes and Muslim revivalism a dominant element in Urdu poetry. His successors were Shibli, Zafar Ali Khan, the editor of the *Zamindar*, Hasrat Mohani, Akbar Allahabadi and Iqbal. Ahmad, *Islamic Modernism in India and Pakistan 1857–1964* (1967), pp. 97–102.   [9] See Appendix II.
[10] *Ibid.*
[11] For instance, Mohsin-ul-Mulk first came to Syed Ahmed's notice when, as a subordinate clerk in the Etawah collectorate, he wrote to Syed Ahmed, after the publication of his commentary on the Bible (*Tabyin al kalam*) in 1862, accusing him of being an infidel. A few years later, Syed Ahmed received the same abuse from Samiullah Khan when he translated for the Scientific Society Elphinstone's *History of India* which calls Mahomed a 'false prophet'.

in 1886,[1] Syed Ahmed extended the scope of Aligarh's influence to Muslims throughout India. In different Indian provinces, various attempts were being made to solve Muslim educational problems; Syed Ahmed's aim was to co-ordinate the various regional solutions and to subject them to the Aligarh way. The emphasis in the Conference's policy was on making government education more acceptable to Muslims and on increasing opportunities for them; many resolutions were passed urging government to introduce religious education into primary schools and to give scholarships to Muslims seeking advanced education in English. At first, attempts at Aligarh imperialism were treated roughly; for instance, Syed Ahmed's resolution at the second Conference that funds intended for private schools in different parts of India should be diverted to Aligarh was defeated.[2] But not for long. A similar resolution was passed a few years later, and from 1898 every session of the Conference discussed and resolved in favour of the establishment of a Muslim University at Aligarh. Indeed, the Conference was little more than an extension of Syed Ahmed's Aligarh campaign. It was aristocratic and shared the same organisation. Aligarh was the headquarters, Aligarh students were often used to put Conference schemes into action. Aligarh staged five of the Conference's first eleven sessions. The Secretaries of the College and its Fund Committee were also Secretary and Treasurer of the Conference. The College was the arena in which Muslim opinion was created and UP Muslim leadership assembled. The Conference was the means by which this opinion was disseminated among Muslims in the rest of India, and this leadership imposed upon them.

The College and its attendant Conference were political organisations in all but name.[3] Their declared aims were educational

---

[1] The Conference began under the title 'Muhammadan Educational Congress'. In 1890, this was changed to 'Muhammadan Education Conference' in an endeavour to remove political suspicion and stress its educational aims, and then in 1895 the title was changed to 'Muhammadan Anglo-Oriental Educational Conference' indicating the nature of its educational aims. Jain, *Aligarh Movement*, p. 79.

[2] *Najmu-l-Akhbar* (Etawah), 4 January 1888, UPNNR 1888.

[3] Concerning the Conference, Syed Ahmed was known to say that, had the Muslims been stronger, he would have founded a political association. Conference sessions usually clashed with those of Congress. Conference propaganda was often aimed against it. Clearly an important aim of the Conference was to oppose the Congress.

because education was 'the passport to political power'.[1] But in addition to this covert political role, they were also the base on which overt political organisations were founded. The M.A.-O. Defence Association was founded at a session of the Educational Conference and the annual sessions of its Council were held at the same time and in the same place as the Conference. Similarly, the All-India Muslim League was founded at a session of the Educational Conference in Dacca, and for several years afterwards the two bodies met together. All UP and All-India Muslim political organisations, until the All-India Muslim League moved to Lucknow in 1910, had their headquarters at Aligarh. The chief importance of the College was that it was the base from which a UP Muslim elite group led a Muslim political party in the province and in India as a whole.

It is questionable whether Aligarh College and its founder would ever have been able to play the important role they did if government's attention had not been focused especially on Muslim affairs. In the late nineteenth century, the fear that had led government to adopt special measures for Muslim education had not diminished. The Wahabi threat had disappeared, but others rose to take its place. In spite of Syed Ahmed's attempts to allay government's suspicions, whenever British forces were engaged against Islamic powers, fears of the pan-Islamic sympathies of the Indian Muslims came to the fore. There is 'little doubt', Lyall wrote to Primrose during the Egyptian war of 1882, 'that the Mahommedans are sympathetic with Arabi Beg'.[2] During the Frontier campaigns and the Turkish crisis of 1897, Macdonnell noticed similar sympathy for the Sultan and went on to suggest that conditions in the UP had the makings of another Mutiny.[3] The plain truth was that the Muslims were not trusted. When, in 1874, the question arose of restoring the Berars to the Nizam of Hyderabad, Salisbury declared 'he [Salar Jung] can hardly imagine that we should look on a Mohammedan and a Native State in the same light. The Nizam is a real danger, and I would never willingly strengthen them [sic].'[4]

[1] *Aligarh Institute Gazette*, 18 November 1890, quoted in Jain, *Aligarh Movement*, p. 91.
[2] Lyall to H. W. Primrose, Private Secretary to the Viceroy, 18 July 1882, Lyall Papers (43), IOL.
[3] Macdonnell to Elgin, 16 July 1897, Confidential, Elgin Papers (71), IOL.
[4] Salisbury, Secretary of State, to Northbrook, 12 June 1874, Northbrook Papers, Vol. II, Part I, No. 15, quoted in S. Gopal, *British Policy in India, 1858–*

Separatism grows among Muslims

In 1877, Northbrook told the House of Lords not only was there 'a disloyal portion of the Indian Mahomedans...' but also that 'a really religious Mahomedan cannot be content with other than Mahomedan rule'.[1] Picking out the elements of danger in the UP, the Army Commission listed 'the lower stratum of the Muhammadan urban population, the dispossessed landholders [many of them, of course, Muslims], the predatory classes, and perhaps the cadets of old Muhammadan families [as]...the only sections of the people who really dislike British rule'.[2] In the 1890s, Macdonnell wrote tirelessly of Muslim fanaticism and of the danger the community represented to the Raj.[3] Such ideas were perpetuated by some Indian officials in prose[4] and others in verse. Describing a game of badminton under the Mughal walls of Delhi, Lyall wrote:

> Near me a Musulman, civil and mild,
> Watched as the shuttlecocks rose and fell;
> And he said, as he counted his beads and smiled,
> 'God smite their souls to the depths of hell'.[5]

Not all, of course, believed in the Muslim danger. Miller, Macdonnell's chief secretary, was doubtful,[6] and Strachey, a close friend of Syed Ahmed, dismissed the fear as 'altogether groundless'.[7] But these were not the attitudes on which government policy was founded.

For a government that was very conscious of the need to deal

1905 (Cambridge, 1965), p. 104. How seriously Muslim native states were regarded is illustrated by the fate of the Nawab of Bhopal when he was suspected of encouraging Jamal al-din al-Afghani, and of fostering Pan-Islamist sentiments of a seditious kind. He was deposed. For an analysis of the affair, see Saeedullah, 'The Life and Works of Muhammad Siddiq Hasan Khan, Nawab of Bhopal (1248/1832 to 1307/1890)' (MLitt thesis Cambridge, 1971), pp. 54–79.

[1] *Hansard*, Third Series (Lords), Vol. CCXLI, 18 July 1878, cols. 1821 and 1825.
[2] *Report of the Special Commission appointed by His Excellency the Governor-General in Council to enquire into the Organization and Expenditure of the Army in India* (Simla, 1879), p. 10. Curzon Papers (259), IOL.
[3] Macdonnell to Elgin, 16 July 1897, Confidential, and 22 August 1897, Confidential, Elgin Papers (71); Macdonnell to Curzon, 18 May 1900, Curzon Papers (201), IOL.
[4] Sir Richard Temple Bart., *India in 1880*, 3rd edn (London, 1881), p. 114.
[5] 'Studies at Delhi, 1876', II, 'Badminton', in Sir Alfred Lyall, *Verses Written in India* (London, 1889), p. 47.
[6] In 1897, Miller told Lyall 'he [Macdonnell] regards a Muhammadan combination as containing possibilities of danger. Personally I don't think there is any special feeling amongst them now.' J. O. Miller, Secretary to Government, NWP and O, to Lyall, 25 December 1897, Lyall Papers (71), IOL.
[7] Sir John Strachey, *India*, new and revised edn (London, 1894), p. 240.

with the Muslim problem, Syed Ahmed's initiatives came like manna from heaven. Both the Viceroy and the lieutenant-governor enthusiastically welcomed the report of the 'Committee for the better diffusion and advancement of learning among Mohammedans in India' and the latter ordered that it should be circulated among the educational officers of the province.[1] Close attention was paid to the report's list of obstructions to Muslim education[2] and action was taken on some, for instance, orders were given that Kempson's Urdu translation of Siva Prasad's *History of India* should be removed from the school curriculum because it was offensive to the Muslims.[3] A month after receiving the report, the Government of India told the UP that 'this movement on the part of the Mahomedans of Upper India is entitled to every encouragement which Government can give',[4] and the local government began well by overruling its Director of Public Instruction's objections to giving Syed Ahmed's College a grant-in-aid.[5] Leading officials heaped favours, personal and public, upon the Muslim effort. Northbrook made a personal donation of Rs. 10,000. Muir arranged for a seventy-four acre site belonging to the government to be sold to the Fund Committee for a derisory sum.[6] His successor, Strachey, donated Rs. 1000, and when local difficulties arose over the possession of the College site, went down to Aligarh and sorted the matter out himself. Muir opened the school in 1875, and the Viceroy, Lytton, laid the foundation stone of the College in 1877. No other institution in India received this kind of treat-

[1] Captain Evelyn Baring, Private Secretary to the Viceroy, to Syed Ahmed Khan, 10 June 1872, and C. W. Muir, Private Secretary to the Lieutenant-governor of the NWP, to Syed Ahmed Khan, 13 June 1872, in Husain, *Documents*, Part II, Nos. 4 and 5, pp. 146–7.

[2] For instance, so concerned was the Government of India about the points brought up by the report of the Benares Committee that it took the rather unusual step of interfering in what normally would have remained a provincial issue and asked the local government to provide information on the points raised. Officiating Secretary to the Government of India to Secretary to Government NWP, 9 August 1872, NWP Educ, June 1873, IOR.

[3] Hassan, 'Educational Movement', p. 292.

[4] Officiating Secretary to the Government of India to Secretary to Government NWP, 9 August 1872, NWP Educ, June 1873, IOR.

[5] The Director of Public Instruction, M. Kempson, urged vigorously that Syed Ahmed's project should not receive a grant-in-aid till it had proved itself. Kempson to Secretary to Government NWP, 28 August 1872, NWP Educ, June 1873, IOR. He was overridden by the lieutenant-governor, A. Colvin, Officiating Secretary to Government NWP, to Secretary to Government of India, 18 April 1873, *ibid.*   [6] Jain, *Aligarh Movement*, p. 160, fn. 2.

ment. Indeed, without it, it is doubtful if Aligarh College would have survived its early years. None of the great donations from the native princes, so essential to its launching, would have been forthcoming.[1] Nor would the bitter opposition of Kempson, who saw in Aligarh College the final victory of Syed Ahmed over government education policy, have been overcome. Theoretically, the College was a private venture – independence of government educational system was the only way it could offer the type of instruction which would attract Muslims – but, if government could help it, this private effort was not going to fail.

Government's conspicuous support for the College did not end with its foundation. To the end of the century, every lieutenant-governor and most Viceroys visited the College. Crosthwaite said what all had to say to the Muslims of Aligarh: 'this institution is one that the government will always foster and support...such assistance as it demands and as it lies in my power and, I venture to say, in the power of my successors, whoever they may be, to give, will always be at its disposal'.[2] Government's patronage of Syed Ahmed and his family as representatives of UP and Indian Muslim interests was no less conspicuous. In 1882, Syed Mahmud was appointed to the Education Commission. In the same year, he became the first native judge of the Allahabad High Court, and when compelled to retire eleven years later most probably because of drunkenness,[3] he was allowed to keep his full pension. In 1894, he was nominated to the provincial legislative council, and after his death in 1903, the government made liberal arrangements for the welfare of his family.[4] Syed Ahmed received marked favour for

[1] The College was very dependent on the generosity of the native princes, none of whom would have supported a cause of which government disapproved, for instance, it received Rs. 90,000 from the Nizam and Rs. 58,000 from the Maharaja of Patiala at its foundation and, in 1898, over forty per cent of its monthly income was derived from their endowments. Note on the Muhammadan Anglo-Oriental College, Aligarh enclosed in LaTouche, Offg. Lieutenant-governor of the NWP and O, to H. Babington Smith, Private Secretary to the Viceroy, 25 May 1898, Elgin Papers (72), IOL.

[2] Crosthwaite's reply to an address from the College, *Aligarh Institute Gazette*, 15 August 1893, quoted in Jain, *Aligarh Movement*, p. 165.

[3] Crosthwaite to Lansdowne, 4 January 1894, Lansdowne Papers (25); Crosthwaite to Lansdowne, 21 December 1892, Lansdowne Papers (23), IOL.

[4] Government took the unprecedented step of making arrangements to look after Ross Masud, Syed Ahmed's grandson, and the widows of his two sons. 'The political effect of any liberality will', LaTouche told Curzon, 'be far-reaching.' LaTouche to Curzon, 7 August 1903, Curzon Papers (208), IOL.

the greater part of his life: rewards for Mutiny services, a gold medal and a C.S.I. for educational work, and the ear of the highest officials. After he turned his attention especially to Muslim interests, there were extra reasons for singling him out. He sat on the Imperial Legislative Council from 1878 to 1882, the Public Service Commission in the NWP, and the Education Commission. In 1887, these honours were capped with the almost unique distinction for a man in his position of a K.C.S.I. Towards the end of the nineteenth century, Syed Ahmed's position and influence in northern India was unrivalled.

By this time, a strange paradox had developed in government's attitude to the Muslims. On the one hand, they were still regarded as dangerous, yet, owing to the success of the Aligarh policy, an important group of Muslims was also regarded as a major support of British rule in north India. 'The better classes of Mohammedans', wrote Strachey, 'are a source to us of strength and not of weakness. They constitute a comparatively small but energetic minority of the population, whose political interests are identical with ours...'[1] Analysing the political structure of the province, Auckland Colvin picked upon the Muslims, with the large landlords, as forces of conservatism; they had been and were to continue to be the main props of the Raj in the UP.[2] No wonder, therefore, that government was worried when, after the death of Syed Ahmed, succession struggles broke out, finances fell to pieces and the College seemed doomed. 'The failure of the Aligarh College', Macdonnell told the Viceroy, 'would be for these Provinces...a disaster of the greatest magnitude',[3] and government took immediate action. Macdonnell mediated in the succession struggle, accountants were despatched to put the finances in order, the Viceroy made a personal donation to encourage the Muslims to pay off the debt, and within the year the College had been saved. Government and Aligarh's interests had become so closely intertwined that even Macdonnell, who wished

---

[1] Strachey, *India*, p. 241.
[2] Note by Auckland Colvin, 11 June 1889, Home Public A, August 1892, 237–52, NAI, and for further analysis of the groups on which government relied for support in the UP see, F. C. R. Robinson, 'Consultation and Control: The United Provinces' government and its allies, 1860–1906', *Modern Asian Studies*, v, Part 4 (October 1971), pp. 313–36.
[3] Macdonnell to Elgin, 19 March 1898, Elgin Papers (72), IOL: LaTouche agreed, LaTouche, Offg. Lieutenant-governor of the NWP and O, to H. Babington Smith, Private Secretary to the Viceroy, 20 June 1898, *ibid.*

to shift the whole basis of government support in the UP from the Muslims to the Hindus, could not ignore the College's claims.

Syed Ahmed was the genius behind Aligarh but it was government's patronage that made the College and its managers a major political force. Without government's aid it is unlikely that the College would have been founded; it is even less likely that it would have been so successful. Without the favour of the Government of India, Syed Ahmed would never have acquired the position and reputation that enabled him to found and lead all-India political organisations. Thus, through government policy, Syed Ahmed, a man from the west UP, where the memory of Muslim power was the strongest, a man from the old Mughal Court with little in common with either the great Muslim peasant populations of Bengal and the Punjab or with the Muslim artisan masses of the UP towns, a man whose religious views were so unorthodox that the majority of his co-religionists branded him an infidel, was raised up as the advocate of his community. His views were accepted by government as Muslim views, and because they were accepted, they found currency among other Muslims who might otherwise have thought differently. By building up the College and Syed Ahmed, government assisted at the birth of a Muslim political party and a Muslim political doctrine.

Such a result smacks of divide and rule. Indeed, it is undeniable that British policy in the second half of the nineteenth century made a great contribution to the development of Muslim separatism. But this is not to say that division was intended. 'Nothing', declared Strachey, 'could be more opposed to the policy and universal practice of our Government in India than the old maxim of divide and rule...'[1] Others said the same.[2] The fact was that the British feared the Muslims. They were thought to be the

[1] Strachey, *India*, p. 241.
[2] For instance, Dufferin told the editor of *The Pioneer* in 1887: 'The diversity of races in India, and the presence of a powerful Mahomedan community, are undoubtedly circumstances favourable to the maintenance of our rule; but these circumstances we found and did not create, nor, had they been non-existent, would we have been justified in establishing them by artificial means. It would have been a diabolical policy on the part of my Government to endeavour to emphasize or exacerbate race hatreds among the Queen's Indian subjects for a political object.' Dufferin to George Allen, editor, *The Pioneer*, 1 January 1887, Dufferin Papers (reel 531), quoted in Gopal, *British Policy*, p. 160. See also note 197, *ibid.*, p. 353.

greatest threat not only to British rule in India but to the British Empire. To deal with them, government adopted special measures and made special concessions. These were aimed not at setting Muslims against Hindus, but at reconciling them to British rule. Their unintended result was to encourage some Muslims to operate in politics as Muslims.

CHAPTER 4

A high point of Muslim separatism
1900-1909

In the last three decades of the nineteenth century, the direction of Muslim politics in the UP depended largely upon an understanding between government and the Aligarh Muslim leaders. The business of the latter was to protect the interests of the Muslims of the Urdu-speaking elite. They supported government so long as administrative reforms were imposed lightly upon them, in deference to their interests, and so long as Hindu revivalist demands were given short shrift. Government wanted allies. It was prepared to support the Aligarh Muslim leaders so long as their politics were compliant and they had the apparent confidence of their politically active co-religionists. Between 1900 and 1909, the conditions in which this understanding worked began to change. The main cause was the cycle of political agitation and government concession, precipitated in part by the impact of administrative reform policies pressed on under Curzon, and in part by government's difficulties in satisfying both the interests these policies disturbed and the aspirations they excited. Concessions to Hindu revivalist agitation in the UP, and Hindu and Congress agitation elsewhere, led Aligarh leaders to fear that the government was deserting them. Young western-educated Muslims were so disillusioned by the poor rewards of political docility that they threatened to join the Congress. Some did. The Aligarh leaders were compelled, in order to remain in contol, to demand more vigorously than ever before that government should protect their interests. Government, in turn, feared that if it did not concede some at least of the Aligarh leaders' demands, it would lose the support of the Muslims, the ally whose hostility it most feared.

The understanding between the Aligarh leaders and the government was first attacked by Macdonnell. Admittedly, the lieutenant-governor's Aligarh salvage operation was true to government form,[1]

---

[1] See pp. 128–31.

but the rest of his Muslim policy was not. Macdonnell felt that the Muslims were too hostile and potentially too dangerous to be encouraged. The majority, Sunnis, had a double allegiance, on the one hand to Britain but on the other hand to their Khalifa, the Turkish Sultan. Moreover, they were too interested in the fate of Turkish and Afghan arms for his peace of mind.[1] He was ever on the watch for signs of Muslim fanaticism. The Nadwat-ul-ulama, probably quite innocent, was branded with sedition,[2] and when disturbances became riots, Macdonnell suspected the hand of the Muslim agitator.[3] Moreover, Muslim government servants were not to be trusted. 'A marked feature of the situation', he told Elgin during the pan-Islamist flurry of 1897, 'has been...the failure of our Mahomedan officials – Tehsildars and Police Officers, to give us any useful or tangible information as to what is going on beneath the surface.'[4] Consequently, one of the first aims of his administrative policy was to shift the basis of government support in the UP from Muslims more towards the Hindus. 'We are', he told Curzon, 'far more interested in [encouraging] a Hindu predominance than in [encouraging] a Mahomedan predominance, which, in the nature of things, must be hostile to us.'[5] The achievement of this aim was helped on by the general trend of government's reform policy, particularly in the bureaucracy. Earlier lieutenant-governors had implemented this policy half-heartedly, and had been concerned to moderate its tendency to reduce Muslim influence. Macdonnell imposed reform with rigour and refused to sugar the pill.

The Muslim service classes could hardly fail to notice the change of emphasis. Persian was removed from the curriculum of Allahabad University. A list of candidates for the post of tahsildar and deputy collector was rejected because it had too many Muslims. An enquiry was conducted to discover why there were more Muslims than Hindus in the Police Department. Orders were issued that not more than three Muslims should be appointed for every five Hindus in any branch of government, and fears for Muslim jobs were in no way soothed when a deputation demanding the replacement of the Persian script by Nagri had an encouraging

[1] Macdonnell to Elgin, 16 July 1897 (Confidential), and 22 August 1897 (Confidential), Elgin Papers (71), IOL.
[2] Macdonnell to Curzon, 21 October 1899, Curzon Papers (200), IOL.
[3] Macdonnell to Curzon, 18 May 1900, Curzon Papers (201), IOL.
[4] Macdonnell to Elgin, 22 August 1897 (Confidential), Elgin Papers (71), IOL.
[5] Macdonnell to Curzon, 18 May 1900, Curzon Papers (201), IOL.

reception.[1] In December 1899, some Muslims of Lucknow
sounded a warning note: 'the conviction was being forced upon
them', they said in a memorial to the government, 'that the activity
of the Congress agitators cannot be adequately counteracted by
following the lines of least resistance and that it is their duty as
loyal citizens no longer to sit with folded hands, while agitators gain
influence over the unthinking masses by monopolising Government appointments, and by getting themselves elected to Municipal Boards, the Legislative Councils and other public bodies.'[2]
A vigorous debate developed in the Muslim press over the
lieutenant-governor's hostility to the community, and some, finding it easy to identify support for Nagri with support for the
national cause, went so far as to accuse him of favouring the Congress.[3] It was hardly surprising that Muslims began to question the
assumption that government was friendly towards them and that
the best way to protect their interests was to eschew agitation.

The Nagri resolution of 18 April 1900 was the last straw.
Aligarh Muslims threw to the winds all the caution that they had
learned at the feet of Syed Ahmed. Mohsin-ul-Mulk[4] reorganised
the Muhammadan Anglo-Oriental Defence Association of Upper
India as the Urdu Defence Association, and at a gathering presided
over by the Nawab of Chhatari[5] it was decided to hold a meeting of
representative Muslims of North India to discuss the resolution
and to present a memorial to the lieutenant-governor.[6] At Allahabad, an Urdu Defence Association founded by English and
Muslim barristers in 1898 sprang into life under the guidance of
Karamat Husein.[7] At Lucknow, most of the leading Muslims, led
by Hamid Ali Khan, were swept into a committee to protect Urdu.

[1] Macdonnell concluded his reply on a hopeful note for those used to interpreting official pronouncements. 'The general conclusion I come to', he told
the deputation, 'is that, while I think that the more general use of Nagri in our
official dealings would be beneficial, and while the tendency of the times makes
me in favour of the change, there is no urgent or overbearing reason why
we should be in a hurry.' *Selections from the Speeches of Sir A. P. MacDonnell,
G.C.S.I., Lieutenant-governor, N.-W.P. and Chief Commissioner of Oudh from
1895 to 1901* (Naini Tal, 1901), p. 64.
[2] 'The Humble Memorial of the Undersigned Residents of the City of Lucknow',
enclosed in J. O. Miller, Chief Secretary to Government, NWP and O, to
Secretary, Government of India, Home Department, 26 January 1900,
L/P&J/6/712, IOR.
[3] *Al Bashir* (Etawah), 19 June 1899, UPNNR 1899.
[4] See Appendix II.   [5] *Ibid.*
[6] Hamid Ali Khan, *The Vernacular Controversy*, p. 101.
[7] See Appendix II.

From these centres, with the assistance of close coverage from the *Indian Daily Telegraph* and the *Pioneer*,[1] both of Lucknow, agitation spread though most of the district towns of the province and beyond right up to Lahore where a meeting was held under the presidency of the ultra-conservative Nawab Fateh Ali Khan Qizilbash.[2] Kayasths and Kashmiri Brahmins[3] joined the Muslims, and the agitation reached its height at a conference at Lucknow in August attended by 400 delegates from the Punjab, Bombay, CP and UP and elsewhere.[4] But this was as far as it went. Macdonnell did not take kindly to opposition.

In the protest against the Nagri resolution, the range of support for Muslim politics was extended far beyond the usual base of Aligarh and its connections. There were Agra landlords, Oudh taluqdars, ulama, civil service hopefuls, lawyers galore and leading Muslim Congressmen such as Hafiz Abdur Rahim of Aligarh, Sajjad Hussain, the editor of *Oudh Punch*, and Hamid Ali Khan of Lucknow. Analysing the Lucknow meeting, the government divided the agitators into the 'men of property and influence' and

[1] The *Pioneer* covered the agitation extensively until 10 June 1900. In the issue of this date, which also happened to be the one in which it announced the extension of Macdonnell's term as lieutenant-governor, the paper declared that it could not publish any more accounts of meetings and demonstrations over the Court character controversy. It seems that the editor of this influential Anglo-Indian paper was nobbled by the government. Hamid Ali Khan, *The Vernacular Controversy*, p. 2.

[2] For Nawab Fateh Ali Khan Qizilbash, see Appendix II. For a detailed description of the development of the Nagri agitation from May to August 1900 with an appendix containing newspaper reports of protest meetings, protest committees and their membership, see Hamid Ali Khan, *The Vernacular Controversy*.

[3] Kayasth and Kashmiri Brahmin service families had almost as much to lose from the upgrading of Nagri as the Muslims. The Kashmiri Brahmins, Pandit Amar Nath, son of Pandit Ajudhia Nath, and Pandit Kedar Nath, played a prominent part in the protest movement in Allahabad and Benares. *Ibid.*, pp. 14 note 1, and 116. The Kayasths already imagined that they were under pressure from what they felt was a government campaign directed against their strong position in the bureaucracy, *Kayasth Reformer* (Bareilly), 2 August 1890, *Hindi Pradip* (Allahabad). 10 July 1898, UPNNR, 1890 and 1898. The Kayasths were in the forefront of the agitation at Farrukhabad, Rudauli (Bara Banki), Rae Bareli, where there were several large Kayasth service families, and Mohan (Unao). Hamid Ali Khan, *The Vernacular Controversy*, pp. 108–9, 115–16 and 120.

[4] Macdonnell to Curzon, 31 August 1900, Curzon Papers (202), IOL; J. O. Miller, Chief Secretary to Government, NWP and O, to J. Hewett, Secretary, Government of India, Home Department, 21 September 1900, Home Judicial B, October 1900, 200–2, NAI, and *Oudh Akhbar* (Lucknow), 18 September 1900, UPNNR 1900.

the 'young gentlemen of progressive tendencies'.[1] It did so with reason because there was a marked difference in the willingness of these two groups to brave government's displeasure. For instance, the Nawab of Pahasu, landlord and Muslim representative on the legislative council, remained mute.[2] A growl from Macdonnell was enough to send most landholders scampering back to their estates.[3] Mohsin-ul-Mulk was made of sterner stuff. In May he ignored a tough warning from the lieutenant-governor,[4] and continued as head of the protest movement, presiding over the August conference in Lucknow. Macdonnell was furious.[5] He summoned the Aligarh principal, Morison, to Lucknow, lectured him and sent him back with a letter setting out the way in which the College Trustees should conduct their relations with the government.[6] When Mohsin-ul-Mulk persisted in associating himself with the agitation, Macdonnell visited Aligarh himself, harangued the Trustees and made it clear that the College secretary must choose between protest and Aligarh's government grant.[7] Mohsin-ul-Mulk chose the College. By 1901, Macdonnell had cut off all the tall poppies and there remained in the protest movement only the 'young gentlemen of progressive tendencies'.

[1] Miller to Hewett, 21 September 1900, Home Judicial B, October 1900, 200-2, NAI.   [2] *Al Bashir* (Etawah), 22 October 1900, UPNNR 1900. *Oudh Akhbar* (Lucknow), 17 September 1900; *Riaz-ul-Akhbar* (Gorakhpur), 20 and 24 September 1900; *Al Bashir* (Etawah), 24 September 1900, UPNNR 1900; and S. M. Ikram, *Modern Muslim India and the Birth of Pakistan (1858–1951)*, 2nd edn (Lahore, 1965), p. 86.

[4] Telegram, Private Secretary to the Lieutenant-governor, NWP and O, to Nawab Mohsin-ul-Mulk Bahadur, 15 May 1900, Hamid Ali Khan, *The Vernacular Controversy*, p. 99.

[5] Mohsin-ul-Mulk's defiance seems to have unbalanced Macdonnell. He wrote to Curzon giving the Aligarh leader a character that was quite out of line with those given him by other government officials and boasting that 'if I went down tomorrow to Aligarh, and called the Trustees together, I have no doubt I could turn Mohsin-ul-Mulk out of his Secretaryship'. Macdonnell to Curzon, 31 August 1900, Curzon Papers (202), IOL.

[6] Macdonnell's letter, sent through his private secretary, is an excellent summary of the way in which government considered not just Aligarh Muslims but all groups should conduct their relations with it. For the full text, which is worth reading, see Captain W. B. Douglass, Offg. Private Secretary to the Lieutenant-governor of the NWP and O, to Theodore Morison, Principal of Aligarh, no date, enclosed in Macdonnell to Curzon, 19 October 1900, Curzon Papers (202), IOL and quoted in F. C. R. Robinson, 'Consultation and Control: The United Provinces' Government and its allies, 1860–1906', *Modern Asian Studies*, v, Part 4 (October 1971), pp. 332–3.

[7] *Riaz-ul-Akhbar* (Gorakhpur), 20 February 1901, *Al Bashir* (Etawah), 1 April 1901, UPNNR 1901; Ikram, *Modern Muslim India*, p. 86.

The 'young gentlemen' were not slow to learn the lessons of this passage of arms. They considered that the Nagri resolution and government's repressive action showed that Syed Ahmed's policy of relying on government was bankrupt. They began to demand more militant action in defence of their interests. Their position was made articulate by one of the ablest Aligarh graduates of the day, Ghulam-us-Saqlain.[1] 'The order of Sir Antony Macdonnell', he wrote in an open letter to Curzon, 'teaches a very serious lesson to the communities of this country. It shows that even a small minority, if it be aggressive and energetic enough, can by sheer persistence succeed in getting such important, indeed revolutionary administrative mandates issued by the Government... This is a ready reward to political agitation, a call upon the people to rise and do the same.'[2] A strong demand developed for the formation of a Muslim political association. In his own monthly journal, *Asr-i-Jadid* or 'Modern Voice', founded in 1903, Ghulam-us-Saqlain gave the following reasons for political organisation:

Intelligent Musalmans will readily admit the necessity for the establishment of a Muhammadan political association. Owing to the want of such an association the interests of the Muhammadan community have already suffered in a variety of ways and are still being trampled under foot; some of the instances being the Hindi–Urdu controversy, the exclusion of Persian from the Allahabad University and the paucity of Musalman members in the Municipal and Local Boards.[3]

He stressed that Muslims could not join the Congress because it stood for the elective principle and competitive examinations, but he felt that they might co-operate with it on other issues. In particular, he saw possibilities of joint action on questions that affected the middle-income professional classes such as reduction in salt duty, raising the limit of taxable income from Rs. 500 to Rs. 1000 and the greater employment of natives in the commissioned ranks of the army. He insisted, no doubt recalling the defection of the landlords in 1900, that the political association ought not to have too many Muslim landowners and taluqdars in it, since 'no association which had a preponderance of Muslim landholders can

[1] See Appendix I.
[2] An 'Open Letter' to Lord Curzon from Ghulam-us-Saqlain, published in the *Punjab Observer* (Lahore), 16 May 1900 and quoted in Hamid Ali Khan, *The Vernacular Controversy*, p. 45.
[3] *Asr-i-Jadid* (Meerut), May 1903, UPNNR 1903.

exist long, the fate of the Aligarh Urdu Defence Association being a good instance'.[1]

If the 'young gentlemen' formed a political association of their own and agitated vigorously against government, they forfeited the special position in government eyes which Syed Ahmed had constructed for the Muslims. If they united with the Congress, they forfeited all possibility of special concessions to Muslims in the future. This was dangerous policy. The 'men of property and influence' went into action to counter it. Morison suggested the formation of a small council of leading Muslims.[2] Mohsin-ul-Mulk vacillated. Sometimes he declared for and sometimes against a moderate Muslim political association, but when he considered the prospect, he insisted that Muslim political representatives should be those who could represent Muslim interests to government in 'a respectful and suitable form as will receive a hearing from the authorities without offending them in any way'.[3] Such milk and water suggestions were unlikely to satisfy the young militants. Only a man whose hands were not tied by broad acres or by the need to ensure a government grant could take the initiative and so Viqar-ul-Mulk, protégé of Syed Ahmed and close friend of Mohsin-ul-Mulk, came out of secluded retirement on the Amroha municipal board to organise a Muslim political association within which the 'young gentlemen' could let off steam. He set out his approach in a letter to the *Pioneer*: 'We start with the firm conviction, and seek to implant it in the mind of every Indian Musalman that our national destiny is now bound up with the presence and permanence of British rule in this country, and that in the government of the day we have got our best and surest friend.'[4] Public agitation was to be avoided but, because the government was confronted with so many conflicting interests, it needed the help of the governed in the shape of 'true representation of facts'. 'We, the Indian Musalmans, being in the minority, have our own especial needs and require some means through which we can place them before the Government.'[5] In October 1901, Viqar-ul-

---

[1] *Asr-i-Jadid* (Meerut), February 1903, UPNNR 1903.
[2] *Aligarh Institute Gazette*, 19 September 1901, cited in Jain, *Aligarh Movement*, p. 149.
[3] Article by Mohsin-ul-Mulk on Muslims and political association, *Aligarh Institute Gazette*, 17 October 1901, UPNNR 1901.
[4] Letter from Nawab Viqar-ul-Mulk to the editor of the *Pioneer*, August 1903, quoted in the *Advocate* (Lucknow), 22 August 1903, UPNNR 1903.
[5] *Ibid.*

Mulk commenced his efforts by calling an informal meeting of Muslim leaders of all complexions[1] at the house of Hamid Ali Khan in Lucknow. After it, Ali Imam, the Bihar Muslim leader, declared that 'all of us who had taken part in it felt the absolute necessity of a political organisation of our own'.[2] This was followed by a couple of political meetings in Moradabad in 1902.[3] But progress was slow. It was not until 1903 that Viqar-ul-Mulk toured the districts of west UP exhorting the inhabitants to form local associations and elect delegates to a general Muslim meeting at Lucknow which would organise a Central Muhammadan Political Association. Meetings were held at Moradabad, Aligarh, Budaun and Bijnor,[4] and political associations were formed in at least two places, Saharanpur[5] and Shahjahanpur.[6] Then, on 22 October 1903, Muslim delegates from the UP, Punjab and Bihar met at Lucknow and agreed to set up a political organisation.[7] The project attracted all sorts of educated Muslims from Ghulam-us-Saqlain who helped Viqar-ul-Mulk on his tour of the west UP[8] to taluqdars who acted as Lucknow representatives of the association.[9]

This attempt to form a Muslim political association came to nothing. In December 1901, the urgent need for it lessened with

[1] The invitation to this meeting addressed to Raja Amir Hasar Khan of Mahmudabad, signed by Viqar-ul-Mulk, Hamid Ali Khan and Munshi Ehtisham Ali and dated 11 September 1901, exists in the private papers of the Mahmudabad family.

[2] Syed Ali Imam, Presidential Address at the Amritsar Session of the All-India Muslim League, 1908, in Syed Sharifuddin Pirzada (ed.), *Foundations of Pakistan: All-India Muslim League Documents: 1906–1947* (Karachi, 1969), Vol. I, p. 49.

[3] Very noticeable about the first Moradabad meeting was Viqar-ul-Mulk's concern to keep the association in the hands of men of standing and on the right side of the authorities; membership of a standing committee formed at Moradabad in February 1902 was limited to men with incomes greater than Rs. 500 p.a. and a copy of the proceedings of the meeting was sent to the local district magistrate. *Uruj* (Bijnor), 28 February 1902, UPNNR 1902.

[4] See reports in *Nizam-ul-Mulk* (Moradabad). 7 February 1903; *Uruj* (Bijnor), 14 July 1903; *Zul Qarnain* (Budaun), 25 July 1903, UPNNR 1903 and Jain, *Aligarh Movement*, p. 150.

[5] *Pioneer* (Lucknow), 31 July 1903, cited in S. R. Wasti, *Lord Minto and the Indian Nationalist Movement 1905 to 1910* (Oxford, 1964), p. 60.

[6] *Edward Gazette* (Shahjahanpur), 26 June 1903, UPNNR 1903.

[7] *Oudh Akhbar* (Lucknow), 10 December 1903, *ibid.*

[8] *Nizam-ul-Mulk* (Moradabad), 7 March 1903, *ibid.*

[9] The representatives included the Raja of Jehangirabad, *Oudh Akhbar* (Lucknow), 10 December 1903, *ibid.*

the end of Macdonnell's term as lieutenant-governor. LaTouche, his successor, was a lieutenant-governor of the traditional mould, and the Muslims came back into favour. The new atmosphere was quickly sensed. Within weeks, Athar Ali, the secretary of the Nadwat-ul-ulama, hurried back from Hyderabad whither he had fled to avoid Macdonnell's persecution.[1] Soon, it was felt that LaTouche was kindly disposed to Urdu, and rightly: 'Sir Antony MacDonnell', he told Curzon, 'went too far in acknowledging Hindi as a language.'[2] Within six months, sheristadars were again being appointed to tahsildarships, and the old ladder of promotion was working in the bureaucracy.[3] By the middle of 1903, no bilingual examinations had been held for clerical officials under clause (3) of the Nagri resolution[4] and government orders in Hindi as well as Urdu were rarely issued.[5] Muslims were finding government jobs easier to get, and, as Hindus pointed out in bitter complaint, Muslim numbers in the bureaucracy were rapidly increasing.[6] With their hands strengthened so handsomely by government the 'men of property and influence' were able to ignore the demands of the 'young gentlemen' for political association. Viqar-ul-Mulk found time to go on the Haj and the Aligarh Muslim leaders went onto the attack, travelling in deputation to Bombay to persuade the local Muslims to boycott the Congress.[7]

Nevertheless, between 1903 and 1906, though they had government favour, UP Muslims were continually reminded that their position was exposed. Urdu was again under attack. The Hindus were now trying to remove Muslim cultural influences from the educational system. Harcourt Butler commented:

The Hindus are now very much up and are trying to eliminate all words of Persian or Arabic origin and our textbook committee has got under the influence of the ultra-Hindi section and are writing primary textbooks in Sanskritized Hindi which the people cannot understand.[8]

Moreover, the principle of election was being extended and Muslims found that they were just as unsuccessful in elections to

---

[1] *Naiyar-i-Azam* (Moradabad), 12 January 1902, UPNNR 1902.
[2] LaTouche to Curzon, 15 May 1902, Curzon Papers (205), IOL.
[3] *Al Bashir* (Etawah), 6 May 1902 and *Hindustan* (Kalakankar), 9 May 1902, UPNNR 1902.   [4] For clause (3) of the Nagri resolution see [ch 2, p. 44].
[5] *Prayag Samachar* (Allahabad), 4 July 1903, UPNNR 1903.
[6] *Indian People* (Allahabad), 5 July 1906.
[7] *Advocate* (Lucknow), 27 November 1904, UPNNR 1904.
[8] Harcourt Butler to Mrs George Butler (his mother), 13 May 1903, Harcourt Butler Papers (6), IOL.

Separatism among Indian Muslims

the University Senates established in 1904 as they were in those to the Provincial Councils. Indeed, the whole nature of democratic politics increasingly disturbed young Muslims. 'How can I keep our boys from agitation,' Mohsin-ul-Mulk asked Harcourt Butler, 'If they see a man like Gokhale treated as equal by the Viceroy... listen, and pass orders[,] be a wise parent, is their idea of a ruler.'[1] But the crisis was precipitated by events outside the province. In 1906, a successful Hindu agitation to dismiss Sir Bampfylde Fuller, the pro-Muslim lieutenant-governor of the newly created province of Eastern Bengal and Assam, was followed by the Secretary of State's announcement in his budget speech that government intended to increase the size and the powers of the legislative councils. Another situation, similar to that created by the Nagri resolution, faced the UP Muslims, but many times worse. They appeared to have lost the favour of the government just at the time that it was to share out more powers among Indians. They had to act.

The 'young gentlemen' threatened to join the Congress. This danger had always been present, kept alive by newspapers such as Sajjad Hussain's *Azad*, Jamaluddin Ahmed's *Hamdard*, and particularly by Hasrat Mohani's[2] *Urdu-e-Moalla*,[3] a journal founded by Aligarh in the wake of the Nagri resolution and advocating joint Hindu–Muslim action in India as the best means of compelling the British to look after Muslim interests in the world at large.[4] In 1905, young Aligarh Muslims such as Tufail Ahmad and Hasrat Mohani attended the Congress held at Benares, and, in May 1906, the Aligarh College Students' Union took an alarming line when it passed by 'overwhelming majorities' motions advocating joint action by Hindus and Muslims in politics.[5] On top of this came Fuller's resignation, and Morley's announcement, seeming to mark the success, even the respectability of agitation. On

[1] Harcourt Butler to H. E. Richards, 28 April 1905, Harcourt Butler Papers (18), IOL.   [2] See Appendix I.
[3] This was an important journal of pan-Islamic sympathies that was to be produced sporadically, largely when Mohani was not in prison, over the next three decades. Its title was that of the form of Hindustani spoken by the Mughal court in Delhi, and it was 'remarkable for elegance of style and for the quality of its composition and versification.' Home Poll. B, August 1912, 120–1, NAI.
[4] Weekly Report of the Director of Central Intelligence (henceforth WRDCI), 24 August 1907, Home Poll. B, August 1907, 135–45, NAI.
[5] *Indian People* (Allahabad), 24 May 1906.

4 August, Mohsin-ul-Mulk advised Archbold, Morison's successor as College principal, that Morley's speech 'will produce a great tendency in them [the young educated Muslims] to join the "Congress"'.[1] He asked if a memorial to the Viceroy would be possible and his suggestion was encouraged.[2] Mohsin-ul-Mulk's correspondence with Archbold sets out the position in which the apparent withdrawal of government favour placed him. He had received letters from all over India telling him that 'Mohammedan feeling is very much changed...people generally say that the policy of Sir Syed and that of mine has done no good to Mohammedans ...that Government has proved by its actions that without agitation there is no hope for any community, and that if we can do nothing for them we must not hope to get any help for the college...'[3] He warned that 'if we remain silent...people will leave us to go their own way...'[4] The memorial was designed to give government an opportunity to affirm publicly its support for the politics of the Aligarh Muslim leaders and to provide them with the means to herd the young Muslim dissidents back into the Muslim fold.

The memorial was drawn up by Mohsin-ul-Mulk with the assistance of another man closely connected with Aligarh, Imad-ul-Mulk, Syed Hosein Bilgrami.[5] Other Muslim leaders, in particular Viqar-ul-Mulk, offered advice, but the memorial was essentially the work of Bilgrami and Mohsin-ul-Mulk.[6] The actual drafting seems to have been done by Bilgrami alone.[7] The result

[1] Mohsin-ul-Mulk to Archbold, 4 August 1906, enclosed in Minto to Morley, 8 August 1906, Morley Papers (9), IOL.

[2] *Ibid.*

[3] Mohsin-ul-Mulk to Archbold, 18 August 1906, enclosed in Archbold to Dunlop Smith, 22 August 1906, Minto Papers (4E383) NLS.

[4] Mohsin-ul-Mulk to Archbold, 4 August 1906, enclosed in Minto to Morley, 8 August 1906, Morley Papers (9), IOL.

[5] See Appendix II.

[6] It is interesting to note how similar the careers and the backgrounds of these two men were. Both had climbed high in the Hyderabad Civil Service, both were connected with Aligarh, both were members of prestigious Syed families the lands and fortunes of which had declined greatly; Imad-ul-Mulk belonged to the Syeds of Bilgram in Hardoi and Mohsin-ul-Mulk to the Etawah branch of the great Barha Syeds.

[7] Three forms of the memorial exist among the Harcourt Butler papers. The first, entitled 'Draft Memorial for private perusal and approval of Members only by Nawab Imad-ul-Mulk, Bahadur'. The second, with slight changes, was the draft that was examined at the Lucknow meeting. The third, with some minor rearrangement, a few additions and deletions here and there, largely

was submitted to Muslim delegates from all over India in the Lucknow Kaiserbagh Bardari on 15 and 16 September 1906, and a slightly amended version was presented to the Viceroy on 1 October 1906.

The memorial claimed to represent the views of all Indian Muslims, but it did not. At the Lucknow discussions, Nawab Salimullah[1] of Dacca and Nawab Ali Choudhury insisted that the memorial should beg assurance that the partition of Bengal would be maintained, but they were ignored by the Muslims of northern India.[2] The memorial, in fact, was not only drawn up by the Aligarh Muslim leaders but also asserted their interests. Its statements were not particularly original. They had been made before in various forms from the M.A.-O. College Fund Committee circular of 1872 to the abortive memorial of 1896. Nevertheless, the memorial did set out more fully than ever before the view that the Muslim members of the Urdu-speaking elite had of their political position, the pressures to which they were exposed and the price of their continued support of government. They reminded their rulers that they had once been the governing class, asked them to 'give due consideration to the position which they occupied in India a little more than a hundred years ago...' and emphasised their 'political importance'.[3] Adverting to the special relationship that they had with government, they warned that it was falling to pieces: 'earnestly as we desire that the Mohamedans of India should not in future depart from that excellent and time-honoured tradition, recent events have stirred up feelings, especially among the younger generation of Mohamedans, which might, in certain circumstances and under certain contingencies, easily pass beyond the control of temperate counsel and sober guidance'.[4]

The memorial went on to deal with the traditional home of power, government service. Recalling, no doubt, the decline in the

designed to give more punch and polish, and two additions strengthening the demand for jobs and begging government's help for a Muslim University, was the final memorial presented to the Viceroy. Harcourt Butler Papers (65), IOL.

[1] See Appendix IV.
[2] Matiur Rahman, *From Consultation to Confrontation: A Study of the Muslim League in British Indian Politics, 1906–1912* (London, 1970), p. 22.
[3] The Muslim address 'To His Excellency the Right Honourable the Earl of Minto...' p. 2, paragraph 5, Harcourt Butler Papers (65), IOL.
[4] *Ibid.*, pp. 2–3, paragraph 6.

number of government jobs held by Muslims since the Mutiny, the authors of the memorial stressed that 'the political importance of a community to a considerable extent gains strength or suffers detriment according to the position that the members of that community occupy in the service of the State. If, as is unfortunately the case with the Mohamedans, they are not adequately represented in this manner, they lose in the prestige and influence which are justly their due.' They pointed out that 'Since...the number of qualified Mohamedans has increased, a tendency is unfortunately perceptible to reject them on the ground of relatively superior qualifications having to be given precedence. This introduces something like the competitive element in its worst form, and we may be permitted to draw Your Excellency's attention to the political significance of the monopoly of all official influence by one class', and prayed that 'Government will be graciously pleased to provide that both in the Gazetted and the Subordinate and Ministerial services of all Indian Provinces, a due proportion of Mohamedans shall always find place.'[1] In the draft presented at Lucknow, this point was played down, but, when it was discussed, the majority present successfully insisted that its importance should be emphasised.[2]

The greater part of the memorial, however, was devoted to securing for the Muslims as strong a position as possible in the new power structure revolving around legislative councils. In doing so the UP Muslims argued from their experience. 'Municipal and District Boards', they stated, 'have to deal with important local interests, affecting to a great extent the health, comfort, educational needs and even the religious concerns of the inhabitants... and it is here that the principle of representation is brought home intimately to the intelligence of the people.' But in many places, they continued, Muslim tax-payers were not adequately represented, and nomination was an ineffective counterweight. The solution was separate representation to be determined in accordance with 'the numerical strength, social status, local influence and special requirements of either Community'.[3] In fact, they set out the lessons that they had learned in municipal self-government in

---

[1] *Ibid.*, p. 4, paragraph 9.
[2] Harcourt Butler to H. E. Richards, Legal Member of the Viceroy's Council, 16 September 1906, Harcourt Butler Papers (18), IOL.
[3] The Muslim address 'To His Excellency the Right Honourable the Earl of Minto...' pp. 5–6, paragraph 11.

west UP and Doab towns, and the solutions which they had demanded, and then applied these, with necessary safeguards, to their position in the development of Council government. They requested that the Muslim position should be protected here as they had found it had to be protected 'in the case of Municipalities and District Boards...'[1]

Finally, the memorialists begged the Viceroy for his assistance in founding a Muslim University – a demand also included as a result of the Lucknow discussions.[2] Aligarh College had enabled them to fight their battles so far. Now they wanted to fulfil Syed Ahmed's dream in order to prepare for the political campaigns of the future.

Minto's reply ignored all but one of the memorial's points. He began by lauding the close and longstanding connection between Aligarh and the government. 'Now', he said, 'when there is much that is critical in the political future of India the inspiration of Sir Syed Ahmed Khan and the teachings of Aligarh shine forth brilliantly in the pride of Mahomedan history, in the loyalty, commonsense, and sound reasoning so eloquently expressed in your address.'[3] Continuing, he mentioned the affairs of East Bengal and Assam, to which the memorial had only referred obliquely, and declared that government's policy with regard to the province, the future of which he hoped was now assured, had 'been dictated solely by a regard for what has appeared best for its present and future populations...'[4] The only issue in the memorial which Minto actually dealt with was the problem of elective government, and here his reply offered little more comfort to the Muslims than his references to Bengal. Pointing out that he had set up a committee to deal with the question, whose conclusions he did not wish to anticipate, he told the deputation that:

The pith of your address, as I understand it, is a claim that in any system of representation – whether it affects a Municipality, a District Board, or a Legislative Council in which it is proposed to introduce or increase an electoral organisation – the Mahomedan Community should be represented as a community, you point out that in many cases electoral bodies as now constituted can not be expected to return a Mahomedan candidate, and that if by chance they did so it could only be at the sacrifice of such a candidate's views to those of a majority opposed to his own community

[1] *Ibid.*, p. 6, paragraph 13.   [2] *Ibid.*, p. 7, paragraph 16.
[3] Lord Minto's reply to the Simla Deputation, quoted in full in Rahman, *Consultation to Confrontation*, Appendix II, p. 300.   [4] *Ibid.*

whom he would in no way represent; and you justly claim that your position should be estimated not merely on your numerical strength but in respect to the political importance of your community, and the service it has rendered to the Empire. I am entirely in accord with you...In the meantime I can only say to you that the Mahomedan Community may rest assured that their political rights and interests as a community will be safe-guarded in any administrative organisation with which I am concerned...[1]

This reassurance, as the reforms took shape, was frequently held up to government as a pledge of specific concessions to the Muslims. It was to be a great embarrassment. Yet in October 1906, Minto promised, and intended to promise, nothing except sympathy.

The memorialists declared themselves satisfied with Minto's reply, and Mohsin-ul-Mulk assured Dunlop Smith that they were grateful for the Viceroy's 'clear and sympathetic recognition of the rights of the Mohammedans of India, as a distinct community, based on a generous appreciation of their political importance...'[2] The Bengal Muslims were pleased with Minto's gratuitous reference to the partition question.[3] But the 'young gentlemen' were not pleased. Many were dissatisfied with the Viceroy's failure to mention the Muslim University and Civil Service and High Court appointments;[4] some did not like the memorial itself.[5] In fine, the Simla deputation failed in one of its major objects, the curbing of the 'young gentlemen'.

The means was soon provided. Nawab Salimullah, smarting after his defeat at Lucknow and the exclusion of Bengal problems from the memorial,[6] decided to go ahead independently. He circulated the members of the Simla deputation with the suggestion that an all-India Muslim political association should be founded. The idea was strongly opposed by the Aga Khan[7] and also by

[1] *Ibid.*, pp. 301–2.
[2] Mohsin-ul-Mulk to Dunlop Smith, Private Secretary to the Viceroy, 7 October 1906, in M. Gilbert, *Servant of India: A Study of Imperial Rule from 1905 to 1910 as told through the correspondence and diaries of Sir James Dunlop Smith* (London, 1966), p. 57.
[3] Rahman, *Consultation to Confrontation*, p. 27.
[4] *Urdu-e-Moalla* (Aligarh), October 1906 and *Awaza-i-Khalq* (Benares), 8 October 1906, UPNNR 1906.
[5] *Rahbar* (Moradabad), 28 October 1906, and *Oudh Akhbar* (Lucknow), 15 and 16 October 1906, UPNNR 1906.
[6] Nawab Salimullah did not join the Simla deputation on the grounds that he was having a cataract operation, an operation that might have been rearranged, Rahman, *Consultation to Confrontation*, p. 27.
[7] See Appendix IV.

Mohsin-ul-Mulk, who no doubt saw a threat in this Bengali-inspired plan to Aligarh Muslim leadership. After some discussion among the Simla deputation, the matter was left till December when the Muslim Educational Conference met at Dacca.[1] But Salimullah was not to be put off. In November, he announced that he was going to found a 'Muslim All-India Confederacy', and asked associations all over India to send delegates to the conference to be held at Dacca.[2] By the end of December, Salimullah's initiative could no longer be resisted. The 'young gentlemen' were clamouring for a political association, so there was every likelihood that the Nawab would succeed and the Aligarh leaders lose all claim to represent Indian Muslims. Moreover, as talk of working with the Hindus to protect Muslim interests had not diminished, there was an argument for helping Salimullah succeed in order to prevent Muslims from joining the Congress. 'They could no longer hold the young men', Mohsin-ul-Mulk told Harcourt Butler; 'they would join the Congress if they were not given a political organisation of their own.'[3] So the Aligarh Muslim leaders, with a large body of 'young gentlemen' from the UP,[4] made the

[1] Rahman, *Consultation to Confrontation*, p. 27.
[2] Salimullah's circular letter setting out the necessity for a Muslim political association, the need to break through the constraints set by Aligarh College into political activity suited to the times, and the lines on which he intended the organisation should run may be found in Pirzada, *Foundations of Pakistan*, Vol. I, pp. xlv–xlix. The objects of Salimullah's association were to be: '(a) To controvert the growing influence of the so-called Indian National Congress, which has a tendency to misinterpret and subvert the British Rule in India, or which may lead to that deplorable situation, and (b) to enable our young men of education, who, for want of such an association, have joined the Congress Camp, to find scope to exercise their fitness and ability for public life.' *Ibid.*, pp. xlviii–xlix and *Indian People* (Allahabad), 13 December 1906. Just before the foundation of the League in Dacca, Mohsin-ul-Mulk went to see Harcourt Butler in Lucknow saying that he could no longer hold the young men. Butler, recalling the occasion for Hardinge in 1913, told him that 'there never was any splendid loyalty. Mohsin-ul-Mulk and others came to me at Lucknow to take my advice. They were quite frank. They could not hold their young men and feared their joining the Hindus, which meant ultimate absorption of the Mahommedans. It was purely in their own interests that they formed the Moslem League.' Harcourt Butler to Hardinge, 3 April 1913, Hardinge Papers (85), CUL.
[4] Among those who travelled to Dacca from the UP who were likely to represent the views of the 'men of property and influence' were the following: Nawab Mohsin-ul-Mulk, Nawab Viqar-ul-Mulk, Hamid Ali Khan, Nawab Imad-ul-Mulk, Munshi Ehtisham Ali, Mahomed Nasim, Raja Naushad Ali Khan, Sahibzada Aftab Ahmad Khan, Mahomed Ishaq, Syed Karamat Husein, Abdur Rauf, Muhammad Muzammilullah Khan of Bhikampur, Abdullah

A high point of separatism

long journey to Dacca where, in a session chaired by Viqar-ul-Mulk, the All-India Muslim League was founded on 30 December 1906. The foundation resolution was proposed by Nawab Salimullah, and seconded and supported by three leading 'young gentlemen', Hakim Ajmal Khan, Zafar Ali Khan and Mahomed Ali.[1] This was both the beginning and the end of Salimullah and Bengal in the Muslim League. Mohsin-ul-Mulk and Viqar-ul-Mulk returned to Aligarh as joint secretaries of a provisional committee, of which nearly forty per cent came from the UP,[2] to frame a constitution for the League. Moreover, the secretaryship, and power in the League generally, was to remain in the hands of Aligarh and UP men for most of its existence.[3]

By capturing the secretaryship at Dacca, the Aligarh leaders were able, perhaps with the help of the Aga Khan and some Punjab Muslims, to fashion the organisation in their own image. The constitution imposed on the League at the Karachi session of December 1907 ensured that it was in the control of the 'men of property and influence'.[4] All-India membership was limited to 400 elected every five years, of which the UP quota was seventy;

Jan, Nawab Abdul Majid, Haji Ismail Khan, Sheikh Abdullah, Dr Ziauddin Ahmad. The following were likely to represent the views of the 'young gentlemen': Syed Nabiullah, Syed Zahur Ahmed, Ghulam-us-Saqlain, Haji Musa Khan, Mahomed Ali, Shaukat Ali, Syed Wazir Hasan, Wahiduddin, Muhammad Yusuf, Sheikh Zahur Ahmad, Hakim Ajmal Khan. Abdur Rahman Siddiqi of Dacca, later to figure prominently in the UP 'Young Party' was also present.

[1] The resolution was proposed by Nawab Salimullah, seconded by Hakim Ajmal Khan (see Appendix I) and supported by Mohamed Ali (see Appendix I) and Zafar Ali Khan, an Aligarh graduate who was later to become editor of the Pan-Islamist newspaper, the *Zamindar* of Lahore. An amendment to the resolution proposed by Aftab Ahmad Khan and Sheikh Abdullah of the UP was withdrawn.

[2] Twenty-one out of fifty-eight committee members represented the UP. Over and above this, there were UP men such as Mahomed Ali representing other areas. Pirzada, *Foundations of Pakistan*, Vol. I, pp. 11–12.

[3] Between 1906 and 1926, the Secretaryship, the key post, remained firmly in UP hands:
1906–April 1907: Nawab Mohsin-ul-Mulk (Aligarh) and Nawab Viqar-ul-Mulk (Aligarh), Joint Secretaries.
April 1907–March 1908: Nawab Viqar-ul-Mulk (Aligarh).
March 1908–February 1910: Major Syed Hasan Bilgrami (Aligarh and London) and Haji Musa Khan (Aligarh), Joint Secretaries.
February 1910–February 1912: Maulvi Aziz Mirza (Lucknow).
February 1912–19: Syed Wazir Hasan (Lucknow).
1919–26: Syed Zahur Ahmed (Lucknow).

[4] For the victory of the 'men of property and influence' see Rahman, *Consultation to Confrontation*, pp. 52–60.

Separatism among Indian Muslims

and only those over twenty-five, literate in an Indian language, in possession of an annual income of more than Rs. 500 and able to pay a yearly subscription of Rs. 25 and an entry fee of the same amount were eligible to join the select band.[1] Thus many of the 'young gentlemen' for whom the League had been brought into being at Dacca were cut out at Karachi.

Aligarh Muslims not only got the type of political organisation they could stomach but they also controlled it. The executive body of the League was a Central Committee of forty elected every three years.[2] This committee, and the day-to-day activity of the League, was largely in the hands of the secretaries who could call meetings when and where they wanted. At the Aligarh session of 16–17 March 1908, Major Syed Hasan Bilgrami,[3] half-brother of Imad-ul-Mulk Syed Hosein Bilgrami and a former I.M.S. officer who had retired to Aligarh, was elected secretary, and Haji Musa Khan,[4] of the great Aligarh Sherwani family, joint secretary. These men, both political disciples of Viqar-ul-Mulk, who had succeeded Mohsin-ul-Mulk as the Aligarh College secretary, compensated for the election of the Aga Khan as President. The Ismaili leader appears to have been chosen for his conservatism, his wealth and his supposed influence with government. It cannot have been for his influence over the Indian Muslims; that was limited. So was his support for the League, financial or otherwise; he did not attend a single meeting till January 1910.

Between 1907 and 1909, provincial Muslim Leagues were founded in all the major provinces.[5] Some had rules and regulations similar to those of the parent association but all were free to frame their constitutions according to local circumstances. The All-India Muslim League claimed no control over the affairs of the provincial leagues, and they had no say in those of the central organisation. The varied political complexions of the provincial associations, some of which had policies at variance with those of the central body, indicates why. The Eastern Bengal and Assam League,

---

[1] *Ibid.*, pp. 52–3.
[2] Representation was divided up thus: the UP, Punjab, E. Bengal, W. Bengal/ Bihar/Orissa had seven members each, Bombay four, Madras, Berar/CP and Indian States two and Burma and the N.W. Frontier/Baluchistan one. *Aligarh Institute Gazette*, 18 March 1908, quoted in Lal Bahadur, *The Muslim League: its History, Activities & Achievements* (Agra, 1954), p. 73.
[3] See Appendix I. [4] *Ibid.*
[5] For an analysis of this process, see Rahman, *Consultation to Confrontation*, pp. 64–85.

founded in 1909, was mainly concerned, naturally enough, with the preservation of Eastern Bengal as a separate province. The Madras League was set up by the young radical Yakub Hasan; he was concerned to block the attempt of Syed Muhammad, a grandson of Tipu Sultan, to capture the Madras Muslims for the Congress.[1] In establishing the Bombay and Bihar Leagues, Congress Muslims played a big part.[2] Indeed, in the Bihar League, the importance of Congressmen such as Hasan Imam and Mazharul Haq,[3] and local Hindu–Muslim alliances, was so great that it declared against the cardinal point of the All-India League's creed, separate electorates.[4] The nature of the Punjab and West Bengal Leagues was closer to that of the parent body. The foundation of both involved a struggle between 'young gentlemen', some of whom had pan-Islamic views, and the 'men of property and influence', in which the latter were victorious.[5] The UP League, founded in June 1909, was almost the last to come into existence. Its inauguration was held up partly because Lucknow and Allahabad Muslims could not agree on where it was to be sited, but mainly because there was little incentive. The needs of UP Muslims, as was always to be the case, were largely catered for by the all-India organisation. The insignificance of the provincial league was a pointer to UP Muslim influence in the All-India League.

Much more important than the provincial leagues, in the short term, was the London branch of the All-India Muslim League. Towards the end of 1907, its foundation was mooted by Ameer

[1] *Ibid.*, pp. 69–72, and for the background to Yakub Hasan's initiative and his political base among the Urdu-speaking Muslims of Madras, see K. Macpherson, 'The Political Development of the Urdu- and Tamil-speaking Muslims of the Madras Presidency 1901 to 1937' (Unpublished MA Thesis, W. Australia, 1968), especially pp. 41–7.

[2] Rahman, *Consultation to Confrontation*, pp. 69–70, 78–9.

[3] See Appendix IV.

[4] Rahman, *Consultation to Confrontation*, p. 143.

[5] In the Punjab, there was a struggle between a group of young men led by Fazl-i-Husain, who had already founded a Muslim League early in 1906, and a group of successful lawyers and landed magnates, centred around the Anjuman-i-Islamia, led by Muhammad Shafi and Shah Din. In Bengal, battle took place between a pan-Islamically minded set of non-Bengalis led by the young Abdullah Suhrawardy and the Bengali Muslim establishment, followers of Ameer Ali and Nawab Abdul Latif, under the direction of Shams-ul-Huda. In the latter case, matters were complicated by a faction with Congress affiliations, but its activities do not seem to have been of great importance. *Ibid.*, pp. 72–7.

Ali,[1] a former judge of the Calcutta High Court who had retired to England. The idea was approved and money voted by the Aligarh session of the All-India Muslim League, and in May 1908 the London branch was inaugurated. The membership consisted mainly of young Muslims either at English universities or reading for the Bar.[2] Ameer Ali was president, a string of British Muslim sympathisers eminent in public life, including Harold Cox, formerly maths master at Aligarh and now MP for Preston, were vice-presidents and young men from the UP, Ibni Ahmad,[3] Sheikh Zahur Ahmad[4] and Masood-ul-Hasan,[5] controlled the secretariat. Ameer Ali had one or two pet enthusiasms such as the reform of Muslim family law in India and the foundation of a mosque in London, but the declared aims of the London branch were: 'To promote concord and harmony among the different nationalities of India; To work in the advancement of the general interests of the country in harmony and concert with the other Indian communities; To advance and safeguard by all constitutional and loyal methods the special interests of the Mahommedan subjects of the King; To bring the Mahommedans so far as possible into touch with leaders of thought in England.'[6]

At each stage in the formulation of the reforms between 1907 and 1909, the All-India Muslim League and its London branch played an important part in fighting to ensure that the price paid for their support for the proposals was high. The first skirmish came after the government of India's reform plans became known in August 1907. The most important part of them concerned the enlargement of the legislative councils. For the centre, an imperial legislative council of fifty-three officials and non-officials was proposed in which the Muslims would have four reserved seats, two chosen by a separate electorate and two nominated by government. For the provinces, government could do no more than suggest the lines on which the provincial governments should draw up their plans; it recommended that 'the general principle to be borne in mind is . . . that the widest representation should be given to classes,

---

[1] See Appendix IV.
[2] There was no shortage of young Muslims in England: in 1903, eighty-eight Muslims from Aligarh alone were there. *Al Bashir* (Etawah), 3 March 1903, UPNNR 1903.   [3] See Appendix II.
[4] See Appendix I.   [5] *Ibid.*
[6] *Report of the Inaugural Meeting of the London Branch of the All-India Moslem League with the President's Address Wednesday, May 6th, 1908*, p. 6.

A high point of separatism

races, and interests, subject to the condition that an official majority must be maintained...'[1] On the subject of Muslim representation government declared that in addition to the small number of Muslims who might be able to secure election in the 'ordinary manner', it seemed desirable, first that in each of the councils it should assign a certain number of seats to be filled exclusively by Muslims (as it had done in the case of the imperial legislative council), and second that in order to fill these seats it should create a special Muslim electorate.[2] The Government of India's suggestions were considered by a subcommittee of the All-India Muslim League. Its reactions showed that the gap between the League's hopes and government plans was large. In the imperial legislative council it demanded ten reserved seats, one for each province and one for the Aligarh Trustees. In the provincial councils, it asked for a fixed number of seats for Muslims in each council, and suggested that there should be at least one Muslim representative for each division. No seats were to be filled by nomination, and in all reserved seats Muslims alone were to have the vote. In addition, the subcommittee wanted reserved seats and separate electorates for Muslims on all municipal and district boards.[3] With these points the League staked out the Muslim claim. In essence its interpretation of the demand for separate representation was that in every elected body Muslims should have a reserved number of seats that took into account both their numerical proportion and their political importance, and that in these seats Muslims only were to vote for Muslims.

The Government of India took note of the Muslim League's comments. The reforms scheme sketched out in its despatch of 1 October 1908 gave the Muslims a fixed number of reserved seats in every council, all of which were to be filled by separate electorates. Only in the Punjab, which was a special case, was nomination retained. The despatch went to some lengths to show how far the Government of India had gone to meet the Muslim League's demands. It illustrated how, in addition to raising Muslim representation on the Imperial Legislative Council from four, two

[1] Circular from the Secretary to the Government of India, Home Department, to Local Governments and Administration, 24 August 1907, Morley Papers (32), IOL.
[2] Ibid.
[3] 'Suggestions on the Councils Reform Scheme of the Government by the All India Muslim League', 24 March 1908, Minto Papers (4E239), NLS.

153

nominated and two elected, to five elected seats, the Government of India had in almost every case improved upon the suggestions for Muslim representation made by the provincial governments.[1] Nevertheless, only in the UP and Madras did the scheme meet the full League demand for representation that took into account both numerical proportion and political importance.[2] But if the Government of India's plans were disappointing, they did at least accept the principle of separate electorates. The Secretary of State's reform scheme, outlined in a despatch of 27 November 1908, denied even this. To gain representation of the Muslim minority, Morley suggested mixed electoral colleges in which a number of seats would be reserved for Muslims on the basis of their numerical proportion, but for these seats both Hindus and Muslims would vote.[3] The cardinal points of the Muslim League position, separate electorates and 'political importance', had been ignored. The League was forced to light the fires of Muslim agitation.

Throughout India, the Muslim press protested against what was regarded as a betrayal of the Viçeroy's promise to the Simla deputation. Muslim activity was, according to the Lucknow *Advocate*, 'simply phenomenal'.[4] In the last week of December, the All-India Muslim League met at Amritsar. In proposing resolutions regarding the Secretary of State's scheme, the president, Ali Imam,[5] attacked the electoral college plan, first for relying on numerical proportions in calculating the political importance of the Muslims,[6] and second as 'a system that will be eminently successful in returning to the Councils mandatories of the majori-

---

[1] Bombay offered the Muslims no seats in its council; India raised this to three. Bengal offered the Muslims no seats; India raised this to two. East Bengal and Assam offered the Muslim one seat; India raised this to two. The UP offered four seats, two nominated and two elected; India changed this to four elected seats. The Punjab offered no Muslim nominations; India gave the Muslims two. Public Despatch No. 21 of 1908 to the Secretary of State for India, 1 October 1908, Morley Papers (33), IOL.

[2] In Madras, where the Muslims were six per cent of the population in 1901, they had ten per cent of the elected members. In the UP where they were fourteen per cent of the population, they had nineteen per cent of the elected members.

[3] Public Despatch No. 193 of 1908 to the Governor-General of India in Council, 27 November 1908, Morley Papers (33), IOL.

[4] *Advocate* (Lucknow), 18 February 1909, UPNNR 1909.

[5] See Appendix IV.

[6] Speech by Syed Ali Imam on moving the first three resolutions of the Amritsar Muslim League session, 30 December 1908, in Pirzada, *Foundations of Pakistan*, Vol. I, pp. 61–3.

ties who are "members" of our community, no doubt, but certainly not "representatives" of our people'.[1] The League's dissatisfaction on these two fundamental points was embodied in its second and third resolutions. The third ended with the threat that the promises of 1906 should be kept or else government would bring about 'the first breakdown of that implicit faith which Musalmans have so long placed in the care and solicitude of Government whose just pride and profession have been to hold the scales even'.[2] The League resolved to send deputations to the Viceroy and to the Secretary of State. A twenty-two man committee was appointed to draw up a memorial. In the middle of January, Ali Imam, the chairman of the committee, saw the Viceroy to arrange the deputations. After the interview the plan was abandoned. What passed is not known, but it is probable that he was informed that the Viceroy was as hostile to the electoral college scheme as the League. Minto had already told Morley that he thought its objections to the scheme 'thoroughly sound'.[3]

Morley was the man who had to be convinced and so the major drive against the electoral college scheme came from the London branch of the Muslim League. Its resolutions on the question, which were similar to those passed at Amritsar, were published in *The Times* of 4 January 1909. They accompanied a report of an interview with Ibni Ahmad and Major Syed Hasan Bilgrami, in which both made it clear that 'if the electoral college scheme was retained in its present form, the non-Moslem majority would absolutely control the elections, and would send the colleges only such Mahomedans as would subscribe to its political doctrines'.[4] The report set going a debate that ranged widely though the British press.[5] In its course, it became evident that the League had considerable support. The electoral college scheme was attacked by retired ICS men of note such as Crosthwaite,[6] the former lieutenant-

[1] *Ibid.*, p. 63.　　　　[2] *Ibid.*, p. 59.
[3] On 12 January 1909, Minto told Morley, 'I will not repeat myself, except to say that the objections raised to the scheme are I am convinced thoroughly sound and that any attempt to introduce it would not only increase the Mahomedan storm that is already raging, but would prove the machinery to be unworkable'. Minto to Morley, 12 January 1909, Morley Papers (19), IOL. See also, telegram, Viceroy to Secretary of State, 8 January 1909, *ibid.* (31).
[4] *The Times* (London), 4 January 1909.
[5] Rahman, *Consultation to Confrontation*, pp. 101–6.
[6] See a letter from Sir C. Crosthwaite in *The Times* (London), 9 January 1909, and also a summary of an article by him in *Blackwood's Magazine*, February

governor of the UP, by *The Times*,[1] by the Parliamentary opposition, and by a section of Morley's own party.[2] Moreover, it was rumoured that, if the Secretary of State did not acknowledge the force of the League's complaint, Ameer Ali would move Lansdowne, the former Viceroy who was now leader of the Conservative opposition in the Lords, to throw out the Indian Councils Bill.[3] Morley had stumbled on a hornets' nest. He was shaken. So shaken, indeed, that when on 27 January the London League presented an address reiterating the Muslim position,[4] his reply made it 'plain enough to anybody accustomed to read between the lines of ministerial statements that the mixed Electoral College is practically dead'.[5] Instead, he hinted that there might be a separate Muslim electoral college and declared that he saw 'no harm...in the principle that population, numerical strength, should be the main factor in determining how many representatives should sit for this or the other community; but modifying influences may be taken into account in allotting the numbers of such representatives.'[6] Nevertheless, the League leaders were not very good at reading between the lines; they were disappointed. Nor were they relieved till 23 February when Morley publicly capitulated. He told the House of Lords that the Muslims demanded the election of their own representatives in councils at all stages by themselves and a number of seats in excess of their numerical strength. 'Those two demands', he declared, 'we are quite ready and intend to meet in full.'[7] The Muslim League had won its first great victory.

If the League leaders imagined that their troubles were over, they were mistaken. The Indian Councils Bill which was then before Parliament in no way met the two demands 'in full'. The discrepancy between Morley's declaration and government's inten-

---

1909, in which he attacked electoral colleges in particular and the reforms in general in *ibid.*, 28 January 1909. See also a letter from Sir Bampfylde Fuller in *ibid.*, 12 January 1909.

[1] See the first leader in *ibid.*, 11 January 1909.
[2] Rahman, *Consultation to Confrontation*, p. 101.
[3] 'The Memoirs of Rt. Hon. Syed Ameer Ali', *Islamic Culture* (July 1932), p. 38 cited in *ibid.*, p. 104.
[4] The London League's address was summarised in *The Times* (London), 27 January 1909.
[5] Morley to Minto, 28 January 1909, Morley Papers (4), IOL.
[6] Lord Morley's reply to the London League deputation published in *The Times* (London), 28 January 1909.
[7] *Hansard*, Fifth Series (Lords), Vol. I, 23 February 1909, col. 125.

tion became evident when the Bill was moved in the House of Commons on 1 April 1909.[1] The legislation was based on the Government of India's despatch of October 1908. Only a few seats were reserved for the Muslims in the Imperial and Provincial Councils over and above those which they might win in the mixed electorates; their number in most cases was less than the Muslims might claim on the grounds of their proportion of the population and they were to be filled in part by separate electorates and in part by nomination. The League appeared to be back where it had started.

The London League launched a strong attack on the Bill,[2] and during the debate about it in committee gained the support of many MPs.[3] Earl Percy, a former Under-Secretary of State for India, pointed out that the Bill was inconsistent with the pledge that the Secretary of State had given to the Muslims on 23 February.[4] In reply, Hobhouse, standing in for Buchanan, the Under-Secretary, first denied the pledge by reading a telegram from Minto stating that some representation would be provided for Muslims through general electorates while a certain number of seats would be reserved which were to be filled by Muslims alone,[5] and then confirmed it.[6] In the face of such inconsistency the opposition had a field day.[7] On 26 April, under pressure in the House of Commons, Hobhouse again confirmed the Secretary of State's pledge saying that 'wherever elections are found possible they shall be conducted on the basis of separate representation of the Mahomedan community'.[8] After this, it at last dawned on the India Office that it was working at cross purposes with the Government of India. Measures taken to resolve the situation made it worse, not better. A worried Morley asked Minto for help.[9] The

[1] See speech by Buchanan, the Under-Secretary of State for India. *Hansard*, Fifth Series (Commons), Vol. III, 1 April 1909, cols. 500–2.
[2] At a meeting of the League on 31 March 1909, the Bill's provisions for Muslim representation were attacked vigorously. *The Times* (London), 3 April 1909.
[3] Rahman, *Consultation to Confrontation*, p. 119.
[4] *Hansard*, Fifth Series (Commons), Vol. III, 19 April 1909, cols. 1307–10.
[5] *Ibid.*, col. 1311.   [6] *Ibid.*
[7] On 26 April, Hobhouse had to weather a storm of criticism from among others: Ronaldshay, Joynson-Hicks, Percy, Balfour and O'Donnell. *Hansard*, Fifth Series (Commons), Vol. IV, 26 April 1909, cols. 33–9, 39–40, 40–2, 51–6, 58–60.   [8] *Ibid.*, col. 51.
[9] On the day after Hobhouse's discomfiture, Morley telegraphed Minto saying that the Muslim question had caused 'serious difficulty', giving details of the problem and asking the Government of India for its views on separate electorates and pledges. Telegram, Secretary of State to Viceroy, 27 April 1909, Morley Papers (33), IOL.

Viceroy replied, denying what any Muslim Leaguer would justi-
fiably infer from Hobhouse's statement: 'I do not understand', he
said, 'any Muhammadan here to claim concession suggested by
Hobhouse, namely that, wherever elections are found possible
they should be conducted on the basis of separate representation
of the Muhammadan community.'[1] On 4 May, Morley read this
to the House of Lords.[2] The London League was furious. They
did not see how it was possible to reconcile Minto's reply to the
Simla deputation, Morley's reply to the London League deputation.
and Hobhouse's statement of 26 April, with the present policy o
the Government of India.[3] Throughout May 1909, the London
League presented its case energetically to the India Office and the
British public.

Effective agitation this time came from India; it was, after all,
the Government of India that had to be persuaded. Nevertheless,
the All-India Muslim League was slow off the mark. One reason
was that the central committee was taken in by Morley's declaration of 23 February 1909, and another that Ali Imam, the chairman
of the Amritsar subcommittee on reforms policy, had moved away
from Muslim League policy as enunciated at the Amritsar session
and committed himself both to the Government of India's scheme
and to a Hindu–Muslim front to help push it through.[4] Moreover,
on 12 April, Ali Imam succeeded in persuading the central committee, assembled at Aligarh, to adopt a more conciliatory attitude
to the Government of India's scheme.[5] These developments, combined with the gradual revelation of the discrepancy between the
government's promises and its plans, did not please most provincial and district leagues. Ali Imam was attacked as a traitor to
the community, and regardless of the new orientation in League
policy, in April and May 1909 League members worked up a
Muslim agitation as never witnessed before. Western-educated and

[1] Telegram, Viceroy to Secretary of State, 2 May 1909, Morley Papers (35), IOL.
[2] *Hansard*, Fifth Series (Lords), Vol. I, 4 May 1909, col. 757.
[3] See, for instance, resolutions 1–3 of the committee of the London branch of
the All-India Muslim League, passed on 6 May 1909, in *The Indian Mahoma-
dans and the Government* (published by the London branch, no date, and sent
to the Secretary of State on 29 May 1909), pp. 51–2.
[4] In early April 1909, Ali Imam joined Gokhale in an attempt to create Hindu–
Muslim support for the Government of India reform scheme. He got support
from the Bihar Provincial Conference, temporary acquiescence from the
Muslim League central committee, but that was all. Rahman, *Consultation to
Confrontation*, p. 117.   [5] *Ibid.*, pp. 116–19.

158

orthodox, Shia and Sunni, landlord, professional man, shopkeeper and priest all joined their voices to the protest. Organisations, public meetings and individuals delivered memorials to the government.[1] The second resolution of a mass meeting held at Lucknow on 28 April is representative of the general complaint. Those present resolved that 'no system of Muhammadan representation in the Provincial and Imperial Councils will be either effective in itself or acceptable to them that does not provide for an adequate number of seats in excess of their numerical strength, and for all such seats to be filled by election by exclusive Muhammadan electorates'.[2]

The League leaders could not ignore views that were expressed so strongly. At an extraordinary general meeting on 23 May they returned firmly to the position they had staked out in 1908. Ali Imam performed a backward somersault, and six weeks after he had declared for the Government of India's scheme proposed the leading resolution which voiced the community's alarm at the government's intention to limit Muslim representation to a few seats, as suggested in the Viceroy's telegram of 2 May, and demanded a 'separate electorate composed entirely of Muhammadan electors' for those seats to be reserved for Muslims on the basis of their numbers and political importance. Moreover, Ali Imam in moving and Muhammad Shafi in seconding the resolution did not mince their words. Muslim good behaviour, they hinted broadly, could not be guaranteed if the government went back on its promises.[3]

Minto was not impressed.[4] But the Reforms Committee of his Council was. Its members felt that the Muslims had a case, and recommended Minto to consult with selected Muslim leaders.[5] On 26 June the two sides met. The Government of India offered to compromise; it would concede a few more Muslim seats here and there, but not the full Muslim League demand. Ali Imam did

[1] *Ibid.*, pp. 121–8; a large number of representations from Muslim organisations, meetings and individuals are collected together in Home Public, August 1909, IOR.
[2] Report in the *Indian Daily Telegraph* of 29 April 1909 enclosed in J. M. Holms, Secretary to Government, UP, to Sir H. Stuart, Secretary to Government of India, Home Department, 5 May 1909, Home Public, August 1909, IOR.
[3] Rahman, *Consultation to Confrontation*, p. 136.
[4] Minto to Morley, 27 May 1909, Morley Papers (20), IOL.
[5] Adamson, Home Member of the Government of India, to Dunlop Smith, 19 June 1909, Minto Papers (4E388), NLS.

another somersault.[1] He was prepared to accept the Government of India's terms. Others, notably Abdul Majid[2] of Allahabad, were not. Ali Imam attempted to force the compromise on the League in two hastily called meetings in Lucknow on 10 and 11 July; he was baulked by Abdul Majid and others from the UP.[3] Consequently, although in the Government of India's despatch to the Secretary of State of 22 July 1909 Muslim representation on the Imperial Council went up from five to six, and was increased by two seats and one seat on the Eastern Bengal and Assam and Bengal councils respectively,[4] the despatch travelled to England without the imprimatur of the All-India Muslim League.

Minto felt that the Muslims had received as much as they deserved, and was disinclined to go further. Morley was less sure. He was unhappy about the pressure they could exert on the government. On 12 September 1909, the Muslim League central committee repeated its usual demands for separate electorates and representation in excess of their proportion of the population.[5] The Aga Khan, Ameer Ali and the London League whipped up considerable parliamentary and public support. Morley cracked. Without the League's support, he feared the Bill would not get through Parliament.[6] Despite great opposition from Minto,[7] he

[1] The twists and turns in Ali Imam's position in 1909 were quite extraordinary. It seems that, as early as February 1909, he may have had some intimation that he was in line for government office which may account for his willingness to compromise with the government. It is undoubtedly the case that at the time he was being considered for three posts, those of Standing Counsel to the Government of Bengal, membership of the Executive Council of the Lieutenant-governor of Bengal, and membership of the Viceroy's Executive Council, the last of which he gained in 1910. Rahman, *Consultation to Confrontation*, pp. 139–46.

[2] For Nawab Abdul Majid, see Appendix II.

[3] For the negotiations between the League leaders and the Government of India on 26 June 1909, and Ali Imam's unsuccessful attempts to force the government's compromise terms on the League, see Rahman, *Consultation to Confrontation*, pp. 137–43.

[4] The despatch contained the Government of India's draft rules and regulations for the reformed councils. Public Despatch No. 12 of 1909 to the Secretary of State for India, 22 July 1909, Morley Papers (34), IOL.

[5] These resolutions are enclosed in a telegram from Haji Mahomed Musa Khan, Offg. Honorary Secretary All-India Moslem League, Aligarh, to the Private Secretary to the Viceroy, 13 September 1909, Home Public, October 1909, IOL.

[6] Telegrams, Secretary of State to Viceroy, 21 October 1909 and 2 November 1909, Morley Papers (35), IOL.

[7] Telegrams, Viceroy to Secretary of State, 24 October 1909 and 3 November 1909, Morley Papers (35), IOL.

A high point of separatism

TABLE IX. *The number of seats reserved for Muslim separate electorates at different stages in the evolution of the Morley–Minto reforms*

Council	Govt. of India and provincial govt. proposals Aug. 1907– March 1908	Proposals of the Govt. of India despatch 1 October 1908	Proposals of the Govt. of India despatch 22 July 1909	Indian Councils 1909	Number of elected members in each Council[a]	Muslim reserved seats as % of total number of elected members	% of Muslims in the population
Imperial	4[b]	5	6	8	28	26.6	22.9
Madras	2	2	2	2	20	10	6
Bombay	0	3	4	4	21	19	20
Bengal	0	2	4	4	25	16	18
UP	4[c]	4	4	4	21	19	14
E. Bengal and Assam	1	2	4	4	17	23.5	53
Punjab[d]	—	—	—	—	5	—	53

[a] Of the total number of elected members, several in each council were Europeans: on the Imperial Council two, in Madras three, Bombay two, Bengal four, UP one and E. Bengal and Assam four. Many calculated the Muslim position not as a percentage of the total number of elected members but as a percentage of the Indian elected members.
[b,c] At this stage, two were to be nominated by the government and two elected by the Muslims.
[d] Because the Punjab was regarded as politically less developed, only 5 out of a maximum of 26 seats were elected. If the Muslims were not able to get their men elected, it was felt that government could use its nominations to redress the balance.
SOURCE: Circular from the Secretary to the Government of India, Home Department, to Local Governments and Administrations, 24 August 1907, Morley Papers (32), IOL; Public Despatch No. 21 of 1908 to the Secretary of State for India, 1 October 1908, Morley Papers (33), IOL; Public Despatch No. 12 of 1909 to the Secretary of State for India, 22 July 1909, Morley Papers (34), IOL; Home Poll. A, August 1909, 182–4, NAI.

reopened the question of Muslim representation and attempted to win over the League leaders. He succeeded. The Aga Khan accepted a compromise in which the number of seats reserved for Muslims on the Imperial Council was raised from six to eight, and undertook to persuade the Muslim League to agree to it. Ameer Ali did not like the compromise but kept quiet. The League submitted reluctantly.[1]

Reluctant the League might have been, but all the same its leaders could look back with satisfaction on a campaign in which they had been markedly successful in turning the nebulous sympathy of Minto's reply to the Simla deputation into hard political currency. Table IX shows how, between the first tentative

[1] Rahman, *Consultation to Confrontation*, p. 148.

6

161

RSA

proposals of 1907/8 and the passing of the Indian Councils Act in 1909, the League won four additional Muslim seats in the Imperial Legislative Council, and in the provincial councils four additional seats in Bengal, four in Bombay and three in East Bengal and Assam. The provisions for nomination disappeared and the Muslims voted in separate electorates for their reserved seats, the only exception being the Punjab where, because the Muslims formed 'the bulk of the population' and because 'the great majority of seats...[were to] be filled by nomination', it was felt that there was little chance of Muslim interests not being secured.[1] In the UP, Madras and Imperial Legislative Councils, the Muslims had representation that exceeded their proportion of the population. In every council election Muslims could also vote in the mixed electorates; so they had, in fact, two votes. Between 1907 and 1909, the All-India Muslim League and its branches succeeded in transforming government's reform proposals from a scheme in which the Muslims received a few reserved seats in addition to what they might be able to gain in the mixed electorates, to one in which in several councils Muslims actually achieved their aim of separate representation taking into account both their proportion of the population and the community's political importance.[2]

Muslims from the different provinces contributed in varying degrees to the formulation of the League's demands and to the agitation designed to win them. But without doubt Muslims from the UP, who from the beginning had done so much to establish the idea of Muslim separateness and specialness, were the chief movers. They arranged the Muslim deputation of 1906 and drew up the general formulation of the Muslim attitude to constitutional progress contained in its memorial. They were also the most influential group when it came to working out the details of constitutional progress. Four UP Muslims (Viqar-ul-Mulk, Syed Hasan

---

[1] Appendix II, 'Muhammadan Representation', in a note entitled 'The New Legislative Councils', Morley Papers (34), IOL.

[2] The full extent of Muslim gains was not revealed until after the first elections under the 1909 Councils Act when, in six out of seven councils, the Muslims gained representation that went way beyond their proportion of the population: in the Imperial Legislative Council the Muslims gained eleven or 39 % of the elected seats, in Bombay eight or 38 %, in Madras three or 15 %, in the UP six or 28.5 %, in Bengal six or 24 %, in the Punjab three or 60 % and only in East Bengal and Assam did they slip below their proportion of the population with six or 35 %. But this was a situation that could not last, and in the ensuing elections the Muslims were quickly edged out of seats voted for by mixed electorates.

A high point of separatism

Bilgrami, Syed Nabiullah, Syed Zahur Ahmed) and three from other provinces sat on the reforms subcommittee of the All-India Muslim League appointed at the Aligarh session of 1908. UP Muslims dominated the secretariat of the London League. More important, they dominated that of the All-India League. The result was that most of the League's committees were held in the province – in 1909, all Central Committee and extraordinary general meetings seem to have been held there[1] – making it easier for UP Muslims to attend them and influence policy. A good example of the pressure that the UP Muslims were able to exert on policy is Abdul Majid's successful baulking of Ali Imam's negotiations of June and July 1909. After obstructing Ali Imam's attempt to compromise with the Government of India on 26 June, he led the UP faction which at Lucknow a fortnight later wrecked the League President's attempt to foist his compromise on the League. Nor was the influence of the UP Muslims restricted to the closed world of the committee: they were also in the van when the need was to agitate. When in April 1909 the League's Central Committee under Ali Imam's maverick leadership threatened to make a compromise with government, by far the greater part of the protest meetings and telegrams for separate electorates and against compromise appear to have come from the UP.[2] In the evolution of the Morley–Minto reforms, Muslims from the UP seem to have been as successful in representing their views as those of all Indian Muslims as they had been in Syed Ahmed's time.[3]

The problem remains, why did government concede so much of the League's demand? Many answers have been put forward. At its crudest, explanation comes in terms of divide and rule,[4] of

---

[1] The Central Committee of the League met in Aligarh on 12 April and 12 September. In addition, two extraordinary general meetings were held in Lucknow on 23 May and 10/11 July.

[2] Of 54 protests from Muslim meetings and associations, 31 came from the UP and, of 151 protests from individuals, 132 came from the UP. Home Public, August 1909, IOR.

[3] It is worth noting that UP influence, if not UP Muslim influence, was just as strong on the government side. Four retired UP lieutenant-governors played a part in the creation of the reforms. Lyall advised Morley at a critical moment, Crosthwaite led the civilian attack on behalf of the Muslims, LaTouche sat on the India Office reforms committee, as did Macdonnell who was later one of the reforms' sternest critics, pp. 171–3.

[4] Gopal, *Indian Muslims*, p. 114; M. N. Das, *India under Morley and Minto: Politics behind Revolution, Repression and Reforms* (London, 1964), p. 242; R. C. Majumdar, *History of the Freedom Movement in India* (Calcutta, 1963), Vol. II, p. 258.

6-2

government consciously dividing 'Indian nationalism by communal electorates'.[1] Most explanations of this type regard the reforms as favouring the Muslims. The extreme Muslim view, on the other hand, claims that 'they were obviously a concession to Hindu sentiment'.[2] The argument of divide and rule in its simple form, however, has little to offer. It has, very properly, been demolished by those seeking to explain the large concessions to the Muslims in terms of the tremendous impact of the League's agitation.[3] The best formulation of this interpretation, perhaps partly to emphasise the success of the Muslim League, stresses the dislike of both Morley and Minto for the eventual extent of Muslim representation, Minto's strong objection to further concessions to the Muslims after the second reading of the Councils Bill, his intense pleasure at any sign of Hindu–Muslim concord, and concludes that 'if there was any divide and rule policy it was in uniting the moderates among Hindu and Muslim leaders as against the extremists among their respective co-religionists'.[4] This argument makes a useful contribution to our understanding of the problem. But even more important is the explanation that draws attention towards the British view of Indian society and divines that 'the real problem confronting British officials, as they saw it, was not how to divide and rule India, but how to rule a divided India', and concludes that 'if British policy exacerbated Indian disharmony, it did so more out of ignorance (or innocence) than malice'.[5]

That there could be so many different explanations suggests that the answer is complex. Nevertheless, it rests primarily on the assumptions that the British made about Indian society. First the assumption that Indian society was a collection of classes and interests – of traders, landlords, government servants, castes and communities. Of all these groups, the Muslims formed the largest and by far the most important. About them, as we have seen, the British made a further series of assumptions: that they were a separate and distinct community, a potential danger to the Raj, and an important conservative force. All these notions contributed

[1] Das, *Morley and Minto*, p. 242.
[2] Abdul Hamid, *Muslim Separatism in India: A Brief Survey 1858–1947* (Oxford, 1967), p. 82.
[3] Wasti, *Lord Minto*, pp. 166–90; Rahman, *Consultation to Confrontation*, pp. 85–155.
[4] Rahman, *Consultation to Confrontation*, p. 155.
[5] S. A. Wolpert, *Morley and India 1906–1910* (Berkeley and Los Angeles, 1967), p. 191.

to the belief that they deserved special treatment. Such assumptions about Indian society in general and Muslims in particular would have been of no more than academic interest had they not seriously influenced the way in which the British ruled. They were behind the government's attempts after the Mutiny to draw together powerful groups such as the taluqdars of Oudh or the Muslims of the Urdu-speaking elite in order to consult with and rule through them. They were also the principles on which the Council reforms of 1892 were constructed.[1] But most important, they seemed to have lingered in the minds of most of those in Simla, Calcutta and London involved in the making of the Council reforms of 1909.

The influence of these assumptions can be seen in the attitudes of officials in India involved in the problems of Muslims and the reforms. Take, for instance, those concerned with the Simla deputation. Archbold, the Aligarh principal, who arranged the deputation with the Government of India on behalf of Mohsin-ul-Mulk, was a Muslim partisan in the tradition of Beck and Morison. He was, he told the Viceroy's private secretary, 'very anxious that the Mohammedans should not put themselves in the wrong; it is just what their enemies would like'.[2] Harcourt Butler, the commissioner of Lucknow, who did his best to advise Mohsin-ul-Mulk on the content of the Simla memorial,[3] though he did not approve of separate electorates,[4] was sure that the Simla deputation should be taken seriously. 'The last time that the Mahm. question was raised as a whole', he told Erle Richards, 'it fizzled out. It will not do that now.'[5] Hare, the lieutenant-governor of East Bengal and

---

[1] These principles are set out in Public Despatch No. 21 of 1908 to the Secretary of State for India, 1 October 1908, Morley Papers (33), IOL.
[2] Archbold to Dunlop Smith, Private Secretary to the Viceroy, 20 August 1906, Minto Papers (4E383), NLS.
[3] Butler's involvement in drawing up the memorial is set out in Harcourt Butler to H. Erle Richards, 16 September and 23 September 1906. By his own account, Butler does not appear to have had much influence. For instance, he thought that the Muslims were 'very short-sighted in raising the question of appointments all over India...I told Mohsin-ul-Mulk that they wd do much better to take this question up in instalments by provinces, so as not to unite the Hindus. They wd get more quietly this way. He agreed yesterday. To-day he tells me that the majority want to "go the whole hog".' Harcourt Butler to H. Erle Richards, 16 September 1906. Harcourt Butler Papers (18), IOL.
[4] Harcourt Butler to H. Erle Richards, 23 September 1906, *ibid*.
[5] Harcourt Butler to H. Erle Richards, 16 September 1906, *ibid*.

Separatism among Indian Muslims

Assam, whose advice Minto used freely in his reply to the deputation,[1] was concerned that government should reassure the Muslims that it would not neglect their interests, and in making his point he emphasised their agitational potential: 'The Mohammedan organisation,' he told Dunlop Smith, 'through the Moulavies, and based on religious practices is far and away in advance of the Hindu organisation, which is only a political organisation, dependent on the engineering of the agitators...'[2] The key figure in the negotiations surrounding the Simla deputation was Minto's private secretary, Dunlop Smith. He was the intermediary between the Viceroy and those involved with the deputation, and it was he who provided Minto with the notes from which he began to draft his reply.[3] A soldier turned civil servant, Dunlop Smith saw most of his service in the Punjab.[4] He knew many Muslims and had a healthy respect for the danger they could present to the Raj.[5] In 1906, he was concerned to help the Muslim leaders control their young men. 'What I want to stop', he wrote in his diary, 'is these young Mohammedans forming small societies all over India. Once they start that game they can make us really anxious.'[6] He attached so much importance to Muslim loyalty that he was thrilled by the success of the deputation. 'It meant', he told Butler a few hours

---

[1] Minto to Hare, 1 October 1906, and Dunlop Smith to Hare, 2 October 1906, Minto Papers (4E383), NLS.

[2] L. Hare to Dunlop Smith, 1 September 1906, enclosed in Minto to Morley, 10 September 1906, Morley Papers (9), IOL.

[3] Dunlop Smith undoubtedly played a part in formulating Minto's reply, though how great it was is difficult to ascertain. Thanking Harcourt Butler for sending him a copy of the memorial he said: 'It was the first copy I had seen & I was able to get to work at some notes on it for H.E. I think I see my way to a satisfactory reply [–] satisfactory i.e. to the Dept.' Dunlop Smith to Harcourt Butler, 20 September 1906, Harcourt Butler Papers (65), IOL.

[4] Dunlop Smith certainly seems to have had the usual preference of soldiers and Punjab civil servants for the 'manly' Muslim. Comparing Gokhale with Mohsin-ul-Mulk, he found the former 'weak and not of the stock that breeds leaders of men' and the latter, though he had not 'one quarter of Gokhale's education', 'a strong, wise man'. Note by Dunlop Smith, 21 October 1907, enclosed in Minto to Morley, 29 October 1907, Minto Papers (4E356), NLS.

[5] Dwelling in his diary on threats to British security, Dunlop Smith recalled Sir Dinkar Rao talking to him 'about the outbreaks at Multan, Etawah and Delhi in 1886, and I can see him now saying: "My boy, you are young and think this is serious. It isn't. What you Sahibs have to fear is first the Mussulman when he preaches Jehad – Holy War. Then, you will be in a worse plight than you were in the Mutiny." Pertab Singh told me the same thing the other day.' Extract from Dunlop Smith's Diary, 10 September 1906, in Gilbert, *Servant of India*, p. 56.   [6] *Ibid.*

166

afterwards, 'that the M's declared to the H's that they would not join the Congress, [and] that they preferred appealing to their Ma-Bap to stumping the country...'[1] Confronted with such views Minto, a Viceroy still unfledged in Muslim affairs, did well to promise the community no more than sympathy.

When it came to working out the details of the reforms, these attitudes were no less important. There was an element in government policy of building up the Muslim League as an ally. 'We have much to gain politically', Minto told Morley in July 1908, 'by our goodwill to Mussulman enlightenment.'[2] But a high regard for the trouble it was believed that the Muslims as a whole could cause appears to have been the most crucial factor in enabling the community to have matters largely their own way. 'It will be a thousand pities', Arundel, the late president of the Government of India's Reforms Committee, told Minto at the height of the electoral college crisis, 'to disgust and alienate the Mahommedan community by deviating a hair's breadth from the promise given to them in 1906...'[3] Ten days after this, Minto told the governor of Bombay, whom he suspected of sympathising with the electoral college scheme, that it might be possible in future to work some other system of representation, 'but for the present the recognition of the Mahommedans as such will alone save us from serious trouble'.[4] And the threat of serious trouble was the argument that Minto used to press home the importance of separate Muslim electorates: 'Mahomedan electorates are absolutely necessary,' he told Morley in April 1909, 'if we retract from that view, we shall have an infinitely worse trouble than anything that can arise from Hindu opposition'.[5]

The threat of Muslim opposition seems to have been no less effective when the League's demands ran counter to Minto's wishes. For instance, he was determined that in the separate electorates the Muslims should not be given the number of seats proportionate to their numbers and 'political importance' which the League demanded. The last thing he wanted was for Muslims to be shut away in a 'water-tight compartment'.[6] Moreover, when

---

[1] Dunlop Smith to Harcourt Butler, 2 October 1906, Harcourt Butler Papers (65), IOL.   [2] Minto to Morley, 29 July 1908, Morley Papers (16), IOL.
[3] Arundel to Minto, 8 January 1909, Minto Papers (4E395), NLS.
[4] Minto to Sir G. Clarke, Governor of Bombay, 18 January 1909, Minto Papers (4E388), NLS.   [5] Minto to Morley, 7 April 1909, Morley Papers (20), IOL.
[6] Minto to Morley, 15 July 1909, Minto Papers (21), IOL.

in April and May 1909 a storm of League-sponsored agitation broke out over the government of India's scheme, he weathered it bravely, making light of the opposition.[1] Nevertheless, by June 1909, he was worried enough by the 'acute Mahommedan dissatisfaction'[2] to give in to the demands of his reforms council that they should be allowed to meet League leaders in order to thrash out a compromise with them. Indeed, for all Minto's efforts to shrug off the League's protests when it was convenient, he does not seem to have forgotten his own dictum 'that though the Mahomedan is silent he is very strong'.[3]

Several important decisions concerning the reforms were made in England. Here the Secretary of State had the largest part to play in dictating their nature and fate. Morley, who went to the India Office with no more knowledge of Indian matters than Minto, seems to have accepted the official view that 'the Mohammedan community is entitled to a special representation on the Governor-General's and local Legislative Councils commensurate with its numbers and political and historical importance'.[4] He was unwilling to challenge 'the broad principle' asserted by the vast majority of Indian civilians 'that Indian society lives, thinks and acts according to castes, races and religions'.[5] But, on the other hand, Morley was strongly opposed to making religion the basis of Indian constituencies.[6] Hence he was keen to find some way of assuring Muslim representation through a territorial rather than a religious franchise, and leapt at the electoral college suggestion. But the Secretary of State's liberal views were not given free rein. First, he had to listen to the advice of his body of experts, the retired Indian civilians who made up his Council. Among them there was between 1906 and 1909 a strong body of opinion, of which Lawrence, LaTouche, Lee Warner, Bilgrami and Morison were the more prominent supporters,[7] that they ought to

---

[1] Minto to Morley, 29 April 1909, Morley Papers (20), IOL.
[2] Minto to Sir E. N. Baker, lieutenant-governor of Bengal, 29 May 1909, Minto Papers (4E388), NLS.
[3] Minto to Morley, 31 December 1908, Morley Papers (18), IOL.
[4] Secretary of State's Despatch, 17 May 1907, Morley Papers (32), quoted in Wolpert, *Morley*, p. 191.
[5] Note by W. Lee Warner, dated 19 April 1907, Morley Papers (32), *ibid.*
[6] *Ibid.*, pp. 192–3.
[7] Lawrence had served in the Punjab government and as Curzon's private secretary. LaTouche was a former lieutenant-governor of the UP with a strong liking for Aligarh. Lee Warner had served in the Bombay Presidency,

go some way towards meeting the League's demands. In the summer of 1909, this view was particularly influential when, with the exception of Lawrence, all sat on the Council's seven-man reforms committee and the most partisan member, Morison, who Morley complained 'would rather have no Reforms at all than such as might be taken to place the M's at a disadvantage',[1] was also 'much the ablest and most active man in all...[the] controversy and in a good many other branches of business...'[2]

The views of the Council, however, though important, were not decisive, for Morley was an autocratic Secretary of State.[3] What mattered more, when it came to the point, was public opinion and the political situation. British public opinion was strongly pro-Muslim. Much was created by retired Indian civilians,[4] many of whom perpetuated traditional attitudes towards the Muslims. 'The *Times* which really informs and leads the mass of newspapers about Indian matters',[5] was a great Muslim partisan, Chirol, the man on the India desk, being hand in glove with Ameer Ali and the Aga Khan.[6] This popular Muslim predilection helped to exacerbate the most important factor in Morley's calculations, the extraordinary situation in Parliament. The Liberal government which came to power in 1906 had a majority only in the Commons, and between 1906 and 1909 much of its legislation had been either rejected or emasculated by the Tory majority in the Lords. In 1906, Education and Plural Voting Bills had been destroyed; in 1907, Land Bills had been cut to pieces; in 1908, a Licensing Bill had been rejected. If Morley wished to preserve peace in India, it was crucial that the Indian Councils Bill of 1909 should not suffer the same fate. Nevertheless, while the League remained dissatisfied, such

had much political department experience and was strongly pro-Muslim. Syed Hosein Bilgrami had been the chief mover in drawing up the Muslim memorial of 1906 and was the half-brother of the secretary of the All-India Muslim League, Major Syed Hasan Bilgrami. Morison was a former Aligarh principal.

[1] Morley to Minto, 20 August 1909, Morley Papers (IV), IOL. Morley's correspondence is full of comments upon Morison's partisan attitude. Morley to Minto, 20 July 1909, 29 July 1909, 6 August 1909, *ibid.*
[2] Morley to Minto, 18 November 1909, *ibid.* Morley was so pleased with Morison's work that he determined to get him a K.C.I.E.
[3] For the relations between Morley and his Council, and also the body's very traditional attitudes, see S. N. Singh, *The Secretary of State for India and his Council (1858–1919)* (Delhi, 1962), pp. 60–1, 160.
[4] Minto to Morley, 10 February and 7 April 1909, Morley Papers (19, 20), IOL.
[5] Morley to Minto, 29 October 1909, Morley Papers (IV), IOL.
[6] Morley to Minto, 7 October 1909, *ibid.*

an end was constantly threatened. 'The Opposition in the person of its leading men [Lansdowne, Curzon, Percy]', Morley told Minto, 'is undoubtedly Mahometan in its partisanship...'[1] Thus it was always important for Morley to damp down the League's opposition before it became so inflamed that the Tory opposition in the Lords could make something of it.

Morley's sensitiveness to the League's agitation is illustrated by his reaction to it during the passage of the electoral college affair. In early January 1909, he became 'very anxious' at the prospect of rousing Muslim sentiment.[2] In early February, after failing to convince the London League deputation of his good intentions, he feared that 'we are in very deep water' regarding Muslim opinion.[3] At this point, he turned to 'the one man', he told Minto, 'to whom I must look for counsel in decisions of real moment – Alfred Lyall, the friend of a lifetime...'[4] In reply, he was given the usual late-nineteenth-century official line. 'The Mahomedans', Lyall advised, 'embody a strong conservative element... [and] would be a substantial support to the Moderate party in India [which]... our policy should be to enlist as allies and auxiliaries on the side of the British government against the extremists. It would be a grave mischance if the Mahomedans were alienated.'[5] Lyall's counsel came on top of similar advice from the Government of India and the press. To insist on a scheme that attracted such hostility was not the way to carry legislation through an uncertain Parliament. Morley was 'keenly alive to the necessity of conciliating the Mahometans' if only he could so do 'without dropping my Hindu baggage'.[6] But within days of uttering this he finally admitted that his cherished electoral college scheme was no hold-all and discarded it.[7] At the third reading of the Bill in autumn

[1] Morley to Minto, 29 October 1909, Morley Papers (IV), IOL.
[2] The diary of F. A. Hirtzel, Morley's private secretary, 11 January 1909, quoted in Wolpert, *Morley*, p. 194.
[3] The diary of F. A. Hirtzel, 2 February 1909, *ibid*.
[4] Morley to Minto, 21 January 1909, Morley Papers (4), IOL.
[5] Lyall to Morley, 4 February 1909, Morley Papers (49), IOL and, on 15 February, he gave Morley the same line in terms of the accepted view of Indian society: 'I do not believe that any system of electing members to the Councils by majorities can profitably produce a fair representation of the Indian people, whose whole society is founded upon divisions of religion and race...' Lyall to Morley, 15 February 1909, *ibid*.
[6] Morley to Lyall, 5 February 1909, Lyall Papers (80), IOL.
[7] Though Morley told Minto on 28 January that the electoral college scheme was 'practically dead', it was not until he had had lunch with Lyall on 13 February

of 1909, similar fears of Muslim League agitation and its effect on
the opposition came into play, though this time, the danger from
the Tory majority in the Lords was greater. The struggle for
power between the Lords and the Commons was nearing its climax
and there was always the danger that the Councils Bill, a hostage to
the jaded spirit of the English constitution, might be cut down out
of sheer spite. 'There is some risk', Morley telegraphed Minto on
21 October, 'of this whole Muhammadan question being used for
purposes of party',[1] and a fortnight later he was compelled to
recognise 'that no scheme will be sanctioned here which does not
either fulfil the pledges, or, without fulfilment of pledges, com-
mend itself to Muhammadan leaders here.'[2] Morley had to square
the League and at the last moment he did so by granting the
Muslims a further two seats on the Imperial Legislative Council.
'If we had not satisfied the Mahometans,' Morley told Minto when
all was done, 'we should have had opinion here which is now with
us – dead against us.'[3]

Few voices were raised in opposition to the assumptions most
Englishmen made about Indian Muslims. A number of retired
Anglo-Indians were opposed. So also, of course, were the British
Committee of the Congress with Lajpat Rai[4] and Romesh Dutt[5] at
their head, though they had to be wary in their opposition as they
did not wish to bring the reforms to a halt. On the India Council,
the 'Muslim bloc' was opposed by Sir L. Jenkins, a 'Congressman' according to Morley,[6] Sir K. G. Gupta, the Hindu member,
and later by Sir T. Raleigh, a former legal member of the Viceroy's
Council. But the really severe opposition came from Lord, formerly
Sir Antony, Macdonnell, who, when it came to reducing Muslim
influence, was determined to carry on in England where he had
left off in India. His attacks on government's policy towards the
Muslims were ceaseless. He criticised Curzon's partition of

and received two letters on the subject from him, that he told Minto that he
had capitulated. Telegram, Secretary of State to Viceroy, 16 February 1909,
Morley Papers (33), IOL.
[1] Telegram, Secretary of State to Viceroy, 21 October 1909, Morley Papers
(35), IOL.
[2] Telegram, Secretary of State to Viceroy, 2 November 1909, *ibid.*
[3] Morley to Minto, 18 November 1909, Morley Papers (IV), IOL.
[4] See, for instance, letter from Lajpat Rai in *The Times* (London), 28 January
1909.
[5] See, for instance, letter from Romesh Dutt, *ibid.*, 9 January 1909.
[6] Morley to Minto, 4 December 1908, Morley Papers (3), IOL.

Bengal,[1] and assailed Minto's reply to the Simla deputation, claiming that the Hindus were the 'real people'.[2] The reforms did not escape his attention. Indeed, in order to curb his tongue, Morley invited him to join the reforms committee of the India Council. 'He may have his uses,' he told Minto, 'and at the worst it may prevent him from raging in the H. of L. against us.'[3] Macdonnell was strongly opposed to the League's demands for a separate Muslim electorate and for greater representation than Muslim numbers justified.[4] So it was not surprising that the reforms committee of late 1908 and early 1909, in which he played the leading part,[5] suggested the electoral college scheme. But this was the only chance he had to cut down Muslim influence from the inside: Morley refused to have him on his reforms committee again.[6] For the remainder of the evolution of the reforms, Macdonnell's activity was restricted to attacks – and he attacked all aspects – in the House of Lords.[7] These assaults greatly annoyed Morley. His correspondence is full of his dislike for 'this good man' whom 'I will pulverise and smash...'[8] But, as far as Muslim questions were concerned, the 'hard-mouthed'[9] and 'wrong-headed'[10]

1 *Hansard*, Fourth Series (Lords), Vol. 198, 17 December 1908, cols. 1996–2000.
2 Morley to Minto, 27 December 1906, Morley Papers (I), IOL.
3 Morley to Minto, 18 September 1908, Morley Papers (III), IOL.
4 Letter from Lord Macdonnell in *The Times* (London), 6 January 1909.
5 Morley to Minto, 7 October and 23 October 1908, Morley Papers (III), IOL.
6 When he assembled the committee of his Council that was to examine Minto's despatch of 22 July 1909, Morley promised the Viceroy that 'it shall not be illuminated by the shining presence of Lord Macdonnell. He did nothing but mischief on the last occasion'. Morley to Minto, 20 July 1909, Morley Papers (IV), IOL.
7 One of Macdonnell's greatest victories, though only temporary, was to persuade the Lords to support a motion of his opposing clause (3) of the reform measure which made provision for the Government of India to create executive councils in provinces where hitherto the lieutenant-governor had ruled on his own.
8 Morley to Minto, 18 December 1908, Morley Papers (III), IOL; and see also, Morley to Minto, 25 February, 5 March, 25 March, 7 April, 6 May and 27 May 1909, Morley Papers (IV), IOL. Morley had not dealt with Macdonnell for long before he felt that 'he might one day become as horrid a bore in the H. of L., as Sir Henry Cotton was, and is, in the H. of C. Along with Cotton, Sir R. Temple, Sir George Campbell, etc., he will be another case of the Indian Eagle moulting and dwindling into the Westminster Parrot or Irish Cocksparrow. Such are the tragedies of Providence'. Morley to Minto, 5 November 1908, Morley Papers (III), IOL.
9 Morley to Minto, 18 December 1908, *ibid.*
10 Morley to Minto, 5 March 1909, Morley Papers (IV), IOL.

A high point of separatism

Macdonnell was unlikely to get much support. His views were quite out of sympathy with prevailing British attitudes to Indian society.

By 1909, a Muslim identity was firmly established in Indian politics. The first stage in the process had been the creation of a Muslim political organisation. In a sense, this had existed for years in Aligarh College and its connections. Nevertheless, important changes were needed to transform the contented client of Syed Ahmed's time into a militant petitioner. One change was the emergence of competition for the leadership of Muslim politics from 'young gentlemen of progressive tendencies', another was a challenge to UP Muslim leadership from Muslims elsewhere in India. These struggles were not self-generated, but were sparked off by the actions of government. Macdonnell's attack on Muslims in government service set them going. Morley's announcement of council reforms, coming soon after the resignation of the pro-Muslim lieutenant-governor of Eastern Bengal, brought them to a head. The result was the foundation of the All-India Muslim League.

The second stage was the winning of a separate Muslim electorate, in which the Muslim League persuaded the government to give Muslims representation which in most councils took into account not only their proportion of the population but also their alleged political importance. This was a remarkable achievement. A wide range of factors played a part in it from the capacity of UP Muslims to lead the All-India Muslim League to the extraordinary situation in the British Parliament. But the key element seems to have been the assumptions that the British made about Indian society and Indian Muslims. The former was regarded as a collection of interests and groups. The latter formed one of these groups and were regarded, quite wrongly as separate, distinct and monolithic. The result was that the Muslims were also seen to be an important and above all dangerous group which had to be kept satisfied. These assumptions were self-sustaining. They were fostered in the twentieth century by Aligarh College and the Muslim League, organisations the growth of which owed much to the influence of these assumptions in the nineteenth century. In the making of the Morley–Minto reforms, which translated the English view of Indian society into formal constitutional arrangements, they prevailed, their very pervasiveness helping to turn Muslim

League protests into Muslim seats. In establishing the Muslims as a separate and special interest in the Indian constitution, the Muslim League was important but government's assumptions about Indian Muslims in general, and its policies towards them, were crucially important.

CHAPTER 5

The struggle for the leadership of the Muslim party in Indian politics
1909-1914

The creation of a protected share of power for Muslims in the Morley–Minto reforms stimulated the further development of Muslim politics. Muslims turned their minds to communal organisation as never before. Many associations were founded to improve aspects of Muslim life and society; the Muslim League gained many new members; Muslim demands for the extension of separate representation to municipal and district boards gained new force; a great campaign for the economic and political re-generation of the Muslims was contemplated; a great campaign for a Muslim University at Aligarh was actually launched. The new energy displayed by Muslims drew a strong response from Hindus who deeply resented the concessions which had been made to the rival community. Local manifestations of communal an-tagonism multiplied; Hindus agitated against the suggestions that separate representation should be extended to municipal and district boards; an All-India Hindu Sabha was founded; a Hindu University campaign was prosecuted with even greater vigour than its rival. The result was that Muslims redoubled their efforts to organise themselves. The most important effect of the new position of the Muslims, however, was that government began to treat them less circumspectly. The Muslims have had a large slice of cake, the feeling went, now it is the turn of others. This change in the government's attitude divided the UP Muslims into two main groups: those who were prepared to defend Muslim interests at all costs, and those who were not. To these groups, and their struggle for the leadership of Muslim affairs, the analysis now turns.

Two main groups among Muslim politicians in the UP had begun to emerge in the decade after Syed Ahmed's death: the 'young gentlemen of progressive tendencies' and the 'men of property and influence'. After 1909, government frequently employed these categories in surveying the political scene[1] and the Muslims used them too, often describing them as the 'Young Party' and the 'Old Party',[2] titles which for the sake of convenience we shall adopt. Nevertheless, the names given to these groupings should not mislead as to their nature. They were in no strict sense parties; there were no subscriptions, no whips, no party organisations. Nor were they particularly united. Successful professional men and large landlords of the 'Old Party' and rabid pan-Islamist journalists and moderate Lucknow lawyers of the 'Young Party' did not invariably agree. Moreover, age is not a wholly reliable guide to party allegiance. Some leading members of the 'Old Party' were young men, Aftab Ahmad Khan, for example, or Sheikh Abdullah who died as recently as 1965; others, of the 'Young Party', Syed Nabiullah or Major Hasan Bilgrami, for example, were old men. However, the majority of the two parties did fit the right age bracket. But these political alignments were not simply a question of age. No less important in shaping political attitudes were social background, prospects of employment and, to a certain extent, education. To understand the political struggles of the time, these aspects must be examined more closely.

'Young Party' men,[3] like those of the 'Old Party', were descended from the Urdu-speaking elite. Nearly all were connected with the landed families of the province. Yet, of the sixty 'Young Party' men whose biographies appear in Appendix I, only four were landowners paying more than Rs. 5000 land revenue;[4] two of them, Haji Musa Khan and Amir Mustafa Khan, were Sherwani Pathans of Aligarh, and the other two were the Raja of Mahmudabad and Prince Hamidullah Khan of Bhopal. Of these, the first

---

[1] See, for instance, Meston to Hardinge, 25 March 1915, Hardinge Papers (89), CUL, and Harcourt Butler to Hardinge, 3 November 1912, *ibid.* (84).

[2] Mahomed Ali's private correspondence and newspapers are littered with references to the 'young' and the 'old' or the 'Young Party' and the 'Old Party', see, for instance, the differences between the 'young' and the 'old' discussed in the context of Aligarh, *Comrade* (Delhi), 28 December 1912, and Mahomed Ali's letter to the editor of the *Daily Graphic* explaining the policy of the 'Young Party' after resignation of the Aga Khan and Ameer Ali from the Muslim League in 1913. Mahomed Ali to the Editor of the *Daily Graphic*, no date but from the address and other internal evidence autumn 1913, Mahomed Ali Papers, JMI.

[3] Biographies of all UP men mentioned in connection with the 'Young Party' will be found in Appendix I.

[4] In 1919, roughly 1000 landowners in the province paid more than Rs. 5000 land revenue.

two were heavily in debt[1] and the party loyalty of the last two weakened under pressure; Mahmudabad became cautious after Meston threatened to take away his taluqdari *sanad* in 1916 and the prince was brought to heel by his mother, the Begum. A few, like Khaliquzzaman or T. A. K. Sherwani, were connected with rich landed families, but this was no guarantee of financial support. The great majority belonged to the class which occasionally had a small pittance in rents from land but generally, in order to survive, had to find employment in service or the professions.

The government described this group as a 'middle class' and they themselves distinguished their party from the wealthier sections of the community. Writing to Mahmudabad in 1917, after the Raja's defection from the 'Young Party', Mahomed Ali discussed the Raja's refusal to support the Ali brothers' latest 'hookah fantasy', the Sultanniah College project, entirely in terms of 'the rich' and 'the poor'. The Muslim University constitution committee, in which the 'Old Party' had gained an ascendancy, had recently accepted the Government's terms for the establishment of the University. This represented a defeat for the 'Young Party' in territory that they held most dear. The 'Young Party' had conceived the Sultanniah project as a last ditch attempt to counter the success of the 'Old Party' by drawing as much of the Muslim University's support as possible away to their new scheme. The intention was to set up another Aligarh, designed for the 'middle classes'[2] and controlled entirely by the members of the 'Young

---

[1] In 1896, the immense Sherwani estates were divided into eleven portions. It is noticeable that those of the family with large, solvent and well-administered portions, for example the Nawab Muhammad Muzammilullah Khan of Bhikampur, who paid Rs. 47,554 land revenue, and Muhammad Habib-ur-Rahman Sherwani of Bhikampur, who paid Rs. 14,147 land revenue, were conspicuous in their loyalty, while those with small, encumbered estates, Amir Mustafa Khan of Kanshirauli, who paid Rs. 7336 and Haji Musa Khan of Datauli, who paid Rs. 5557, were vigorous supporters of extremist politics. The evidence is suggestive. The clue to the political allegiances of the Sherwanis could well lie in the internal politics and prosperity of the family. Revenue and Agriculture, 1918, 578, UPS.

[2] 'There is, moreover, the great difficulty of expenses, which have, of recent years, risen to such proportions that it is becoming increasingly difficult for Musalmans of the middle classes to send their boys to these colleges. And these boys, the most promising and diligent ones of the community, boys on whom the future of the community principally depends, are thus often denied the benefits of higher education', declared Raja Ghulam Husain's 'Young Party' paper in making out the case for the Sultanniah College in 1917. *New Era* (Lucknow), 5 May 1917.

Party'. The Raja, apparently, had objected to the class bias of the scheme, but Mahomed Ali was uncompromising:

> I am against all class warfare and would not encourage anything suggestive of class prejudice. But I cannot obviously help it if the actions of the rich themselves should compel those who do not share their wealth or their weaknesses to give the new institution the character of a poor Man's college for the poor and managed by the poor...But I own that experience has only too painfully and too well convinced me also that every gift horse from a richman's stable must be carefully examined, not so much in the mouth, as with a view to ensure that it is we that would ride it and not it that would bestride us. I own that the largest and in the aggregate the greater part of the subscriptions to the Moslem University have come from the rich. But I would nevertheless contest with anyone who desires to establish it the truth of any assumption that the greater part of the thought and energy and selflessness that went to shape the project and carry it into execution was the contribution of the rich.[1]

Clearly, the 'Young Party' thought of themselves as the poorer section of the community. Mahomed Ali had only his salary to live on, as an angry letter from his elder brother Shaukat bears witness: 'Your financial affairs are always in such a condition that one had to notice them. You get 400/- a month and yet can't manage to live in it. It is your own look out and nobody else can help you.'[2] Some of the professional men did have small supplementary sources of income, but most of them, like Mahomed Ali, had nothing more than their wits to keep them in pan.

Powerful influences on the attitudes of the 'Young Party' were where they had been educated and what they had studied. Something is known about the higher education of forty of the sixty whose biographies are set out in Appendix I. At least twenty studied in England, fifteen at the forcing houses of nationalist political talent, the Inns of Court. At least thirty-one graduated from Aligarh and three from other colleges affiliated to Allahabad

---

[1] Mahomed Ali to the Raja of Mahmudabad, 6 April 1917, Mahomed Ali Papers, JMI.

[2] Shaukat Ali to Mahomed Ali, no date although the text indicates that the year was probably 1909, *ibid*. Mahomed Ali did in theory hold a share in a zamindari estate in Rampur worth Rs. 15,000 p.a., but it was heavily encumbered with his father's debts and whatever income remained had to be shared with his mother and four other brothers. By all accounts he received no income from it at all, as on no occasion did he refer to it in his various computations of his income. Indeed, the only occasion when it was mentioned was when he was forced to sell part of the estate in order to raise money during his wartime internment.

University. Limited though the information is, it is clear that the bulk of the 'Young Party' were educated at Syed Ahmed's college and had experienced the remarkable *esprit de corps* that the institution seemed to develop. Many were imbued with its mission to regenerate the Indian Muslims. Some of the younger graduates had grown up in the atmosphere of rebellion that was such a marked feature of the College in the two decades after Syed Ahmed's death, and in 1907 both Raja Ghulam Husain and T. A. K. Sherwani had been expelled for their part in a college strike against the principal, Archbold. Such struggles with the 'Old Party' men who ran Aligarh provided an early baptism for many. But, if the young Aligarh man avoided those student exercises in politics, he found it hard to escape the attentions of the older members of the 'Young Party', the Ali Brothers and Dr Ansari, who were for ever prowling around the precincts and regaling wide-eyed students with chimaerical plans for anything from a take-over of the college to an armed insurrection against the British.[1] In this fashion, Khaliquzzaman, Abdur Rahman Siddiqi and Shuaib Qureshi were drawn into the party while still undergraduates.

At least thirty-nine of the 'Young Party' had BAs, which meant that they had studied modern subjects, had been taught by English teachers and spoke English. Only one or two, such as Hakim Ajmal Khan or Zafar-ul-Mulk Alvi, were traditionally educated. Many had read European history and were able to place Islam in a wider framework than their traditionally educated brethren. They knew about Islam's past glories and were painfully aware of its present decline. Moreover, at Aligarh, this awareness was heightened by the teaching of Shibli and Arnold. Indeed, many of these modern Muslims had been educated to think in pan-Islamic terms.

Thus, most of the 'Young Party' had a common educational experience. Since the party was not formerly organised, this tie was important. Crucial, of course, was the fact that so many had been to Aligarh. In 1911, the Old Boys' Association boasted 800 members. Shaukat Ali was secretary and also proprietor of the *Old Boy*, their magazine.[2] Such an old-boy network was no mean

---

[1] For a graphic account of the Ali brothers' methods, see Choudhry Khaliquzzaman, *Pathway to Pakistan* (Lahore, 1961), pp. 30–1.

[2] Shaukat Ali was elected secretary in 1911. It is not clear whether the *Old Boy* was the official organ of the association or of the 'Reform League' within the association which was aimed at reforming the Aligarh trustees.

foundation for a political party. It launched Mahomed Ali as a leading journalist and helped to launch him as the foremost agitational politician of his day.

The first aim of most Muslims who graduated was to find a job in government service. They attached much more importance to this, Harcourt Butler declared, than to getting seats in Council.[1] But it was becoming increasingly difficult to get into government service, and in 1912 no leading member of the 'Young Party' held an official post. Most of those in Appendix I were professional men: thirty-three were lawyers, sixteen in Lucknow alone, and twelve were journalists. For many of these men, a career in law or journalism was a second best. Mahomed Ali was a case in point. He had had high hopes and a high estimate of himself. In 1898, he had won a government scholarship to Oxford where, in 1902, he got a second in Modern History, 'missing a First, as I learnt subsequently from my tutor, by a very narrow margin'.[2] But, when he came to seek a job, he discovered that the world did not feel that it owed him a living. He failed to enter the ICS. He was ploughed in the Allahabad Bar examination and turned down when he applied for a job at Aligarh. So, he had to opt for the second choice of many of his fellows, a career in a Native State civil service. He went into the educational department of his home state, Rampur, but soon left it for the prospects of large opportunities in the Gaekwar of Baroda's service. Here his overweening ambition and consuming vanity stood in his way; he annoyed his superiors by bombarding them with fanciful projects and was regarded with suspicion by his fellow officers.[3] In spite of doing his job badly, as he himself admitted,[4] he constantly demanded

[1] Commenting on the discussion of the Simla memorial at Lucknow in September 1906, Harcourt Butler noticed that the lawyers and professional classes attached 'much more importance to getting more appointments than to getting more seats in Council'. Harcourt Butler to H. E. Richards, 16 September 1906, Harcourt Butler Papers (18), IOL.

[2] Mahomed Ali to Dewan Tek Chand, survey and settlement commissioner Baroda, no date but the text suggests 1909, Mahomed Ali Papers, JMI.

[3] Mahomed Ali complained in his letter of resignation to the Gaekwar of Baroda: 'In spite of being an Indian and having received a very similar education to the rest of the Baroda officials, I found that I differed from them in almost everything, and that it was difficult if not impossible for me to be received by them as one of their own number.' Mahomed Ali to the Gaekwar of Baroda, no date but the text suggests 1912, *ibid.*

[4] Shaukat Ali to Mahomed Ali, 4 February 1909, *ibid.*

more pay.[1] His brother, Shaukat, had little time for his troubles or his methods and urged him to 'curb yourself a little – you have to work with certain people and you can't always have your way. – If I was your *boss*, I would strongly object to your nature of correspondence. It borders on insubordination.'[2] By the middle of 1909, Mahomed had been heavily defeated in the internal politics of the Baroda bureaucracy and was desperate to leave.[3] Encouraged by a tip from Shaukat that the Home Member, Sir Harold Stuart, was not disinterested in him,[4] he threw all he had into an attempt to join the ranks of the 'heaven born'. But, in October, he was turned down for an Assistant Secretaryship in the Home Department of the Government of India,[5] in November the Governor of Bombay did 'not think that the expense of an Indian Private Secretary would be justified at present'.[6] In December, he was told that the Assistant Directorship of Criminal Intelligence was 'booked'.[7] He was rejected all round.

Few had as high-flying ambitions as Mahomed Ali, but many met similar disappointments. Competition for posts was becoming increasingly tough, and the Muslims as a community were not holding their own. Between 1887 and 1913, the proportion of Muslims decreased from 44.8 per cent to 41.3 per cent in the provincial executive service and from 45.9 per cent to 24.8 per cent in the judicial service.[8] This displacement of Muslims, particularly in the judicial service, was the object of bitter complaint from 'Young Party' men before the Public Services Commission in 1913.[9] They spoke for the able and ambitious young Muslims who would have preferred to enter government service as their forebears had done before them but found they were unable to do so.

---

[1] After five years in the service of the Gaekwar Mahomed Ali was earning a mere Rs. 350 p.m. He demanded to be put on to a salary scale similar to that of members of the provincial executive services. Mahomed Ali to Dewan Tek Chand, no date but text suggests 1909, *ibid.*
[2] Shaukat Ali to Mahomed Ali, 4 February 1909, *ibid.*
[3] Mahomed Ali to the Gaekwar of Baroda, no date but the text suggests 1912, *ibid.*   [4] Shaukat Ali to Mahomed Ali, 31 March 1909, *ibid.*
[5] H. A. Stuart to Mahomed Ali, 31 October 1909, *ibid.*
[6] Sir George Clarke to Mahomed Ali, 2 November 1909, *ibid.*
[7] H. A. Stuart to Mahomed Ali, 10 December 1909, *ibid.*
[8] Calculated from *PSC 1886–7*, Report, *P.P.* 1888, XLVIII, p. 55 and *PSC 1913*, Report, Appendix VIII, *P.P.* 1916, VII, p. 604.
[9] Evidence of Syed Riza Ali and Syed Nabiullah given before the Public Service Commission, *PSC 1913*, Evidence taken in the United Provinces, *P.P.* 1914, XXIII, pp. 1030 and 1124.

Separatism among Indian Muslims

If they failed to get a government job, the law was traditionally the main alternative. But by 1912 the Bar was seriously over-crowded. Motilal Nehru, writing to his son at Cambridge, made this very clear:

It is becoming more and more difficult every day for a beginner to push his way through. I have been trying my utmost to help Shamji Mushrao an abler and more hardworking Junior than whom it is impossible to conceive but I have so far failed to render him any material assistance. Jagmohan...is literally starving – He is now trying to get a Munsifi! [A legal post of the lower grade – the limbo into which the failed lawyer usually fell]...The great Jagmandarlal Jaini who was made so much of by you all is as great failure as the others. It is impossible for you to succeed, however able you may be, within a reasonable time if you are left to your own resources.[1]

For Muslim lawyers the early years were even more difficult. Macdonnell's Nagri resolution cut down the number of briefs going to Muslims. Then the amount of work they could expect was further reduced by the increase in communal tension. As feeling mounted, the boycotting of lawyers of the rival community became a favoured tactic.[2] Muslims found it hard to make a living. This is reflected by their numbers in the profession. In 1873, there were more Muslim lawyers than Hindu and they were the leaders of the Bar. But by 1909 their number had reached its peak, while the number of Hindu lawyers continued to increase at a rapid rate. The growth of the profession is set out below:

TABLE X. *Hindu and Muslim membership of the legal profession in the UP, 1873–1929*

	1873	1889	1899	1909	1919	1929
Hindu	88	608	890	1222	1620	1847
Muslim	98	335	402	455	453	460

SOURCE: *Thacker's Bengal Directory* for 1873 which later became *Thacker's Indian Directory* and was employed in calculating the figures for the years 1889, 1899, 1909, 1919 and 1929.

[1] Motilal Nehru to Jawaharlal Nehru, 6 January 1911, Nehru Papers, NMM.
[2] Letter from E. H. Radice, Commissioner of Lucknow, 24 May 1909, quoted in Home Poll. A, October 1913, 100–13, NAI.

Not many Muslims found it possible to make a success of the law. Shah Muhammad Sulaiman[1] and Wazir Hasan,[2] at the Allahabad and Oudh Bars respectively, reached the top of their professions but perhaps the career of one member of the 'Young Party', Qazi Bashiruddin Ahmed of Meerut, was more typical. After the heady excitements of the Red Crescent Mission, he returned to discover that all he could become was a 'bald-headed munsiff'.[3] 'Work is very dull, nowadays', he told Mahomed Ali, 'all the elite of Aligarh sit in a room in the Court and talk the whole day over. Nice Profession.'[4] The less successful lawyers had plenty of time to sit around in the Bar library and discuss politics; Khaliquzzaman and Bashiruddin Ahmed were more prominent as politicians than as lawyers. With a few exceptions, the really successful lawyer tended to have little time for such activities. Mahomed Wasim, Khaliquzzaman's cousin, who did well by specialising in the extremely lucrative Oudh Estates Act, only occasionally dabbled in politics. As his legal career got under way, Wazir Hasan gradually opted out of politics. Shah Muhammad Sulaiman never entered them.

Yet as opportunities for Muslims in the Provincial Civil Service grew smaller and remained static in the Bar, the number of Muslims qualified to enter these professions was increasing. In 1902, eighteen per cent of those in colleges were Muslims; in 1907, twenty per cent; and in 1912, twenty-three per cent.[5] The problem

---

[1] Shah Muhammad Sulaiman: born Jaunpur 1886; educated Muir Central College Allahabad, Christ's College Cambridge, Middle Temple; quickly came to dominate the Allahabad Bar; knighted 1929; Chief Justice of the Allahabad High Court 1932.

[2] The legal career of Wazir Hasan was as remarkable as that of Shah Sulaiman. He also came from Jaunpur though he did not have the advantage of education in England. He began practice in his home town, later moved to Partabgarh and then to Lucknow. He rose rapidly, being one of the four vakils to be made advocates in 1914. He was appointed Second Judicial Commissioner in 1921, being the first Indian member of the Oudh Bar who was not a Barrister to be raised to the Bench. He became a Puisne Judge of the Chief Court after its inauguration in 1925, Chief Judge of the Court in 1930 and retired in 1934. He was knighted in the same year, being the first Indian member of the Oudh Bar to receive the honour. See also Appendix I.

[3] Bashiruddin Ahmed to Mahomed Ali, 24 August 1916, Mahomed Ali Papers, JMI.

[4] Bashiruddin Ahmed to Mahomed Ali, 17 August 1919, *ibid.*

[5] Calculated from *RDPI (UP), 1901–02*, General Table IIIA, p. 42; *RDPI (UP), 1906–07*, General Table IIIA, p. 8A; *RDPI (UP), 1911–12*, General Table IIIA, p. 8A.

of how to employ these men seriously occupied Muslim leaders. At the Aligarh Old Boys' annual dinner in March 1913, this question was taken up by the Honorary Secretary:

Gentlemen, the first and foremost problem is 'what to do with our boys'...We all know that at present the field of service is becoming daily congested in this country, the bar is overcrowded, and the straitened circumstances of our community have placed an embargo on us regarding Commerce and Industry. It is therefore my ambition to draw the attention of our youths to service outside this country and to agricultural and commercial training.[1]

The Honorary Secretary's ambitions were laudable, but for many they came rather late and anyway they did not amount to very much. Thus, in the early twentieth century, the UP contained a large number of educated Muslims with high aspirations and low expectations in service and the law. The briefless vakil had to retreat to a minor judicial post in the mofussil, and the hopeful graduate had to accept a poorly-paid post in the administration of a petty native state. What they were looking for was some new occupation in which they could satisfy their pretensions and retrieve some of their prestige and that of their community. That occupation was politics.

Opportunities for full time political activity opened up with the Morley–Minto reforms. Heightened communal consciousness produced a wide range of schemes for communal regeneration. The most important was the Muslim University project which at last seemed likely to become a reality. This new situation provided the context in which young Muslims such as the Ali brothers were able to leave the jobs which they despised and make a mark for themselves elsewhere. In December 1910, Shaukat Ali became private secretary to the Aga Khan, the president of the Muslim University Association. In January 1911, Mahomed Ali founded the *Comrade*, a weekly journal in English published from Calcutta, with the aim of promoting Muslim interests in general and the Muslim University in particular. Neither Shaukat nor Mahomed Ali was sure how his new career would develop and both left themselves with a safety-net. Shaukat Ali obtained extended leave from the Opium Department,[2] and Mahomed Ali kept his name on the Baroda

---

[1] Speech of Muhammad Ishaq Khan at the Old Boys' annual dinner, 21 March 1913, *Aligarh Institute Gazette* (Aligarh), 26 April 1913.
[2] This point was mentioned in an undated note by Shaukat Ali on the formation of the Anjuman-i-Khuddam-i-Kaaba, Mahomed Ali Papers, JMI.

Civil List.[1] Neither had to return. A new breed of Muslims had
been born. They were men who gained their living entirely from
politics. They were financed from three sources: political journalism, public subscription and the patron.

From 1909, the political newspaper was not only a major source
of financial support for the politician but also the major means
through which he carried on a dialogue with his supporters, his
opponents, and the Government. In a province in which the politically aware were thinly scattered over a wide geographical area,
it was the only really effective way of creating an organised public
opinion. Twelve 'Young Party' men appeared to make something
of a living by this means.[2] Of these, Mahomed Ali was the most
influential and his fortunes demonstrate how it was possible to
make politics pay. Within six months of its first issue, it became
clear that the *Comrade*, however well produced, was not going to
survive on the minor excitement of the Muslim University.
Desperate to keep his venture going, Mahomed Ali circularised
the Aligarh old boys, who formed the hard core of his readership,
asking them to suggest how the *Comrade*'s sales might be increased.
Suggestions included everything from love stories[3] to moving the
offices to Lucknow so that he could capitalise on reporting Shia-

[1] Dewan Tek Chand to Mahomed Ali, 30 December 1911, *ibid.*
[2] These were:
  Mahomed and Shaukat Ali: *Comrade* (Calcutta and Delhi), 1911–14 and
  Hamdard (Delhi), 1912–15.
  Raja Ghulam Husain: *Comrade* (Calcutta and Delhi), 1911–14; *Indian Daily
  Telegraph* (Lucknow), 1915–16; *New Era* (Lucknow), 1917.
  Wahid Yar Khan: *Nai Roshni* (Allahabad), 1917.
  Syed Shabbir Hasan: *Muslim Gazette* (Lucknow), 1912–13; *Saiyara*
  (Lucknow), 1914–15; *Nai Roshni* (Allahabad), 1917.
  Wahiduddin Salim: *Muslim Gazette* (Lucknow), 1912–13; *Saiyara* (Luck-
  now), 1914–15.
  Zafar-ul-Mulk Alvi: *An Nazir* (Lucknow).
  Hasrat Mohani: *Urdu-e-Moalla* (Aligarh), founded in 1903 and appeared
  irregularly until the 1930s.
  Syud Hussain: *Bombay Chronicle* (Bombay), 1917–19; *Independent* (Allah-
  abad), 1919–20.
  Qazi Abdul Ghaffar: *Hamdard* (Delhi); *Tarjuman* (Calcutta); *Sadiqat*
  (Calcutta), 1916–18; *Jamhur* (Calcutta), 1918; *Akhuwat* (Lucknow), 1919–20.
  Syed Jalib Delhavi: *Hamdard* (Delhi); *Hamdam* (Lucknow), 1917–18.
  Shuaib Qureshi: *Comrade* (Delhi), 1913–14; *New Era* (Lucknow), 1917;
  Young India (Bombay), 1921–22; *Independent* (Allahabad), 1922.
  Two others, Ziauddin Ahmad Barni and Abdur Rahman Siddiqi, also worked
  as journalists for a brief period, both of them on Mahomed Ali's papers.
[3] S. Sadiq Husain, a probationary sub-registrar in Gonda, to Mahomed Ali,
31 July 1911, Mahomed Ali Papers, JMI.

Sunni quarrels.[1] None was particularly constructive. What saved
the *Comrade* from liquidation and Mahomed Ali from ignominious
return to the obscurity of Baroda were the Balkan wars, when
Turk was attacked by Christian. Turkish wars were usually a
boon to the Muslim press in the UP. In 1877 and 1897 they
brought about considerable expansion,[2] and in 1912 they did so
again. The *Comrade* was immediately filled with news on Turkey,
its pages were crammed with reports, supplements and pictures
documenting in minute detail the progress of the war and lingering
over horrors perpetrated by the infidel Christian on the chosen of
Islam. The paper dropped its mild tone for one of rabid sensa-
tionalism. Indian news was largely ignored. From this moment the
Comrade never looked back. The number of advertisements multiplied and the paper grew in size. By the middle of 1912, Mahomed
Ali felt in a strong enough position to resign from the Baroda
service[3] and found an Urdu daily, the *Hamdard*, to address a wider
audience. Financially, it would appear, he had made a big improvement in his position; in 1909, he had been earning Rs. 5400 a year,
but by 1914 he claimed that in spite of the well-known reluctance
of Muslims to pay newspaper subscriptions, and even after he had
paid interest on Rs. 60,000 borrowed capital, Shaukat and he
together were earning Rs. 27,500 a year.[4] The Ali brothers had
acquired some of the fame they sought and they had become self-
supporting politicians. Not everyone was as successful as these,
the leaders of the 'Young Party', but several managed to make
a living out of political journalism.

The Turkish wars and the development of pan-Islamist politics
also stimulated a rash of public subscriptions. The cry of 'Islam in
danger' could always be guaranteed to persuade the poor to surrender their pice in the name of religion. The *Comrade* launched

[1] Abdul Hamid to Mahomed Ali, 25 July 1911, *ibid.*
[2] The Muslim press in northern India gave the Russo-Turkish war of 1877
and the Graeco-Turkish war of 1897 considerable coverage. The former
created enough interest for 'single sheets of paper giving the latest telegraphic
news [to be] published at many places to meet the local demand for intelligence
of the war'. *NWP&O Administration Report 1877–78*, p. 270. In the latter
war, government felt that the amount of journalistic interest stimulated was
'a striking evidence as to the interest that struggle, crowned as it was by the
final success of the Muhammadan power, has aroused among the Musulmans
of India.' *NWP&O Administration Report 1899–1900*, p. 194.
[3] Mahomed Ali to the Gaekwar of Baroda, no date but the text suggests 1912,
Mahomed Ali Papers, JMI.
[4] Mahomed Ali to Moazzam Ali, 27 March 1919, *ibid.*

appeal after appeal for which the money was collected but no satisfactory accounts rendered.[1] Rs. 80,000 of the Cawnpore Mosque Fund in the keeping of the Bihari lawyer–politician, Mazharul Haq, stayed with Haq and never reached the mosque;[2] the Anjuman-i-Khuddam-i-Kaaba, apparently designed to collect funds so that poor Muslims could perform their holy duty, the haj, split over the Shaukat Ali's management of the finances;[3] on his visit to England in autumn 1913, Mahomed Ali lived in grand style, purchased many luxuries and paid off his Oxford bills. The funds were legion, the accounts few and in financial matters, the politicians, the Ali brothers in particular, came to be trusted by no one. They lived well. It is a fair assumption that they lived well on the proceeds of pan-Islamic politics.[4]

[1] In 1920, a Budaun Muslim newspaper called the Ali brothers to task for their failure to render accounts of the following funds raised between 1907 and 1920:

1. Bait-ul-Malk fund collected to send Master Mohamad Husain [Raja Ghulam Husain] the martyr of the Aligarh College strike of 1907 to Europe for higher studies.

2. The Turkish Relief Fund which was considerably mismanaged and utilized in utter disregard of the wishes of the donors.

3. The Turkish colonization fund organised by Mahomed Ali and Dr Ansari.

4. The Cawnpore Mosque fund.

5. The Ghalib Tomb Fund – nothing has been done to improve the condition of the tomb.

6. The Hamdard Debenture Fund.

7. The Khuddam-i-Kaaba fund.

Zul Qarnain of Budaun quoted in the *Leader* (Allahabad), 20 November 1920.

[2] History sheet of Mazharul Haq, Home Poll. A, July 1917, 408–10, NAI.

[3] An open letter from Hafiz Abdur Rahim of the Delhi branch committee of the anjuman carried the following indictment of Shaukat Ali: 'the Anjuman has about 16,000 members and the total of subscriptions for the past three years should be about Rs. 48,000. The rules allow the expenditure of $\frac{1}{4}$ of this in connection with the organisation of the Anjuman. Is this all that has been spent and where is the balance of the Rs. 36,000? How much to the Holy Places? Is it a fact that the Anjuman has only Rs. 2–3,000 in hand? Were the expenses of Shaukat Ali's trip to Bombay paid out of the funds of the Anjuman? Has he ever accounted for the Rs. 1,000 he wired for from Bombay? Has he paid into the funds of the society his commission as pilgrim broker? Is it not a fact that the Commission which examined the accounts of the Society found defalcations and this is why they have never been published?' Weekly Report of the Director of Central Intelligence [henceforth WRDCI], 20 April 1915, Home Poll. B, April 1915, 416–19, NAI.

[4] Hearing rumours of the embezzlement of Red Crescent Funds, Harcourt Butler exclaimed, 'No Mahommedan can collect public funds apparently without this imputation! This is pan-Islamism!' Harcourt Butler to Hardinge, 30 April 1913, Hardinge Papers (85), CUL.

The patron was a third source of financial support. He could support the politician by direct gifts of money, by employing him or by putting him in the way of business. Notable patrons of the period included Prince Hamidullah Khan of Bhopal, Mahomed Nasim, a rich lawyer, and even Mahomed Ali, who gave jobs to several young Muslims on his newspapers. But perhaps the best example was the Raja of Mahmudabad. He paid cash[1] and provided sinecures.[2] It certainly paid the briefless Muslim vakil to cease his idle gossip in the Oudh Bar library and take a rickshaw for the 200-yard ride up to No. 1 the Kaiserbagh, where the Raja dispensed hospitality to those who were prepared to chat about politics or applaud the wit of his favourite companion, Bom Bahadur Shah.[3] Mahmudabad held the second largest taluqdari estate in Oudh, while Bom Bahadur Shah was the manager of the largest, Balrampur; amidst the gup and ghazals, there was always the chance of netting a fat brief. These lawyers and sycophants, whom Meston characterised as the Raja's 'vile entourage',[4] were the nucleus of the 'Young Party' in Lucknow and the source of his influence in Muslim League politics. They gorged his vanity and he fed them from his purse. They gained a living and he acquired a voice in young Muslim politics. For as long as the Raja could combine his reactionary taluqdari position with his progressive political allegiances, Mahmudabad made it possible for several young men to have time for politics.

In order to stay in business, the politician had to keep politics alive. Unemployment encouraged Abdur Rahman Siddiqi and Shuaib Qureshi to play politics and they became involved in the Ali brothers' newspapers, the internment agitations and the Sultanniah College. Wherever there was an opening, an agitation to organise, a newspaper to run, they were there immediately. But when, in 1918, the political tempo slowed down, they were at a

[1] In 1917, for instance, the Raja sent Khaliquzzaman with Rs. 6000 to the Ali brothers who were interned at Chhindwara. Chowdry Khaliquzzaman, *Pathway to Pakistan*, p. 38.

[2] When he left Aligarh, the Raja provided Khaliquzzaman with the post of Education Secretary in his service. Khaliquzzaman described it as a sinecure; 'There was hardly any work for me worth the name.' *Ibid.*, p. 35.

[3] Bom Bahadur Shah was the constant companion of Mahmudabad and a close friend of Harcourt Butler. A great organiser, he fixed everything from the arrangements for the local hockey and tennis tournaments to a Viceroy's visit to Lucknow. He was a leading figure in Lucknow society and a renowned wit.

[4] Meston to Hardinge, 25 March 1915, Hardinge Papers (89), CUL.

loss as to what to do.[1] Moreover, their political activities made it difficult for them to find a job in anything but politics. Abdur Rahman Siddiqi, for instance, tried for a post as Assistant Professor of History at Aligarh in 1915 but was turned down for political reasons.[2] Issues apart, politics just had to be kept going. The newspaper editor was subject to similar pressures. Circulations only thrived on political sensation. The *Comrade* became profitable as soon as it adopted a rabidly pan-Islamist line. It inflated every religious issue. Islam was to the Muslim press what sex is to the western press. In this way the Cawnpore municipality's action over the Macchli Bazaar mosque was hit upon and turned by the *Comrade* into a *cause célèbre*. The gamble paid off handsomely, enabling the *Comrade* to open agencies throughout the UP and to extend its sales in Bengal.[3] The logic of newspaper economics led this type of editor towards constant agitation. Thus, politicians were beginning to make politics as much as politics made politicians.

The professional politicians, the shock troops of the 'Young Party', and their followers, the unemployed and the potentially unemployed, were dominated by Mahomed Ali, 'the popular hero', Meston told Hardinge, 'of every Islamic school and college in the province'.[4] The party's home was the *Comrade* office in Delhi and its reunions the Aligarh Old Boys' dinner. Its politics were pan-Islamic and their pace frenetic. But under Mahomed Ali's wing there nestled another leader, Wazir Hasan, 'who has', Meston said, 'always been to Mahomd [sic] Ali as a twin-brother'.[5] Twins they may have been, but they were not identical. Wazir Hasan commanded a second 'Young Party' nucleus at Lucknow. His supporters were young lawyers at the Oudh Bar, members of the sophisticated intercommunal Rifah-i-Am club and those for whom he could persuade Mahmudabad to open his money-bags. His aims were moderate and his methods temperate – though he never shrank from making capital out of the pan-Islamic ploys of his less temperate allies. While Mahomed Ali was free, Wazir Hasan played second fiddle. When Mahomed Ali was interned, he rose to

[1] Abdur Rahman Siddiqi to Mahomed Ali, 24 March 1919, Mahomed Ali Papers, JMI.
[2] Abdur Rahman Siddiqi to Mahomed Ali, 6 July 1915, *ibid*.
[3] Shaukat Ali to Mahomed Ali, 24 October 1913, *ibid*.
[4] Meston to Hardinge, 25 March 1915, Hardinge Papers (89), CUL.
[5] Meston to Hardinge, 10 June 1915, Hardinge Papers (89), CUL.

lead the 'Young Party' and to direct it to his more moderate ends.

The 'Old Party'[1] like the 'Young Party' was drawn from the descendants of the Urdu-speaking elite, but their social and economic background was rather more varied. At least seventeen of the forty-four 'Old Party' men whose biographies appear in Appendix II could count themselves among the magnates of the province, those paying Rs. 5000 p.a. in land revenue. They included some of the richest landowners and certainly the richest Muslims in the province. Among their number were the Nawab of Rampur, the Oudh taluqdars, Jehangirabad, Pirpur and Qizilbash and the rich landlords of Aligarh, Chhatari, Bhikampur and Pahasu. Almost all were members of families which had been prominent for some years, which thought of themselves, and were recognised by others, as the aristocracy. In the absence of much information on the background of the remainder, it is difficult to place them firmly in social and economic terms. Many, however, such as the Justices Mahomed Rafique and Syed Abdur Rauf and the grandsons of Syed Ahmed, Syed Ross Masud and Syed Mahomed Ali, appear to have come from the same impoverished circumstances as the 'Young Party'. The 'Old Party', therefore, falls into two groups: the rich and well-born, and the men who had had to make their way in service and the professions.

Just as the background of the 'Old Party' had rather more variety, so did its educational experience. There was no solid phalanx of Aligarh men; it is possible to mark only twelve as having been there. As a group they were more concerned with the administration of the institution, twenty-eight being trustees, four secretaries and one principal of the college. Some of them, for instance, Mohsin-ul-Mulk and Viqar-ul-Mulk, who had played a big part in founding the college, had had a purely orthodox Muslim education; others, particularly the landed aristocrats, had been educated privately or at Colvin Taluqdars College; a few had been to Muir Central College or to other institutions. Fourteen of the younger men had been to England; seven had attended English universities and all but one had been called to the Bar. As was to be expected, there were fewer BAs and more who spoke little or no English. Indeed, the group represented a wide range

[1] Biographies of all UP men mentioned in connection with the 'Old Party' will be found in Appendix II.

of educational experience and had neither the *esprit de corps* nor the pan-Islamic outlook of the large proportion of the 'Young Party' which had been educated at Aligarh.

There were no unemployed among the 'Old Party', no members were struggling for jobs. They represented the rich, the successful, those who had 'arrived'. Most of the landed aristocrats were involved in the management of their estates, nearly all of which were in excellent condition.[1] Those who were not landed aristocrats were divided between service, the law, journalism and teaching. Many older men had served in Hyderabad, the plum of the native state services; Nawab Sarbuland Jung had been an official member of the Hyderabad Legislative Council, Syed Hosein Bilgrami the Director of Public Instruction, and Aziz Mirza Home Secretary. These and others retired to the UP to live off the fortunes they had accumulated. Others had made careers in the Indian civil services. There was the worthy Syed Jafar Husain, a retired engineer; Sheikh Mohammad Habibullah of the Provincial Civil Service, who managed the Mahmudabad estates and kept an eye on the Raja; and Nawab Ishaq Khan, a successful Indian Civil Servant. The lawyers were no less successful. Three of them reached the pinnacle of their profession; Mahomed Rafique and Syed Karamat Husein were Justices of the Allahabad High Court and Syed Abdur Rauf of Allahabad was, in 1918, appointed to the bench of the Punjab High Court. The two journalists ran newspapers which had good circulations and whose politics government looked upon with favour.[2] Even the one teacher, the brilliant mathematician, Ziaud-

[1] One point stood out from an examination into the condition of the landed estates in Agra and Oudh paying over Rs. 5000 land revenue, ordered by Harcourt Butler in 1918, and that was that the property of the large Muslim landowners who formed the nucleus of the 'Old Party' was invariably solvent and well-managed, and the owner affluent. In this respect they were far superior to the average representative of their class. Revenue and Agriculture, 1918, 578, UPS and see also Appendix II.

[2] Their papers, the *Al Bashir* of Etawah and the *Mashriq* of Gorakhpur, were the two most prominent conservative Muslim papers of the province. There is a distinct possibility that they may have at some stage received government subsidies. In 1913, Meston in urging the government of India to consider the possibility of press subsidies mentioned *Mashriq* as representative of the type of paper which deserved encouragement. A note by Meston for the government of India on security, 21 July 1913, Meston Papers (15), IOL. While the chief secretary to the UP government, R. Burn, supported a suggestion that *Al Bashir* should be upgraded with government assistance from being a weekly to being a daily. Burn to Meston, 4 June 1914, Meston Papers (6), IOL. In a letter to Meston of May 1914 Nawab Fateh Ali Khan Qizilbash actually

din Ahmad, received a CIE at the early age of thirty-six and became principal of Aligarh four years later. All these men were either rich or sickeningly successful. 'Young Party' men galled by their failure in the competition for jobs could hardly be blamed for attacking them for being smug and lethargic in their politics.[1]

The constraints on the political activities of the 'Old Party' were considerable. The landed magnates tended to be landowners first and Muslims second. Their ventures into Muslim politics were cautious and qualified. For instance, some were restricted by the supra-communal taluqdari bond; when the Muslims met in Lucknow in September 1906 to discuss their memorial to the Viceroy, Mahmudabad and Jehangirabad did not attend for fear of offending their fellow Hindu taluqdars.[2] After the Morley–Minto reforms, when communal feeling reached new heights, this same concern to preserve taluqdari solidarity played its part in elections in which landlords pushed their own candidates regardless of community.[3] But the major curb on the landlords' freedom of action was their dependence on government for the maintenance of their social and economic position. As far as the taluqdars were concerned, what the government had given, it could take away; Meston's warning to Mahmudabad in 1916 can have been lost on no one. Such threats, however, were not made everyday. As a rule what mattered was to be 'in' with government; official favour gave a man position with his tenants and standing in society. So landlords competed for the Rajaships, knighthoods and other distinctions that the Raj doled out to mark them off from other men. In

stated that the government had agreed to help support conservative Muslim newspapers. 'A[n] extract journal of a tour in the United Provinces of Agra and Oudh, during March and April 1914', by Nawab Fateh Ali Khan Qizilbash and dated 19 May 1914, enclosed in Nawab Fateh Ali Khan Qizilbash to Meston, 19 May 1914, Meston Papers (6), IOL. Whether or not these newspapers received subsidies in the form of money, it is highly likely that they received hidden subsidies, of a kind acceptable to the Government of India, in the form of preference in government advertising and the purchase of large numbers of copies for distribution to government offices.

[1] The government servants of the 'Old Party' were attacked for displaying the 'insolence of office' in a leader entitled 'The Young and the Old', *New Era* (Lucknow), 14 April 1917, while the landed aristocrats came in for their share of abuse in *ibid*, 26 May 1917.

[2] Harcourt Butler to H. E. Richards, 16 September 1906, Harcourt Butler Papers (18), IOL.

[3] See, for instance, the way in which Hindu and Muslim taluqdars worked together to hoist their man into the chairmanship of the Fyzabad municipal board in 1910. Francis Robinson, 'Muslim Separatism in the United Provinces', *Modern Asian Studies*, VII, 3 (1973), pp. 423–6.

addition, several had particular interests the success of which depended on government: some supported schools, others, for instance the Shias Qizilbash and Pirpur, a Shia College. Government was eager to build up the landlords and to bring them forward as the 'Natural Leaders' of society. They equally, regardless of the cruel satire that was flung at them by the 'Young Party',[1] were keen to have the marks of favour that came their way. As Muslims they might have wanted to criticise the government but as landlords there was no point in not supporting it loyally.

The successful professional men were described by an observer as the 'independent conservatives', 'the men who follow very faithfully in the political footsteps of Sir Saiyid Ahmad...men of a conservative turn of mind who sincerely desire to co-operate with Government, but only as independent allies, not as tools'.[2] Puppets they may not have wished to be, but when it came to the point, their movements were much influenced by what they hoped for from government. Powerful local leaders such as Asghar Ali Khan and Mufti Haidar Husain, vice-chairmen of the Bareilly and Jaunpur municipal boards respectively, were not going to fritter away in politics that bore little relevance to their localities the high esteem they had in government's eyes. Men who had spent their lives in government service were not going to sacrifice in the pursuit of pan-Islamist chimaera the reward they had, or hoped to receive, of a Khan Sahib or Bahadurship. Men like Maulvi Bashiruddin and Sheikh Abdullah, who were involved in educational schemes, were not going to forego the government aid which was crucial to their success.[3] Moreover, almost everyone, professional

---

[1] Thus, for instance, Vilayat Ali, the Bara Banki lawyer who wrote a satirical column entitled 'Gup' under the pen name 'Bambooque' in both the *Comrade* and the *New Era*, mocked the 'Natural Leader':

'The "Natural Leader" principally subsists on decorations and titles, and unlike the proverbial bread, a title, big or small – even a Khan Sahib ship – can sustain an aristocratic life. He has no illusions about the aim and object of human life. Man is born to flatter and be flattered, to bore and be bored, to entertain Big Sahibs and tip their be-turbanned chaprasies, to despise an untitled neighbour and fawn on a bigger one, to value all settlements as sacred, to avoid old taxes and vote for the new, and – to hate the politician like the Devil.' *New Era* (Lucknow), 26 May 1917.

[2] Sir Theodore Morison, 'Notes on the Mahomedan Situation', Meston Papers (15), IOL.

[3] Sheikh Abdullah was an enthusiast for female education, a project so unpopular among Muslims that it was only likely to succeed with government support. Bashir-ud-din ran the Islamia High School of Etawah, the top Muslim

and magnate alike, was caught up in the community's pet project, Aligarh. The college depended on its government grant. Opposition to government was out of the question.

The 'Old Party', therefore, was distinguished by its reliance on government. Its dependence is yet further illustrated by its inability, after the death of Mohsin-ul-Mulk in 1907, to produce a leader. Viqar-ul-Mulk had some of Mohsin-ul-Mulk's broad appeal but he was too old to be effective. As it was, Aftab Ahmad Khan led those interested in education, and Qizilbash tried to organise the party as a whole, but neither could create a general front. In fact, such leadership as the 'Old Party' had came from government. It was the government party.

In the new and live political atmosphere that followed the Morley–Minto reforms, communal feeling increased greatly. 'Never in my experience', wrote Harcourt Butler, 'has Hindu–Mahommedan antagonism been so intense as it now is in Northern India. People there are beginning to ask for separate courts of justice, separate schools etc...., for the two communities. Most municipal elections turn on this question. The Mahommedans have got too much, say the Hindus; we must get back a bit.'[1] Throughout the province the Hindus attacked their rivals where they could. Hindu taluqdars dismissed Muslims from their service.[2] Hindu merchants considered stopping credit.[3] Muslim pleaders and physicians were boycotted[4] and the Hindus of Agra even went so far as to renounce the charms of their Muslim courtesans.[5]

By the autumn of 1910, communal antagonism had become so bad that Congress leaders suggested to the Aga Khan, a pronounced supporter of Hindu–Muslim conciliation,[6] that community leaders should meet to discuss their differences. On the last day of the year, over one hundred Hindus and Muslims met at

secondary school in the province – a kind of prep school for Aligarh – which was no less dependent on government aid.
[1] Harcourt Butler to Sir James DuBoulay, Private Secretary to the Viceroy, 25 November 1910, Hardinge Papers (81), CUL.
[2] Letter from the Commissioner of Lucknow, 18 May 1909, quoted in Home Poll. A, October 1913, 100–18, NAI.
[3] Letter from the Commissioner of Agra, 21 February 1911, quoted in *ibid*.
[4] *Ibid*.   [5] GAD, 1910, 442, UPS.
[6] At the Delhi session of the Muslim League in January 1910, the Aga Khan took the line that, now that the Muslims had been given an assured share of power, they could begin to work together with the Hindus for the good of India. He maintained this position throughout the year.

Struggle for leadership

Allahabad. The signs had not been auspicious. Resolutions passed at the Nagpur session of the Muslim League, but three days before, had strongly demanded the extension to local bodies of separate representation and deplored the attempts of Hindus to replace Urdu as an official vernacular with Hindi in the UP and with Punjabi in the Punjab.[1] Equally the Congress, in session at Allahabad, patronised the Common Script and All-India Shuddhi conferences[2] and passed a resolution objecting strongly to separate representation in local bodies. Not surprisingly the conference was a disaster. It could not even decide on what subjects the communities were and were not able to agree to differ. All that emerged was a committee of nine Hindus and eight Muslims[3] which was instructed to discuss and make recommendations on points that had arisen during the conference. The committee did nothing. Conciliation was far from the minds of most Hindus. A few weeks later, Madan Mohan Malaviya, one of the committee members, spoke for most of his co-religionists when he complained in a speech before the Imperial Legislative Council that the Muslims were overrepresented in the councils and attacked the idea of Muslim 'political importance'.[4] No less representative of the Hindu mood was the action of the Hindus who, just before the Allahabad conference, had founded a provincial Hindu Sabha to 'do for the Hindus...what the Muslim League has done for the Mahomedans'.[5] This hostility was in part a reaction to the triumphs of

[1] Resolutions VI and VIII of the fourth annual session of the All-India Muslim League at Nagpur, 28 and 30 December 1910, Pirzada, *Foundations of Pakistan*, Vol. I, pp. 177 and 194.

[2] The Common Script conference, which supported Nagri and the All-India Shuddhi conference, the object of which was to consider methods of converting Muslims and others to Hinduism, were allowed to use the Congress Pandal at Allahabad.

[3] The Hindu members of the committee were Gokhale, Maharaja of Darbhanga, Ganga Prasad Varma, Saroda Charan Mitra, Surendranath Banerjee, Madan Mohan Malaviya, Harchand Rai Vishindas, Lala Munshi Ram and Lala Harkishen Lal. The Muslims were Syed Nabiullah, Syed Muhammad, Muhammad Shafi, Rafiuddin Ahmad, Ibrahim Rahimtullah, Shamsul Huda, Nawab Abdul Majid and Aziz Mirza. Syed Nabiullah and Ganga Prasad Varma of Lucknow were secretaries. *Leader* (Allahabad), 3 January 1911.

[4] Speech by Madan Mohan Malaviya, 24 January 1911, *Proceedings of the Council of the Governor-General of India, assembled for the purpose of making Laws and Regulations from April 1910 to March 1911* (Calcutta, 1911), pp. 134–7.

[5] 'Faith' to the Editor, *Leader* (Allahabad), 22 February 1911. In the same number, a leading article entitled 'The Hindu Sabha and the work before it' stressed the development of Hindu organisations in reaction to Muslim successes.

the Muslims in the Morley–Minto reforms but it was no less a response to the remarkable communal energy that reforms seemed to have drawn out of them.

Regeneration was the cry of Muslims in 1910. In January, at the third annual session of the All-India Muslim League, it was the main theme of Ameer Ali's presidential address. He warned the unprecedented number of 300 delegates and 4000 visitors, who gathered in Delhi, that 'a steady process of disintegration and de-moralization, partly induced by circumstances and forces beyond our control, has been going on in our midst',[1] urged them to consider 'how best to prevent the impoverishment of Musalmans and the passing of Musalman estates into other hands, how to foster industries among them to encourage trade and commerce, a better and more practical use of academic learning',[2] presented a programme of economic regeneration and suggested the establish-ment of a committee, divided into Economic, Political, Educational and Sociological sections, to put it into operation.[3] In the months that followed, there were many indications of how widely the new mood was spread. In February, Syed Karamat Husein published 'A scheme for the Progress of Muhammadans'. He stressed the importance of education and the fostering of communal conscious-ness.[4] In April, Mushir Husain Kidwai announced the formation of a 'Central Islamic Society'. He offered a pan-Islamist solution.[5]

---

[1] Because Ameer Ali had just been appointed to the Judicial Committee of the Privy Council, he was not able to leave England in order to preside over the Delhi session of the Muslim League. His address was read at the session by Mian Muhammad Shafi. Address of Ameer Ali to the third annual session of the All-India Muslim League, 29 January 1910, Pirzada, *Foundations of Pakistan*, Vol. I, p. 112.

[2] *Ibid.*, p. 114.   [3] *Ibid.*, p. 118.

[4] Karamat Husein laid especial stress on the development of communal con-sciousness. Section (d) of his plan recommended the following: 'Every Mahomedan has to know his creed and to develop a consciousness that he is a unit of an organised Mahomedan community and that his well-being is indissolubly bound up with the well-being of his community.

This is to be effected through mosques, clubs, associations, lectures, addresses and papers demonstrating the advantages of such consciousness creating a sympathetic interest in the community and rousing the feelings of the Mahomedans in favour of such interests.'

To put his plan into operation he suggested that a body of 'Servants of Islam' should be formed. First published 18 February 1910 and republished at the instance of Mirza Samiullah Beg in the *Leader* (Allahabad), 18 October 1913.

[5] Kidwai appears to have been attempting to produce an eclectic society on the model of the Theosophical movement, WRDCI, 24 May 1910, Home Poll. B, August 1910, 1–9, NAI.

Struggle for leadership

Local Muslim communities began to look at their condition more carefully. In June, a Muhammadan League was set up in Jhansi. It was strictly non-political, claiming to have the overall aim of looking after education and all things Muslim in the district.[1] In August, leading Muslims of Allahabad, with similar aims, organised themselves into an Allahabad Muslim Club.[2] And in October the *Leader* reported that in Lucknow 'there is no Mahommedan merchant, worth the name, who is not busy in collecting donations to the One Anna Fund', which had been started by the local Muslim League for keeping old mosques in repair.[3]

This burst of Muslim activity was not all hot air and uncoordinated action. In 1910, for the first time, the Muslim League had overall direction of considerable vigour. Aziz Mirza, who was elected secretary of the Delhi session, devoted all his energies to the League. In his first year of office he travelled 20,000 miles, visited most of the major cities of India and Burma, gave pep-talks to provincial league leaders and published pamphlets on League policy. Most important, however, he attempted to put into practice the leading resolutions of the League sessions.

The object of one of Mirza's first initiatives was the waqf question, a problem closely tied to the community's economic backwardness. Judicial decisions of 1887, 1890 and 1894 had made substantial inroads into the right in Muslim personal law to create waqfs (irrevocable settlements to safeguard property for a charitable purpose) for the benefit of their descendants or religious institutions. It had been British policy to leave Muslim personal law untouched. The Muslims claimed that this change had destroyed the financial resources of many of their old families.[4] In the

[1] WRDCI, 4 July 1910, Home Poll. B, August 1910, 18–25. NAI.
[2] *Leader* (Allahabad), 16 August 1910.
[3] *Ibid.*, 21 October 1910. It is interesting to note that the Shias became concerned about the economic condition of their community before the Muslim League launched its great campaign. At its 1908 session, the All-India Shia Conference introduced an ambitious scheme for technical and agricultural education 'to awaken the interest of our co-religionists in the pursuits of arts, industries, agriculture and commerce' which was to be implemented by a committee headed by Rampur, Mahmudabad, Qizilbash and Pirpur. Resolution VIII of the Second All-India Shia Conference, Lucknow 1908, xv, 1909, 728, LCA.
[4] In a letter to the Government of India enclosing the Waqf resolution, resolution IX of the Delhi Session of the All-India Muslim League, Aziz Mirza stressed that the courts' misinterpretation of Muslim personal law 'had led to the disintegration of many well-to-do Muhammadan families and is striking

Separatism among Indian Muslims

1880s, and 1890s Syed Ahmed and Ameer Ali had made protests but
it was not until 1910 that Muslims were able to generate enough enthusiasm to be effective. Aziz Mirza introduced a resolution on the
subject at the Delhi League session, pestered the government about
the problem, and laid the foundation on which Jinnah was able to
introduce legislation validating Muslim waqfs into the Imperial
Legislative Council, and in 1913 pilot it to a successful conclusion.

Other League initiatives involved Muslims in government
service, separate representation on local bodies, and the position of
Urdu. The League made the inevitable complaints to the Government of India about the inadequate number of Muslims in government service. On the subject of separate representation feeling was
strong. 'We regard, in the present state of India,' Mahomed Ali
pontificated in the *Comrade*, 'separate electorates to be the only
logical conclusion of a separation only too patent.'[1] Many Muslims
felt that the 1909 reforms would not be complete until separate
representation was extended to all elected bodies. Moreover, they
felt they had a strong case. The Decentralisation Commission had
endorsed their claim and they believed that Morley and Minto
supported it. Aziz Mirza, local leaders and the Muslim press
nagged the government for action.[2] At the same time, steps were
taken to protect Urdu against the gathering strength of Hindi. In
April 1910, the League secretary presided over the first UP Urdu
Conference at Budaun, which demanded that Urdu should be
introduced into the Allahabad University examinations and
launched a campaign to ensure that, in the 1911 Census, Urdu-
speaking people were returned as speaking Urdu alone.[3]

Nothing, it was thought, played a bigger part in the cause of

at the root of their national prosperity.' Aziz Mirza, Honorary Secretary of the
All-India Muslim League, to Secretary, Government of India Home Department, xv, 1909, 728, LCA.
[1] *Comrade* (Calcutta), 18 February 1911.
[2] Demands for the extension of separate representation to local bodies were the
annual product of the League sessions. Resolution VI of the Nagpur session
is typical. 'The All-India Muslim League once again records its deliberate
opinion that in the interests of the Musalman community, it is absolutely
necessary that the principal [sic] of communal representation be extended to
all self-governing public bodies, and respectfully urges that a provision for the
adequate and effective representation of the Musalmans on municipal and
district boards is a necessary corollary of the application of the same principle
to the Imperial and Provincial Legislative Councils and, at the same time,
essential to the successful working not only of the Reform Scheme, but also
of those public bodies themselves.' Pirzada, *Foundations of Pakistan*, Vol. I,
p. 177.   [3] *Advocate* (Lucknow), 7 April 1910, UPNNR 1910.

198

communal betterment than education. It was not remarkable, therefore, that this great outpouring of communal energies was eventually subsumed in a campaign to realise Syed Ahmed's dream, the raising of Aligarh College to the status of a university. The idea of a Muslim University had always been connected with Aligarh. Even before the College was founded, Syed Mahmud had produced an elaborate university scheme for the consideration of the College Fund Committee. From time to time, the idea was brought up but it did not become credible until it was given official recognition by Macdonnell in a speech at Aligarh in 1896. Plans were drawn up by Beck and Morison which were adopted by the Muslim Education Conference at Lahore in 1898. Financial crises and factional squabbles, however, prevented the scheme from gaining momentum. It became a hardy perennial among the Educational Conference resolutions; it was included in the Simla memorial of 1906, but not until 1910 did it get under way. At the Delhi Muslim League session it was resolved to turn Aligarh into a Muslim University.[1] The move was supported on all sides. Within a year, a Muslim University Foundation Committee had met, and by the second month of 1911 fund-raising deputations were fanning out all over the subcontinent. The Muslims of the UP were in the forefront. They had most Aligarh old boys and most to gain from the establishment of a Muslim University in their province.[2]

[1] Resolution VIII of the third annual session of the All-India Muslim League at Delhi, January 1910, Pirzada, *Foundations of Pakistan*, Vol. I, p. 135.
[2] The following was the state of collections for the Muslim University Fund on 31 October 1911:

	Rs.	As.	Ps.
Burma	8,175	4	0
East and West Bengal	20,308	15	0
Behar	42,543	8	6
UP including Rampur State	5,49,962	2	11
Punjab	1,58,361	5	5
Frontier Province and Baluchistan	24,863	11	6
Sind and Bombay	4,21,616	11	0
Madras	37,632	12	3
Central Provinces	22,483	0	9
Native States	3,09,059	2	7½
Unlocated and Outside India	13,098	3	3
Total realised	16,08,683	9	5½

Beyond this a further Rs. 30,46,050 10 4 had been promised.
Calculated from 'Collections for the Moslem University Fund up to 31 October 1911', *Comrade* (Calcutta), 25 November 1911.

Separatism among Indian Muslims

The Muslim University campaign was dressed up as a purely educational affair: there was no mention of it at the Nagpur session of the League and the appeal to the Muslims of India for financial support came from the Educational Conference at Rangoon. But this was no more than a device to win government support. In inspiration the drive to found a Muslim University was no less a political movement than the campaign to found the Muhammadan Anglo-Oriental College forty years before. It derived its impetus in general from the heightened communal rivalry that marked the first years of the Morley–Minto Councils and in particular from the news that the Hindus themselves were planning a denominational university. What the Hindus were going to do tomorrow, the Muslims should do today. 'Aligarh is destined to be the focus of all Muhammadan intelligence and activity in India', the collector of Aligarh warned the government, 'begun as a defensive move it is already acquiring an offensive character...The Muslims are not thinking of education in itself at all, but of more boys, more subscriptions, more candidates for government employment, more lawyers to fill seats in Council, and more political power generally.'[1] The President of the Delhi League session made no bones about it. The movement was, he said, 'as intimately connected with the fortunes of the political movement in the community as with its educational or social advancement'.[2] Mahomed Ali was even more candid. Once rulers, he wrote in the *Comrade*, the Muslims were now the ruled. They had distinctive religious and cultural traditions which they wished to preserve. They had 'every ambition to live and act as patriotic Indians and work for a nationality of which they would be a component yet conscious part. But they dread the position of the second fiddle which the new-fangled "Nationalism" of some Indian public men and newspapers assigns to them: a "Nationalism" which is avowedly Hindu in sympathies and

[1] Note by W. S. Marris, 17 May 1911, Education, 111, 1909, UPS.
[2] Speech by Ghulam Muhammad Ali, Prince of Arcot, at the Delhi League session, January 1910, Pirzada, *Foundations of Pakistan*, Vol. I, p. 107. Any doubts about the political character of the movement must be dispelled finally by the composition of the Foundation Committee. The Aga Khan, the League President, was its President, Viqar-ul-Mulk, a former League secretary, was its secretary, League members provided sixteen of its twenty-one vice-presidents and, in 1911, the university movement so embraced the energies of its supporters that the League secretary had to admit in his annual report that other communal affairs had been neglected. Rahman, *Consultation to Confrontation*, pp. 214–15, 220.

aspirations, has developed Hindu symbolism and battlecries and formula of faith, and draws its energising forces from Hindu religion and mythology.' For this reason they were organising higher education on a communal basis, to enable them 'to participate on something like equitable terms in the vast process of political and social change which is going on in this country'.[1] Communal feeling was in full flow. Never had Muslims been so vigorous in looking after their interests as a community.

Amidst this perfervid activity, 'Young Party' Muslims quickly began to play a bigger part in politics. At the Delhi League session, Wazir Hasan and Haji Musa Khan were elected joint secretaries, Hakim Ajmal Khan was chairman of the Reception Committee and Masood-ul-Hasan, Syed Riza Ali and Syed Zahur Ahmed were prominent in the proceedings. At Nagpur, Nabiullah was president and 'Young Party' men dominated the session as they were to dominate League meetings for a long time to come. In 1911, men such as the Ali brothers, Mustafa and Musa Khan Sherwani, Mahmudabad, Nabiullah, Riza Ali and Wazir Hasan toured the country with the Muslim University deputations. But the most powerful evidence of their rising importance lay in the press. The period was distinguished by the rise of the extremist Muslim newspaper. In 1911, Mahomed Ali left his unrewarding work in Baroda to found the *Comrade*, with the help of subventions from the Aga Khan and Ali Imam,[2] and then later, the *Hamdard*. These were the most notable papers in the UP. But, there were others: the Aligarh old boy, Zafar Ali Khan's *Zamindar* of Lahore, Khwaja Hasan Nizami's *Tauhid* of Meerut, Syed Wahiduddin's *Muslim Gazette* of Lucknow and Abul Kalam Azad's *Al Hilal* of Calcutta. Through papers such as these the 'Young Party' came to exercise considerable influence: 'the extremist group has been immensely helped in its activities by a most powerful press',[3] Nawab Fateh Ali Khan Qizilbash told Meston as, in 1913, he struggled to get together a Muslim government party. But the lieutenant-governor

---

[1] *Comrade* (Calcutta), 19 August 1911.
[2] 'He [Mahomed Ali] soon turned on the former [Ali Imam]', Harcourt Butler told Hardinge, 'who gave him only a lump sum. Aga Khan gives him a regular subvention still, I believe.' Harcourt Butler to Hardinge, 3 November 1912, Hardinge Papers (84), CUL.
[3] Note by Qizilbash on 'The Moderate Muslim Organisation' enclosed in Nawab Fateh Ali Qizilbash to Meston, 26 December 1913, Meston Papers (6), IOL.

knew. He had already told the Viceroy that 'the danger centre is
the press...If the press were properly warned and regulated the
the excitement here would soon be negligible.'[1]

Not only did communal fervour sweep 'Young Party' men into
prominence, it also swept one man to their head. That man was
Mahomed Ali; the vehicle, his two newspapers. Other papers had
nothing to approach their influence in the province. The *Zamindar*,
although it had considerable weight in west UP, and was said to
be 'sold in Meerut by the cartload',[2] was still essentially a Punjab
Muslim paper; *Tauhid*, *Muslim Gazette* and *Al Hilal* all inclined
towards ulama thinking. The *Comrade*, however, was the paper of
the young educated Muslims. It was, for instance, the only one of
these papers taken by the Rifah-i-Am, the Lucknow club to which
many of them belonged.[3] The only paper in English, like the
'Young Party', it was largely an Aligarh concern. It was founded
on the old-boy network and was full of Aligarh cricket scores,
gossip about the Trustees and information about the Old Boys'
Association. In the absence of any formal political organisation, it
performed the important role of providing a framework for the
uneasiness and dissatisfaction of the Muslim educated elite
scattered throughout the district bars and low-paid government
jobs of the province. It moulded their attitudes towards government and towards other groups in the community. Instead of
discontent being dissipated over a multitude of petty incidents, the
whole weight of young Muslim feeling was focussed on specific
issues. At the same time, the 'Young Party' began to look to
Mahomed Ali as their leader. 'No paper has so much influence
with the students as the *Comrade*, and no individual has the
authority over them which is exercised by Muhammad Ali',[4]
the provincial government declared in 1914. When, at the
beginning of his internment, Mahomed Ali wanted to stop the
Hamdard, Vilayat Ali wrote begging him not to do so: 'I
don't approve of your decision and I don't think many will...

[1] Meston to Hardinge, 11 September 1913, Hardinge Papers (86), CUL.
[2] Minute on the 'Causes of Muhammadan discontent' by R. Burn, Chief
Secretary to the Government of the UP, 17 September 1913, enclosed in
Burn to Secretary to Government of India, Home Department, 17 September
1913, Home Poll. A, October 1913, 100–18, NAI.
[3] Proceedings Book of the Rifah-i-Am Association, 1910–16, entry for 1912.
Mss. Records of the Rifah-i-Am Association, Lucknow.
[4] Fortnightly Report [henceforth FR] (UP), Home Poll. D, December 1914,
31, NAI.

You can't imagine what the loss of Hamdard will mean to us – the Musalmans.'[1]

Just at the moment, however, when the Muslims were fairly united and their communal efforts were moving into top gear, they experienced three sharp checks. The first was the repartition of Bengal. At the Delhi Durbar of December 1911, the King announced that the province of East Bengal and Assam created in 1905 was to be reabsorbed into the Presidency of Bengal, that a new province of Bihar and Orissa was to be formed, and that the capital was to be moved from Calcutta to Delhi. The blow came unheralded. The Muslims were stunned. They had come to regard the existence, in spite of Bengali terrorism, of the Muslim-dominated province of East Bengal and Assam as a touchstone of the government's willingness to defend their interests. Now, government seemed to have sacrificed Muslim interests to Hindu agitation and administrative convenience.[2] Muslims quickly asserted the need for more positive action to protect their interests. Mahomed Ali concluded that government's action justified the use of vigorous protest: 'agitation', he declared, 'is acknowledged by the Government to be the only effective method of converting them...'[3] Other 'Young Party' men such as Riza Ali, Samiullah Beg and Mushir Husain Kidwai, went so far as to suggest that the Muslims should join the Congress.[4] The 'Old Party' leader,

[1] Vilayat Ali to Mahomed Ali 20 August? (most probably 1915), Mahomed Ali Papers, JMI.

[2] The suggestion for the repartition of Bengal came from the King, who wished to make some gesture of imperial magnanimity at the Delhi Durbar; he hoped that the measure would flatter the Bengalis, allay discontent and stop sedition. Though the idea had the full support of the Secretary of State, from February to June 1911 Hardinge opposed it forcefully. It was not till he received a memorandum from Jenkins, the Chief Justice of the Calcutta High Court, suggesting that repartition should be linked with the creation of a new imperial capital at Delhi, that he was prepared to acquiesce. Once converted, the Viceroy became the scheme's strongest advocate. The decision was kept secret with great success with the result that its announcement at Delhi in December 1911 had considerable impact. Rahman, *Consultation to Confrontation*, pp. 231–7.

[3] *Comrade* (Calcutta), 3 February 1912, quoted in Rahman, *Consultation to Confrontation*, p. 245.

[4] Samiullah Beg wrote an article in the *Muslim Review* suggesting that the Muslims should join the Congress, *Muslim Gazette* (Lucknow), 21 January 1912, UPNNR 1912. Syed Riza Ali, as secretary of the Moradabad Muslim League, published a statement denying Muslim separatism and supporting unity with the Hindus, *Leader* (Allahabad), 17 January 1912. Kidwai recommended a similar course, *ibid.*, 27 January 1912.

Viqar-ul-Mulk, was no less adamant that strong action was required. 'It is now manifest like the midday sun', he wrote a few days after the announcement, 'that after seeing what has happened lately, it is futile to ask the Muslims to place their reliance on Government. Now the days for such reliances are over. What we should rely on, after the grace of God, is the strength of our right arm...'[1] Nevertheless, he was no less sure that the Muslims 'should not destroy their political existence by joining the Congress movement' and should not antagonise the government. He declared:

We cannot reside in India on any terms of enmity with the British Government. To try to establish Government on a firm footing and to co-operate with it are to strengthen the Muhammadan community, and therefore we should not entertain any ill-feeling against Government.[2]

The second blow came with the realisation that the British seemed to be no more prepared to protect Muslim interests in the world at large than those in India. As soon as war broke out between Italy and Turkey in Tripoli in autumn 1911, Mahomed Ali made clear what many Muslims expected Government to do: 'One of the ideals', the *Comrade* announced, 'which the Indian Muhammadans have cherished for long is that the British Government, which rules over the largest number of Mussalman subjects, should be bound in an alliance with Muhammadan powers and Kingdoms so that their own territorial loyalty and extra-territorial patriotism should work in the same direction.'[3] Yet the British did nothing to check the Italian invasion of Tripoli, remained immobile when the Russians bombarded Meshed and, worse, actually exulted in the invasion of Turkey by the Balkan States. Mahomed Ali found 'the Balkan war...prolific in many lessons for the Mussalmans of India. Its origin, its character, its cries, the ways of European diplomacy and the attitudes of Christian Europe have all combined to teach the Mussalmans of India...the futility of relying on anything else but their own God and the strength that he may choose to grant them.'[4] In June 1912, the Commissioner of Lucknow

[1] Viqar-ul-Mulk's article entitled 'The Fate of Muslims in India', published in the *Aligarh Institute Gazette* of 20 December 1911, quoted in *Tazkirah-i-Viqar*, pp. 340–1 and requoted in Ikram, *Modern Muslim India*, p. 118.
[2] An excerpt from the same article by Viqar-ul-Mulk, *Aligarh Institute Gazette* (Aligarh), 20 December 1911, UPNNR 1911.
[3] From an article entitled 'Great Britain and the Moslem Kingdoms', *Comrade* (Calcutta), 14 October 1911.   [4] *Comrade* (Delhi), 12 April 1913.

sensed how the Muslims were being affected. He told the UP
government:

I do not see how any one, who is in frequent contact with Muhammadans
interested in politics, can be of opinion that our prestige with them stands
where it did a year ago. At the same time they are well aware that their
interests are bound up with ours. What we have to anticipate from them
is far more active and persistent agitation to gain their objects than we
have ever experienced in the past...[1]

The bitter disillusionment of the repartition was still fresh in the
mind, and government's refusal to befriend the beleaguered Turkey
was causing increasing discontent, when in August 1912 the third
blow fell. The Muslim University scheme was rejected. Fundamental to Muslim ambitions for a university as the engine for the
regeneration of the whole Indian Muslim community was the
right to affiliate colleges outside the province. Government made
little objection to this proposal or to any of the others that were put
forward by the Muslim University Constitution Committee. Indeed, the whole business was amicably executed, relations with
the Government of India being exceptionally smooth owing to the
friendship between the president of the Foundation Committee,
the Raja of Mahmudabad, and the Education Member, Harcourt
Butler. The Secretary of State, however, would not accept several
points, including affiliation.[2] The Government of India pressed on
London, 'with all the force at our command, the political necessity
of granting powers of affiliation'.[3] But the Secretary of State would
not budge. Thus the Government of India's proposals, communi-
cated to Mahmudabad in August 1912,[4] ignored a central concern
of the Muslims in their Muslim University ambitions. The great
project, in which so much Muslim energy and money had been
invested, juddered to a halt. All were disappointed, but Mahomed
Ali and his followers, whose cherished dream it was, were especially
disappointed.

Such rebuffs from government had an inevitable effect on Muslim

[1] H. Verney Lovett, Commissioner of Lucknow, to Chief Secretary, Government of the UP, 14 June 1912, Home Poll. A, March 1913, 45–55, NAI.
[2] Theodore Morison, the former Principal of Aligarh, who was on the Secretary
of State's Council, was thought to have played a big part in placing the veto
on affiliation.
[3] Telegram, Viceroy (Education Department) to Secretary of State, 24 June
1912, Home Education A, July 1913, 4–12, NAI.
[4] Harcourt Butler to Mahmudabad, 9 August 1912, *ibid.*

politics. As increasingly the government appeared to be hostile, the dynamic drive to prepare the Muslims to face the challenge of a Hindu-dominated India slowed down. As the British ignored each shibboleth of Muslim politics – East Bengal, Turkey, the Muslim University project – the credibility of the policy of collaboration declined and the reputation of the politics of protest increased. Simultaneously, the reputations of the two major groupings among UP Muslims changed. 'Old Party' men, whose wealth, success and ambitions inclined them towards the government, lost influence. 'Young Party' men, whose poverty, lack of employment, lack of success and suppressed ambition seemed but a reflection of their community's position were encouraged to assert themselves. They took the line that government must be compelled to recognise and to protect Muslim interests by whatever means were available.

'Young Party' men had two main approaches to the problem of forcing government to attend to Muslim concerns. Agitation was the first. Violent articles, demagogic speeches and pressing petitions were used to draw attention to Muslim interests in India and the world at large. Agitators sought to associate government with projects to protect Muslim interests in Islamic countries and to persuade it to acknowledge these interests in India itself. Their tone was hostile and, if necessary, they were ready for a trial of strength. They gained inspiration mainly from the *Comrade* and leadership mainly from Mahomed Ali. The second approach was more constitutional. 'Young Party' men set out to capture all the organisations of Muslim society so that theirs would be the views represented to government. Mahomed Ali's agitations did much to help men gain these more limited objectives. But the more subdued politics of organisations were not suited either to his temperament or to his finances and leadership here fell into the hands of Wazir Hasan and his lawyer band from Lucknow.

Intense Muslim consciousness of the fate of their co-religionist abroad owed its development to the professional politicians. 'Pan-Islamism', observed the government, 'had very little footing in India till 1912 when Mr. Muhammad Ali removed his paper *The Comrade* to Delhi and stirred up the feelings of your Muhammadans there in favour of Turkey.'[1] But it should not be imagined that,

[1] 'Sedition in the United Provinces', UP secretariat note by S. H. Fremantle, December 1917, p. 2, Meston Papers (15), IOL.

because there was in pan-Islamic politics a boost for Mahomed Ali's image, an obvious return for his newspapers and a definite political purpose, that there was not also a great deal of very real feeling. 'If he is genuine about anything', the collector of Chhindwara said of Mahomed Ali, 'he is first and last a fanatical Muslim.'[1] 'Shaukat Ali', observed Theodore Morison who knew him well, 'was filled with josh [fervour] for Islam and rage at its impotence during the Balkan war'; he felt 'he must *do something* for Islam. . .'[2]

The Red Crescent Mission was the first project. Shaukat Ali suggested it in the first Delhi edition of the *Comrade*[3] and Dr Ansari later gave it form.[4] Their plan was that a group of Muslim doctors and assistants should go to the Turkish front as a medical mission. It was entirely a 'Young Party' affair.[5] The scheme received government support. High-ranking officials contributed generously. The Viceroy saw the party off from Delhi and Dr Ansari, at least, was perfectly happy with the government's attitude to the scheme.[6] The Red Crescent Mission was a genuine response by young Muslims concerned to do something for their co-religionists in Turkey. In Turkey their work was purely medical; but their mission was a product of their politics in India and it kept their papers in good copy.

Other projects for Islam were tried. Mahomed Ali was in contact with the Ottoman Minister of the Interior and tried both to foster Indo-Turkish trade[7] and to set up an Indo-Ottoman Colonization

---

[1] WRDCI, 6 October 1917, Home Poll. B, October 1917, 43–5, NAI.

[2] Sir Theodore Morison, 'Notes on the Mahomedan Situation', *ibid*. Morison taught Shaukat Ali when he was at Aligarh.

[3] *Comrade* (Delhi), 12 October 1912.

[4] *Ibid*., 26 October 1912.

[5] The following 'Young Party' men went on the Red Crescent Mission: Khaliquzzaman, Dr M. A. Ansari, Dr M. N. Ansari, Shuaib Qureshi, Abdur Rahman Siddiqi and Bashiruddin Ahmed.

[6] Just before the mission set out, Dr Ansari wrote to Mahomed Ali: 'So far the Govt. of India have not in any way shown any dislike for our human[e] Mission, nor should I think they are likely to do so. My own impression has been that they have been very fair to us and have given every legitimate help and support.' Dr M. A. Ansari to Mahomed Ali, 28 November 1912, Mahomed Ali Papers, JMI.

[7] There is in the Mahomed Ali papers an unsigned copy of a letter, the tone of which would suggest that it was from the Ali brothers, addressed to 'His Excellency Talaat Bey, Minister of the Interior, His Imperial Majesty the Sultan of Turkey, Constantinople', 8 July 1914. The letter recommended the strengthening of Indo-Turkish trade ties and the establishment of Turkish consulates in Delhi and Calcutta. *Ibid*.

Separatism among Indian Muslims

Society, which had the aim of starting a pan-Islamic settlement at Adana composed of Indian and Turkish Muslims.[1] But the most effective project in action, as well as the most significant in method, was the Anjuman-i-Khuddam-i-Kaaba. This organisation, designed to protect the holy places, was conceived by several persons at about the same time.[2] The first blueprint was produced by Mushir Husain Kidwai and Maulana Abdul Bari of Lucknow, who hoped to achieve their end by collecting a crore of rupees in order to build dreadnoughts and airships and maintain armed forces.[3] In March 1913, Shaukat Ali publicly announced the scheme. It was soon seen to be impractical. In a later draft of May 1913 and in the final constitution of early 1914, peaceful replaced warlike means.[4] The objects too were broadened. The subscription, which every member of the anjuman paid, was divided into three parts; one half was to go to support the independent Muslim power in control of the holy places, one quarter was to be used for administrative expenditure and the remainder was to be kept in reserve for use in

[1] Possibly money was sent to Turkey to aid this project. A mysterious letter in the Mahomed Ali papers contains the following: 'Cheque above enclosed. This is another instalment of the contribution of the *Comrade* Fund to the Indo-Ottoman Colonization Society for their Col at Erzine in the Vilayat of Adana. More money will be sent later, and in the meantime we trust details of the work done hitherto would be sent to the *Comrade* for the publication so that the interest of the Indian Mussalmans in the Colony may be fully maintained. As these are received money will be forwarded from time to time.' Mahomed Ali to 'Dear Friend' [most probably Talaat Bey], 16 July 1914. On this occasion the money was not sent; still with the letter in its envelope was a cheque, payable to Talaat Bey for £998-9-11. *Ibid.*

[2] Note signed by Abdul Bari on the aims of the Anjuman-i-Khuddam-i-Kaaba, Urdu Mss. undated, *ibid.*

[3] R. Burn, Chief Secretary to Government, UP, to H. Wheeler, Government of India, Home Department, 10 June 1913, Home Poll. D, July 1913, 7, NAI.

[4] The following were the means which the anjuman intended to use: '3. To attain this object the *Anjuman Khuddam-i-Kaaba* shall:
(a) preach the aims and objects of the Anjuman to Musalmans generally; invite them to join it; and induce them to render sincere service to *harmain sharifain* (holy places);
(b) spread Islamic ethics in the neighbourhood of the *harmain sharifain*; and invite the attention of the inhabitants of those places to a knowledge of the religion; promote intercourse and unity among them; and persuade them to the allegiance and assistance of the *Khadim-i-harmain-i-sharifain* (guardian of the holy places);
(c) promote relations between the Musalmans and the *harmain-i-sharifain* and extend and facilitate the means of communication with the holy places.' Quoted from 'Complete Rules (*Dasturul-Amal*) of the Society of Servants of Kaaba (*Anjuman-i-Khuddam-i-Kaaba*) published at the commencement of 1914', Home Poll. A, May 1914, 46, NAI.

connection with the haj and other religious duties.[1] To pursue the activities of the society a complete administrative hierarchy was set up, with circle, district, provincial and all-India organisation.[2] There were two types of membership. Those who paid their subscriptions and swore allegiance to the objects of the anjuman were entitled to style themselves Khadim-i-Kaaba (servants of the Kaaba).[3] Those who promised to devote their lives to the service of the Kaaba and undertook to wear a splendid green uniform adorned with a yellow crescent badge, were privileged to become Shaidaian-i-Kaaba (votaries of the Kaaba), and, if they were poor, to be supported with their families from society funds.[4]

The composition of the Central Committee was representative of the make-up of the society as a whole; it contained 'Young Party' men and ulama.[5] But not all ulama joined. Those connected with the Firangi Mahal and Budaun schools did so, but Deoband declared against the anjuman. Try as he might, Abdul Bari could not extract from Maulana Habibur Rahman, the leading Deobandi, anything more than very grudging approval.[6] Rahman had no intention of having much to do with a society in which the Firangi Mahalis were in command. But, even if only some ulama joined, their support had much to do with the anjuman's success. Indeed, their potential in Muslim political organisation was revealed. In proselytisation the power of the mosque was fully employed.

---

[1] *Ibid.*, clause 30. The May 1913 constitution devoted one third of the society's capital to 'orphanages, and schools and Islamic missionary societies'. See the rules and regulations of the anjuman published in the *Muslim Gazette* (Lucknow), 21 May 1913, UPNNR 1913.

[2] 'Complete rules', clauses 11–28, Home Poll. A, May 1914, 46, NAI.

[3] 'Complete rules', clause 4, *ibid.*

[4] 'Complete rules', clauses 6–10, *ibid.*

[5] The following were the members of the anjuman's central committee: Maulana Maulvi Abdul Bari of Firangi Mahal, Lucknow, Khadim-ul-Khuddam (Servant of the Kaaba); Hakim Abdul Wali, Lucknow; Mohamed Ali, Delhi; Maulvi Ghulam Mohiuddin, Kasur; Maulvi Ghulam Muhammad, Hoshiarpur; Nawab Viqar-ul-Mulk, Amroha; Dr Naziruddin Hasan, Lucknow; Maulana Maulvi Shah Ahmad Ashraf, Kachocha; Maulana Maulvi Abdul Majid Qadri, Budaun; Maulana Mian Khwaja Ahmad, Rampur; Dr M. A. Ansari, Delhi; Nawab Bashiruddin Ahmad, Hyderabad, Deccan; Qazi Wahiduddin, Barabanki; Mushir Husain Kidwai, Lucknow; Shaukat Ali, Rampur. 'Complete rules' clause 31, *ibid.*, and see also notice in Urdu of a meeting to be held on 19 April 1914, Abdul Bari Papers, File 1, Firangi Mahal [henceforth FM].

[6] Maulana Habibur Rahman Deobandi to Maulana Abdul Bari, 1 Safar 1332 and also 14 Rabi'ul-Awwal 1332 [1914], in Urdu, Abdul Bari Papers, File 1, FM.

Women too, among them the mother of the Ali brothers and the wife of Dr Ansari, were brought into a public movement for the first time.[1] In the first eighteen months of its existence, the anjuman's membership grew from twenty-three in May to 3413 in September,[2] and 17,175 a year later.[3] There were members in every district of the UP bar five, and branches in at least eleven.[4] The organisers were disappointed with the number of recruits, but they ought not to have been because, by 1914, the anjuman had grown faster and extended further than any other Muslim politico-religious organisation yet to exist.

The growth of the anjuman might have been impressive, but this was not matched by its activities. It failed to obtain official recognition.[5] Government was suspicious, wished the anjuman dead[6] and refused Abdul Bari's importunate demands for a letter of recommendation.[7] No money was sent to Turkey.[8] Nothing was done for Muslim orphans. No schools were built to fill the gaps in the government educational effort. Indeed, only in work concerned with the haj was anything achieved. Reports were issued on the state of the route.[9] Shaukat Ali set himself up in Bombay as a pilgrim-broker. He put off his sharply cut western-style clothes, ignored 'his pretty taste in silk shirts',[10] donned the green livery

[1] Printed notice of a ladies' meeting of the anjuman in Delhi, 6 November 1913, Abdul Bari Papers, File 1, FM. See also an undated note in Urdu, Mahomed Ali Papers, JMI.
[2] Undated note by the Assistant Director of Intelligence, Home Poll. A, May 1914, 46, NAI.
[3] WRDCI, 1 June 1915, Home Poll. B, June 1915, 549–52, NAI.
[4] Undated note in Urdu on the Anjuman-i-Khuddam-i-Kaaba and its centres. The text suggests that it was written in 1914. Mahomed Ali Papers, JMI.
[5] Abdul Bari tried hard to get government recognition for work concerned with the haj. Abdul Bari to Private Secretary to the Viceroy, 17 March 1914 and 28 May 1914, Home Poll. D, July 1914, 7, NAI and Hardinge Papers (87), CUL.
[6] Note by R. H. Craddock, Home Member, 4 May 1914, Home Poll. A, May 1914, 46, NAI.
[7] Private Secretary to the Viceroy to Maulana Abdul Bari, 10 June 1914, Home Poll. D, July 1914, 7, NAI and Hardinge Papers (87), CUL.
[8] WRDCI, 1 June 1915, Home Poll. B, June 1915, 549–52, NAI.
[9] A draft for inclusion in the newspaper of the anjuman went thus: 'A. K. Ghaznavi when travelling through the Hedjaz experienced many difficulties – all Muslims are angry with Government of Usmania because it has not built the Hedjaz railway and the pilgrims are thus hindered. The real problem is the failure to maintain peace essential for the performance of the haj.' etc.... Translation from Urdu, Mahomed Ali Papers, JMI.
[10] Afzal Iqbal (ed.), *My Life, A Fragment: An Autobiographical Sketch of Maulana Mohamed Ali* (Lahore, 1942), p. 68.

of the anjuman and grew a shaggy beard 'which, as he himself used to say was his fiercest protest against Europe and Christendom'.[1] He attempted to break into the European monopoly of the pilgrim trade and set up, with Turkish aid,[2] a wholly Muslim shipping company. His efforts seem to have had some impact. 'Last year', Obeidullah Sindhi told Abdul Bari, 'Shaukat Ali did much to improve the condition of the pilgrims.'[3]

The anjuman, however, fell foul of the sickness which appeared to attack every islamic organisation, embezzlement. Clause eight of the rules permitted Shaukat Ali and the Shaidais (votaries or workers) to live at the anjuman's expense. They appeared to be living too well. In 1915, the Delhi branch committee under the leadership of Hafiz Abdur Rahim rebelled. They exposed the peculation in the finances of the central organisation, threatened legal action and published a stream of pamphlets emphasising that the anjuman was more than just a religious affair: 'How is it that a purely religious society attracts so many young men of the new political school and so few men learned in religion?'[4] asked one pamphlet. Young Muslims had been attracted to the society as a source of support. Shaukat conceived of the Muslim shipping company as a means of creating employment; 'there will be a new profession for our boys',[5] he wrote to his brother in July 1914. For ulama and men of religious outlook the closing of the haj route as a result of World War One had destroyed much of the *raison d'être* of the organisation. Hafiz Abdur Rahim closed down the Delhi office of the anjuman for the duration of the war[6] and the society fell to pieces amid squabbles over money and objectives.

The interest of the anjuman lies as much in what it portended as in what it set out to achieve. Here were all the materials of the Khilafat movement: the religious issue and the union between young, western-educated, Muslims and the ulama. The close

---

[1] *Ibid.*

[2] Unsigned copy of a letter, most probably from the Ali brothers, to 'His Excellency Talaat Bey, Minister of the Interior, His Imperial Majesty the Sultan of Turkey', 8 July 1914, Mahomed Ali Papers, JMI.

[3] Obeidullah Sindhi to Maulana Abdul Bari, 5 August 1915, translation from Urdu, Abdul Bari Papers, File 1, FM.

[4] WRDCI, 25 May 1915, Home Poll. B, May 1915, 855–8, NAI.

[5] Shaukat Ali to Mahomed Ali, 16 July 1914, Mahomed Ali Papers, JMI.

[6] Printed notice signed by Hafiz Abdur Rahim, undated but surrounding correspondence suggests early 1915, Abdul Bari Papers, File 1, FM.

alliance between Abdul Bari of Firangi Mahal and the Ali brothers was established. From henceforth they regarded the maulana as their pir (spiritual guide).[1] Access to the Muslim masses was achieved by 'Young Party' men through the most powerful unifying forces of the community: Islam, the mosque and the connections of the ulama. The financial and employment possibilities of the politics of religion were discovered. But, just as the advantages of an organisation of ulama and young Muslims were revealed, so were its drawbacks. Like the Anjuman-i-Khuddam-i-Kaaba, the Khilafat movement was also to divide over the embezzlement of funds and the essential differences of aim between the politicians and the ulama.

In the way that the Anjuman-i-Khuddam-i-Kaaba and the Red Crescent Mission were attempts to protect Muslim interests outside India, the Cawnpore Mosque agitation aimed to achieve the same object within India. But, whereas the pan-Islamic projects merely tried to involve government in Islamic affairs, the mosque agitation actually set out to coerce government to recognise Muslim interests. 'The entire forces', Meston told Hardinge, 'of the new Mahommedan machinery for agitation were being dishonestly used on the false cry of religious sentiment to show that the demagogues, who now aspire to lead the Mussalman community, can defeat the Government and wring concessions from it...'[2] The agitation developed as the British set about imposing their own capital over the Mughal Imperial city. As the navvies moved in to obliterate the relics of the Muslim raj and replace them with the symbols of British power, Mahomed Ali fought a desperate rearguard action. Each mosque, each graveyard was the scene of a bitter battle Howls of execration were raised when buildings were demolished and graveyards levelled.[3] Shouts of jubilation greeted the news that the Commissioner had agreed to supply full compensation for the destruction of a mosque.[4] The results of Mahomed Ali's defence can be seen to this day in some of the bends and roundabouts of the New Delhi road system. In the midst of this struggle, there came the news that the Cawnpore municipality was

---

[1] Interview with Mufti Reza Ansari of Firangi Mahal, 29 May 1968.
[2] Meston to Hardinge, 25 August 1913, Hardinge Papers (86), CUL.
[3] See, for instance, *Comrade* (Delhi), 24 May 1913.
[4] W. Hailey, the Chief Commissioner of Delhi, agreed to give full compensation for the destruction of the Mosque of Maulana Shah Abdul Haq, a renowned traditionalist of Delhi, *ibid.*, 21 June 1913.

determined to remove the lavatory of the Macchli Bazaar Mosque
in order to straighten out a road as part of the town improvement
scheme. The local mutawalis (mosque board of management) were
satisfied with the authorities' offer to rebuild the structure at
another part of the mosque. But to the professional politicians it
was another example of the government's disregard for Muslim
interests, and this feeling was enhanced by the fact that a re-
alignment had been made to miss a Hindu temple but not to avoid
the mosque.[1] In private correspondence with Meston, Mahomed
Ali tried to have the municipality's decision reversed. He failed.[2]
In May, a memorial was presented on behalf of the Raja of
Mahmudabad.[3] It was rejected. The more 'the young and turbulent party' appeared to be interested in the affair, the more
Meston dug in his heels: 'surrender to them', he told Hardinge,
'would have meant...great and permanent embarrassment to
Government...'[4] Finally, in August, the weavers, a most bigoted
and turbulent community, were brought into the city on their free
day and a riot occurred which was only quelled by police guns.
The *Comrade* splashed the incident across its columns, revelling
in every detail from the screams of the dying to the blood-
bespattered pavement.[5] A 'Cawnpore Mosque Fund' was, of
course, set up. On 16 August the Raja of Mahmudabad led a
second deputation, largely composed of men of the 'Old Party', to
wait on the lieutenant-governor and to demand that the demolished portion of the mosque should be restored.[6] Again, he was
refused. Muslim lawyers, 'Young' and 'Old', led by Mazharul
Haq[7] of the Bankipur Bar, poured into Cawnpore to make their

[1] Minute by Meston on the Cawnpore Mosque Affair, Home Poll. A, October 1913, 100–18, NAI.
[2] See the following correspondence: Mahomed Ali to Meston, 15 May 1913, telegram; Meston to Mahomed Ali, 15 May 1913, telegram; Mahomed Ali to Meston, 16 May 1913, telegram; Meston to Mahomed Ali, 23 May 1913; Mahomed Ali to Meston, 9 June 1913; Meston to Mahomed Ali, 2 July 1913, republished in *Comrade* (Delhi), 6 July 1913.
[3] The memorial was presented on 6 May 1913 by Sheikh Shahid Husain.
[4] Meston to Hardinge, 16 September 1913, Hardinge Papers (86), CUL.
[5] *Comrade* (Delhi), 9 August 1913.
[6] The following signed the Raja of Mahmudabad's address: Maulana Abdul Bari, Raja of Jehangirabad, Raja of Pirpur, Nawab Ishaq Khan, Nawab Muzammilullah Khan, Hon. Syed Abdur Rauf, Hon. Sheikh Shahid Husain, Hon. Khwaja Ghulam-us-Saqlain, Hon. Syed Riza Ali, Syed Nabiullah, Maulvi Mahomed Habib-ur-Rahman, Maulvi Mahomed Nasim and Munshi Ehtisham Ali; *Comrade* (Delhi), 9 August 1913.
[7] See Appendix IV.

names in the trial of the rioters which promised to be sensational.[1] Agitation developed throughout the province, led by 'Young Party' men, supported by the ulama and stimulated by the newspapers of the politicians. It pervaded the mosques.[2] It insinuated itself into the zenanas.[3] It embraced Muslims of all shades of opinion. 'This Cawnpore business', Harcourt Butler told the Governor of Bengal, 'gave us a lot of thought. I...was greatly impressed by the feeling among the loyal Muhammadans in Northern India that there was a change of policy. I have never seen such real feeling...'[4] The intransigence of the provincial government over the mosque came to be seen as a symptom of the new hardness of the government towards Muslim interests. It was not until the Viceroy descended into the Cawnpore arena from the heights of Simla, invited Mazharul Haq and Mahmudabad to lunch, and engineered a compromise in which the government stepped down, that the Muslims were mollified. The replacement of a lavatory was a small victory compared with the repartition of Bengal, but the 'Young Party' men had shown that agitation worked, and in so doing made a strong claim to the leadership of the community.

This style of politics was created by professional politicians. Their financial dependence on politics almost as much as their genuine feelings put drive and bite into their activities. The Cawnpore mosque affair would never have become an issue but for the journalist Mahomed Ali's search for agitational issues. The Anjuman-i-Khuddam-i-Kaaba would never have had the impact it did but for its paid servants: pilgrim broker, Shaukat Ali, and the shaidais. The development of agitational politics brought more professionals into the game. Azad Sobhani, the leading local agitator of the Cawnpore affair, discovered, as a result, what fame and rupees were to be won by pouring fanatical vitriol into the

[1] The following lawyers took part in the defence: Mazharul Haq, Syed Ross Masud, Khwaja Abdul Majid, Dr Naziruddin Hasan, Tassaduq Ahmed Khan Sherwani, Dr Syed Mahmud, Syed Nabiullah, Gholamur Rahman, Mian Muhammad Shafi and Aftab Ahmad Khan; *Comrade* (Delhi), 20 September 1913.

[2] Extracts from demi-official letters for September 1913, quoted in Home Poll. A, October 1913, 100–18, NAI.

[3] Harcourt Butler regarded this as very significant of the depth of the agitation: Harcourt Butler to Carmichael, Governor of Bengal, 21 October 1913, enclosed in Harcourt Butler to Lady Griffin, 22 October 1913, Harcourt Butler Papers (24), IOL.

[4] *Ibid.*

columns of the press. He left his billet as a teacher in the Madrasa Ilahiat, joined the Anjuman-i-Khuddam-i-Kaaba as a shaidai and became one of its major preachers.[1] The politico-religious crisis of Islam in India and the world brought the professionals into politics and sustained them. Meston described the process and the groups involved:

> The true nature of the agitation is not, in my opinion, far to seek. The troubles of Turkey have, among other unfortunate consequences, brought to the front a type of young Muhammadan in India who will always be a problem to us. He has little to do, and little to live upon, a poor education and no stability of character. Excitement is everything to him, and agitation provides a congenial and frequently a remunerative employment. The sufferings of Turkey and the atrocities of her enemies, coupled with the supposed indifference or hostility of the British Government, give him the text for fervid speeches at public meetings or in mosques, or for unbalanced newspaper articles, which have a considerable effect on a comparatively illiterate audience. Side by side with this type, we have the unforgiving religious bigot, who draws from the Turkish defeats a revival of his smouldering dislike of Christians and of the British ascendancy in India. Finally, we have – and this at present is the most powerful member of the combination – a group of energetic, clever, ambitious, sometimes personally embittered men, whose aim is to displace the natural leaders of the Muhammadan community, and to become for a time the leaders themselves. Their motives are probably mixed, but are certainly not free from a large ingredient of self-aggrandizement. Their weapons are invective, a multiplication of racial grievances, and opposition to the Government. By invective they beat down the attempts of the older-fashioned, moderate but extremely sensitive leaders of the community to resist their domination. By racial grievances they hope to unite the Muhammadans in allegiance to themselves. By opposition to the Government they believe, that they will eventually wring out concessions which will prove to their community that they, and not the loyalists, are the leaders who may profitably be followed.[2]

The Cawnpore Mosque triumph, however, was the zenith of the 'Young Party' agitators' achievement. Government saw that the press and the professional politicians lay at the root of their influence. It first attacked, using the Press Act. In May 1913,

---

[1] Advanced copy of a paragraph to appear in the UP Secret Abstract, 19 June 1915, Municipal, 1915, 230 E, UPS. Azad Sobhani ran the Anjuman-i-Khuddam-i-Kaaba office in Cawnpore. In February 1914, he toured eastern UP and Bihar. Fazl-ur Rahman to Shaukat Ali, 20 February 1914, translation from Urdu, Mahomed Ali Papers, JMI. In May 1914, he was lecturing on the anjuman in Delhi, WRDCI, 2 June 1914, Home Poll. B, July 1914, 124–8, NAI. He later became a leading Khilafatist.

[2] Minute by Meston on the Cawnpore Mosque affair, Home Poll. A, October 1913, 100–18, NAI.

Hasrat Mohani's *Urdu-e-Moalla* was forced out of business. Soon after, *Tauhid* had its security confiscated. In August, the *Comrade* was forced to deposit security and, in September, the *Muslim Gazette* was closed. The outbreak of the First World War and the involvement of Turkey, though ostensibly it gave the pan-Islamists greater cause to agitate, strengthened government's hand. Most men were careful not to appear disloyal and it became possible for government to be much more firm; more rigorous wartime legislation was introduced. In November 1914 *Al Hilal* and *Comrade* were closed, and in May 1915 the *Hamdard*. Then came the turn of the editors. In April 1915 the Ali brothers were interned, and in 1916 Hasrat Mohani and A. K. Azad. Gagged and bound, the agitators were silenced.

While from 1912 'Young Party' men were attacking the government, they were also doing their best to oust government's supporters from the organisations of Muslim society. But to imagine that the struggle for power was suddenly joined everywhere would be wrong. In some institutions, the need to take control was evident already and the onset of apparent government disfavour merely made it more urgent. At Aligarh College, for instance, the problem had been for some time who should have the final say in administrative decisions, the staff or the trustees. Theoretically, final power rested with the trustees. Yet the interests of efficient management demanded that the principal and the English staff should have considerable control, and in Syed Ahmed's time wide powers had been statutorily conferred upon them. Under Mohsin-ul-Mulk these powers had grown. With these developments, the trustees, most of whom were landed magnates or successful government servants, did not quarrel. But for young men who wished to have a say in the education of their community they were intolerable. Matters came to a head when, in 1907, the principal expelled a student for striking a policeman. The Ali brothers immediately began to plot to gain control of the trustees. Two routes were open to them. The first was to overwhelm the 'Old Party' element on the trustees. In October 1907, four Aligarh old boys,[1] with minor posts in the jungly district of Bahraich, produced a scheme of reform for the trustees in which life

---

[1] The four old boys were: Badrul Hasan, Trustee of Aligarh and Munsif, Bahraich; Shaukat Ali, additional Opium Agent, Bahraich; Md. Masna, Deputy Collector, Bahraich; Md. Hasan Khan, Munsif, Bahraich.

trusteeship was to be abolished, trustees were to be elected every five years and the number of trustees was raised from seventy to one hundred, the greater part of whom were to come from the professions and the old boys.[1] Little room was left for the landed magnates.[2] But to put this plan into effect, the 'Young Party' needed to gain a majority among the trustees. This was a hopeless task. Each year the trustee elections were vigorously contested but Shaukat Ali was not elected till 1913,[3] Mahomed Ali till 1915 and of the eighty-four trustees elected between 1909 and 1918 only about thirty were 'Young Party' men.[4] The second method was rougher. Day-to-day decisions regarding the College tended to be made by those trustees who lived on the spot and here the great Aligarh and Bulandshahr landowners, led by the lawyer Aftab Ahmad Khan, dominated. Much, it was thought, might be achieved by beating the local men at their own game. So the *Comrade* launched attack after attack on the 'inner cabinet'[5] and Mahomed Ali gathered around himself a small clique of local trustees, two Sherwanis, Haji Musa Khan and Haji Swaleh Khan, Safaraz Khan, a sub-registrar, Khwaja Abdul Majid and Major Hasan Bilgrami. But all Mahomed Ali succeeded in doing was making a nuisance of himself. The government and most Muslims were too determined that Aligarh should succeed to allow the 'Young Party' to have its way.[6]

[1] 'A new scheme for the selection of Trustees for the M.A.-O. College Aligarh, from members of the Old Boys' Association', dated Bahraich, 22 October 1907, translation from Urdu, Mahomed Ali Papers, JMI.

[2] Of the one hundred trustees, thirty were to come from the professions (education, engineering, medicine, religion being mentioned by name) and a further thirty-five from the old boys, which would mean almost entirely professional representation. *Ibid.*

[3] Shaukat Ali was a trustee for a brief period in 1905 but, because of a quarrel which he had with Sheikh Abdullah in which he knocked him down, he was forced to resign.

[4] 'List of the Trustees as it stood on the 1st June 1919', *Education*, 1919, 140, UPS.   [5] For instance, *Comrade* (Calcutta), 29 July 1911.

[6] For instance, when, in December 1913, Md. Ishaq Khan arranged an emergency meeting of the trustees in order to make a declaration of the trustees' loyalty to government, Meston wrote personal letters to 'Old Party' men to persuade them to attend and wrote to superior officers asking them to release trustees who were government servants. Meston to Md. Israr Hasan Khan, Meston to Nawab Fateh Ali Khan Qizilbash, Meston to Nawab Abdul Majid, Meston to Nawab of Pahasu, Meston to Raja of Jehangirabad, Meston to Brownrigg, Commissioner of Allahabad, and Meston to Sir H. Richards, Chief Justice of the Allahabad High Court; all 22 December 1913, Meston Papers (6), IOL.

Separatism among Indian Muslims

The struggles which raged at Aligarh from 1907 anticipated in microcosm those which broke out in other areas of Muslim public life from 1912. Take, for instance, the Muslim University scheme. Muslims, 'Young' and 'Old', from Dr Ziauddin to Mahomed Ali were agreed on the essentials of a Muslim University. But, when government rejected the scheme, they divided. 'Old Party' men were prepared to accept government's terms, 'Young Party' men were not. The 'Young Party' wanted the original plan, especially affiliation, an all-India organisation being fundamental to their plans for regenerating the community; 'if the University is to be deprived of the power of guiding Moslem education throughout India by a well-planned system of affiliation', declared Mahomed Ali, 'the main object underlying the Moslem University movement falls to the ground.'[1] It was affiliation, or no University. To prevent a compromise being reached the 'Young Party' broke up a meeting of the Constitution Committee at Lucknow in December 1912.[2] Three months later, they compelled a small committee appointed to negotiate terms with the Government to resign.[3] When the whole matter was referred back to the Foundation Committee, which met in Aligarh on 26–7 July 1913, they used the vague terms of membership of the Committee, that is anyone who had donated money to the Muslim University Fund to pack the meeting. 150 came from the outstations; 500 from Aligarh, many of whom were 'of the common mob'.[4] In a turbulent meeting, the 'Young Party' forced through each point of their programme.[5]

[1] *Comrade* (Calcutta), 20 July 1912.
[2] R. Burn, Chief Secretary to Government, UP, to Secretary, Government of India Home Department, 17 September 1913, Home Poll. A, October 1913, 100–18, NAI.
[3] *Ibid.*
[4] Extract from the advance copy of a paragraph to appear in the UP Secret Abstract, 16 September 1913, Educ, D, January 1916, 13, NAI. To promote their cause, the 'Young Party' formed the 'National Liberal Party' under the titular presidency of Major Syed Hasan Bilgrami. 'By the National Liberal Party', explained the *Muslim Gazette*, 'is meant that section of the community which, according to the desire of the majority of Muhammadans, want an independent University, possessing powers of affiliation. The party of leaders or conservatives is opposed to the Liberal party, does not care for the wishes of the community, and is willing to accept unhesitatingly whatever form of University, Government may choose to give.' *Muslim Gazette* (Lucknow), 6 August 1913, Educ, D, January 1916, 13, NAI.
[5] Most of the resolutions at this meeting were proposed by Mahomed Ali, Mazharul Haq, Syed Hasan Bilgrami and Wazir Hasan. A Committee was elected to decide what future action should be taken; it had a straight 'Young

Members of the 'Old Party' hardly dared to raise a dissentient voice. When they did, 'they were hissed and hooted and made to sit down'.[1] But it was a hollow victory. The Government had now come to an agreement with the Hindus over Benares Hindu University, which also had all-India aspirations, and would receive no representations from the Muslims unless they first accepted the decisions on questions of principle reached with the Hindus.[2] The 'Young Party' lost the battle and the internment of their leaders set the seal on their defeat. In 1916, with no one to raise a voice in opposition, Mahmudabad, and with him Ansari, defected and accepted the University on the government's terms. To this humiliation the Sultanniah College scheme, the eagerness with which educational non-co-operation was espoused by young Muslims and ultimately the foundation of the National Muslim University itself all owed their origin.

In local government, 'Young Party' men could make even less impression than they did on the community's educational projects. The use of municipal and district boards as electorates for the provincial council did extend the horizons of local politics but still their pattern was dictated by local needs. This restricted the 'Young Party's' opportunities. These opportunities, however, were further restricted by the kind of people they were. They had little prestige or local influence. They were educated, but then their western learning, their foreign clothes and their Urdu, sometimes marred by a multitude of incongruous anglicisms, could often be offensive to the locals. Moreover, they had no wealth and elections could be expensive. In district boards which were dominated by landed wealth, there were no openings for them. In municipal boards, on the other hand, there were some but these varied according to the urban power structure of the two major areas of the province.

In east UP and Oudh, Kayasths and Muslims of the landed interest were as unlikely to include in their alliances jumped-up young Muslims of advanced views as Hindu traders of Congress tendencies. Before 1916, no young Muslim, apart from Syed Nabiullah in

Party' majority. It consisted of Mahmudabad, Mazharul Haq, Major Syed Hasan Bilgrami, Mian Muhammad Shafi, Aftab Ahmad Khan and Nawab Ishaq Khan. *Comrade* (Delhi), 2 August 1913.
[1] Extract from the advance copy of a paragraph to appear in the UP Secret Abstract, 16 September 1913, Educ, D, January 1916, 13, NAI.
[2] Harcourt Butler to Raja of Mahmudabad, 24 September 1915, *ibid*.

Lucknow, appears to have held a municipal seat. In 1910 Wazir Hasan tried for a Lucknow seat, but failed. The problem was that 'Young Party' men just did not have the wherewithal to break into local politics. What hope had they against the accumulated wealth of merchants and money lenders? What could they do when Pirpur's word was law in Tanda and Jehangirabad strewed his riches around Fyzabad? In west UP and Doab, however, where more Muslims lived in the towns and Muslim landowners had less power, there were some opportunities for 'Young Party' men. This was particularly the case in the large cities, where the lawyer could cut as good a figure as the landowner.[1] Some 'Young Party' men had already established themselves as local leaders, for example, Syed Ali Nabi was vice-chairman of the Agra municipal board and Fazlur Rahman and Hafiz Hidayat Husain had a big say in politics in Cawnpore. Generally, however, Muslim politics still tended to be in the hands of the unreconstructed rais. Generally too, though Shia and Sunni would invariably divide, in the bitter communal politics of the area 'Young' and 'Old' tended not to compete but to co-operate.

It was not till the Municipalities Act of 1916, when the introduction of separate representation assured Muslims of their local position, that 'Young Party' men were able to make a serious bid for urban power. In east UP and Oudh, the new circumstances made little difference. Although 'Young Party' men no longer had to compete with the Hindus, wealth, particularly landed wealth, still ruled. Raja Salamat Khan put in his nominees in Azamgarh, Mufti Haidar Husain dominated Jaunpur and Shah Badr Alam had Ghazipur under his thumb. In the large cities of west UP, on the other hand, Bareilly, Meerut, Moradabad, major battles were fought for local power. Qazi Bashiruddin wrote excitedly to Mahomed Ali:

The separate representation on Municipal Boards has produced very keen interest in the electorate. Effort was made that the Mohammedans here should unanimously elect the candidates but the 'old, vested interests', could not be persuaded and hence, the men of 'new light'

[1] A really successful lawyer could build up a considerable position. The Kashmiri Brahmin Prithvi Nath Chak of Cawnpore, for instance, became so influential in the city that he was known popularly as the 'King of Kanpur'. G. F. M. Buckee, 'An Examination of the Development and Structure of the Legal Profession at Allahabad, 1866–1935' (Unpublished PhD thesis, London, 1972), p. 312.

are contesting every seat. Ismail (Barrister), Mohammad Husain, Salam, Ismail Hanifi (old Boy), Mustohsin, (Deputy Mud. Husain Shauq's son and 'my Lords' nephew) A. Bari (Haider's Brother) and myself, are the young men's candidates.[1]

Every trick in the electoral game was employed. The Commissioner reported that 'the old party is incensed with the young pleader lot...'[2] They first used the number of Muslim voters as a device to increase Muslim representation, and then shamelessly went on to strike many of the 'Old Party' supporters off the electoral rolls. But, in spite of such electoral chicanery, they were defeated at almost every turn and 'Moradabad', Syed Riza Ali wrote to Mahomed Ali, 'was the only place in these provinces where everything was in the hands of the young party'.[3] As late as 1916, the 'Young Party' had won local power in Moradabad, and in Moradabad alone.

'Young Party' men had little success in capturing the seats of local power. Up to 1914 they did not have much more success in making their way into the provincial councils. In the general electorates their weakness in the localities handicapped them. The results of the 1909 and the 1913 elections show that in the eight municipal constituencies,[4] which elected four members alternately, 'Old Party' men such as Nawab Asadullah Khan and Munshi Asghar Ali Khan were successful in Meerut and Bareilly respectively. But no 'Young Party' man won a seat. In the eight divisional constituencies, which elected representatives at each election, weakness at the local level was again a barrier. Divisional representatives were elected by electoral colleges, which were in turn elected from the municipal and district boards of the divisions. Here the only Muslims who had a chance of winning a seat were big landlords such as the Raja of Jehangirabad, who was elected for the Fyzabad constituency in 1909 by the narrow margin of one vote. 'Young Party' men could not hope to compete with the 'Old Party' in constituencies based on municipal and district

[1] Bashir (Qazi Bashiruddin) to Mahomed Ali, 24 August 1916, Mahomed Ali Papers, JMI.
[2] Extract from a fortnightly demi-official letter, dated 27 August 1916, from the Commissioner of Meerut, Municipal, 1915, 230E (81), UPS.
[3] Syed Riza Ali to Mahomed Ali, 24 March 1919, Mahomed Ali Papers, JMI.
[4] The municipal constituencies were: Allahabad, Agra, Meerut, Lucknow, Fyzabad, Benares, Bareilly and Cawnpore. The municipal boards of the first four elected members in 1909 and the second four in 1913.

boards. But then as a rule they did not want to; it made no sense for them to split the Muslim vote. As it was, by 1916 Hindu communal consciousness had grown so much that no Muslim was returned for a general electorate. ·

In the four Muslim reserved constituencies, however, 'Young Party' men did have an opportunity. This was created in part by the increasing attractiveness of the 'Young Party' politics of protest, in part because in separate electorates there was no need to keep the community's ranks united and in part because the franchise increasingly favoured 'Young Party' candidates. Prima facie, this last development seems unlikely. Most of the electoral qualifications favoured the wealthy, the successful and the loyal; titleholders, pensioned government servants, those who paid land revenue of not less than Rs. 3000 a year or income tax on earnings of not less than Rs. 3000 a year. But there was one qualification which did work markedly in favour of the 'Young Party': graduates of five years' standing were given the vote.[1] Between 1902 and 1912, the number of Muslims taking university courses in the UP increased well over three times[2] and the steady inclusion of large numbers of Muslim graduates must have had some effect on the leanings of constituencies in which 400 or less usually voted. Yet, by 1914, as Table XIII shows, 'Young Party' men filled no more than two of the eight seats held by Muslims in the UP legislative council.

[1] The following were the electoral qualifications for the Muslim constituencies:
(*a*) Ownership of land of which the land revenue was not less than Rs. 3000 p.a.
(*b*) Ownership of land free of land revenue but which would otherwise pay Rs. 3000 p.a.
(*c*) Payment of income tax on an income of not less than Rs. 3000 p.a.
(*d*) Membership of the Provincial Legislative Council.
(*e*) An ordinary or honorary fellowship of Allahabad University.
(*f*) Trusteeship of M.A.-O. College Aligarh.
(*g*) Possession of any title conferred or recognised by the Government of India.
(*h*) The receipt of a pension for service as a gazetted or commissioned officer of the Government.
(*i*) Those who were Honorary Assistant Collectors, magistrates and munsifs.
(*j*) Graduates of five years' standing of any university in the British Empire.
'Regulations &c., for giving effect to the Indian Councils Act, 1909', *P.P.*, 1910, LXVII, p. 981.
[2] In 1902, there were 337 Muslims at Arts Colleges in the UP, and, in 1912, 1155. *RDPI (UP), 1901–02*, General Table IIIA, p. 42 and *RDPI (UP), 1911–12*, General Table IIIA, p. 8A.

Struggle for leadership

TABLE XI. *'Old Party' and 'Young Party' representation in the UP legislative council from 1909 to 1919*

1909–12		1913–16		1916–19	
'Old Party'	'Young Party'	'Old Party'	'Young Party'	'Old Party'	'Young Party'
Nominated members					
Nawab of Rampur, Nawab of Pahasu	—	Nawab of Rampur, Nawab of Pahasu, Raja of Jehangirabad	—	Nawab of Rampur, Nawab of Pahasu, Raja of Jehangirabad	Mirza Samiullah Beg
Elected members					
Nawab Abdul Majid, Raja of Jehangirabad, Sheikh Shahid Husain, Aftab Ahmad Khan, Munshi Asghar Ali Khan, Nawab Asadullah Khan	Syed Ali Nabi	Sheikh Shahid Husain, Munshi Asghar Ali Khan, Syed Abdur Rauf	Syed Riza Ali Ghulam-us-Saqlain[a]	Nawab Abdul Majid	Syed Riza Ali Syed Wazir Hasan, Syed Ali Nabi
Total members					
8	1	6	2	4	4

[a] Gulam-us-Saqlain died in 1915 and Syed Ali Nabi gained his seat in the by-election.

SOURCE: GAD, 1912, 550, UPS and GAD, 1916, 115, UPS.

The Muslim League was the most important organ of Muslim opinion, and here the most crucial battles were fought. As the All-India League was dominated by UP men, the UP Muslim League was 'small and comparatively negligible...'[1] The sum

[1] Note on the UP Muslim League, GAD, 1917, 593, UPS.

total of its early work was to advocate separate representation.[1] The officers of the League were chosen, five from Agra and five from Oudh, in order to balance the rivalry of the two provinces.[2] But, as in the case of most provincial associations, it was really controlled by the men of the locality where the organisation had its headquarters. It was established in Lucknow on 26 June 1909, but was moved to Allahabad in 1910 at the instigation of the Aga Khan, when the All-India Muslim League office was moved to Lucknow. Thus the organisation was moved from the centre of Oudh Muslim culture to the home of the Malaviyas and Tandons, the most belligerent supporters of Hindu interests. It was transplanted from the seed-bed of Hindu–Muslim conciliation to the field of Hindu–Muslim antagonism. In Allahabad, the League fell into the hands of the most aggressive defenders of Muslim interests in the province. Syed Abdur Rauf became the president and Ibni Ahmad the secretary. But for all its fighting talk, the UP League was a sleepy affair: no provincial session was held between 1909 and 1913. When it did bestir itself, it was to deny the follies of the 'Young Party'. It was temperate over the Balkan Wars,[3] equivocal about the Cawnpore Mosque[4] and begged Ameer Ali not to resign from the London League.[5] The organisation was ripe for capture, and the attack was made when the second provincial sessions were

[1] For example, the demand for separate electorates formed the bulk of the resolutions passed at a 'Special General Meeting' of 6 September 1909, xv, 1909, 786, LCA; it was the object of an Executive Council meeting of 27 November 1909, *ibid*. After the municipal elections of 1910, separate electorates were demanded in local government as 'a logical and necessary corollary to the application of the principle in the case of the Imperial and the Provincial Legislative Councils'. Resolution of the Hon. Nawab Abdul Majid, *Leader* (Allahabad), 24 April 1910; Ibni Ahmad, Secretary of the League, addressed the government on the question in November 1910, Ibni Ahmad to Chief Secretary to Government UP, 30 November 1910, and urged Mahomed Ali to push the matter in the *Comrade*, Ibni Ahmad to Mahomed Ali, 10 June 1911, Mahomed Ali Papers, JMI.

[2] The following were elected officers of the UP Muslim League in 1909: President, Nawab Abdul Majid (Agra); Vice-Presidents, Raja of Salimpur (Oudh), Munshi Ehtisham Ali (Oudh), Syed Ali Nabi (Agra), Syed Abdur Rauf (Agra); Secretary, Raja Naushad Ali Khan (Oudh); Joint Secretary, Syed Zahur Ahmed (Oudh); Assistant Secretaries, Azhar Ali (Agra) and Shaikh Shaukat Ali (Oudh); Auditor, Syed Awat Ali (Agra). xv, 1909, 786, LCA.

[3] Sheikh Zahur Ahmad to Editor, 14 January 1914, *Leader* (Allahabad), 16 January 1914.

[4] Statement of the UP Muslim League, *ibid*., 1 November 1913.

[5] Statement of the League Council, *ibid*., 12 May 1913.

held at Agra in 1913 under the presidency of Syed Ali Nabi. The 'Young Party' of Allahabad, headed by Sheikh Zahur Ahmad, his father Shaikh Abdur Raoof,[1] his brother Nazir Ahmad[2] and Kamaluddin Jafri descended on the city of the Taj to see if they could force through the self-government resolution of the parent league and push themselves into power by capturing the local organisation. The attempt aroused furious opposition and they lost.[3] On his return, Sheikh Zahur Ahmad wrote angrily to the *Leader* of one of the Honorary Vice-Presidents (most probably Syed Abdur Rauf), who had 'formed a clique at Allahabad and literally captured the League'.[4] He exposed the manner in which the meeting had been managed in order to exclude 'Young Party' men: notices of the event had been sent only to selected members while 133 others had been removed, contrary to Rule 10 of the League's constitution for failure to pay their subscription in time. He warned that the League must either change its policy or the 'Young Party' would form a new organisation.[5] Though the broad political struggle between 'Young' and 'Old' was being pursued here, clearly, as in many other cases, local rivalries were also involved.

The provincial league, however, was an unimportant trophy to lose because, by 1913, the most important battle had already been won. The 'Young Party' had captured the All-India Muslim League. This success was in part a result of the new mood created by the rebuffs the Muslims received from government in 1912 and in part the result of changes within the League. To realise the significance of the latter, it is important to understand the mechanics of power in the League. Policy was laid down by the members at the annual sessions. Changes in the constitution made at the Delhi session of 1910 strengthened the 'Young Party' position. The membership limit was increased from 400 to 800, the age limit reduced from twenty-five to twenty-one, entrance fees were abolished and subscriptions lowered from twenty-five to twenty rupees p.a. with provision for payment on an instalment

---

[1] Shaikh Abdur Raoof was a zamindar of Mau Aimma in Allahabad district who paid Rs. 6205 land revenue.
[2] Nazir Ahmad was the editor of the Urdu weekly, *Masawat*.
[3] The history of the attempt is contained in two letters to the *Leader*: Sheikh Zahur Ahmad to Editor, 14 January 1914, *Leader* (Allahabad), 16 January 1914; and Khwaja Abdul Majid to Editor, undated, *ibid.*, 24 January 1914.
[4] Sheikh Zahur Ahmad to Editor, 14 January 1914, *ibid.*, 16 January 1914.
[5] *Ibid.*

plan.[1] By June 1911 membership had increased by twenty-three per cent, and the majority of the new recruits were professional men, men likely to take the 'Young Party' line.[2] But such changes in the composition of the League were of little use without control of the central organisation. Here much power lay with those who lived close to the League headquarters, and above all with the Secretary. He could dictate the League's policy. He was its executive. He had to take the initiative in any new situation, and he could always do nothing if he wished. If he needed the approval of the League Council, a hurriedly called meeting ensured that only local, or at least provincial representatives, were present. If the wrong people turned up, another meeting could be held at short notice. Then if it appeared that these tactics were earning him the disapproval of many League members, it was usually possible, through manipulation of the League Council, to ensure that an annual session was held at a place where it could be packed with his men.

In the League's early years it was controlled by Aligarh men, but they were forced to surrender this control by the Aga Khan and the lieutenant-governor of the province. In one of the interminable contretemps between the European staff and the Aligarh trustees, Sir John Hewett had in 1908, as patron of the College, taken his stand with the staff, but in the wrangles that followed he was forced to step down. From this moment he determined to remove the control of the Muslim League from Aligarh. Early in 1909, Hewett suggested the move to some League leaders, but there was no reaction.[3] Later he put the matter to the Aga Khan,[4] and at the Delhi League session of January 1910 the Ismaili leader, despite very strong opposition from Viqar-ul-Mulk and Aftab Ahmad Khan, pushed through the decision to transfer the League organisation to Lucknow.

It would have been better if the government and the leader of Muslim conservatism had stuck to the devil they knew, than committed themselves to one they did not. At Aligarh, the League was

[1] Rahman, *Consultation to Confrontation*, p. 171.
[2] Many of the new members were recruited by League members while on deputations engaged in raising funds for the Muslim University. The twenty-three per cent increased occurred between June 1910 and June 1911 and was calculated by M. Rahman, *ibid.*, pp. 221–2.
[3] Hewett to Dunlop Smith, 3 October 1908, Minto Papers (4E387), NLS.
[4] Hewett to Minto, 3 February 1910, Minto Papers (4E390), NLS.

dominated by 'Old Party' men with communal predilections. At Lucknow, however, it was at the mercy of a large group of the 'Young Party'. 'Lucknow', declared one 'Old Party' man attempting to counter 'Young Party' politics, 'was the most difficult place to deal with.'[1] 'Being one of the biggest centres of Muslim political activities and having a large population, extremely lethargic, who are mostly the members of old families as well as [the] *extremely* and mischievously active who are mostly upstarts and of the lawyer class...'[2] Sixteen of the sixty-four 'Young Party' men in Appendix I practised at the Oudh Bar in Lucknow and another nine made the city the centre of their activities. Their politics were less anti-Hindu than elsewhere; in the culture of Oudh and the cities of east UP, the quarrels that disturbed Muslim politicians were not so much those between Hindu and Muslim as those between Muslim and Muslim, between Shia and Sunni. Thus the lieutenant-governor's pique and the Aga Khan's myopia shifted the League from the 'Old Party's' sanctuary to the 'Young Party's' preserve, and unwittingly did much to help the 'Young Party' to capture the very body which had been formed to discipline them.

Setting up the League office in a bungalow on the Lalbagh Road in the spring of 1910, however, did not give the 'Young Party' automatic control. Aziz Mirza, the first tenant of the secretary's chair, continued to give policy an Aligarh slant. But in February 1912 he died, and Wazir Hasan, the assistant secretary, stepped into his shoes. From 1912 to 1919, Hasan's hold over the League and its organisation was so tight that it came to be nicknamed the 'Waziri League'.[3] With his assumption of the secretaryship, the foundations of 'Young Party' dominance were finally laid.

Just one week after Aziz Mirza's death, the League met at Calcutta. The sessions were overshadowed by the implications of the repartition of Bengal. The air was full of demands for a re-assessment of the League's composition and its policy towards government. Consequently, the first task the new secretary undertook was an examination of the constitution.[4] Theoretically the

---

[1] 'A[n] extract journal of a tour in the United Provinces of Agra and Oudh, during March and April 1914', by Nawab Fateh Ali Khan Qizilbash and dated 19 May 1914, enclosed in Nawab Fateh Ali Khan Qizilbash to Meston, 19 May 1914, Meston Papers (6), IOL.
[2] *Ibid.*
[3] *Al Bashir* (Etawah), 24/31 July 1917, UPNNR 1917.
[4] Rahman, *Consultation to Confrontation*, p. 256.

8-2

work was to be done in consultation with the branch leagues, but the whole process was in Wazir Hasan's hands. A draft of a revised constitution emerged which placed the stamp of 'Young Party' policy on the League's objectives and would enable it to consolidate its position in power. The annual subscription was reduced from twenty rupees to six,[1] the educational qualification was lowered to 'Literate' with no definition,[2] the number of members of the League Council increased from forty to 300[3] and provision was made for the affiliation of any Muslim association inside or outside British India.[4] Encapsulated in the revised aims of the organisation was the 'Young Party' protest at the way the League had connived at the government's failure to protect Muslim interests. Alterations to clauses (a) and (b) of the old objects of the League wiped out collaborationist phrases.[5] A new clause (d) proclaimed the aim of

[1] 'Revised constitution and rules of the All-India Muslim League', Section 6, Home Poll. A, February 1913, 85–6, NAI.
[2] Students, however, were barred from membership, Section 3 (c), *ibid.*
[3] Section 12, Rule 1, *ibid.*
[4] Sections 8 (7) and 30, *ibid.*
[5] The following were the aims of the League drawn up at the Dacca session of 1906:

'(a) To promote, among the Musalmans of India, feelings of loyalty to the British Government, and to remove any misconception that may arise as to the intention of the Government with regard to any of its measures.

(b) To protect and advance the political rights and interests of the Musalmans of India, and to respectfully represent their needs and aspirations to the Government.

(c) To prevent the rise, among the Musalmans of India, of any feeling of hostility towards other communities, without prejudice to the other aforementioned objects of the League.' Wasti, *Lord Minto*, p. 79.

The following were the revised aims drawn up by Wazir Hasan and approved by the Lucknow session of March 1913:

'(a) To maintain and promote among the people of this country feelings of loyalty towards the British Crown.

(b) To protect and advance the political and other rights and interests of the Indian Musalmans.

(c) To promote friendship and union between the Musalmans and other communities of India.

(d) Without detriment to the foregoing objects, attainment, under the aegis of the British Crown, of a system of self-government suitable to India, through constitutional means by bringing about, amongst others, a steady reform of the existing system of administration, by promoting national unity, by fostering public spirit among the people of India and by co-operating with other communities for the said purposes.'

'Revised constitution and rules of the All-India Muslim League', Section 2, Home Poll. A, February 1913, 85–6, NAI. It should be noted that there are

the League to work with other groups for 'a system of self-government suitable to India' with the important proviso that this should be done 'without detriment' to the protection of Muslim interests.[1] Thus the 'Young Party' brought the objects of the League close to the Congress and opened the way for working with it.

This manifesto of 'Young Party' politics was scheduled to be presented to the full body of the League, under the presidency of Ameer Ali, at Lucknow in December 1912. No doubt this leader of Muslim conservatism got wind of what the secretary and his friends were up to, because with the Aga Khan he telegraphed from London urging postponement of the session as a 'token [of] mourning [at the] grave peril [of] Islam'.[2] An emergency meeting of the League Council at Lucknow was not impressed with this plea. It refused to call off the session. Ameer Ali, supported by the London League, made a second attempt to stop the session. This time a meeting of the League Council at Lucknow on 12 November 1912 agreed by a majority vote to postponement. This was clearly not good enough for Wazir Hasan and his followers, and a third meeting of the League Council was held at Bankipur on 31 December 1912. The secretary invited several non-members. His followers dominated the meeting and approved the new constitution and creed. The changes were ratified by the League in full session held in Lucknow on 22–3 March 1913 and the 'Young Party' were in power.[3]

Of all the positions of power and influence in Muslim society, the All-India Muslim League was the only one from which 'Old Party' men were ousted. They launched a counter attack. But their attempts to recapture the League and throw out the self-government clause were not a success. Without the ties of common experience that held the 'Young Party' together, they found it

different versions of the punctuation and word order of the revised creed. Compare the above, for instance, with that reproduced by Pirzada from the *Pioneer* of 2 January 1913, Pirzada, *Foundations of Pakistan*, Vol. I, p. 248. Nevertheless, the sense remains the same.

[1] 'Revised constitution and rules of the All-India Muslim League', Section 2 (d), Home Poll. A, February 1913, 85–6, NAI.

[2] Syed Wazir Hasan to Editor, *Pioneer Mail* (Lucknow), 13 December 1912, Rahman, *Consultation to Confrontation*, p. 271.

[3] For the details of the way in which the new creed was pushed through the League, see *ibid.*, pp. 271–5. It should, however, be noted that the League Council meeting of 31 December 1912 was held at Bankipur and not at Lucknow as Rahman suggests.

difficult to operate as a group. Another obstacle was their lack of courage: 'they live', Meston told Hardinge, 'in deadly terror of Mohamed Ali and his gang'.[1] They bent like reeds before the 'Young Party's' blasts of communal enthusiam. 'It almost invariably happens', Butler told Hardinge, 'that the young Mahommedans carry away the old ones at meetings, and afterwards the old ones gain some ascendancy.'[2] Lack of political conviction was also a problem. Many, particularly the successful professional men, were no less disappointed than the 'Young Party' by the apparent loss of government favour. They sympathised with the 'Young Party's' desire to represent Muslim interests more effectively and differed only over the means. Even then many signed Mahmudabad's address to the Viceroy demanding that the demolished portion of the Cawnpore Mosque should be restored, and some, such as Ehtisham Ali, actually declared themselves in favour of the self-government clause.[3] Lack of political concern, however, was just as much a problem. It was particularly hard for landed aristocrats secure in their mofussil mansions, sure of official favour, honoured at the provincial Durbar and consulted by officialdom, to imagine that government would desert those whom it had supported for years in favour of the raucous pleaders and clamorous editors of the 'Young Party'. Their activities were tiresome, but no threat to the 'Old Party' political position.

During 1913, the 'Old Party' campaign to discredit the young leaders of the Muslim League and to revoke the new policy got slowly under way. In April, Nawab Abdul Majid toyed with the idea of starting a rival organisation to the Muslim League.[4] In July, Nawab Fateh Ali Khan Qizilbash addressed a letter to all members of the League urging that the self-government clause be abandoned.[5] In September, 'Old Party' determination was given

---

[1] Meston to Hardinge, 6 January 1914, Hardinge Papers (87), CUL. For instance, in the autumn of 1913, attacks from the *Hamdard* and *Zamindar* drove Ishaq Khan, the Secretary of Aligarh, to the point of resignation. Muhammad Ishaq Khan to Meston, 20 November 1913, Meston Papers (6), IOL.

[2] Harcourt Butler to Hardinge, 3 November 1912, Hardinge Papers (84), CUL.

[3] See Munshi Ehtisham Ali's speech as chairman of the reception committee of All-India Muslim League meeting at Lucknow, March 1913, *Leader* (Allahabad), 25 March 1913.

[4] Harcourt Butler to Hardinge, 3 April 1913, Hardinge Papers (85), CUL.

[5] Confidential letter sent by Nawab Fateh Ali Khan Qizilbash to all members of the All-India Muslim League, dated Lahore, 7 July 1913 and enclosed in Nawab Fateh Ali Khan Qizilbash to Meston, 3 January 1914, Meston Papers (6), IOL.

a boost when Meston advised district officers to encourage local men of influence to work together to resist 'Young Party' agitators.[1] The first move was made a few days later when the Nawab of Rampur, a personal friend of the lieutenant-governor, made a rare excursion onto the political platform to chair a Delhi meeting of 'Old Party' members of the League.[2] The aim was to disown Mahomed Ali and Wazir Hasan who had travelled to England to represent the new Muslim politics. Some 'Young Party' men managed to gain entrance, and led by Riza Ali and Muhamuad Shafi wrecked the meeting.[3] The Nawab scuttled back to Rampur, and from then on reserved his political effusions for the ear of the lieutenant-governor.

From this moment the 'Old Party' counter-attack was in the hands of Qizilbash, a Shia with property in Lahore and the Oudh district of Bahraich. His letter of July 1913 is worth examining because it reflects the dual political interests of this type of 'Old Party' man: they were both landlord and Muslim. As a Muslim he reiterated the policy of Syed Ahmed. Muslims would always be in a minority; it would take them years to rival the Hindus in wealth and education, and even when they managed to do so,

they should on principle refrain from subscribing to a political creed which differs in no way from the ideal of autonomy for which the Congress has been agitating and from which Muhammadans have so far recoiled in horror. Self-government in any form whatsoever and under any circumstances means our death as a distinct community and the sooner the League clears its position on this momentous and far-reaching issue, the better for the cause of Islam in India.[4]

The new Muslim politics were doomed to failure: 'so long', he prophesied, 'as Hindu and Muslim interests clash over the vexed question of separate electorates and adequate representation – and clash they must always – all talk of Hindu and Muslim co-operation

[1] Meston to all district officers, 9 September 1913, enclosed in Meston to Hardinge, 11 September 1913, Hardinge Papers (86), CUL.
[2] Kurshaid Ali to Mahomed Ali, 25 September 1913, Mahomed Ali Papers, JMI, and a memorandum describing the Muslim meeting at Delhi, 1 October 1913, enclosed in the Nawab of Rampur to Hardinge, 7 October 1913, Hardinge Papers (86), CUL.
[3] Mahomed Yusuf to Syed Wazir Hasan, 2 October 1913, Mahomed Ali Papers, JMI.
[4] Confidential letter sent by Nawab Fateh Ali Khan Qizilbash to all members of the All-India Muslim League, dated Lahore, 7 July 1913, and enclosed in Nawab Fateh Ali Khan Qizilbash to Meston, 24 August 1913, Meston Papers (6), IOL.

is in my humble opinion, little better than can't [sic].'[1] As a land-lord Qizilbash made it clear that landed support was vital to the Muslim League but, because government had begun to distrust the organisation, 'the aristocratic classes...have perforce to sever their connection with an organisation which at its birth was in-tended to be a pillar of strength to Government and to display a loyal and contented attitude throughout its proceedings'.[2] The message was that landlords could not belong to a political associa-tion that was hostile to government.

In December 1913, Qizilbash toured the political centres of the UP and the Punjab to rally League members for an attack on the self-government clause in the coming League sessions at Agra. On the 10th, he gave a dinner to the Muslim leaders of the Punjab. On the 23rd, he made the rounds of the UP leaders in Lucknow, and, from the 27th, began to bring pressure to bear on delegates as they arrived at Agra.[3] He went on to make a vicious public attack on Wazir Hasan published in the *Civil and Military Gazette* of Lahore, the *Pioneer* of Allahabad and the *Morning Post* of Delhi, on the day before proceedings began.[4] It was a tribute to the power which Wazir Hasan had acquired in the organisation. Qizilbash regarded him as the source of all evils, the man 'on whom is also primarily fixed the responsibility of formulating an ideal, which from the very nature of its being, is not only impossible of attain-ment but positively dangerous and ruinous to the cause of Islam in India'.[5] Wazir Hasan was urged to resign and Qizilbash sug-gested that 'it might be made a rule that none who has not com-pleted the age of 45 years should ever be made Secretary. The blood of youth is impulsive and uncontrollable, and can never be safe when indulging in the politics of a *great* community.'[6] Syed

[1] *Ibid.*   [2] *Ibid.*
[3] 'Review of the present political attitude of some of the so-called leaders of the extreme wing of the All-India Muslim League', by Nawab Fateh Ali Khan Qizilbash, 3 January 1914 and enclosed in Nawab Fateh Ali Khan Qizilbash to Meston, 3 January 1914, Meston Papers (6), IOL.
[4] Article entitled, 'The All-India Muslim League and its Secretary' and signed 'A Muslim', 25 December 1913, enclosed in Nawab Fateh Ali Khan Qizilbash to Editor, *Civil and Military Gazette* (Lahore); the *Pioneer* (Allahabad); the *Morning Post* (Delhi), 25 December 1913, Meston Papers (6), IOL.
[5] Article entitled, 'The All-India Muslim League and its Secretary' and signed 'A Muslim', 25 December 1913, enclosed in Nawab Fateh Ali Khan Qizilbash to Editor, *Civil and Military Gazette.* etc..., 25 December 1913, Meston Papers (6), IOL.
[6] *Ibid.*

Karamat Husein was put forward as a suitable replacement. In the League Council at Agra, Qizilbash succeeded in expunging several progressive resolutions and,[1] as he wrote for Meston's benefit, 'our party rose as one against the amendment' that the League should withdraw its support from the principle of separate representation.[2] But the 'Old Party' did not have the numbers or the courage to brave 'the ready tongue and fulsome abuse...of the Pleader and Editor class'.[3] They failed to unseat Wazir Hasan and to throw the self-government clause out of the League's creed.

As a result of his experiences at Agra, the Nawab came to the conclusion that either 'strenuous efforts be made to reform the present League' and 'to this end all the taluqdars and members of the Indian aristocracy be persuaded to join the League...[or] if they do not succeed in reforming the League they be asked to join the separate organisation'.[4] The Nawab had drawn up a scheme for a moderate Muslim organisation, and had sent it to Meston before the Agra sessions of the Muslim League. He envisaged a body entitled 'The Moderate Muslim Senate' and based on the landlord interest. He urged that to ensure success, 'vigorous Government help secretly given is absolutely necessary' and that 'Government should through the agency of its Collectors and District Officers revive the aristocratic and conservative forces and make them take active interest in the Moderate Senate proposed'.[5] A moderate press was to be set up to combat that of the extremists.

---

[1] The following were the resolutions that the Nawab claimed to have removed from the programme for the Agra session:
'1. [paragraph 2] The All-India Muslim League is of opinion that a body of voluntary workers working in a spirit of self-sacrifice and abnegation be organised to further its work and mission on the lines of the Servants Of India Society established by the Hon'ble Mr. Gokhale.
14. Protest against English Ministers' conduct towards Messrs. Wazir Hasan and Muhammad Ali.
15. Protest against the members of the League being called an Extremist.
16. An appeal might be sent to Amir of Kabul to have mercy on Muhammad Husain and Abdul Ghani.' Resolutions to be proposed at the Agra Sessions of the All-India Muslim League, December 1913, enclosed in Nawab Fateh Ali Khan Qizilbash to Meston, 3 January 1914, Meston Papers (6), IOL.
[2] Review of the present political attitude...' enclosed in *ibid*.
[3] Nawab Fateh Ali Khan Qizilbash's plan for 'The Moderate Muslim Organization', enclosed in Nawab Fateh Ali Khan Qizilbash to Meston, 26 December 1913, Meston Papers (6), IOL.
[4] 'Review of the present political attitude...' enclosed in Nawab Fateh Ali Khan Qizilbash to Meston, 3 January 1914, Meston Papers (6), IOL.
[5] 'The Moderate Muslim Organisation', Nawab Fateh Ali Khan Qizilbash to Meston, 26 December 1913, Meston Papers (6), IOL.

In order to get the organisation moving, Government was requested to make an initial grant of one lakh of rupees and give the Nawab assistance in prising open the coffers of rich Muslim landowners. The body's declared aims were to reassert the old policy of the Muslim League.[1]

Throughout the early months of 1914, the Nawab kept in constant contact with the moderate leaders, Ibni Ahmad, Hamid Ali Khan and the Nawab of Rampur. By March, he appeared to have decided in favour of a separate organisation. His decision was hastened by an increase of Shia–Sunni trouble at Aligarh which drove the Shias to think in terms of a separate college. A Shia college could only be set up with considerable government aid. After several interviews with the lieutenant-governor on 13 and 31 March and 2 and 5 of April, the Nawab noted that 'a vast vista of immense political potentialities'[2] had been revealed, and that the following deal had been made:

To make a short business of it His Highness the Nawab of Rampur, the Raja of Jehangirabad, the Nawab of Pahasu and the Raja of Pirpur's moral and material supports and a liberal contribution from the Government towards Muslim moderate organs and organisations were ensured. (2) The attention of the Rampur Darbar had been invited to the danger and undesirability of the power and influence enjoyed by the relatives of Muhammad Ali, Editor, *Comrade*, by whom the Rampur State offices are over run. (3) I would get replies to my previous papers in writing for my guidance. [e.g. The Moderate Muslim Organisation plan] (4) Pressure would be brought to bear upon such members of the League as pointed out by me to assist me in having the ideal of self-government cancelled. (5) The Shias shall be supported in securing their rights in the Muhammadan Anglo-Oriental College, Aligarh. (6) His Honour Sir James S. Meston will preside over the first meeting to be held for starting a Shia College. (7) Government will make a liberal grant to the Shia College in contemplation.[3]

[1] The principal objects of the Senate were to be:
   '(1) to safeguard and advance the Muslim interests in India;
   (2) to maintain relations of mutual good will and trust between the Muslims on one hand and the Government on the other, to secure the co-operation of both in matters of public weal and to take all such measures as may be necessary for the maintenance of peace, order and good government, to remove all misunderstandings between the rulers and the ruled by explaining to the people the point of view of the Government and vice versa and to point out unhesitatingly to them when they go wrong.' *Ibid.*
[2] 'A[n] extract journal of a tour in the United Provinces of Agra and Oudh, during March and April 1914', by Nawab Fateh Ali Khan Qizilbash and dated 19 May 1914, enclosed in Nawab Fateh Ali Khan Qizilbash to Meston, 19 May 1914, Meston Papers (6), IOL.   [3] *Ibid.*

The stage appeared to be set for a massive 'Old Party' reaction, powered by the landed interest, supercharged by Shia bigotry and lubricated by the government.

But it all came to nothing. There was no moderate drive. The whole show was the work of Qizilbash who, apart from wanting to dish the 'Young Party', hoped for personal reward from government (he dropped a broad hint about the acceptability of a baronetcy)[1] as well as a reward for his Shia community. 'Old Party' men, many of whom lacked courage, energy and political conviction, were not very promising material for the Nawab to work with. Moreover, as a group, they were far less cohesive than their young rivals. They were not bound together by common background, organisation, education or profession. United action was difficult. The glorious conception of Muslim collaboration with government – 'The Moderate Muslim senate' – was never launched and the energies and ambitions of its promoter were diverted into the Shia College project. Such obstacles apart, however, there was no real reason in 1914 to expect a vigorous moderate drive. In the struggle of the previous two years, the 'Old Party' had warded off almost all the 'Young Party' attacks. Moreover, in the second half of the year the need for counteraction declined as the outbreak of the World War brought declarations of loyalty from all sides and gave government the opportunity to take a tougher line with political dissidents. 'Old Party' men knew that they had government on their side and were sure that, while this was so, they had no reason to anticipate a threat to their political position from pleader and editor control of the All-India Muslim League. In the event, they reacted to their loss of power in the League by resigning from it. Between 1914 and 1916, League membership dropped from 800 to 500.[2]

[1] *Ibid.*
[2] Estimates made by the UP CID, 12 March 1919, GAD, 1917, 423, UPS.

CHAPTER 6

The 'Young Party' victorious
1914-1916

In 1914 the 'Young Party' was weak. 'Young Party' men had demonstrated the bankruptcy of the 'Old Party' politics of un-questioning loyalty. They had shown that agitation worked, vindicating their politics of protest. Yet, in the battles to capture the positions of power among Muslims, they had been out-gunned almost all along the line. Only in the All-India Muslim League had they had some success, though even here the gilt was quickly being rubbed off as its more prominent members resigned. It was clear that to defend Muslim interests successfully and to bolster their own political position they needed help. For this they had already begun to turn to the Congress.

This was a natural course for young Muslims to take. For many, educated in English and secular in approach, the 'Old Party's' slavish reliance on government had never seemed the only way to protect Muslim interests. Indeed, events such as the Nagri Reso-lution of 1900 and the setbacks of 1906 had quickly set them look-ing to Congress as an ally. Young Muslims such as Naziruddin Hasan, Khwaja Abdul Majid and Tassaduq Ahmad Khan Sher-wani had extra reasons for adopting this line; they had just returned from England where they had belonged to the Indian Majlis at Cambridge or the circle of intellectuals that flittered around Saro-jini Naidu,[1] groups full of national idealism rather than communal claptrap. Others too, such as Hyder Mehdi and Kamaluddin Ahmed Jafri at the Allahabad Bar or Wazir Hasan and Azhar Ali at the Lucknow Bar, found themselves daily working alongside Congressmen, such as Motilal Nehru and Tej Bahadur Sapru or A. P. Sen and Jagat Narain Mulla, with whom they had much greater affinity than the landlords and the ulama of their own

---

[1] The concerns of these groups are well illustrated by the correspondence of Syed Mahmud of Bihar with W. S. Blunt, Ameer Ali, Ali Imam and Sarojini Naidu. The affairs of Jinnah and Mazharul Haq were frequently mentioned. Syed Mahmud Papers, NMM.

community.[1] As soon as they found themselves baulked by the government, rapprochement with the Congress seemed the obvious as well as the most congenial course for many western-educated leaders of the Muslim League to take.

The Congress had already begun to sweep the way clear for rapprochement. In 1912 it had met at Patna. Mazharul Haq was chairman of the reception committee and the president, R. N. Mudholkar, recognised the expediency of adopting communal representation for Muslims.[2] In 1913 it met for the first time in the Muslim city of Karachi, Nawab Syed Muhammad was President, only the third Muslim president, and the resolutions tactfully ignored the question of separate representation.[3]

These contributions to rapprochement were matched by the Muslim League. Every move was planned by the League secretary, Wazir Hasan, and supported by an obedient clique of 'Young Party' men mainly from Lucknow. He completed the first step by bringing the League creed into line with that of the Congress. He followed this, in May 1913, by addressing the UP Congress Committee on the possibility of a joint Hindu–Muslim conference.[4] Three months later, he led a contingent of young Muslims from Lucknow to Allahabad to attend the foundation meeting of the UP Elementary Education League.[5] Then he brought the League behind the Congress in an agitation over the condition of Indians in South Africa,[6] and in December 1913 he attempted

[1] This point was strongly made by *Al Bashir* (Etawah), 8 June 1915, UPNNR 1915.
[2] *Report of the Proceedings of the Twenty-Seventh Indian National Congress. Held at Bankipur, December 26–28th, 1912* (Bankipur, n.d.), p. 19.
[3] *Report of the Twenty-Eighth Indian National Congress held at Karachi on the 26th, 27th and 28th of February 1913* (Karachi, n.d.), pp. 59–118.
[4] Wazir Hasan to the Secretary, the UP Congress Committee, 1 May 1913, published in the *Leader* (Allahabad), 18 May 1913. Wazir Hasan suggested that four prominent men of each community should meet in Lucknow in September. At a meeting on 15 July 1913 the UP Congress Committee reacted favourably, but the matter appears to have been left at that. *Leader* (Allahabad), 9 July 1913. Mahomed Ali also followed this affair, *Comrade* (Delhi), 17 and 31 May 1913.
[5] *Leader* (Allahabad), 29 July 1913. The following Muslims from Lucknow attended the Conference: the Raja of Mahmudabad, who was made vice-president of the League, Wazir Hasan, Sheikh Shahid Husain, Samiullah Beg, Nawab Sadiq Ali Khan, Syed Zahur Ahmed and Syed Mir Jan. The only other Muslims to attend were: Hafiz Hidayat Husain, Manzar Ali Sokhta, Sheikh Zahur Ahmad and Nawab Ishaq Khan. *Ibid.*, 2 August 1913.
[6] *Ibid.*, 2 December 1913.

to remove a resolution demanding separate representation in local bodies from the programme of the League's Agra sessions.[1]

These political developments drew an unpromising reaction from the Hindu politicians of the UP. True, the *Leader* hailed the presence of the Lucknow Muslims at the Allahabad Elementary Education Conference declaring that 'possibly for the first time, Hindu and Mahomedan leaders – the representatives of the National Congress and the Muslim League – were there together, holding identical views and animated by common hopes and aspirations'.[2] But more typical, even of the *Leader*, was a general arming to meet the new Muslim strength. Everyone was impressed by the 'Young Party's' victory in the Cawnpore Mosque affair. 'The self-sacrifice and zeal displayed by our Mahomedan brethren in the cause of their co-religionists at Cawnpore', commented one Hindu, 'should serve to open our eyes.'[3] The power of the rallying cry 'Islam in Danger' and the unity that had been displayed was compared with the divisions among the Hindus in matters such as the Ajodhia riot case.[4] More communal organisation was needed to resist Muslim initiatives: 'our Musalman brothers have led the way for us with their great League', Bhagwan Das declared at the inaugural meeting of the Kashi Hindu Sabha; 'it behoves us also therefore, and urgently, to set out house in order...'[5] Any suggestions that concessions to the Muslims for the national good would be acceptable, particularly in the field of separate representation, were slapped down. Malaviya's *Abhyudaya* deplored the failure of the Karachi Congress, after the objection of Muslim delegates, to reaffirm the resolution against separate representation.[6] When Sapru, as president of the Meerut Provin-

---

[1] 'Review of the present political attitude...' enclosed in Nawab Fateh Ali Khan Qizilbash to Meston, 3 January 1914, Meston Papers (6), IOL and Ch. 5, p. 233.　　[2] *Leader* (Allahabad), 29 July 1913.

[3] *Ibid.*, 6 December 1913; the Muslim agitational success at Cawnpore was often referred to by leading Hindus in urging Hindu organisation; for example, Radha Kishen Das, Moradabad, to Editor, *ibid.*, 19 November 1913; speech by Lala Lajpat Rai at Allahabad, 19 February 1914, *ibid.*, 22 February 1914 and speech by Pandit Bishen Narayan Dar at the inaugural meeting of the Kashi Hindu Sabha, *ibid.*, 4 March 1914.

[4] Ajodhia came under the Fyzabad municipal board. A Hindu–Muslim riot occurred there in 1913 in which local Hindu attitudes were, as usual, be-devilled by the rivalry between the Balak Ram and Manohar Lal factions.

[5] Speech by Bhagwan Das at the inaugural meeting of the Kashi Hindu Sabha, *Leader* (Allahabad), 4 March 1914.

[6] *Abhyudaya* (Allahabad), 3 January 1914, UPNNR 1914.

cial Conference in April 1914, suggested that he would not mind the Muslims 'getting wherever they are in a minority of 14 per cent or less [in local boards] up to 20 or 21 per cent of the seats provided the same consideration is shown to the Hindus wherever they may be in a similar minority',[1] he was chastised by the provincial press[2] and rebuked by the conference which passed an uncompromising resolution against separate representation.[3]

The outlook for rapprochement in 1914 seemed limited. The Muslim demand for separate representation was the bogy. Muslim League leaders were prepared to ditch it. Congress leaders were willing to accept it. But in the UP, the province where it mattered most, no local leader was ready to compromise. All the talk, however, about separate representation was speculative. In 1914, Indian leaders knew from the recommendations of the Decentralisation Commission and from the Delhi Despatch of 25 August 1911[4] that the general trend of government policy was towards providing further measures of local self-government. But the real chance of a further devolution of power, either in local boards in the UP or in provincial councils throughout India, seemed to belong to the distant rather than the near future.

The situation was drastically changed by the outbreak of World War One. The first reaction of nearly all Indians was one of loyalty. The trustees of Aligarh offered the services of 500 students as an ambulance corps,[5] the members of the Imperial Legislative Council vied with one another in expressing their allegiance to the

[1] Presidential Address of Tej Bahadur Sapru to the Meerut Provincial Political Conference, April 1914, *Leader* (Allahabad), 11 April 1914. Sapru, himself, had moved from a position of hostility to Muslim claims. In 1909, at the Agra Provincial Conference, he had strongly opposed concessions to the Muslims on the grounds that they had never worked with the Congress, their claims were insulting and it was senseless to make sacrifices for a 'false notion of unity'. Speech by Sapru proposing an amendment to Resolution 3 (the separate representation resolution) of the Third UP Political Conference, Agra, April 1909. *Indian People* (Allahabad), 15 April 1909. Sapru further developed his attitude in a letter to the press, Sapru to Editor, *ibid.*, 30 May 1909.
[2] Leading article in the *Leader* (Allahabad), 11 April 1914.
[3] Local self-government resolution of the Meerut Provincial Conference, April 1914, Section (c), *ibid.*, 10 April 1914.
[4] Government of India to the Secretary of State, 25 August 1911. The relevant passage is quoted in C. H. Philips (ed.), *The Evolution of India and Pakistan 1858–1947* (London, 1962), pp. 90–1.
[5] FR (UP), Home Poll. D, September 1914, 3, NAI.

Raj[1] and the government was overwhelmed by declarations of loyalty and support for the Empire. At the end of October the Muslim League decided not to hold its annual sessions in order not to embarrass the government in wartime.[2] So confident was the Viceroy of Muslim loyalty that he declared 'I am not even afraid of the attitude of the Mahomedans in the event of war with Turkey'.[3] His judgement was good. On 4 November Turkey declared war against Britain. Two days later, the Muslim League passed another loyalty resolution.[4] Indeed, so remarkable was the effusion of Muslim feeling for the government that even the most ardent pan-Islamists of the previous two years, such as Mahomed Ali and Dr Ansari, were to be found, for a little while, urging loyalty.[5] The feeling was strong enough to enable government to withstand the effects of a rapid rise in prices, and in March 1915 to push through the Imperial Legislative Council without trouble a Defence of India Ordinance enabling it to intern men without trial.

At the same time as Indians were voicing their loyalty, their appreciation of Britain's position in the world and India's position in the Empire was changing. The passage of the war made it clear, suddenly, that Britain was no longer the giant of Victorian times but just one of several fairly equal leading world powers. More important, Indians developed a 'new sense of self-esteem'.[6] India was providing large quantities of men and materials to fight the war. In France, Indian regiments helped to bring the best trained army in the world to a halt. Indians felt that the survival of the British Empire was in part due to their efforts. They found themselves eulogised in the British press. British ministers solemnly pledged their gratitude, and within three months of the outbreak of war the Under-Secretary of State for India declared that India's 'partnership with us in spirit and on the battlefields cannot but alter the angle from which we shall all henceforward look at the problems of the government of India'.[7] Inevitably, India's new

[1] Hardinge to Crewe, 9 September 1914, Hardinge Papers (120), CUL.
[2] *Leader* (Allahabad), 30 October 1914.
[3] Hardinge to Sir T. Holderness, 21 October 1914, Hardinge Papers (120), CUL.
[4] *Leader* (Allahabad), 6 November 1914.
[5] FR (UP), Home Poll. D, December 1914, 31 and 32, NAI.
[6] This was the phrase used to describe the impact of the war on Indian morale by the Montagu–Chelmsford Report, *P.P.*, 1918, VIII, pp. 142–3.
[7] Speech by C. Roberts, Under-Secretary of State for India, in the House of Commons, *Hansard*, Fifth Series (Commons), vol. LXVIII, 26 November 1914, col. 1357.

sense of self-esteem was accompanied by a broadening of political horizons. The feeling quickly began to emerge that, after the war had finished, Indian politicians need no longer confine themselves to their pre-war concerns, such as ending the indentured labour system or acquiring preferential tariffs, but could reasonably aspire to a further grant of political power.

The new possibilities created by the war were quickly understood. In February 1915, Wazir Hasan announced that the Muslim League was preparing a schedule of political demands to be made after the war.[1] In March 1915, the political testament of Gokhale who had died in the previous month became known, in which the Maharashtrian leader demanded provincial autonomy and the reduction of the Secretary of State's control over the Government of India.[2] In April, Mrs Besant, aiming to carve a place for herself in all-India politics, told the UP provincial conference that it should claim self-government for India within the British Empire after the war and presented it with a detailed plan of reforms.[3] The conference endorsed her aim.[4] By mid-1915, Indian politicians had come to believe that political reforms were imminent and were acting on that assumption.

The feeling that a grant of further political power was not far away had a dramatic effect on Indian politics. It helped to bring together the two Maharashtrian factions whose disputes had weakened the Congress since the Surat split of 1907; at the Bombay Congress of 1915 the constitution passed at Allahabad in 1908 was amended to enable Tilak and his followers to return to the Congress platform. More important, it gave the budding friendship between the 'Young Party' leaders of the Muslim League and the Congress a definite object towards which the two organisations could work together. Indeed, almost as soon as this object came into view, the crucial importance of unity was demonstrated by proceedings in the House of Lords. The issue was whether or not the lieutenant-governor of the UP should have an Executive Council.[5] The province wanted one. The lieutenant-governor and

[1] FR (UP), Home Poll. D, March 1915, 56, NAI.
[2] Pencilled draft in Gokhale's hand in the Gokhale Papers (Reel 9), NAI.
[3] Annie Besant, *U.P. Provincial Conference Presidential Address* (Madras, 1915), pp. 22–9.
[4] Resolution 5 of the Gorakhpur Provincial Political Conference, April 1915, *Leader* (Allahabad), 25 March 1915.
[5] The UP with other more 'backward' provinces had not been given an Executive Council under the Morley–Minto reforms. At the time, UP politicians

the Viceroy were prepared to have one. So was the Secretary of State. But the House of Lords was not. The proposal was thrown out by the Tory majority under the leadership of Macdonnell and Curzon. The Executive Council was represented as the demand of the educated alone; 'all [their] reasonable ambitions', Macdonnell declared, 'have...been adequately provided for at the present and for a long time to come...'[1] An Executive Council was also represented as doomed to failure; it would not survive the hostility of Hindu and Muslim.[2] These were inflammatory arguments to use against Indians who had just begun to scent the possibility of more power. Hindu and Muslim leaders sprang into life in order to demonstrate how widely political reform was demanded and how united the two communities were in demanding it. Joint parties went into the districts. Wazir Hasan Samiullah Beg, Jagat Narain Mulla and Gokaranath Misra toured Oudh.[3] Former irreconcilables such as Rai Debi Prasad and Fazlur Rahman of Cawnpore came together.[4] On 30 May, nearly 500 men from forty-one districts braved the hot weather – the temperature was 111° – to attend a special provincial conference at Allahabad under the presidency of Mahmudabad. Rarely had there been such widespread agitation and never had there been such wholehearted co-operation between the Hindus and Muslims of the UP.

Simultaneously the Muslim League leaders had begun to make preparations for taking the unprecedented step of holding the annual Muslim League sessions in Bombay at the same time and in the same place as the Congress. The Congress was going to discuss the subject of reforms after the war; 'Young Party' Muslims wanted to join them in this. As in the local rapprochement in the UP in 1913, the major initiative came from the 'Lucknow gang',[5] 'the small clique, which Wazir Hassan [sic] organises and Mahmudabad feeds...',[6] and events were stamped with their determination to succeed at all costs.

The idea of holding the League session in Bombay was first

were disappointed, but did not agitate. However, when the newly created province of Bihar received the privilege in 1912, the men of the UP felt that they had just cause for complaint.
[1] *Hansard*, Fifth Series (Lords), Vol. XVIII, 16 March 1915, cols. 771–2.
[2] Speeches by Macdonnell and Curzon in *ibid.*, cols. 770–2 and 787.
[3] *Leader* (Allahabad), 16 May 1915.
[4] *Ibid.*, 30 April 1915.
[5] FR (UP), Home Poll. D, December 1915, 26, NAI.
[6] Meston to Hardinge, 23 December 1915, Hardinge Papers (90), CUL.

mooted at Delhi in the middle of March 1914 by the Aga Khan in consultation with Mahmudabad, Nabiullah and Wazir Hasan.[1] Fazulbhoy Currimbhoy went immediately to Bombay to arrange for a formal invitation to be made by the Bombay Provincial League. Two months, however, passed before the formal invitation arrived and, when it did arrive, it came from M. A. Jinnah, a Bombay barrister, not Currimbhoy. The invitation was included by Wazir Hasan in the agenda for the League Council meeting of 6 June, which was circulated on May 15, and forty-one of the forty-three members of the League Council who replied said they were in favour of accepting it.[2] At this point opposition to the proposal came to a head. Two of the signatories, Casim Mitha and Currimbhoy, withdrew their support on the grounds that they had signed the invitation under a misapprehension.[3] At the same time, opposition to Wazir Hasan, Mahmudabad and the 'Young Party' in the UP became more vociferous. A massive campaign was launched against them by the 'Old Party' press.[4] *Al Bashir* chastised the 'Muhammadan barristers and vakils who live in bungalows isolated from their community, who are ignorant of its condition and of the harsh and improper treatment of the Hindus, [and] foolishly join with the Congressmen in demanding political rights'.[5] Wazir Hasan must resign, declared *Al Mizan*: 'Muhammadans can get their separate rights only by identifying themselves with Government...'[6]

The Muslim League Council did not accept Jinnah's invitation in June: it decided it would be wiser to wait. Instead Wazir Hasan went to Bombay to try and win over the opposition. He failed and, as the Aga Khan now declared himself against the proposal,[7]

[1] Note by Wazir Hasan appended to the announcement of the meeting of the Council of the All-India Muslim League at Lucknow, 10 November 1915, to decide whether or not the League should meet at Bombay. *Leader* (Allahabad), 5 November 1915.   [2] *Ibid.*

[3] In a letter of 25 May Casim Mitha gave Hasan 'a definite assurance that if the League comes to Bombay the bulk of the Mahomedans will have nothing to do with it, and may do their utmost to minimise the importance of the sessions.' *Ibid.*

[4] *Al Mizan* (Aligarh), 12, 22, 26, 29 May, 12, 19, 30 June, 10 July, 18 September 1915; *Al Bashir* (Etawah), 8 June, 20 July 1915; *Mashriq* (Gorakhpur), 20 July, 9 November 1915, UPNNR 1915. FR (UP), Home Poll. D, August 1915, 28, NAI.

[5] *Al Bashir* (Etawah), 8 June 1915, UPNNR 1915.

[6] *Al Mizan* (Aligarh), 19 June 1915, *ibid.*

[7] WRDCI, 17 August 1915, Home Poll. B, August 1915, 552–6, NAI.

matters became worse. There was nothing for it but to force the proposal through. 'According to the rules and constitution of the All India Moslem League', Wazir Hasan pointed out in a note appended to the agenda for the League Council meeting at Lucknow on 10 November, 'the Council of the League is the sole authority competent to determine and decide all matters relating to the annual meeting of the League...'[1] The meeting, dominated by the UP, and to a lesser extent the Bihar members,[2] accepted Jinnah's invitation. Immediately Wazir Hasan, Azhar Ali and Raja Ghulam Husain went to Bombay to make preparations. Tension grew between the Bombay League leaders, who were Sunnis, and the All-India League leaders, who had Khoja support. The situation was only resolved by a conference called by the Bombay leaders, and chaired by the Governor of the presidency who was eager to cut down the growing friction among the Muslims. The result was a compromise. The Bombay leaders agreed to support the League's sessions in their city to discuss political reforms. The All-India League leaders promised that those present would pass a resolution of loyalty to the government.[3]

The 'Young Party' men who travelled to Bombay were politically among the most extreme of the city's visitors in the last week of December 1915. At a meeting to inaugurate the Home Rule League they 'joined the Hindu extremists in supporting the proposal to found a Home Rule League without delay'.[4] The

[1] *Leader* (Allahabad), 5 November 1915.

[2] Note marked '*Strictly Confidential*' on the All-India Muslim League drawn up by the UP C.I.D., dated Allahabad 12 March 1919, Section VI (a), GAD, 1917, 423, UPS. A breakdown of the voting may be found in Hugh F. Owen, 'Negotiating the Lucknow Pact', *Journal of Asian Studies*, xxxi, No. 3 (May 1972), p. 571.

[3] The meeting agreed to the following terms:
'The All-India Moslem League do hold its sessions at Bombay and pass a resolution of Loyalty to the Government.
The League may also, if it so desires, proceed to appoint a Committee which shall have power to confer with such political and other organisations as they may deem fit with a view to forming a scheme of reform having due regard for the needs of Muhammadans. The report of the Committee to be presented at the next annual sessions of the All-India Moslem League.'
FR (Bombay), Home Poll. D, January 1916, 35, NAI. Having won one point, Wazir Hasan tried to win more. On 18 December 1915 he produced an agenda for the League's annual session which went way beyond the spirit of the compromise. He was forced to withdraw it. FR (Bombay), Home Poll. D, January 1916, 36, NAI.

[4] WRDCI, 4 January 1916, Home Poll. B, January 1916, 541–4, NAI.

presidential speech of Mazharul Haq, on the first day of the League meeting, to an audience full of Shias, Hindus and delegates from Upper India made S. P. Sinha's Congress address seem very tame.[1] By the second day the local Sunnis had had as much as they could stand. Casim Mitha, who had been at the heart of the Presidency League's opposition, infiltrated a body of Pathans, Julahas and local roughs into the session, and at a critical moment broke it up with cries of 'This is the Congress' and 'They want to join the Congress'.[2] The leaders retired to the Taj Mahal hotel, where in a session at which attendance was by invitation only they passed the crucial resolution of the meeting, appointing a committee to frame a reform scheme and where necessary to confer with other communities and organisations. Then, to cap Lucknow's triumph over Bombay, the Raja of Mahmudabad was elected League president in the place of the Aga Khan.

As the 'Young Party' recorded this singular victory, an element of discord threatened the harmonious progress of Congress and League towards the formulation of a joint scheme of reforms. In July 1915, the UP government introduced a municipalities bill into its legislative council. The product of a massive effort to increase non-official participation in local government and make it more efficient, the legislation was the *pièce de resistance* of Meston's lieutenant-governorship. At the outbreak of the war his government had been willing to postpone the bill. But, as soon as it realised that the war was raising the level of political aspiration and threatening its chances of passing the type of legislation it wanted, the UP government introduced the bill without more ado. The draft legislation aimed to remove official influence from municipal boards and to separate executive from deliberative functions, but it made no provision for separate representation. Meston had discarded his predecessor's recommendation that the Muslims be given separate representation and a large weighting[3] because it would 'arouse a storm of indignation among the Hindus which will do us more harm with them, than good it will do us with the Muhammadans'.[4] Instead, the bill merely contained the provisions

---

[1] *Ibid.*

[2] *Leader* (Allahabad), 3 January 1916.

[3] Hewett's recommendation would have raised the proportion of Muslim-elected members of municipal boards from 30.3 per cent, the proportion on 1 April 1911, to 46 per cent.

[4] Private note by Meston, 6 September 1913, Meston Papers (6), IOL.

of the 1900 Municipalities Act which empowered government in particular cases to make rules regarding representation by notification. The effect, therefore, of introducing the bill was to raise, in the home territory of the League leaders, the question of separate representation for Muslims.

This spelt danger for the Congress–League rapprochement. There was no doubt that the UP Muslims were going to insist on the insertion of separate representation in the bill. They felt that they had been promised it by Minto in his reply to the Simla deputation, and they knew that it had been recommended by the Decentralisation Commission. Separate representation in local bodies had been demanded by every Muslim League meeting since the organisation's foundation,[1] it had been demanded by every Muslim municipal commissioner who replied to the Burn circular of 1911,[2] and moreover Muslims in many municipalities in the province stood to gain something from its introduction on the basis of the communal proportions of the town population, and much more if weighting was added to allow for the community's alleged political importance.[3] Syed Ali Nabi, 'Young Party' sympathiser and President of the UP Muslim League, uttered what was evident when he warned the local government on 19 October 1915 that 'there has never been such a consensus of opinion among all the Musalmans on any political question as there exists today among them on the question of separate representation in local bodies'.[4]

The chances of the UP Muslims unbending on the question were slight. No Muslim member of the legislative council could compromise on this issue without jeopardising his seat at the next election. Nor could any member of the 'Young Party' clique, which ruled the Muslim League, interfere without risking a Muslim agitation which would reveal just how unrepresentative were those, who with the Raja of Mahmudabad declared, 'We are

---

[1] For these resolutions in the seven League sessions before 1915 see Pirzada, *Foundations of Pakistan*, Vol. I, pp. 32, 77, 129, 177, 256, 280–1, 315.

[2] The Burn circular of 22 April 1911 asked every municipal and district board in the UP for its views on the questions of separate electorates for Muslims and the proportion of seats they should receive. For the replies see Home Educ, Municipal A, April 1914, 22–31, NAI.

[3] In 1911 the Muslims had over 38 per cent of the municipal population but only just over 30 per cent of the municipal seats.

[4] Syed Ali Nabi to Secretary, Government of UP, 19 October 1915, Municipal 1915, 230 E No. 58, UPS.

The 'Young Party' victorious

Indians first and Muhammadans afterwards'.[1] All Hindu politicians, on the other hand, were strongly opposed to granting
separate representation to the Muslims. They were unwilling
both to admit any further concession to the community's claim to
be special and to make the sacrifice of municipal seats that this
would entail. Indeed, as the Congress began to make concessions
to the Muslims, the Hindus of the UP organised to resist them,
founding an all-India Hindu Sabha in April 1915 and a provincial
Hindu Sabha in December 1915. As soon as the municipalities
bill was introduced, therefore, there was the danger that the
developing Congress–League alliance would founder on the rocks
of communal prejudice in the UP.

UP Muslim agitation against the refusal of the Hindus to accept
separate representation in the home of the League would most
probably kill the Congress–League front over political reform.
UP Hindu agitation over the acceptance of separate representation
would not. It was evident that it was the Hindus who had to make
concessions to the Muslims. The men who took the lead in thus
sacrificing local interests to national ends were three Kashmiri
Brahmins, Motilal Nehru, Tej Bahadur Sapru and Jagat Narain
Mulla. Moreover, they were the only members of the UP Legislative Council who were prepared to do so. They realised that separate representation was the most important problem they had to
solve. 'It is', declared Sapru, 'a commonplace of Indian politics
that the evolution of India to higher and freer political institutions
...depends...wholly upon a satisfactory re-adjustment of intercommunal relations between the two communities in this country
...I believe', he continued, 'we are destined to rise to higher
political powers in no distant future and I do not want any domestic
quarrels to defeat or delay that destiny.'[2]

The three Kashmiri Brahmins showed their readiness to settle
this domestic quarrel straightway. Between the first and second
readings of the municipalities bill, July and December 1915, the
select committee of a non-official UP conference on municipal reform, chaired by Sapru, and the select committee of the legislative

[1] Speech of the Raja of Mahmudabad at the Special Provincial Conference on
the Executive Council question, May 1915, *Al Bashir* (Etawah), 20 July 1915,
UPNNR 1915.
[2] *Proceedings of the Council of His Honour the Lieutenant-Governor, United
Provinces of Agra and Oudh, assembled for the purpose of making laws and
regulations, 1916* [henceforth *UPLC*] (Allahabad, 1917), pp. 217–18.

247

council, led by Nehru and Mulla, both declared their willingness to concede the principle of separate representation. But the concession of the principle was only a beginning: the real test came in the negotiations over the details. The problem was first explored by Sapru's committee which recommended that Muslims should have a fixed proportion of seats, according to their proportion of the population in each town, for which both Hindus and Muslims would vote. The committee was prepared to go further and partially concede the Muslim demand for weighting. It suggested that the fixed proportion of Muslim seats could be larger than the Muslim proportion of the population in those towns in which the Muslims formed less than one-quarter of the total population.[1] But this was no more than kite-flying. The decisions were to be made by the select committee of the legislative council on which Nehru and Mulla sat with five officials, Hindu Sabha man, Lala Sukhbir Sinha, and 'Old Party' man, Asghar Ali Khan. Here Nehru took the lead and was prepared to concede a separate electorate, in which Muslims alone voted, provided they were not given the right they had in legislative council elections of voting in the general electorates as well. In addition, he was willing to concede that the Muslims should have thirty per cent weighting in excess of numerical proportion providing that this in no case gave them more than one-third of the number of seats. Both concessions were advances on the Sapru terms. Asghar Ali Khan agreed to the first, which became a substantive part of the bill, but not to the second. Nehru's offer came nowhere near the Muslim League demand of fifty per cent of the seats or his own of fifty per cent weighting providing it did not result in giving more than fifty per cent of the seats. Meston tried desperately hard to find a compromise, but neither side would budge. So, after it had had its second reading, the bill, including separate electorates but with the proportion of Muslim representation unresolved, was sent to the Government of India for approval.[2]

In March 1916, the Government of India sent the bill back to the UP saying that it would sanction the legislation only if the

---

[1] Representation of the Sapru Committee on the municipalities bill, to Secretary, Government of UP Municipal Department, *Leader* (Allahabad), 29 October 1915.

[2] Based on a note by A. W. Pim, 27 October 1915, Municipal 1915, 230 E No. 62, UPS, and 'Report of the Select Committee on the United Provinces Municipalities Bill', 25 December 1915, *U.P.Gazette Extraordinary, 1915*.

non-official members of the Council could arrive at an agreement that was acceptable to government over the proportions of Muslim representation.[1] By this time, a compromise was from the Hindu nationalists' point of view not only desirable but necessary. The success of the Congress and League meetings in Bombay, and the agreement to prepare a joint reform scheme, made the possibility of further devolution of power seem much closer. Letting the matter ride, as they had done in the inconclusive meetings of the committee, would no longer do. But when on 13 March Meston explained the situation to council members, it was not the Kashmiri Brahmins, but Syed Riza Ali, one of the two 'Young Party' men on the Council, who came forward with a suggestion. He recommended that minorities above forty per cent should get no additional seats, that those between twenty-five and forty per cent should have forty per cent of the seats, and that those under twenty-five per cent should have a ratio of seats equal to their proportion of the population plus one-third.[1] Nehru took up the offer immediately, and when on the following day Ali's recommendation was being discussed by the Hindus, put forward a similar formula to which most agreed.[2]

At the next meeting of the Council, the Raja of Jehangirabad introduced the formula as an amendment to the bill. It was bitterly attacked both by Hindus and Muslims of the right. 'Old Party' man Syed Abdur Rauf demanded equal representation declaring that the amendment 'is a great concession they [his Muslim colleagues on the Council] have made'.[3] Babu Brijnandan Prasad, on the other hand, a Hindu extremist from Moradabad, where communalism was endemic, poured scorn on his 'nationalist friends [who] are willing to make every concession in the pious hope of having a glimpse, distant and hazy though it be, of the millennium when separation will lead to compact union'.[4] Nehru and Sapru did their best to ward off these attacks[5] and finally succeeded in leading six of the nine Hindus who voted into the lobby in favour of the amendment.

[1] A. Muddiman, Secretary, Government of India Legislative Department, to Secretary, Government of UP Municipal Department, 10 March 1916, Municipal 1916, 230 E. No. 74, UPS.
[2] For the Nehru formula, background and details of the making and the passage of the municipalities bill see Francis Robinson, 'Muslim Separatism in the United Provinces' in *Modern Asian Studies*, VII, 3 (1973), pp. 428–41.
[3] *UPLC, 1916*, p. 229.   [4] *Ibid.*, p. 167.
[5] *Ibid.*, pp. 217–19, 228.

Separatism among Indian Muslims

By negotiating the concession of separate representation in UP towns, the exposed rear of the Muslim League had been saved. But this did not mean that the Congress–League front was free from local opposition. As soon as the municipalities bill was passed, a massive agitation was launched by the Hindu right. It was supported by Hindu Sabha men such as Bhagwan Das and Lala Sukhbir Sinha, 'who', Sapru told a friend, 'every now and again reminds me that the Municipal Act has "ruined" (he uses no other word) the Hindus...'[1] It was led by bigoted Brahmins from Allahabad, Chintamani and Madan Mohan Malaviya, who whipped up support through the columns of the *Leader*, through the paper's network of correspondents and by appeals to 'narrow prejudices against Muhammadans...'[2] The Kashmiri Brahmin trio were bitterly attacked. In Cawnpore, it was said that they were 'little better than Muhammadans and they have sold their Hindu brethren'.[3] In Lucknow, Sapru and Jagat Narain were burnt in effigy.[4] Hindu members of municipal boards were urged to resign as a symbolic gesture of protest. They did so – if it suited their local interests.[5] Meeting after meeting was held against the Jehangirabad Amendment, culminating in a grand provincial conference at Benares in August which recorded 'its sense of injustice' at the concession of 'not only separate but excessive representation' to the Muslims.[6] The whole agitation was instinct with hostility towards the Muslims and towards the idea that there should be any composition with them except on Hindu terms.[7] 'To some of our friends who are heading this agitation...', Sapru wrote despon-

[1] Sapru to Sita Ram, 10 August 1916, Sita Ram Papers, NAI.
[2] Motilal Nehru to Jawaharlal Nehru, 24 June 1916, Nehru Papers, NMM.
[3] Extract from the diary of the Superintendent of Police, Cawnpore, 8 April 1916, Municipal 1915, 230 E No. 70, UPS.
[4] C.I.D. Memo No. 3304, Allahabad 17 April 1916, *ibid.*
[5] Thus in Gorakhpur and Jaunpur, where the amendment put the Hindus back in power, they kept quiet but in west UP towns, such as Moradabad, Bijnor and Deoband, where Hindus lost power, or big political centres, such as Allahabad and Lucknow, where Hindus lost seats, they agitated.
[6] Resolution 1 of the Hindu Conference at Benares, 20 August 1916, Home Municipal A, March 1917, 3–4, NAI.
[7] The agitation 'is confined', Meston noted in May 1916, 'to a certain section who are in their hearts opposed to any *rapprochement* with the Muhammadans, or at least who resent any composition with Muslims except on their own terms.' Note by Meston, 7 May 1916, Municipal 1915, 230 E, (Confidential) UPS. See also A. W. Pim, Secretary to Government UP, to Secretary to Government of India Department of Education, 10 February 1917, Home Municipal A, March 1917, 3–4, NAI.

dently to Sita Ram, 'it matters little what effect this agitation has on the larger issues which will arise at no distant date. I understand that some of them don't feel at all keen about the Congress or Home Rule or anything of the sort. – To them the Jehangirabad amendment sums up everything worth living and dying for.'[1]

Sapru was despondent, with reason. In the autumn of 1916, the bitter UP Hindu opposition to political compromise with the Muslims was affecting wider issues. Mrs Besant was rapidly emerging as the figurehead and the most vociferous agitator of the Home Rule movement. For a Congress meeting that was to place its imprimatur on a scheme of reforms she was the obvious candidate for president. For an occasion that was to celebrate Hindu–Muslim unity she had the merit of being neutral. The Lucknow Reception Committee put her forward to the All-India Congress Committee.[2] The recommendation was turned down; Chintamani and Malaviya were known to be strongly opposed.[3] More serious than this, however, was the effect the Hindu agitation was having on the Muslims. On 5 October 1916, Syed Riza Ali wrote to the *Indian Daily Telegraph* asking 'is this the Self-Government, is this the Home-Rule, is this the *Swaraj* which is worth striving for by the Mussalmans?' and threatened that 'if the Allahabad politicians do not call a halt to the present agitation, the Mussalmans owe it to themselves to boycott the forthcoming Congress'.[4] Riza Ali's stand struck a sympathetic note in many provincial papers,[5] and to emphasise his point Muslims in various UP towns gave deputations from the Congress Reception Com-

---

[1] Sapru to Sita Ram, 10 August 1916, Sita Ram Papers, NAI.
[2] This was not the job of the Reception Committee. It was the task of the Provincial Congress Committees to elect the President. When three committees voted against Mrs Besant, the Lucknow Reception Committee attempted to force the hand of the remaining six, by holding a public meeting which resolved in her favour, When this had no effect, the Reception Committee overruled the vote of the provincial congress committees – an unprecedented action – and recommended her to the All-India Congress Committee.
[3] *Leader* (Allahabad), 18 August 1916. Apart from political strategy, the Hindu right had other reasons for being wary of Mrs Besant. She had fallen out with Malaviya in an attempt to control the Hindu University movement and with Bhagwan Das over dirty work among the theosophists. They knew she needed careful watching; Bhagwan Das described here as 'a sixty horse-power motor car requiring good driving'. FR (UP), Home Poll. D, August 1917, 35, NAI.
[4] Syed Riza Ali to the Editor, *Indian Daily Telegraph* (Lucknow), 5 October 1916, a cutting in Municipal 1915, 230 E No. 83, UPS.
[5] For instance, *Mashriq* (Gorakhpur) and *Hamdam* (Lucknow), 17 October 1916 and *Al Bureed* (Cawnpore), 25 October 1916, UPNNR 1916.

mittee a cool reception.[1] On 11 November, a large Muslim meeting
was held in Lucknow supporting the Municipalities Act and
attacking the Hindu agitation for imperilling Congress–League
unity over political reforms.[2] The Hindu extremists got the message.
They shut up.

While other groups were manoeuvring for advantage in the
province, the League was attending to its own political position.
Matters even more than before were in the hands of the Lucknow
'clique'. In February the Lucknow leaders gained new allies by
helping the Punjab 'Young Party' outdo Shafi and capture the
provincial Muslim League.[3] Their real effort, however, was concentrated on developing their connections with Congress. They
played a big part in the Congress Reception Committee and joined
its deputations to rally support. So great was their influence that
the Committee was 'said to have been controlled by a party of
young Kashmiris and Muslims...'[4] Moreover, in the attempts to
force Mrs Besant on the Congress as president their voice appears
to have been supreme.[5] On 11 October, links with the Congress
were further strengthened by deciding to hold the annual session
at Lucknow and by electing Jinnah as president. The former
decision was inevitable, the latter inspired. The Bombay barrister,
who had joined the League only in 1913, was still seen much more
as a Congressman. He brought to the League leadership important
connections with All-India Congress circles and the distinction of
having been a close friend of Gokhale.

Only eight men were present at the League Council meeting
which made the important decisions of 11 October, seven from
Lucknow and one from Allahabad.[6] Only nine men, all from Lucknow, had attended the League Council meeting at Mahmudabad
House, Lucknow, on 21 August, which considered the League
reforms scheme for the first time.[7] The scheme had been drafted by
Wazir Hasan in consultation, or so he claimed, with members of

[1] FR (UP) Home Poll. D, January 1917, 42, NAI.
[2] Municipal 1915, 230 E No. 83, UPS.
[3] WRDCI, 21 February 1916, Home Poll. B, February 1916, 515–18, NAI.
[4] WRDCI, 16 September 1916, Home Poll. B, September 1916, 652–6, NAI.
[5] Report of a public meeting in Lucknow to consider the question of the president of the Lucknow Congress. *Leader* (Allahabad), 11 August 1916.
[6] Note by the UP C.I.D., 12 March 1919, Section VI (b), GAD 1917, 423, UPS.
[7] They were: Syed Wazir Hasan, the Raja of Mahmudabad, Mirza Samiullah
Beg, Dr Naziruddin Hasan, Shaikh Sakhawat Ali, Maulvi Asghar Ali, Munshi
Ehtisham Ali, Hakim Abdul Qazi and Hakim Abdul Wali; *ibid.*, Section III.

the Reforms Committee.[1] It was similar in every respect to the one already prepared by the Congress except for the introduction of separate representation. It asked for fifteen reserved Muslim seats out of sixty-five elected seats in the Imperial Council, twenty out of seventy-five in the provincial councils, and it appeared to be understood that the Muslims would vote in the general electorates as well.[2] As in the UP municipalities bill, separate representation was clearly going to be the point of negotiation. League leaders had sound reason to believe their demand would be accepted in principle: Congress had shown its hand in the UP municipalities' affair. Moreover, if Wazir Hasan had any doubts, these must have been dispelled when a memorandum on reforms submitted to the Viceroy by the nineteen elected members of the Imperial Legislative Council, including several leading Congressmen, proposed that wherever Muslims or Hindus were in a minority they should be 'given proper and adequate representation having regard to their numerical strength and position'.[3]

Thus far the influence of the 'Young Party' leaders of the UP appears to have been paramount. It was not much less when the Congress and League schemes were considered by their Joint Reform Committee. At the Committee's Calcutta meeting of 17–18 November 1916, more than three-quarters of the Muslim delegates came from Bengal and the UP.[4] Their dominance was displayed in the proceedings. Members were agreed on almost all points. Separate representation was conceded by the Hindus provided the Muslims had no vote in the general electorates. This the Muslims accepted. It remained to negotiate the proportions of representation. In five provinces, the position was quickly settled. Only in the case of Bengal, where the Bengali Hindus offered the

---

[1] Report of the League Reform Committee, appointed at Bombay, 1 January 1916, presented by Wazir Hasan at the Lucknow League session, December 1916; Pirzada, *Foundations of Pakistan*, Vol. I, p. 378.

[2] Note by UP C.I.D., 12 March 1919, Section III, GAD 1917, 423, UPS and Owen, 'Lucknow Pact' in *Journal of Asian Studies*, xxxi, No. 3 (May 1972), p. 575.

[3] 'Memorandum submitted by the undersigned elected Members of the Imperial Legislative Council with regard to the proposed reforms', enclosed in Chelmsford to Chamberlain, 6 October 1906, Chelmsford Papers (2), IOL.

[4] There were twenty Muslim Leaguers among the seventy-one present: twelve from Bengal, four from the UP, one each from Bihar, N.W.F.P., Madras, and one unknown. Mazharul Haq achieved the feat of representing both the Congress and the League. Note by UP C.I.D., 12 March 1919, Section IV, GAD 1917, 423, UPS.

Muslims twenty per cent as against their claim of fifty per cent, and the UP, where the Hindus refused to agree to the League Reform Committee's suggestion of thirty-three and a third per cent, was no settlement achieved.[1] The matter was postponed to a second meeting before the League and Congress sessions at Lucknow. On this occasion, the Joint Committee lost its Bengali Muslim majority and was reinforced with UP Muslims.[2] The difficulties over Bengal were rapidly despatched. On the other hand, it took four sittings between 25 and 28 December for Mrs Besant, Bhupendranath Basu, Tilak and Jinnah to persuade the UP Hindus, Malaviya and Chintamani, to give up their proposal of twenty-five per cent, the UP Muslims to sacrifice their claim to thirty-three and a third per cent and all to agree to a suggestion of thirty per cent put forward by those masters of compromise Nehru and Sapru. Even then, this figure was only settled subject to a further provision that any measure which was opposed by two-thirds of either Hindus or Muslims should be dropped.[3]

[1] Some sources give the impression that 33⅓ per cent was conceded to the UP Muslims at Calcutta and agreed to. Fazlul Haq to Mahomed Ali, 23 November 1916, Mahomed Ali Papers, JMI, and WRDCI, 25 November 1916, Home Poll. B, November 1916, 452–3. Yet it is clear that a satisfactory arrangement was not made because the matter was raised again at Lucknow.

[2] Note by UP C.I.D., 12 March 1919, Sections V and VI, GAD 1917, 423, UPS.

[3] Based on *ibid.* and FR (UP), Home Poll. D, January 1917, 45, NAI. The following are the proportions of Muslim representation that were agreed to:

Province	Muslims in population (%)	Number of Muslim legislative seats (%)
Bengal	52·6	40·0
Bihar and Orissa	10·5	25·0
Bombay	20·4	33·3
Central Provinces	4·3	15·0
Madras	6·5	15·0
Punjab	54·8	50·0
United Provinces	14·0	30·0

The pattern of the negotiations went thus. On 25 December the joint committee met. Bhupendranath Basu of Bengal proposed a 40 % basis for Bengal Muslim representation to which all agreed. For the UP Muslims Malaviya proposed a 25 % basis. Syed Riza Ali demanded 33⅓ %. Chintamani supported Malaviya and there was no decision. On 26 December the Hindus led by Sapru and Nehru offered a 30 % basis (government suggests that Malaviya made this proposal; this, however, seems unlikely and more probable is the suggestion put forward by Owen, and based on reports in the *Hindu* (Madras),

The 'Young Party' victorious

This compromise came to be known as the Lucknow Pact. It originated in the move that the UP 'Young Party' leaders of the Muslim League had made towards the Congress from 1913 in order to improve their political position – a move which acquired a new significance when the war transformed political reform from a remote possibility into an imminent reality. These unusual circumstances enabled the 'Young Party' leaders to barter their support for political reform against Congress support for separate representation.

The terms of the pact and the limited support it received from Indian Muslims at Lucknow illuminate the role of the UP 'Young Party'. The proportions of representation negotiated for Muslims in the Muslim majority provinces were poor value. Only in the minority provinces, particularly the UP and Bihar, were good bargains struck. Muslim attendance at the League and Congress sessions to ratify the Hindu–Muslim agreement on reform makes the same point. Of the 433 Muslims who went to the Congress, over 400 were stooges from Lucknow packed into the session at the last moment.[1] At the League meeting, 'apart from the President Mr. Jinnah, there were few delegates from Bombay. Madras was almost entirely unrepresented and the delegates from Bengal were few. Important sections in the United Provinces were quite unrepresented.'[2] Meston who visited the League meeting when

that Nehru and Sapru took the lead in offering the 30% compromise). The Muslims would not budge. Malaviya made it clear that he conceded 30% against his better judgement, but, even then, the secretary of the Muslim League would not step down from 33⅓%. On 27 December there was another unsuccessful meeting. On 28 December the UP Muslims agreed to accept Jinnah's proposal of the previous day that they should have a proportion of 30% with the proviso vesting a veto in a two-thirds minority opposition. Forty voted for and eleven, including Malaviya and Chintamani, against the settlement. GAD 1917, 140, UPS and Owen, 'Lucknow Pact' in *Journal of Asian Studies*, XXXI, No. 3 (May 1972), p. 578.

[1] Figures given by Swami Shraddhanand, who was on the Lucknow platform, in B. R. Ambedkar, *Pakistan or the Partition of India* (Bombay, 1946), p. 141 and cited in Khalid B. Sayeed, *Pakistan: The Formative Phase 1857–1948*, 2nd edn (London, 1968), p. 40. The printed delegate lists of the Congress session support the Swami's assertions as to the poverty of Muslim attendance from outside Lucknow, although they do not immediately corroborate his suggestions regarding the strength of representation from the city itself; only seventeen Muslim delegates were elected by the various associations of the city. They would, however, support the Swami's argument that the majority of the Muslims attending the Congress were stooges packed in for the occasion.

[2] FP (UP), Home Poll. D, January 1917, 45, NAI.

'the Home Rule Resolution was in full blast', told the Viceroy that 'there were many empty benches. Very few of the audience were men of over 40; and I could see nobody of any position except the handful on the platform.'[1] This pact, therefore, which was to mean so much to the makers of the Montagu–Chelmsford reforms, nationalists and historians, was not an agreement between the representatives of the Congress and the Muslims of all India, or even the Muslims of the UP, but a deal between the Congress and the UP 'Young Party' leaders of the Muslim League.

[1] Meston to Chelmsford, 11 January 1917, Chelmsford Papers (18), IOL.

PLATE 1

The Struggle for a Place, *Oudh Punch* (Lucknow) May 1881

Oudh Punch shows the relative position of four leading communities in India and illustrates their major characteristics with terse Hindustani colloquialisms. The Englishman, well-mounted and a good rider, 'progresses like the wind'. The Parsi 'gets on fairly well without much fuss'. The Bengali, well-mounted on a steady ambling horse and with fish hung from the crupper of his saddle, 'even though no great rider, by persevering gets on well somehow or other and carries his food with him so that he may persue his object with greater determination'. The well dressed Muslim of the modern sort, with the reins in his mouth and a whip in both hands, is 'doing his best to keep pace with the rest, but is so poorly mounted [i.e. his education is so poor] that he is in danger of being left behind'.

PLATE 2
Syed Ahmed Khan flanked by men of Aligarh.

PLATE 3

Standing: Shaukat Ali (left), Mahomed Ali (right). Seated: their mother, who was one of the few Muslim women of position prepared to be seen unveiled in public, and Shaukat Ali's son.

؛ دوستو دلدل میں پھنسنا بہ نسبت بَہ جانے کے بائیمیتے ‟

PLATE 4

Gandhi and Civil Disobedience, *Oudh Punch* (Lucknow) March 1922
Gandhi declares to the Indian leaders around him, among them most
probably Hakim Ajmal Khan, Hasrat Mohani and A. K. Azad (first, second
and third from the left), 'friends, it is better to be stuck in the mud than
swept away by the current'.

CHAPTER 7

Religious reinforcements for the Muslim party

1917-1918

Political action up to 1916 had been determined increasingly by the prospect of further reform of the legislative councils. In August 1917, the Secretary of State, Montagu, declared that the British government had decided to take 'substantial steps' in the direction of the 'progressive realisation of responsible government in India as an integral part of the British Empire'.[1] In April 1918, together with the Viceroy, he published a report which recommended the devolution of considerable power to Indians in the provinces. These two events, which assured many Indian politicians that power was not very far from their grasp, had an important effect on political alignments.

The 'Old Party' disappeared. In future, the province was going to be governed by those who could command a majority in the provincial council. It was clear that the policy of relying on government to protect Muslim interests, for which the 'Old Party' stood, was unlikely to be effective. Nevertheless, 'Old Party' men did not allow reform to go through without a fight. When the government called for memorials on reforms, two leaders of the UP Muslim League, Ibni Ahmad and Syed Abdur Rauf of Allahabad, and the large Muslim landlords of Aligarh, led by Muzamilullah Khan of Bhikampur, organised with government encouragement a UP Muslim Defence Association. The association's address presented to Montagu and Chelmsford declared 'that any large measure of self-government which might curtail the moderating and adjusting influence of the British Government would be nothing short of a cataclysm', and demanded that, if devolution took place, Muslims should have fifty per cent representation.[2] This line was

---

[1] The Secretary of State's announcement, 20 August 1917, C. H. Philips (ed.), *The Evolution of India and Pakistan 1858 to 1947: Select Documents* (London, 1962), p. 264.

[2] Address of the United Provinces Muslim Defence Association, GAD, 1917, 553, UPS; Addresses presented at Delhi No. 16, Montagu Papers (35), IOL.

257

supported by the memorials of three other Muslim groups and by resolutions passed by meetings of Muslims all over the province.[1] But British influence was being curtailed and there was no chance of Muslims being given equal representation. The lack of reality in the Defence Association's policy, even as a bargaining position, indicates that the 'Old Party' had reached the end of the road. 'Old Party' men now began to leave the mainstream of Muslim politics. Aftab Ahmad Khan joined the Secretary of State's Council, Syed Abdur Rauf became a judge of the Punjab Chief Court, and Ibni Ahmad disappeared from view. The large land-lords began to emphasise their landlord as much as their Muslim status. When landlord associations presented memorials in 1917, Muslim magnates were prominent among those involved: Jehang-irabad in the British Indian Association, Nawab Abdul Majid in the Agra Zamindars' Association, Pahasu and Nawab Ishaq Khan in the Muzaffarnagar Zamindars' Association, and Chhatari, Bhikampur and Talibnagar actually organised a deputation from a new group known as the 'Zamindars of the Province of Agra not belonging to the [Agra Zamindars] Association'![2] The prospect of a severe reduction of British power in the province rendered impracticable the great alliance of Muslim landed and service interests with government which had been built up in the nineteenth century.

Several 'Young Party' leaders also left the mainstream of Muslim politics. Wazir Hasan's aim, after his great achievement at Lucknow in December 1916, was to ensure that political reforms were carried out. This required that his hold over the Muslim League should remain tight. Yet in 1917 it was coming increasingly under attack. Opposition came in a subtle form with the demand, which developed among 'Young Party' men from May 1917, that the League should launch a campaign to secure the release of Mahomed Ali and the other Muslim internees. Wazir Hasan re-sisted as long as he could; he realised that Mahomed Ali at large, embittered by his and Mahmudabad's treachery over the Muslim University and wielding considerable authority over 'Young Party' men, would limit his capacity to keep the Muslim League

---

[1] The Muslim Association for the protection of the Mohammadans of Gorakhpur, the Anjuman-i-Islamia of Saharanpur and the Mohammedans of Rohilkhand, organised by Abdul Wadud who was the secretary of the Islamia school, Bareilly. GAD, 1917, 553, UPS.
[2] *Ibid.*

behind the reforms.[1] Simultaneously, he had to face a direct assault on his control of the League from Lucknow itself. Raja Ghulam Husain, Mahomed Ali's follower, was its organiser; his newspaper, the *New Era*,[2] the vehicle. In a series of articles entitled 'Reconstruction', he launched a campaign for the transformation of the League into an 'efficient vehicle for the expression of the will of the Muslim community'.[3] He did not deny Hasan's liberal policies, but the secretary had placed a dead weight on the development of Muslim politics:

> The All-India Moslem League in its framework and organisation has inevitably led to the growth of political despotism – an exclusive ring of a few favoured personalities, who have coalesced into a form of dictatorship and have suppressed, however unconsciously, all healthy development of political thought in the democracy of Islamic India. The result is that Moslem politics is split into 'warring cliques' revolving around masterful and self-seeking personalities.[4]

There were to be no more Wazir Hasans. In his blueprint for the new League, Husain recommended that the same man should be eligible for the post of secretary only every other year.[5]

Wazir Hasan warded off these attacks, but they did not diminish. When the Montagu–Chelmsford Report was published in April 1918, 'Young Party' opposition to Hasan crystallised around it. Most thought they had little chance of winning seats or ministries in the new councils. Moreover they were concerned by the Report's hostility to separate representation, and were being increasingly alarmed by the fate of Turkey in the war. With nothing to gain from supporting reforms, they joined the Congress in condemning them. Their alliance was cemented by a new and real participation in Congress affairs. T. A. K. Sherwani and Manzar Ali Sokhta

---

[1] Note by the UP CID, 12 March 1919, section (d), GAD, 1917, 423, UPS; WRDCI, 19 May 1917, Home Poll. B, May 1917, 445–8, NAI.
[2] Published from Lucknow, the first issue of *New Era* appeared in April 1917. Ghulam Husain had worked for some time on the *Comrade* staff, which would explain why the format of this English weekly should resemble it closely. It was stopped under the Press Act at the end of the year. Its aim was to fill the gap left in 'Young Party' politics by the death of the *Comrade* and 'restore to educated Moslem opinion a unity of aim and direction and endeavour to create a lasting basis for the united and progressive development of "Young India"'. GAD, 1917, 140, UPS.
[3] *New Era* (Lucknow), 16 June 1917.
[4] *Ibid.*, 9 June 1917.
[5] Clause 10 of a draft constitution for the All-India Muslim League published in *New Era* (Lucknow), 16 June 1917.

9-2

became prominent in provincial Congress activities; Ansari, Asaf Ali and Hakim Ajmal Khan gained leading positions in the Delhi Congress Committee; while Khwaja Abdul Majid and Syed Hyder Mehdi were elected to the All-India Congress Committee.

Wazir Hasan had to tread warily to keep the League on the side of the reforms. When in May 1918 it looked as if the Congress, which meant the League as well, was about to hold a special session to discuss the Montagu–Chelmsford Report in either Allahabad or Lucknow, both hotbeds of extremism, he insisted that Lucknow would be 'too hot' – he really meant too hot for him – and urged the merits of Bombay.[1] The wheel had turned full circle. The man who had brought the League to Lucknow in 1916 to win the Muslim support for the Congress–League scheme now wished to retreat to Bombay to keep reforms on the table and himself in power. Even then, he was dubious about holding a full League session. 'We do not think', he told the Congress secretary, 'that we should hold a special meeting of the All-India Moslem League but we would call a meeting of the Council of the All India Moslem League to confer with the Congress...'[2] Hasan still felt he could control the Council but was uncertain of his command of a full session. He won his point over Bombay, but had to accept a full session. The Congress leaders were eager to hurry, but in July he told the Congress secretary that, if they wanted the support of Mahmudabad and himself, the earliest they could have a joint session was the first week in September. They wanted time 'to gauge fully the public opinions as well as the views of the Press'.[3] In the meantime, Harcourt Butler, recently installed as lieutenant-governor of the UP, is said to have made Mahmudabad's support for the reforms certain by promising him, if he behaved himself, the Home Membership in the first government formed under the new dispensation.[4] Whether true or not, the Raja did behave him-

---

[1] Wazir Hasan to Ramaswami Aiyer, 22 May 1918, All-India Congress Committee Papers [henceforth AICCP], 1918, 2, NMM.

[2] *Ibid.*

[3] Wazir Hasan to Ramaswami Aiyer, 9 July 1918, AICCP, 1918, 2, part III, NMM.

[4] So went the story told by the Raja's second son. There is possibly a good measure of truth in it as it suits both the political methods of Harcourt Butler and the very special relationship that he had with the Raja. And, of course, the Raja did become the first Home Member of the UP. Series of interviews with the Maharajkumar of Mahmudabad, Lucknow and Mahmudabad, June 1968.

self, and the Special sessions of the League over which he presided in September refused to join the Congress in condemning the reforms Report.[1] As a result, attacks on Hasan, and now the Raja, intensified.[2] They came to a head at the Delhi Muslim League sessions in December 1918. In the subjects committee, Hasan, with the help of Nabiullah and Jinnah, bravely defended his policy against the assaults of Hakim Ajmal Khan and Ansari urging that 'nothing which might injure their interests in India or which might compromise their national position should be done...'[3] In the League Council, Hasan still had enough influence to get the Raja and himself re-elected as president and secretary, and to defeat an attempt to change the constitution.[4] But in the League sessions, he and his patron came in for such a drubbing that Mahmudabad, having received treatment ill-befitting a taluqdar and a nobleman, 'left Delhi in disgust'.[5] They resigned from the League. They could no longer reconcile the growing hostility to government and to themselves of many League members with their own hopes of receiving the rewards of collaboration, and their own views of what was best for the Muslims. In the following two years, the Lucknow clique, like many of the Congress leaders with whom they had made the joint reform scheme, left the front line of nationalist politics. Mahmudabad was appointed Home Member of the UP and Vice-Chancellor of Aligarh Muslim University; Mirza Samiullah Beg became Chief Justice of Hyderabad State; Dr Naziruddin Hasan also entered the Nizam's service; Wazir Hasan became the first member of the Oudh Bar to be appointed Assistant Judicial Commissioner of Oudh.

As the old leaders left the League at Delhi, new supporters arrived, the ulama. The odd alim had attended sessions before, for instance, Shibli had come to press the waqf question, but never before had a session been graced by so many of the religious leaders of Indian Islam. They had been invited by Ansari in order to add their weight to his protests regarding the Khilafat. In the sessions they were fêted, being given a paean of praise in welcome and

[1] FR (UP), Home Poll. D, October 1918, 31, NAI; *Leader* (Allahabad), 2 September 1918.
[2] WRDCI, 9 November 1918, Home Poll. B, December 1918, 158–9, NAI.
[3] Report by Tassaduq Hussein, 1 January 1919, Home Poll. A, March 1919, 251–9, NAI.
[4] FR (UP), December 1918, Home Poll. D, January 1919, 42, NAI.
[5] Report by Tassaduq Hussein, 1 January 1919, Home Poll. A, March 1919, 251–9, NAI.

a prominent place on the platform. One of them, Maulvi Ghulam Mohiuddin of Kasur, replied saying that 'up to this time the *Ulemas* had considered the religion and politics of Musalmans were two different things but in fact they were one and the same in Islam. Their politics was their religion.'[1] Ansari and Hakim Ajmal Khan took up this theme by trying, without success, to alter the aims of the League from protecting the rights of Indian Muslims to protecting the religious as well as the political rights of Muslims both outside and inside India.[2] Not all 'Young Party' men, however, approved of this attempt to connect religion with politics. Khaliquzzaman told an intelligence agent 'that they were playing with fire in uniting with the *Ulemas*. They would either be swept off their legs or carry the whole of Muslim India with them.'[3] Khaliquzzaman's warning was not far wrong. Over the next four years, the ulama were to be a powerful force in both Muslim and Indian politics. They must be examined more closely.

Five times a day the azaan rang out over the housetops. Five times a day the thoughts of Indian Muslims turned towards their religion. 'Their talk is continually (without hypocrisy) of religion...'[4] commented one sympathetic observer. The mosque, declared Mahomed Ali, is 'the humming hive of the Muslims, the more devout of whom at least gather there oftener and with greater regularity than do the habitués of Clubs and Cafés...'[5] Religion lay at the centre of their existence. Religious law, the sharia, regulated minutely every aspect of life, admitting no distinction between religious, ethical and legal considerations. Under British rule, the effective sphere of religious law had been cut back vigorously in the direction of dealing purely with private, religious and family affairs; yet for the Muslim artisans who thronged the bazars of mofussil towns, for the Muslim amla who populated the government offices, for the Muslim women who spent their lives confined

---

[1] Home Poll. A, March 1919, 251–9, NAI; WRDCI, 18 January 1919, Home Poll. B, January 1919, 160–3, NAI.

[2] This attempt was defeated by Wazir Hasan with the help of the Bengal and Bombay delegates. FR (Delhi), December 1918, Home Poll. D, January 1919, 42, NAI.

[3] Report by Tassaduq Hussein, 1 January 1919, Home Poll. A, March 1919, 251–9, NAI.

[4] T. W. Arnold, *Preaching of Islam*, p. 413, quoted in Afzal Iqbal (ed.), *My Life A Fragment: An Autobiographical Sketch of Maulana Mohamed Ali* (Lahore, 1942), pp. 13–14. [5] *Ibid.*, p. 11.

to the zenana, indeed, for the majority of Indian Muslims, the sharia continued to exercise great influence over their daily lives.

The ulama interpreted the sharia. In theory Islam does not tolerate the existence of a clergy, who might presume to intervene between God and Man, yet almost inevitably a body of interpreters has emerged in every Islamic society. The typical alim was a distinctive figure:

He wore a shirt and paijama of home-spun, a cane cap brownish in colour and dirty at the edges, and a bandana over his shoulder. His head was close-cropped and made his forehead look broader. His expansive fan-shaped beard was dyed red with henna, and his moustaches were shaved on the upper lip in accordance with Islamic law. His nose was big, jutting out on his face like a rock, and a callosity had formed on his forehead on account of constantly rubbing it on the ground at prayer, and shone ashy grey from a distance on his dark face.[1]

Ulama called the faithful to prayer and led mosque services. They preached the Friday sermon in the mosque and gave private guidance to those who wanted it. They taught the Koran in the local maktab and madrassa, explained fatwa, and, if very eminent, issued them. They had great sway in Muslim society.

But who were the ulama? What made them a distinct group? The following assessment is useful:

They were certainly not a hierarchy or an order; if they were a professional body, they were without, so to speak, a registration council or a court of discipline. They were a class by their education,... They did not possess equal qualifications or individual parity of esteem. Not much more than pretension united the product of one of the great teaching centres, say the Farangi Mahal in Lucknow, and the village *mulla* who, though he could recite the Qur'an in Arabic, could hardly understand what he was reciting... As long as a man followed a traditional syllabus of study (here the eighteenth century *Dars-i-Nizami* taught under the aegis of the Firangi Mahal [sic] had great but not exclusive prestige) and accepted the *ijma* of his learned predecessors, he would be accepted as an *alim*.[2]

The ulama, therefore, were those who had followed the traditional education of Islam.

It has been asserted on the basis of a random sample of 100 biographies of nineteenth-century ulama, most of whom were village and small town mullas and maulvis, that they were 'an open-ended

---

[1] Ahmad Ali, *Twilight in Delhi*, 2nd edn (Oxford, 1966), p. 92.
[2] P. Hardy, 'The ulama in British India', unpublished seminar paper, School of Oriental and African Studies, London, 1969, p. 8.

petit-bourgeoisie of pre-industrial society'.[1] True, many had fairly humble backgrounds, but some of the leading ulama of the first quarter of the twentieth century appeared to come from backgrounds little different from those of 'Old' and 'Young Party' men. Shibli's father was a big zamindar and leading vakil of the Azamgarh bar. His son Muhammad Hamid Nomani became a Naib Tahsildar. One brother, Muhammad Ishaq, was the leading Muslim vakil in the Allahabad High Court until his death in 1914, another, Muhammad Junaid, was a munsif at Cawnpore.[2] Abdul Bari was considered a suitable husband for one of Mahmudabad's relations.[3] Habibur Rahman Khan Sherwani, later head of the Hyderabad State Ecclesiastical Department, owned land paying Rs. 14,147 land revenue[4]. There is enough evidence to suggest that, far from being a group with a distinct social and economic background, the ulama were drawn from all ranks of society.

Most ulama depended on religion to make their living. A few eked out an existence in industry or trade;[5] early in its history the Deobandi school, suspecting that it would be hard to find work for its graduates, opened a department teaching small handicraft industries.[6] Some had alternative means of support. Shibli inherited wealth from his father and received a grant from the Nizam;[7] Nasrat Husain, one of Mahmud-ul-Hasan's companions during his Malta internment, owned 'a comfortable little estate in Fatehpur District';[8] Salamatullah of Firangi Mahal owned property in

---

[1] *Ibid.*

[2] 'History sheet of Shibli Nomani Shams-ul-Ulama', GAD, 1914, 55, UPS.

[3] Interview with Mufti Reza Ansari (the grandson of Maulana Salamatullah, see Appendix III) of Firangi Mahal, 29 May 1968.

[4] See Appendix II.

[5] The following list of services rendered by the graduates of Deoband during the period 1867–1967 shows the sources of support found by ulama: spiritual guides, 536; writers, 1164; debaters, 1540; orators and missionaries, 4288; teachers, 5888; muftis, 1784; journalists, 684; tabib, 288; industry and trade, 748; As there were 7417 graduates during the century, some have probably been listed under two occupations. Source: *Hundred Years of Darululoom Deoband*, pamphlet prepared by the Department of Tanzeem Abnae Qadeem Darululoom, Deoband, 1967.

[6] This experiment did not succeed, most probably because it was not needed. Ziya-ul-Hasan Faruqi, *The Deoband School and the Demand for Pakistan* (London, 1963), pp. 38–9.

[7] 'History sheet of Shibli Nomani Shams-ul-Ulama', GAD, 1914, 55, UPS.

[8] Statement by Nasrat Husain, 14 December 1917, Home Poll. D, January 1916, 47, NAI.

Lucknow and Abdul Bari held a small zamindari.[1] But most derived all their income from activities concerned with their religion, and there was clearly a living to be had. Some were journalists and writers, like Maulvi Habibur Rahman of Deoband,[2] but the great majority were missionaries or teachers. In the early twentieth century, most eminent ulama were teachers. They were supported by gifts from the faithful, by fees for taking boys through the Koran, and by waqf endowments[3] while Abdul Bari, as a leading pir, received large enough donations in the form of nazra to pay for running his Madrassa Nizamia with its 300 students.[4] Men so dependent on the reverence and contributions of the faithful could lose power and income if they failed to take a popular line on a religious issue. Equally, religious agitation could help them to improve their position. It was 'reported from Nawabshah, during the Khilafat agitation, that 'the agitation is making rapid progress, [and] that the Maulvis and *pirs* have regained their influence through it...'[5] Between 1917 and 1922, Maulvi Khalil-ur-Rahman changed his *Al-Khalil* of Bijnor from a weekly into a bi-weekly and improved its circulation from 450 to 3000.[6] As an alim won fame and riches, he sometimes developed a taste for the things of this world. At the height of the Khilafat agitation in 1921, Abdul Bari treated himself to a Chevrolet.[7]

The ulama looked to no governing body or hierarchical chief for guidance. Nevertheless, they were not without organisation. They had all been taken through the Dars-i-Nizamia at one of the schools, and the particular training they received imposed something of a pattern upon their thinking and action. Ulama organisation, therefore, tended to be derived from the schools. In the UP there were three schools of primary importance: Maulana Ahmad Reza Khan's school at Bareilly, Firangi Mahal tucked away in an alley

[1] Interview with Mufti Reza Ansari of Firangi Mahal, 29 May 1968.
[2] A leading maulvi of the Dar-ul-ulum, Deoband, who edited two Urdu monthlies, *Al-Qasim* and *Al-Rashid*.
[3] The receipt of any permanent income was strongly opposed by the Deobandis who were thus completely dependent on subscriptions. Faruqi, *The Deoband School*, pp. 25–6.
[4] Interview with Mufti Reza Ansari of Firangi Mahal, 29 May 1968.
[5] WRDCI, 10 May 1920, Home Poll. D, June 1920, 78, NAI.
[6] Quarterly list of reported newspapers and periodicals, 1917, UPNNR 1917, and half-yearly list of reported newspapers and periodicals, corrected up to May, 1922, UPNNR 1922.
[7] Bombay Garage to Maulana Abdul Bari, June 1921, Abdul Bari Papers, File 18 (Urdu), Firangi Mahal [henceforth FM].

of the Chowk at Lucknow,[1] and the dar-ul-ulum at Deoband,[2] which Meston described in 1915 as 'a most impressive place, very like what one imagines some of the great universities of the middle ages to have been...'[3] At his school the youthful alim, sitting at the feet of a teacher, learnt his lessons on Islamic law (fiqh) and the traditions (hadith), and learnt to revere great teachers such as Mahmud-ul-Hasan, Shibli and Abdul Bari. On occasion, the pupil elevated his teacher to the rank of pir (religious guide) and became his disciple. Maulana Ahmad Reza Khan of Bareilly was the pir of Abdul Halim, head of the Anjuman Qasim-ul-Ma'arif, Mainpuri.[4] Maulana Abdul Bari, a pir from a long line of pirs, possessed immensely wide influence that stretched beyond his immediate pupils, and included the Rani of Jehangirabad, the Ali brothers and many other prominent families and politicians in the province and outside.[5]

[1] Firangi Mahal was the oldest of the leading schools in the UP. It was founded in the house of a French merchant (hence Firangi Mahal) in Lucknow with a grant given by Aurangzeb. The Mughal Emperor, it is said, had taken pity on the relatives of an eminent alim, Mulla Qutbuddin, who had been killed by jealous rivals. The fame of the institution developed with the teaching of Qutbuddin's son, Mulla Nizamuddin. He was the creator of the Dars-i-Nizamia, the curriculum employed in one form or the other in most of the madrassas of India. Firangi Mahal was never a school in the sense that Deoband was, apart from the years 1908–26 when Abdul Bari's Madrassa Nizamia flourished, but merely the quarters in which the descendants of Mulla Qutbuddin, most of whom were maulvis, lived. Interview with Mufti Reza Ansari of Firangi Mahal, 29 May 1968; Faruqi, *The Deoband School*, pp. 27–8; W. C. Smith, *Modern Islam in India* (London, 1946), p. 296.

[2] Deoband was founded in 1867, when a small 'Arabi maktab' was raised to the status of a dar-ul-ulum. The maktab had been started shortly after 1857 in the Jama Masjid of Deoband by Hafiz Syed Abid Husain. Its leading lights are said to have been survivors from the battlefields of the Mutiny. Next to Al Azhar of Cairo, it is the most important and respected theological seminary of the Muslim world. Faruqi, *The Deoband School*, pp. 22–4; W. C. Smith, *Modern Islam*, pp. 335–6.

[3] Meston to Hardinge, 25 March 1915, Hardinge Papers (89), CUL.

[4] Shaukat Ali to Abdul Bari, 23 January 1914, Abdul Bari Papers, File 1 (Urdu), FM.

[5] The following were among those who regarded Abdul Bari as a pir:
   – The Rani of Jehangirabad, originally a disciple of Abdul Bari's grandfather Abdul Razzaq, but on his death transferred her devotions to his grandson.
   – The Kidwais of Gadia, Bara Banki; Saidur Rahman Kidwai was his secretary while Mushir Husain Kidwai was closely involved with his Pan-Islamic activities.   – The Chaudhris of Paisa, Bara Banki.
   – Some of the Sherwanis of Aligarh.
   – The wife and sister of Khwaja Abdul Majid of Aligarh, Begum Abdul Majid was extremely active during the Khilafat movement, among other things editing the Urdu weekly, *Hindi*.
   – The Ali brothers.

Religious reinforcements

On completing his course, the alim went out into the world to find religious employment and carry on the traditions which he had been taught. Whatever he did, he carried the influence of his school with him. The reverence he excited in mosque or maktab was power for his school.[1] He tended to look to the old school for religious guidance[2] and would observe the fatwa and follow the lead taken by its eminent ulama. The schools, in turn, manipulated the strings of a remarkable old boy network, which increasingly they attempted to weld into a stronger, more unified organisation. The press was one means. For example, in 1915 Abdul Bari started *Al-Nizamiya*, an Urdu monthly designed to appeal to members of his school and dealing with all the latest theological developments.[3] But if the network was there to be used by the accepted leaders of a school, it was also accessible to aspirants to leadership. In 1909 Deoband divided apparently on ideological grounds.[4] The challengers of authority formed an Old Boys' Association, the Jamiat-ul-Ansar, in order to put the weight of Deoband ulama opinion behind them.[5] Just as in Aligarh the party out of power formed the Old Boys into a pressure group, so in Deoband, only a year later, the same tactic was employed. The

- Mahomed Mian Chotani, the rich Bombay timber merchant and financier of the Khilafat organisation.
- Syed Jalib Delhavi.   – Dr M. N. Ansari.
Interview with Mufti Reza Ansari of Firangi Mahal, 29 May 1968; GAD, 1917, 553, UPS; Ali brothers to Viceroy, 24 April 1919, Home Poll. A, July 1919, 1, NAI.
[1] According to the Deoband records, old pupils founded the remarkable number of 8934 maktabs and madrassas in the years 1867–1967. *Hundred Years of Darululoom Deoband*. Two of the most prominent founded in this fashion were the Mazahirul-Ulum at Saharanpur and the Qasimul-Ulum at Moradabad. Both owed their foundation to Maulana Nanautavi, the early Deoband leader, and were designed as feeders for the school. Faruqi, *The Deoband School*, pp. 23–4.   [2] *Ibid.*, pp. 23–4.
[3] Advertisement for *Al-Nizamiya*, an Urdu monthly published at Firangi Mahal, edited by Maulana Shahid and supported by Abdul Bari. Files of the paper for the years 1915–19 are in Abdul Bari's library at Firangi Mahal. Abdul Bari Papers, File 12 (Urdu), FM.
[4] Statement of Maulana Mahmud-ul-Hasan, 11 December 1917, Home Poll. B, July 1918, 92–101, NAI.
[5] Faruqi suggests that the Jamiat-ul-Ansar was formed by Mahmud-ul-Hasan, but the statements of Hasan and Nasrat Husain in 1917 made it quite clear that it was founded by Obeidullah Sindhi (see Appendix III), an alim of radical and anti-government views, in order to bend college teaching to his pan-Islamist outlook. Faruqi, *The Deoband School*, pp. 56–8; statements of Maulana Mahmud-ul-Hasan, 11 December 1917 and Nasrat Husain, 14 December 1917, Home Poll. B, July 1918, 92–101, NAI.

attempt failed, but it illustrated the possibilities that existed in turning the informal allegiances of the ulama into formal organisation. As political consciousness among this group developed, the leading ulama tried harder to acquire a tighter control over their own religious followers.

The influence of a school was greatest where its students had been successful in setting up their own institutions and where its leading ulama were recognised as pirs. It is not clear where the Bareilly school had its strongholds but the *Mashriq* of Gorakhpur and *Al Bashir* usually took note of the pro-government fatwas of Ahmad Reza Khan, and it seems that the school's permissive thinking on Islamic practice appealed especially to certain low status groups in Muslim society.[1] Deoband's influence was primarily in west UP and the Punjab, although its pupils were recruited from, and its graduates later operated throughout, the Islamic world.[2] Firangi Mahal too had a pan-Islamic reputation, but its influence was particularly strong in central and east UP and Bihar. Prominent divines of this area, for example Maulana Mahomed Quaim Abdul Quayum, Dean of the Madrassa Hanafia Jaunpur, Abul Khair of Ghazipur and Shah Badruddin Sulaiman of Phulwari, Shahabad, the leading alim of Bihar, had all studied under the ulama of Firangi Mahal.[3]

The elements of organisation among the ulama were also sources of division. Apart from a natural rivalry, religious schools were at loggerheads with each other over education and doctrine. Deoband concentrated on the traditions, textual commentary (tafsir) and disputation; Firangi Mahal on Islamic law and its methodology (usul-i-fiqh). Deoband accepted the old Islamic order in principle and tried to revive and purify it; the school rejected any reinterpretation of the canon law (ijtihad).[4] Firangi Mahal on the other hand

---

[1] The school adhered to corruptions of Islam such as saint worship and intercession at tombs; these were common among converts, particularly in rural areas, where often there were considerable similarities between Hindu and Muslim practices.

[2] In the 100 years 1867–1967 pupils came to Deoband from the following countries: *India* (UP, 1896, Bihar and Orissa, 780, Assam and Manipur, 265, East Punjab, 196, Rest of India, 658); *Pakistan* (West Pakistan, 1519, East Pakistan, 1672); Afghanistan, 109; Burma, 144; Russia and Siberia, 70; Rest of the world, 108. Source: *Hundred Years of Darululoom Deoband.*

[3] Interview with Mufti Reza Ansari of Firangi Mahal, 29 May 1968.

[4] Deoband resisted obstinately all innovation. It defended polygamy and resolutely opposed compulsory education for Muslim girls. W. C. Smith, *Modern Islam in India*, p. 336.

attempted to compromise with modern developments: it permitted reinterpretation.[1] Deoband and Bareilly were forever locked in the most bitter doctrinal battles. Although Bareilly, like Deoband, was of the Hanafi school of jurisprudence and rejected reinterpretation, its support of worship and intercession at tombs and its belief in the miraculous powers of saints were naturally anathema to the puritanical Deobandis.[2] The ulama of Firangi Mahal also objected to the Bareilly dogma.[3] The Sunni schools of ulama were prepared to ally only in doing down their hated sectarian rivals, the Shia mujtahids. Much more 'fatwa-power' was expended in trying to get the better of rival schools than in tackling the implications of British rule for the faithful.[4] A united ulama platform was immensely difficult to achieve.

In much the same way within individual schools ulama were divided over doctrinal issues, and their differences were sharpened by bitter personal rivalry. The Nadwat-ul-ulama of Lucknow was for many years rent by struggles between orthodox and reformist parties, and in 1913 Shibli almost destroyed the institution in a petty attempt to score off a doctrinal rival.[5] Deoband was divided over the question of its curriculum, and also by a straightforward struggle for power between rival factions. 'Ubaid Ullah and his friends', wrote Mahmud-ul-Hasan, principal from 1890 to 1914, 'wished to teach Arabic history, not Indian. I did not approve of it. I thought it would have a bad effect. It [the Deoband school] was founded to promote piety and religion and bringing in a secular

---

[1] Firangi Mahal accepted reinterpretation, thus recognizing the existence of the need to adapt to change, but its solutions were conservative and cautious. *Ibid.*, pp. 336–7.

[2] P. Hardy, 'The Ulama in British India', p. 9; Faruqi, *The Deoband School*, p. 40.

[3] Shaukat Ali to Abdul Bari, 23 January 1914, Abdul Bari Papers, File 1 (Urdu), FM.   [4] P. Hardy, 'The Ulama in British India', pp. 9–10.

[5] At the height of Muslim disturbance over the Balkan Wars, when Shibli was pouring poems instinct with hostility to the British Government into the pan-Islamic press, a teacher at the Nadwa, Maulvi Abdul Karim Khan, published a virulent article on jehad in the college paper, *An Nadwa*. Shibli took the remarkable course of bringing the piece to the notice of the Deputy Commissioner and inducing the board of the Nadwa to suspend Abdul Karim Khan. His action was not the result of a sudden feeling of loyalty, nor even an attempt to wheedle a bigger grant for the school, but merely an attempt to score off an old theological opponent. The vernacular press had no illusions about Shibli's motives. Note by Meston, 22 April 1915, GAD, 1914, 55, UPS; *Muslim Gazette* (Lucknow), 9 April 1913, 16 April 1913 and *Rohilkhand Gazette* (Bareilly), 16 April 1913, UPNNR 1913.

subject like history would injure it in the minds of its supporters. I told Ubaid Ullah and his friends they had no money. The school which was for "namaz rauza", would become an ordinary school."[1] Having failed to achieve reform from within, Obeid Ullah Sindhi left the college and attacked it from without. He formed the Jamiat-ul-Ansar 'to improve the management of the college...'[2] This meant cutting down the powers of the superintendent, Hafiz Mohamed Ahmad, who naturally resented this and issued a fatwa declaring Obeidullah a Kafir (unbeliever).[3] The college divided into factions and remained divided against itself throughout the period.

Firangi Mahal split irreparably over the question of what its attitude to government should be. Two parties developed when the Balkan Wars broke out, their positions hardened during the First World War and were maintained during the Khilafat movement. The first, known as the 'Madrassa Party', consisted of Abdul Bari, his disciples, relations and pupils of the Madrassa Nizamia. The second, known as the 'Bahr-ul-ulum Party', consisted of the two brothers, Maulvis Abdul Majid and Abdul Hamid, and their followers.[4] Abdul Majid and his party strongly objected to the extreme line taken by Abdul Bari over the Balkan Wars and resigned from the Madrassa Nizamia. The rivalry between the two groups, if it did not stem from personal considerations, rapidly became imbued with them. The bad blood it created lay behind many of the conspiracies among Lucknow ulama. In 1916, for example, government requested the Raja of Jehangirabad to dismiss Mahomed Bashir, a follower of Abdul Bari. Bashir, the maulvi in charge of a mosque under the Raja's control, had, encouraged by Abdul Bari, permitted a fanatical divine to include the Sultan of Turkey in the Friday sermon (Khutba).[5] Poor Jehangirabad found

[1] Statement of Maulana Mahmud-ul-Hasan, 11 December 1917, Home Poll. B, July 1918, 92–101, NAI.
[2] Statement of Nasrat Husain, 14 December 1917, Home Poll. B, July 1918, 92–101, NAI.
[3] *Ibid.*
[4] Interview with Mufti Reza Ansari of Firangi Mahal, 29 May 1968; 'The humble Memorial of Md. Barkatullah Raza of Firangi Mahal, Lucknow', Abdul Bari Papers, File 1 (English), FM.
[5] The Khutba was delivered or read out before Friday prayers. The declaration of war on Turkey had made the mention of the Sultan's name a problem. Government decided to be guided by custom. In several important mosques in the UP the practice was normal, but not in Lucknow or Allahabad. Secretariat note, 4 April 1917, GAD, 1916, 436, UPS.

himself caught on the horns of a dilemma. Directives from his zenana, where Abdul Bari was much admired, instructed him to do nothing. The government, on the other hand, considered it 'intolerable that in a mosque in the charge of the most loyal taluqdar of Oudh, prayers should be publicly recited for the victory of the Turkish Sultan'.[1] The Raja took to a diplomatic bed. He prevaricated. But eventually he had to take action. The 'Madrassa Party' were furious at 'what they regard as a victory for Abdul Hamid and Abdul Majeed...'[2] They attempted to revenge themselves by drawing public attention, through the columns of the *Indian Daily Telegraph*, to the 'scandalous' condition of the Lucknow Idgah, of which Abdul Majid was the prayer leader (pesh-Imam).[3] The 'Bahr-ul-ulum Party' countered by opposing all the doings of Abdul Bari and his gang. In 1918, with government aid, they set up a rival school in Firangi Mahal, the Madrassa Qadima.[4] In 1919, they appear to have had a hand in the internment for the dissemination of seditious pamphlets of Barkatullah Raza, a member of the staff of the Firangi Mahal Khilafatist paper, *Akhuwat*.[5] For every fatwa Abdul Bari produced in favour of the Khilafat movement, non-co-operation and Hindu–Muslim unity, they fired off one in opposition. The Lucknow battle of the fatwas achieved all-India importance when the 'Bahr-ul-ulum Party' furnished the major government fatwa refuting 'The Religious Fatwa of the Ulamas of All India' (Muttaffiqa Fatwa), which made non-co-operation mandatory on all Muslims.[6] For their activities the brothers, Abdul Hamid and Abdul Majid, were well rewarded by the government. Medals denoting the title of Shams-ul-ulama dangled from their turbans, while for his anti-Khilafat work Abdul Majid was one of the

---

[1] Note by Meston, 10 August 1916, GAD, 1914, 718, UPS.
[2] Note by Jopling, Deputy Commissioner of Lucknow, 7 August 1916, *ibid.*
[3] *Ibid.*
[4] Abdul Hamid was granted Rs. 3000 for the year 1918 'for building a school in Firangi Mahal, Lucknow'. Education, 1918, 315, UPS. The Madrassa Qadima, or Old Madrassa, exists to this day under the title Jamia Bahr-ul-ulum and is in charge of Abdul Hamid's son. Interview with Mufti Reza Ansari of Firangi Mahal, 29 May 1968.
[5] Barkatullah Raza's memorial to the lieutenant-governor was built entirely around the suggestion that he had been framed as part of the long battle between the two Firangi Mahal parties. 'The humble Memorial of Md. Barkatullah Raza of Firangi Mahal, Lucknow', Abdul Bari Papers, File 1 (English), FM.
[6] Home Poll. 1921, 137: 1922, 699, NAI.

most rewarded men in the province. At a provincial durbar in 1922, he received from Harcourt Butler both a robe and a sword of honour.[1]

The old school turban was the passport to organisation among the ulama. But it also exacerbated their natural divisiveness. They were incapable of working together. Loyalty to the teacher undermined loyalty to the school. Loyalty to the school made it difficult for ulama to take a united stand over larger issues; they could not even present a united front to the secularising processes introduced by British rule. For every alim who issued a fatwa that India was dar ul-harb there would be one who declared that it was dar ul-Islam. For every alim who opposed the government there would be one who declared his loyal support. When the ulama entered the politics of the Muslim League, it could not be all ulama, only particular factions. Nevertheless, their entry was received with considerable foreboding: even factions of ulama had influence which secular politicians feared. Islam was their stock in trade. All Muslims came within their ken, political or non-political, literate or illiterate, male or female. They could reach far beyond the English columns of the *Comrade* or the Urdu vituperation of the *Hamdard*. Other groups had not a tithe of their wide-ranging influence. English-speaking lawyers in their western suits, ignorant of the Koran but knowledgeable about a chota peg, verged on the status of Kafirs. Landed magnates, stuffy about their status and tough on their tenants, were attractive only to their toadies and dependants. The appeal of a group of ulama, however, could transcend many of the divisions of Islamic society.

Evidently the alliance of a group of ulama with some of the leading Muslim League politicians, which was heralded at Delhi in 1918, was likely to extend greatly the depths of Muslim society which political agitators could plumb. But it is important to know why ulama should become involved in League politics and from what groups they came.

There were excellent reasons for ulama to be discontented with British rule. Theoretically every Muslim activity was subject to their approval, yet the whole tendency of government was to interfere with their authority and steadily to reduce their influence in

---

[1] 'Grants of awards in connection with meritorious public service', GAD, 1921, 347, UPS.

Religious reinforcements

Muslim society. The immense growth of administrative activity both encroached on those aspects of government over which they had power and created new areas over which they had none. Ulama preserves – mosques, shrines, religious practice and susceptibility – were all beginning to come within the purview of local bureaucracy. Moreover this bureaucracy, through the increasing association of local interests with local government by means of elections, was coming under the control of Muslims who had had secular training, and of Hindus. Government was also interfering with Muslim personal law. Indeed, by legislating against the Muslim right to make waqfs, it limited an important source of ulama income. But by far the most important encroachment was the establishment of a government educational system which taught mainly secular subjects. These subjects became essential for most forms of employment, and so Muslim boys were steadily enticed away from the religious education of Islam. Immediately, as Muslim parents began to pay their school fees to the state instead of the mosque, this meant a decline in priestly income. In the long term, moreover, the drain of boys from traditional schools attacked ulama influence in Muslim society at its very roots.

Logically then, the most persistent of the early ulama responses to British rule came in the field of education. They attacked most bitterly the protagonists of English education and secular values, Syed Ahmed Khan and the Aligarh school. At the same time they tried to reinforce Islamic education against the new influences. Their endeavours took two forms: a puritanical assertion of the traditional forms of education and an attempt to come to terms with western learning. Deoband represented the first response. Soon after the Mutiny, a group of ulama from Shamli in Muzaffarnagar, who had fought against the British, decided that now the important victories were going to be won not on the battlefield but in the classroom. 'It is known', their leader Maulana Nanautavi declared, '...that the ancient disciplines never, not even in the former days of the sultans, enjoyed, on such a large scale, the generous patronage modern sciences are receiving through the increasing number of government institutions...There is no doubt that the Islamic sciences have declined tremendously...'[1] To revive and strengthen the Islamic sciences, the Shamli group

---

[1] Speech of Maulana Nanautavi at the first convocations of the dar-ul-ulum in 1874. Faruqi, *The Deoband School*, p. 30.

273

TABLE XII. *Hindus and Muslims attending private schools as a percentage of all Hindus and Muslims attending school in the UP, 1890/91–1920/21*

Year	Hindu	Muslim
1890/91	18.2	47
1900/01	13.3	39.7
1910/11	7.4	26.6
1920/21	3.8	16.4

Calculated from: *RDPI (NWP&O), 1890/91,* Table III, pp. 52–3. *RDPI (NWP&O), 1900/01,* Table IIA, p. 45. *RDPI (UP), 1910/11,* Table III, p. 7A. *RDPI (UP), 1920/21,* Table IIIA, p. 8A.

founded, in 1867, the dar-ul-ulum at Deoband. They established a syllabus which contained only traditional Islamic learning – though they were not entirely opposed to modern knowledge – and tried to set up branch institutions elsewhere in the province. The founders of Deoband believed, in the tradition of the Wahabis, that the salvation of the Muslims lay in strict adherence to the sharia. The dar-ul-ulum of the Nadwat-ul-ulama, founded in Lucknow about thirty years later, represented the second response. Here, in addition to the traditional syllabus, students were compelled to learn English. Shibli, the major force in the institution, insisted on this: a knowledge of English was vital, he believed, if the ulama were to maintain their proper role in modern Muslim society.

Traditional Islamic education was bound eventually to be over-whelmed by the new western learning. But the ulama resisted the process with some success. Even as late as 1890 nearly half of the Muslims going to school were going to private schools and there was always a much larger proportion of Muslims in the latter than Hindus.

Moreover the top institutions of traditional learning became more popular. In the first decade of the twentieth century, they expanded rapidly in the same way as did Aligarh. In 1908, Abdul Bari set up the Madrassa Nizamia at Firangi Mahal; up to this point the Lucknow school had played little part in the educational effort. Between 1907 and 1912, enrolment at Deoband leapt from 267 to 600 and the dar-ul-ulum buildings were extended.[1] At the

[1] *General Report on Public Instruction in the United Provinces of Agra and Oudh for the quinquennium ending 31st March 1912* (Allahabad, 1913), p. 99.

274

Religious reinforcements

same time, the Nadwa authorities pressed vigorously for expansion,[1] and on 1 December 1908 the lieutenant-governor laid the foundation stone of an ambitious building project.

The strengthening and expansion of traditional education, however, was not enough to ward off all the attacks on ulama influence in Muslim society. By the 1890s, some ulama had begun to perceive that the growth of elective government and modern politics meant further restriction on their influence. So they began to organise in order to make their views heard. Two years after the 1892 Councils Act, the first Nadwat-ul-ulama (Congress of Muslim theologians) met. 'Many believed', recorded Syed Suleman Nadvi, 'that this would lead to the establishment of the Government of the Maulvis.'[2] Shibli, then a dissatisfied assistant professor of Arabic at Aligarh, quickly joined the movement. He hoped, according to a friend, that 'by becoming head of religious Ulama, he would get a status and authority, which was even beyond Syed Ahmed Khan'.[3] In his first address to the Nadwat-ul-ulama in 1894, he showed how the organisation was to solve the problem of the decline of ulama authority:

Gentlemen! In the days of the Muslim rule the worldly as well as the religious affairs of the Muslims were in the hands of the ulama. In addition to indicating regulations regarding prayer, fasting, etc., the ulama decided judicial cases. They punished criminals and passed orders, awarding capital punishment or ransom. In short, the reins of the affairs of the community relating both to this and the next world were in the hands of the ulama. Now that things have changed, and worldly affairs have come under the authority of (the British) Government, we have to see what relationship the ulama have with the community, viz., what powers have been taken over by the Government, and what have been left over and are within the domain of the ulama, in which Government itself does not wish to interfere.

Attacking the notion that the role of the ulama was purely religious and concerned only with regulations regarding fasting and prayer, he insisted that 'a very large part of the national life is in the ulama's right of ownership (haqq-i-malkiyat) and they alone have or can have absolute sway (mutliq-ul-inan) over it'. He urged the ulama to join the Nadwa which 'would then be so powerful that the entire Muslim community will be governed by its injunctions.

[1] Education, 1908, 260, UPS.
[2] S. M. Ikram, *Modern Muslim India*, p. 134.
[3] *Ibid.*

275

Separatism among Indian Muslims

People will have to bow to the religious verdicts of Nadva, and will be powerless to defy its decisions.'[1] But the ulama were too divided and the government too hostile for the organisation to work, and within a few years it subsided into insignificance.

The Morley–Minto reforms, and the great outburst of political activity that surrounded them, brought forth another ulama organisation, the Majlis Muid-ul-Islam.[2] It was based entirely on Firangi Mahal and its connections. Its constitution stated that it was 'an Islamic association which seeks to promote the way of the shariat for the benefit of the Muslims. By means of this organisation, the ulama of Firangi Mahal can join with other ulama of their persuasion to work among the Islamic people.'[3] Its aims were declared to be:

(a) To try to work for the religious progress of the Islamic community within the laws of the current government, and to help the Islamic community.

(b) To help the Muslims attain progress in worldly matters, while keeping in mind the injunctions of the shariat.

(c) To propagate the injunctions of the shariat among the Islamic community and to overcome opposition to it.[4]

Membership cost Rs. 3 p.a.[5] but the right to join was a privilege restricted to associates of Firangi Mahal.[6] Members were to avoid 'any matter of business...which might be the cause of doctrinal disputes or which might cause factional quarrels within the association'.[7] They were to eschew free thinking.[8] Branch associations were to be formed wherever possible.[9] The Majlis was to meet once a month, not necessarily in Lucknow, and the remarkable provision was made that the occasion could take the form of a general meeting open to non-members, both Muslim and non-

[1] *Khutbat-i-Shibli*, pp. 29–33, quoted in *ibid.*, pp. 139–40.
[2] The Majlis Muid-ul-Islam was a more ambitious version of another society founded earlier in 1910 called the Majlis-e-Islah (Society of Reform).
[3] 'The constitution of the Majlis Muid-ul-Islam', dated Firangi Mahal, Lucknow, 1328 AH (1912), article 1. Urdu leaflet in the private library of Mufti Reza Ansari of Firangi Mahal.
[4] *Ibid.*, article 2. Section C of article 2 was elaborated in article 7; 'It is incumbent upon the members of the Majlis to work for the reform of the religious, moral, and social conduct of the Muslims, to give their serious attention to principles and customs which are contrary to the sharia, and make efforts to set them on the right path.'
[5] *Ibid.*, article 19.
[6] *Ibid.*, article 3.
[7] *Ibid.*, article 8.
[8] *Ibid.*, article 9.
[9] *Ibid.*, article 18.

Muslim.[1] Abdul Bari was appointed president and Salamatullah, secretary. The Majlis was important because, for the first time, a formal organisation was imposed over the connections and allegiances of an ulama school.

Simultaneously Shia ulama, the mujtahids, asserted themselves. But they did not need to found an organisation. They captured one. The foundation of the Sunni-dominated All-India Muslim League in 1906 had encouraged the Shias to organise, and in 1907 they established the All-India Shia Conference. Secular men took the lead in its early sessions, passing resolutions on the need for more western education, the development of technical education and industries.[2] But from the beginning the mujtahids made their presence felt and the Conference passed resolutions insisting that religious education be given a place in government schools[3] and that a theological college should be founded.[4] By the 1910 Conference at Amroha, early secular enthusiasm had died. The deadweight of religious orthodoxy had smothered the reforming zeal of the young, educated Shias, and the mujtahids had captured the organisation. They put forward most of the resolutions, and regarded it to be a right that one of their number should act as president. Men such as Ghulam-us-Saqlain, who had taken a vigorous part in early meetings, resigned. The young, English-educated Shias, such as the Raja of Mahmudabad, Wazir Hasan, Riza Ali and Ali Nabi were conspicuous by their absence.[5] The emphasis of the Conference changed from the furtherance of western science and learning in the community to the reinforcement of orthodox Shiism,[6] an emphasis which was reflected in the Shia College, founded in 1918, in which not an iota of modern learning was to be had without a strong antidote of Shia doctrine.

These attempts to organise in order to meet the threats which modern education and politics presented to priestly authority were the work of the leading ulama from the great schools of the province.

---

[1] *Ibid.*, article 11.
[2] Resolutions VIII and IX of the All-India Shia Conference, Lucknow, 1908, xv, 728, 1909, LCA.
[3] Resolution VII of the All-India Shia Conference, Lucknow, 1908, *ibid.*
[4] Resolution XVI of the All-India Shia Conference, Lucknow, 1909, *ibid.*
[5] Syed Riza Ali to Editor, *Leader* (Allahabad), 26 March 1920.
[6] For example, Syed Ali Hairi, mujtahid of the Punjab, devoted the whole of his Presidential speech to the 1914 All-India Shia Conference at Lucknow to urging the necessity of reinforcing orthodox Shiism in education. *Ibid.*, 21 October 1914.

But not all ulama were affiliated to the great schools and not all who were affiliated were moved by their initiatives. Many, in fact, had to live and get on in local society, on which they often depended for their income, and could not afford the luxury, however much they regretted it, of preaching rigid adherence to orthodox Islam. The sajjada-nashins (sitters on the carpet or head ulama) of the Diara Shah Hajatullah at Allahabad, Mahomed Husain and his son Wilayat Husain who succeeded him, are a case in point. Far from attacking Aligarh and all its works, Mahomed Husain appears to have been influenced by it. Certainly, when he opposed the Congress in February 1888, he merely repeated in parrot fashion the arguments concerning representation and entry into government service which Syed Ahmed had used two months earlier in his great set piece at Lucknow, 'On the Present State of Indian Politics'. Of course, he and his followers did not attend the 1888 Congress, while the Deobandi ulama did. In the same way, Mahomed and Wilayat Husain do not seem to have shared the fundamental hostility to government of many of their clerical colleagues. True they did agitate against the Nagri resolution but generally they worked closely with the local authorities in controlling the city's Muslim population, and for this Wilayat Husain received the title Khan Bahadur in 1911. Indeed, the activities of the sajjada-nashins of the Diara Shah Hajatullah owed more to the political needs of the minority community they led in Allahabad than any general perception of what ulama should do.[1]

The considerable development of communal awareness from 1910, derived mainly from the Morley–Minto reforms and to a lesser extent from the growth of pan-Islamism, helped to bridge the gaps between the ulama of the leading schools and other groups in Muslim society. Contacts between leading and local ulama became more frequent. Groups in Firangi Mahal and Deoband began to organise potential support, and ulama in the localities responded to these initiatives. Abdul Wadud of Bareilly and Azad Sobhani of Cawnpore followed the Firangi Mahal lead in the mosque agitation of 1913. When four years later the Majlis Muid-ul-Islam arranged a deputation to present an address to the Viceroy and Secretary of State, it persuaded ulama of as varied points of view as Abdul Majid of Budaun, Wilayat Husain of

---

[1] C. A. Bayly, 'The Development of Political Organization in the Allahabad Locality, 1880–1925' (unpublished D.Phil. thesis, Oxford, 1970), pp. 168–80.

Allahabad, Ahmad Reza Khan of Bareilly, and the two leading
Shia mujtahids of Lucknow, to join. But the most dramatic evidence of the drawing together of the ulama lay in the membership
of the Anjuman-i-Khuddam-i-Kaaba. The organisation was based
on Firangi Mahal; the leading ulama of Deoband and Bareilly
opposed it.[1] Not surprisingly, the anjuman could call on the
support of the school's usual associates such as Abdul Majid of
Budaun, Moinuddin of Moradabad and Shah Sulaiman of Phulwari. But it also attracted priests of all kinds: ulama of local
importance such as Abdul Jalil of Benares and Mian Khwaja
Ahmad of Rampur: ulama of different schools and sects such as
Shibli, Obeidullah Sindhi, the renegade Deobandi, Abdul Halim
of Mainpuri, who followed the Bareilly line, as well as the leading
Shia mujtahids of Lucknow and Lahore: ulama from all over
India – Calcutta, Hyderabad, Bombay and Sind. Membership was
not just a matter of being a name on a list. Many headed local
branches and Abdul Bari corresponded personally with them.[2] Of
course, this did not mean that all these ulama would invariably
follow the Khadim-ul-Kaaba's dictates. Nor did it mean that all
these contacts were being made for the first time. Nevertheless, it
does indicate the growth of connections among the ulama after
1910, many of which were to bear fruit in the Khilafat agitation.

No less significant for the future of Muslim politics was the
development of connections between the leading ulama schools
and the young western-educated Muslims. Remarkably, the first
attempts at rapprochement appear to have been made between
those deadly enemies, Aligarh and Deoband. Of course, these did
not take place while Syed Ahmed was alive: he adhered too strongly
to his belief in modern education and was too well-hated by the
ulama. But the secretaries of Aligarh, who succeeded Syed Ahmed,

---

[1] In 1913, the Deoband ulama issued a fatwa, published in *Mashriq* (Gorakhpur),
against the movement, Nawab Ishaq Khan to Meston, 5 January 1914,
Meston Papers (6), IOL, and the Deoband leader, Habibur Rahman, repeatedly
refused to join the anjuman. Maulana Habibur Rahman Deobandi to Abdul
Bari, 1 Safar 1332 and 14 Rabi'Awwal 1332, Abdul Bari Papers, File 1 (Urdu),
FM. In the summer of 1913, Ahmad Reza Khan issued a fatwa against the
anjuman, Nawab Ishaq Khan to Meston, 5 January 1914, Meston Papers (6),
IOL, and again in 1914 when he declared 'that the Anjuman by admitting to
membership adherents of all kinds of unorthodox sects, is really subversive
of Islam and is therefore unworthy of support'. WRDCI, 15 June 1915,
Home Poll. B, June 1915, 549–52, NAI.
[2] Abdul Bari Papers, Files 1 and 3 (Urdu), FM, and file on the Anjuman-i-
Khuddam-i-Kaaba in the Mahomed Ali Papers (Urdu), JMI.

did take steps to make a compromise with the ulama and orthodox education. Mohsin-ul-Mulk set up an Arabic department[1] and made overtures to the ulama; Abdul Bari, his biographer, praised him highly for his diplomacy.[2] Viqar-ul-Mulk increased the religious content of the Aligarh syllabus. Students had to pass a paper on 'Islamic Religion', and if they played truant from daily prayers they were threatened with expulsion.[3] Some ulama were so pleased by these developments that they began to deliver sermons at the College and send their children there.[4] By 1910, relations were so friendly that Aftab Ahmad Khan was able to lead an Aligarh deputation to attend a Deoband Jalsa-i-Dastarbandi, where arrangements were made for the exchange of students.[5] But enthusiasm for such manifestations of good will evaporated after the first two Aligarh visitors to Deoband turned out to be secret agents.[6]

As secular leaders attempted to give effect in the Aligarh curriculum to their rapprochement with the ulama, some ulama attempted to give it tangible form within the orthodox system. Under the patronage of Hakim Ajmal Khan and Viqar-ul-Mulk, Obeidullah Sindhi, who had been asked to leave Deoband for his unorthodox ideas on the curriculum, set up the Nazarat-ul-Maarif-ul-Qurania (Academy of Koranic learning) in the Fatehpuri Mosque at Delhi. He aimed to redress the balance of secular education by teaching the Koran to English-educated Muslims, and hoped to establish his system on an all-India basis.[7] The school operated successfully until Sindhi's involvement in the 'Silk Letters Conspiracy'[8] forced him to leave the country.

[1] Home Examinations, D, July 1904, 31–5; Home Education, A, November 1904, 35–6 and November 1905, 30–1, NAI.
[2] S. M. Ikram, *Modern Muslim India*, p. 85.
[3] *Ibid.*, p. 210.
[4] *Ibid.*, p. 121, and today the sons of Firangi Mahal ulama still go to Aligarh.
[5] A leading article entitled 'The Moslem University and the Ulama', *Comrade* (Calcutta), 11 February 1911.
[6] Faruqi, *The Deoband School*, p. 58, footnote 2.
[7] 'The Rules of the Nazarat-ul-Maarif-ul-Qorania', published in *Mashriq* (Gorakhpur), 1 July 1913, UPNNR 1913.
[8] A plot, in which Obeidullah Sindhi, Mahmud-ul-Hasan, A. K. Azad, Hasrat Mohani, Hakim Abdur Razzak Ansari, and perhaps Dr Ansari, Abdul Bari and the Ali brothers, were involved, to raise the tribes on the North-West Frontier, with Turkish and German help, against the British during the First World War. The plot was given the name 'Silk Letters Conspiracy' because communications between plotters in Afghanistan and India were made by means of letters written on bales of silk.

Religious reinforcements

Deoband and Aligarh, however, were too far apart in aim as well as in geography for these tentative approaches to result in united political action. The effective rapprochement between secular and religious leaders occurred in Lucknow, between 'Young Party' men and the ulama of Firangi Mahal. It is probable that there had always been connections between the leading ulama of Firangi Mahal and the prominent men of the Nawabi city. Important 'Young Party' men certainly had associations with the school. The Raja of Mahmudabad was a distant relative of Abdul Bari and, of course, helped to finance its political activities.[1] Mushir Husain Kidwai regarded Abdul Bari as a pir and his brothers, Ehsanhur and Saidur Rahman, were to work for the maulana during the Khilafat movement. Dr Naziruddin Hasan is said to have been Abdul Bari's closest adviser, almost an éminence grise, and he was involved in all the early 'Young Party' and ulama campaigns, though he avoided the limelight.[2] When, from 1912, 'Young Party' men began to cast around for means of forcing government to take account of Muslim interests, such contacts helped to win Firangi Mahal and its influence for their politics of protest. Firangi Mahal ulama were soon to be found following the initiatives of the Ali brothers. The Majlis Muid-ul-Islam worked for the Red Crescent Fund:[3] it warned the government to abstain from putting diplomatic pressure on Turkey.[4] Abdul Bari played a leading part in the Cawnpore Mosque agitation and settlement.[5] At the same time, with Mushir Husain Kidwai, he concocted the Anjuman-i-Khuddam-i-Kaaba scheme and sold it to Shaukat Ali, who put it into operation. Abdul Bari, the president of the Majlis Muid-ul-

[1] 'Akhtar' to Abdul Bari, 20 May 1916, Abdul Bari Papers, File 8 (English); Series of interviews with the Maharajkumar of Mahmudabad, Lucknow and Mahmudabad, June 1968; Interview with Mufti Reza Ansari of Firangi Mahal, 29 May 1968.
[2] Interview with Mufti Reza Ansari of Firangi Mahal, 29 May 1968.
[3] A leaflet taking the form of an appeal to Indian Muslims from the Majlis Muid-ul-Islam, Firangi Mahal, asking them to contribute to the fund they were collecting to carry on the work of the organisation against the Turko-Balkan Wars and to help the unfortunate Turkish and Arab victims. Muslims were asked to send their contributions to the *Comrade* (Delhi), the *Zamindar* (Lahore), The Red Crescent, Lucknow, or the Majlis Muid-ul-Islam, Firangi Mahal. Abdul Bari Papers, File 8 (Urdu), FM.
[4] Report of a meeting in the *Advocate* (Lucknow), 30 January 1913, Home Poll. B, March 1913, 44–55, NAI.
[5] *Muslim Gazette* (Lucknow), 13 August 1913; *Zul Qarnain* (Budaun), 21 October 1913; *Rohilkhand Gazette* (Bareilly), 8 December 1913, UPNNR 1913.

Islam, became Khadim-ul-Khuddam, and in the framework of the anjuman 'Young Party' men and ulama worked together.

During World War One, the 'Young Party' leaders maintained their close association with the Firangi Mahal ulama. At the outbreak of the war, Deoband and the Nadwa passed fervent resolutions of loyalty,[1] and maintained this stand throughout the war. But Abdul Bari and Firangi Mahal, again under the influence of the 'Young Party', were more diffident. In September 1914, the maulana and Mahmudabad sent telegrams to the Sultan begging him to remain neutral or join Britain.[2] The Sultan was not impressed. When Turkey actually entered the war, Abdul Bari played the same devious game as the 'Young Party'. Confronted with the prospect of a public meeting which would announce their loyalty to the British, 'Mahmudabad behaved like a petulant child. He shuffled and prevaricated', while 'Abdul Bari shut his doors and would not receive the invitation to it; then he consented to come if there were no speeches; finally he agreed to bring his faction if the word "Turkey" were not used at the meeting'.[3] At the beginning of 1915, Abdul Bari allowed the Ali brothers to write a series of letters in the *Hamdard* under his signature, refuting Abdul Haq of Calcutta's fatwa which had laid down that Turkey's war was political, and therefore did not concern good Muslims.[4] When the Sherif of Mecca revolted, the maulana, despite considerable private reservations (he was a personal friend of the Sherif), fully supported the Muslim League's resolution of condemnation,[5] and tried to wheel Deoband in behind him. For his pains he was snubbed with the suggestion that he was 'a busybody who could not read his Koran rightly'.[6] Whenever there was a crisis, when-

[1] Deoband passed a 'fervent resolution of loyalty'. FR (UP), Home Poll. D, October 1914, 61, NAI; after the entry of Turkey into the war the Nadwa declared that India was dar-ul-Islam. WRDCI, 29 September 1914, Home Poll. B, January 1915, 278–82, NAI.
[2] FR (UP), Home Poll. D, October 1914, 61 and November 1914, 34, NAI.
[3] Meston to Hardinge, 25 March 1915, Hardinge Papers (89), CUL. Moreover Abdul Bari got his way, There were neither speeches at the meeting nor any reference to Turkey. It just passed resolutions of loyalty. FR (UP), Home Poll. D, December 1914, 32, NAI.
[4] Meston to Hardinge, 25 March 1915, Hardinge Papers (89), CUL; WRDCI, 2 February 1915, Home Poll. B, February 1915, 777–80, NAI; FR (UP), Home Poll. D, March 1915, 55, NAI.
[5] WRDCI, 8 July 1916, Home Poll. B, July 1916, 441–5, NAI, and for the text of Abdul Bari's telegram to the Viceroy on this occasion, Abdul Bari Papers, File 10 (English), FM.
[6] FR (UP), Home Poll. D, September 1916, 17, NAI.

ever the voice of orthodoxy was needed to add weight to the politics of protest, Abdul Bari could be relied upon to play his part, It was an alliance without precedent: Aligarh's brightest sons and Lucknow's most learned divines stood shoulder to shoulder on the issues of the day. Syed Ahmed Khan must have turned in his grave.

The 'Young Party's' advantage in being able to switch on the voice of orthodox Islam is obvious, but what was in it for Abdul Bari? When he began to support 'Young Party' politics, those who knew him were surprised. 'I may be wrong', Harcourt Butler commented, 'but I have known him for many years and believe him to be well-disposed.'[1] Government could only conclude that he was 'a sincere man, but is ignorant and bigoted and probably an unwilling tool of politicians such as Muhammad Ali'.[2] There is much truth in this assessment. Abdul Bari, as an apprentice in politics, was confused, suggestible and easily manipulated. 'He was', he told the commissioner of Lucknow in September 1914, 'often perplexed what to believe.'[3] On the other hand, Abdul Bari certainly revelled in the fame he gained through politics, and was concerned to use it to extend his influence as an alim; he is, Meston declared, 'the most pestilent of all our prelates. Eaten up with vanity and conceit his ambition is to beome the spiritual director of the "Young Turk" party in India...'[4] In spite of these earthly ambitions, however, the maulana's primary concern was his faith. His religious outlook tended to be pan-Islamic, a result perhaps of his student days in Constantinople. His religious beliefs he held fanatically, indeed, on occasion he appeared to seek martyrdom.[5] When he had to choose between the paths of religion and those of Muslim politics, there was no doubt that he would take the former.

Abdul Bari's religious rather than political aims made him potentially a difficult ally for 'Young Party' men. To this was added a second problem; as the maulana became more experienced

---

[1] Note by Harcourt Butler, May 1914, Home Poll. A, May 1914, 46, NAI.
[2] R. Burn, Chief Secretary to Government, UP, to H. Wheeler, Home Department, Government of India, 10 June 1913, Home Poll. D, July 1913, 7, NAI.
[3] Note on a conversation between H. V. Lovett, Commissioner of Lucknow, and Maulana Abdul Bari, 19 September 1914, FR (UP), Home Poll. D, November 1914, 34, NAI.
[4] Meston to Chelmsford, 11 August 1916, Meston Papers (1), IOL.
[5] FR (UP), Home Poll. D, August 1915, 2, NAI.

in politics, he became more independent. The difficulties which his essentially different aims and his growing independence could create are illustrated by his reaction to the Shahabad riots of October 1917, when many Muslims were killed by Hindus.[1] For the 'Young Party' men who had made the Lucknow Pact, it was crucially important, in view of the Secretary of State's impending visit, that this event should not be allowed to mar the appearance of communal harmony. Abdul Bari, however, on hearing news of the riots, became by his own account 'beside himself'.[2] Regardless of the consequences, he rose at a Lucknow meeting 'and proclaimed *Jehad* against the Hindus. About 50 men rose and offered to follow him. Fortunately there were no Hindus present excepting the editor of the Advocate, who disappeared...'[3] The enraged maulana was persuaded to take a less drastic course. Nevertheless his reaction to the riots was damaging. He telegraphed his intention to the Lahore ulama:

Mussalmans nominal leaders and outward coreligionists are in delusion of union with infidels. If ulema keep silent Mussalmans will suffer great loss. The matter must be consulted over and a deputation of ulemas presented before Sec of State.[4]

He followed this by calling all ulama to a meeting of the Majlis Muid-ul-Islam on 30 October at Lucknow. His circular leaflet began with the statement that 'we are Muslims first and Indians second'.[5] The 'Old Party' were delighted with this denial of 'Young Party' policy. Jehangirabad jumped in and offered to pay all the expenses of the ulama deputation on condition that it declared against Home Rule.[6] With such impeccable support, the organisers of the deputation could hope to give it a very broad base. The deputation was to include Shia mujtahids as well as Wilayat Husain of Allahabad and Ahmad Reza Khan of Bareilly.

[1] These were one of the most severe outbreaks of communal rioting that took place under the British in India. In the Shahabad district of Bihar, 143 Muslim villages were attacked by rioters, in Gaya, thirty-one, and in Patna, two. Vast bands of Hindus up to 50,000 strong rampaged over the country. It took ten days to bring Shahabad district under control.

[2] Abdul Bari to Editor, *Hamdam* (Lucknow), 16 December 1917, UPNNR 1917.

[3] FR (UP), Home Poll. D, January 1918, 1, NAI.

[4] Abdul Bari to Tajuddin, 13 October 1917, copy of the text of a telegram, Abdul Bari Papers, File 10 (English), FM.

[5] Leaflet issued by Abdul Bari calling a meeting of ulama in Lucknow, dated 26 Zil-hijja 1335 (1917), Abdul Bari Papers, File 6 (Urdu), FM.

[6] *New Era* (Lucknow), 10 November 1917.

The Deobandis, characteristically, objected 'strongly to coming in with the Lucknow lot, who call themselves the Muid-ul-Islam but belong to Firangi Mahal and Abdul Bari'.[1] The remainder, however, followed the Firangi Mahal lead.[2] A draft address was prepared, uncompromising and instinct with hostility towards the Hindus.[3] 'Young Party' men were desperately worried. The man who had been their tool, whom they could not credibly disown, was jeopardising the Congress–League scheme – the whole of their political achievement. The Lucknow leaders called up their cohorts in order to swamp the meeting in which the ulama were to discuss the draft. Hakim Ajmal Khan and Ansari came down from Delhi, Khwaja Abdul Majid from Aligarh. Mahmudabad summoned Syed Mahmud from Bihar. 'To avert a disaster,' he told Mahmud, 'it is absolutely necessary that the point of view of educated Mohammadans should be presented and pressed in the meeting.'[4] The 'Young Party' stormed into the meeting of the 30th

[1] R. Burn, Chief Secretary to Government, UP, to W. S. Marris, Secretary to the Reforms Deputation, 11 November 1917, GAD, 1917, 553, UPS.

[2] Those who finally formed the Majlis Muid-ul-Islam deputation were: Abdul Aziz and Abdul Bari of Firangi Mahal, Abdul Majid of Budain, Wilayat Husain of Allahabad, Ahmad Reza Khan of Bareilly, Aga Hasan and Nasir Husain, mujtahids of Lucknow, and Nawab Maulvi Abdul Majid of Jaunpur.

[3] 'A separate department should be created for all the Moslem trusts with necessary offices in each province, division and district that Musalmans may easily get necessary information about them and have facilities in matters relating thereto. This department should be under the supervision of Moslem Committees with a fair number of Moslem Ulemas in it and that laws should be made for the sanctity of the religious places of the Musalmans. (2) Wine drinking and adultery are to be considered crimes for Mahomedans. (3) This meeting of Ulemas announces that it is our principle that whenever an act of *Sunnet* is prohibited by force it becomes compulsory for Mahomedans to do it, and on account of poverty cow sacrifice also becomes compulsory on some occasions, and under the circumstance we consider cow sacrifice a doctrine of Islam and its protection is essential. We draw the attention of the Government to safeguard the doctrine of Islam against any interference. (4) The committee expects all Mahomedans to ardently help our brethren who have suffered and express every sympathy with the sufferers. The committee requests them not to accept any help from the class which has committed the crime of disparaging Islam as acceptance is itself of the an [sic] insult. (5) This meeting of Ulemas suggest that the Government may be requested to issue instructions against recurrence of the trouble which the Mahomedans have received at the hands of non-Moslems for the purpose of safeguarding the right of sacrifices and respect of mosques. (6) This meeting requests the Government that all enquiries in connexion with the case of the riots be conducted by non-Hindus.' Report in the *Indian Daily Telegraph* (Lucknow), 6 November 1917, GAD, 1917, 553, UPS.

[4] Raja of Mahmudabad to Syed Mahmud, 27 October 1917, Syed Mahmud Papers, NMM.

and succeeded in removing the highly provocative clauses (3), (5)
and (6) of the draft and replacing them with the more diplomatic
clause (*d*) of the address.[1] Its whole tone was altered. It was no
longer an attack on the Hindus, but an assertion of the sharia
against the administrative activity of the Government. However,
the ulama stood firm by clause (4) of their draft address. The
'Young Party' leaders left Lucknow, leaving a supposedly
chastened Abdul Bari to remove the offending clause.[2] He did so.[3]
They were mollified.[4] The address of the representatives of orthodox Islam, instead of being an attack on the Hindus and making
a nonsense of Hindu–Muslim unity, appeared, as government
described it, as 'a nakedly impracticable demand for the pre-
domination of priestly influence', in which respect it bore little
difference from the address of the ulama of Deoband.[5]

[1] By the time the 'Young Party' had finished with it, the address of the Majlis
Muid-ul-Islam looked very different:
'(a) The Musalmans of India should be allowed to enjoy complete religious
freedom, and that at no time and in no wise their religious rights and usages
should be interfered with by the Government.
(b) That in legislation regard should always be had that no law or part of law
affecting the Musalmans of India should be contrary to the tenets of Islam.
(c) All cases and disputes relating to the religious rights of the Musalmans of
India, for instance, marriage, divorce, succession, *waqf* and pre-emption,
etc., should be decided in accordance with the laws of Islam by such Muslim
judicial officials who may possess the knowledge of such laws, and that the
recognised Alim or Mujtahid of each section, as the case may be, should have
the power of revision over those decisions.
(d) Other religious communities of India should not be permitted to make a
departure from the customs and usages hitherto adopted by them in the performance of their religious rites affecting the Musalmans of India, and that
they should have no right to interfere with, or obstruct the exercise of, our
customary and prevalent religious rites.
(e) Drinking and fornication should be declared crimes as against the
Musalmans.
(f) The Government and its representatives should, as promised, respect the
sanctity of Muslim Holy places under all circumstances, and that they should
be kept immune from the ravages of war.'
GAD, 1917, 553, UPS; Montagu Papers (35), IOL.
[2] The Delhi leaders, Ajmal Khan and Ansari, appear to have left Abdul Bari
with an ultimatum to change clause (4), but, unfortunately, there is no hint
of what it was. Abdul Bari to Hakim Ajmal Khan, 2 November 1917, telegram,
Abdul Bari Papers, File 10 (English), FM.
[3] Abdul Bari to Hakim Ajmal Khan, 2 November 1917, a second telegram,
Abdul Bari Papers, File 10 (English), FM.
[4] Hakim Ajmal Khan and Dr Ansari to Abdul Bari, 2 November 1917, telegram,
Abdul Bari Papers, File 10 (English), FM.
[5] Note by the UP government for the information of the Reforms Deputation
on the address of the Majlis Muid-ul-Islam, undated, GAD, 1917, 553, UPS.

Religious reinforcements

Abdul Bari was unabashed by this rebuff, and in 1918 he developed markedly as an agitator. In January he tried to re-organise the Anjuman-i-Khuddam-i-Kaaba. The headquarters were to be set up under him in Lucknow and the object was to agitate for the release of the Muslim internees.[1] But though he was careful to state that Shaukat Ali, who was of course still interned, would not be allowed to get his hand in the till, the reputation of the organisation was so bad that no one would have anything to do with it.[2] Nevertheless, throughout the year the maulana continued to work for the release of his disciples. In addition, he attacked the Nadwat-ul-ulama for failing to try either to unify the ulama or to assert the Sharia.[3] He eulogised the spotless record of the Firangi Mahal ulama in protecting Muslim rights, and true to his boast, when ulama in Bengal called him down to Calcutta to agitate over an unfortunate newspaper article which had likened the prophet's tomb to the gutter,[4] he and his Firangi Mahal followers went with alacrity. So, when in December 1918 Ansari and Ajmal Khan wanted religious sanction for the demands they wished the Muslim League to make concerning the Khilafat and Holy Places, though they must have had qualms about their ability to control him, Abdul Bari was their man. They invited the ulama of Firangi Mahal and Deoband. The latter refused,[5] but Abdul Bari and his followers came, the maulana himself taking a hand in writing Ansari's welcoming speech which ran close to being an incitement to jihad.[6] Indeed, government noticed that the 'only maulvis who attended the Muslim League meeting in Delhi were Abdul Bari and his immediate associates'.[7] Thus, when ulama entered modern

[1] FR (UP), Home Poll. D, March 1918, 39, NAI; *Nai Roshni* (Allahabad), 11 January 1918, and *Hamdam* (Lucknow), 27 January 1918, UPNNR 1918.

[2] *Hamdam* (Lucknow), 6 February 1918, UPNNR 1918; FR (UP), Home Poll. D, March 1918, 39, NAI.

[3] Article by Abdul Bari in *Hamdam* (Lucknow), 11 May 1918, UPNNR 1918.

[4] Ghiasuddin, general secretary of the Muinul-Islam, to Abdul Bari, 17 August 1918, Abdul Bari Papers, File 4 (Urdu), FM.

[5] Hafiz Mohamed Ahmed to Hakim Ajmal Khan and Dr Ansari, no date, a copy in Abdul Bari Papers, File 16 (Urdu), FM.

[6] Report by Tassaduq Hussein, 1 January 1919, Home Poll. A, March 1919, 251–9, NAI.

[7] FR (UP), Home Poll. D, February 1919, 41, NAI. The ulama were: Ibrahim of Sialkot, Sanaullah of Amritsar, Kifayatullah of Delhi, Koramanullah, Abdul Latif, Abdul Hasan, Azad Subhani of Cawnpore, Ahmad Said of Delhi, Salamatullah and Abdul Bari of Lucknow.

Muslim politics, it was not the representatives of all ulama, but the Firangi Mahal faction which was led by Abdul Bari.

Any alliance between ulama and secular Muslim politicians rested on shaky foundations. Their interests, as the Majlis Muid-ul-Islam address indicates, were fundamentally different, if not opposed. Secular Muslim politicians were interested in cutting out a share of power for themselves in the framework of elective government being set up by their rulers. But the ulama simply were not interested in this system of government, which would maintain the secular control of Muslim society established by the British. Abdul Bari stated their view exactly: the only true 'Home Rule' for the Muslims, he declared, would be the enforcement of the sharia.[1] Ulama were interested in protecting traditional Islam and their position within it. They were prepared to ally with secular Muslim politicians only when the latter were concerned to press Muslim religious interests on government or to oppose the regime as a whole.

[1] *Jadu* (Jaunpur), 21 May 1918, UPNNR 1918.

CHAPTER 8

Religion overwhelms politics
1919-1920

The growth of the alliance between the 'Young Party' leaders and the Congress, and the increasing involvement of the ulama in the politics of the Muslim League, were the most remarkable developments in UP Muslim politics during the war. The first led to the Lucknow Pact of 1916 and the second to the attendance of the ulama at the 1918 League session. The two years that followed the war were to bring changes that were no less notable. Ulama became much more than useful agitational tools to be deployed by western-educated politicians, indeed from time to time they took the lead in Muslim politics. The Muslim League, the home of Muslim politics, disappeared from view completely, being overwhelmed by the new all-India Khilafat organisation. Hindus began to play a much bigger part in Muslim affairs. Arya Samajists such as Swami Shraddhanand and Pandit Neki Ram were to be found addressing Muslim meetings, while for a time the overall direction of Muslim politics, once the charge of Syed Ahmed, Mohsin-ul-Mulk and Viqar-ul-Mulk, lay in the hands of a Hindu bania, Mahatma Gandhi. Muslims, on the other hand, began to play a greater part in the Congress. Indeed, so great did their influence become in the organisation that they were mainly responsible both for the powerful position that Gandhi attained in Indian politics by September 1920 and for the Congress's decision to boycott the new reformed councils.

At the beginning of 1919 such extraordinary developments seemed unlikely. The major issues in Muslim politics were the council reforms and the Khilafat. Anticipation of the former had already increased the divisions among UP Muslim politicians, attracting landlords and some professional men away from the Muslim League and its anti-government politics. And more were to go the same way over the next two years as their prospects of getting into the new councils became brighter. But at the beginning of 1919 all that was to be known about the forthcoming reforms was in the Montagu–Chelmsford report. This agreed reluctantly to communal representation for Muslims and remained equivocal in its attitude to the crucial point for UP Muslims, the proposals of the Congress–League scheme for extra representation to allow for their 'political importance'.[1] The Muslims were worried by what they felt was a change in government's attitude to their claims. 'The question of separate electorates and communal representation', Dr Ansari reminded government at the Muslim League's 1918 session, 'is the life and soul of all our political activities of the present day', and he went on to emphasise most strongly the value that the community placed on the principle of 'political importance' which had been acknowledged in the Morley–Minto reforms and confirmed by the Lucknow Pact.[2]

The doubts which the Montagu–Chelmsford report raised in the mind of Muslim politicians concerning government's sensitivity to their demands were massively increased by government's attitude to the Khilafat and the Holy Places of Islam. For some Indian Muslims it was, and others discovered it could become, an article of faith that the spiritual head of Islam, the Khalifa, who was the Sultan of Turkey, should wield enough temporal power to defend the faith and the faithful; that the Jazirat-ul-Arab, Arabia as defined by the Muslim religious authorities, should according to the prophet's dying injunction remain in Muslim hands; and that the Holy Places, Mecca, Medina, Jerusalem and the Holy Shrines, Najaf, Kerbella, Sammerra, Kaziman and Baghdad should remain not only in Muslim hands but subject to the Khalifa.[3] Whenever, in the nineteenth and early twentieth centuries, there had been threats to Turkish control over these areas, Indian Muslims had protested. The most recent and most vigorous agitation had been that which had raged between 1911 and 1915. For most of World War One, however, the partial success of Ottoman arms, the rigid provisions of the Defence of India Act, and the promises of the British and American governments that

[1] Report on Indian Constitutional Reforms, 1918, *P.P.*, 1918, VIII, pp. 256–7, 307–10.
[2] Speech by Dr Ansari as chairman of the Reception Committee of the Delhi sessions of the All-India Muslim League, December 1918. Home Poll. A, March 1919, 251–9, NAI.
[3] Manifesto adopted in resolution (10) of the third All-India Khilafat Conference at Bombay, 15–17 February 1920, FR (Bombay), Home Poll. D, July 1920, 89, NAI, and statement by Mahomed Ali to the editor of *Britain and India*, which was quoted in the *Independent* (Allahabad), 8 May 1920.

Turkish sovereignty would be respected[1] kept protest in check. But in October 1918 Turkey was overcome by Allenby's armies. Soon after Constantinople was occupied by the Allies, the British Prime Minister, hotly supported by the Archbishop of Canterbury, began to use the language of the crusades, and in August 1920 by the Treaty signed at Sèvres, the Sultan was reduced to the status of a British puppet and the Ottoman Empire shared out between Britain, France, Greece, Italy and the Arabs. This settlement, and those that followed it, were not the result of any lack of sensitivity to Muslim demands on the part of those responsible for Indian affairs. The Government of India emphasised continually and strongly their disastrous effect on the Indian Muslims. The Secretary of State ruined his health and his political career in urging the cabinet to adopt the Turkish cause.[2] But all to no avail. Turkish affairs, like council reforms and other matters that concerned Indian Muslims, were not decided finally by the India Office but by the British Parliament.

The agitation to preserve the Khilafat and the Holy Places of Islam from their fate initiated the last climactic phase of Indian pan-Islamism. It revealed more clearly than any other agitation those who supported pan-Islamism and the reasons why they found it attractive. Most Muslims were to some extent moved by the demise of the last great Muslim power, even though the Khalifa was to many no more than a name – in many mosques in the UP he was not even mentioned in the Khutba.[3] But their willingness to agitate for the Khilafat was directly related to their political position in India. 'Old Party' men, who expected to gain power under the coming reforms, were not prepared to go beyond empty expressions of concern. 'No one can deny that every Muslim is concerned about the future of Turkey . . .', Ibni Ahmad told Ansari in December 1919; 'we differ only on one point, i.e. how to convey our feelings to the authorities.'[4] The 'Young Party' leaders who

---

[1] On 5 January 1918, Lloyd George declared that the Allies would not challenge the maintenance of the Turkish Empire in lands of Turkish race with a capital at Constantinople, and three days later Point Twelve of President Wilson's famous Fourteen Points promised much the same. J. M. Brown, *Gandhi's Rise to Power: Indian Politics 1915–1922* (Cambridge, 1972), p. 193.

[2] S. D. Waley, *Edwin Montagu* (Bombay, 1964), pp. 239–51.

[3] Note by Jopling, Deputy Commissioner of Lucknow, 7 August 1916, GAD, 1916, 436, UPS.

[4] Ibni Ahmad to Dr Ansari, 20 December 1919, in Urdu, Mahomed Ali Papers, JMI.

left the Muslim League at Delhi in 1918, and those who followed
them over the next two years, took up much the same position on
the issue as 'Old Party' men. Mahmudabad led a moderate party
over the Khilafat question. Those who agitated vigorously were
'Young Party' men and the ulama. Most 'Young Party' men had
no chance of influence in the new councils. They needed the weight
of the Muslim identity in order to compensate for their weakness.
Their object in agitating over the Khilafat was to ensure that the
Muslim identity remained the powerful guise to adopt in Indian
politics that it had been. Much of the 'political importance' of the
Muslims, it was felt, stemmed from the formidable military power
of their co-religionists outside India and their capacity to create
embarrassing political complications. 'The important consideration', Mahomed Ali insisted, 'is the temporal power of the Khalif,
as one of his chief functions is to defend the Faith and to put into
jeopardy the strength of those who put us into jeopardy.'[1] Ulama,
of course, were not interested in power in India as a whole. They
just wanted to control Indian Muslims. Those who agitated did so
for religious reasons, though some found that agitation could
improve their personal positions and many came to hope that
through it they would be able to restore their influence in the
community generally.

Despite the essential differences in aim between the ulama and
'Young Party' men, their alliance was the key to the extraordinary
vigour of the Khilafat agitation. 'Young Party' men provided a
guiding hand, but the ulama were the driving force behind the
agitation and its ever more radical development. The Khilafat
campaign was in effect launched by Dr Ansari and Hakim Ajmal
Khan who, in their speeches to the 1918 League and Congress
sessions respectively, voiced the concern about Turkey which had
grown amongst the Muslims during the year. Words, however,
were translated into deeds by Abdul Bari. As soon as the Delhi
conferences had finished, he went into action trying to draw as
many Indian ulama as possible behind him. In January, he issued
an istifta (questionnaire)[2] designed to obtain opinions on the
Khilafat. Ansari helped to distribute it, using his influence to make

---

[1] Statement by Mahomed Ali to the editor of *Britain and India*, which was
quoted in the *Independent* (Allahabad), 8 May 1920.
[2] This was circulated to ulama for their opinions. Once these had been collected
and collated, a fatwa was then issued.

sure the Deobandis received a copy.[1] Those who signed were
largely of the Firangi Mahal connection.[2] The most radical opinion,
part of which argued that 'if there is any danger of infidels gaining
possession of the holy places, all Muhammadans must fight. Jehad
is as imperative as praying and washing', came from eleven Firangi
Mahal ulama either related to or closely associated with Abdul
Bari.[3] Abdul Bari was opposed by some ulama of Allahabad,
Cawnpore[4] and Delhi,[5] and as usual by Ahmad Reza Khan of
Bareilly, Maulvis Abdul Hamid and Abdul Majid of Firangi Mahal
and all the ulama of Deoband.[6] Hafiz Ahmad of Deoband took the
position that 'the Indian Muslims were not obliged to help their
co-religionists against the British Government with which they
entered into a contract'.[7]

After issuing his fatwa, which enjoined the faithful to perform
jihad if there was any danger of the infidel controlling the Khalifa
or the Holy Places, Abdul Bari tried to arrange a meeting of ulama
of different schools. He was supported by Ansari and Hakim Ajmal
Khan,[8] and some Delhi ulama, but opposed by Deoband,[9] and the
meeting did not immediately materialise. Meanwhile, he tried to
organise a village campaign in the UP[10] and with the help of a
professional editor founded a radical journal, the *Akhuwat*.[11] In
April 1919, the maulana was spilling ideas all over the place: an
Indian Muslim mission to Islamic countries,[12] a deputation to the
Viceroy[13] and an All-India Conference of Muslims to meet in
Lucknow to discuss the Khilafat problem.[14] His own paper became
increasingly anti-Christian and anti-government, and from time

[1] Ansari to Abdul Bari, 27 January 1919, in Urdu, Abdul Bari Papers, File 16, FM.
[2] Home Poll. A, August 1919, 415–16, NAI.
[3] WRDCI, 10 March 1919, Home Poll. B, April 1919, 148–52, NAI.
[4] FR (UP), Home Poll. D, April 1919, 48, NAI.
[5] FR (UP), Home Poll. D, March 1919, 16, NAI.
[6] Endorsement No. 1696, 11 March 1919, from UP CID, Home Poll. A, August 1919, 415–26, NAI; FR (UP), Home Poll. D, March 1919, 17, NAI.
[7] FR (UP), Home Poll. D, March 1919, 17, NAI.
[8] Ansari to Maulana Salamatullah, 12 February 1919, in Urdu, Abdul Bari Papers, File 16, FM.
[9] FR (UP), Home Poll. D, March 1919, 17, NAI.
[10] FR (UP) Home Poll. D, April 1919, 48, NAI.
[11] WRDCI, 18 March 1919, Home Poll. B, April 1919, 148–52, NAI.
[12] *Akhuwat* (Lucknow), 1 April 1919, UPNNR 1919.
[13] *Ibid.*
[14] FR (UP), Home Poll. D, July 1919, 47, NAI.

to time hinted at jihad.[1] Even the ever-confident Harcourt Butler began to be concerned about the way the maulana was using his influence. The lieutenant-governor thought that he required very careful handling. He wrote to the Viceroy:

I am trying to influence him through the people on whom he relies financially. My problem is to keep the Musalman women right. If they get a handle, as they did over the Cawnpore mosque incident, they will force their husbands and male relations to do something for Islam. No Government in the East can control a combination of priests and women. Hence the importance of not making a martyr of Abdul Bari.[2]

At this point, the editor of the *Akhuwat* made a mistake; he tried attacking the Shias instead of the government. This gave the administration an excuse to act. It moved rapidly, invoked the Press Act and locked away some of the minnows in the Abdul Bari 'gang'.[3] A month later, it managed to intern Barkatullah Raza of Firangi Mahal who was suspected of being the author of leaflets encouraging jihad.[4] The government need not have concerned itself about Abdul Bari's capacity for martyrdom. He had feet of clay. The sight of the C.I.D. poking around Firangi Mahal unnerved him. He rushed up to Naini Tal to see Butler, professed his innocence, protested his loyalty, and at the end of the interview broke down completely.[5]

While Abdul Bari and his followers had already pressed far enough ahead to get entangled with the law, others were beginning to move. In March a Khilafat Committee had been founded in Bombay City under the presidency of M. M. Chotani, one of Abdul Bari's disciples, and most of the committee, including the president, were drawn from the rich Muslim merchants of the city. The committee conducted meetings and organised a deputation to the Governor. In London, three Khilafat deputations waited on Lloyd George in as many weeks. Even the All-India Muslim League, which had been very quiet since Syed Zahur Ahmed took over the secretaryship from Wazir Hasan, began to act. It supported the deputations to the Prime Minister, commanded its branches to do so, and, taking up Abdul Bari's idea, organised an all-India conference at Lucknow on 21 September to 'demon-

[1] WRDCI, 19 May 1919, Home Poll. B, June 1919, 494–7, NAI.
[2] Harcourt Butler to Chelmsford, 20 April 1919, Chelmsford Papers (22), IOL.
[3] FR (UP), Home Poll. D, July 1919, 49, NAI.
[4] FR (UP), Home Poll. D, August 1919, 51, NAI.
[5] *Ibid.*

strate...the true depth and intensity of Musalman feelings for the Sultan of Turkey and his Empire'.[1]

The Lucknow conference was a remarkable occasion. Seldom had so many Muslims (between 300 and 400) attended a meeting from outside the province and never had so many ulama attended a meeting under the auspices of the Muslim League. Indeed the occasion seems to have been dominated by ulama. Apart from those actually working in the Firangi Mahal seminary, leading divines such as Khwaja Hasan Nizami of Delhi, Mahomed Fakhir of Allahabad, Abdul Majid Sharar of Madras, Mahomed Sajjad of Bihar and Abdul Majid of Budaun were there.[2] In the subjects committee, Abdul Bari, who had recovered from the wigging Butler gave him in May, used his ulama supporters to try and capture the presidency from a moderate party led by Mahmudabad, and for half the conference he was successful.[3] In the sessions themselves, ulama such as Syed Suleman Navdi set the tone, their dirges on the decline of Islam reducing those present to paroxysms of grief.[4] Maulvi Sanaullah of Amritsar introduced the chief resolution 'that the spiritual position of the Sultan as Khalifa was indissolubly bound up with his temporal power and that the creation of small states out of the component parts of the Turkish Empire, with non-Muslim powers as mandatories, was an intolerable interference with the Khilafat'.[5] And the Firangi Mahal ulama had a hand in the most important resolution of the conference, introduced by Chotani, which fixed Friday 17 October as Khilafat Day and established an All-India Central Khilafat Committee in Bombay with branches throughout India. The Firangi Mahalis, with Khaliquzzaman's help, drew up the committee's constitution.[6]

The Lucknow conference illustrates just how influential the ulama had become in Muslim politics since the Muslim League

[1] A large advertisement for the Lucknow conference on 21 September placed by the secretary of the All-India Muslim League, Syed Zahur Ahmed, in the *Independent* (Allahabad), 7 September 1919.
[2] Of the prominent visitors to the conference, at least one-third were ulama: *ibid.*, 25 September 1919.
[3] *Leader* (Allahabad), 24 September 1919; FR (UP), Home Poll. D, November 1919, 15, NAI.
[4] *Leader* (Allahabad), 25 September 1919.
[5] FR (UP), Home Poll. D, November 1919, 15, NAI.
[6] Resolution seven of the Lucknow conference reported in the *Leader* (Allahabad), 25 September 1919; Khaliquzzaman, *Pathway to Pakistan*, p. 46.

meeting nine months before, when they had been displayed on the platform more as trophies than as allies. In December 1918, Ansari and Ajmal Khan had introduced Abdul Bari and his followers in order to make political capital out of them. But, as Khaliquzzaman prophesied, in doing so they had unleashed forces which could overwhelm them. By September 1919, the ulama were beginning to take the lead in Muslim politics, and the creation of the Central Khilafat Committee at the Lucknow conference gave them the means by which they might well take control of them.

By deciding to hold Khilafat Day, the Lucknow conference brought Gandhi to a prominent position in Muslim politics. Just a week before, Gandhi had displayed his willingness to exert himself for the Khilafat. At a Muslim mass meeting in Bombay he had berated his audience for being so lackadaisical.[1] Moreover his interest was soon felt in more than words. The idea of holding a Khilafat day on which 'all Muslims should fast and pray and suspend all their business and close their shops... and hold monster meetings and pass resolutions of protest against the contemplated betrayal of Turkey',[2] was most probably his. It was his style of politics. He was certainly the organising genius behind it. Money and instructions flooded out of Bombay while posters under the signature of Abdul Bari urged Muslims to take part.[3] In the event, the 'Day' was not a great success, but nevertheless it heralded a degree of organisation in the Khilafat movement of a new order.

It may seem odd that the help of this Hindu bania, who was in many ways identified closely with traditional Hinduism, should have been accepted so readily by the Muslims. It was, however, very natural. Of all Hindu leaders, Gandhi had the longest and most creditable association with Muslims. In South Africa he had been a Muslim leader to an extent which provoked opposition from Hindus.[4] When he returned to India in 1915, he came with the intention of working with and for Muslims, and his popularity among them was very great.[5] In 1918, his concern for the Khilafat

[1] FR (Bombay), Home Poll. D, November 1919, 15, NAI; the speech that was later published in *Young India* was more temperate. *The Collected Works of Mahatma Gandhi* (in process of publication in Delhi and hereafter cited as *CWG*), Vol. XVI, pp. 151–2.
[2] A message from Gandhi to all Muslims published in the *Independent* (Allahabad), 12 October 1919.
[3] FR (Bombay), Home Poll. D, November 1919, 14, NAI.
[4] Brown, *Gandhi*, pp. 9–11, p. 9 note 2.
[5] *Ibid.*, p. 47.

Religion overwhelms politics

and the release of the Ali brothers brought him into prominence as a Muslim spokesman, and at the Muslim League session of that year Ansari declared that Gandhi had 'by his noble actions, endeared himself, as much to Musalmans as to Hindus'.[1]

Since his return to India, Gandhi had further strengthened his connections with the Muslims by sedulously cultivating the friendship of Mahomed Ali and Abdul Bari. Gandhi first met Mahomed Ali at Aligarh and Delhi in 1915.[2] Soon after Mahomed Ali was interned, he wrote to him offering his services: 'It was during the Congress sessions that I was able to get your address. I wanted to write to you to say how my heart went out to you in your troubles. Pray let me know if I can be of any service to you.'[3] Although government would not let Gandhi visit Mahomed Ali at Chhindwara, he corresponded with him through a local lawyer, Ghate, and the 'Young Party' man, Shuaib Qureshi.[4] In correspondence in 1918 and 1919, the Ali brothers impressed on Gandhi the importance of the issue of the Khilafat and Holy Places,[5] and Gandhi in return took up the question of the Ali brothers' release. He told Mahomed Ali that 'in the proper solution of the Mahomedan question lies the realization of swaraj',[6] but he exacted a promise from the brothers that they would make no political move

[1] Speech by Dr Ansari as chairman of the reception committee of the Delhi sessions of the All-India Muslim League, December 1918, Home Poll. A, March 1919, 251–9, NAI.
[2] Speech by Gandhi at the reception of the Khilafat delegation at Bombay, 2 August 1920, *CWG*, Vol. XVIII, p. 110.
[3] Gandhi to Mahomed Ali, 9 January 1916, Mahomed Ali Papers, JMI.
[4] A police raid on the Ali Brothers' bungalow revealed the following correspondence: Gandhi to Mahomed Ali, 9 January 1916; Mahomed Ali to Gandhi (copy), 9 January 1916; Gandhi to Ghate, 16 February 1916; Mahomed Ali to Gandhi (copy), 20 February 1918; Gandhi to Ghate, 6 August 1918; Mahomed Ali to 'Mahatmaji' (copy), 19 September 1918; Gandhi to Mahomed Ali, 10 November 1918; Gandhi to Ghate, 31 January 1919; Mahomed Ali to 'Mahatmaji' (copy), 9 May 1919; Gandhi to Ali Brothers 23 May 1919; Ali Brothers to 'Mahatmaji' (copy), 28 May 1919; and an Urdu draft setting out the views of the Ali Brothers on Satyagraha. Counterfoil issued by the police to Mahomed Ali for property seized from him under section 523 of the Criminal Procedure Code, *ibid*. But this was not the full extent of Gandhi's correspondence with the Brothers. If Gandhi's letter to Mahomed Ali of 18 November 1918 (*CWG*, Vol. XV, pp. 63–4) could escape the police search, so could others, and this is supported by Gandhi's statement that he was using Shuaib as an intermediary for correspondence. Gandhi to Ghate, 6 August 1918, Mahomed Ali Papers, JMI.
[5] Mahomed Ali to Gandhi, 20 February 1918 and 25 May 1919, *ibid*.
[6] Gandhi to Mahomed Ali, 18 November 1918, *CWG*, Vol. XV, pp. 63–4.

towards this solution without consulting him first. He gave them instructions and Mahomed Ali acknowledged this arrangement. When Gandhi complained of their failure to consult him, Mahomed Ali replied: 'Ever since we received your message a year and a half ago we have unreservedly consulted you at every stage, and have exercised considerable restraint and allowed much suspense in forming our opinions, in expressing them and in taking action upon them'.[1] Gandhi assiduously developed his relations with the doyen of the 'Young Party', and, despite the occasional tiff which was inevitable in dealing with such a hothead, by 1919 he had acquired considerable ascendancy over him.

Gandhi cultivated Abdul Bari in a similar fashion. It is said that he first came to hear of the maulana in England in 1914 from his disciple, Mushir Husain Kidwai, and was introduced to him during the Lucknow Congress sessions of 1916.[2] Their first recorded meeting was in work for the release of the Ali brothers.[3] When Gandhi wrote to the Viceroy about the 1918 War Conference, he tacked on a paragraph about Muslim feelings over the Holy Places,[4] and this impressed Abdul Bari. He wrote to Gandhi:

The Imperial War Conference contained many official and non-official Muslims. The Provincial War Conference was attended by Muslim leaders including Mujtahids of Lucknow and the ulama of Deoband but none of them expressed the feelings of Muslims. GOD LEFT THIS FOR GANDHI.[5]

In 1919, Gandhi continued to foster his relations with Abdul Bari. In March, he stayed with the maulana and his maulvis in Firangi Mahal. Gandhi sought Abdul Bari's support for the Rowlatt Satyagraha, and in return he offered Hindu assistance for the Khilafat protest.[6] The maulana followed this interview with an obedient statement in the *Akhuwat* expressing his 'great regard and respect for Mr. Gandhi', his entire agreement with his views, and urged Muslims to follow the Mahatma's example.[7]

[1] Mahomed Ali to Gandhi, 28 May 1919, Mahomed Ali Papers, JMI.
[2] Interview with Mufti Reza Ansari of Firangi Mahal, Lucknow, 29 May 1968.
[3] FR (Delhi), Home Poll. D, May 1918, 22, NAI; Shuaib Qureshi helped to make the meeting possible; telegrams, in English, Shuaib to Abdul Bari, 20 February 1918 and 22 March 1918, Abdul Bari Papers, File 10, FM.
[4] Gandhi to Viceroy, 29 April 1918, *CWG*, Vol. xiv, p. 379.
[5] A letter from Abdul Bari to Gandhi published in the *Hamdam* (Lucknow), 12 May 1918, UPNNR 1918.
[6] FR (UP), Home Poll. D, April 1919, 49; WRDCI, 18 March 1919, Home Poll. B, April 1919, 148–52; WRDCI, 12 May 1919, Home Poll. D, June 1919, 494–7, NAI.   [7] *Akhuwat* (Lucknow), 14 March 1919, UPNNR 1919.

Religion overwhelms politics

However, after the Rowlatt Satyagraha, their roles were reversed. It was Abdul Bari who now courted Gandhi. He was eager to get him more closely involved with the Khilafat protest. Throughout the summer of 1919, he bombarded the Mahatma with suggestions for the release of the Ali brothers,[1] a scheme for Hindu–Muslim unity,[2] and pleas that Gandhi should adopt Satyagraha for Muslim grievances.[3] In return, he promised Gandhi that he would stop Muslims sacrificing cows.[4] But if Gandhi appeared to be playing hard to get, it was only because he was waiting for the right moment to move. When he did in September 1919, he was clearly accepted as leader by Abdul Bari. The maulana, in boasting of having won the mahatma for the Khilafat cause, spoke of his submission:

> ...I have made Mahatma Gandhi to follow us in the Khilafat question while I have accepted his support in getting our aims fulfilled and for that purpose I think it is necessary to follow his advice.[5]

Not every Muslim appeared to appreciate such subservience. 'You made Gandhi your Peshwa and became his disciple. You called him greater than your own self', one anonymous letter-writer told Abdul Bari; 'all the papers condemned you but you did not abstain from evil doing... In view of all these points you are declared a damn, impudent fellow and to pray behind you is unlawful.'[6] Such cranks apart, however, most Muslims found Gandhi's leadership very welcome.

The adherence of Gandhi to the Khilafat campaign strengthened it immensely. The mahatma's reputation in the summer of 1919, though a little tarnished by the disasters of the Rowlatt Satyagraha, was still very great, and his support a priceless asset to any cause. Unlike other Indian politicians, Gandhi belonged to no organisation

---

[1] Abdul Bari to Gandhi, 16 June 1919, 4 August 1919 and 20 August 1919, Gandhi Papers, nos 6663, 6788, 6812, NAI.
[2] Abdul Bari to Gandhi, 27 April 1919, Gandhi Papers, no. 6567, NAI.
[3] Abdul Bari to Gandhi, 10 May 1919, 3 September 1919, Gandhi Papers, nos. 6603, 6845, NAI.
[4] WRDCI, 29 September 1919, Home Poll. B, September 1919, 454–7; Home Poll. D, April 1921, 67, NAI.
[5] A statement made by Abdul Bari, undated but internal evidence suggests that it was made for the Jamiat-ul-ulama meeting at Delhi in November 1920. Abdul Bari Papers, English File, FM.
[6] The writer continued: 'Considering all these points, the Muslim community has decided to honour you with a robe of honour perfumed with dung and a garland of fifty shoes. Take help of Gandhi and your other supporters...' Khadiman-e-Islam wa Shaidaiyan to the Son of Gandhi, undated but text suggests 1921, in Urdu, Abdul Bari Papers, File 21, FM.

and had no regional political base, yet this did not limit his influence. He had a large band of followers drawn from all regions and all groups. He was known and admired by almost every major politician in the country. He was respected by many members of the bureaucracy, and, Rowlatt apart, he had already conducted several successful agitations. All these factors made Gandhi a powerful ally for the ulama and 'Young Party' men to have won, but the most important was that through him there was a chance of persuading Hindus to join their protest over the Khilafat. For Gandhi, on the other hand, there were also advantages. The support of large numbers of Muslims, particularly ulama and 'Young Party' men, who had little to hope for from the contemporary structure of Indian politics, greatly strengthened his position in dealing both with the government and with Congress. Indeed, he hoped it would help him further several of his most prized ambitions:

I hope by my 'alliance' with the Mohammedans to achieve a threefold end – to obtain justice in the face of odds with the method of satyagraha and to show its efficacy over all other methods, to secure Mohammedan friendship for the Hindus and thereby internal peace also, and last but not least to transform ill will into affection for the British and their constitution which in spite of its imperfections has weathered many a storm.[1]

In the weeks following the first Khilafat Day, the UP Khilafatists became increasingly dissatisfied with the limited vigour with which the Bombay leaders of the Khilafat organisation prosecuted the agitation. They decided to snatch the initiative themselves and, early in November 1919, the Delhi Khilafat committee announced that they would hold an All-India Khilafat conference at Delhi on 23 November to determine how Muslims should protest against the dismemberment of Turkey. This was to be followed on 24 November by a joint Hindu–Muslim conference. Gandhi was the only Hindu invited to both conferences. His invitation informed him 'that not only the Khilafat question but the question of cow protection as well would be discussed at the conference, and it would, therefore, afford a golden opportunity for a settlement of the cow question'.[2] The intention of the Delhi Muslims

---

[1] *Young India*, 5 May 1920, *CWG*, Vol. XVII, p. 391.
[2] A letter from Hakim Ajmal Khan, Asaf Ali and others to Gandhi summarised in M. K. Gandhi, *An Autobiography: The Story of my Experiments with Truth*, translated from the Gujarati by Mahadev Desai, paperback edn (London, 1966), p. 398.

was obvious: they hoped to do a deal with Hindu leaders over cow-protection in order to win their support for their new Khilafat agitation plans, and Gandhi was to help them do this.

The majority of those who attended the conference of 23 November were UP Muslims[1] – the 'prominent leaders' who 'frankly confessed...that an equally representative gathering of the Musalmans of India had not yet met anywhere within their memory...'[2] must have had their tongues in their cheeks – and it was swayed by the fanaticism of the ulama, particularly Abdul Bari and his followers.[3] Surprisingly, their attempts to move the headquarters of the Khilafat organisation to Lucknow or Delhi failed. Nevertheless, they forced through resolutions instinct with their extremism. They resolved to send a deputation immediately to England to make their case regarding the Khilafat and Turkey one last time; to boycott the Peace Celebrations planned by government for 13 December; progressively to boycott British goods; and 'in the event of a satisfactory settlement of the Turkish question not taking place...progressively [to] withhold all co-operation from the British Government'.[4] Two committees were appointed to make suggestions to the next Khilafat conference about the practical working of the last two resolutions. Their composition illustrates the prominence of the ulama and UP men generally. The boycott of British goods committee consisted of Syed Zahur Ahmed, Hasrat Mohani, Zafar-ul-Mulk Alvi, Maulvi Akram Khan, Maulvi Munirazzaman, Seth Abdullah Harmi, Haji Ahmed Khattri, Maulana Sanaullah, Agha M. Safdar, Maulana Arif Havsi, Tajuddin and Maulvi Mahomed Sajjad, of whom at least three came from the UP and five were ulama. The non-co-operation committee consisted of Maulanas Abdul Bari, Abdul Majid, Sanaullah and Wilayat Husain, plus Hakim Ajmal Khan, Syud Hussain, Riza Ali, Hasrat Mohani, Kamaluddin Jafri, Mumtaz Hussain, Fazlul Huq and Seth Abdullah Harmi, of whom four were ulama, six were 'Young Party' men and nine came from the UP.[5]

[1] The numbers of delegates from each province were: UP 161, Delhi 40, Rajputana and Sindh 35, Punjab 20, Madras 4, Bombay 8, CP 8, Bengal 18. *Leader* (Allahabad), 27 November 1919.
[2] *Independent* (Allahabad), 2 December 1919.
[3] FR (Delhi), Home Poll. D, January 1920, 5, NAI.
[4] *Independent* (Allahabad), 28 November 1919.
[5] *Ibid.*, and *Leader* (Allahabad), 28 November 1919.

Gandhi supported the decision to boycott the Peace Celebrations; it was in line with his own policy which he had already announced.[1] He also supported the resolution to withhold co-operation from the government, coining the word 'non-co-operation' to describe the measure.[2] But it should be noted that, despite this and all Gandhi's past and future association with techniques of non-co-operation, the idea on this occasion stemmed from the Muslims and the Mahatma was merely following their lead. However, as far as progressive boycott of British goods was concerned, Gandhi was not prepared to follow their lead. Over three-quarters of Bombay's Muslim merchants, many of whom financed the Khilafat agitation, did business in British goods. Boycott would ruin them. Gandhi was not prepared to help the Khilafat agitators commit suicide.[3]

On 23 November the UP Khilafatists won Gandhi's approval for part of their programme. But on 24 November he was very cautious about the kind of Hindu–Muslim action he was prepared to support. For a start he would be a party to no communal bargain. He rejected the offer, made by Abdul Bari, Asaf Ali and others, to stop cow-slaughter in return for Hindu support for the Khilafat. The Muslims, he argued, should only stop cow-slaughter of their own free will just as Hindus should only join the Khilafat protest of their own free will. He was no less firm when, just before the Hindu–Muslim Conference, Swami Shraddhanand, Hasrat Mohani and Shankerlal Banker tried to persuade him to link the Khilafat issue with government action under martial law in the Punjab. The Punjab affair, Gandhi objected, was a local issue. When they threatened to decide the matter by a majority vote, Gandhi warned them that, if they did not accept his decision, he would have nothing more to do with the agitation.[4] As far as joint action was concerned Gandhi was prepared to support only one item in the Muslim programme resolved upon the day before. Boycott of British goods he pilloried as 'ridiculous'. Non-co-operation he hailed as a 'sublime decision', but would go no further. Only boycott of the Peace Celebrations gained his un-

---

[1] FR (Bombay), Home Poll. D, December 1919, 5, NAI; *Leader* (Allahabad), 3 November 1919.
Gandhi, *Autobiography*, pp. 401–2; *Navajivan*, 16 May 1920, *CWG*, Vol. XVII, pp. 415–16.
[3] Brown, *Gandhi*, pp. 202–4.
[4] *Ibid.*, p. 203; Gandhi, *Autobiography*, pp. 399–400.

qualified approval.[1] Resolutions on this and thanking the Hindus were the only ones passed by the joint conference. Gandhi had his way. The *Independent* called it 'Gandhi's day',[2] and the Muslims discovered that the Mahatma was no easy tool to manipulate.

So much for the UP Khilafatists' first attempt to capture the Khilafat organisation, rally the Hindus behind them and drive the Khilafat protest into a higher gear. Hindu support for their boycott of the Peace Celebrations, which did admittedly cause 'a serious curtailment of the programme of celebrations and gave great prominence to the Khilafat question throughout India',[3] was all they gained. At the end of 1919, the council reforms became law and the Khilafatists did not have to be very perceptive to see that most Hindu politicians, like many Muslim politicians, were much more interested in these than the Khilafat. In addition the resolutions of the Delhi conference regarding the boycott of British goods and non-co-operation came to nought. The Bombay-dominated Central Khilafat Committee opposed them and told the chairman of the next All-India Khilafat conference, to be held at Amritsar in Congress week, that it should reach no decision on the matter and that the non-co-operation sub-committee should be enlarged to include representatives of Muslim commercial interests.[4] Muslim merchants from Bombay, notably the Central Khilafat Committee president Chotani, financed the agitation both in north India and in England.[5] The UP Khilafatists, with as yet few alternative resources, were powerless to resist. Moreover, they had to stand by silent as the Bombay hold over the Khilafat organisation was confirmed. In the constitution adopted in February 1920, Bombay held over one-quarter of the seats on the Central Khilafat Committee and every seat on the working committee bar one.[6]

If the Muslims had any doubts as to the ineffectiveness of their agitation, these were confirmed in January 1920. At the Amritsar Khilafat conference it was resolved to send a deputation to the Viceroy to place before him their threefold demand regarding the Khilafat and Holy Places, and to obtain permission for deputations

[1] Speech by Gandhi at the Delhi Khilafat conference, 24 November 1919, *CWG*, Vol. XVI, 307–12.
[2] *Independent* (Allahabad), 2 December 1919.
[3] WRDCI, 12 April 1920, Home Poll. D, April 1920, 103, NAI.
[4] FR (Bombay), Home Poll. D, January 1920, 5, 45, NAI.
[5] *Ibid.*   [6] FR (Bombay), Home Poll. D, July 1920, 89, NAI.

to go to England and America. Permission was granted. But the Khilafat, Chelmsford told the Muslims, was their own affair. Moreover, he did not encourage them in their hopes for the Holy Places. He could not. The demand that Turkey should preserve the sovereignty and dominions which she possessed before the war was one, he declared 'we cannot reasonably hope will be recognised by the Allied Powers in Conference'.[1]

Tied by the financial strings of the Central Khilafat Committee, given not a spark of hope by the Viceroy, the Muslims of Upper India were not daunted. If the government would not take notice, it had to be forced to take notice. In January and February 1920 they pressed forward the agitation with renewed vigour. In doing so they were assisted by two developments. The first was the creation of the basis of better ulama organisation. Two days after the Delhi Khilafat conference, the ulama delegates had met to discuss ways of overcoming their ineffectiveness. They were ineffective, they decided, because they were divided. Ulama of different schools, they felt, should make another attempt to unite and so they voted to form the Jamiat-ul-ulama-i-Hind (the Society of Indian Theologians).[2] The basis of the common front which Abdul Bari had been toiling so long to form was at last created and he was president of its first conference at Amritsar in the last week of 1919. The demands of the ulama concerning the Khilafat, the Holy Places, and their own position in Muslim society, were no longer to be voiced in politics just by Firangi Mahalis and the Majlis Muid-ul-Islam but through a more representative organisation which even the leading Deobandi ulama were eventually willing to join.[3] The second development was the release, as a

[1] Chelmsford's reply to the Khilafat deputation of 19 January 1920, enclosed in Chelmsford to Montagu, 22 January 1920, Montagu Papers (10), IOL.
[2] *Mukhtesat Halat-e-Ine'-qad-e-Jamiat-ul-Ulema-i-Hind* (Delhi, 1920), pp. 3–4.
[3] The aims and objects of the Jamiat were laid down as follows:
'1. To guide the followers of Islam in their political and non-political matters from a religious point of view.
2. To protect Islam, centres of Islam (Hijaz and the Jazirat-ul-Arab) and Islamic customs and practices and defend Islamic way of life against all odds injurious to it.
3. To struggle for the complete independence of the country.
4. To achieve and protect the religious and national rights of the Muslims.
5. To promote and protect the rights and interests of other communities of the country.
6. To organise the ulama on a common platform.
7. To establish good and friendly relations with the non-Muslims of the country.

result of the amnesty which accompanied the Royal Proclamation of the Montagu–Chelmsford reforms, of those Muslims interned during the war. The release of Abdul Kalam Azad,[1] Shibli's most prized pupil, brought to Muslim politics an alim who, though less influential than Abdul Bari, was intellectually his superior and capable to a far greater extent than any other alim of appreciating both the religious and the political sides of a problem. The release of the Ali brothers brought those masters of Muslim agitational politics to the head of the Khilafat campaign.

In early 1920, therefore, the Khilafat agitation reached a new level of intensity. Leaders went on a series of agitational tours throughout northern India, a whole rash of provincial Khilafat conferences were held and the Ali brothers' Purse Fund was launched – the first of many appeals for money which were to help to reduce the extremists' dependence on Bombay financial support. The UP Khilafatists' methods of making the government take notice remained the same as those they had advocated at Delhi in 1919. They wished to force the Khilafat organisation into adopting non-co-operation and to persuade, with Gandhi's aid if possible, Hindu politicians to follow them. In speeches on tour and at conferences, Shaukat Ali, Abdul Bari, Azad and others stressed the importance of fostering Hindu support. Gandhi joined in and he was no less strong in advocating Hindu support for the Khilafat, though he maintained his line of refusing to endorse any bargain over religious practice.

The main effort, however, was devoted to persuading the Khilafat organisation to adopt measures of non-co-operation. A strong attack was launched during the third All-India Khilafat conference held at Bombay on 15, 16, and 17 of February. Twice in the month before it was held, Shaukat Ali and Abdul Bari toured the backward Muslim province of Sind, and with fanatical Sindhi pirs and mullas at their backs they descended upon the conference. Fourteen resolutions were passed, among them the adoption of the Central Khilafat Committee's constitution, an appeal for thirty lakhs of rupees for the Committee's Fund and a manifesto, said to

8. To establish *Mahakim-i-Shariyah* (religious courts) to meet the religious needs of the community...
10. To propagate Islam, by way of missionary activities, in India and foreign lands.'
Jamiat-ul-Ulema-i-Hind (A Brief History) (Meerut, 1963), p. 4.
[1] See Appendix IV.

have been drawn up by Gandhi, which stated the Khilafat claim
and threatened government that, if it was not met, 'it is futile to
expect peace in India...' But the Committee still would not accept
a measure of non-co-operation. The decisive action came in the
subjects committee where the following questions were considered:
the proposed boycott of English goods combined with a withdrawal from co-operation with Government; whether or not it
was haram for a Musalman to serve in the Indian Army; and
the evacuation of the Jazirat-ul-Arab. The delegates from outside
Bombay demanded an extreme course of action, those from within,
moderation. When the temper of the conference was tested with
a resolution on the third subject, it was discovered to lean towards
the extremists. The resolution was passed. The moderates tried to
wriggle out of the situation by submitting the question of army
service to the ulama. This was a bad move. The ulama session was
chaired by Azad Sobhani, and immediately, under the inspiration
of Abdul Bari, it was decided that, as there was no guarantee that
the army would not be used against Muslim forces, it was haram
(forbidden) for Muslims to belong to it. Notices were issued to
those present asking for the circulation of fatwas among the troops.
When some objected, they were told that in this matter the sharia
should prevail. Nevertheless it was clear to the extremists that they
were not going to be able to carry the Bombay moderates with
them, and, as they could not afford to do without them, they had
no alternative at the end of the conference but to accept Bhurgri's
compromise that the questions of the army, boycott and non-
co-operation should be left until it was seen what success Mahomed
Ali's deputation achieved in England.[1]

A few days later a speech by the Archbishop of Canterbury
denouncing Turkey with crusading zeal was reported in India.
Bombay financiers notwithstanding, the UP Khilafatists were no
longer prepared to wait for the results of Mahomed Ali's deputation. At the Bengal Provincial Khilafat conference in Calcutta,
Abdul Bari wanted nothing less than an eye for an eye from the
Anglican primate. He told his audience:

They could sacrifice every Christian's life and property; they could burn
them, and even if they stole their property he would give them a Fatwa

[1] FR (Bombay), Home Poll. D, July 1920, 89, NAI. Mahomed Ali, with Syud
Hussain and the alim Syed Suleman Nadvi, left India on 1 February in a final
attempt to persuade the Imperial government to see the Indian Muslim point
of view concerning the Khilafat.

in justification...He declared that had cannon and guns been at his disposal he would have declared war and would have burnt the Christians after saturating them with Kerosine oil...[1]

Azad, the conference president, concentrated on more practical means of revenge and in his address raised plain non-co-operation into the Islamic doctrine Tark-i-malavat, surrounding it with wreaths of quotations from the Koran. Then the conference re-solved to boycott British piece goods immediately, to withdraw co-operation from government if the Khilafat decision was un-favourable, and to observe Friday 19 March as a Khilafat Day with a hartal.[2]

The Calcutta resolutions become the instrument of an extremist coup within the Khilafat organisation. The Bengal Khilafat con-ference was a mere provincial affair, and had no right to declare for the whole of India a hartal, boycott of British goods and non-co-operation. The extremists were offering Khilafatists the alterna-tive of either joining them or opposing them. Their seizure of the initiative was very successful. Gandhi was forced to follow them. The Mahatma had attended the Bengal conference. He had witnessed Abdul Bari's fury. He had been unable to prevent the boycott resolution – indeed he had to swallow the fact that, despite his known disapproval, it had been implemented straightway in Calcutta.[3] He had heard the great chorus of approval of the resolu-tions that had been voiced in north India.[4] He knew that, if he was to continue to influence the Khilafatists, he must go with them. A week after the conference, he issued a manifesto on Khilafat agitation. He stressed that there should be no violence, no boycott of British goods and no confusion of the Khilafat with other questions. He supported the hartal of 19 March, declared that if Muslim demands were not granted 'non-co-operation is...the only remedy left open to us', and hazarded a few suggestions as to its form.[5] All these things he had said before. They were un-important. What mattered was that he had shown his willingness to keep up with the extremists. But there was a greater success than this. The Central Khilafat Committee also, very reluctantly,

[1] WRDCI, 15 March 1920, *ibid.*   [2] *Independent* (Allahabad), 3 March 1920.
[3] *Ibid.*, 6 and 12 March 1920.
[4] *Hamdam* (Lucknow), 17 March 1920; *Medina* (Bijnor), 17 March 1920, UPNNR 1920.
[5] Manifesto on the Khilafat question issued by Gandhi on 7 March 1920, *Young India*, 10 March 1920, *CWG*, Vol. XVII, pp. 73–6.

fell into line. Why they did so is not clear, though Abdul Bari did exert immense pressure to persuade Chotani to support the Calcutta resolutions,[1] and Gandhi undoubtedly stressed the importance of a united front. However that may be, on 7 March, the Central Khilafat Committee, with a few dissentients, approved of the 19 March hartal.[2] On 14 March, the Central Khilafat Committee actually endorsed non-co-operation. It agreed that, when action next became necessary, non-co-operation should be begun and that, according to a plan drawn up by a committee of which Gandhi was a member, it should take effect in three stages: first, return of titles and honours: second, resignation of council seats and withdrawal from private and public service (including the police and army); third, non-payment of taxes.[3]

On 22 March at Delhi, fifteen Muslims and Gandhi discussed this non-co-operation plan with nine Hindu leaders, among them Lajpat Rai, Madan Mohan Malaviya and Tilak, with the aim of gaining their support.[4] The Hindu politicians were not impressed: Malaviya doubted that many Muslims would implement the policy; Lajpat Rai was more interested in Swadeshi; Tilak thought it was all nonsense. Even some of the Muslims were not entirely in

---

[1] Abdul Bari to Chotani, 12 March 1920 and 13 March 1920, telegrams, Abdul Bari Papers, English File, FM; FR (Bombay), Home Poll. D, July 1920, 90, NAI.

[2] FR (Bombay), Home Poll. D, July 1920, 90, NAI.

[3] Brown, *Gandhi*, pp. 207–8.

[4] There is some confusion as to exactly when this Hindu–Muslim conference on non-co-operation took place. According to Azad, after the Khilafat deputation to the Viceroy on 19 January 1920, Gandhi, Azad, the Ali brothers, Hakim Ajmal Khan and Abdul Bari met Hindu leaders in Delhi in order to determine what the Muslims should do next, and a non-co-operation plan was formulated, discussed and announced at a Meerut Khilafat conference a few days later. A. K. Azad, *India Wins Freedom: An Autobiographical Narrative* (Bombay, 1959), pp. 8–10 and a statement describing the Hindu–Muslim conference on 20 January attributed to Azad in D. G. Tendulkar, *Mahatma*, new edn (Government of India Publications Division, 1960), Vol. I, pp. 283–4. The editors of Gandhi's collected works appear to follow Azad, *CWG*, Vol. XVII, p. 507, note 1.
It is true that the Muslim leaders did meet Gandhi at Delhi during the third week in January and that the Mahatma did attend a Khilafat meeting at Meerut a few days afterwards and it is very possible that the subject of non-co-operation was discussed. But there is no evidence for Hindu leaders having attended the meeting or for any announcement of non-co-operation at the Meerut Khilafat meeting, an event that would not have been missed either by the government or by the press, so it would appear that Azad confused the events of the meeting of 20 January with those of the meeting of 22 March, the circumstances of which were very similar.

favour of the Central Khilafat Committee's plan: Abdul Bari jibbed at the restriction of non-violence; Hakim Ajmal Khan was diffident – non-co-operation put an end to his hopes of a government grant for his beloved Tibbia (medical) college.[1] Nevertheless a committee composed of Gandhi, Lajpat Rai, Ajmal Khan, Shaukat Ali and Azad examined the Central Khilafat Committee's programme, and two days later at a Khilafat conference at Meerut, Gandhi announced a non-co-operation programme to be implemented if the Turkish peace terms were not favourable, which was substantially the same as that of the Central Khilafat Committee.[2] Though they had yet to win much Hindu support, the UP extremists had scored a great victory. Within five weeks of the disappointments of the Bombay Khilafat conference, they had turned the tables on the Bombay moderates and committed them, and Gandhi, to the extreme political measures they wanted.

Once non-co-operation was agreed upon, the UP Khilafatists set about preparing to put it into action. They were determined that government should realise that Gandhi's Meerut announcement was no idle threat. At the Meerut Khilafat conference it was proposed to form committees of ulama to organise agitation.[3] Ten days later, a conference of UP ulama, under Abdul Bari, set up a central co-ordinating body for these committees at Budaun under Abdul Bari's disciple Abdul Majid Budauni.[4] Two weeks afterwards, a Khilafat Workers conference, attended by delegates from all over India, was held at Delhi to decide upon ways and means of putting the non-co-operation programme into effect. UP leaders helped to stiffen morale elsewhere in India. Azad Sobhani and Abdul Majid attempted to stir up the Bihar ulama.[5] Shaukat Ali, with Abdul Bari in attendance, presided over the Madras Khilafat conference, and ten days later made the major speech at the Bihar Khilafat conference.[6] But there was a price to pay for all this activity and preparation: Muslim feelings became increasingly strong. The resolutions of the ulama conference went beyond the content and the spirit of the programme of non-violent non-co-

---

[1] Home Poll. A, February 1921, 341–54; FR (Delhi), Home Poll. D, April 1920, 4, NAI; Brown, *Gandhi*, pp. 209–10.
[2] *Independent* (Allahabad), 27 March 1920.
[3] *Ibid.*, 25 March 1920.   [4] *Ibid.*, 9 April 1920.
[5] FR (Bihar), Home Poll. D, July 1920, 95, NAI.
[6] *Independent* (Allahabad), 20 and 28 April 1920.

operation, approving of Abdul Bari's Calcutta speech.[1] The Khilafat Workers conference went further. It advocated hijrat and many were disappointed that preparations for jihad were not to commence at once; 'with few exceptions', it was noted, 'the delegates were determined not to follow Mr. Gandhi's peaceful instructions'.[2] The Bombay moderates were attacked mercilessly and even Abdul Bari came in for a share of abuse. Matters were getting out of hand. By early May, Muslims in several UP districts had begun to non-co-operate of their own accord.[3] It was clear that UP Khilafat leaders were having difficulty in controlling the leaders of local agitation, particularly the ulama.

Just as it was difficult for UP leaders to prevent local agitation from getting out of hand so they had problems in preventing the Central Khilafat Committee from wriggling out of its commitment to non-co-operation. Understandably, the moderate men of Bombay were alarmed by the increasing fanaticism of the agitation in northern India. They showed their displeasure by refusing to affiliate to the Khilafat organisation the Khilafat Workers League and the UP Provincial Khilafat Committee. Then, encouraged by declarations from the Aga Khan and Mahmudabad, they suggested that the non-co-operation programme ought to be reconsidered.[4] It seemed in late April that the UP Khilafatists' victory of March was about to be reversed. They reacted sharply. 'I want Hakim Sahab and Maulana Majid [Hakim Ajmal Khan and Abdul Majid Budauni] to be here', Shaukat Ali told Asaf Ali, so 'that we could thoroughly work up the Bombay Moslems.'[5] The committee was bombarded with letters of objection from Sind, Madras, UP and Bengal. Kidwai told Chotani that the time when the Turkish peace terms were in the final stages of negotiation was not the moment to water down the non-co-operation programme. Indeed, he would secede from the Central Khilafat Committee if it did so. Now was the time to convince government that India meant business and simultaneously give an opportunity to make concessions at the eleventh hour. The advocacy of Kidwai and the others

---

[1] *Ibid.*, 9 April 1920.
[2] WRDCI, 3 May 1920, Home Poll. D, June 1920, 78, NAI.
[3] Muslims in Bara Banki, Cawnpore and Jhansi, *Independent* (Allahabad), 8 May, 1920.
[4] Report of the Commissioner of Police, Bombay, 10/11 May 1920, Home Poll. A, February 1920, 341–54, NAI.
[5] Shaukat Ali to Asaf Ali, 22 April 1920, Mahomed Ali Papers, JMI.

prevailed.[1] On 12 May the Central Khilafat Committee decided to adhere to its non-co-operation programme, with the change that it should be implemented in four stages instead of three, and appointed a sub-committee consisting of Chotani, Shaukat Ali, A. K. Azad, Haji Ahmed Khattri and Mahomed Ali of Dharavi to work out in detail a plan for starting it. Consequently several leading Bombay moderates, Badruddin Abdullah Koor, Fazulbhoy Currimbhoy and Rahimtulla Chinoy, resigned. Gandhi was elected to the Committee in Chinoy's place.[2]

On 14 May the terms of the proposed treaty between Turkey and the Allies were published in India. The Allies' conditions were tough. Apart from the Jazirat-ul-Arab, which was left in Muslim hands, the demands of the Indian Muslims were ignored. The frontiers of the once great Ottoman Empire were cut back to Constantinople and the predominantly Turkish areas of Asia Minor; the Holy Places of Islam were removed from the Khalifa's custody; and the power with which he was supposed to defend the Faith and the Faithful was reduced to risible proportions – 50,000 policemen, seven sloops and six torpedo boats.[3] The Firangi Mahal ulama condemned these terms straightaway and demanded that non-co-operation should be implemented at once. But two days later their political sense got the better of them and they modified their stand. Abdul Bari and Kidwai sent a telegram to the press declaring, 'Turkish Peace terms outrageous situation desperate Muslims should be patient till ulemas and Central Khilafat Committee decides actions'.[4] Gandhi described the terms as 'a staggering blow to the Indian Mussulmans...non-co-operation', he declared, 'is the only effective remedy', and hoped that the Central Khilafat Committee would call a joint conference of Hindus and Muslims to consider what ought to be done.[5] Shaukat Ali in a press communiqué supported Gandhi, though he was not prepared to admit that non-co-operation was the only remedy, and

[1] M. H. Kidwai to Chotani, 4 May 1920, enclosed with the report of the Commissioner of Police, Bombay, 10/11 May 1920, Home Poll. A, February 1921, 341–54, NAI.

[2] Extract from the weekly letter of the Commissioner of Police, Bombay, 17/18 May 1920, Home Poll. D, June 1920, 112, NAI.

[3] The Turkish peace terms, *CWG*, Vol XVII, Appendix I, pp. 541–2.

[4] Telegram to the press from Abdul Bari and M. H. Kidwai, 16 May 1920, Abdul Bari Papers, English File, FM.

[5] Statement to the press by Gandhi on the Turkish peace terms, *Bombay Chronicle*, 18 May 1920, *CWG*, Vol. XVII, pp. 426–7.

recommended that the next Central Khilafat Committee meeting to consider policy should be held in northern India.[1] When on 24 May this body's working committee considered Shaukat Ali's suggestion, there was strong opposition from the Bombay moderates to this overt attempt to force their hand. Nevertheless, it was agreed that the Central Khilafat Committee would meet at Allahabad from 1 to 3 June, which was immediately after the All-India Congress Committee meeting at Benares. Moreover, Hindu leaders of all shades of opinion were to be invited to join in the deliberations in order to hear the Muslim case and to give advice.[2]

At the Hindu–Muslim conference in June, Khilafat leaders were going to try and win Hindu support for the non-co-operation programme. They realised that non-co-operation was less likely to be a success without it. However important it might be to press forward the Khilafat protest, few were likely to resign honours and jobs if they saw that these were immediately snapped up by Hindus. Equally they felt that their action would make little impact on the government if it was restricted to the Muslim minority. So Khilafat leaders laid heavy stress on the need for Hindu–Muslim unity; Kidwai's presidential speech to the Oudh Khilafat conference concentrated on this point, and Shaukat Ali did not appear to consider starting non-co-operation without our 'Hindu brethren'.[3]

Soft words from the Khilafatists carried little weight with Hindu politicians. Any real hope they had of gaining Hindu support lay with Gandhi. By June 1920, the mahatma, who had skirted round the edge of Indian politics for the past five years, was coming to be a leading politician in his own right. He had developed strong associations with Hindu revivalism in north India. He had special relationships with trading groups such as the Marwaris and Bombay Muslims. He had cultivated pockets of support in the areas where he had championed causes: Champaran in Bihar, and Kaira and Ahmedabad in Gujarat. He was beginning to assert himself in

[1] Statement to the press by Shaukat Ali, 17 May 1920, *Independent* (Allahabad), 20 May 1920.
[2] Message from Shaukat Ali, *Tribune* (Lahore), 26 May 1920.
[3] 'Presidential address of M. H. Kidwai to the Oudh Khilafat conference at Fyzabad, 1 May 1920', in Urdu, pamphlet from the private library of Mufti Reza Ansari of Firangi Mahal, and statement to the press by Shaukat Ali, 17 May 1920, *Independent* (Allahabad), 20 May 1920.

Religion overwhelms politics

Religion overwhelms politics

Congress affairs: he was the leading member of the subcommittee
on the Punjab disturbances and powerful enough to postpone an
All-India Congress Committee meeting twice. Moreover, on
28 April 1920, he had joined, and become president of, the All-
India Home Rule League. In the policy statement he issued on
the same day, he referred specifically to Swadeshi, the adoption of
Hindustani as the *lingua franca* of India, the reorganisation of the
provinces on the basis of language, and the abolition of untouch-
ability – all issues which would appeal to political undercurrents in
the Congress. The one group that Gandhi deliberately ignored were
the Nationalist leaders who had come to power in the Congress
with the Home Rule movement and the secession of the Liberals –
Tilak, C. R. Das and Motilal Nehru.[1]

Gandhi was very willing to play the Khilafatists' game. Indeed,
he had been playing it for some time, though of course it did also
suit his own idealistic ends. In April and May 1920, he urged
closer Hindu co-operation with the Khilafat movement. Soon after
he joined the All-India Home Rule League, he declared that he
wished 'to engage every member...in Khilafat work'.[2] Three days
later, he hinted that Hindus should join Muslims in non-co-
operation.[3] When the Turkish peace terms were announced he
declared that 'the Hindus are bound to join in non-co-operation'.[4]
But when he tried to bind the nationalist leaders to non-co-operation, he found them unwilling. Gandhi explained his programme,
that agreed by the Central Khilafat Committee on 12 May, to the
All-India Congress Committee at Benares. The discussion of the
subject was perfunctory, its tone hostile: the nationalist leaders
were much more interested in settling the role which the Congress
was to play in the forthcoming council elections. Thus all that was
agreed was to submit the principle and programme to the provincial congress committees and to defer the decision to adopt non-
co-operation to a special session of the Congress, which was to be
held not later than the middle of September, to discuss the

[1] Letter from Gandhi to the members of the Home Rule League, entitled 'Why
I have joined the Home Rule League', *Navajivan*, 2 May 1920, *CWG*,
Vol. XVII, pp. 369–71; R. A. Gordon, 'Aspects in the History of the Indian
National Congress, with special reference to the Swarajya Party, 1919–1927'
(Unpublished D.Phil. thesis, Oxford, 1970), pp. 22–6.
[2] 'Why I have joined the Home Rule League', *Navajivan*, 2 May 1920, *CWG*,
Vol. XVII, pp. 369–71.
[3] *Young India*, 5 May 1920, *ibid.*, p. 390.
[4] *Navajivan*, 16 May 1920, *ibid.*, p. 416.

Turkish peace terms, the government's action regarding the Punjab atrocities, and the rules and regulations of the new councils.[1]

The Central Khilafat Committee's sessions at Allahabad were dominated in spirit though not in number by the extremists of Upper India and their followers. Abdul Bari had spent the previous days whistling up as many of his ulama contacts as possible.[2] Two-fifths of those who attended the first meeting in Sheikh Zahur Ahmad's house on 1 June were from the UP.[3] Many were very bitter when they heard that the Congress would not support them straightaway in non-co-operation: Abdul Bari accused the Hindus of 'playing' with the Muslims and 'excitedly held Gandhi to his pledge of support'.[4] If the Khilafatists had any doubts about the Congress decision on non-co-operation these were removed by the meetings held with the Hindus in the Railway Theatre. Only twenty-five Hindus bothered to attend, and important Congress leaders such as Tilak and Das did not come at all. Most of those that did attend supported Motilal Nehru and Madan Mohan Malaviya when they made it quite clear that they were not convinced of the practicability of non-co-operation, or of the need for the whole of Gandhi's programme, and that they wanted to consider the question much more fully. At the second joint meeting on 2 June, the extremist Muslims really ran wild. Hasrat Mohani promised to join any Afghan army which might invade India to drive out the British. Then Hindus promptly demanded an explanation, whereupon Shaukat Ali jumped up.

—and in an aggressive tone said that their holy places had already been snatched away, that attempts were being made to obliterate Islam and there was nothing left. If any Moslem invader came for support of the

[1] Resolutions 14 and 15 passed by the All-India Congress Committee at Benares, 30/31 May 1920, *The Indian National Congress 1920–1923* (Allahabad, 1924), p. x.
[2] 'Bring Sind ulema to Allahabad Conference particularly Pirjhandi's son and Maulana Taj Mohamed.' Abdul Bari to Abdullah Haroon, 25 May 1920; 'Urgently required at Allahabad on thirtieth June. Reach unfailingly.' Abdul Bari to A. K. Azad, 28 May 1920; 'Meet Alld. 1–2 June. Kindly attend with other delegates.' Abdul Bari to Md. Abdullah, Secretary of the Anjuman-i-Islam, Sylhet, 28 May 1920; 'Ulemas of all sects should particularly and earnestly invited for first second June Khilafat meeting.' Abdul Bari to Kamaluddin Jafri and Abdul Bari to Shaukat Ali, 28 May 1920. All telegrams in Abdul Bari Papers, File of telegrams, FM.
[3] The following attended from the various provinces: UP 50, Bombay and Sind 20, Bihar and Orissa 10, Punjab 6, Madras 6, Delhi 5, Calcutta 5, CP 5, Rest of India 18. 'Report from the Commissioner of Police, Bombay', Home Poll. B, July 1920, 109, NAI. [4] *Ibid.*

Religion overwhelms politics

Khilafat cause and punish the British [sic], the Mussalmans would join hands with them. The British, he said, deserved such punishment for their injustice and high-handedness towards Islam. So saying he dropped into his seat and tears began to flow.[1]

Azad Sobhani and Zafar Ali Khan strongly supported this stand. But speeches such as these were not likely to encourage the Hindus to ally themselves with the Muslims. Lajpat Rai warned them that, at the first sign of the Muslims pursuing the course set out by Shaukat Ali, the Hindus would oppose them.[2] The Muslims did not win Hindu support for non-co-operation.

It was clear to the Khilafatists that, if they were going to non-co-operate, they would have to do so by themselves. The thought must have deterred many, because, when the Central Khilafat Committee met on 3 January, only forty attended. After the resolution to implement non-co-operation had been proposed, Gandhi was asked to explain his programme and the terms on which he would assist. According to an intelligence report:

He said that if he were allowed to lead the Mohammedans who would then form a small committee of such whole-hearted workers who would have to leave themselves *at his mercy and who would have to behave in any manner he directed them to do.* He would not limit the number but those who joined him whether few or many should be such people who would sacrifice their very lives if he asked for them. He would then get through all the stages in four or five months one by one. [stages of non-co-operation] *He would himself be sort of a dictator.* The committee would work in the cause of the Khilafat but *would not be dependent to any other committee. Even the Central Khilafat Committee would not be allowed to guide this Committee.*[3]

Shaukat Ali declared that the Muslims were ready to submit to Gandhi's dictatorship. 'There was a dead silence and people did not dare to speak one way or the other as they did not approve of placing themselves blindly under Gandhi.' Eventually Riza Ali, supported by Bombay moderates and some UP 'Young Party' men who together amounted to a majority of those present, put forward an amendment which would have limited non-co-operation to the first stage. But Shaukat Ali and Abdul Bari with their customary vigour and religious fanaticism quashed all dissent.[4] Consequently, Gandhi was made chairman of a committee composed of A. K. Azad, Ahmed Hasan of Bihar, Mahomed Ali of Dharavi, H. S. Khatri, Shaukat Ali, Saifuddin Kitchlew and Hasrat Mohani,

[1] *Ibid.*   [2] *Ibid.*   [3] *Ibid.*   [4] *Ibid.*

315

which was answerable to no one, not even the Central Khilafat Committee, and was to have complete charge of putting non-co-operation into practice 'without further delay'.[1]

'Take great care', the *Independent* of Allahabad warned its readers on the morning of 3 June, 'that the control of the Khilafat movement does not fall entirely into the hands of theologians and divines, without any appreciation of the great national and international issues involved in it.'[2] Yet this was the very thing that most of the 'Young Party' Muslims and the Bombay moderates, by permitting themselves to be bullied into acquiescence by Abdul Bari and Shaukat Ali, allowed to happen. In getting the upper hand the UP extremists were helped by men from the Punjab, Sind and Madras. But this had happened before. What was important on this occasion was that the Khilafat organisation had become less dependent on Bombay financially.[3] By June 1920 it was tapping funds from all over India, and anyway Chotani, the major financial backer, though reluctant, still provided support, probably as a result of Abdul Bari's spiritual guidance. Thus the UP extremists were able to shake off the leading reins of the Bombay moderates, ignore the opposition of the less advanced Khilafatists of their own province, and commit the Khilafat organisation to putting non-co-operation into practice. Their failure, as yet, to win substantial Hindu support was a great disappointment. But they had done enough to persuade Gandhi to commit himself to their cause and to lead them.

The leaders of the Khilafat protest now submitted themselves completely to Gandhi's control. At his dictation they appealed to their rulers once more. On 22 June they addressed a memorial to the Viceroy asking him either to get the Turkish peace terms revised or to resign. They gave him till 1 August to take action, failing which they would commence progressive non-co-operation.[4] Non-co-operation was launched on 1 August.

The impact of the introduction of non-co-operation was not startling, either in the UP or in India as a whole. A few lawyers resigned their practices and a few titleholders returned their

---

[1] Resolution of the Allahabad Khilafat conference, 3 June 1920, *Independent* (Allahabad), 8 June 1920.
[2] *Independent* (Allahabad), 3 June 1920.
[3] Brown, *Gandhi*, p. 216.
[4] Representation of the Central Khilafat Committee, enclosed in Gandhi to Private Secretary to the Viceroy, 22 June 1920, Chelmsford Papers (24), IOL.

honours. The commencement of the programme at this stage was partly a sop to the extremists, but mainly a tactical expedient. Between June and September 1920, the basic aim of Gandhi and the Khilafatist leaders was to line up enough support to persuade the Calcutta Special Congress to support their non-co-operation plans. Gandhi was the architect of the campaign. In June he began to use two levers to edge Congressmen into the non-co-operation camp – the Punjab and the reformed councils. The Hunter Report on the Punjab disturbances of 1919 was published on 28 May. It criticised the author of the Amritsar massacre, condemned some minor aspects of the martial law administration but yet gave general approval to the martial law policy in the area. This made many Indians angry. Gandhi immediately attempted to associate this protest with non-co-operation. 'If we are worthy to call ourselves a nation,' he declared in his first comment on the report on 9 June, 'we must refuse to uphold the Government by withdrawing co-operation from it.'[1] By 30 June he had lumped the Punjab problem together with the Khilafat – a policy which he had strongly opposed seven months before – and, if Indians failed to get satisfaction on either issue, non-co-operation was to be their course of action.[2]

The Hunter Report came at a fortunate time. But, emotive though the Punjab issue was, few were likely to make the sacrifices of non-co-operation on that account. The reformed councils were a much more effective lever. Indian politicians did not know precisely what their opportunities were under the new reforms until they saw the council rules and regulations. These were published in draft form in early May 1920. Those for the Punjab showed that Hindus who lived in the towns of the province, the very groups whose political expression had been limited for so long by government, would have little chance of power. The Punjab Congress Committee, though full of protest, had at first seemed willing to work the new council, and at the Benares All-India Congress Committee meeting of the end of May its spokesman, Lajpat Rai, had been among the strongest opponents of non-co-operation. Three weeks after the publication of the Hunter Report, however, he executed a volte-face. He called for a boycott

---

[1] *Young India*, 9 June 1920, *CWG*, Vol. XVII, p. 483.
[2] Press statement issued by Gandhi on boycott of the reformed councils, *Bombay Chronicle*, 30 June 1920, *ibid.*, pp. 521–2.

of the reformed Punjab council: first, because the statements of the Government of India and the Secretary of State on the Hunter Report implied that they condoned the Punjab government's policy of silencing the 'educated community', and the rules and regulations of the reformed council 'partake of the same character'; second, because the officers responsible for the martial law excesses were still in the government, some would sit on the reformed council, and in such circumstances it would not be possible to work the reforms in the proper spirit.[1] Gandhi saw the opportunity straightaway and in his statement of 30 June, which united the Punjab and Khilafat issues, included council boycott, not just for the Punjab but for all India, in the non-co-operation programme. Immediately afterwards he gained the approval of the Central Khilafat Committee's non-co-operation subcommittee and it appeared as part of an enlarged programme announced on 7 July.[2] Council boycott had been included in the Central Khilafat committee's first non-co-operation programme of 14 March, but had not been part of either the three stages announced on 24 March or the four stages agreed to on 12 May. But from now till the council elections non-co-operation centred round this issue; it was, Gandhi declared, 'the most important programme facing the country now...'[3] With it he aimed to sweep all those who were discontented with their lot under the reforms into the non-co-operation camp. Signs of how effective it would be came as the non-co-operation programme was considered by the provincial congress committees in August. Non-co-operation was approved in principle by all; but all, to various degrees, opposed the programme. Council

[1] Statement published by Lajpat Rai in his own vernacular paper, *Bande Mataram*, in mid-June 1920. This was summarised in the *Tribune* (Lahore), 24 June 1920, and translated in the *Bombay Chronicle* (Bombay), 28 June 1920. R. A. Gordon suggests that Lajpat Rai changed his stance on council boycott after seeing the Punjab council rules and regulations which, he states, were published in the second week of June 1920. Gordon, 'Aspects in the history of the Indian National Congress', pp. 35–7. This seems unlikely. First, because the draft proposals for the council rules and regulations were published not in June but in the first week of May 1920, and there were no further developments concerning them till the Joint Select Committee of Parliament published its reports on 6 July and 10 August 1920. *P.P.*, 1920, VI, pp. 1087–100. Second, because Lajpat Rai stressed both in his *Bande Mataram* statement and in a letter to the *Tribune* of 3 July 1920 that it was the Hunter Report which had led him to take up his new position regarding the Councils.

[2] Statement issued by the non-co-operation committee, *Young India*, 7 July 1920, *CWG*, Vol. XVIII, pp. 13–14.   [3] *Navajivan*, 18 July 1920, *ibid.*, p. 55.

boycott, in particular, was rejected out of hand by the CP, Bengal and Madras. It was approved by the UP and Bihar, but with strong opposition from leading politicians, and accepted unanimously only by Sind. Bombay, Punjab and Andhra, which were hostile at heart, postponed decision till the Special Congress.[1] Up to September, therefore, Gandhi's use of the Punjab and council issues appeared to have had limited success.

Simultaneously Gandhi and the Khilafat leaders made a direct bid to persuade their supporters to go to Calcutta and vote for non-co-operation. Gandhi courted his Gujarati supporters with a hurriedly held Gujarat Political conference just before the Special Congress. He told his audience that he was 'going to Calcutta to get non-co-operation accepted by it'.[2] He wooed his Marwari followers by emphasising the concern of leading Khilafatists for cow-protection.[3] To make the point Abdul Bari, Hakim Ajmal Khan, Azad and the Central Khilafat Committee all issued statements enjoining Muslims to abstain from cow-slaughter on the Bakr Id, which fell a few days before the Congress.[4] Their real search for support, however, was directed towards the Muslims. In July Gandhi and Shaukat Ali toured the Muslim areas of Punjab and Sind, in August those of Bombay and Madras. They spoke mainly to the Muslims, explaining non-co-operation and emphasising that it was the only answer to the Khilafat problem. The pursuit of votes also went on elsewhere. In Bengal, the Khilafat Committee asked Muslims to go to Calcutta in large numbers and offered free board and lodging to encourage them.[5] In Bihar, Mazharul Haq and Nurul Hasan helped to push the provincial conference into approving the non-co-operation programme. In the UP, leading ulama formed a propaganda subcommittee of the provincial Khilafat organisation and toured the province. A free trip was offered to all ulama who wished to attend the Special Congress.[6]

All these preparations bore fruit at Calcutta. The real fight over the Central Khilafat Committee subcommittee's non-co-operation

---

[1] Gordon, 'Aspects in the history of the Indian National Congress', pp. 39–42.
[2] Speech on non-co-operation at the Gujarat Political conference, 28 August 1920, *Gujarati*, 5 September 1920, *CWG*, Vol. XVIII, p. 201.
[3] Articles on cow-protection in *Young India*, 4 August 1920, and *Navajivan*, 8 August 1920, *ibid.*, pp. 117–19. 127–9.
[4] *Hamdam* (Lucknow), 11 and 19 August 1920, UPNNR 1920; *Amrita Bazar Patrika* (Calcutta), 25 August 1920.
[5] *Amrita Bazar Patrika* (Calcutta), 25 August 1920.
[6] *Independent* (Allahabad), 29 July 1920; *Leader* (Allahabad), 23 August 1920.

programme took place in the subjects committee. Once the decision was reached here, victory in the full Congress was a foregone conclusion. Three hundred members of the subjects committee were crammed into the Indian Association's rooms in Bow Bazar. In the discussions three groups emerged: Gandhi, Shaukat Ali, Yakub Hasan, Saifuddin Kitchlew and Jitendralal Banerjee, who were out and out supporters of non-co-operation; C. R. Das, B. C. Pal and Madan Mohan Malaviya, who were only partial supporters; Jinnah, Mrs Besant and Jamnadas Dwarkadas, who were strongly hostile. The real struggle was between Das and Gandhi. The Mahatma presented the following plan of non-co-operation: (a) surrender of titles and honorary posts; (b) refusal to attend levées and durbars; (c) withdrawal of children from government schools; (d) boycott of British courts by lawyers and litigants; (e) refusal to serve in Mesopotamia; (f) withdrawal from council elections; (g) boycott of foreign goods. Refusal to participate in government loans and interference in recruitment for the army and police, which had been included in the programme announced on 7 July, were omitted. Das and his party were prepared to adopt the programme with the exception of (c), (d) and (f), which reduced it to little more than an endorsement of the principle of non-co-operation. Gandhi stood firm against all attempts to whittle down his programme. For three days in stifling heat the argument raged back and forth. A session of the Congress had to be postponed. The only concession that Gandhi was prepared to make was the substitution of 'gradual' for 'immediate' in sections (c) and (d). More than once, when the drift of the debate seemed to be going against him, Gandhi stopped his opponents in their tracks by declaring that, whatever they did, he would put non-co-operation into effect. Shaukat Ali was Gandhi's staunchest supporter. He blasted Fazlul Huq off the fence into the non-co-operation camp with a volley of abuse, and was only narrowly prevented from forcing non-violent non-co-operation on Jinnah with his fists. When on 7 September the vote was finally taken, Gandhi's resolution passed by the narrow margin of 148 to 133. With the meeting still in session, Shaukat Ali leapt to a window and announced the result to the crowds outside to a swelling cry of 'Gandhi Ki Jai'. That evening the Congress voted. The resolution passed by 1885 to 883 votes.[1]

[1] FR (Bengal), Home Poll. D, September 1920, 70, NAI; *Amrita Bazar Patrika* (Calcutta), 6, 7, 8, September 1920; *Leader* (Allahabad), 9 September 1920;

Religion overwhelms politics

Only one leading Congressman, Motilal Nehru, supported Gandhi; it was an amazing victory. Its explanation lies in part in the membership of the subjects committee. No list of members appears to exist, but nevertheless some important facts about its composition can be ascertained. It was elected by the delegates from the various provinces and these contained a remarkable number of non-co-operation sympathisers. There were personal supporters of Gandhi: Khadder-clad Punjabis from Ludhiana, Bhatias from Gujarat and Madras, Marwaris from Calcutta and Upper India.[1] But the major group were Muslims. Mazharul Haq led a personal following of fifty Muslims from Bihar, Chotani, a similar number from Bombay, while 'Khilafat Specials' from Bombay and Madras brought hundreds of Muslims to Calcutta. The *Leader* reckoned that over 2000 of the 5500 delegates were Muslims.[2] Never had so many Muslims attended a Congress. These newcomers did their utmost to ensure that only supporters of the non-co-operation programme were elected. In the Bengal camp, advantage was taken of the claim for special representation for Muslims and Marwaris to introduce a larger number of non-co-operation supporters.[3] In the Madras camp, the elections were fixed by Rajagopalachariar and Abdul Hamid Khan. Seven of the fifteen delegates they were allowed to return were Muslim, and not one of the pro-council entry party led by Kasturiranga Iyengar was elected.[4] Evidence is not available for the elections from the other provincial camps, but the loud complaints that followed them suggest that the large numbers of Muslims and other supporters of non-co-operation, who flocked to Calcutta in September, made a concerted and successful attempt to pack the subjects committee with their men.

Independent (Allahabad), 14 September 1920. The figures given for those voting are the ones reported by government, FR (Bengal), Home Poll. D, September 1920, 70, NAI. Many different figures exist, Brown, *Gandhi*, p. 266, n. 4. The reason why so few of the Congress delegates voted is because they were asked to vote either for Gandhi's resolution or for another proposed by B. C. Pal, which also recommended a form of non-co-operation. The result was that the opponents of non-co-operation could do no more than abstain from voting. *Ibid.*, pp. 266–7.

[1] *Amrita Bazar Patrika* (Calcutta), 4, 6 September 1920; WRDCI, 30 August 1920, Home Poll. D, August 1920, NAI.
[2] *Amrita Bazar Patrika* (Calcutta), 4 September 1920; *Bombay Chronicle* (Bombay), 10 September 1920; *Independent* (Allahabad), 1 September 1920; *Hindu* (Madras), 6 September 1920; *Leader* (Allahabad), 1 September 1920.
[3] *Hindu* (Madras), 6 September 1920.   [4] *Ibid.*

Separatism among Indian Muslims

The Muslims were the core of Gandhi's party, but his victory was narrow enough to make every source of support important. Here the council boycott element of the non-co-operation programme played an important part. Whatever the provincial congress committees may have determined beforehand, Congress politicians at Calcutta decided whether or not to support non-co-operation according to their estimate of the Congress's chances of winning a majority at the elections in their provinces. Thus Congressmen from Maharashtra, CP and Bengal, who fancied their chances, were most strongly opposed to non-co-operation. But those from Madras, where Rajagopalachariar's Brahmin faction feared defeat, from Bihar, where they knew they would be squashed by the landed interest, and from the UP, where a similar result was anticipated, supported it. Crucial, probably, in swinging the UP delegation behind the programme was the defection during the discussions of Motilal Nehru. Das thought so. Gandhi certainly thought so; it was for him he made his one concession.[1]

This was a great victory for Gandhi. By persuading the Congress to join the Central Khilafat Committee in non-co-operation he had gone some way towards achieving his ambitions of Hindu–Muslim unity and proving the efficacy of Satyagraha as a means of obtaining justice. But Gandhi, for all his political shrewdness, was an idealist. In crude political terms, this was a much greater victory for the Khilafatists. For months they had been trying to win Hindu support to strengthen their Khilafat protest. For months the Congress chiefs had resisted them. Now they had with Gandhi's aid tossed them to one side, and as Lajpat Rai put it, 'tacked' the Congress on to the Khilafat Committee.[2]

This Khilafatist victory was primarily the work of the 'Young Party' men and the ulama of the UP. They had led the movement, and led it into ever more radical paths. But not all had worked with equal enthusiasm. Many 'Young Party' politicians were wary of association in politics with fanatical ulama. Moreover, their wariness grew as non-co-operation became increasingly the favoured tactic of the Khilafat leaders: they, like many of their Congress contemporaries, did not want to relinquish their legal practices, however small they might be, their chances of winning

---

[1] Gordon, 'Aspects in the history of the Indian National Congress', pp. 44–7.
[2] Lajpat Rai's closing address as president of the Calcutta Special Congress, *Leader* (Allahabad), 12 September 1920.

a council seat or their hopes of government patronage. So, as the
steady revelation of the reforms assured them that the Muslim
claims of separate representation and 'political importance' were
not in danger and as the influence of the ulama in politics increased
and non-co-operation seemed a likely form of protest, many
'Young Party' men became more circumspect in their agitation
for the Khilafat. Ajmal Khan and Ansari, who had launched the
agitation at Delhi in 1918, refused to assist either the Delhi Khilafat conference of November 1919 or the extreme Khilafat Workers
conference of April 1920.[1] After the draft rules of the new UP
council were published in May 1920, several 'Young Party' men
fancied their chances of getting a seat, among them Ansari,
Kamaluddin Ahmed Jafri, Riza Ali, Ali Nabi, Haji Musa Khan,
Hyder Mehdi, Sheikh Zahur Ahmad and Syed Zahur Ahmed.[2]
Attitudes to the Khilafat agitation became influenced by the
council entry question. For electoral reasons 'Young Party'
politicians had to appear to support the Khilafat agitation whole-
heartedly but, when at the Allahabad conference Riza Ali gave
them a chance to limit non-co-operation to harmless items, several
of them seized it. Right up to the Calcutta Congress they kept
their options open. When they were forced to choose, those who
knew they could win council seats, like Riza Ali and Ali Nabi,
abandoned the Khilafat agitation; most of those who knew they
could not made the best of a bad job and supported non-co-operation. These were not the men to force the non-co-operation programme through the Calcutta Congress.

The only 'Young Party' men wholly behind the Khilafatist drive
to implement non-co-operation were the pan-Islamist rump of
Mahomed Ali's pre-war following. They were few in number:
Hasrat Mohani, Mushir Husain Kidwai, plus one or two new
recruits such as Syed Mahomed Husain and Ismail Khan who
helped to run the UP Khilafat Committee, and they joined hands
in other provinces with Kitchlew, Zafar Ali Khan, Mazharul
Haq and Yakub Hasan. Their doyen was Shaukat Ali, tireless
agitational tourer, bombastic orator and committee lion, with the
useful knack of being able to bludgeon opponents into submission.
Such men formed, according to the Intelligence Department, the

[1] FR (Delhi), Home Poll. D, January 1920, 5; Home Poll. D, April 1921,
67, NAI.
[2] *Independent* (Allahabad), 18 May, 15, 17 June, 4 July 1920.

11-2

'...growing class of men who make politics a means of livelihood because they have no other'.[1] Non-co-operation had no terrors for them. They welcomed it because it meant the continuance of the agitational politics off which, as in the pre-war period, they fed.[2]

The Muslims, however, who made the Khilafatist victory were the ulama. They tried to push the movement in a radical direction faster than the 'Young Party' politicians wished to go. They, for instance, founded the Delhi Khilafat Workers association in order to force the hands of Ansari and Ajmal Khan. They originated the idea of non-co-operation and put constant pressure on the Central Khilafat Committee to adopt it and put it into practice. The extent of their involvement is indicated by the closeness with which the non-co-operation programme had, by 7 July, been tailored to fit their interests; they hoped to replace legislative councils with committees of ulama, courts of infidel law with bodies that would

[1] WRDCI, 13 September 1920, Home Poll. D, September 1920, 71, NAI.
[2] Mahomed Ali lived like a prince off Khilafat funds on his six-month-long deputation to Europe. FR (Bombay), Home Poll. D, December 1920, 66, NAI. Shaukat Ali had immense difficulty in getting the Khilafat accounts audited to his taste. The accountants, Messrs. A. H. Billimoria & Co., refused to certify payment of two and a half lakhs of rupees alleged to have been spent on propaganda work. Billimoria himself remained unimpressed when Shaukat Ali took him into his confidence and said that the money had been used for bribing the Indian Army which had sworn to follow him against the British whenever he gave the word. Home Poll. 1922, 155, NAI. When a committee investigated the Khilafat accounts it revealed that Shaukat Ali and his cousin Moazzam Ali had used their positions as secretaries to live in great style: 'We called for the travelling allowance bills for checking expenditure under this head, but after a good deal of search only three bills were produced before us. A perusal of these has resulted in a strange revelation. These bills are a compound mixture in which the competent physican has entered remedies for all needs, i.e. dhobi, barber, medicine, telegrams (on which large sums have been spent), subsidy to papers, reward, bakshish, press message, formidable motor hire, and above all a long string of unknown persons entertained during the journey...It would appear from the details of the expenditure given above that when the Secretary travels the cloud of his bounty showers rupees on all sides. Mahajirs, deserving persons, newspapers, servants, all are fully satiated from the fountain of generosity and for the complete satisfaction of the auditor the following words are caused to be entered "help for Khilafat – Name to be kept secret".' 'Report of the Khilafat Account Enquiry Committee', Home Poll. 1923, 15, NAI. To cap it all Chotani abused his position as president of the Central Khilafat Committee by investing sixteen lakhs of its funds in his own financial ventures. FR (Bombay), Home Poll. 1923, 25, NAI. Journalists and newspaper owners benefited too. Between 1917 and 1922, the circulation of papers in English in the UP nearly tripled and that of Urdu papers nearly doubled. F. C. R. Robinson, 'The Politics of U.P. Muslims 1906–1922' (Unpublished PhD thesis, Cambridge, 1970), Table XXXV, 'Growth of the Press by Language, 1912–22', p. 399.

interpret the sharia and government schools with Muslim madras-sas. What could have appealed more to a band of private school-masters (for that is what most of them were), who were fast losing business to state schools, than smashing the rival system, winning back their pupils and reviving their trade. The ulama had most to gain from driving the Khilafat agitation more extreme. It was not surprising that they lay at the heart of its organisation. They dominated the UP provincial Khilafat Committee: Azad Sobhani was president and Abdul Majid and Nazir Ahmed ran its propa-ganda. They presided over district, provincial and all-India con-ferences and their followers were usually a large part of the audience. Nor were they any less prominent in other provinces. Maulvis Akram Khan and Ghiasuddin ran the Bengal Khilafat Committee, Mahomed Sajjad was the leading worker in Bihar and Abdul Majid Sharar the organiser in Madras.

These ulama, who dominated the early stages of the Khilafat agitation both in the UP and in India as a whole, were mainly followers of Abdul Bari.[1] The Lucknow maulana's influence, not only as head of the school which most ulama politicians followed but also as the pir of most leading lay Khilafatists, was immense. He organised the first great fatwa on the Khilafat question as well as those which reinforced the various developments in the agitation. These fatwa moved Muslims all over India, and their practical power was considerable: his Hijrat fatwa sent 10,000 Sindhis to their deaths in the Khyber Pass. Abdul Bari led most of the ulama who attended such important occasions as the Delhi Khilafat conference of November 1919 or the Allahabad meetings of June 1920. His followers were mainly responsible for the large Muslim attendance at the Calcutta Congress in September, which transformed non-co-operation from a dream into a practical poli-tical proposition.

[1] During most of 1920, the Khilafat agitation was strongly opposed by most of the leading schools of ulama apart from Abdul Bari's section of Firangi Mahal. Neither the ulama of the Nadwa nor those of Deoband would support it, despite considerable pressure. WRDCI, 3 May 1920, Home Poll. D, June 1920, 78, NAI; *Iqbal* (Moradabad), 7 September 1920. The divines of the Barh-ul-ulum section of Firangi Mahal, and of Thana Bhavan (Saharanpur), issued fatwa against non-co-operation. *Aligarh Institute Gazette* (Aligarh), 15 Decem-ber 1920, and *Al Bashir* (Etawah), 23 November 1920, UPNNR 1920. Ahmad Reza Khan of Bareilly issued fatwa declaring India to be Dar-ul-Islam, making it a sin for Muslims to associate with infidels, and declaring it scandalous that they allowed themselves to be duped by Gandhi. *Mashriq* (Gorakhpur), 7 October, 25 November 1920, UPNNR 1920.

CHAPTER 9

The Muslim party disintegrates

1920-1923

For most 'Young Party' politicians the alliance with the ulama was a grave embarrassment. The failure of the allies to make peace with Turkey had enabled the ulama, with the help of Gandhi and 'Young Party' agitators, to transform the Khilafat protest. Thus, what had been begun as a tactical move to strengthen the Muslim League's claims during the making of the Montagu–Chelmsford reforms had become the major concern of Muslims in politics. In consequence, the influence of the Muslim League, the spokesman of secular Muslim politics, declined while that of the Khilafat Committee and the Jamiat-ul-ulama, which stood for Islamic politics, rose. The politicians had been hoist by their own petard.

At the Nagpur Congress in December 1920, the victory that had been won at Calcutta in September was confirmed. The non-co-operation programme which was adopted owed more to Das than to Gandhi, and indeed several Congress leaders who had been among the opposition at Calcutta now joined them. For once the first elections to the reformed councils had taken place at the beginning of December, it made sense for politicians who did not have council seats to join the non-co-operation movement and control it.[1] 'Young Party' politicians accepted non-co-operation for many of the same reasons. They did not believe that it would bring the government down; they could see that in any case the experiment was for a strictly limited period. If full swaraj was not won in a year, they would have to content themselves with a more modest step towards it by fighting the next council elections in 1923. Non-co-operation was viable only if the Congress supported it, and 'Young Party' men were sure that Congress politicians would not, a second time, allow themselves to be tricked out of using the reformed councils. In the meantime they tried to extract what political advantage they could out of the situation, and their main task was to resist the growing challenge of the priest in their affairs.

[1] Gordon, 'Aspects in the history of the Indian National Congress', pp. 51–7.

The Muslim party disintegrates

The striking feature of 1921 and 1922 was the increasing influence of the ulama. 'The influence and prestige of the Moulvies,' wrote Jawaharlal Nehru, who was in the thick of things, 'which had been gradually declining owing to new ideas and a progressive Westernisation, began to grow again and dominate the Muslim community.'[1] He might have added that this gave the ulama a powerful voice in Muslim politics, and, because they were the driving force behind non-co-operation, a new importance in Indian politics as a whole. For most Hindus non-co-operation was a matter of politics. For most Muslims the ulama helped to make it a matter of religion. In November 1920, the Jamiat-ul-ulama, prompted by Abdul Bari, made giving funds for anything to do with non-co-operation zakat, that is a religious duty as obligatory as praying or fasting. Muslims were now supposed to devote two and a half per cent of their income to the cause. At the same session a fatwa was issued, the muttaffiqa fatwa which was signed eventually by 500 ulama, making non-co-operation a duty and declaring it lawful to ally with Hindus and to follow Gandhi.[2] These injunctions from the great assembly of Indian ulama were broadcast in the press and preached in the countryside by missionaries from the leading schools. In February 1921, the ulama of Firangi Mahal toured the eastern districts of the UP. Later in the year the students of the Nadwat-ul-ulama and Deoband went out to rally the faithful. Local priests also did their bit with fatwas, sermons and face-to-face persuasion. And if local priests were not effective, the Khilafatists turned to the leading divines: 'Please send fatwa containing authorities on educational non-co-operation', telegraphed the Lahore Khilafat committee to Abdul Bari.[3] As a result the agitation came increasingly to be a crusade and the more religious it became the more the influence of the ulama grew. By the time non-co-operation reached its climax in February 1922, the UP government singled out as the real danger 'the Mahomedan population of numerous small towns [which] is very hostile and is controlled by fanatical Maulvis'.[4]

[1] Jawaharlal Nehru, *An Autobiography* (London, 1936), p. 72.
[2] Statement by Abdul Bari, undated but most probably published in November 1920, Abdul Bari Papers, English File, FM; Home Poll. 1921, 137, NAI.
[3] Lahore Khilafat Committee to Abdul Bari, 30 October 1921, Abdul Bari Papers, File of telegrams, FM.
[4] Telegram, Viceroy to Secretary of State, 28 February 1922, Home Poll. 1922, 18, NAI.

By 1921 most of the leading ulama schools had declared for non-co-operation. Until September 1920 most ulama kept their options open, just as the secular politicians had done, and paid little heed to the Central Khilafat Committee's adoption of non-co-operation. But when the Congress approved Gandhi's programme, the dam burst: almost immediately the Nadwat-ul-ulama refused its government grant; Shah Abdul Sulaiman of Phulwari, the leading alim of Bihar and the most cautious of Abdul Bari's disciples, made public his support for non-co-operation; and the Deobandis signed the muttaffiqa fatwa.[1] Even the Shias were persuaded to join in with the ulama. In March 1921, persuaded by a brilliantly stage-managed rumour that the sacred shrine at Najaf had been bombarded by the British, the leading Lucknow mujtahid, Syed Yusuf Husain, issued a fatwa in favour of non-co-operation. Some Shias now joined their Sunni brethren, a most uncommon example of co-operation between the religious leaders of the two major sects of Islam.[2] How united the ulama were in backing non-co-operation in 1921 was revealed when the government tried to arrange a fatwa to refute the muttaffiqa fatwa. The Raja of Jehangirabad spent a lot of money to this end but he had little to show for it. 'I tried my best', replied another helper to the government, 'but found it very difficult to persuade them.'[3] In the event, the only ulama of any standing, who could be induced to sign were Abdul Majid and Abdul Hamid, Abdul Bari's mortal Firangi Mahal enemies. By 1921, non-co-operation was no longer supported just by Abdul Bari and his Firangi Mahal gang, but by the vast majority of Indian ulama, briefly united, regardless of sect and school. One consequence of this unprecedented unity was that Abdul Bari no longer dominated the scene; another was that the ulama became a yet more potent political force.

A sure sign of the ulama's growing confidence was that they now began to do something about their dreams of reinstating their old dominance in Muslim society. Four years earlier, while the politicians petitioned Montagu for separate electorates and reserved

---

[1] Educ, 1921, 211, UPS; *Independent* (Allahabad), 5 November 1920; *Hamdam* (Lucknow), 5 November 1920, UPNNR 1920; Home Poll. 1921, 137, NAI.

[2] FR (UP), Home Poll. D, June 1921, 63, 65, NAI; *Al Khalil* (Bijnor), 28 March 1921; *Jadu* (Jaunpur), 22 March 1921; *Al Bashir* (Etawah), 29 March 1921; *Ittihad* (Amroha), 1 April 1921, UPNNR 1921.

[3] Kazi Azizuddin to W. Vincent, 18 December 1921, Home Poll. 1922, 699, NAI.

seats on councils, the ulama demanded that Indian Muslims be governed according to the principles of the Koran. In 1917 this had been a total chimaera; but now this ambition seemed to be entering the realm of practical politics. Already in 1918 there had been talk of a Shaikh-ul-Islam, or religious head, for all India,[1] and Abdul Bari who coveted the post had even offered Gandhi a bargain built around his hopes.[2] In June 1920, the Lucknow divine tried again, and at the Allahabad conferences the Firangi Mahal ulama did their best to secure his election.[3] By 1921, some ulama were ready to set up organisations to administer the sharia. In Bihar, for example, a conference dominated by Abul Kalam Azad and Azad Sobhani set up a system of religious courts in the districts, each headed by an Amir-i-shariat, which were to administer the sharia. These were subject to a provincial council, which was also headed by an Amir-i-shariat, who was to be Shah Sulaiman Phulwari. It was, according to a local police observer, 'a scheme for the complete organisation of the community throughout the country under selected religious leaders and under the general control of one religious head'.[4] Abdul Bari at first opposed the scheme;[5] he was jealous of Azad, who was now the favourite for the top post of Shaikh-ul-Islam. Later, however, he changed his mind when he discovered that even the Deobandi ulama would rather support his election than be subject to Azad, whose political views were thought to run too close to those of the secular politicians.[6] And

---

[1] *Ifada* (Agra), April 1918; *Jadu* (Jaunpur), 21 May 1918; *Al Bureed* (Cawnpore) 25 July 1918, UPNNR 1918. Shaikh-ul-Islam was the title applied to the mufti of Constantinople, the supreme law-giver of the Ottoman government.

[2] Abdul Bari's bargain with Gandhi was struck early in 1919. Abdul Bari is said to have arranged to call a conference of ulama and Muslims at the height of the Mahatma's Rowlatt satyagraha at which he would be elected Shaikh-ul-Islam and Muslim demands regarding the Khilafat would be formulated. Gandhi and the Hindus would support these demands and Abdul Bari in turn would use his new-found position to ban cow-slaughter. The deal, however, came to nothing. 'A note on political agitation in Delhi with special reference to the activities of volunteers corps', Home Poll. D, April 1921, 67 NAI.

[3] The position, in this case, was wali or religious ruler, not Shaikh-ul-Islam. 'Report from the Commissioner of Police, Bombay,' Home Poll. B, July 1920, 109, NAI.

[4] 'Report received from D.I.G. of Police, Crime and Railways, B & O, of a Conference of Ulemas held at Patna on 25 & 26th June 1921', Home Poll. 1921, 180, NAI.

[5] Abdul Bari to Editor, *Hamdam* (Lucknow), 24 July 1921, UPNNR 1921.

[6] D-O letter from the Commissioner of Police, Bombay, 24 January 1922, Home Poll. 1922, 551, NAI.

here was the rub. The purpose of the Amir-i-shariat scheme was to elevate the ulama to the position of political as well as religious leadership, 'to bring them out of the madrassas to the field of action....'[1] In such an organisation the leadership of a priest who openly listened to the advice of laymen was bound to be unwelcome. It meant too that the policies of men such as the Ali brothers and Gandhi would only be tolerated so long as they coincided with those of the ulama.

From the middle of 1921, it became increasingly difficult for the politicians, whose attention was diverted to Gandhian spinning wheels and homespun, to contain the ulama. At the Meerut All-India Khilafat conference in April, some ulama objected strongly to the alliance with the Hindus and demanded that its scope be defined according to religious rules. Not surprisingly, Khilafat leaders found it difficult to paper over such cracks in the non-co-operation front.[2] In June Abdul Bari warned that the Muslims were ready to desert Gandhi and adopt violent methods.[3] As Britain and Turkey drifted towards war, the ulama became more militant. In July at the Karachi All-India Khilafat conference, an extremely aggressive resolution was passed. It congratulated the Turks on their recent victories, forbad Muslims to serve in the Army, threatened that, if the British went to war with Turkey, the Muslims would, 'carrying the Congress with them', both launch civil disobedience and proclaim India an independent republic.[4] By now the agitator and the priest were clearly making the running. The government was forced to intervene; it arrested, tried and imprisoned all those who were prominent in backing the resolution, among them Hasan Ahmed Madni, the new leader of Deoband, Pir Gulam Mujadid, a Sindhi follower of Abdul Bari, and the Ali brothers. Soon afterwards it proscribed the muttaffiqa fatwa, which had also forbidden Muslims to serve in the army.

The events which followed illustrate the increasing differences between the political and religious wings of the agitation. The

---

[1] Speech by Azad Sobhani at the Patna ulama conference, 25/26 June 1921, Home Poll. 1921, 180, NAI.
[2] WRDCI, 11 April 1921, Home Poll. D, June 1921, 54; FR (UP), Home Poll. D, June 1921, 51, NAI.
[3] Statement by Abdul Bari entitled 'We are forced to revise our programme', 11 June 1921, Home Poll. 1921, 45, NAI.
[4] Resolution 6 of the All-India Khilafat Conference at Karachi, 8–10 July 1921, FR (Bombay), Home Poll. 1921, 18; Home Poll. 1922, 155, NAI.

The Muslim party disintegrates

Delhi ulama immediately asked to be allowed to begin civil disobedience, but were persuaded to put the matter off until the Central Khilafat Committee and the Jamiat-ul-ulama met in Delhi on 21 and 22 September. At the Khilafat meeting it 'was urged that the verses of the Qoran were proscribed and their respected leaders were being arrested for preaching the commandments contained in the holy Qoran and it was the last straw to break the camel's back and there was nothing left but for them to have recourse to civil disobedience.'[1] By now the ulama were in full cry, and Azad and Hakim Ajmal Khan were hard pressed to resist their demands for a full-blooded campaign of civil disobedience. The temper of the meeting was militantly Muslim; so little store was set on Hindu support that it voted funds for the Malabar Muslims who in August had risen against the Hindus, killing and forcibly converting many of them. It was left to Azad, who understood the political facts of life, to insist on an amendment which offered Rs. 10,000 to the Hindus who had been the victims of the Muslim attack. At the Jamiat-ul-ulama meeting, Azad again had to stand against immense pressure for civil disobedience. He reminded his audience that the question was political and could only be decided at the next meeting of the Congress in December at Ahmedabad. With difficulty he persuaded the ulama to be content with a resolution which declared that the proscribed muttaffiqa fatwa should continue to be printed and distributed.[2]

The ulama, however, did not have to wait until December. Gandhi was clearly worried by their increasingly independent and extreme attitude, and as before he altered his policy to curb it. On 4 October he issued a manifesto, signed by leading Congressmen, Khilafatists and ulama, which endorsed the resolution of the Karachi Khilafat conference. A month later he piloted a resolution through the All-India Congress Committee which authorised the

[1] Report by Tassaduq Hussein on the Central Khilafat Committee and Jamiat-ul-ulama meetings at Delhi on 21/22 September 1921, Home Poll. 1921, 137, NAI.

[2] *Ibid.* Judith Brown suggests that Azad, far from being a moderating force on this occasion, actually took the lead in calling for immediate civil disobedience. Brown, *Gandhi*, pp. 334–5. This view is based on letters from the Chief Commissioner of Delhi, C. A. Barron to the Secretary of the Government of India Home Department, S. P. O'Connell, 24 September 1921 and 1 October 1921. But the Chief Commissioner's portrait of Azad as a fanatical extremist is quite out of character, and for this reason the detailed report of Tassaduq Hussein, which shows the maulana as a moderate politician determined to hold the agitation together, has been followed.

provinces to begin mass or individual civil disobedience on their own responsibility and in the way they thought most fit. Here was permission for civil disobedience with limited liability. Moreover, after government's wholesale imprisonment of Congress and Khilafat leaders in November and December 1922, Gandhi had no choice but to confirm this decision to allow civil disobedience at the Ahmedabad Congress.

By the end of 1921, however, mere civil disobedience was no longer enough for the ulama. Now their aim was to sever the British connection with India completely, if necessary by force. Azad Sobhani and Hasrat Mohani[1] were the spokesmen at Ahmedabad. Throughout the proceedings they were resisted by the politicians. When Hasrat Mohani made his demand in the Khilafat conference, the president, Hakim Ajmal Khan, did not allow the resolution to go forward. When in the All-India Congress Committee and the full Congress session Hasrat Mohani tried to insert in the Congress creed the words 'The object of the Indian National Congress is the attainment of *swaraj* or complete independence, free from all foreign control, by all legitimate and peaceful means', Gandhi had to intervene to prevent him getting his way. In the All-India Muslim League sessions Mohani presided and got his own back by telling the Mahatma to his face that he scorned his methods and favoured violence. But when Azad Sobhani, supported by Maulvis Abdul Majid Budauni and Daud Ghaznavi, put forward in the subjects committee another resolution advocating complete independence, he was strongly opposed by the political wing. By marshalling their forces, Ansari, Riza Ali, Hakim Ajmal Khan and Syed Zahur Ahmed defeated him by thirty-six votes to twenty-three.[2]

During January and February 1922, all control over the movement began to break down. For one thing, many of the local leaders of non-co-operation had been put in jail. For another, the movement's propaganda began to strike home amongst the people. In the UP it looked as if unrest in both town and country was on the point of boiling over in indiscriminate and insensate violence. In Sultanpur the Raja of Amethi became so alarmed that he took to the jungle with his family and his gold.[3] In Bara Banki a Muslim

---

[1] Hasrat Mohani, of course, was an Aligarh old boy, although by this time he was barely distinguishable in attitude from the ulama.
[2] *Leader* (Allahabad), 4 January 1922; Home Poll. 1921, 461, NAI.
[3] FR (UP), Home Poll. 1922, 18, NAI.

zamindar marched 1200 of his co-religionists into the district town, surrounded the headquarters, abused the government and declared independence. Even the ever-confident Harcourt Butler began to get anxious. 'The fanatical Mussalman party is out of hand', he told a friend.[1] Violence, of course, did eventually occur; on 5 February twenty-one policemen were burned to death by a rural mob at Chauri Chaura in Gorakhpur district. Gandhi reacted immediately. Seven days later at Bardoli he suspended all civil disobedience. Instead, his followers were ordered to concentrate on a constructive programme. In place of civil disobedience they were to collect funds, encourage temperance, spin cotton and teach in national schools.[2] It was now clear that it would be a long time before Gandhi launched another civil disobedience campaign. The Mahatma was abused for his decision by his allies and by his friends; to many he seemed to have dashed the cup of success from their lips. But Gandhi realised that he had lost control of non-co-operation, and he was not prepared to lead a violent insurrection which would only be bloodily suppressed by government. A month later the government saved him further embarrassment by placing him under arrest.

For Gandhi the abandonment of civil disobedience was a political and moral necessity, for the ulama it was no less a necessity to continue to protest with every means at their disposal. The Khilafat question remained unresolved. The Turkish nationalists were still fighting for their lives against the Greeks, while the British led by a blatantly anti-Turkish Lloyd George stood by ready to intervene. Right up to the signing of the Treaty of Lausanne in July 1923, the ulama continued to fight to save the Khilafat and, by the same token, to improve their own status in Indian Muslim society. 'Young Party' politicians reacted to Gandhi's decision rather differently. On the one hand, they were not averse to continuing to exploit the political potential of religious issues: 'Ansari and Ajmal Khan do not wish the complete settlement of [the] Turkish question', Chotani complained when they refused to allow him to thank the Viceroy and Secretary of State for their support over Turkey, in order 'to keep Musalmans

<hr>

[1] Harcourt Butler to H. E. Richards, 12 January 1922, Harcourt Butler Papers (21), IOL.
[2] Resolutions passed by the Working Committees at Bardoli on 11 and 12 February 1922, *The Indian National Congress*, pp. 176–82; *Young India*, 16 February 1922, *CWG*, Vol. XXII, pp. 377–81.

hanging on to the national movement'.[1] But on the other hand these politicians knew that in the last resort their future lay with those groups in the Congress which wanted political solutions, not revolution, and in the end to enter the councils. Thus, when the Congress withdrew from the brink of mass civil disobedience, so did the 'Young Party' Muslims, and the Khilafat Committee fully endorsed their change of policy.[2]

Over the next two years, as the Congress slowly extricated itself from the travail of non-co-operation, the ulama were to remain difficult to control. They were infuriated by the Bardoli Resolutions and showed their feelings in a Jamiat-ul-ulama conference at Ajmere a few days before Gandhi's arrest. They wanted to use violence, but were opposed by the 'Young Party' leaders Ansari, Sheikh Zahur Ahmad and Syed Mahmud of Bihar. Abdul Bari, in his closing speech as president, attacked both the Bardoli Resolutions and non-violence. 'Mahatma Gandhi', he said, 'had exhausted all the items of his programme and no arrow was now left in his quiver. The Mussalmans would not remain silent like a woman but need some forward programme for the achievement of their aims...he was ready to commit violence by hand, teeth and by all the implements available.'[3] Ansari was furious and called the maulana a 'brainless, insincere, notoriety hunter'. There was consternation, and it looked as if priest and politician would go their separate ways. But the inevitable divorce was postponed once more. The Mahatma was sent for. He hastened to Ajmere and extracted a temporary recantation from the fiery alim.[4]

But the ulama did not remain quiet for long. In June the Jamiat-ul-ulama, the Central Khilafat Committee and the All-India Congress Committee met for a joint conference in Lucknow. The executive committee of the Jamiat were in great excitement. The Koran, ulama complained, was daily insulted, the Khilafat question was still unsolved, and Kemal Pasha was on his last legs: 'If they wished to save Islam they should not depend on the Bardauli programme.' Their followers were ready for radical

[1] Report by Tassaduq Hussein on the All-India Congress Working Committee at Ahmedabad on 17/18 March 1922, Home Poll. 1922, 601, NAI.
[2] Resolutions of the All-India Khilafat Committee 25/26 February 1922, Home Poll. 1922, 632, NAI.
[3] Description, sent by 'Justice' to Tassaduq Hussein, 20 March 1922, of Abdul Bari's speech to the All-India Ulama conference at Ajmere, 5 March 1922, Home Poll. 1922, 501, NAI.   [4] *Ibid.*

solutions. The people of Gorakhpur, Basti and Azamgarh, declared Azad Sobhani, had asked him to be allowed to rise. Twelve UP and eight Madras districts, added Abdul Majid Budauni, were game for anything. With these arguments, the Jamiat persuaded the Khilafat working committee to join them in putting before the Congress working committee resolutions demanding (1) the right to retaliate as private individuals, (2) the extension of the principle of boycott, and (3) the definition of swaraj as complete independence. When the three committees met the first two subjects were deferred for further consideration and the third was left undecided. Some ulama were invited to the full meeting of the All-India Congress Committee and here they continued their assault. Congress leaders, pressed by strong demands from the body of the committee for mass civil disobedience, had already compromised with their extremists by appointing a committee to examine the country's preparedness for such a campaign and by agreeing to decide on the matter on 15 August. The ulama said this was not enough: they wanted to commence mass civil disobedience straight away, and, if this was not possible, at least to agree upon a firm date when it would begin. But the Congress committee had made its decision; it was not to be moved. Two days later the ulama tried to commit the Central Khilafat Committee to beginning civil disobedience without the Congress, but Hakim Ajmal Khan dissuaded them on the grounds that the Muslims could not win such a campaign by themselves. Their sole and paltry achievement was to prevent the Khilafat Committee from sending yet another deputation to England.[1] Nevertheless their anger, combined with the impatience of the large number of Congressmen who wanted extreme measures, was enough to make Hakim Ajmal Khan and Ansari feel that they would not be able to stall for long. In the weeks that followed, both showed signs of wishing to abandon politics altogether.[2]

The two Delhi leaders, however, were able to stay in politics. Between June and December 1922, the demand for mass civil

[1] Home Poll. 1922, 868; Report by Tassaduq Hussein, 19 June 1922, Home Poll. 1922, 941, NAI.

[2] Ansari was reported to be showing signs of yielding to his wife's demands that he should give up politics and Hakim Ajmal Khan is reported to have said that he would withdraw from the movement; 'it is all right to go to jail for a year or 18 months, but he was not prepared to go to the gallows'. Report by Tassaduq Hussein, 18 June 1922, Home Poll. 1922, 941, NAI.

disobedience slackened, in part because the evidence given before the Congress and Khilafat Enquiry Committees revealed that no part of India was ready for it,[1] and in part because the unreasoning fury of the ulama abated as the tide of battle turned in Turkey, the Kemalists drove the Greeks into the Aegean and the British government seemed willing to come to terms. By November 1922, the main issue was no longer whether to revive civil disobedience but whether to fight the Council elections of 1923. The Khilafat Enquiry Committee opposed Council entry, only Sheikh Zahur Ahmad voting in favour. The Congress Enquiry Committee divided equally over the question; Hakim Ajmal Khan, Motilal Nehru and V. F. Patel were for council entry and Ansari, Kasturiranga Iyengar and Rajagopalachariar were against. When the All-India Congress Committee met in November, Nehru and T. A. K. Sherwani tried to make Council entry the official Congress policy. But, since the All-India Congress Committee could not agree, the matter was put off until the Gaya Congress. The Central Khilafat Committee also agreed to postpone its decision until December.[2]

At Gaya the influence of the ulama, which had declined somewhat in the second half of 1922, revived. The peace negotiations at Lausanne, and the abolition of the temporal power of the Khilafat by the Turks in November, were both religious questions. Muslims again looked to the ulama for a lead. Another factor strengthening their hand was the readiness of Congressmen to woo them in order to preserve Hindu–Muslim unity. This unity, which had already been endangered by the Moplah riots, was now further threatened by communal rioting in northern India. Congressmen were prepared to make sacrifices to maintain the appearance of communal harmony; 'should the Ulemas come to the conclusion that under the present circumstances it would be an offence against their religion to enter the Councils,' Das declared in his presidential address, 'the Congress should unhesitatingly accept their de-

---

[1] The reports of the Enquiry Committees, which were both supposed to appear at the beginning of August, were not published till the beginnings of November. Congress leaders, such as Motilal Nehru and probably Hakim Ajmal Khan, who wished to put an end to civil disobedience ambitions, played an important part in causing the delay. *Leader* (Allahabad), 6 September and 21 October 1922. Similarly, the All-India Congress Committee session, which was supposed to discuss the Enquiry Committee report, was postponed from 15 August to 20 November.

[2] Gordon, 'Aspects in the history of the Indian National Congress', pp. 83–4; *Leader* (Allahabad), 29 November 1922.

cision, because no work in this country towards the attainment of Swaraj is possible without the hearty co-operation of both Hindus and Mussulmans'.[1] One indication of the swing towards the ulama was that the Muslim League did not meet. Another was the claim by the Jamiat-ul-ulama's president, Habib-ul-Rahman of Deoband, that it was superior to 'all other Muslim organisations or conferences in India...'[2] The Jamiat's policy was to boycott the councils. The Khilafat conference now voted overwhelmingly against council entry. In the Congress, the council boycott party won in the end by a large majority after a keen debate. It won largely because of support from the Muslim extremists. 'If a Hindu–Muhammadan split was to be avoided', government reported, 'the Congress had to follow the lead of the Muhammadans who in their turn were largely in the hands of their religious leaders, the *ulemas*.'[3] In September 1920 the ulama had helped to force the Calcutta Congress to boycott the councils; in December 1922 they ensured that the Gaya Congress continued the boycott.

Gaya marked the apogee of ulama power in Indian politics, and in 1923 their influence swiftly declined. There were several reasons for this. Their religious grievance against the government became less acute. While the Turks thrashed out a peace at Lausanne with the Allies, and the Urdu press bitterly complained about the harshness of the British terms,[4] the ulama were able to keep Muslim agitation at a high pitch. 'Every political line of action', the *Leader* commented in April 1923, 'is now put to the test of religion and the fatwas of the Ulema are supreme.'[5] But once the Treaty of Lausanne had been signed in July, and a strong and independent Turkey emerged upon which the spiritual authority of the Khilafat might rest, the main ostensible Muslim grievance against their

---

[1] *Leader* (Allahabad), 28 December 1922. Das's statement caused a furore; it was too much for the Congress to be told that it was being dictated to by the ulama. On the following day, he did his best to restore the situation by publishing a correction replacing the word 'Ulemas' in his address with 'Khilafat Conference'. *Ibid.*, 29 December 1922. The *Leader* was not impressed. It commented on this 'significant correction': 'Whatever it is the Ulemas, the high ecclesiastics of Islam or whether it is the Khilafat politicians the fact is that it is one or the other or both who have got the whip hand and it is for them to say what Congressmen shall do or not do.' *Ibid.* 30 December 1922.   [2] *Ibid.*, 28 December 1922.
[3] FR (Bihar), Home Poll. 1922, 18, NAI.
[4] UPNNR, 3 February 1923, 10 February 1923, 17 February 1923, 3 March 1923.
[5] *Leader* (Allahabad), 8 April 1923.

Separatism among Indian Muslims

rulers was removed. Of course, the ulama were not completely satisfied. Only part of their threefold Khilafat demand had been met, and some, notably Abdul Bari, tried to keep the agitation going on the ground that parts of the Jazirat-ul-Arab were still in foreign hands. But they had little success. From July 1923, the Indian ulama lost the religious lever which they had used with such success to assert their leadership over the Muslim community.

Another reason why the influence of the ulama declined was the growth of communal antagonism. By 1923 the trend of recent events had given Hindus cause for alarm. They had discovered that Muslims had loyalties outside India: 'At present the fear is only too real in the mind of many a Hindu', declared the *Leader* in January, 'that the leanings of the average Indian Mussalman are not national but extra-territorial, and that fear is obviously a bar to true national solidarity.'[1] They had also discovered that many Muslims placed communal loyalties higher than national unity. The Jamiat-ul-ulama, for instance, had quite shamelessly supported the Moplahs who converted Hindus by force. They were perturbed at the political power which Muslim priests had acquired: 'they cannot be permitted', protested one Hindu after Gaya, 'to control public policy affecting the rights, liberties, political and economic interests of the composite Indian people in the name of their communal religion or scripture.'[2] Moreover, they were alarmed at the recent growth of specifically communal organisation among the Muslims. 'The Khilafat agitation', continued the same Hindu, 'has helped to make the Mahomedan community as a whole much stronger than the Hindu community ...The Hindus must apply themselves seriously to organise their forces and resources just as the Mahomedans have done.'[3] This the Hindus did, reviving the organisations of Hindu self-defence that had sprung up after the Morley–Minto reforms. Towards the end of 1922 the Hindu Sabha was refounded as the Hindu Mahasabha. In the spring of 1923, Swami Shraddhanand, the Arya Samajist who had preached in the Delhi Juma Masjid in 1919, launched a campaign in Agra and neighbouring districts to reclaim for Hinduism the Malkana Rajputs, a Rajput sub-caste which had been converted to Islam under Aurangzeb. Though the reclama-

[1] *Ibid.* 20 January 1923.
[2] A letter from B. C. Pal to the editor of the *Englishman* which was republished in *ibid.*, 31 January 1922.
[3] *Ibid.*

338

tion campaign was small, the issue was blown up to immense proportions by the vernacular press, and the tensions it created contributed to the many communal riots that broke out in northern India during the summer of 1923.[1] Some ulama, for instance Azad Sobhani, now vice-president of the UP Congress Committee, felt that they should not interfere with the Arya Samaj campaign.[2] But for most of them there was only one reply to this Hindu counter-attack on Islam – vigorous defence. The Jamiat-ul-ulama immediately launched a propaganda campaign. It sent missionaries to the disturbed areas and appealed for funds, forcing the Central Khilafat Committee, much against the will of its more politically-minded members, to donate Rs. 50,000.[3] Abdul Bari, the erstwhile apostle of Hindu–Muslim unity, came to the fore again. Now he spoke the language of the zealot. He urged Muslims to sacrifice cows without regard for Hindu feelings, and declared: 'If the commandments of Shariat are to be trampled under foot then it will be the same to us whether the decision is arrived at on the plains of Delhi or on the hilltops of Simla. We are determined to non-co-operate with every enemy of Islam whether he be in Anatolia or Arabia or at Agra or Benares.'[4] In these circumstances, 'Young Party' politicians and Congressmen were forced to loosen their links with the ulama.

The chief cause of the decline of ulama influence, however, was the imminence of the 1923 council elections. Immediately after their defeat at the Gaya Congress, the council entry group, led by Nehru and Das, formed a Congress–Khilafat–Swarajya party as a 'party within the Congress'. 'Young Party' leaders were prominent in the Swarajya organisation, among them Khali-quzzaman, who was party secretary, Hakim Ajmal Khan, T. A. K.

---

[1] FR (UP), March, April, May, June and August, Home Poll. 1923, 25 NAI; Home Poll. 1925, 140, NAI; UPNNR, 7, 28 April, 16, 23, 30 June, 14, 21 July; 4 August, 8 September 1923.

[2] *Hamdam* (Lucknow), UPNNR, 26 May 1923; *Leader* (Allahabad), 18 May 1923.

[3] *Leader* (Allahabad), 24 March and 9 April 1923; UPNNR, 7 and 21 April 1923.

[4] Statement by Abdul Bari, most probably September 1923, as it refers to the Delhi Special Congress, in English, Abdul Bari Papers, File 24; for the maulana's activities see also Abdul Bari to Moulvi Latif Ahmad Minai of the Nizam of Hyderabad's Ecclesiastical Department, 9 June 1922, and a memorial to Abdul Bari from the Majlis Numandagam-e-Tabligh, Agra, 3 March 1923, in Urdu, Abdul Bari Papers, File 23, FM; UPNNR, 23 June, 15, 21 July, 22 September 1923.

Sherwani and Syed Zahur Ahmed.[1] Ansari alone of the really
prominent men did not join: he continued to take the line that
council boycott was the way to preserve Hindu–Muslim unity.
During 1923, the Swarajist bandwagon gathered way amidst a
flurry of attempts at compromise with those opposed to entering
the councils. By May the All-India Congress Committee had
decided to cease its propaganda against council entry. Ansari
himself, followed by Moazzam Ali and Khwaja Abdul Majid, began
to move towards the Swarajists as he came to realise that Hindu–
Muslim unity had to exist between politicians and not between
politicians and priests.[2] By August the Swarajists felt strong
enough to ignore the All-India Congress Committee and attack
the ulama.[3] All the ulama could do, once the 'Young Party'
politicians had deserted them and the Congress had begun to edge
towards council entry, was to complain, as Abdul Bari did, that
'those who pretended to be our friends at one time and made
a catspaw of the ulama now seem anxious to get rid of them'.[4]

Abdul Bari read the situation correctly. The ulama may have
once been, as he put it, 'the soul of the Khilafat Committee...
[which] infused new life into the Congress',[5] but now, with their
insistence on non-co-operation as a religious duty, they stood in the
way of a Congress compromise over council entry. They had to be
abandoned. Their last hope was Mahomed Ali. When he came out
of prison at the end of August, he declared against council entry.[6]
But three weeks later, it was he who proposed the compromise

---

[1] *Leader* (Allahabad), 3 January 1922.
[2] In the Congress Working Committee meetings of 23/28 May 1923 at Bombay,
Sarojini Naidu, T. Prakasan, Ansari and Moazzam Ali brought forward a
resolution suspending the Gaya resolution on Council Boycott in an attempt
to bridge the gulf that lay between the Congress and the Swarajists, *ibid.*,
26 May 1923.
[3] In a public meeting at Lucknow in August, for instance, Motilal Nehru
regretted that 'his Moslem brethren had given so much latitude to their
Ulemas in politics' and urged that 'they should insist in future that the
Ulemas refrain from meddling in politics'. *Ibid.*, 20 August 1923.
[4] Statement to the Press by Abdul Bari (in reply to Motilal Nehru's assault
on the ulama in politics), 20 August 1923, in English, Abdul Bari Papers,
File 24, FM; see also, *Hamdam* (Lucknow), UPNNR, 25 August 1923.
[5] Statement to the Press by Abdul Bari, 20 August 1923, in English, Abdul
Bari Papers, File 24, FM.
[6] On being released on 29 August 1923, Mahomed Ali was asked to persuade
the ulama to withdraw their fatwa against council entry. He replied: 'If
cooperation was "haram" according to the Islamic law two years ago, it
cannot become "halal" today...' *Leader* (Allahabad), 1 September 1923.

The Muslim party disintegrates

resolution at the Delhi Special Congress which enabled Congressmen, who had 'no religious or other conscientious objections',[1] to enter the councils. The Swarajists were now the dominant party in the Congress. The ulama were totally defeated. Their council entry fatwa was ignored and even the Jamiat-ul-ulama meekly accepted the fact. 'At Delhi', the *Leader* was delighted to announce, 'the once powerful voice of theocracy was drowned in the passionate appeals for unity.'[2]

The ulama had been the driving force behind the remarkable non-co-operation agitation of 1920 to 1923. It was their involvement that gave Muslim politicians their crucial role as brokers between the predominantly Hindu Congress and its new allies, the Muslim priests. Thus, in the UP Azad Sobhani, Kamaluddin Ahmed Jafri, T. A. K. Sherwani and Khwaja Abdul Majid all rose to a new importance on the Provincial Congress Committee,[3] their co-religionists filled leading positions on many Town and District Congress Committees[4] and also played a large part in the provincial political conferences. 'Old familiar faces were mostly invisible', complained the *Leader* of the 1920 conference, and 'a large number of Mahommedan delegates...were present.'[5] The role of the Muslim politician as a broker was particularly marked in Congress politics at an all-India level. It was best reflected in the marked change in the choice of Congress president. Between 1885 and 1920, only four Muslims had held the position. Between 1921 and 1923, three out of four Congress presidents were Muslims, Hakim Ajmal Khan, Abul Kalam Azad and Mahomed Ali, and the fourth, C. R. Das, was replaced by Dr Ansari during his year of office.[6] Moreover, all these Muslims, with the exception of Azad, were from the UP. Since most of the leaders of the ulama and of the Khilafat organisations came from the UP, it was natural that the province provided the architects of an intercommunal non-co-operation movement.

[1] *Ibid.*, 19 September 1923.   [2] *Ibid.*, 20 September 1923.
[3] In 1923, for instance, Sobhani was vice-president, Jafri a secretary and Khwaja Abdul Majid and Sherwani members of the Executive Council. *Ibid.*, 2 December 1923.
[4] Ten of the twenty-two local Congress committees which returned the names and positions of officers arrested during November 1921 had Muslim presidents or vice-presidents. 'Repression report for the U.P.', by Vishwambhar Dayal, 16 February 1922, enclosed in Superintendent UPPCC (Allahabad) to Gandhi, 18 February 1922, Gandhi Papers, no. 7771/113, NAI.
[5] *Leader* (Allahabad), 14 October 1920.   [6] Nehru, *Autobiography*, pp. 107–8.

When the ulama lost their political influence, this extraordinary Muslim role in Congress politics also came to an end. But it also meant the end of the Muslim front which had been such a powerful force in UP and Indian politics since the days of Syed Ahmed Khan. After the ulama were edged off the stage in 1923, there was no solid Muslim base from which 'Young Party' politicians could operate. Indeed, the marvellous growth of Muslim influence in Indian politics between 1919 and 1923 merely disguised the fact that the Montagu–Chelmsford reforms had finally smashed the old alignment of UP Muslim politicians. An alliance between 'Young Party' men and ulama was useful as a temporary tactic, but it could never be the basis of a permanent Muslim political party. This basis still had to be in an alliance between the 'Young Party' and the 'Old Party, particularly its landlord members. But in the council reforms government's concern for the landed interest was turned into the solid benefit of council seats. Muslim landlords now saw they would do better if they operated primarily as landlords rather than as Muslims, a fact which the zamindar party majority in the first two council elections underlined. Moreover, as soon as they entered the new councils, these Muslim landlords found that there were good reasons for emphasising their landlord status because the three major pieces of legislation undertaken by government in the early twenties, the Oudh Rent bill, the District Boards bill and the Agra Tenancy bill, all threatened some landlord privileges. Thus, many who had been Muslim politicians during the first two decades of the century became landlord politicians in the third. During the non-co-operation movement Mahmudabad was Home Member with the embarrassing task of throwing many of his former 'Young Party' cronies into gaol. Jehangirabad helped government get its fatwa against the muttaffiqa fatwa which had the strong support of his wife's pir, Abdul Bari. Sheikh Shahid Husain of Bara Banki district, Pirpur of Fyzabad, Masood-uz-Zaman of Banda, Bhikampur of Aligarh and many other Muslim magnates threw their weight behind the Aman Sabhas, or security leagues, designed to combat non-co-operation in the districts. Nawab Abdul Majid took the leading role in organising the Agra zamindars to campaign for more landlord council seats, and the Nawab of Chhatari played the same part in trying to organise the landlords as a political force both outside and inside the legislature. Communal alignments were played down, and only on one occasion in the early 1920s, over communal proportions on district boards, did the Muslim landlords vote as a communal bloc.

This left 'Young Party' politicians at the end of 1923 without a strong Muslim political base. They went different ways in their search for allies. Some moderates opted for the Muslim League, which had a brief resurrection during the 1920s. Former Khilafatists, such as Nawab Ismail Khan, Syed Mohammad Husain and Hafiz Hidayat Husain, found themselves back in harness not only with 'Young Party' men such as Syed Riza Ali and Syed Ali Nabi, who had defected in 1920, but also with their 'Old Party' enemies, professional men such as Aftab Ahmad Khan, Sheikh Abdullah, Ziauddin Ahmad and Mohammad Yakub, whose only platform was the Muslim League. The Ali brothers clung to the Central Khilafat Committee. Azad, Khaliquzzaman and Mushir Husain Kidwai wanted to close down the organisation and merge it with either the Congress or the Muslim League, but the Ali brothers were determined to keep it as a separate entity.[1] Their Islamic fanaticism surpassed that of all other secular Muslim leaders. So did their dependence on Islamic politics for their income; they needed their Khilafat organisation as a political platform, and they needed Islamic issues to keep body, soul and platform together. As time passed, the brothers became more communal, more reactionary, more estranged from Congress, and more out of touch with the mainstream of Indian Muslim politics. One of the Khilafat Committee's last acts was to support the Arabs against the Jews in the Wailing Wall Commission affair in 1929–30. Some 'Young Party' politicians abandoned separate Muslim politics altogether. An important group, which included Hakim Ajmal Khan, Dr Ansari, T. A. K. Sherwani, Khaliquzzaman and Khwaja Abdul Majid, decided to remain in the Congress. They had joined the Congress during the Khilafat movement and had risen to positions of power within the organisation which, nationalist ideals apart, they saw no point in sacrificing.

For a while there had been a strong separate Muslim political front in the UP. It had attracted, at different times and for different reasons, support from 'Old' and 'Young', professional and landlord, alim and agitator, all of whom had at least the common bond of their religion. It had spoken for the Muslims of

---

[1] *Leader* (Allahabad), 25 June 1923 and 10 February 1924.

all India and had dominated Indian politics during a crucial period of change. This front had now broken up. Once its leaders had gone their different ways, all that remained were politicians, who happened to be Muslim, but pursued their aims however they could, and a handful of specifically Muslim politicians whose platform had disintegrated. Khaliquzzaman declared from the vantage point of Pakistan:

The history of the next sixteen years of Muslim India is a mass of confusion and a chapter of political benightedness. The disruption of the Khilafat organization was like a breach in the embankment of the flowing stream of Muslim mass emotion, which diverted it into several petty streams, some leading to desert lands there to dry up, some flowing by zig-zag routes to meet the original bed in their headlong march and some others rushing towards the mighty flowing ocean to drown themselves. To try to find any consistency, sound reasoning or logical method in Muslim politics during that period would be utterly futile. We were divided between ourselves, some rushing recklessly towards the Congress, without sufficient safeguards for the Muslims of India, some others raising their head to cling to the British raj with redoubled satisfaction.[1]

[1] Khaliquzzaman, *Pathway to Pakistan*, p. 74.

CHAPTER 10

Conclusions

Were the Indian Muslims a separate nation? This study of the UP Muslims suggests that, by most of the standards applied to modern European nations, they were not. They had no racial homogeneity, little common history and many conflicting interests. Some were descended from converts, others from Arabs, Turks, Persians, Afghans and Central Asians. Some spoke Urdu, others the various dialects of the province – Braj, Bhojpuri and Awadhi. Some families had been in India for over 1000 years, others for less than 100. Many shared more interests with Hindu groups than with their co-religionists, a fact which their political activities frequently illustrated. Indeed, there was little that the depressed artisan had in common with the great magnate, or the English-educated official with the orthodox-educated priest, except the fact that they were Muslim. Being Muslim, of course, did not make them a nation. But being Muslims under British imperial rule did give them some common experience. It was within this context that they all grappled with the problems which they were set by the secular and modernising culture of their conquerors.

That Muslims had some common religious experience is self-evident, and must lie at the base of any explanation of why some Muslims organised for politics on a communal basis. But it is not the sole or even the chief cause of why they did so. Further explanation is provided by the responses to British rule of UP Muslim landlords and professional men. They constituted a powerful group in their province, in part because of their good position in land-ownership, but in the main because of their very great strength in government service. Throughout the period, however, their power was weakening. Muslim landlords sold more land than they bought, while the power of landed magnates in general was cut down as government took over more and more of their administrative functions. The proportion of Muslims in government service fell from just over two-thirds in 1857 to just over one-third in 1914

345

as government tried to improve the standards of its officials, to gain firmer control over them, and to limit the number who were Muslim. The introduction of elective government threatened their power further, modifying the influence of the bureaucracy, where they were strong, by that of elected bodies, in which they tended to be weak; and by the last years of the nineteenth century the implications of this change for Muslims on many elected municipal boards in the west UP and Doab were clear. Muslim landlords and government servants in the UP organised to meet these challenges. Aligarh College and the All-India Muslim League were founded to preserve a strong position, not to improve a weak one.

This conclusion has an important bearing on the theory of Muslim backwardness. The argument runs that because Muslims were slow to go to government schools, they fell behind in getting their share of power under the British and so they demanded government favour, a reserved proportion of jobs, and separate arrangements in elective government. The problem is that this argument, derived by Hunter from the failure of Bengali Muslims in the race for power, and deployed by many others, does not fit the circumstances of the UP Muslims who made most of the demands. Taking the UP Muslims as a whole, they were certainly slow in going to government schools, but it is not clear that this affected their capacity to get government jobs. Indeed, when they mainly attended traditional Islamic schools, they did well in getting official posts, but when they mainly went to government schools, they did less well. If anything it was the threat of becoming backward, rather than backwardness itself, which encouraged UP Muslims to organise for politics, and their power in the province helped them to do so with such effect.

Hindu revivalism, the demands of which often cloaked direct competition for government jobs or seats on elected bodies, was another pressure which encouraged Muslims to organise on a communal basis. An important argument of this study has been that in the mid-nineteenth century Muslim landlords and professional men in the UP were just part, though the largest part, of an Urdu-speaking elite which was defined basically by an association, past or present, with government. Syed Ahmed Khan's Ghazipur Translation Society, his Aligarh Scientific Society, and his British Indian Association of the North Western Provinces, were all replies from this Urdu-speaking elite to the threats government issued to its position in the 1860s. But this supra-communal response was challenged by Hindu revivalists, some of them from this very Urdu-speaking elite, who insisted that the language of the Vernacular University planned by the British Indian Association should not be Urdu but Hindi, and its script not Persian but Nagri. One effect was that many Hindus of the Urdu-speaking elite deserted its organisations: they could not resist the call of communal loyalty. Another was that Syed Ahmed Khan turned his attention to working purely for Muslims at the very moment when government was beginning to turn its mind to their needs. The supra-communal connections of the Urdu-speaking elite were not totally destroyed; they appeared time and time again in the politics of the landlord and the professional men of the province. But an important change had taken place. Once some Muslims had begun to organise on a communal basis, Hindu revivalism had extra fuel to feed its fires, and its various manifestations in turn reinforced Muslim communal activity. Further Hindu agitation for the introduction of the Nagri script encouraged Muslims to organise to resist it, Hindu campaigns for a Hindu University spurred Muslims in their campaign for a Muslim University, and Hindu opposition to Muslim separate electorates only made Muslims want them more. Overall, the frequently close association of Hindu revivalism with the Congress made it difficult for Muslims to join the organisation of Indian nationalist politics.

The tendency of some Muslims in the UP to organise as Muslims was not just a reaction to threats to their power from government and Hindu revivalists. Muslims also reached back into their cultural past to reinforce their attempts to come to terms with the challenges of British rule, and in their turn produced a form of Muslim revivalism. Syed Ahmed Khan's attempts, from 1870, to preserve the power of the Muslim members of the Urdu-speaking elite, came to be given the greater aim of an endeavour to preserve Muslim power in India as a whole. Moreover, many of those who helped to create the spirit of Muslim revivalism around Aligarh, such as Hali or Shibli, were inspired by or involved in Syed Ahmed's work. But it should be noted that Muslim revivalism was more the creation than the creator of the Muslim politics of the UP Muslim landed and service elite in the nineteenth century, and it had no important political impact until the great outburst of communal energy that followed the Morley–Minto reforms.

Separatism among Indian Muslims

These arguments help to explain why some UP Muslims tried to organise on a communal basis, but they do not explain why they were successful. This problem introduces the crux of our explanation of the growth of Muslim separatism up to 1909 – the role of government. A prominent feature of British rule in the nineteenth century was a tendency to see its Indian subjects primarily not as members of different races, nor as speakers of different languages, nor even as representatives of different interests, but as the followers of different faiths. Men were recognised first as Parsis, Sikhs, Hindus or Muslims. This would not have been particularly important but for the fact that the British were mortally afraid of the Muslims. The followers of Islam were regarded as the greatest threat to imperial security. Hence the witch-hunt launched against them after the Mutiny, and, when it was discovered that this policy was counter-productive, the subsequent attempts to woo them. For the last thirty years of the century, the UP Muslims came high on the government's list of patronage. This is of crucial importance. Aligarh College, the heart of Muslim communal organisation, would have been unlikely to overcome either the short term opposition of the provincial Education Department, or the long term hostility of the Muslim orthodox, but for the immense political and financial support which it received both officially and unofficially from the government of India. It would certainly not have grown so great, nor its founder so influential, had it not played an important part in government's scheme of political control. Two results flowed from this policy in the early twentieth century. First, the leaders of Aligarh had such great prestige and such broad connections that they were able to organise a powerful deputation of Indian Muslims to the Viceroy at Simla in 1906 and found an all-India political organisation to support its demands. Second, these Muslims, far from being regarded as the major threat to British rule, came to be seen as such an important pillar of it that government felt it must submit to their demands concerning the council reforms of 1909. The foundation of the All-India Muslim League, and the fixing of special electorates for Muslims in the constitution, established a separate Muslim identity in Indian politics.

Does this mean that the British divided and ruled? In the crude sense, no. There was no deliberate attempt to foster communal hostility; indeed, the aim was to avoid it. Nevertheless, policy

348

makers did need to divide Indian society in order to govern; they had to isolate areas of opposition and discover areas of support. Then, with these divisions in mind, they had to formulate policies and to hand out patronage. Inevitably, the effect of imperial rule was to exacerbate some divisions and to break down others. Because of their view of Indian society, and their particular fear of the Muslims, the divisions the British fostered were communal ones. There can be no doubt that British policy played the main part in establishing a separate Muslim identity in Indian politics by 1909.

It would be wrong, however, to see government's marked susceptibility to Muslim pleas as a constant factor in the growth of Muslim separatism, because, from 1909, government came to regard Muslims as politically less important. Instead, Muslims themselves became increasingly effective in sustaining their separate identity in politics.

The feeling that government favour had been withdrawn invariably caused tension in the Muslim alliance of landlord and professional men which Syed Ahmed Khan build up around Aligarh College. After the 1892 Councils Act, the Nagri resolution and Morley's announcement of further political reforms in 1906, fissures opened. But these did not become serious till the period after 1911, when Britain's vocal hostility to a Turkey enmeshed in Balkan Wars, coupled with the imperial government's revocation of the partition of Bengal and its refusal to meet Muslim wishes for their University project, forced the alliance into two loose but distinct parties: the 'Old Party', a group of large landlords and successful professional men, and the 'Young Party', a group of educated men who hoped for success in the professions. The difference between them was that 'Old Party' men were well-established, reliant on government and often had other political platforms as landlords, educationalists or Shias. They did not want to risk much in opposition to government, and it would have been unwise of them to do so. 'Young Party' men, on the other hand, still had to make their way, and a separate Muslim politics was their sole effective platform, whether it had government support or not. Thus, they had to protest against the government riding roughshod over Muslim interests because it was crucial to their own political survival that government should continue to respect them. They had to capture the organisations of Muslim politics from 'Old Party' men because it was clear that government was not to be moved by the latter's diffident complaints. Moreover, once they had taken over the All-India Muslim League, and 'Old Party' men had begun to leave it, they had to drive it towards areas where it would find fresh political support because government was even less likely to be moved by the clamour of insignificant lawyers and journalists.

Seen in this light the All-India Muslim League's move towards the Congress from 1913 makes good sense. It explains why Muslims should have been such active parties in the rapprochement and why two years later they should have been the initiators of the deal with the Congress over political reform. 'We will not lose', Mahomed Ali told an anxious friend, 'by conferring with the Hindus as to the future, but by sitting with folded hands and allowing others to settle that future for us.'[1] The Lucknow Pact which resulted was less a victory for nationalist altruism, at least on the Muslim side, than a triumph for the 'Young Party'. The results of this agreement were momentous. First, it helped the UP capture the initiative in Congress politics, shifting the focus of all-India politics from the seaboard to the centre where it was henceforth to remain. Second, in the next round of political devolution, it vastly strengthened Muslim claims concerning separate representation and their 'political importance', which Montagu and Chelmsford would have been delighted to have been able to ignore.

'Young Party' politicians also sought to strengthen their position by allying with ulama. Muslim priests were persuaded to support 'Young Party' Campaigns, like the Red Crescent Mission, and the potential of the alliance was quickly realised when government was forced to retreat before the Cawnpore Mosque agitation. It was the same kind of victory that Dr Ansari and Hakim Ajmal Khan were looking for when they made much of the Khilafat issue at the Delhi Muslim League session of 1918 and invited Abdul Bari and his followers to add ecclesiastical weight to their agitation. The Montagu–Chelmsford report voiced general disapproval of Muslim claims and particular hostility to the concept of Muslim 'political importance'. No help could be expected from 'Old Party' men, nor from Congressmen, who would have been pleased

---

[1] Mahomed Ali to Moulvi Abdullah Ahmad, 19 November 1915, draft letter, Mahomed Ali Papers, JMI.

to have political reforms without concessions to Muslims, so agitation about the Khilafat with ulama in the van was to be the means to jog British memories. The problem was, of course, that the plan went awry. What was to be a brief and clean campaign to make a point during the formation of the reforms turned out to be a long and messy struggle which threatened to wreck them. The Khilafat remained in danger for much longer than can ever have been anticipated, and the ulama released political and organisational energies about which 'Young Party' men cannot have dreamed. Within a year Muslim priests had seized the initiative in Muslim politics; within a further two years they had done the same in Congress politics. They certainly made the 'Young Party's' point about Muslim 'political importance', but it was at the expense of the seats 'Young Party' men wished to win in the first elections to the new councils.

From 1920 the Muslim identity in Indian politics was sustained mainly by ulama. The Khilafat issue, increasingly no more than rhetoric for 'Young Party' politicians, was central to ulama interests. The Khalifa was head of the orthodox scheme of Muslim society of which they were part. A concession from the imperial government towards the need to preserve the Khilafat would be support for their own waning influence in Indian Muslim society. Ulama may have been moved by religious fervour, but their basic reasons for agitating about the Khilafat were involved as much with problems of their power in India as were those of the 'Young Party'. The only difference was that the former were worried about their power among Indian Muslims and the latter more about their power in India as a whole. The political tactics of the ulama were also similar to those of the 'Young Party'. They needed allies to press their point and this was why Abdul Bari tried to win Gandhi for the Khilafat agitation, and through him the Congress. The Mahatma, who had just burned his fingers at Amritsar, was willing to help but less eager to drive the protest to extremes. Eventually, after pressing him for months and threatening to take the law into their own hands, ulama, with the help of 'Young Party' agitators fresh from prison, committed Gandhi to leading them in a campaign of non-co-operation with the government. Then, with boycott of the reformed councils as the centrepiece of the programme, they played the main part in helping him win Congress for this policy. What immensely successful tactics these were!

The ulama diverted the whole organisation of Indian nationalist politics away from the enjoyment of the power for which it had fought, and placed it, till the next council elections at least, behind their own Khilafat agitation.

The analysis of the activities of the ulama has clarified several points in the very confused politics of the Khilafat-non-co-operation movement. First, the ulama themselves were no solid phalanx of orthodoxy moving in harmony with a single interpretation of the sharia. The fact that their religious authority was generally threatened did not mean that they moved in unison to defend it. Indeed, the rivalry between and within the various schools was so great that they could only move at different times. So Abdul Bari's section of Firangi Mahal led the first phase of the Khilafat movement, and it was not until the Congress was captured that Deoband joined in. Secondly, Gandhi does not appear to be just the masterly politician in search of allies, but also the ally who is sought, and occasionally even manipulated. It is true that ulama were vital in helping him impose his own idiosyncratic ideas on the Congress, but beyond this they either used or ignored him. Few cared for homespun or spinning wheels, many tried to drive the movement towards bloodshed, and it was the steady growth of the violence which they urged that forced Gandhi to call off civil disobedience in 1922 and accept imprisonment with relief. Weighing the balance of gain, Gandhi had the help of the ulama for a few moments at Calcutta and Nagpur, but the ulama had Congress support for nearly three years. The Mahatma, in fact, was won for the Muslims and not the Muslims for the Mahatma. Thirdly, it would be wrong to see non-co-operation as a specifically Gandhian tactic. It was first advocated by ulama, for whom boycott of the secular system of government could only bring advantage, and the many non-co-operation programmes were closely adapted to their needs. In view of this it is hardly surprising that ulama came to have such influence in all-India politics. So long as non-co-operation was at the heart of Congress policy between 1920 and 1923, they were at the heart of Congress activity. Moreover, while this was so, 'Young Party' politicians also had a role in the Congress. However much they disliked Islamic politics, they had an important part to play as brokers between ulama and Congress politicians, a part which brought them to the very pinnacle of influence within the Congress machine.

Conclusions

The roles of the politician and the priest in the Khilafat movement illuminate the nature of Muslim separatist politics. The activities of Muslim politicians were separatist only in a limited sense; they were concerned with a wide range of provincial, class and sectarian interests many of which knew no communal divisions. In their endeavours to promote these specific interests different Muslim politicians adopted the Muslim identity when it was useful, and discarded it when it had served their purpose. Being a Muslim was less an article of political faith than a useful weapon in their political armoury. For the ulama, on the other hand, being a Muslim was something which set them apart from other men, and much of their activity can be seen as a struggle to preserve a separate Muslim society. Though they were divided as to how to achieve it, they all sought a regime in which their interpretation of the sharia would be the ruling fiat. Towards this end their demand for non-co-operation with the British raj, and their establishment of an Amir-i-Shariat organisation, were important steps. The truth was, that if there were two nations in India, they were divided not by religion but by education. The division, in fact, lay not between Hindus and Muslims but between orthodox Muslims and the rest, both Hindu and Muslim. But if the Khilafat movement illustrated the differences of approach between the two nations in the Muslim community, it also showed that they could ally despite their conflicting ends. Moreover, it also demonstrated the immense political potential of such an alliance. The campaign for Pakistan was to be pressed forward by a similar mixture of politicians, who happened to be Muslim, in search of power, and Muslim priests in search of a theocratic ideal.

There are some larger conclusions which spill over the boundaries of Muslim politics. For instance, the period from 1909 saw a considerable increase in the importance of professional politicians or agitators as government regarded them, that is men who relied on politics for the greater part of their living. The staple of this breed were young graduates from Aligarh unable to find employment to match their aspirations. They were joined by others, notably ulama, who found politics a satisfactory way of improving their waning prestige and flagging finances. The professional politicians par excellence were, of course, Mahomed and Shaukat Ali. As a group these politicians must be distinguished from men such as Hakim Ajmal Khan and Dr Ansari or Wazir

Hasan and Riza Ali, who derived adequate incomes from their vocations as doctors and lawyers. The latter left their jobs for politics when the situation called for it, but the professional politicians had continually to manufacture issues and to whip up agitations to keep their newspapers going, their organisations active and their coffers full. The Cawnpore Mosque Fund, the Khilafat Fund, the Angora Fund, the names trace the path trodden by India's political gold-diggers. The issues were religious, usually pan-Islamic: these were the only sure sources of the money they needed. The result was that agitations were sometimes manufactured, could be maintained at a high intensity, lasted longer and became harder for government to smother. Often the only way of gagging a professional politician was to put him in jail.

Another general conclusion is that it is important to study politics in localities in order to understand them at higher levels. Different patterns of municipal politics derived from different social and economic conditions have, for instance, shown why communalism, and demands for separate representation, were much stronger in the west of the UP than in the east. Amongst the ulama, important differences were less regional than educational. A detailed analysis of the various schools has revealed that up to 1921 the politics of the Jamiat-ul-ulama-i-Hind were those of one section of Firangi Mahal, though afterwards they came increasingly to be dominated by Deoband. However, the proposition which this work has supported with much fresh proof is that all-India politics can be understood only in terms of provincial politics. All-India Muslim politics were almost entirely those of the UP Muslims. Indeed it is often hardly possible to distinguish between the two levels of activity. Their growth must be understood in the interplay between government policy and the many threats to the power of the province's Urdu-speaking elite, their changes of direction in the new pressures to which different Muslim groups were exposed, and their decline in the impact of the Montagu–Chelmsford reforms on the political alignments of the province. Important developments such as the Lucknow Pact or the Khilafat alliance of priest and politician have acquired new meaning in the provincial context. Examination of the grammar of local politics explains the language of all-Indian politics.

At all levels of politics Indians strove for the power available to them under the British. They sought it in all forms: jobs in government service, membership of municipal boards, places on university senates and seats on provincial councils. Evidence of how strong the competition was lies in affairs such as the battles over the introduction of Nagri into government, the squabbles over Muslim proportions of representation, and the great surges of political activity which preceded each major piece of devolution in 1892, 1909 and 1920. There is perhaps no better proof of the politicians' concern about their power than the way in which politics between 1916 and 1923 took shape around the Montagu–Chelmsford reforms. While these constitutional changes were being formulated, politicians were concerned about putting pressure on government to protect their interests. When they were forced to choose between standing for council seats and non-co-operation, they made their decisions according to their chances of entering the councils and influencing them. When the time came to abandon non-co-operation and cut down ulama influence in the Congress, the event which governed the timing of the decision was not the abolition of the Khilafat in 1924 but the second elections to the reformed councils in 1923. The corollary of this is that government, which decided who should have the powers it was ready to share, had considerable influence on the pattern of politics. Its fear of the Muslims contributed much to the rise of Muslim organisation. Later, its greater interest in other groups in Indian society broke this organisation. Government's changing concerns were reflected in the lives of the various parties of Indian politics.

The politics of Indian Muslims illuminate more generally the politics of modernisation in Muslim societies. In the nineteenth and twentieth centuries, particular groups in these societies, whether they were trying to ward off the foreign invader or throw off the foreign ruler, found they had to arm themselves with modern learning and modern technology. The result has been that they have drawn apart from the education and outlook of their orthodox brethren, creating what amounts to two societies, one arranged according to the needs of the modern industrial state and the other according to the laws of Islam. Nevertheless, from time to time, they have had to galvanise both societies in pursuit of their political objectives. To this end they have found the common bond of religion invaluable, and they have emphasised Islamic issues when convenient and ignored them when not. Thus 'Young Party' politicians took advantage of the ulama from

1913, and dropped them after 1923. Thus a powerful religious agitation was launched for the Islamic republic of Pakistan, but small place was found for Islam in the ordering of Pakistan's national life. Thus declarations of jihad accompany the advance of Muslim armies in the middle east, but the states which they defend do scant justice to the injunctions of Koranic law. There are dangers in such tactics. Occasionally, as in the Khilafat movement, the modern politician has been overwhelmed by religious passion, and has been deflected from his purpose. Yet, as Muslims tackle the challenges of the modern world with increasing success, and the gap between the emancipated Muslim and the orthodox Muslim widens, there are still few Muslim politicians who can afford to ignore the unifying power of Islam.

Appendices

Appendices I, II, and III contain biographies of men who were prominent in politics in the UP between 1900 and 1923. Entries under the heading 'Occupation' simply state what the subject normally did for a living. Those under 'Sect' state whether the subject was a Shia or a Sunni, and, when it is known, to which alim or school he looked for guidance, but this kind of information is hard to uncover. In Appendices I and II, entries under 'Education' say where the subject was educated, the type of education he had, and the level attained. In Appendix III, this heading has been replaced by 'School' on the grounds that an alim's school was much more than just the place in which he was educated, and sometimes taught, but usually the focus of all his theological and political loyalties. 'Home Town' states where the subject normally lived during the period. 'Background' sets out the wealth, connections and general standing of the subject and his family. 'Career' shows his activities as a politician up to 1923, though occasionally information on his subsequent doings has been added.

357

APPENDIX I

THE 'YOUNG PARTY'

Men have been included in this appendix if, for all or part of the time up to 1923, they followed the various political leads given by the Ali brothers, Wazir Hasan, the Raja of Mahmudabad, Dr Ansari or Hakim Ajmal Khan. The general background to 'Young Party' men and their families has been drawn mainly from the following: *District Gazetteers of the United Provinces of Agra and Oudh*, Volumes I to XLVIII (Allahabad, 1903–11); Nurul Hasan Siddiqi, *Landlords of Agra & Avadh* (Lucknow, 1950), and a file in the UP Secretariat Archives which analysed the financial condition of the more important landed estates in the province in 1918, Revenue and Agriculture, 1918, 578, UPS. Newspapers provided the main source of information on political careers, in particular: *Indian People* (Allahabad), 1903–9; *Leader* (Allahabad), 1909–23; *Comrade* (Calcutta and Delhi), 1911–14; *New Era* (Lucknow), 1917; *Independent* (Allahabad), 1919–21; and the UP Native Newspaper Reports for the whole period. Further information has been gleaned from the Mahomed Ali papers, from government files and history sheets in the National Archives of India, the archives of the UP Secretariat and the Commissioner of Lucknow, and the following articles and books: D. Lelyveld, 'Three Aligarh Students: Aftab Ahmad Khan, Ziauddin Ahmad and Muhammad Ali', *Modern Asian Studies*, Vol. VIII (1974); Afzal Iqbal (ed.), *My Life A Fragment: An Autobiographical Sketch of Maulana Mohamed Ali* (Lahore, 1942); Shaikh Ali Hasan, *Tarikh-i-Mahmudabad* (hand-written Urdu mss., Mahmudabad House, Lucknow, n.d.); Choudhry Khaliquzzaman, *Pathway to Pakistan* (Lahore, 1961); G. Natesan, *Eminent Musalmans* (Madras, 1925); S. K. Bhatnagar, *History of the M.A.O. College Aligarh* (Aligarh, 1969); M. Mujeeb, *The Indian Muslims* (London, 1967); *The Allahabad High Court: Centenary Volume of the Allahabad High Court, 1868–1968* (Allahabad, 1968).

Biographies of the following will be found below, and names in capitals indicate cross-references within the Appendix:

Ahmad, Sheikh Zahur
Ahmed, Syed Zahur
Ahmed, Qazi Bashiruddin
Ali, Azhar
Ali, Mahomed
Ali, Moazzam
Ali, Syed Riza
Ali, Shaukat

Ali, Shaikh Shaukat
Ali, Vilayat
Alvi, Mahomed Sakhawat Ali
Alvi, Zafar-ul-Mulk
Ansari, Abdul Aziz
Ansari, Dr Mukhtar Ahmad
Ansari, Dr Mahomed Naim
Barni, Ziauddin Ahmad

The 'Young Party'

Beg, Mirza Samiullah
Bijnori, Abdur Rahman
Bilgrami, Major Syed Hasan
Delhavi, Syed Jalib
Ghaffar, Qazi Abdul
Ghulam-us-Saqlain
Halim, Hafiz Mahomed
Hasan, Dr Naziruddin
Hasan, Syed Shabbir
Hasan, Syed Wazir
Hayat, H. M.
Husain, Raja Ghulam
Husain, Hafiz Hidayat
Husain, Haji Syed Mohammad
Hussain, Mumtaz
Hussain, Syud
Jafri, Kamaluddin Ahmed
Jan, Syed Mir
Khaliquzzaman, Choudhry
Khan, Hakim Ajmal
Khan, Prince Hamidullah of
  Bhopal
Khan, Sheikh Yusuf Husain
Khan, Nawab Ismail
Khan, Wahid Yar
Kidwai, Rafi Ahmed
Kidwai, Mushir Husain
Mahmudabad, Raja Muhammad Ali
  Muhammad
Majid, Khwaja Abdul
Masood-ul-Hasan
Mehdi, Syed Hyder
Mohani, Hasrat
Nabi, Syed Ali
Nabiullah, Syed
Qureshi, Shuaib
Rahman, Syed Fazlur
Salim, Wahiduddin
Sherwani, Tassaduq Ahmad Khan
Sherwani, Haroon Khan
Sherwani, Haji Musa Khan
Sherwani, Amir Mustafa Khan
Siddiqui, Abdur Rahman
Sokhta, Manzur Ali
Wali, Hakim Abdul
Wasim, Mahomed

Sheikh Zahur Ahmad

Home Town
Allahabad.

Sect
Sunni.

Background
From a family of long-standing, his grandfather was Sheikh Nasiruddin, a taluqdar in the Allahabad district, his father was Sheikh Abdur Raoof, a zamindar of Mau Aimma who paid Rs. 6205 land revenue, and his younger brother was Nazir Ahmad, the editor of *Khilafat-e-Usmaniya* and *Masawat*.

Education
BA, Aligarh, and Barrister-at-Law.

Occupation
Lawyer at the Allahabad High Court.

Career
Zahur Ahmad entered politics during the anti-Nagri agitation of 1900. A founder member of the All-India Muslim League, he went to England to read for the Bar in 1907, became joint secretary of the London Muslim League in 1908 and a member of the Council of the All-India Muslim League on his return to India in 1910. In 1915, he was elected an Aligarh trustee. A prominent member of the Allahabad Muslim League, he was elected to the Allahabad Municipal Board in 1916 and worked as secretary of the board in the 1920s. He assisted the defence in the Cawnpore Mosque Trials. He was involved in all 'Young Party' activities in Allahabad: the Home Rule Leagues, the Khilafat movement etc.... When

359

he non-co-operated, Zahur Ahmad claimed to have sacrificed a practice worth Rs. 2000 p.m. But if Zahur Ahmad lost one source of income as a result of his adherence to non-co-operation, and it is unlikely that he lost anything nearly as large as he claimed, he gained two others. First he was recruited by Tassaduq Hussein, who was most probably at Aligarh with him, as a Central Intelligence Department spy, being paid Rs. 200 p.m. at the beginning and Rs. 500 p.m. when his reports became more valuable. From the moment of his recruitment he was never far from the centre of events. The important Khilafat meetings of early June 1920 were held in his Allahabad bungalow; in 1921 and 1922, he was head of the Central Khilafat Committee's Propaganda Department; he attended the All-Indian Khilafat Conferences; moreover in 1922 he was also a member of the Khilafat Committee's Civil Disobedience Enquiry Committee, being the only man in favour of council entry. When the non-co-operation movement came to an end he was little use as an intelligence agent and kept on a retainer of Rs. 100 p.m. which was not terminated till 1928. His spying activities were never exposed, and no doubt help to explain the government's very detailed reports of high level Khilafat Committee and ulama meetings between 1921 and 1925. Second, as head of the Central Khilafat Committee's Propaganda Department, he was in charge of the department in which most financial mismanagement was revealed both by the auditors and by the Khilafat Accounts Enquiry Committee. 1923–6, he held the legislative council seat for the Allahabad-cum-Benares Muslim urban constituency, and was described by government in 1923 as 'not a very reputable barrister who is reported to have done well out of the Khilafat funds. Held in little esteem among his own class.'

Syed Zahur Ahmed
Home Town
Lucknow.
Sect
Sunni.
Background
He passed his early years in Allahabad.
Education
BA, LL.B, Muir Central College, Allahabad.
Occupation
Lawyer.
Career
Zahur Ahmed entered politics in 1900, taking a leading part in the Nagri agitation. He was a foundation member of the All-India Muslim League, a leading member of its council and involved, from the beginning, with important activities such as the subcommittee appointed in 1908 to formulate the League's attitude to the government's reform proposals. He was joint secretary of the UP Muslim League and took part in the 1909 agitation over separate electorates. Considered standing for the legislative council in 1920. Secretary of the All-India Muslim League from 1919 to 1926 and its effective leader from 1919 to 1923. He joined the Swarajists in 1923. Described by another Muslim as 'one of the most sincere and silent·workers in our community'.

The 'Young Party'

Qazi Bashiruddin Ahmed
Home Town
Meerut.
Sect
Sunni.
Education
BA, LL.B, Aligarh.
Occupation
Lawyer at the Meerut Bar.
Career
He took part in the Red Crescent Mission from 1912 to 1913 and corresponded with MAHOMED ALI during his wartime internment. With NAWAB ISMAIL KHAN he was a leading member of the 'Young Party' in Meerut and secretary of the Syed Munzil Club, an Aligarh Old Boy's club under the patronage of SHAUKAT ALI. He was involved in all 'Young Party' activities in the locality; the Home Rule Leagues, the Rowlatt protest and the Khilafat movement.

Azhar Ali
Home Town
Lucknow.
Sect
Shia.
Education
BA, LL.B, Allahabad.
Occupation
Lawyer at the Lucknow Bar.
Career
He was assistant secretary of the UP Muslim League and played a leading part in the 1909 agitation for separate electorates, organising protest meetings in the districts of Oudh. He was also joint secretary of the All-India Muslim League and did much to help WAZIR HASAN arrange the important session at Bombay in 1915. He was very active in Lucknow during the years 1916–17. After this, he opted out of politics. He was a member of the Rifah-i-Am.

Mahomed Ali (1878–1931)
Home Town
Rampur.
Sect
Sunni; he regarded Abdul Bari (q.v. Appendix III) as his pir.
Background
The youngest son in his family, he suffered from diabetes. For the rest of his background see under SHAUKAT ALI.
Education
BA, Aligarh, Gold Medallist and government scholar. He attended Lincoln College, Oxford from 1898 to 1902, where he got a second in Modern History, 'missing a First, as I learnt subsequently from my tutor, by a very narrow margin'.

Appendix I

Occupation
Civil servant and later journalist and politician.

Career
Mahomed Ali's early attempts to find employment equal to his aspirations were not successful; he failed the ICS examination, the Allahabad High Court Bar examination and was refused a position as a teacher at Aligarh. After a short spell in the Rampur Education Department, he became an Opium Agent in the Baroda Service, 1904–12. In 1909, when defeated in the internal politics of the Baroda bureaucracy and further progress depended on success in departmental examinations he grew restless. He applied without success for three high-ranking positions under the British. After these setbacks, though remaining on the Baroda civil list till 1912, he devoted himself to politics and journalism. On this second career, he was already well-embarked. He made his political debut with a speech on the Muslim University at Ahmedabad in 1904 and learned about journalism as correspondent on Aligarh affairs for the *Times of India*. Founder member of the All-India Muslim League; supported the students against the staff in the Aligarh College strike of 1907. In the same year he published his *Thoughts on the Present Discontent* and made a short tour of the UP delivering two lectures entitled 'The Present Political Situation' and 'The Muhammadan Programme'. In January 1911, he founded the *Comrade*, a weekly, and the first All-India Muslim journal in English. Soon afterwards, he founded the *Hamdard*, an Urdu daily. These newspapers enabled him to establish himself as leader of the 'Young Party', a position which was strengthened by his Cawnpore Mosque agitation, his bid to control Aligarh and the Muslim University movement. In 1913, he visited England with WAZIR HASAN and in 1915 became an Aligarh Trustee. During World War One, his pan-Islamic writings led him into serious conflict with government and he was interned with SHAUKAT ALI, May 1915 to December 1919. Gandhi corresponded with him during this period. January to September 1920, he led a Khilafat deputation to Europe, then until September 1921 played a leading part in working up the Khilafat agitation. 1921–3, he was imprisoned for sedition. President of the Coconada Congress 1923 and revived the *Comrade*, 1924–5, but his political influence declined steadily throughout the 1920s. He died in January 1931 while attending the Round Table Conference in London. 'Jauhar' was his takhullus as an Urdu poet. Apart from his general political importance, Mahomed Ali is interesting as the prime example of a new breed of men who in the second decade of the twentieth century found they could make a living out of politics. His interests were Islamic rather than nationalist. Any alliance with the Hindus was a 'mariage de convenance', as he described it, out of which the Muslims must get the best deal they could; while 'constitutions', he declared, 'like pretty women are meant to be violated'.

Moazzam Ali
Home Town
Rampur.
Sect
Sunni.

362

The 'Young Party'

Background
Related to the ALI BROTHERS.
Education
BA, Aligarh, and Barrister-at-Law.
Occupation
Lawyer and politician.
Career
Moazzam Ali started practice in Patna and then moved to Moradabad where in 1917 he led the local agitation against the internment of the ALI BROTHERS. Aligarh trustee, 1919. He was much involved in the Khilafat and non-co-operation movements and gave up his legal practice in 1920. He succeeded SHAUKAT ALI as secretary of the Central Khilafat Committee in 1921, and was a member of the Khilafat Civil Disobedience Enquiry Committee in 1922. In 1922–3 he was a secretary of the Congress, and a member of its Working Committee in 1923. He became a professional politician in 1920 and followed in the footsteps of his more famous relations.

Syed Riza Ali (1882–)

Home Town
Kondarki in Moradabad district, but settled in Allahabad from 1916.
Sect
Shia.
Background
From a small zamindari family, he was the first member to be educated in English.
Education
BA, LL.B, Aligarh.
Occupation
Lawyer. He began practice at Moradabad in 1908, but soon moved to work at the High Court.
Career
Riza Ali was involved in all 'Young Party' activities down to 1920. He was the leader of the Khilafat agitation in Allahabad in 1919 and early 1920, and acted as leading defence counsel in the trial of the editors of the *Akhuwat* in 1919 and Hamid Ahmed, an alim who had gone too far, in 1920. But, as soon as council boycott became Khilafat policy, he was forced to choose between the Khilafat and his council seat, he chose the latter. 1912, secretary of the Moradabad District Muslim League; member of the Council of the All-India Muslim League; 1912–25, sat on the UP legislative council; 1921–6 sat on the Council of State; 1915, elected Aligarh trustee; gave evidence before the Islington Commission, 1913, and the Southborough Committee, 1918; led Muslim delegations to the Viceroy over Turkey in 1922 and 1923; President of the All-India Muslim League, 1924; member, Indian government deputation to South Africa, 1925–6; agent of the Government of India in South Africa, 1935; knight and CBE. Riza Ali was described by Meston in 1914, rather unfairly, as a 'plausible but very third-rate member of the young Muhammadan party'. He was much more than this. He was the strongest advocate of specifically Muslim interests in the UP legislative council and the major protagonist of UP Muslim interests in the UP

Municipalities Bill compromise and the Lucknow Pact. His talent was to sit on the middle ground in politics, and he was usually instrumental in making whatever compromise had to be reached.

Shaukat Ali (1873–1938)
Home Town
Rampur.
Sect
Sunni; he regarded Abdul Bari (q.v. Appendix III) as his pir.
Background
The elder brother of MAHOMED ALI, in the Mutiny his father's family received a large property in Moradabad district for saving English lives, but his mother's family lost eighty-two villages. His father, who with Shaukat's uncles worked in the Rampur state service, had a zamindari income of Rs. 1250 p.m., but died while Shaukat was young leaving him and his mother, Begum Abadi Bano, with the task of bringing up a large family. Another brother, Zulfiqar Ali, was an Ahmadiyya, a disciple of the poet Dagh and worked in the Rampur state service.
Education
BA, Aligarh.
Occupation
Civil servant, and later, politician.
Career
Shaukat Ali was a sub-deputy Opium Agent till 1912. He took long leave in 1910, became private secretary to the Aga Khan in 1911 and by 1912 had found a new career in politics. Most of his activity up to this date had been concerned with Aligarh. He was elected a trustee in 1905, but was forced to resign in the same year after assaulting Sheikh Abdullah (q.v. Appendix II); founder member of the All-India Muslim League; organised the Aligarh Old Boys' Association in 1907; proprietor of *Old Boy*, an Urdu monthly with a circulation of 1000 and aimed at promoting fellowship among Aligarh old boys; organised Muslim University Fund collections; re-elected a trustee of Aligarh, 1913; founded with Abdul Bari (q.v. Appendix III) and M. H. KIDWAI the Anjuman-i-Khuddam-i-Kaaba, 1913; involved with MAHOMED ALI in the publication of the *Comrade* and *Hamdard*; interned with his brother, May 1915 to December 1919; the leading Khilafat agitator in 1920–21, he toured the subcontinent tirelessly speaking at meetings and imposing his forceful personality on conferences, as at Allahabad in June 1920 and Calcutta in September 1920, to force through more radical measures; secretary of the Central Khilafat Committee till interned with his brother in September 1921; president of the All-India Khilafat Conference at Coconada, 1923; bad reputation with money; lost influence after the Khilafat movement; a Muslim representative at the Round Table Conference, 1931; member of the legislative assembly, 1935. Six feet two inches tall, and very broad, Shaukat Ali was known to his friends as 'big brother'. Endowed with immense energy, he was a great organiser, but his politics were those of MAHOMED ALI to whom he played second fiddle.

The 'Young Party'

Shaikh Shaukat Ali
Home Town
Lucknow.
Sect
Sunni.
Background
From a zamindari family in the Lucknow district.
Education
BA, LL.B.
Occupation
Lawyer at the Lucknow Bar.
Career
A member of the Rifah-i-Am and assistant secetary of the UP Muslim League in 1909, he moved into politics in a big way during the Khilafat movement, becoming president of the Lucknow District Congress Committee and secretary of the District Khilafat Committee. He was imprisoned towards the end of 1921.

Vilayat Ali (1885–1918)
Home Town
Bara Banki.
Sect
Sunni.
Background
A member of the great Kidwai clan, and uncle and guardian of RAFI AHMAD KIDWAI.
Education
BA, LL.B, Aligarh.
Occupation
Lawyer.
Career
A close friend of the ALI BROTHERS, SHUAIB QURESHI, GHULAM HUSAIN and KHALIQUZZAMAN, he was a member of both the local Congress Committee and the Council of the Muslim League; regularly contributed to the *Comrade* and to *New Era* under the pen-name of 'Bambooque'; was the hub of Muslim politics in Bara Banki; played a leading part in organising the Besant internment agitation of 1917.

Mahomed Sakhawat Ali Alvi
Home Town
Lucknow.
Sect
Sunni.
Background
His father, Himayat Ali Alvi, sat on the Lucknow municipal board, held a small zamindari, owned flour mills in the city, and was an influential Sunni. His brother was ZAFAR-UL-MULK ALVI.
Occupation
Lawyer.

Appendix I

Career
Sakhawat Ali was active in Lucknow politics; agitated for separate electorates in 1909; member of the Council of the All-India Muslim League; one of the Lucknow 'Young Party' group which brought the Congress–League rapprochement to fruition in 1916; vice-president of the Anjuman-i-Islamia, Lucknow; secretary of the Anjuman Islahub Muslimeen, Lucknow; proprietor of the *An Nazir* newspaper.

Zafar-ul-Mulk Alvi
Home Town
Lucknow.
Sect
Sunni.
Background
See under MAHOMED SAKHAWAT ALI ALVI.
Occupation
Journalist.
Career
Zafar-ul-Mulk edited his brother's paper, the *An Nazir*, a literary journal which published poems and advocated female education; took the 'Young Party' side in the Nadwat-ul-Ulama question, 1913; member of the Anjuman-i-Khuddam-i-Kaaba; entered politics in 1918 with the growth of the Khilafat issue; 1919–20, a leading Khilafat agitator in Lucknow; proposed the non-co-operation resolution during Khilafat Day, 1 August 1920; sentenced to two years' hard labour in October 1920 for seditious writing.

Abdul Aziz Ansari
Home Town
Settled at Bara Banki.
Sect
Sunni.
Background
A cousin of DR M. A. ANSARI.
Education
BA, LL.B, Aligarh.
Occupation
Lawyer at the Bara Banki bar.
Career
Contemporary of KHALIQUZZAMAN at Aligarh; Red Crescent Mission, 1912–13; corresponded with MAHOMED ALI during his internment; involved in litigation with the RAJA OF MAHMUDABAD; does not appear to have been politically active until the Khilafat movement; jailed 1921; member of the Muslim Nationalist Party.

Dr Mukhtar Ahmad Ansari (1880–1936)
Home Town
Yusufpur in Ghazipur district, but settled in Delhi, 1910.
Sect
Sunni.

366

The 'Young Party'

Background
Small zamindari background, one brother was Abdul Wahhab Ansari, another, an elder brother, Hakim Abdur Razzak Ansari. What distinguished the family was its close connections with Deoband. Abdul Wahhab was a follower of Rashid Ahmad Gangohi. Abdur Razzak was a close friend and adviser of the Shaikh-ul-Hind, Mahmud Hasan of Deoband. He instigated Hasan to leave India in 1915, paying for the maulana's trip to the Hedjaz and his family's expenses while he was away. Abdur Razzak was also involved in the Silk Letters Conspiracy.
Education
Queen's College, Benares; Government School, Allahabad; Muir Central College, Allahabad; Nizam's College, Hyderabad; BA, Madras, 1900; went to England in 1901 where he was the first Indian house surgeon in the Charing Cross hospital.
Occupation
Doctor and politician.
Career
Ansari began his practice in Delhi in 1910. He had attended the Madras Congress in 1898 but did not enter politics, either in England or India, till MAHOMED ALI and the *Comrade* arrived in Delhi in 1912. He led the Red Crescent Mission to Turkey in 1912–13; appointed a Trustee of Aligarh, 1915; member of the Central Standing Committee of the Muslim Educational Conference; member of the Muslim University Association; member of the Council of the All-India Muslim League; founded the Home Rule League at Delhi in 1917 and elected its President; founded the Provincial Congress Committee in Delhi in the same year; chairman of the Reception Committee of the Muslim League, Delhi, 1918; invited ulama to the occasion; his own address to the session was proscribed; appeared to oppose non-co-operation till the Calcutta Special Congress, 1920; considered standing for the Legislative Assembly from the eastern districts of the UP in 1920; gave effective support for non-co-operation after September 1920; president of the Muslim League at Nagpur, 1920; president of the All-India Khilafat Conference at Gaya, 1922; member of the Congress Civil Disobedience Enquiry Committee, 1922, and opposed council entry till mid-1923; took over from C. R. Das as president of the All-India Congress Committee 1923; chairman of the Reception Committee of the Special Congress at Delhi, September 1923; president of the Congress, 1927; leading member of the Muslim Nationalist party. One of the front rank pan-Islamist leaders of the 'Young Party', Ansari was a strong supporter of Hindu–Muslim unity. With his Delhi ally, HAKIM AJMAL KHAN, he was from 1920 a leading engineer of political unity between Muslim groups and the Congress. This role of political broker made him an important member of the Congress high command in the 1920s and 1930s.

Dr Mahomed Naim Ansari
Home Town
Lucknow.
Sect
Sunni.

Appendix I

Occupation
Doctor.
Career
He resigned his government position of Assistant Civil Surgeon in 1912 to go on the Red Crescent Mission. He later set up in private practice in Lucknow where he had considerable influence, but was not prominent in city politics. He was a disciple of Abdul Bari (q.v. Appendix III), a member of the Council of the All-India Muslim League and a member of the Legislative Assembly, 1923–6, holding the Lucknow cum Benares Muslim seat.

Ziauddin Ahmad Barni

Sect
Muslim theosophist.
Occupation
Journalist and teacher.
Career
Friendly with MAHOMED ALI, he was a subeditor of the *Hamdard* for twenty-five months. Afterwards he became a teacher in the Cawnpore Theosophical School, and was much involved in the Home Rule movement in the city. A pan-Islamist, and a strong advocate of Hindu–Muslim unity, he disappeared from UP politics after 1918.

Mirza Samiullah Beg

Home Town
Lucknow.
Sect
Sunni.
Education
BA, LL.B.
Occupation
Lawyer.
Career
Beg started practice at the Lucknow Bar in the mid-1890s. He was a leading man in the agitation against the Nagri Resolution of 1909 and for separate electorates in 1909. He was involved in all 'Young Party' activities in Lucknow up to 1918 and was a leading advocate of Hindu–Muslim unity and the Lucknow Pact; member of All-India Congress Committee, 1916–17; general secretary of the Reception Committee of the Lucknow Congress, 1916; prominent in the Home Rule and internment agitations, 1917. He was a member of the Lucknow municipal board, of the Senate of Allahabad University and was nominated to the UP legislative council, 1916–19. Though a coming provincial politician, he put his legal career first. In 1918, he left politics when he was appointed Chief Justice of the Hyderabad High Court, – he had been one of the four vakils who were appointed advocates of the Oudh Court in 1914. Later he became president of the Hyderabad Privy Council and was given the title Mirza Yar Jung Bahadur.

The 'Young Party'

Abdur Rahman Bijnori (–1918)
Education
Aligarh.
Occupation
Civil servant in Bhopal.
Career
Expelled from Aligarh after the 1907 College strike, but allowed to return later.
He conceived the Sultanniah College project.

Major Syed Hasan Bilgrami
Home Town
Settled in retirement at Aligarh.
Sect
Sunni.
Background
Half-brother of Nawab Imad-ul-Mulk, Syed Hosein Bilgrami (q.v. Appendix II).
Education
A doctor and linguist, he spoke French, German, Persian, Arabic, English and
Urdu.
Occupation
Retired from the Indian Medical Service.
Career
Secretary of the All-India Muslim League, March 1908 to February 1910;
member of the Reforms Subcommittee, 1908; member of the London Muslim
League, 1908; education member of the Aligarh College syndicate, 1913;
president of the short-lived 'Young Party' organisation, 'The National Liberal
Association', 1915. In this year Theodore Morison urged that he was the only
man capable of becoming College secretary in place of Nawab Ishaq Khan (q.v.
Appendix II), but the UP government considered him to be a tool in the hands
of MAHOMED ALI. He disappeared from politics after 1915.

Syed Jalib Delhavi (–1930)
Home Town
Delhi.
Sect
Sunni: he regarded Abdul Bari (q.v. Appendix III) as his pir.
Occupation
Journalism.
Career
A subeditor of MAHOMED ALI's Urdu daily, *Hamdard*; editor of the RAJA OF
MAHMUDABAD's Lucknow Urdu daily, *Hamdam*, 1917–18, and very active in
Lucknow 'Young Party' politics during the same period. Attended the Jamiat-
ul-ulama sessions as a guest in 1919 and was prominent at the Oudh Khilafat
Conference of May 1920.

Qazi Abdul Ghaffar
Home Town
Moradabad.
Sect
Sunni.

Appendix I

Occupation
Journalism.
Career
Began as a journalist on MAHOMED ALI's *Hamdard*; later went to Calcutta to work first on the *Tarjuman* and then on its successor the *Sadiqat* which was founded in 1916; last Calcutta assignment was as editor of *Jamhur*; externed from Bengal after the Calcutta riots of 1918; corresponded frequently with MAHOMED ALI; member of the Council of the All-India Muslim League; said to have written DR M. A. ANSARI's Reception Committee speech at the Delhi Muslim League session, 1918; editor of the short-lived Firangi Mahal Khilafatist paper, *Akhuwat*, 1919; staunch Khilafatist.

Ghulam-us-Saqlain (–1915)
Home Town
Meerut, but settled at Lucknow.
Sect
Shia.
Education
BA, Aligarh.
Occupation
Lawyer and journalist.
Career
Founded the Ikhwan-us-Sufa at Aligarh in 1890, an association to promote physical and moral reform; inspector of schools at Hyderabad and pleader at Meerut in the 1890s; 1900, came to prominence in the agitation against the Nagri Resolution; 1903, founded the *Asr-i-Jadid* which advocated the setting up of a Muslim political organisation which specifically excluded the territorial aristocracy; joined Viqar-ul-Mulk (q.v. Appendix II) in his west UP tour designed to form a Muslim political association; active in the All-India Muslim League; attended early meetings of the All-India Shia Conference, proposing resolutions on education, till the attempts of the mujtahids to assert their authority drove him to resign in disgust; member of the provincial legislative council, 1913–15; recommended by the chief secretary of the UP government to succeed Viqar-ul-Mulk as Aligarh secretary; strongly urged that the Hindu depressed castes should be converted to Islam in 1914; of great independence of mind, even as a student 'he was chaffed for his zeal and quaint ideas'.

Hafiz Mahomed Halim
Home Town
Cawnpore.
Sect
Sunni.
Occupation
Hide merchant.
Career
A prominent citizen and honorary magistrate, Halim first appeared in politics in the agitation for separate electorates in 1909. He was prominent in the Cawnpore Mosque affair and a member of MAHMUDABAD's deputation to

370

The 'Young Party'

Meston. He was a member of the municipal board and was elected an Aligarh trustee in 1916. He normally tried to press forward 'Young Party' interests in local politics.

Dr Naziruddin Hasan
Home Town
Lucknow.
Sect
Sunni.
Education
BA, Aligarh; in 1910 at Trinity College, Dublin; Barrister-at-Law.
Occupation
Lawyer.
Career
Helped to defend the accused in the Cawnpore Mosque case; elected trustee of Aligarh, 1915; involved in the Home Rule and internment agitations, 1917; on the board of management of the Nadwat-ul-ulama; a close friend and adviser of Abdul Bari (q.v. Appendix III); essentially a supporter rather than a leader of 'Young Party' activities in Lucknow; around 1918 he went into the Hyderabad service, eventually rising to become Chief Justice and to bear the title Nawab Nazir Jar Jang; after retiring from Hyderabad service, rejoined the All-India Muslim League, and was hailed by KHALIQUZZAMAN as 'the best speaker in Urdu I have ever heard...'

Syed Shabbir Hasan
Sect
Shia.
Background
Small zamindari family of Macchlishahr, Jaunpur district, and younger brother of SYED WAZIR HASAN.
Occupation
Journalist.
Career
Editor with WAHIDUDDIN SALIM of the 'Young Party' *Muslim Gazette* (Lucknow), 1912–13, and the *Saiyara* (Lucknow), 1914–15; involved with WAHID YAR KHAN in the publication of another 'Young Party' paper, the *Nai Roshni* or 'New Light' at Allahabad in the years 1916 to 1918; Khilafatist and jailed in 1921.

Syed Wazir Hasan (1874–1947)
Home Town
Settled in Lucknow.
Sect
Shia.
Background
Small zamindari family of Macchlishahr, Jaunpur district: had five brothers of whom one was SHABBIR HASAN, the journalist; related by marriage to SYED RIZA ALI, whose daughter married Mir Nazir Hussain, a relation of Hasan, who became private secretary to the RAJA OF MAHMUDABAD in 1918.

Appendix I

Education
Aligarh and Muir Central College, Allahabad.
Occupation
Lawyer.
Career
Began practice in Jaunpur, moving later to Partabgarh and then to Lucknow; rose rapidly, being one of the four Vakils to be made Advocates in 1914. He rose in politics as rapidly as he did in the law; foundation member of the All-India Muslim League, 1906; helped to squash Ali Imam's move to accept the government of India's reform compromise proposals in July 1909; assistant secretary of the All-India Muslim League, 1910–12; secretary, 1912–19; member of the All-India Congress Committee, 1919; accompanied MAHOMED ALI to England, 1913; a close friend, both personal and political, of the RAJA OF MAHMUDABAD; dominated Muslim League policy, 1913–16, when he directed Congress–League rapprochement; member of the UP legislative council, 1916–19; gradually edged out of Muslim League politics with MAHMUDABAD as the extent of the Montagu–Chelmsford reforms became clear; resigned in 1919; then he became a government man, he was president of the Lucknow Aman Sabha – and left politics. Hasan's legal career continued to develop impressively: appointed Second Judicial Commissioner in 1921 being the first Indian member of the Oudh Bar, who was not a barrister, to be raised to the Bench; one of the Puisne Judges of the Chief Court after its inauguration in 1925; Chief Judge of the Court, 1930; retired, 1934; knighted in the same year. In 1936, he returned to politics as president of the All-India Muslim League at Bombay. Two years later, in contrast to most other Muslims, he joined the Congress.

H. M. Hayat
Home Town
Settled in Aligarh.
Sect
Sunni.
Background
Brought up in Lahore.
Education
BA, Aligarh, 1907–12.
Occupation
Teacher.
Career
Master at Aligarh from 1912 to 1920, resigning in accordance with the non-co-operation programme; member of the Red Crescent Mission; kept MAHOMED ALI informed on events at Aligarh; went to England as secretary to MAHOMED ALI in the Khilafat deputation of 1920.

Raja Ghulam Husain (1882–1917)
Sect
Sunni.

The 'Young Party'

Background
Punjabi Muslim, and most probably from impoverished circumstances as subscription had to be raised for his wife and family after his early death.
Education
Aligarh.
Occupation
Journalist.
Career
Leader of the Aligarh College strike of 1907; expelled but reinstated; subeditor of *Comrade*, 1911–14; editor of the RAJA OF MAHMUDABAD's *Indian Daily Telegraph*, 1914–16; 1917, founded his own *New Era* in Lucknow on the model of the *Comrade* to operate as the organ of the 'Young Party' in its attempts to strengthen its hold on the Muslim League and to achieve political reform. A fine writer of English, he was the most articulate exponent of 'Young Party' policy, and is a good example of the new breed of man who make his living out of political journalism. He died in the autumn of 1917 after being knocked down by a runaway horse.

Hafiz Hidayat Husain (–1936)
Home Town
Cawnpore.
Sect.
Sunni.
Education
BA and Barrister-at-Law.
Occupation
Lawyer at the Cawnpore Bar.
Career
Involved in the agitation for separate electorates, 1909; prominent in the Executive Council agitation, 1915; collected funds for the relief of the Muslim victims of the Shahabad riots, 1917; Home Rule Leaguer; president of the Cawnpore Khilafat Committee; member of the legislative council from 1923; chairman of the reception committee of the Fatehpur district Tanzim conference, 1925; a leading member of the committee to formulate UP Muslim demands to be submitted to the Indian Statutory Commission, 1928; member of the UP legislative council committee appointed to co-operate with the Simon Commission, 1928; secretary of the All-India Muslim League in the 1930s and president of the Delhi session in 1933.

Haji Syed Mohammad Husain
Home Town
Meerut.
Sect
Sunni.
Education
Barrister-at-Law.
Occupation
Lawyer.

Appendix I

Career

Successful in the 'Young Party' attack on the Meerut municipal board in the 1916 elections; involved in the Meerut Rowlatt protest, 1919; secretary of the provincial Khilafat Committee based at Meerut and very active in the organisation of the early Khilafat agitation in the province; worked closely with NAWAB ISMAIL KHAN; 21 November 1920, after being attacked in the press, resigned from the Khilafat Committee; founded the Anti-Shuddhi League with ISMAIL KHAN in 1923; a leading member of the All-India Muslim League in the 1930s.

Mumtaz Hussain (–1920)

Home Town

Lucknow.

Sect

Sunni.

Background

Son of Sajjad Hussain who was editor of *Oudh Punch* (Lucknow), a leading Urdu literary paper of the province; his grandfather was a deputy collector in Hyderabad; the family, which he had founded in 1877, was one of several leading service families established at Kakori, in Lucknow district.

Education

BA, Aligarh; became a Barrister-at-Law in 1901.

Occupation

Lawyer.

Career

Took part in the agitation for separate electorates in 1909; tried unsuccessfully for the legislative council in 1909 and 1912; member of Muslim University Constitution Committee; vice-president of the Oudh Khilafat Committee, 1919; involved in all 'Young Party' activities in Lucknow; he was a strong advocate of Hindu–Muslim unity.

Syud Hussain

Home Town

Came from Calcutta.

Sect

Sunni.

Background

Son of Nawab Syud Mohammad of Dacca and Calcutta; cousin of Shahed and Abdullah Suhrawardy and uncle of Begum Ikramullah.

Education

BA, Aligarh, and was in England with KHWAJA ABDUL MAJID and Dr Syed Mahmud.

Occupation

Journalist.

Career

Member of the Council of the All-India Muslim League; *Bombay Chronicle* staff, 1917–19; editor of Motilal Nehru's *Independent*, 1919 – the paper was run from Anand Bhavan, Allahabad; involved in all the city's extremist politics in 1919 with Jawaharlal Nehru and KAMALUDDIN AHMAD JAFRI; late 1919, when

The 'Young Party'

Motilal and Jawaharlal Nehru were involved in the Punjab trials, is said to have eloped with Motilal's eldest daughter, to have been married according to Muslim rites by Maulana Fakhir of Allahabad and on the news coming to light to have been compelled by the Nehrus to perform a Muslim divorce; Syud Hussain was sent to England with the Khilafat deputation, allegedly with a large pay-off, and thence went to America.

Kamaluddin Ahmed Jafri (–1933)
Home Town
Allahabad.
Sect
Shia.
Background
Father, Maulana Muhammad Muhiuddin Jafri, a professor at Muir Central College, Allahabad; brother, Dr S. N. A. Jafri of the UP civil service.
Education
BA, Muir Central College, Allahabad; Barrister-at-Law.
Occupation
Lawyer.
Career
Edited the *Islamic Review* in England; on his return practised in the Allahabad High Court; member of the Allahabad District Muslim League; like his fellow Shia, HYDER MEHDI, frequently worked with Hindu groups in local politics; made strong attempts ro reconcile the two communities in the Allahabad municipal board quarrel of 1917, though was still keen to protect the Muslim position in the locality; prominent Home Rule Leaguer; leading Allahabad Khilafatist, being secretary of the Allahabad Khilafat Committee and publishing a series of pamphlets on the Khilafat; considered standing in the legislative council on May 1920 against Nawab Abdul Majid's (q.v. Appendix II) son; worked closely with Jawaharlal Nehru in organising extremist politics in Allahabad; jailed 1921.

Syed Mir Jan
Home Town
Lucknow.
Sect
Shia.
Education
BA, LL.B.
Occupation
Lawyer
Career
Practised at the Oudh Bar; proprietor of the Urdu weekly, the *Muslim Gazette* (Lucknow), edited by WAHIDUDDIN SALIM and SHABBIR HASAN, which was the voice of the Lucknow 'Young Party' from 1912 till it was closed under the Press Act in September 1913; active in the politics surrounding the Congress–League rapprochement and the Lucknow Pact, 1915–16.

375

Appendix I

Choudry Khaliquzzaman (1889–1973)

Home Town
Lucknow.
Sect
Sunni.
Background
Father, Shaikh Mohammad Zaman, a naib tahsildar; related through him to the taluqdars of Subeha, through his mother to taluqdars of Bhilwal, and both taluqdari families were heavily in debt; immediate family were not wealthy, apart from his mother's brother, Mahomed Nasim (q.v. Appendix II), who was leader of the Oudh Bar, 1894–1917; Nasim's son, MAHOMED WASIM, was of course, his cousin.
Education
Jubilee School, Lucknow; Aligarh, 1907–16, BA, LL.B.
Occupation
Lawyer and politician.
Career
Belonged to the SHUAIB QURESHI, ABDUR RAHMAN SIDDIQUI, HAMIDULLAH KHAN and BASHIRUDDIN AHMED set at Aligarh; Red Crescent Mission, 1912–13; strongly influenced by the ALI BROTHERS; after leaving Aligarh employed as Education Secretary by the RAJA OF MAHMUDABAD; joined the Congress in 1916 acting as a member of the Lucknow Reception Committee; became joint secretary of the All-India Muslim League in the same year, appointing HAKIM ABDUL WALI as his assistant; began practice in April 1917 as junior to Mahomed Nasim (q.v. Appendix II) and MAHOMED WASIM; Home Rule Leaguer; from 1917, leader of the 'Young Party' in Lucknow; opposed the entry of the ulama into Muslim politics in 1918; claimed to have organised the Lucknow Khilafat Conference of September 1919 and, with the ulama of Firangi Mahal, to have drawn up the constitution of the Central Khilafat Committee; elected president of the Lucknow Congress Committee, March 1920; gave up practice, October 1920; important Khilafat leader in Lucknow; jailed for defying government resolution on Volunteers, December 1921; joined the Swarajists, January 1923; chairman, Lucknow municipal board, 1923; a leading UP Muslim politician in the 1930s and 1940s; after independence, governor of East Pakistan.

Hakim Ajmal Khan (1863–1928)

Home Town
Delhi.
Sect
Sunni.
Background
Family came from Kashgar, Turkestan, and held important positions under the emperor, Babur; produced a long line of physicians of which the most famous was Hakim Sharif Khan, Ajmal's grandfather; family received jagirs from Mughal emperors, which were confiscated in 1857; his father, Hakim Mahmud Khan, had a very large practice in Delhi and north India; Ajmal had two brothers, Hakim Abdul Majid Khan and Hakim Wasil Khan; the former established a school to teach the Unani system of medicine in order to preserve

it, published a journal, *Akmal-ul-Akhbar*, and associated himself with the educational movement of Syed Ahmed Khan.

Education
Traditional education in Arabic and Persian, learned medicine from his family, and spoke English only with hesitation.

Occupation
Hakim

Career
The leading hakim of northern India, he was personal physician to the Nawab of Rampur, 1892–1901, and treated many other leading Muslims; founder member of the All-India Muslim League, 1906; Board of management of the Nadwat-ul-ulama; president of the Nadwat-ul-ulama annual session, 1909; set up the Unani Tibbia organisation, 1909; chairman of the Reception Committee of the All-India Muslim League, Delhi, January 1910; vice-president, All-India Muslim League; trustee of Aligarh; 1911, visited England, made the acquaintance of DR ANSARI, toured hospitals and attended the Coronation; on the way back he visited Constantinople and Al Azhar; became increasingly interested in politics after his return to India which coincided with the outbreak of the Turkish wars and the removal of the capital of the empire to Delhi; a close friend of the Viceroy, Hardinge, after whom he named the hospital he founded; operated closely with DR ANSARI and involved in all 'Young Party' politics from 1917; president of the All-India Muslim League at Amritsar, 1919; took part in the Khilafat agitation, and was the first man to hand back his titles in April 1920, but was unhappy about the extremism of those who wanted more extensive forms of non-co-operation; strongly opposed to the attempts of the ulama to gain predominant influence in Muslim politics; appointed Chancellor of the Jamia Millia Islamia, November 1920; chairman of the Reception Committee of the Hindu Mahasabha conference, Delhi, November 1921; president of the Congress and All-India Khilafat conference, Ahmedabad, December 1921, in which he did much to curb the extremists, a role which he was to continue to play throughout 1922; member of the Congress Civil Disobedience Enquiry Committee and voted in favour of council entry; joined the Swarajists, January 1923; strove manfully in 1922–3 to keep the alliance between the Congress and the various Muslim groups in being; retired from politics in 1925 because of ill-health; a man of many parts, in addition to being a physician and a politician, he was a poet, a calligraphist, a wrestler, a billiard and a card-player, moreover he was the nearest the Muslims had to Gandhi in terms of breadth of political appeal: he was highly regarded by government, respected in the Congress, and amongst Hindus generally, and was one of the few Muslims who could feel equally at home among ulama, Nawabs and Aligarh graduates. He was known as 'the uncrowned King of Delhi'.

Prince Hamidullah Khan of Bhopal (1894–   )
Home Town
Bhopal.
Sect
Sunni.

Appendix I

Background
Third son of the Begum of Bhopal and heir to the throne.
Education
BA, Aligarh.
Career
Contemporary of KHALIQUZZAMAN at Aligarh; trustee of Aligarh, 1917; important patron of 'Young Party' activities; several Aligarh contemporaries were employed in Bhopal service, among them ABDUR RAHMAN BIJNORI; supported the Sultanniah College scheme; helped to pay for SHUAIB QURESHI and ABDUR RAHMAN SIDDIQUI to go to England; his support for the 'Young Party' led to his right of succession being strongly disputed by the government of India; succeeded in 1926.

Sheikh Yusuf Husain Khan
Home Town
Lucknow.
Sect
Shia.
Education
Barrister-at-Law.
Occupation
Lawyer.
Career
Active in all 'Young Party' politics up to the Lucknow Pact; regularly attended the UP provincial conference; frequently contributed articles on Hindu–Muslim unity to the *Leader*; disappeared from politics after 1918.

Nawab Ismail Khan (1884–1958)
Home Town
Meerut.
Sect
Sunni.
Background
For this, see his father, Nawab Ishaq Khan (q.v. Appendix II).
Education
Aligarh.
Occupation
Lawyer.
Career
Leading light with BASHIRUDDIN AHMED in the Syed Manzil Club, the Aligarh graduates club in Meerut; entered politics in the Besant internment protest, 1917; organised the Rowlatt protest in Meerut with Sita Ram; a leading member of the Meerut Congress Committee, also of the Meerut Provincial Khilafat Committee and very energetic in Khilafat activities in Meerut up to 1922; founded the Anti-Shuddhi League with HAJI SYED MOHAMMAD HUSAIN, 1923; in the same year government summed Ismail Khan up thus: 'A keen Muslim and far more concerned with Muslim interests than with national politics...His part is that of an organiser.' Represented the Meerut Muhammadan Rural constituency in the legislative council, 1924–6; prominent All-India Muslim League politician in the 1930s and 1940s, remained in India after partition.

The 'Young Party'

Wahid Yar Khan
Home Town
Agra.
Sect
Sunni.
Education
BA.
Occupation
Journalist.
Career
Proprietor and publisher of the *Nai Roshni* or 'New Light', a 'Young Party' paper published in Allahabad between 1916 and 1918, and described by government as a 'rag'; SHABBIR HASAN worked on the editorial side; involved in Home Rule League activities, 1917–18; and Cawnpore Khilafat agitation, 1919–20; described by the Allahabad district magistrate in 1917 as 'being rather stupid and having no political sense as we understand it'.

Rafi Ahmed Kidwai (1896–1954)
Home Town
Masauli in Bara Banki district.
Sect
Sunni.
Background
A Kidwai Shaikh, his father, Imtiaz Ali was a government servant; Rafi Ahmed was strongly influenced by VILAYAT ALI who brought him up from the age of ten.
Education
Aligarh.
Occupation
Politician.
Career
Involved in the agitation against Towle, the principal of Aligarh; on Dr Ziauddin's (q.v. Appendix II) black list of rebel students; attended the Lucknow Congress, 1916; much impressed by Mrs Besant and took part in the internment agitation, 1917; left Aligarh and became a Congress regular in 1920.

Mushir Husain Kidwai (1878–   )
Home Town
Lucknow.
Sect
Sunni; he regarded Abdul Bari (q.v. Appendix III) as his pir.
Background
A Kidwai Shaikh of Gadia in Bara Banki district; from a petty zamindari family; his brother was Maqbul Husain, a deputy collector, and he had many well-to-do relations including Shaikh Shahid Husain (q.v. Appendix II) of Gadia.
Education
Barrister-at-Law.
Occupation
Lawyer and politician.

379

Appendix I

Career

Much interested in pan-Islamism, and one of the founders of the Anjuman-i-Khuddam-i-Kaaba; family had close contacts with Abdul Bari and one brother acted as the maulana's private secretary; in 1913, government summed up Kidwai thus: 'A crank...Contributions to the press are frequent but moderate in language. Regarded by the Muslim community as well-intentioned, but unpractical and his political influence is correspondingly limited.' In England, 1913–20, where he was closely involved with the Woking Mosque; president of the Oudh Khilafat Conference, May 1920; in spite of his apparent concern for the Khilafat, he ignored non-co-operation, enrolling as an advocate of the Allahabad High Court in 1921 and becoming adviser to the British Indian Association; president of the Socialist group of legislative assembly members formed in March 1924; three times member of the Council of State; combined a legal career, which culminated in the Senior Judgeship on the Lucknow Bench, with an international reputation in the 1930s as an ultra-radical; president of the non-communal All-India Independent League; author of *Swaraj and How to Obtain it* (Lucknow, 1924) and *Pan-Islamism and Bolshevism* (London, 1937); hobby, rose-growing, and his name is immortalised in the 'Kidway' rose.

Muhammad Ali Muhammad, Raja of Mahmudabad (1879–1931)

Home Town
Mahmudabad in Sitapur district.

Sect
Shia.

Background
Family claimed to be descended from Qazi Nasrulla, a Siddiqi Sheikh of Baghdad, who came to India in the thirteenth century; ancestors appeared in Oudh in the fourteenth century and settled at Mahmudabad in the sixteenth; Mahmudabad's grandfather, Nawab Ali Khan, greatly increased the Mahmudabad estates in the last two decades of Nawabi rule in Oudh, played a prominent part in the Mutiny and submitted shortly before his death in 1858; Mahmudabad's father, Raja Sher Mohammad Amir Hasan Khan, was one of the leading men of the province in the late nineteenth century, being elected vice-president of the British Indian Association in 1871, and president 1882–92. He was also a member of the Viceroy's council and received many titles from government. Estate paid Rs. 2,43,198, in Sitapur district, Rs. 46,640 in Bara Banki and there were other large estates in Kheri.

Education
Private tutor.

Occupation
Politician.

Career
Fellow of Allahabad University, 1906; Aligarh trustee, 1906; UP legislative council, 1904–9; Governor-general's council, 1907–20; did not attend the Lucknow meeting of September 1906 which approved the Simla memorial for fear of offending Hindu taluqdars; entered agitational politics in the protests over separate electorates in 1909; a close friend of SYED WAZIR HASAN and vigorous supporter of 'Young Party' politics from 1913 to the Lucknow Pact; took the

The 'Young Party'

'Young Party' line in the Muslim University Association till 1916; leading role in the agitations over the Cawnpore Mosque and the UP Executive Council; president of the All-India Muslim League, 1915–19; Meston became very hostile after the Cawnpore incident, actually threatening to remove his sanad in 1916, and from this moment the Raja steadily withdrew from 'Young Party' politics; president of the Bureau for the release of the Muslim internees, 1917; president of the All-India Muslim League session at Calcutta, 1917; president of the special session of the All-India Muslim League at Bombay, 1918; quarrelled with Abdul Bari (q.v. Appendix III), 1919; the arrival of the Raja's close friend, Harcourt Butler, as lieutenant-governor in 1918 finally pulled him out of 'Young Party' politics; home member UP government 1920–5; president of the British Indian Association, 1917–21, 1930–1; vice-chancellor of Aligarh Muslim University, 1920–3; personal title of Maharaja, 1925; president of the Calcutta session of the All-India Muslim League, 1928; during his involvement with 'Young Party' politics, the Raja, though in debt to the Bank of Bengal to the tune of Rs. 20 lakhs, played the important part of paymaster and employer, helping to support among many others: the ALI BROTHERS, RAJA GHULAM HUSAIN and KHALIQUZZAMAN.

Khwaja Abdul Majid (1885–1962)
Home Town
Aligarh.
Sect
Sunni.
Background
Son-in-law of Nawab Sarbuland Jung (q.v. Appendix II).
Education
BA, Aligarh, Christ's College, Cambridge; Barrister-at-Law.
Occupation
Lawyer and politician.
Career
Member of the Council of the London Muslim League, 1908; prominent in the Indian Majlis at Cambridge; close personal friend of Ross Masud (q.v. Appendix II) and Dr Syed Mahmud of Bihar; on his return to India set up practice first at Aligarh and then at Patna; elected trustee of Aligarh, 1912; succeeded SHAUKAT ALI as secretary of the Aligarh Old Boys Association, 1915; fought with the 'Young Party' throughout the struggles over the Muslim University, but not even in local politics till the Khilafat agitation, when he gave up his practice at Patna; principal of the Jamia Millia Islamia, 1922; jailed, 1922; the women of his family regarded Abdul Bari (q.v. Appendix III) as their pir, and his wife ran an Urdu weekly *Hindi* to support Congress and Khilafat; secretary of the Congress Working Committee, 1923; chairman of the Aligarh municipal board, 1923; Swarajist; 1923, stood for the legislative council against Dr Ziauddin (q.v. Appendix II), but without success; member of the Muslim Nationalist Party; described by government in 1913 as 'a pushing young lawyer to whom notoriety is gain'.

Appendix I

Masood-ul-Hasan (‑1937)
Home Town
Moradabad.
Sect
Sunni.
Education
BA, Barrister-at-Law.
Occupation
Lawyer.
Career
On the council of the London Muslim League and also of the All-India Muslim League; in the second decade of the twentieth century one of Moradabad's radical Muslims and a strong personal rival of Mahomed Yakub (q.v. Appendix II); involved in all local 'Young Party' activities from the Home Rule Movement to the early stages of the Khilafat movement; resigned from the Moradabad Khilafat Committee, January 1920; chairman of the Rohilkhand divisional political conference, May 1920; chairman of the Moradabad municipal board, 1919–23; later he became chief minister of Rampur state.

Syed Hyder Mehdi
Home Town
Allahabad.
Sect
Shia.
Background
Son of Moulvi Muhammad Mehdi, pleader, a prominent member of the Allahabad district bar who died in 1913.
Education
BA, LL.B.
Occupation
Lawyer.
Career
A leading Shia of Allahabad; practised at the Allahabad High Court; member of the UP Congress Committee; member of the All-India Congress Committee, 1919–21; worked closely with Jawaharlal Nehru and KAMALUDDIN AHMED JAFRI in most agitation in Allahabad; Home Rule Leaguer; Khilafatist; considered standing for the legislative council, 1920, but non-co-operated; stood for the legislative assembly in 1923.

Hasrat Mohani, alias, Fazl-ul-Hasan (1877–1951)
Home Town
Mohan in Unao district, but settled in Cawnpore.
Sect
Sunni; he regarded Abdul Bari's (q.v. Appendix III) father, Abdul Wahab, as his pir.
Background
Petty zamindari family in Unao.

The 'Young Party'

Education
Early education on traditional lines in the local maktab; later attended the government school, Fatehpur, but in his free time learned Persian and Arabic from local maulvis; went to Aligarh 1895, BA, 1903.
Occupation
Journalist and politician.
Career
1903, founded *Urdu-e-Moalla*, an Urdu weekly which was published intermittently until the 1930s; its pan-Islamic and virulently anti-British views had a strong influence on Aligarh students in the first decade of the twentieth century; sentenced to two years' imprisonment, which was reduced to one, for publishing an article entitled 'The Educational policy of the English in Egypt' which had been written by an Aligarh student, 1908; published an edition of Ghalib's works and many of his own poems; as a poet made an important contribution to the refinement and development of the modern Urdu ghazal; an admirer of Tilak, he attended the Surat Congress as an extremist; member of the council of the All-India Muslim League; important agitator in the Cawnpore Mosque affair; a leader in the Silk Letter Conspiracy, hoping to become a major-general in the 'Army of God', he was arrested on his way to Kabul and imprisoned from 1916 to the end of the War; during the Khilafat movement he associated increasingly with the ulama, coming to be called 'our mad Mullah' by the ALI BROTHERS, and was usually in the forefront when extreme measures were being demanded; introduced the non-co-operation resolution at the Khilafat conference at Delhi, 23 November 1919; president of the Khilafat workers conference, Delhi, April 1920; declared that he was willing to join an Afghan invasion of India at the Allahabad joint conference, June 1920; demanded complete independence for India at the All-India Khilafat conference and the Congress at Ahmedabad, December 1921; president of the All-India Muslim League at Ahmedabad, December 1921; imprisoned 1922; mid-1920s, associated with well-known Communists such as Satya Bhakta and Saklatvala; prominent at the Communist conference at Cawnpore, 1925, and led a group which stormed the Congress pandal; resigned from the Jamiat-ul-ulama, 1929; much involved in civil disobedience, 1930; a leading All-India Muslim League worker from 1937.

Syed Ali Nabi (-1928)
Home Town
Agra.
Sect
Shia.
Education
Agra College.
Occupation
Lawyer.
Career
President of the Anjuman-i-Islamia, Agra, and leader of the city's Muslims; vice-chairman of the Agra municipal board; Khan Bahadur for public service, 1909; agitated for separate electorates for Muslims, 1909; member of the

383

legislative council, 1909–12 and 1916–23; chairman of the Reception Committee of the All-India Muslim League session at Agra, December 1913; president of the UP Muslim League; elected Aligarh trustee, 1916; vice-president of the District Congress Committee, 1916, and president, 1919; president, Agra Home Rule League, 1917; took part in the early stages of the Khilafat agitation, resigning his title, but refused to forgo his council seat; in 1921 was active in organising the Aman Sabha movement in Agra on the grounds that non-co-operation was likely to lead to lawlessness.

Syed Nabiullah (–1925)
Home Town
Kara in Allahabad district but settled at Lucknow.
Sect
Sunni.
Background
Held a small zamindari estate in Allahabad district.
Education
BA, Aligarh, Barrister-at-Law, returning from England in 1885.
Occupation
Lawyer.
Career
Foundation member of the All-India Muslim League; on the Reforms Sub-committee of the League, 1908; president of the Nagpur session of the League, 1910; chairman of the Reception Committee of the Lucknow session of the League, 1916; elected trustee of Aligarh, 1907; member of the Muslim University Association; member of the committee of the Rifah-i-Am club and the Jalsa-e-Tahzib, Lucknow; took part in all 'Young Party' activities in Lucknow up to the Khilafat movement; though not involved in the Khilafat agitation, did not join the anti-non-co-operation movement or the Liberal League; chairman of the Lucknow municipal board, 1916–23.

Shuaib Qureshi
Home Town
Rae Bareli.
Sect
Sunni.
Background
Married a daughter of MAHOMED ALI.
Education
BA, LL.B, Aligarh.
Occupation
Journalist and politician.
Career
While still at Aligarh, took part in the Red Crescent Mission, 1912–13; assistant secretary of the Aligarh Old Boys' association under SHAUKAT ALI; active in Rae Bareli politics, 1913–15; worked for the Sultanniah College scheme in Bhopal, 1916; succeeded RAJA GHULAM HUSAIN as editor of *New Era*, 1917; but soon lost his job when government proceeded against the paper because of

'objectionable' articles on the Muslim internees; member of the Council of the All-India Muslim League; Home Rule Leaguer; a messenger between Gandhi and the ALI BROTHERS during their internment; in 1919, HAKIM AJMAL KHAN, PRINCE HAMIDULLAH KHAN of Bhopal and HASRAT MOHANI paid for him to go to England with ABDUR RAHMAN SIDDIQUI; joined Cambridge University, but left in June 1920 to devote himself to Khilafat work; went to Switzerland, late 1920, to publish a pan-Islamic newspaper there; retired to India, 1921, and edited *Young India*; 1922, edited the *Independent*, but was prosecuted in June for seditious writing; described by Motilal Nehru in 1928 as a bigot 'disguised as a socialist'; friendship with PRINCE HAMIDULLAH KHAN stood him in good stead as in the end he entered the Bhopal service becoming a member of the State Council.

Syed Fazlur Rahman
Home Town
Cawnpore.
Education
BA, LL.B, Aligarh.
Occupation.
Lawyer.
Career
In practice at the Cawnpore bar, he first entered politics in the Mosque affair; member of the Council of the All-India Muslim League; leader of 'Young Party' politics in Cawnpore; Home Rule Leaguer; moderate Khilafatist; member of All-India Congress Committee, 1921; member of Cawnpore municipal board, 1916–26.

Wahiduddin Salim (1863–   )
Home Town
Settled in Lucknow.
Occupation
Journalist.
Career
Leading 'Young Party' editor of Lucknow from 1912 to 1915; with SHABBIR HASAN edited both the *Muslim Gazette*, owned by SYED MIR JAN, which lasted from 1912 to 1913, and the *Saiyara*, which lasted from 1914 to 1915; both were shut down by government.

Tassaduq Ahmad Khan Sherwani (–1935)
Home Town
Aligarh.
Sect
Sunni.
Background
A member of the Bilona branch of the Sherwani Pathan family – see Muzammilullah Khan (q.v. Appendix II); eldest son of Haji Abdul Rashid Khan; one brother, Nisar Ahmad Khan, became a superintendent of post offices, resigning his post in the non-co-operation movement, and another, Fida Ahmad Khan,

managed a sugar factory in Etah. It is not clear whether Tassaduq Ahmad held any land.
Education
BA, Aligarh; direct contemporary of Jawaharlal Nehru at Cambridge; Barrister-at-Law.
Occupation
Lawyer and politician.
Career
Expelled from Aligarh after the 1907 College strike, but reinstated later; leader of 'Young Party' politics in Aligarh district from 1913; followed MAHOMED ALI in the Aligarh and Muslim University struggles; elected trustee of Aligarh, 1916; member of the Council of the All-India Muslim League; Home Rule Leaguer; member of District Congress Committee; member of the Provincial Congress Committee and the All-India Congress Committee, 1919; organised the first Aligarh District Conference, 1920; leading Khilafatist and non-co-operator; secretary of the Jamia Millia Islamia; member of the Khilafat civil disobedience enquiry committee, 1922; joined Swarajists, January 1923; firm Congressman and devoted admirer of Motilal Nehru; took part in the civil disobedience movement of 1930; president of the UP Congress Committee, 1931; member of the Congress Parliamentary Board, 1934; throughout the early 1930s worked closely with Jawaharlal Nehru.

Haroon Khan Sherwani
Home Town
Aligarh.
Sect
Sunni.
Background
A member of the Datauli branch of the Sherwani Pathan family – see Muzammilullah Khan (q.v. Appendix II); the son of HAJI MUSA KHAN SHERWANI.
Education
BA, Aligarh, Oxford, Barrister-at-Law.
Occupation
Lawyer and historian.
Career
Trustee of Aligarh; took a similar line to TASSADUQ AHMAD KHAN SHERWANI in politics up to the Khilafat movement, though restricted to an Aligarh base. Later became head of the department of History and Political Science at Osmania University, Hyderabad.

Haji Musa Khan Sherwani (1872–   )
Home Town
Aligarh.
Sect
Sunni.
Background
A member of the Datauli branch of the Sherwani Pathan family – see Muzammilullah Khan (q.v. Appendix II); father, Nawab Haji Mohammad Faiz Ahmad

The 'Young Party'

Khan who migrated to Mecca after the Mutiny and acquired so great a position in the Hedjaz that the Ottoman government gave him a salute of eight guns; son, HAROON KHAN SHERWANI; owned the smallest of the Sherwani estates, it was based on Datauli, paid Rs. 5557 land revenue and was heavily encumbered.
Education
Aligarh.
Occupation
Scholar and politician.
Career
Returned to India in 1878; elected trustee of Aligarh, 1891; toured northern India with Syed Ahmed Khan in 1890, 1892 and 1895 in order to popularise the Muslim Educational Conference; played a leading part in the anti-Nagri agitation of 1900; member of the Aligarh College Syndicate, 1909; member of the Muslim University Foundation Committee; active in all early All-India Muslim League politics; member of the Reforms Sub-committee, 1908; joint-secretary of the League, 1908–18; very active in 'Young Party' politics in Aligarh up to the Khilafat agitation; involved in the establishment of the Jamia Millia Islamia; wrote books on the history of Islam, the Khilafat movement and the life of the Prophet.

Amir Mustafa Khan Sherwani (–1936)
Home Town
Aligarh.
Sect
Sunni.
Background
A Sherwani Pathan descended from Nawab Yusuf Khan; his father was Haji Mustafa Khan of Burha Gaon; Amir Mustafa held a zamindari estate at Kanshirauli in Aligarh district which paid Rs. 7336 land revenue but was heavily encumbered.
Education
BA, Aligarh.
Occupation
Landowner.
Career
Played a leading part in the agitation against the Nagri resolution, 1900; a trustee of Aligarh; secretary of the Aligarh Old Boys' association from 1918; involved in 'Young Party' politics, but purely on a local basis.

Abdur Rahman Siddiqui
Home Town
Dacca in east Bengal, but lived in Aligarh and Delhi for much of the period.
Sect
Sunni.
Education
BA, LL.B, Aligarh.
Occupation
Journalist and politician.

387   13-2

Appendix I

Career
Founder member of the All-India Muslim League and a member of its council; president of the Aligarh Students Union; worked on the *Comrade* staff in Calcutta, 1911; returned to Aligarh to read law, 1912; general manager of the Red Crescent Mission, 1912–13; close friend of DR ANSARI and lived with him in Delhi; managed MAHOMED ALI's affairs while he was interned and kept him in touch with politics; much involved with the agitation for MAHOMED ALI's release, 1917–18; supported the Sultanniah College scheme; at a loss what to do in 1918 and in debt; in 1919, HAKIM AJMAL KHAN, PRINCE HAMIDULLAH KHAN of Bhopal and HASRAT MOHANI paid for him to go to England with SHUAIB QURESHI; unlike his companion, he remained in England during the 1920s and 1930s, becoming a successful businessman; later he became governor of East Pakistan.

Manzur Ali Sokhta
Home Town
Allahabad.
Sect
Sunni.
Background
Father was the manager of the Nehru household and lived in a house in the Nehru compound, which was where Manzur Ali was brought up.
Education
BA, LL.B.
Occupation
Lawyer.
Career
Delegate of the UP Congress Committee at the Lucknow Congress, 1916; joint secretary of the Allahabad Home Rule League; involved in all Khilafat and Congress activities in Allahabad and worked closely with KAMALUDDIN JAFRI, SYED HYDER MEHDI and Jawaharlal Nehru; he was to become very powerful on the UP Congress Committee in the early 1930s.

Hakim Abdul Wali (1884–   )
Home Town
Lucknow.
Sect
Sunni.
Background
Son of Moulvi Abdul Ali.
Education
BA.
Occupation
Hakim.
Career
Part proprietor, with Moulvi Syed Sulaiman of Bihar, of the *Al Bayan*, an Arabic–Urdu monthly of Lucknow which published articles on Arabic literature and in praise of the Ottoman government; Abdul Wali owned the Asi Press of Lucknow on which his paper and the *An Nadwa*, the journal of the Nadwat-

ul-ulama, were published; involved in all 'Young Party' activities in Lucknow; member of the Lucknow clique which pushed the League towards the Congress; employed by KHALIQUZZAMAN as assistant secretary of the All-India Muslim League from 1916: joint secretary of the Oudh Khilafat Committee, 1920; imprisoned with KHALIQUZZAMAN for defying the government order regarding volunteers, 1921; member of the Lucknow municipal board, 1920–6.

Mahomed Wasim

Home Town
Lucknow.
Sect
Sunni.
Background
For details see his father, Mahomed Nasim (q.v. Appendix II).
Education
BA, Aligarh, went to England in 1904; Barrister-at-Law, 1908.
Occupation
Lawyer.
Career
Member of the Council of the All-India Muslim League; not very actively involved in politics but always prepared to vote with and support the 'Young Party'; taking over his father's practice, he became an extremely successful lawyer; concentrated on the Oudh Estates Act and became the 'idol of every Taluqdar'; Advocate General of the UP; Attorney General of Pakistan; KHALIQUZZAMAN started as his junior.

APPENDIX II

THE 'OLD PARTY'

'Old Party' men were marked by their reliance on government, so men have been included in this appendix if, for all or most of the period, they acted on the assumption that government was the best defender of their interests. The sources of these biographies are the same as for those in Appendix I with the addition of the following: *History of Services of Gazetted Officers employed under the Government of the N.-W.P. and Oudh corrected up to 1st January 1881* (Allahabad, 1881), and volumes in the same series for 1890, 1909 and 1920; Darogah Haji Abbas Ali, *An Illustrated Historical Album of the Rajas and Taluqdars of Oude* (Allahabad, 1880); *Rajahs and Nawabs of the North-Western Provinces* (Allahabad, 1877); *Manual of Titles United Provinces of Agra and Oudh* (Allahabad, 1917); C. E. Buckland, *A Dictionary of Indian Biography* (London, 1906); Sir R. Lethbridge, *Golden Book of India* (London, 1900); *Who's Who in India* (Newal Kishore, Lucknow, 1911); Al-Haj Mahomed Ullah ibn S. Jung, *Leaves from the Life of Al-Haj Afzal-ul-Ulema Nawab Sarbuland Jung Bahadur, M. Hameed-Ullah Khan, M.A. (Cantab), Barrister-at-Law, formerly Chief Justice H.E.H. the Nizam's High Court, Hyderabad (Deccan)* (Allahabad, 1926).

Biographies of the following will be found below, and names in capitals indicate cross-references within the Appendix:

Abdullah, Sheikh
Ahmad, Ibni
Ahmad, Dr Ziauddin
Alam, Moulvi Maqbul
Alam, Shah Munir
Ali, Munshi Ehtisham
Ali, Syed Mahomed
Bashir-ud-din, Muhammad
Bilgrami, Syed Hosein, Imad-ul-Mulk
Chhatari, Nawab Hafiz Ahmad Said Khan
Habibullah, Sheikh Mohammad
Haidar, Syed Agha
Hasan, Nawab Mehdi Ali, Mohsin-ul-Mulk
Hasan, Syed Mehdi
Husain, Mufti Haidar

Husain, Syed Jafar
Husain, Nawab Mushtaq, Viqar-ul-Mulk
Husain, Sheikh Shahid
Husein, Syed Karamat
Jehangirabad, Raja Tassaduq Rasul Khan
Khan, Munshi Abdul Karim (alias Hakim Barham)
Khan, Sahibzada Aftab Ahmad
Khan, Munshi Ashgar Ali
Khan, Hamid Ali
Khan, Moulvi Haji Mahomed Hamidullah, Nawab Sarbuland Jung
Khan, Masood-us-Zaman
Khan, Nawab Mahomed Ishaq

390

The 'Old Party'

Khan, Nawab Muhammad
  Muzammilullah
Khan, Raja Naushad Ali
Majid, Nawab Maulvi Abdul
Masud, Syed Ross
Mirza, Aziz
Nasim, Mahomed
Pahasu, Nawab Muhammad
  Faiyaz Ali Khan
Pirpur, Raja Syed Abu Jafar

Qizilbash, Nawab Fateh Ali Khan
Rafique, Mahomed
Rampur, Nawab Hamid Ali Khan
Rasul, Moulvi Syed Iltifat
Rauf, Syed Abdur
Sherwani, Habibur Rahman
  Khan
Talibnagar, Nawab Muhammad
  Abdus Samad Khan
Yakub, Mohammad
Zainuddin, Syed

Sheikh Abdullah (1878–1965)

Home Town
Aligarh.
Sect
Sunni.
Background
A Kashmiri Brahmin converted to Islam.
Education
Aligarh BA, LL.B.
Occupation
Lawyer with a large practice at Aligarh.
Career
His foremost interest was female education and with the aim of cultivating concern for a subject unpopular with the Muslims he edited a newspaper, *Khatun* (Aligarh), and regularly proposed resolutions on female education at the Mahomedan Educational Conference. In November 1906, he started a girls' school at Aligarh which was supported by government in dribs and drabs up to 1917 when Abdullah made a big bid for a Government subvention of a more substantial kind. In July 1917, despite very strong opposition on educational grounds from the Director of Public Instruction, Meston promised support. A few months later Abdullah organised the Muslim Defence Association at Aligarh, which was merged into the UP Muslim Defence Association, with the aim of representing the moderate Muslim point of view to the Viceroy and the Secretary of State. The coincidence is suggestive but Abdullah had been interested in 'Old Party' Politics for some time. He had taken part in the agitation against the Nagri Resolution, he attended the foundation session of the Muslim League at Dacca and was a director of *Al Mizan* (Aligarh), a paper published in 1915 and 1916 with the aim of opposing and exposing the 'Young Party'. In 1925, he was chairman of the Reception Committee of the All-India Muslim League sessions at Aligarh. But, like his close friend AFTAB AHMAD KHAN, Abdullah was primarily interested in education. He was elected an Aligarh trustee in 1904 and was a member of the College Syndicate. He organised the Aligarh Exhibition in 1905 and for his pains was knocked down by Shaukat Ali (q.v. Appendix I). He was a member of the Aligarh Elementary Education League of 1913 and followed the 'Old Party' line closely in the struggle for the control of the College. A fervent Muslim, in 1908, in response to the Arya Samaj proselytisation campaign, he founded the Aligarh Society for the propagation of Islam. Abdullah

was a typical 'independent conservative'. His daughter is now principal of the Aligarh Ladies' College which grew out of his endeavours.

Ibni Ahmad
Home Town
Allahabad.
Sect
Sunni.
Background
Landowner of Budaun described as 'rais'.
Education
BA, and Barrister-at-Law.
Occupation
Lawyer practising at the Allahabad High Court.
Career
Secretary of the Muslim hostel, Allahabad; Honorary Secretary of the London branch of the All-India Muslim League, 1908–10, and involved with Major Syed Hasan Bilgrami (q.v. Appendix I) in the Muslim League's negotiations with Morley. He succeeded RAJA NAUSHAD ALI KHAN as Honorary Secretary of the UP Muslim League in 1910 and was elected an Aligarh trustee in 1916. In February 1917, he supported the Allahabad nationalists' resolution in favour of the Congress–League scheme, but this was only a minor aberration, because by November 1917 he was acting as Honorary Secretary of the UP Muslim Defence Association. He was a strong advocate of separate representation for Muslims.

Dr Ziauddin Ahmad (1878–1947)
Home Town
Aligarh.
Sect
Sunni.
Background
A Kamboh Sheikh from a network of intellectual families of Marehra, Amroha, Bareilly and Meerut in west UP, Ziauddin was related to VIQAR-UL-MULK and MUHAMMAD BASHIRUDDIN. He came from Meerut. His grandfather had owned land in Bareilly but had lost it in a family dispute. His father was a tahsildar. His elder brother was also a revenue official.
Education
Aligarh MA 1898, D.Sc 1901; Trinity College, Cambridge, MA and PhD; FRAS and member of London Mathematical Society, 1904; Gottingen PhD, 1906; studied in Paris, Bologna and Al Azhar, 1906–7.
Occupation
Teacher.
Career
Joined Aligarh as Professor of Mathematics, 1907; member of Industrial Conference; member of Calcutta University Commission, 1916; Principal of Aligarh, 1918; first Pro-Vice-Chancellor, 1921. Ziauddin was regarded by Meston as a very important steadying force at Aligarh and he kept Harcourt Butler in touch with College affairs. He was the arch-enemy of the 'Young Party' in their attempts to take over Aligarh and the Muslim University project. In 1924, he resigned

his post at Aligarh to represent the Muslim constituency of Mainpuri, Etah and Farrukhabad in the legislative assembly. In 1926 he returned to Aligarh and was Vice-Chancellor for most of the next two decades. He was a member of the Skeen and Shea Committees on the Indianisation of the Army. Awarded a CIE in 1914, Ziauddin was described by government as 'moderate and a strong Islamist who is opposed to Hindu–Muslim unity. Of outstanding intellect and reputation.'

Moulvi Maqbul Alam
Home Town
Benares.
Sect
Sunni.
Education
BA, LL.B.
Occupation
Lawyer practising at Benares.
Career
Alam was the leading Muslim lawyer of Benares in the early twentieth century and secretary of the Bar Library. In 1900 he organised meetings in Benares against the Nagri resolution and later became secretary of the Benares District Muslim League. In 1913, he tried for the provincial legislative council but his staunch defence of Muslim interests lost him the Hindu vote and the election. In 1916, he competed unsuccessfully with Babu Moti Chand, a leading Agarwala banker, for the chairmanship of the Benares municipal board. In 1917, he organised the Anti-Home Rule League movement in Benares and joined the UP Muslim Defence Association. In 1921, he was a committee member of the Benares Aman Sabha. His politics and his standing were acknowledged by government in the award of the title of Khan Bahadur. With ASGHAR ALI KHAN of Bareilly and MUFTI HAIDAR HUSAIN of Jaunpur, Alam is a good representative of the successful local politician type in the 'Old Party'.

Shah Munir Alam
Home Town
Mianpura in Ghazipur district.
Sect
Sunni.
Background
Alam traced his descent from an Arab immigrant, Shah Junaid Qadri. His estate paid Rs. 20,000 land revenue and his family had owned land in Ghazipur for a long time and more property in Ballia and Azamgarh. He had many relations in government service.
Education
BA, LL.B.
Occupation
Government servant and landowner.
Career
A member of the Provincial Service, Alam was elected an Aligarh Trustee in 1916 and was a safe 'Old Party' vote. During 1921 he was very active in the Aman Sabha movement in Ghazipur district.

Appendix II

Munshi Ehtisham Ali (1867–)
Home Town
Kakori in Lucknow district.
Sect
Sunni.
Background
A zamindar of Kakori, Ali came from a family that had been highly placed in the service of the rulers of Oudh. His father was Munshi Imtiaz Ali who had been a minister in the Bhopal state and a Congressman.
Education
Literate in Persian, Urdu and Arabic.
Occupation
Landowner.
Career
Having taken a leading role in the agitation against the Nagri resolution of 1900, Ali was also closely involved with VIQAR-UL-MULK and HAMID ALI KHAN in an attempt to form a Muslim political association in 1901. He was on the board of management of the Nadwat-ul-ulama and its financial secretary. In 1906, he was a signatory of the Muslim memorial and a member of the deputation to the Viceroy. In 1909, he played a leading part in the Lucknow agitation for separate electorates and became vice-president of the UP Muslim League on its foundation in the same year.

Syed Mahomed Ali (1863–
Home Town
Aligarh.
Sect
Sunni.
Background
Grandson of Syed Ahmed Khan's elder brother and married to his second cousin, Syed Ahmed Khan's granddaughter by his son Syed Hamid.
Education
BA, Aligarh.
Occupation
Government servant.
Career
Elected a trustee of Aligarh in 1886 and acted as Syed Ahmed Khan's private secretary until his appointment by the Government of India as an Assistant Magistrate and Collector under the Statutory Civil Service rules. Ali held subordinate judicial posts in a range of UP districts until he became Judge of Banda in 1907. Soon after retiring from government service he became secretary of Aligarh (1918–20), steering the College through the period when 'Young Party' attacks were at their most dangerous.

Muhammad Bashir-ud-din (1857–)
Home Town
Etawah.
Sect
Sunni.

The 'Old Party'

Background
A Kamboh, he was a relation of Ruhullah Khan, Khan Bahadur, rais of Etawah, NAWAB MUSHTAQ HUSAIN, VIQAR-UL-MULK, and ZIAUDDIN AHMAD.
Occupation
Newspaper editor.
Career
In the late nineteenth century, Bashir-ud-din was editor of the *Najm-ul-Akhbar* (Etawah). In 1899, soon after this paper closed down, he founded the *Al Bashir* (Etawah). The paper was strongly opposed to the Congress and attacked the Government when Muslim interests appeared to be ignored, for instance, towards the end of 1919 for a brief period it strongly attacked the Government over the Khilafat question. A weekly, in 1911 the circulation of the paper was over 1000 but, during the Khilafat period, this fell to 600 and by 1921 the paper had been closed down. During its twenty-two years of existence *Al Bashir* was regarded as one of the most influential papers in the province and a reliable guide to conservative Muslim thinking. A close associate of Syed Ahmed Khan, Bashir-ud-din was the manager of the Islamia School, Etawah, the most highly regarded Muslim High School in the province and stepping stone to Aligarh. He was also a member of the Central Committee of the All-India Muhammadan Educational Conference and, in 1914, founded a District Muslim League at Etawah to counteract the influence of the 'Young Party'. In 1911, Bashir-ud-din was granted certificates by government for his services in the cause of education and, as a press representative, was the guest of government at the Coronation Durbar. A Muslim before all things, Bashir-ud-din's aim was to maintain and develop the policies first set out by Syed Ahmed Khan.

Syed Hosein Bilgrami, Imad-ul-Mulk (1844–1926)
Home Town
Hyderabad.
Sect
Sunni.
Background
Ancestors came from Wasit in Mesopotamia. His grandfather represented the King of Oudh at the Governor-general's Court. His father and uncle both held high positions in British service. His uncle, Saiyid Azam-ud-Din Husain, served on the staff of Lord William Bentinck, took part in the defence of Arrah House in the Mutiny, was political agent in Sind and finally a member of the Bengal legislative council. His brother, Saiyid Ali Bilgrami, rose high in Hyderabad service and eventually retired to England. His half-brother was Major Syed Hasan Bilgrami of the Indian Medical Service (q.v. Appendix I). Bilgrami's second wife, whom he married in 1897, was an Englishwoman.
Education
Presidency College, Calcutta.
Occupation
Government servant.
Career
After holding the post of Professor of Arabic at Canning College, Lucknow, 1866–73, Bilgrami entered the service of the Nizam. He was first private

secretary to Sir Salar Jung and then to the Nizam himself. From 1887 to 1902 he was Director of Public Instruction of the Hyderabad State. In 1901–2 he was a member of the Universities Commission. Soon afterwards he was appointed a member of the Imperial Legislative Council and from 1907 to 1909 he was a member of the Secretary of State's Council. In 1886, Bilgrami was elected an Aligarh trustee and, in 1906, drafted the great part of the Muslim memorial. A holder of the CSI, he was a safe vote for the 'Old Party'.

Nawab Hafiz Ahmad Said Khan of Chhatari (1888–   )
Home Town
Chhatari, in Aligarh district.
Sect
Sunni.
Background
A Lalkhani Rajput, and for the family history, see his cousin TALIBNAGAR. He was also related to PAHASU. The estate was very wealthy and paid Rs. 59,612 land revenue.
Education
Aligarh.
Occupation
Landowner.
Career
Elected an Aligarh trustee in 1911 and a safe vote for the 'Old Party'. Member of the deputation of 'Zamindars of the Province of Agra not belonging to the Association', 1917. President, All-India Muslim–Rajput Conference, 1923; member of UP Legislative Council, 1920–5; first elected non-official Chairman of the Bulandshahr district board, 1922–3; minister of Industries, UP, 1923–5; Home Member UP, 1926–33; Acting Governor, 1928 and 1933; member of the first and second Round Table Conferences; Prime Minister of Hyderabad, 1941. Awarded the title of Nawab (personal) 1915 and (hereditary) 1919. Awarded an MBE and a CIE during World War One, a KCSI in 1928 and a KCIE in 1933. Chhatari was the leader of the Zamindar Party in the UP legislative council in the 1920s, and was the most influential Muslim landlord politician in the 1920s and 1930s.

Sheikh Mohammad Habibullah (1871–   )
Home Town
Lucknow.
Background
A taluqdar of Saidanpur in Bara Banki district who paid Rs. 7366 land revenue, the estate did not carry any debt and was well managed. The Saidanpur family of Sheikhs claimed to have held their land since the fifteenth century. Habibullah's father, Sheikh Inayat Ullah took a prominent part in the annexation of Oudh and was one of the founder members of Canning College, Lucknow.
Education
BA, Colvin Taluqdars' College.
Occupation
Government servant.

The 'Old Party'

Career
Joined the provincial civil service in 1893. He was a deputy collector in Benares and Aligarh but, in 1905, was sent to Sitapur as manager of the Mahmudabad Estate, a post which he held for the rest of his official life. Corresponded with both Harcourt Butler and Meston in order to keep them informed of the general run of feeling among the Muslims and the particular activities of the Raja of Mahmudabad (q.v. Appendix I). In the 1920s twice returned unopposed to the UP legislative council from the Muslim constituency of Sitapur and Lakhimpur. For some time Vice-chancellor of Lucknow University, he was awarded an OBE. Appears to have supported government policy throughout except during the Cawnpore Mosque affair.

Syed Agha Haidar
Home Town
Allahabad.
Sect
Shia.
Background
Described as a 'rais' of Saharanpur.
Education
BA, Cambridge and Barrister-at-Law.
Occupation
Lawyer practising at the Allahabad High Court.
Career
He was a leading member of the All-India Shia Conference – being chairman of the Allahabad Session of 1915 – and a member of the UP Muslim Defence Association of 1917. He led the Saharanpur Rowlatt Protest in 1919 but nevertheless entered the provincial legislative council in 1920. Haidar was noted for his independence of mind.

Nawab Mehdi Ali Hasan, Mohsin-ul-Mulk (1837–1907)
Home Town
Aligarh.
Sect
Sunni.
Background
A Shia by birth, converted to Sunnism, Mohsin-ul-Mulk belonged to the Etawah branch of the Barha Syed family, which had provided many Mughal administrators. His mother came from the Abbasids of Sheikhapur, Farrukhabad. His immediate forebears were poor but noble.
Education
Educated in Persian and Arabic at home and under Moulvi Inayat Husain of Phapund, Etawah.
Occupation
Government servant in the UP and Hyderabad.
Career
Poverty compelled him to enter a government office on the low salary of Rs. 10 p.m. He was loyal in the Mutiny and soon afterwards made a peshkar and

a sheristadar. In 1861, he was made a tahsildar in Etawah in which capacity he impressed A. O. Hume, the Collector. In the early 1860s, he wrote two vernacular works on Criminal and Revenue Law. In 1867, he was appointed a deputy collector and posted to Mirzapur. In 1874, he went to Hyderabad where, eventually, he was appointed Inspector-General of Revenue, Commissioner of Settlement and Survey department, Revenue Secretary and, in 1884, Financial and Political Secretary. He introduced Urdu instead of Persian as the court language throughout Hyderabad, and represented the Nizam in London before a special committee looking into Sirdar Dilar Jung's case. He was forced to leave Hyderabad in 1893 after being worsted in a factional dispute. Mohsin-ul-Mulk's connection with Syed Ahmed Khan dates back to 1863 when he accused him of apostasy for his critical commentary on the Bible. However, as soon as he met Syed Ahmed Khan, he was won over by him, becoming a major contributor to the *Tahzib-ul-Akhlaq* and winning first prize in the essay competition organised by the Committee for the Better Diffusion and Advancement of Learning among the Muhammadans of India in 1871. In 1893, he settled in Aligarh, revived the *Tahzib-ul-Akhlaq* and the *Aligarh Institute Gazette*, played a big part in the College Debating Society and infused new life into the Muhammadan Educational Conference. In addition, he did much to win the ulama over to Aligarh and the Educational Conference. He was secretary of Aligarh College from 1898 to 1907 and reorganised the Urdu Defence Association in 1900 in response to Macdonnell's Hindi resolution. Greatly disturbed by the growing dissatisfaction among young Muslims, he played a leading role in organising the Muslim memorial, deputation and League of 1906. He drew up the Muslim memorial with fellow Hyderabad civil servant, SYED HOSEIN BILGRAMI, IMAD-UL-MULK. Joint secretary of the All-India Muslim League, 1906–7, he was known as 'Manjhoo Sahib' or 'the helmsman'. In 1907, he was to be awarded a KCIE but died before he could receive it. His major aim was the continuation of the policies set out by Syed Ahmed Khan.

Syed Mehdi Hasan
Home Town
Lucknow.
Sect
Shia.
Occupation
Naib Tahsildar on the Mahmudabad Estate.
Career
Secretary of the All-India Shia Conference and a member of the UP Muslim Defence Association of 1917. He was involved in the Shia College scheme and his interests appear to have been closely connected with government.

Mufti Haidar Husain
Home Town
Jaunpur.
Sect
Shia.
Background
He came from a very old family which had provided Muftis for the Sharqi Kings

of Jaunpur. At one time members of the family had been large landholders but now the estates were much subdivided.

Education
Most probably traditional.

Occupation
Mukhtar and landowner.

Career
He was the leading Muslim in Jaunpur politics and for a long time vice-chairman of the district board and vice-chairman and secretary of the municipal board. With Muhammad Yahia he seems to have run local politics until the non-co-operation movement and there were several complaints over the number of his supporters and clients in the local administration. He was a member of the Jaunpur Shia College Committee. He worked with the government in opposing 'Young Party' activities and was a member of the UP Muslim Defence Association. He was made an Honorary Magistrate in 1883. Later he became a Khan Sahib and a Khan Bahadur and, in 1922, received a Sanad from the Governor for Aman Sabha work. A local politician marked for his loyalty to the government.

Syed Jafar Husain

Home Town
Lucknow.

Occupation
Engineer in government service.

Career
A Khan Bahadur and elected an Aligarh trustee in 1908. He was a fairly safe 'Old Party' vote in the struggle for the control of Aligarh and a member of the UP Muslim Defence Association of 1917.

Nawab Mushtaq Husain, Viqar-ul-Mulk (1841–1917)

Home Town
Aligarh.

Sect
Sunni.

Background
A Kamboh Sheikh related to ZIAUDDIN AHMAD and MUHAMMAD BASHIRUDDIN, Viqar-ul-Mulk belonged to an old Amroha (Moradabad district) family, several of whom had gained distinction in government service. He had an estate of five mahals, four of which were revenue-free.

Education
He was educated in Persian, Urdu and Arabic, and at no stage does it seem that he understood English.

Occupation
Government servant.

Career
He commenced work as a temporary assistant teacher on a salary of Rs. 10. He came to Syed Ahmed Khan's notice in 1861 as a result of his work in the Moradabad famine and Syed Ahmed Khan, when he was sub-judge at Aligarh,

Appendix II

employed him as a reader. When Syed Ahmed Khan was transferred to Benares he also worked under Moulvi Samiullah Khan the Syed's foremost assistant in founding Aligarh. Viqar-ul-Mulk was both a leading member of the Aligarh Scientific Society and a leading contributor to the *Tahzib-ul-Akhlaq*. From 1875 to 1892 he held high appointments in the Hyderabad civil service till he was compelled to resign owing to local intrigue. In retirement he sat on the Amroha municipal board until 1900 when he entered politics after his Hyderabad contemporary MOHSIN-UL-MULK, was forced to resign from the Urdu Defence Association as a result of official pressure. He was the leader in the attempt to form Muslim political associations between 1901 and 1906. During the drafting of the Muslim memorial in 1906, he corresponded with MOHSIN-UL-MULK and IMAD-UL-MULK. He was also a member of the Simla deputation and chairman of the foundation session of the All-India Muslim League at Dacca in 1906. He was joint secretary of the League, 1906–7, secretary, 1907–8, and a member of the Reforms Subcommittee of 1908. He resigned as secretary in 1908 because the death of MOHSIN-UL-MULK had resulted in his appointment as secretary of Aligarh, a post which he held 1907–13 and resigned because of illness. In his reign of office he took steps to deepen the religious content of education at Aligarh, for instance, he made it obligatory for all students to pass a paper on 'Islamic Religion'. This approach resulted in (1) visits of ulama to Aligarh, including Abdul Bari of Firangi Mahal who chose the college for his own children, (2) the preparation of the ground for the pan-Islamic outbursts of the 'Young Party', and (3) the hostility of the Shias towards Aligarh. Over attitudes to college administration he quarrelled with both MOHSIN-UL-MULK and AFTAB AHMAD KHAN. He was a Fellow of Allahabad University and was awarded the personal title of Nawab in 1908. Recently he has been described thus: 'More conscientious, more painstaking, more vigorous, more self-willed [than Mohsin-ul-Mulk], he seldom swerved from his resolve when once he had made up his mind. Sir Syed had once written...that he believed that Viqar-ul-Mulk would not change his opinion even if God revealed Himself against it.' He corresponded with Mahomed Ali (q.v. Appendix I) and often veered close to the 'Young Party' line, but his concern for the protection of Muslim political interests within India as conceived by Syed Ahmed Khan led him to look to the government for support.

Sheikh Shahid Husain (1878–1924)
Home Town
Lucknow.
Sect
Sunni.
Background
A member of the ancient Kidwai family and taluqdar of Gadia in Bara Banki district, an estate paying Rs. 11,865 land revenue. The estate carried some debt but was well-managed. It had been acquired as recently as 1843 and had been partitioned. Sheikh Shahid was related to Mushir Husain Kidwai (q.v. Appendix I).
Education
Canning College, Lucknow, BA, Cambridge, and Barrister-at-Law.

400

The 'Old Party'

Occupation

Landowner and lawyer.

Career

In 1905, he endowed an annual scholarship of Rs. 120 for the Oudh student at Aligarh who took Arabic as his second language. In 1909, he was involved in agitation for separate electorates. From 1909 to 1916, he was a member of the provincial legislative council. In 1916, he supported the Jehangirabad Amendment less as a Muslim than as a taluqdar who did not wish to offend the government. In the same year, he stood for the Imperial Legislative Assembly and expected government to order Hindu landlords to vote for him; he was unsuccessful. From 1908, he was joint secretary of the British Indian Association and in 1914 he was appointed secretary. In 1921, he joined the Liberals, A. P. Sen, Gokaranath Misra and Syed Wazir Hasan (q.v. Appendix I) in founding the Lucknow Aman Sabha. In 1923, he was elected to the legislative council from the Lucknow and Unao Muslim rural constituency. He was chairman of the Education Committee of the Lucknow municipal board, a member of the boards of management of Canning, Colvin Taluqdars and Lucknow Medical College and a director of the Upper India National Bank Ltd. and the Baib and Wood Pulp Manufacturing Co. of Lucknow. He had a good practice at the Oudh Bar and in 1924 the government assessed him thus: '...difficult to ascertain his real views. Is well educated and a fluent speaker and is possibly a conservative at heart. Is ambitious and if given office would come down definitely on the side of Government.'

Syed Karamat Husein (1852–1917)

Home Town

Allahabad.

Sect

Shia.

Background

A minor taluqdar of Sandila in Hardoi district, he traced his descent from Musa Kazim, the seventh Imam. His grandfather was a Sadr Amin in Meerut and his father a munsif and later a Diwan in a native state.

Education

Studied Arabic under his uncle Saiyid Hamid Husain, Mujtahid of Lucknow, then western languages and science and completed his education in England, being called to the Bar in 1889.

Occupation

Lawyer practising at the Allahabad High Court.

Career

Before going to England, he was mir munshi to the Political Agent in Bundelkhand and also Diwan of the Narsingarh State. From 1891 to 1897, in addition to his legal practice, he taught law at Aligarh for Rs. 300 p.m., a post in which he was succeeded by AFTAB AHMAD KHAN. In 1907, he was appointed an Honorary and Special Magistrate and Honorary Munsif at Allahabad and from 1907 to 1912 he was a Judge of the High Court. He was a fellow of Allahabad University, author of several books in Arabic and a great supporter of female education. His political career began in 1898 when he founded an organisation in Allahabad to

Appendix II

protect Urdu. In 1900, he played a leading part in the anti-Nagri agitation, and in 1906 he was a signatory of the Muslim memorial. He was a member of the provincial committee of the All-India Muslim League appointed at Dacca in 1906 and involved in agitation for separate electorates in 1909. In 1910, he produced 'A Scheme for the Progress of Mahomedans' and later was regarded by NAWAB FATEH ALI KHAN QIZILBASH as a moderate Muslim who objected to the self-government resolution of the All-India Muslim League. As a member of the UP provincial legislative council in 1916, he demanded equal representation for Muslims and refused to vote for the compromise Jehangirabad amendment.

Tassaduq Rasul Khan, Raja of Jehangirabad (1851–1921)
Home Town
Lucknow.
Sect
Sunni.
Background
A Kidwai Sheikh, the same family as the taluqdars of Mailaraiganj (RAJA NAUSHAD ALI KHAN), Gadia (SHEIKH SHAHID HUSAIN), Sahabpur and Partabganj. Holder of an estate of 193 villages based on Jehangirabad in Bara Banki district and paying Rs. 1,10,209 land revenue. He was very affluent. His uncle, Farzand Ali, the previous Raja, had been high in the favour of Wajid Ali Shah, the last King of Oudh. In the Mutiny, however, he submitted early and added to his possessions by purchase. Jehangirabad was the uncle of RAJA NAUSHAD ALI KHAN.
Education
Said to be literate only in Urdu.
Occupation
Landlord.
Career
For most of the period, the Raja was the leading Muslim nobleman of Oudh. In 1897, he was created KCSI and made a hereditary Raja. In 1900, he took part in the anti-Nagri protests and from 1902 to 1903 was a member of the UP legislative council. He was a liberal supporter of Aligarh and was elected a trustee in 1904. There was strong rivalry between him and the Raja of Mahmudabad (q.v. Appendix I) and they competed for positions both within Muslim organisations and the British Indian Association. They were usually to be found on opposite sides of any issue although as taluqdars both avoided the meeting in Lucknow, 16 September 1906, which passed the Muslim memorial. Nevertheless, he did become a vice-president of the Muslim League and, in 1909, was involved in the agitation for separate electorates. From 1909 to 1912, he was a member of the provincial legislative council for the Fyzabad Division seat; he was elected from a general constituency as a result of his successful manipulation of a Kayasth/Muslim/landlord alliance. In the 1913–16 council, he was nominated by government and achieved particular fame by introducing the amendment to the UP municipalities bill which contained the Hindu–Muslim compromise over communal proportions in municipal boards. In 1913, joined the Lucknow South Africa protest and was involved in the Cawnpore Mosque deputation to Meston. In 1915, attended the special provincial conference on the Executive Council question. At the Lucknow session of the All-India Muslim

The 'Old Party'

League in 1916, he proposed the resolution to adopt the Congress–League reforms scheme. In 1917, he helped to organise the Muid-ul-Islam deputation of maulvis of various shades of opinion which was designed 'to represent orthodox Islam and the safeguards it demands' before the Viceroy and the Secretary of State. His wife was much under the influence of Maulana Abdul Bari of Firangi Mahal, regarding him as her pir, and it was through the Firangi Mahal connection that the effort was organised. In 1923, he gave strong support to her anti-Shuddhi agitation. Jehangirabad was a landlord first and a Muslim second in politics. His son, Maharaja Sir Mohammad Ejaz Rasul Khan, followed the same political line into the 1920s and 1930s, Jehangirabad was described by Hewett as 'a man of particularly acute judgement'.

Munshi Abdul Karim Khan, alias Hakim Barham (1863–   )
Home Town
Gorakhpur.
Sect
Sunni.
Background
A Pathan from the village of Fatehpur in Bara Banki district.
Education
Literate in Persian, Urdu and Arabic.
Occupation
Newspaper editor.
Career
First heard of as an Inspector of Police in Bhopal State. After being dismissed from this post, he appeared in Gorakhpur in 1905 to practise as a physician. He was engaged by Riyaz Ahmad to subedit his weekly paper the *Riyaz-ul-Akhbar*. He also edited the *Sulah Kul* for Subhanullah, a Gorakhpur rais, and, in addition, started papers of his own called the *Fitnah* and the *Itra Fitnah*. Owing to some misunderstanding between them, Riyaz Ahmad took the *Riyaz-ul-Akhbar* to Lucknow, and in 1907 Abdul Karim founded another paper of his own, *Mashriq*. This Urdu weekly, together with *Al Bashir*, came to be regarded by government as the voice of Muslim conservatism, In 1911, it was assessed thus: 'Its tone is thoroughly loyal, though its criticisms are frequently strikingly independent.' Its circulation was about 1000 in 1911 and had risen to 1400 by 1922. Abdul Karim had a personal feud with Munshi Narsingh Prasad, a leading Kayasth zamindar and lawyer of Gorakhpur. His paper reported frequently the fatwa and views of the Bareilly school of ulama and Abdul Karim organised the first conservative Muslim reaction to the Lucknow Pact in Gorakhpur in the spring of 1917. He was a member of the UP Muslim Defence Association and an Honorary Magistrate. His policy was that the interests of the Muslim members of the Urdu-speaking elite were best protected by a stance of loyalty to the government.

Sahibzada Aftab Ahmad Khan (1867–1930)
Home Town
Aligarh.
Sect
Sunni.

Appendix II

Background

Aftab Ahmad was born in the casbah of Kunjpura in Karnal just north of Delhi. This early-eighteenth-century town had been founded by an ancestor who had also established a dynasty of semi-independent Nawabs. Aftab's great-grandfather lost his land in an early British settlement and so his grandfather became an ill-paid courtier at the Kapurthala court. After 1857, Aftab's father, Ghulam Ahmad Khan, sought his fortune in the princely states, first as a clerk in Tonk and later acquiring wealth and power in Gwalior. Aftab's mother came from a Pathan family of Muzaffarnagar. His elder brother was Sultan Ahmad Khan who was, like his father, a Gwalior official.

Education

BA, Aligarh and Cambridge, and Barrister-at-Law.

Occupation

Lawyer practising at Aligarh.

Career

In 1900 he took a leading part in the agitation against the Nagri resolution, and in 1909 in the agitation for separate electorates. However, his main concern was education. While still at Cambridge he had decided that this was the key to the regeneration of the Indian Muslims. In 1890, he founded the Duty Society at Aligarh to raise funds for the college by begging from door to door. In 1896, he was elected a college trustee. At Syed Ahmed Khan's suggestion he settled at Aligarh and, soon afterwards, he was secretary of the Syed Memorial Fund and, 1905–17, Honorary Joint Secretary of the Muslim Educational Conference. He was very determined to keep Aligarh as a purely educational institution and he fought bitterly all attempts to bring politics into its management and development. He had a personal feud with NAWAB VIQAR-UL-MULK and was regarded by the Ali Brothers (q.v. Appendix I) as the major enemy of their attempts to win control of Aligarh. In 1906, he was a signatory of the memorial and a foundation member of the League. He dropped out of the League after 1913. Between 1909 and 1912, he represented the Agra and Meerut Muslim constituency in the provincial legislative council. He was an ardent supporter of the Muslim University Scheme and prepared to work it on government lines. He was a member of the Aligarh Elementary Education League of 1913 and attended the special provincial conference on the Executive Council affair in 1915. In 1916, he was strongly opposed to the Lucknow Pact. In 1917, he was made a member of the Secretary of State's council. In 1919, he represented the Indian Muslims, with the Aga Khan and Abdullah Yusuf at the Paris peace conference. On his return from England, he became Honorary Vice-Chancellor of the Muslim University. In 1923 he was president of the All-India Muslim Educational Conference, and in 1925 president of the UP Muslim Educational Conference. Too independent a thinker and operator to be altogether pleasing to government, he was regarded as the 'éminence grise' of Aligarh politics. SHEIKH ABDULLAH was his chief follower.

Munshi Asghar Ali Khan

Home Town

Bareilly.

Sect

Sunni.

The 'Old Party'

Education
BA.

Occupation
Lawyer practising at Bareilly.

Career
In 1909, he was elected to the provincial legislative council from the Rohilkhand general constituency and, in 1912, from the Bareilly municipal board; he was very popular in Bareilly and able to command Hindu support. 1915–16, he was a member of the select committee of the legislative council on the municipalities bill. In 1916, he voted for the Jehangirabad amendment; it did not affect his position either way. He had been vice-chairman of the Bareilly municipal board and from 1916 to 1919 he was its first chairman. In 1917, he was a member of the UP Muslim Defence Association. He was an Honorary Magistrate, a Fellow of Allahabad University and, in 1909, he received a Khan Bahadur for his public services. Like MUFTI HAIDAR HUSAIN and MOULVI MAQBUL ALAM, he was primarily a local politician.

Hamid Ali Khan

Home Town
Lucknow.

Sect
Shia.

Background
A muafidar from Amroha in Moradabad district.

Education
BA, Aligarh, and Barrister-at-Law.

Occupation
Lawyer practising in Lucknow.

Career
He was an eager Congressman until the late 1890s attending the Allahabad Congresses of 1888 and 1892 and standing as the Congress candidate for the Lucknow municipal board seat in the provincial legislative council in 1893 and 1895. By 1900 he seems to have entered the Aligarh camp. He played a leading part in the agitation against the Nagri resolution both organising meetings and publishing a tract. In 1901, he was involved with VIQAR-UL-MULK and MUNSHI EHTISHAM ALI in an attempt to form a Muslim political association. He was a member of the provisional committee of the All-India Muslim League appointed at Dacca in 1906 and, in 1907, became an Aligarh trustee. In 1914, he was regarded by NAWAB FATEH ALI KHAN QIZILBASH as a safe 'Old Party' vote. In 1885, he published in London *The Bulwark for India* with the aim of improving relations between Indians and Englishmen and a little later *Farewell to London*. In 1900, he published *The Vernacular Controversy*.

Moulvi Haji Mahomed Hamidullah Khan, Nawab Sarbuland Jung

(1864–   )

Home Town
Allahabad.

Sect
Sunni.

405

Appendix II

Background
Father, Samiullah Khan (q.v. Appendix IV); he came from the same area of Old Delhi (the Tiraha Bairam Khan section) as Syed Ahmed Khan, the families being related on the female side.
Education
BA, Aligarh and Cambridge, and Barrister-at-Law.
Occupation
Lawyer and government servant.
Career
1886–95, practised at the Allahabad High Court; played an important role in helping his father establish the Muslim Boarding House at Allahabad; 1890–95, edited the *Allahabad Review*; 1895–1904, Puisne Judge of the Hyderabad High Court; 1904–6, Secretary to the Hyderabad Cabinet and Legislative Department; 1906, Home Secretary, Hyderabad; soon afterwards, Chief Justice, Hyderabad; about 1910, he retired from the Nizam's service and in 1911 was elected an Aligarh trustee; 1913, president of the Kashmiri Muslim Conference at Gujranwalla; 1918, president of the All-India Muslim Kashmiri Conference at Rawalpindi; contributed to many European and Indian journals on oriental subjects; a safe 'Old Party' vote in the struggle for the control of Aligarh College and the Muslim University Project.

Masood-us-Zaman Khan (1891–   )

Home Town
Banda.
Sect
Sunni.
Background
A Sheikh of the same clan as the Kidwais, Mahmudabads and Jehangirabads. His grandfather, Shaikh Shafiuz-Zaman, aided the British in the siege of Lucknow and bought the rebel Nawab of Banda's property at a nominal sum. His father, Yusufuz-Zaman, was government pleader of Banda, Honorary Magistrate and Honorary Secretary of the municipal board. He died in 1915. The estate, which was well managed, paid Rs. 9143 land revenue in Banda district and Rs. 1000 in Lucknow.
Education
Colvin Taluqdars' School, Lucknow, BA, Aligarh and Cambridge, and Barrister-at-Law.
Occupation
Landowner and lawyer practising at Banda.
Career
In 1914, returned from England. In 1915, he attended the special provincial conference on the Executive Council affair. In 1920, he formed a People's Association to work the reforms. He was president of the Banda Khilafat Committee but resigned in August 1920 in opposition to non-co-operation. In the same year, he was elected to the provincial legislative council from the Jhansi division Muslim rural seat. In 1921, he formed an Aman Sabha, one of the most active in the province. Such was his influence that both the president of the District Congress Committee and his successor as president of the Khilafat

Committee resigned their posts in order to join him. A member of the Allahabad University Senate, an Honorary Magistrate and chairman of the municipal board, he was a member of the provincial council until 1928. He was awarded a Khan Bahadur in 1925, and after independence became deputy speaker of the provincial legislative council. He was primarily a local politician.

Nawab Mohamed Ishaq Khan (1860–1918)

Home Town
Meerut.

Sect
Sunni.

Background
He was a descendant of Murtaza Khan, a Bangash Afghan and son-in-law of General Ismail Bey Khan Hamadani, a Mughal general and risaldar in Scindia's army. He received the jagir of Palwal in Gurgaon from Lord Lake and purchased the estate of Jehangirabad in Meerut at an auction sale in 1813. His son, Mustafa Khan, was related to the rebel Walidad Khan, who fought against the English in the Mutiny, corresponded with the Emperor of Delhi, was imprisoned but pardoned. He was the poet whose *takhullus* was in Urdu, *Shefta*, and in Persian, *Hasrati*, and who was a close friend of Ghalib and patron of Hali. Mustafa Khan was Ishaq Khan's father, but before the estate reached him it was held by his eldest brother, Nawab Muhammad Ali Khan, who was additional member of the Imperial Legislative Council and Revenue member of the Council of Regency of Bharatpur, then by another brother from 1899 to 1914, and then only did it pass to him. In 1917, Ishaq Khan had three sons: Muhammad Ismail Khan (q.v. Appendix I) who was a barrister at Meerut, Muhammad Ibrahim Khan who was at Clare College, Cambridge, and Ghulam Alauddin, who was ADC to the Nawab of Rampur.

Occupation
Government servant.

Career
He was appointed to the Statutory Civil Service in 1884 and, apart from four years on loan to Rampur State as a minister, remained there till he retired in January 1913 as a district and sessions judge. VIQAR-UL-MULK's choice as his successor, he was secretary of Aligarh, 1913–18. He worked very closely with Meston in the battles for the control of the College and the University movement. He was willing to push through a purely non-political programme but, being a weak man, found it difficult to swallow the constant personal and political attacks of the 'Young Party'. He was given the title Nawab in 1913.

Nawab Muhammad Muzammilullah Khan (1865–1938)

Home Town
Bhikampur in Aligarh district.

Sect
Sunni.

Background
A Sherwani Pathan from a family which came from Jalalabad in Afghanistan in the sixteenth century. The ancestors of the Nawab obtained high office from the Kings of the Lodi dynasty and one of them was Sikandar Lodi's Wazir. The

family continued to be powerful under the Mughals and Shujat Khan was Commander-in-Chief under Shahjahan. In 1803, when the Mahrattas were defeated by Lord Lake, Baz Khan, the then head of the family, threw in his lot with the British and gained the right to farm many villages. The family remained loyal during the Mutiny and helped maintain peace. A third cousin of HABIBUR RAHMAN KHAN SHERWANI, his estate paid Rs. 35,599 land revenue in Aligarh district and 12,055 in Etah. It was solvent, progressive and well-administered.

Education
Literate in Persian, Arabic and English.

Occupation
Landowner.

Career
He was elected an Aligarh trustee in 1886 and was joint secretary of the College from 1899. From 1910 to 1913, while VIQAR-UL-MULK was very ill, he was virtually secretary of the College. Throughout he resisted strongly the 'Young Party' attack on Aligarh and the Muslim University project. He was a signatory of the Muslim memorial in 1906 and was involved in agitation for separate electorates in 1909. 1916–19, he was a nominated member of the UP legislative council. In 1917, he was president of the UP Muslim Defence Association and also went in deputation to Montagu representing the views of the 'Zamindars of the Province of Agra not belonging to the Association'. Later, he was a nominated member of the Viceroy's Council of State and twice Home Member of the UP government. He was a special magistrate, a Fellow of Allahabad University and exempted from the Arms Act. He was awarded the title of Khan Bahadur in 1904, of Nawab in 1910 and later an OBE and a KCIE. In politics he was as much a Muslim as a landlord.

Raja Naushad Ali Khan

Home Town
Lucknow.

Sect
Sunni.

Background
A Kidwai Sheikh, of the same family as the taluqdars of Jehangirabad (RAJA TASSADUQ RASUL KHAN), Gadia (SHEIKH SHAHID HUSAIN), Sahabpur and Partab-ganj, Naushad Ali Khan held the Mailaraigunj estate in Bara Banki district paying Rs. 9464 land revenue. He was JEHANGIRABAD's nephew.

Occupation
Landowner.

Career
He attended the foundation session of the All-India Muslim League at Dacca in 1906 and was appointed a member of its provisional committee. From 1907 to 1909, he campaigned with VIQAR-UL-MULK and Mahomed Ali (q.v. Appendix I) for the foundation of District Muslim Leagues. He was the first secretary of the UP provincial Muslim League after its foundation in June 1909. In the same year, he agitated against separate electorates and took part in the July 1909 discussions of the Government of India's compromise proposals. Supported by JEHANGIRABAD in 1909 as a candidate for the Oudh Muslim seat on the provincial

The 'Old Party'

legislative council. Described by Hewett as 'a disreputable Talukdar' he faded from politics after the Morley–Minto reforms.

Nawab Maulvi Abdul Majid (1859–1924)
Home Town
Allahabad.
Sect
Sunni.
Background
He was head of the Jaunpur family of Maulvis which was said to be of great antiquity. It was founded by Bandagi Shah Jalal-ul-Haq Nizam-ud-din the grandson of the Wazir of Shah Ibrahim of Jaunpur. The descendants held revenue-free and altamgha grants under the Mughals but eventually became ordinary zamindars. At the beginning of the nineteenth century, Abdul Majid's grandfather, Syed Haji Imam Bakhsh, acquired a considerable fortune through dealing in indigo. He was for a time in government service at Ghazipur but retired and during the Mutiny sided with the government enabling the district officers to escape from Jaunpur. For this action, he was persecuted by the rebels but government rewarded him with a grant of land assessed at Rs. 5000. He died in 1861. His son, Maulvi Muhammad Haidar Husain, the leading vakil at the High Court both at Agra and afterwards at Allahabad, succeeded. He added largely to the estate by purchase of lands in Jaunpur, Azamgarh and Ballia and, after his death in 1875, was succeeded by Nawab Abdul Majid. The property became subject to litigation and part of it was granted to the daughter of Imam Baksh and, at the beginning of the twentieth century was in the hands of Maulvi Abdul Jalil, Barrister-at-Law, and Maulvi Abdul Aziz, Deputy Collector, and was worth at the time of separation Rs. 16,235 land revenue. Abdul Majid considerably enlarged his share of the property and during the period was the largest and most influential landowner in the eastern districts of the UP. In Jaunpur he held land in every tahsil and paid Rs. 69,827 land revenue. His estate was solvent and prosperous although he was regarded as a very harsh manager.
Education
BA, Aligarh, and Barrister-at-Law.
Occupation
Landowner and lawyer practising at the Allahabad High Court.
Career
The most successful Muslim lawyer at the Allahabad High Court, he was considered in 1907 by government with SYED KARAMAT HUSAIN as a candidate for the sixth puisne judgeship but rejected because he had made a partition of family estates very much in his favour and because he had been disqualified from the Allahabad vakil's exam for cheating – which was why he was called to the Bar in England. As a politician he was rather more successful. He attended the foundation session of the All-India Muslim League at Dacca in 1906, was a vice-president of the League and the first president of the UP Muslim League founded in June 1909. He was involved in agitation for separate electorates in 1909. Chosen by government as a representative Muslim to discuss compromise over reforms at Simla in summer 1909, he was the leader of the UP bloc that insisted

409

on separate electorates with extra weightage to allow for political importance and refused to compromise. Member of the Committee elected by the Allahabad Hindu–Muslim unity conference of 1910. In 1912, he was elected president of the Allahabad District Muslim League and in 1915 chaired an Allahabad meeting to elect delegates to the special provincial conference on the Executive Council affair. In 1916, he led the Allahabad Muslims in supporting the Jehangirabad Amendment. He was a᷑ member of the Imperial legislative council 1910–12 and of the provincial legislative council, representing the Allahabad/Jhansi/Benares/Gorakhpur Muslim seat 1909–12 and 1916–19. From 1913 to 1916 the seat was held by his close personal rival, fellow Allahabad barrister and member of the 'Old Party', SYED ABDUR RAUF. The founder, with Raja Ragho Prasad Narain Singh of Baraon, of the Agra Province Zamindars' Association in 1914, he represented their case before the Viceroy and Secretary of State in 1917. His son Nawab Sir Muhammad Yusuf, also a barrister, was a member of the provincial legislative council from 1921 to at least 1951, a minister in the UP government from 1926 to 1937 and president of the Agra Province Zamindars' Association. A waqf set up by Imam Bakhsh and managed by Abdul Majid cared for the fine Muslim buildings of Jaunpur and supported an Arabic Madrassa, the Madrassa Hanafia which provided free board and lodging and books to students of Arabic theology. Majid was elected an Aligarh trustee in 1886. His family owed its 'rise to British rule and he consistently supported it.

Syed Ross Masud (1889–1937)
Home Town
Aligarh.
Sect
Sunni.
Background
Grandson of Syed Ahmed Khan and son of Syed Mahmud.
Education
BA, Aligarh and Oxford, Barrister-at-Law.
Occupation
Government servant.
Career
Brought up by Theodore Morison after the early death of his father in 1903. On his return from England he was elected a trustee of Aligarh and entered the Indian Educational Service. He was headmaster of the Patna High School, a professor at Ravenshaw College, Cuttack and a fellow of Calcutta, Madras and Osmania universities. From 1916 to 1928 he was Director of Public Instruction in Hyderabad State. In 1918, he was desperately keen to take over Towle's position as Principal of Aligarh but the job went to DR ZIAUDDIN. However, he achieved his ambition to follow in his grandfather's footsteps later by becoming Vice-chancellor of Aligarh Muslim University. He was awarded the title of Nawab Jung Bahadur by the Nizam and knighted in 1933. Though a friend and frequent correspondent of Mahomed Ali (q.v. Appendix I), Khwaja Abdul Majid (q.v. Appendix I) and Dr Syed Mahmud of Bihar, he strongly opposed

The 'Old Party'

their extremist politics. A friend too of E. M. Forster, he was the man to whom *A Passage to India* was dedicated. He was a safe 'Old Party' vote.

Aziz Mirza (1865–1912)
Home Town
Aligarh and Lucknow.
Sect
Sunni.
Background
A Chagtai, his father served in the Indian police in the 1840s.
Education
BA, Aligarh.
Occupation
Government servant.
Career
The ringleader of the first Aligarh strike of 1887, he addressed meetings and wrote articles against Syed Ahmed Khan and the College. He was, however, allowed to take his BA and in 1888 made a public apology to Syed Ahmed Khan. Soon after, he joined the staff of Sir Asman Jah, Prime Minister of Hyderabad, and rose to be Home Secretary and also a Judge of the High Court. In 1909, he retired from the Nizam's service and settled at Aligarh. He became a trustee and member of the College Syndicate. In 1910, he was elected secretary of the All-India Muslim League and was the first man to make it a full time job. He opened the central office of the League in Lucknow and, during the first year of his secretaryship, travelled more than 20,000 miles covering most of the important cities in the UP and India. He was particularly keen on the waqf question and produced several brochures in Urdu and English on the aims of the League, notably, *A Talk on Muslim Politics* (Lucknow, 1910). He was also a prominent numismatist. His death in February 1912, facilitated the swift rise to eminence of the 'Young Party' in 1913.

Mahomed Nasim (1859–1953)
Home Town
Lucknow.
Sect
Sunni.
Background
He was the younger son of Choudhri Riyasat Ali, taluqdar of Bhilwal in Bara Banki district, whose estate paid Rs. 28,500 land revenue but was in debt to the tune of Rs. 16 lakhs. Despite the family's straitened circumstances, Nasim's elder brother, Mahomed Yusuf, succeeded in giving him a good education. Nasim had three sons: Mahomed Wasim (q.v. Appendix I), Mohammad Habib, who became professor of History at Aligarh Muslim University and Mahomed Mujib who became Vice-chancellor of the Jamia Millia Islamia. Choudhry Khaliquzzaman (q.v. Appendix I) was his nephew.
Education
Literate in English.
Occupation
Lawyer practising at the Oudh Bar.

Appendix II

Career

He started practice in 1890 and from 1894 to his retirement in 1917 was regarded as the leader of the Oudh Bar. In 1900, he took part in the agitation against the Nagri resolution. In 1906, he was a member of the provisional committee of the All-India Muslim League and later a member of its Council. In 1909 he took part in the agitation for separate electorates, and in the same year defeated Syed Nabiullah (q.v. Appendix I), MUNSHI EHTISHAM ALI and RAJA NAUSHAD ALI KHAN in the election for the Oudh Muslim seat but then withdrew. In 1913, he was involved in the South Africa protest and in 1915 in the Executive Council agitation. He was regarded by NAWAB FATEH ALI KHAN QIZILBASH as a moderate Muslim and in 1917 joined the UP Muslim Defence Association. In September 1919, he paid the organisational expenses of the Lucknow meeting to discuss the Khilafat situation at which the All-India Khilafat Committee was found. A man more interested in his profession than his politics, nevertheless he was prepared to forsake his law books at high points of Muslim political activity.

Muhammad Faiyaz Ali Khan, Nawab of Pahasu (1851–1922)

Home Town

Aligarh.

Sect

Sunni.

Background

His father, Nawab Sir Muhammad Faiz Ali Khan (1821–94) – son of Murad Ali Khan who died in 1858 – was Paymaster and Commander in Chief of the Jaipur forces; aided the British at Delhi in the Mutiny; guarded the ferries of the Ganges; rewarded with a large grant of land and the title of Khan Bahadur; Prime Minister Jaipur state 1863; CSI 1870; KCSI 1876; member of the Baroda Commission 1874; Superintendent of Kotah State; Attaché to the Foreign Office 1877; Fellow of Allahabad University; member of both the Governor-general's and the provincial legislative council. Pahasu, therefore, had a good start in life. In addition he was hereditary head of the Lalkhani Rajputs, had a wealthy landed estate in Bulandshahr paying Rs. 33,721 land revenue and more property in Jaipur state.

Education

Literate in English.

Occupation

Landowner.

Career

He was a nominated member of the provincial legislative council 1898–1902 and 1909–19, and of the Governor-general's council 1898–1900. He was Foreign Minister of the Jaipur State Council in 1901 and represented the UP at Edward VII's coronation in 1902. He was a trustee of the Lady Dufferin Fund, founded an Anglo-vernacular school in 1899 and was president of the Aligarh trustees. He was a firm vote for the 'Old Party' in the struggle for the control of Aligarh and the Muslim university movement. In 1917, he appeared in deputation to the Viceroy and Secretary of State not as a Muslim but as a landlord, as a member of the Muzaffarnagar Zamindars' Association. He received the following titles and medals from the government: CSI, MBE, Khan Bahadur, KCIE and KCVO.

The 'Old Party'

Syed Abu Jafar, Raja of Pirpur (1872–1927)
Home Town
Pirpur.
Sect
Shia.
Background
The family was said to have been founded by one Syed Suleman, a merchant of
Khorassan, who came to Oudh in 1403 and married a local Syed. It held for
many generations the post of hereditary Chaudhri of the pargana of Akbarpur
and gradually acquired proprietary rights. The estate in Fyzabad, Azamgarh
and Sultanpur districts paid Rs. 1,43,738 and was very well managed.
Education
Educated in Arabic literature and Philosophy in Arabia and in English by
private tutors at Pirpur.
Occupation
Landlord.
Career
He was a generous supporter of education. He built and endowed a students'
boarding house at Tanda, gave Rs. 20,000 to the Muslim University fund, spent
Rs. 3000 p.a. in grants to poor students and his main benefaction was the Jafria
School which gave free education. He was elected an Aligarh trustee in 1915.
A member of the All-India Muslim League he was involved in agitation for
separate electorates in 1909. In 1912, he defeated NAWAB ABDUL MAJID, the
retiring member, in the election for the Muslim landholders' seat on the Imperial
legislative council. He was a strong supporter of the Shia College movement and
a member of the UP Muslim Defence Association of 1917. He tended to use his
influence in municipal, district and council elections in favour of the landed
interest. His son represented the Taluqdars of Oudh at the Second Round Table
Conference in 1931.

Nawab Fateh Ali Khan Qizilbash (1862–   )
Home Town
Lahore.
Sect
Shia.
Background
The family were said to have come from Turkistan with Nadir Shah and settled
in Kandahar. Raza Khan, Qizilbash's grandfather, helped the British in the
First Afghan War. He returned with the British army to India and with his
brothers distinguished himself serving in the Sikh Wars and the Mutiny. Raza
Khan was given confiscated estates as a reward and became a taluqdar of Oudh
and a jagirdar of the Punjab. Qizilbash's uncle, a hereditary Nawab and member
of the Governor-general's council, succeeded his grandfather, and in 1897 he
succeeded his uncle. As well as his large estates in the Punjab, Qizilbash possessed
the Aliabad estate in Gonda district, paying Rs. 45,710. The lands were prosperous and well-managed and Qizilbash was in the process of buying up the
lands of poorer Shias in the district, e.g. the Waira Qazi estate of Syed Ali
Haidar.

413

Appendix II

Education
Proficient in English.
Occupation
Landowner.
Career
He was elected an Aligarh trustee in 1897, represented the Punjab at the Famine Conference, and in 1900 was admitted to the privilege of a private entrée to the Viceroy. He was a vice-president of the All-India Muslim League, president of the Punjab Muslim League and the Punjab Chiefs' Association, Life President of the Anjuman-i-Islamia Punjab and patron of the Punjab Muslim Club. Between 1913 and 1917, he was the leader of the Shia College movement and the moderate Muslim reaction in northern India. Throughout he was in close correspondence with the lieutenant-governor, Meston. Qizilbash hoped to receive a baronetcy for his efforts but died, it would appear, with no more than the CIE he received in 1903.

Mahomed Rafique (1863–   )
Home Town
Allahabad.
Sect
Sunni.
Education
Barrister-at-Law.
Occupation
Government servant.
Career
Began practice at Lucknow in 1886 but entered government service in 1892. He became a District and Sessions Judge in 1898 and rose to become the first Indian Additional Judicial Commissioner of Oudh in 1910. In 1912, he was appointed a Judge of the Allahabad High Court and, after retiring in 1923, became a member of the Council of the Secretary of State. Elected a trustee of Aligarh in 1897, he was a safe vote for the 'Old Party' in the Muslim University struggle.

Hamid Ali Khan, Nawab of Rampur (1875–1930)
Home Town
Rampur.
Sect
Shia.
Background
Ruler of the surviving remnants of Rohilla power, the annual revenue of his state was Rs. 49,17,023. The family had a tradition of loyalty to the British. His great-grandfather, Usuf Ali Khan, had been loyal during the Mutiny and served on Lord Elgin's council. His grandfather, Kalb Ali Khan, served on Lytton's council.
Education
Private tutors, H. O. Budden of the Indian Educational Service and Captain Colvin.

414

The 'Old Party'

Occupation
Administration.

Career
The ruler of the most important native state in the UP, he succeeded his father, Mushtaq Ali Khan, in 1889 and assumed personal control of administration in 1896. He was patron of Aligarh but withdrew his large grant to the College in 1913 when its politics began to appear extreme. In the same year he attempted to create the nucleus of a moderate Muslim party in an attempt to discredit the new policy of the Muslim League in general and Mahomed Ali (q.v. Appendix I) and Syed Wazir Hasan (q.v. Appendix I) who had gone in deputation to England in particular. He had the pleasure of interning Mahomed Ali in Rampur in 1915 and worked with NAWAB FATEH ALI KHAN QIZILBASH to get the Shia College scheme off the ground. From 1909 to 1919 he was a nominated member of the UP provincial legislative council and, when he attended, a safe government vote. A personal friend of Meston, he looked after the lieutenant-governor's furniture when he visited England in 1918.

Moulvi Syed Iltifat Rasul (–1920)

Home Town
Jalalpur.

Background
He belonged to an ancient Syed family which settled in Oudh in the fourteenth century. His grandfather took the government side in the Mutiny and was rewarded with considerable additions to his property. The estate, mainly in Hardoi, paid Rs. 35,300 land revenue.

Occupation
Landowner.

Career
President of the Hardoi District Muslim League, he was involved in the agitation for separate electorates. He supported the Muslim University scheme and was a strong supporter of the co-operative movement, He was a Khan Bahadur, Honorary Munsif and Magistrate.

Syed Abdur Rauf

Home Town
Allahabad.

Sect
Sunni.

Education
Lawyer practising at the Allahabad High Court.

Career
In 1900, he took part in the agitation against the Nagri resolution. In 1906, he was a signatory of the Muslim memorial and a member of the League's provisional committee. He was active in early Muslim League politics and was a member of the UP group that squashed Ali Imam's attempts to accept government's compromise terms in the negotiations over the council reforms in July 1909. He was vice-president of the UP Muslim League in 1909 and later president. In the same year he was elected an Aligarh trustee. From 1913 to 1916

he represented the Allahabad/Jhansi/Benares/Gorakhpur Muslim constituency in the UP provincial legislative council and lost his seat in the 1916 election to his personal rival, fellow barrister and member of the 'Old Party' NAWAB MAULVI ABDUL MAJID. An important reason for Rauf's defeat was his opposition to the Cawnpore Mosque agitation. In 1913, he supported the Turkish Relief Fund and was a member of the South Africa Committee. In 1915, he attended the special provincial conference on the Executive Council affair. He was uncompromising in the defence of Muslim interests. In the April 1916 Council debates on the UP municipalities bill, with SYED KARAMAT HUSAIN, he demanded equal representation for Muslims on municipal boards. In 1917, he organised with IBNI AHMAD the UP Muslim Defence Association which made similar demands for Muslims on provincial councils. He held the title of Khan Bahadur and was made a judge of the Punjab Chief Court in 1918. He was described by Theodore Morison as a typical Muslim of the 'independent conservative' variety.

Habibur Rahman Khan Sherwani
Home Town
Aligarh.
Sect
Sunni.
Background
For his family background see entry under NAWAB MUHAMMAD MUZAMMILULLAH KHAN, his third cousin. Habibur Rahman owned an estate paying Rs. 14,147 land revenue.
Education
Literate in Persian, Arabic and Urdu.
Occupation
Landowner and scholar in Islamic theology.
Career
He was elected an Aligarh trustee in 1897, was a member of the University Court and was in charge of Sunni theology at the College. A member of the Nadwat-ul-Ulama, Lucknow, he twice presided over its annual sessions. He was a Fellow of Allahabad University, and in 1917 was appointed Joint Secretary of the All-India Muslim Educational Conference. He was a signatory of the Muslim memorial and, in Aligarh affairs, a safe 'Old Party' vote. He eventually became head of the ecclesiastical department of the Hyderabad state and was awarded the title of Nawab Sadar Yar Jung. His son was a member of the UP legislative council from the 1920s to the 1950s.

Nawab Muhammad Abdus Samad Khan of Talibnagar (1862–   )
Home Town
Aligarh.
Background
A Lalkhani Rajput, he traced his descent from one Lal Singh who was given the title of Lal Khan by Akbar. The clan was converted to Islam in the time of Shahjahan. The major landowners in the family were all descended from Mardan Ali Khan of Chhatari who received the estates from the British after they

confiscated them from his rebellious cousin Dunde Khan. He was a cousin of
PAHASU and CHHATARI. His estate was solvent and paid Rs. 7304 land revenue in
Aligarh district and Rs. 27,000 in Bulandshahr district.

Career

He was elected an Aligarh trustee in 1909 and was a safe vote for the 'Old
Party'. In 1917, he was a leading member of the UP Muslim Defence Association
and was a member of the deputation of the 'Zamindars of the Province of Agra
not belonging to the Association' to the Viceroy and Secretary of State. He was
an Honorary Magistrate, Vice-chairman of the district and municipal boards
and was given the personal title of Nawab in 1913. In politics he tended to
follow the lead of men like PAHASU.

Mohammad Yakub (1879–

Home Town

Moradabad.

Sect

Sunni.

Education

BA, Aligarh and Barrister-at-Law.

Occupation

Lawyer.

Career

An office-holder in the London Muslim League in 1908 and a member of the
Council of the All-India Muslim League. He played a prominent part in the
League meetings of 1910 and was a leading member of the Moradabad District
Muslim league. In the second decade of the century he was primarily a local
politician. His main rival was another barrister, Masood-ul-Hasan (q.v. Appendix I). He was a member of the Moradabad municipal board and its first
non-official chairman. He was an active journalist in the vernacular press and
took part in most local agitations from the protest concerning the Executive
Council for the province to that concerning the Rowlatt Bill. He was a member
of the UP Muslim Defence Association in 1917 and went into the provincial
legislative council in 1920. In the 1920s, though retaining local interests such as
the vice-chairmanship of the Moradabad district board, he became more of an
all-India figure. In 1927, he was president of the All-India Muslim League and
later became its secretary. He was a member of the Age of Consent Committee
in 1928 and the Indian Franchise Committee in 1932. In 1930, he became president of the legislative assembly. He was elected an Aligarh trustee in 1913, was
a member of the University Court and sat on the Central Standing Committee
of the Muslim Educational Conference. He held the honour of a knighthood.

Syed Zainuddin (1873–   )

Home Town

Aligarh.

Background

He was the son of Syed Zain-ul-Abdin (born 1851) who joined government
service in 1879 and rose to become a District and Sessions Judge.

Education

MA, Aligarh.

Appendix II

Occupation
Government servant.

Career
He joined the provincial service in 1896 serving in various districts as a deputy collector. In 1906–8, he was placed at the disposal of Bhopal State. In 1897 he was elected an Aligarh trustee. In 1913 he competed unsuccessfully with Shaukat Ali (q.v. Appendix I) for the secretaryship of the Aligarh Old Boys' Association. Later he received a sanad from the governor for work in combating the non-co-operation movement. He was a safe vote for the 'Old Party'.

THE ULAMA

The sources on which the following biographies are based are the same as for Appendices I and II, with the addition of information acquired from the Abdul Bari papers and an interview on 29 May 1968 with Mufti Reza Ansari of Firangi Mahal, the grandson of Salamatullah and present head of the institution.

Biographies of the following ulama will be found below, and names in capitals indicate cross-references within the Appendix:

Bari, Abdul	Majid, Abdul (of Firangi Mahal)
Hamid, Abdul	Nomani, Shibli
Husain, Wilayat	Salamatullah
Khan, Ahmad Reza	Sindhi, Obeidullah
Madni, Hasan Ahmad	Sobhani, Azad
Majid, Abdul (Budauni)	Wadud, Abdul

Abdul Bari (1878–1926)

Home Town

Lucknow.

Sect

Sunni, a Qadri Sufi.

School

Firangi Mahal, Madrassa Nizamia section.

Occupation

Teacher, writer and pir.

Background

A Siddiqi Shaikh and descendant of Mulla Nizamuddin, the founder of Firangi Mahal, his father was Abdul Wahab, his grandfather, Abdul Razzaq, and his wife a relation of the Raja of Mahmudabad (q.v. Appendix I). His sources of income were varied: he received a grant of Rs. 200 p.m. from the Nizam, he received large donations from his disciples as Nazra, and he owned a small zamindari and property in Lucknow.

Career

He received his early education from his father. Later, he was a student in Constantinople with the man later to become the Sharif of Mecca. As a student he also met HASAN AHMAD MADNI in Medina. In 1908, he founded the Madrassa Nizamia in Firangi Mahal, which was supported by the contributions he received from disciples and, surprisingly, by subventions from large Shia magnates, Nanpara, Mahmudabad (q.v. Appendix I) and Rampur (q.v. Appendix II). Abdul Bari took part in the Muslim agitation for separate electorates in 1909, but up to the Balkan wars was considered well-disposed by government. In 1910, he was president of the newly founded Majlis Muid-ul-Islam, in 1912, a member of the Anjuman Hila-e-Amar. In 1913, with Mushir Husain Kidwai (q.v. Appendix I), he hatched the Anjuman-i-Khuddam-i-Kaaba, was elected Khadim-ul-Kaaba and took a leading part in the Cawnpore Mosque agitation and compromise. In 1917, he organised the Muid-ul-Islam deputation to Montagu. In 1918, he was involved in speculation concerning a religious head for Indian Muslims and agitations concerning the Muslim internees and insults to Islam. In the same year he led the first band of ulama to attend a Muslim League session. In 1918 and 1919, he developed connections with Gandhi and pressed him to introduce Satyagraha on behalf of the Khilafat issue. In September 1919, he led the extremist party at the Lucknow All-India Khilafat conference and, according to Khaliquzzaman, ulama from his school produced the plan for the Central Khilafat Committee. Certainly, ulama under his influence dominated the Delhi Khilafat meeting of November 1919 and in the following month he was elected the first president of the Jamiat-ul-ulama-i-Hind. Up to the Calcutta special Congress he and his followers were the main influence in drumming up political support for non-co-operation. After September 1920, his political fortunes declined. The entry of Deoband into the agitation reduced Firangi Mahal influence and the increasing importance of Azad also reduced that of Abdul Bari. Abdul Bari opposed Azad's plan for an Amir-i-Shariat organisation until Deobandi's made it clear that they would prefer him to Azad as the religious head of Indian Muslims. In 1921 and 1922, Abdul Bari and his followers increasingly drew apart from the political wing of the agitation, particularly over the question of violence. In 1922 and 1923, the gap became wider as a result of the growth of communalism. In 1923 and 1924 Abdul Bari continued to agitate over the Khilafat and the Jazirat-ul-Arab, though the politicians had dropped them as dead issues. As time went on, he drew closer to the government: 'Towards the end', it was reported of his last illness, 'he repeatedly advised his friends to remain loyal to the British Government and said that he felt his past policy had been mistaken.'

Abdul Bari was on the boards of management of the shrine of Muin-ud-Din Chishti at Ajmere and the Nadwat-ul-ulama at Lucknow. He wrote over 100 books, some of them on hadith and the life of the Prophet but others on secular subjects such as a biography of Mohsin-ul-Mulk and an Urdu translation of the works of Bishop Berkeley, the eighteenth-century English philosopher. As a pir he had a considerable following which included the Rani of Jehangirabad, the Kidwais of Bara Banki, the Chaudhris of Paisa in Bara Banki, some Sherwanis of Aligarh (q.v. Appendix I), the wife and sister of Khwaja Abdul Majid (q.v. Appendix I), Shaukat and Mahomed Ali (q.v. Appendix I), Syed Jalib (q.v. Appendix I), and M. M. Chotani. Though a man of unstable temperament and vacillating policy, he appears to have been the most influential alim of his time. Possessed of deep religious conviction he was ambitious for the protection of Muslim rights, for the assertion of ulama power and his own elevation to the religious leadership of Indian Muslims.

The Ulama

Abdul Hamid (–1932)
Home Town
Lucknow.
Sect
Sunni.
School
Firangi Mahal, Bahr-ul-ulum section.
Occupation
Teacher.
Background
A Siddiqi Shaikh and descendant of Mulla Nizamuddin, the founder of Firangi
Mahal, he was the younger brother of Abdul Majid.
Career
He taught in ABDUL BARI's Nadrassa Nizamia until 1912 when he quarrelled with
the maulana over his opposition to the government. In 1918, he founded, with
a grant of Rs. 3000 from the government, a rival school to the Madrassa Nizamia,
the Madrassa Qadima or 'Old Madrassa', which exists to this day in the charge
of his son and under the title Jamia Bahr-ul-ulum. He remained loyal to government throughout World War One and the Khilafat movement, issuing fatwas
both in support of government and in opposition to the pronouncements of
Abdul Bari. He was rewarded for his pains with a shams-ul-ulama. Like his
brother, ABDUL MAJID, he was consistently pro-government and anti-ABDUL
BARI.

Wilayat Husain
Home Town
Allahabad.
Sect
Sunni.
School
Diara Shah Hajatullah.
Occupation
Teacher and Sajjada-nashin or head of the Diara Shah Hajatullah.
Background
A Siddiqi Shaikh, his family was traditionally associated with the Diara Shah
Hajatullah. His father was Shah Mahomed Hussain (d. 1904), the leading
Muslim of Allahabad in the late nineteenth century, and his son Maulvi Mahomed
Mian is today a prominent member of the Congress Party.
Career
As head of the Diara Shah Hajatullah, he was the most influential Muslim in
Allahabad and an important ally of government in its attempts to maintain order
in the city. His authority did not go unchallenged. From about 1907 his influence
was contested by a follower of ABDUL BARI, Mahomed Fakhir, who was head of
a rival Diara, the Diara Shah Ajmal. Mahomed Fakhir constantly attempted to
lead the Muslims of the city into a radical stance. But Wilayat Husain successfully led a conservative and dominant party. He supported the government
during the Cawnpore Mosque affair and chaired meetings proposing loyalty
resolutions at the beginning of World War One. In 1917, he joined the Muid-ul-

Islam deputation to the Viceroy. In the early part of the Khilafat agitation he opposed the government and returned his title as a gesture of non-co-operation. But, by 1921, had returned to his usual attitude of loyalty.

Ahmad Reza Khan (1855–1921)
Home Town
Bareilly.
Sect
Sunni.
School
Bareilly.
Occupation
Teacher and leader of the Bareilly School.
Career
He was a consistent theological opponent of both Firangi Mahal and the Deoband School, attacking ABDUL BARI, for instance, for acquiescing in the compromise reached with government over the Cawnpore Mosque. Nevertheless, his normal stance was one of support for government and he supported it throughout World War One, the Khilafat Movement, and in 1921 organised a conference of anti-non-co-operation ulama at Bareilly. He had considerable influence with the masses but was not favoured by the educated Muslims.

Hasan Ahmad Madni (1879–1957)
Home Town
Deoband.
Sect
Sunni.
School
Deoband.
Occupation
Teacher.
Background
Of Indian stock, his family received twenty-four villages from the Mughals of which eighteen remained at the time of the Mutiny. He claimed that his father had been so victimised by the Raja of Bhiti in Fyzabad district that he was eventually compelled to leave the area. Madni was brought up in Medina and was thus a Turkish citizen.
Career
Madni knew Enver and Jamal Pasha in Medina, and was interned with the Shaikh-ul-Hind, Mahmud-ul-Hasan, on Malta during World War One. He was very hostile to the British and took part in the 'Silk Letters Conspiracy'. His return to India towards the end of 1920 contributed to Deoband's move into non-co-operation. In September 1921 Madni was tried at Karachi with the Ali brothers (q.v. Appendix I) and imprisoned. Given the title Shaikh-ul-Islam by the Jamiat-ul-ulama, he presided over its fifth session, and every session from the twelfth to the nineteenth. He was principal of the Dar-ul-ulum, Deoband, from 1926 to 1957.

The Ulama

Abdul Majid Budauni (–1931)
Home Town
Budaun.
Sect
Sunni, a Qadri Sufi.
School
He usually followed the lead taken by ABDUL BARI and belonged to the Madrassa Qadria at Budaun.
Occupation
Teacher.
Career
He first came to prominence during the Cawnpore Mosque agitation. He was a member of the Central Committee of the Anjuman-i-Khuddam-i-Kaaba and a frequent correspondent of ABDUL BARI and SALAMATULLAH. In March 1915, after an altercation in Delhi's Chandni Chowk, he knocked out the front teeth of a member of the Delhi District Anjuman-i-Khuddam-i-Kaaba who complained about Shaukat Ali's misuse of the central Anjuman's funds. He signed the Deoband fatwa urging Muslims to give zakat to the Red Crescent Fund, the Muid-ul-Islam address to Montagu, ABDUL BARI's Jazirat-ul-Arab fatwa and the Muttaffiqa fatwa. He was secretary of the first UP Ulama Conference, April 1920, and in charge of its organisation; president of the propaganda subcommittee of the UP Provincial Khilafat Committee; toured the province as an agitator between 1920 and 1922; president of the Calcutta All-India Khilafat conference, September 1920. A leading figure at the Jamiat-ul-ulama-i-Hind meetings and a member of the Central Khilafat Committee, he was a very vigorous supporter of Civil Disobedience in 1921 and 1922. He sat on the Khilafat Committee's Civil Disobedience Enquiry Committee in 1922. During the Khilafat period he emerged as one of the leading ulama politicians of the subcontinent and himself wrote a history of the Khilafat Movement.

Abdul Majid (–1922)
Home Town
Lucknow.
Sect
Sunni.
School
Firangi Mahal, Bahr-ul-ulum section.
Occupation
Teacher and Pesh Imam of the Lucknow Id-gah.
Background
Siddiqi Shaikh and descendant of Mulla Nizamuddin, the founder of Firangi Mahal, he was the elder brother of ABDUL HAMID.
Career
He first came to prominence as a Sunni agitator in the Lucknow Shia–Sunni clashes of 1905–8, as a result of which he was banned from Government House garden parties. With his brother, ABDUL HAMID, he taught in ABDUL BARI's Madrassa Nizamia till 1912 when he quarrelled with the latter over his hostile attitude to the government. Then he became a lecturer at Canning College,

14-3

Lucknow. He remained loyal throughout World War One and the Khilafat movement, issuing fatwa both in support of the government and in opposition to the pronouncements of ABDUL BARI. Odd comments let fall by both government and other Firangi Mahal ulama suggest that he and his brother informed on the anti-government members of the school. He was heavily rewarded by government, receiving a shams-ul-ulama, a Khillat and a sword of honour.

Shibli Nomani (1857–1914)
Home Town
Azamgarh.
Sect
Sunni.
School
Nadwat-ul-ulama.
Occupation
Teacher and scholar.
Background
From non-ashraf stock, his father was leading member of the Azamgarh bar and a large zamindar with business interests. He inherited some money from his father and in 1914 was receiving a grant of Rs. 300 p.m. from the Hyderabad government. His brothers were both professional men; Mahomed Ishaq was educated in England and became leader of the Muslims at the Allahabad bar, Mahomed Junaid was a munsif in Cawnpore. Shibli's son, Mahomed Hamid Nomani was also in the provincial service.
Career
He was educated in the orthodox Muslim fashion at Azamgarh, Ghazipur, Rampur, where he studied in the madrassa of Maulvi Abdul Haq, Lahore, where he read Arabic literature under Maulvi Faizul Husain and Saharanpur, where he studied hadith under Maulvi Ahmad Ali. In 1876 he performed the haj and on his return tried his hand at the law and government service with no satisfaction and decided to set up as a free-lance writer. It was in this capacity that, while visiting his brother at Aligarh in 1882, he got a post as professor of Persian. He became a close friend of Syed Ahmed Khan and of T. W. Arnold to whom he taught Arabic in exchange for French lessons. At Aligarh he wrote *Subah-Umeed* [The Dawn of Hope], which described the efforts of Syed Ahmed Khan to rouse the Muslims, and other works describing the glories of Islam. In 1892, he visited Constantinople, where his work for Islam received recognition from the Sultan. In 1894, he presided over the first session of the Nadwat-ul-ulama. In 1899, he resigned from Aligarh and was employed by Syed Ali Bilgrami in the Hyderabad Education Department. In 1904, he returned to Lucknow and taught in the madrassa of the Nadwat-ul-ulama, where both Syed Suleman Nadvi and Abul Kalam Azad came under his influence. He was the only well-known alim to attend the early sessions of the Muslim League and strongly supported action over the waqf question at the 1910 session. In the same year dissension arose in the Nadwa over the content of his teaching and in the struggles that followed he succeeded in getting himself elected secretary of the school. His position in the school remained unchallenged for another three years until in an attempt to score over a doctrinal opponent, Maulvi Abdul

The Ulama

Karim, he brought to the notice of government an article that the maulvi had written on jihad, and in the resulting furore was forced to resign. The dissensions which divided the school centred around Shibli's attempt to modernise the curriculum of the traditional madrassa to meet modern demands through the introduction of English, logic, history, mathematics and geography. In 1913, he retired to Azamgarh where he founded what was later to be called the Darul-Musannafin or Shibli's Academy of Letters. Member of the Lucknow Red Crescent Society, 1912; member of the central committee of the Anjuman-i-Khuddam-i-Kaaba; shams-ul-ulama, 1892; fellow of Allahabad University; member of the Simla committee for the advancement of oriental learning, 1911. Shibli's importance lay in the influence of his Islamic revivalism over students at Aligarh such as Mahomed Ali, the influence of his views on the role of the ulama on men such as Azad, and his popularisation of the political poem as a literary form.

Salamatullah
Home Town
Lucknow.
Sect
Sunni.
School
Firangi Mahal, Madrassa Nizamia section.
Occupation
Teacher.
Background
Siddiqi Shaikh and descendant of Mulla Nizamuddin, the founder of Firangi Mahal, he owned property in Lucknow City. His grandson, Mufti Reza Ansari, is the present head of Firangi Mahal.
Career
Secretary of Anjuman Muid-ul-Islam and later president; member of Anjuman-i-Kuhddam-i-Kaaba; closely involved with ABDUL BARI in all his religious and political activities. He attended the Delhi session of the Muslim League, 1918, signed ABDUL BARI's Jazirat-ul-Arab fatwa, 1919, and the Muttaffiqa fatwa, 1920. Prominent speaker at the UP Ulama Conference April 1920; jailed 1921-2; president of the second session of the Ajmere Khilafat conference, March 1922. President of Oudh Khilafat Committee, 1920, but resigned in 1923 over differences with 'Young Party' politicians. He acted as ABDUL BARI's second-in-command, did much organising work and on his leader's death became head of Firangi Mahal. He was a member of the Muslim Nationalist Party in 1930.

Obeidullah Sindhi (1872–1944)
Home Town
Born in the Punjab.
Sect
Sunni.
School
Deoband.

Occupation
Teacher and scholar.

Background
Of Sikh parents, he rebelled against his family as a boy, became a Muslim and in 1889 entered the Dar-ul-ulum at Deoband.

Career
The leader of a radical group within Deoband, he attempted to reform the syllabus by introducing secular subjects. He was opposed by the administrator and forced to leave. He organised the Jamiat-ul-Ansar in 1909–10 and the Nazarat-ul-Maarif-ul-Qorania in 1913. A correspondent of ABDUL BARI, he was involved in the 'Silk Letters Conspiracy' and escaped to Afghanistan in 1915. For the next twenty-four years he lived in Afghanistan, the USSR, Geneva, Turkey and the Hedjaz, lost his vocation as a Muslim, and became a nationalist and a secularist. He was permitted to return to India in 1939.

Azad Sobhani (c. 1873–   )
Home Town
Cawnpore.

Sect
Sunni, a Qadri Sufi.

School
Usually followed the lead given by ABDUL BARI, and belonged to the Madrassa Ilahiat at Cawnpore.

Occupation
Teacher and professional politician.

Background
Born in Ballia.

Career
He rose to prominence in the pan-Islamist agitations of 1913–14. He was the leading local agitator during the Cawnpore Mosque agitation, being acquitted in the subsequent trial; he joined the Anjuman-i-Khuddam-i-Kaaba and became a full-time lecturer and journalist. He attended the Muslim League session at Delhi in 1918, signed ABDUL BARI's Jazirat-ul-Arab fatwa and the Muttaffiqa fatwa. In 1920, he set up the Halqa-i-Adabia in Cawnpore to promote Urdu literature. He presided over the ulama session of the Bombay All-India Khilafat Conference in February of the same year and replaced ABDUL MAJID BUDAUNI as president of the Calcutta All-India Khilafat conference in September 1920. He was president of the UP Provincial Khilafat Committee and frequently presided over district Khilafat conferences. He was a most articulate exponent of the need for ulama to take charge of Muslim politics; at the foundation of the Bihar Amir-i-Shariat organisation in 1921 he declared that 'it was necessary to establish the position of the ulemas and to bring them out of the madrassas to the field of action (maidan e amal).' In January 1922 he moved the resolution demanding complete independence at the All-India Muslim League session and in July organised the Moplah Relief Fund. Then he became vice-president of the UP Congress Committee and his views appeared to undergo a transformation; he abandoned his extreme Muslim orthodox line in favour of a secular and political approach. In 1923, for instance, his report on the Shuddhi movement in the UP

The Ulama

recommended that the Muslim should not interfere with the Arya Samaj campaign. Sobhani was an alim who became a professional politician. He was very much in the limelight in 1922–3, and when the Khilafat movement collapsed, became a labour agitator in Cawnpore. By the mid-1920s, he was professing communist views.

Abdul Wadud

Home Town
Bareilly.
Sect
Sunni.
School
Usually followed the lead taken by ABDUL BARI, and belonged to the Madrassa Ishaat-ul-ulum at Bareilly.
Occupation
Teacher.
Career
Wadud sat on the Bareilly municipal board and was secretary of the District Muslim League. A member of the Anjuman-i-Khuddam-i-Kaaba, he came to the fore in the Cawnpore Mosque agitation and worked up feeling in Bareilly. He maintained contact with ABDUL BARI, signed the maulana's Jazirat-ul-Arab fatwa, was a member of the Jamiat-ul-ulama-i-Hind and helped to bring some Shia ulama into the non-co-operation movement. In the non-co-operation period, he became president of the Bareilly Town Congress Committee and was arrested in 1922. In 1914, Wadud, supported by the Nawab of Rampur, begged for a title from Meston. The lieutenant-governor, who liked the maulvi, was not persuaded.

APPENDIX IV

OTHER MEN OF IMPORTANCE

This Appendix contains the biographies of men who played an important part in all-India Muslim politics, but do not qualify for any of the categories in Appendices I to III.

Ahmad, Hafiz Nazir	Khan, Aga
Ali, Syed Ameer	Khan, Nawab Sir Salimullah
Ali, Chiragh	Khan, Samiullah
Azad, Abul Kalam	LaTouche, Sir James John Digges
Butler, Sir Spencer Harcourt	Lyall, Sir Alfred Comyn
Colvin, Sir Auckland	Macdonnell, Sir Antony Patrick
Crosthwaite, Sir Charles Hawkes	Mahmud, Syed
Hewett, Sir John Prescott	Meston, Sir James Scorgie
Haq, Mazharul	Prasad, Raja Siva
Hussain, Altaf	Zakaullah, Mahomed
Imam, Sir Ali	

Hafiz Nazir Ahmad (1836–1912); a good representative of the Urdu-speaking elite; a native of Bijnor, he was connected by marriage with a family of erudite Delhi maulvis; attended the oriental section of Delhi College and then entered government service rising to become a deputy inspector in the education department, a tahsildar and a deputy collector; 1861, helped to translate the Indian Penal Code; 1869, received the largest prize of Rs. 1000 in the government's recently instituted vernacular literature competition for his novel, *The Bride's Mirror*, and in the following years his novels and translations continued to carry off the best prizes; 1877, entered the Hyderabad service and rose to become the Revenue Member; retired to Delhi and was closely involved in the activities of Aligarh College; titles, Khan Bahadur, Shams-ul-Ulama, LL.D, Edinburgh.

Syed Ameer Ali (1849–1928); born at Chinsura, the son of Syed Saadut Ali of Mohan, Oudh; descendant of a soldier of Nadir Shah's army of 1739; family prominent in the service of the Nawabs of Oudh till shortly before the annexation; educated at Hooghly College; won a government scholarship to England and was one of the first Indian Muslims to read for the Bar; 1873, set up practice in Calcutta; 1874, elected a fellow of Calcutta University; 1876, founded the Central National Mahommedan Association of which he was secretary for twenty-five years; 1876–1904, president of the Hooghly Imambara Committee; 1878–81, Presidency Magistrate; 1879, member of the Commission to enquire into the affairs of the ex-king of Oudh; 1878–83, member of the Bengal legislative council; 1883–5, member of the Imperial legislative council: CIE, 1887;

428

Other men of importance

1890–1904, High Court Judge; 1904, retired to England with his English wife; 1908, founder and president of the London branch of the All-India Muslim League and was the life and soul of Muslim agitation in England; 1909, Privy Councillor; author of many books on historical, religious and legal subjects: *Critical examination of the Life and Teachings of Mohammad*; *Spirit of Islam*; *Ethics of Islam*; *A short History of the Saracens* etc.

Chiragh Ali (1844–95); son of a sheristadar in the Saharanpur collectorate; entered government service as a subordinate clerk in the treasury at Basti; 1872, deputy munsarim in the Court of the Judicial Commissioner, Lucknow, and later tahsildar in Sitapur; 1877, selected for service in Hyderabad on Syed Ahmed Khan's recommendation and appointed Assistant Revenue Secretary under Mohsin-ul-Mulk (q.v. Appendix II); ultimately rose to the post of Revenue and Political Secretary. He was a considerable pamphleteer in English and Urdu, and an important supporter of Syed Ahmed Khan's advanced religious ideas.

Abul Kalam Azad (1888–1958); the son of an eminent pir, Maulana Khairuddin Ahmad (d. 1909), who worked in Calcutta under the patronage of a wealthy Surati merchant, Haji Zachariah. Khairuddin had considerable influence among the wealthier classes of Muslims who used the Nakhoda Mosque, Calcutta. Azad inherited this influence which was increased by the fact that his sister married Maulvi Irshad Qadri of Midnapore, who had many disciples in Bengal. Azad was educated at the Calcutta Madrassa and the Nadwat-ul-ulama, Lucknow, where he was the favourite pupil of Shibli (q.v. Appendix III). In 1907, he edited the *Vakil* (Amritsar) and *An Nadwa* (Lucknow), the journal of the Nadwat-ul-ulama. Between 1907–1, he wrote and edited educational books for the Rifah-i-Am press, Lahore. In 1911, he settled in Calcutta and, in the following year, under the patronage of Nur Muhammad Zachariah, one of the mutawalis of the Sundariapati Mosque and the son of his father's patron, he started his pan-Islamic journal *Al-Hilal*. In July 1914, he founded the Jamiat-i-Hizballah (Society of God), the aims of which were similar to those of the Anjuman-i-Khuddam-i-Kaaba. From 1916 to 1920, he was interned in Ranchi. After his release, he became the most articulate supporter of non-co-operation among the Muslims, and the major rival of Abdul Bari (q.v. Appendix III) in all-India leadership of the ulama. In later life, he became a leading nationalist Muslim, acting as president of the Congress from 1938 to 1947 and as Education Minister after Independence. Azad was married to the daughter of Manglu Khansamah of Kalinga, Calcutta, who, as Khansamah (house steward) of the Grand Hotel, Calcutta, made a fortune through hiring out carriages.

Sir Spencer Harcourt Butler (1869–1938): educated at Harrow and Balliol Oxford; entered ICS, 1890; 1890–2, assistant magistrate and collector, Allahabad and Roorkee; 1892–3, junior secretary, board of revenue; 1893–8, assistant settlement officer, Sitapur; 1898–1900, settlement officer, Kheri; 1900–1, secretary to the Famine Commission; 1902–3, Director of Land Records, UP; 1903–6, third secretary, UP government; 1906–7, deputy commissioner, Lucknow; 1908–10, secretary to the foreign department, government of India; 1910–15, council of the Governor-general; 1915–18, lieutenant-governor of Burma; 1918–20, lieutenant-governor and 1920–3 governor of the UP; 1923–6 governor of Burma; 1928, chairman of the Indian States Committee; a close friend of the of Mahmudabad (q.v. Appendix I); the leading advocate of pro-landlord policy; in the running for the Viceroyalty in 1921 and widely regarded as the ablest ICS man of his generation; published *Oudh Policy: The Policy of Sympathy* in 1906, and often wrote to the press in his earlier years under the pseudonym, 'Indophilus'.

Sir Auckland Colvin (1838–1908); son of John Russell Colvin, Lieutenant-governor of the North-West Provinces, 1853–7; grandson of James Colvin, Calcutta merchant; educated at Eton and Haileybury; entered the ICS in 1858; 1859, assistant magistrate, Bijnor; 1860–4, assistant settlement officer, Muzaffarnagar; 1864–5, under secretary, government of India home department; 1866–70, assistant settlement officer in Etah and Allahabad; 1870–5, secretary, board of revenue, North-West Provinces; 1875–9, various appointments in the government of India; 1880–2, comptroller-general, Egypt; 1882–3, financial adviser to the Khedive; 1883–7, financial member, supreme council; 1887–92, lieutenant-governor, North-West Provinces and Oudh; published *John Russell Colvin* in 1895 and *The Making of Modern Egypt* in 1906.

Sir Charles Hawkes Todd Crosthwaite (1835–1915); educated at Merchant Taylors and St John's College, Oxford; entered the ICS in 1857; 1858–63, assistant magistrate and collector at Banda, Bareilly and Budaun; 1864–8, assistant settlement officer Etah; 1869–74, settlement officer at Etawah and Moradabad; 1874–7, secretary, board of revenue; 1877–81, on loan to the Central Provinces; 1881 and 1890–1, member of the Governor-general's council; 1883–4 and 1887–90, chief commissioner, Burma; 1886, public service commission; 1892–5, lieutenant-governor of the North-West Provinces and Oudh; 1895–1905, member of the Council of India; published several books including *Notes on the N.W. Provinces of India* in 1870.

Sir John Prescott Hewett (1854–1941); educated at Winchester and Balliol, Oxford; entered the ICS in 1877; 1877–80, assistant magistrate and collector in Allahabad, Agra, Bulandshahr, Muttra; 1881–2, assistant commissioner, Tarai; 1883–4, in charge of the provincial gazetteer; 1884–5, junior secretary, board of revenue; 1886–90, under secretary to government of India home department; 1890–3, deputy secretary to the home department; 1894–1902, secretary to the home department; 1893–4, Royal Commission on Opium; 1898–9, plague commissioner; 1902, chief commissioner of the Central Provinces; from 1904, member of the Governor-general's council; 1907–12, lieutenant-governor of the UP.

Mazharul Haq (1866–1929); grandson of Maulvi Sakhawat Ali Khan a deputy collector, and great nephew of the biggest indigo planter in Saran District, Bihar; educated at Patna College school, 1876–84, Patna College, 1884–7, and Canning College, Lucknow, 1887–8; 1888, ran away to England where he was supported by ALI IMAM, and in 1891 was called to the Bar; 1891, began practice at Bankipur; 1892, enrolled as a munsif; 1896, resumed practice at the Chapra district Bar; 1906,

Other men of importance

moved to Bankipur and became leader of the Bar; member of the Chapra municipal board; 1909–12, member of the Imperial legislative council; he was involved
in the foundation of the All-India Muslim League in 1906, the Bihar Muslim
League in 1908 and the Bihar Provincial Association in the same year; he was
president of the fourth session of the Bihar Provincial Conference at Gaya in
1911, of the Village Panchayat Association in 1913, of the Bombay session of the
All-India Muslim League in 1915, of the Bihar Home Rule League in 1916, and
the special session of the Bihar Provincial Conference in 1918; much involved
in the organisation of the Khilafat and non-co-operation protests in Bihar;
reputation marred by his peculation in Khilafat funds, 1921; chairman of the
Saran district board in the early 1920s; in 1915, the Bihar Special Branch
assessed him thus: 'Mazharul Haq is, I think in all respects a professional politician, with no principles and no real influence with orthodox Muhammadans.
He is clearly very anxious not to prejudice his position permanently with the
authorities, and by this time he has probably realised that little is to be gained
by espousing the cause of the Turks. My impression of him is that he is entirely
unscrupulous, that he is dependent upon his wits from month to month for his
income...'

Altaf Hussain, takhullus 'Hali' (1837–1914); born in Panipat; family came
originally from Herat; traditionally educated; 1856–7, petty post in the Hisar
collectorate; 1857–61, left government service in order to continue to educate
himself; 1861–9, companion to Nawab Mustafa Khan of Jehangirabad, the
'Shefta' of Ghalib's correspondence; the remainder of his life he spent first as
a translator in the government book department, Lahore, and then as a teacher
in the Delhi Anglo-Arabic school; he was, before all things, a poet and his
Musaddas, recited aloud at political and educational conferences, featured on
the front page of journals and learnt by most young Muslims, summed up for
generations what Muslim revivalism was about.

Sir Ali Imam (1869–1932); from a distinguished Syed family; one ancestor was
tutor to Aurangzeb; great grandfather, Syed Imdad Ali, subordinate judge of
Patna; grandfather, Syed Wahid-ud-din, the first Indian to be made a district
magistrate; father, professor of history and Arabic at Patna College and an Urdu
poet; educated at Arrah Zilla school and Patna College; went to England in 1887
and was called to the Bar in 1890; much involved with the Congress delegation
to England in 1890; after he returned to India, built up a very big practice;
member of Patna district and municipal boards; 1903, elected a trustee of
Aligarh; 1909, Fellow of Calcutta University; April 1908, president of the first
session of the Bihar Provincial Conference; December 1908, president of the
Amritsar session of the All-India Muslim League and, in 1909, the leader in the
League's negotiations with the government of India; 1910–15, member of the
Viceroy's executive council; 1917, judge of the Patna high court; 1919–22
president of the Nizam's executive council; 1920, represented India at the
League of Nations.

Aga Khan (1875–1958); head of the Ismailis, who devoted one-tenth of their
income to his support; grandfather married a daughter of the Shah of Iran;

431

Appendix IV

father, one of the claimants to the Persian throne, was offered asylum at Bombay, and a pension of Rs. 10,000 p.m., by the British in recognition of the assistance he had given; the Aga Khan also received the pension; 1902–4, member of the Imperial legislative council; 1903, presided over the Muslim Educational Conference; 1906, led the Simla deputation; 1907–13, president of the All-India Muslim League; president of the Muslim University Association; an organiser of the Hindu–Muslim unity conference of January 1910; 1915, published Gokhale's 'testament' on political reforms – he was a close friend of the Maharashtrian leader; chairman of the British delegation to the round table conferences of 1930 and 1931; led the Indian delegation to the League of Nations, 1932, 1934–7; president of the League of Nations, 1937.

Nawab Sir Salimullah Khan (1884–1915); head of the great Dacca Nawabi family, he was the premier Muslim zamindar of East Bengal; brought into politics by the Hindu agitation against East Bengal in 1906; invited Muslims to Dacca to found an all-India Muslim political association in 1906; president of the All-India Muslim Educational Conference at Amritsar in 1908; president of the All-India Muslim League at Calcutta in 1912; room for manoeuvre in politics much restricted by heavy debts to government and he left politics after the repartition of Bengal.

Samiullah Khan (1834–1908); 1858, munsif in Cawnpore and Aligarh; 1862–73, practised as a pleader in the Allahabad high court; 1873–87, subordinate judge in Aligarh, Allahabad, Moradabad, Farrukhabad, and Rae Bareli; 1887–9, district judge in Rae Bareli. His main interest was education. Traditionally educated himself, his first educational project was to found an Arabic school in Delhi. Later he teamed up with Syed Ahmed Khan, became a member of the Aligarh District Education Committee and, while Syed Ahmed Khan was stationed in Benares, was the heart and soul of the campaign for Aligarh College. He devoted his energies to the College till 1889 when he quarrelled with Syed Ahmed Khan. He differed with him both over administrative policy and personally – a girl intended for Samiullah's son, Hamidullah Khan (q.v. Appendix II), married SYED MAHMUD instead. Samiullah then had nothing more to do with Aligarh and set up a Muslim hostel at Muir Central College, Allahabad.

Sir James John Digges LaTouche (1844–1921); educated Trinity College, Dublin; 1867, joined ICS; 1867–71, assistant magistrate and collector, Meerut, Aligarh, Bareilly; 1871–5, settlement officer, Ajmere; 1875–8, district superintendant of police, Bulandshahr, Jhansi, Muttra; 1879–82, district officer Moradabad, Banda, 1882–3; joint magistrate Banda; 1883–4, settlement officer, Gorakhpur; from 1886, a commissioner in Burma; 1891, member legislative council, North-West Provinces and Oudh; 1893–1901, chief secretary to government North-West Provinces and Oudh; 1901–6, lieutenant-governor, UP.

Sir Alfred Comyn Lyall (1835–1911); educated Eton and Haileybury; 1855, entered Bengal Civil Service; 1856–8, assistant magistrate and collector, Bulandshahr; 1858–73, joint magistrate and deputy collector, Shahjahanpur, Pilibhit, Bareilly and Agra; 1861–3, ill; 1864–6, deputy commissioner of the Central

432

Other men of importance

Provinces; 1867–73, commissioner West Berar; 1873–4, secretary to the government of India in the home department; and in the foreign department, 1878–82; 1874–8, agent of the governor-general in Rajputana; 1882–7, lieutenant-governor, North-West Provinces and Oudh; 1888–1903, member, Council of India; correspondent and friend of John Morley, giving important advice to the Secretary of State during the Muslim separate electorate agitations of 1909; publications: *Verses written in India*; *British Dominion in India*; *Asiatic Studies*; *Life of Warren Hastings*; *Life of Marquis of Dufferin*.

Sir Antony Patrick Macdonnell (1844–1925); educated Queen's College, Galway; 1865, entered ICS; 1866–72, assistant magistrate and collector in Monghyr, Nadia, Hazaribagh, Pabna, Mymensingh; 1874–81, joint magistrate and deputy collector, Tirhut, Darbhanga, Saran; 1881–6, various posts in the Bengal secretariat; 1886–9, secretary, government of India home department; 1889, acting chief commissioner, Burma; 1891–3, chief commissioner, Central Provinces; 1893, acting lieutenant-governor, Bengal; 1893–5, member of supreme council; 1895–1901, lieutenant-governor, North-West Provinces and Oudh; 1902, Council of India; elevated to peerage, 1908, and with Curzon the bastion of conservatism on Indian matters in the Lords; 1902–8, Under Secretary of State for Ireland; 1917–18, member of the Irish Convention; published *Food-grain Supply and Famine Relief in Bihar and Bengal* in 1876.

Syed Mahmud (1850–1903); eldest son of Syed Ahmed Khan; educated at Government College, Delhi, Queens' College, Benares, and Christ's College, Cambridge, where he read oriental and classical languages; 1872, called to the Bar and, on returning to India, joined the Allahabad Bar; 1879, joined the ICS as a district judge; 1882, member of the Education Commission; 1884–93, first puisne judge and then judge of the Allahabad high court; 1893, forced to retire because of drunkenness; 1896–7, member of the North-West Provinces and Oudh legislative council; 1898, for a short time succeeded his father as secretary of Aligarh College till he was replaced on account of his unpopularity with the community and his manifest unsuitability; the formulator of the first Muslim University scheme in the early 1870s, he was one of the project's strongest advocates; published *A History of English Education in India (1781–1893)* in 1895.

Sir James Scorgie Meston (1865–1943); educated at Aberdeen Grammar School, Aberdeen University, Balliol College, Oxford; 1885, entered ICS; 1885–9, assistant magistrate and collector Saharanpur, Basti, Moradabad, Partabgarh; 1889–90, assistant commissioner, Jhansi, Lalitpur and Jalaun; 1891–2, joint magistrate Jalaun; 1892–7, settlement officer, Jhansi, Budaun; 1897–8, Director of Land Records; 1899–1903, third secretary to government, UP; 1905–6, lent to the government of the Cape of Good Hope; 1906–12, secretary to the government of India, finance department; 1912–18, lieutenant-governor of the UP; 1917, represented India in the Imperial War Conference; 1919, finance member of the governor general's council; vice-chairman of the Supervisory Commission, League of Nations; president of the Liberal Party organisation, 1936; elevated to the peerage, 1919; published *Nationhood for India* in 1931.

Appendix IV

Raja Siva Prasad (1823–1895); almost as important in the history of late-nineteenth-century UP as Syed Ahmed Khan; his career is a good example of the kind of influence that a determined and single-minded man might wield through an office in government. An Oswal Vaishya by caste, he was descended from the same family as the Jagat Seth of Murshidabad. His grandfather fled to Benares after his two cousins had been killed by the Nawab of Murshidabad (part of his marked hostility towards Muslims could well have sprung from family memory of this event); his father, Gopi Chand, owned land in Benares and Gorakhpur; Siva Prasad was educated at Benares College; 1839, vakil to the Maharaja of Bhartpur; 1840, naib mir munshi under W. Edwards in the foreign department; 1848, when Edwards became superintendent of the Hill States, he became mir munshi of the Simla Agency; 1852, mir munshi of the Benares Agency; 1856, joint inspector and later inspector of schools in the North-West Provinces education department; 1878, retired; 1870, CSI; 1874, Raja; 1877, hereditary Raja; 1883, member of the governor-general's legislative council; fellow of Allahabad University; wrote poetry under the takhullus, 'Wahbi'; author of thirty-two books, eighteen in Hindi and fourteen in Urdu. He was described by a missionary, who knew him, as the man 'who, by his personal labours as Joint Inspector of Schools, and by the many valuable books he has written, has done more, perhaps, for the education of the people than any other native in the North-West Provinces of India'. Rev. M. A. Sherring, *The Sacred City of the Hindus: An account of Benares in ancient and modern times* (London, 1868), p. 339.

Mahomed Zakaullah (1832–1910); son of a tutor to the children of the last Mughal emperor; attended Delhi College and was a class fellow of NAZIR AHMAD; on leaving, taught mathematics at Delhi College and then Persian and Urdu at Agra College; 1855–69, deputy inspector of schools in Bulandshahr and Moradabad; 1869–72, head teacher, Delhi Normal School; 1872–86, Professor of Persian and Arabic at Muir Central College, Allahabad. His contribution was as an author and a publicist; his works number 143. He translated many mathematical text books from English into Urdu, wrote several histories, including a ten-volume History of India under Muslim rule, and contributed to a wide range of newspapers and journals including the *Aligarh Institute Gazette*, *Tahzib-ul-Akhlaq* and *Zamana*; titles, Khan Bahadur and Shams-ul-Ulama.

Glossary

alim: *the singular of ulama, meaning one who possesses the quality of ilm, knowledge, learning, science in the widest sense, though normally used to denote a Muslim priest.*

Amir-i-shariat: *commander of the path to be followed, or the divine law of Islam.*

amla: *pl. subordinate officials.*

anjuman: *an association, usually of Muslims.*

Anjuman-i-Khuddam-i-Kaaba: *The Society of the Servants of the Holy Place.*

ashraf: *pl. of the Arabic sharif meaning honourable, the term usually used to describe those Muslims descended from immigrants into India.*

azaan: *call to prayer.*

babu: *originally a term of respect, but often used disparagingly by the British in India for the English-educated Bengali and for Indian clerks who used English.*

Bahr-ul-ulum: *'sea of sciences', one section of the Firangi Mahal school of ulama at Lucknow.*

Bania: *a Hindu of the trading castes.*

Brahmin: *the priestly or highest caste of Hindus.*

chaprasie: *a peon or orderly.*

chaukidar: *a watchman.*

chota peg: *Anglo-Indian slang, meaning a small drink.*

crore: *one hundred lakhs or ten millions.*

dar-ul-harb: *'land of war', a territory in which the sharia (q.v.) is not observed and which in, according to classical Muslim jurisprudence, believers should choose between jihad (q.v.) and hijrat (q.v.).*

dar-ul-Islam: *'land of Islam', a territory in which the sharia (q.v.) is observed.*

dar-ul-ulum: *'the abode of sciences', a Muslim theological seminary such as Firangi Mahal or Deoband.*

dars-i-nizamia: *traditional curriculum, emphasising Arabic, philosophy and jurisprudence, laid down by Mulla Nizamuddin of Firangi Mahal and used in most Muslim madrassas (q.v.) and dar-ul-ulums (q.v.) in India.*

durbar: *a public audience or levee held by a native prince, or by a high-ranking British official.*

fatwa: *a formal opinion, given by a mufti (q.v.) or an alim (q.v.) of standing, on a point of Islamic law.*

fiqh (fickah): *'understanding, knowledge, intelligence', the technical term for the science of Islamic jurisprudence.*

Glossary

Gandhi Ki Jai!: '*Victory to Gandhi*'.

gharry: *a box-like carriage with small wheels.*

ghazal: *poetry in the form of rhyming couplets.*

gotra: *an exogamous group, descended from a common ancestor, within the endo-gamous caste.*

gup: *Anglo-Indian slang, meaning gossip.*

hadith (hadees): *the traditions, the record of the sayings and doings of the Prophet Muhammad.*

haj: *the annual pilgrimage to Mecca.*

haji: *a pilgrim or, as a title, one who has performed the haj (q.v.).*

hakim: *a doctor practising one of the orthodox systems of Muslim medicine.*

haram: *forbidden by the sharia (q.v.).*

hartal: *strike.*

Hedjaz: *name normally used by Muslims to describe Arabia.*

hijrat: *act of migration by Muslims to dar-ul-Islam (q.v.) after the territory in which they are living has been declared dar-ul-harb (q.v.).*

hookah: *an Indian tobacco pipe.*

huzur: '*presence*', *title of respect given to a superior.*

ijma: *consensus of religious opinion.*

ijtihad: '*exerting oneself to the utmost degree to attain an object*', *i.e. the utmost effort to understand points of Islamic law.*

istifta: *a questionnaire circulated to ulama (q.v.) for their opinion on a point of Islamic law; it forms the prelude to the issue of a fatwa (q.v.).*

jagir: *the right to collect state revenues from a specified area which was usually given in Mughal times instead of a salary.*

jalsa-i-dastarbandi: *the graduation ceremony at a dar-ul-ulum (q.v.), at which a turban (the symbol of learned status) is tied on the head of a student who has qualified to become a teacher.*

Jazirat-ul-Arab: '*the island of Arabia*', *the area bounded by the Mediterranean, the Red Sea, the Indian Ocean, the Persian Gulf and the Rivers Tigris and Euphrates.*

jihad (jehad): *holy war, a religious duty which may be performed to establish the the sway of Islam over the world, or to defend the dar-ul-Islam (q.v.).*

josh: *religious fervour.*

Kaaba: *the shrine of the sacred stone at Mecca situated in the centre of the great Mosque.*

kafir: *one who is ungrateful to God, hence an unbeliever.*

kanungo: *subordinate official in Mughal and British revenue administrations, the immediate superior of the patwari (q.v.).*

Kayasth: *clerical caste, usually found in Bengal and northern India outside the Punjab.*

khadder (khadi): *hand-spun and hand-woven cloth.*

Khadim-ul-Khuddam: '*Servant of the Servants*', *the title born by the head of the Anjuman-i-Khuddam-i-Kaaba.*

Glossary

Khalifa: '*Caliph*', *the successor to the Prophet Muhammad as head of the Muslim community, and in recent times, that is up to 1924, the Sultan of Turkey.*

Khan Bahadur: *a title bestowed by government upon Muslims (the version given to Hindus being Rai Bahadur), it was the highest honour which a local politician could normally expect to receive.*

Khattri (Khatri): *a mercantile caste, originally from the Punjab, but widespread in northern India.*

Khilafat: '*Caliphate*', *the office which the Khalifa (q.v.) filled.*

khoja: *a Muslim of the Shia Ismaili sect, most of whom were traders.*

khutba: *a bidding prayer or sermon delivered before the congregation in a mosque on Fridays, in which God's blessings on the reigning prince are invoked, thus constituting a symbolic acknowledgement of sovereignty.*

kotwal: *the chief police officer of a city or town under both the Mughals and the British.*

lakh: *one hundred thousand.*

ma-bap: *mother and father.*

madrassa (madrasa): *a secondary school or college for Muslims.*

majahir (muhajir): *an emigrant, one performing hijrat (q.v.).*

majlis: *gathering, assembly.*

maktab: *a school for teaching children the elements of reading, writing and Quranic recitation.*

marwari: *a trading sub-caste found throughout India.*

maulana (moulana): *title usually applied to an alim, but, during the Khilafat movement, also assumed by, or given to, leading western-educated Muslim politicians.*

maulvi (moulavi, moulvi): *a title equal to maulana (q.v.).*

maund: *measurement of weight which varied from place to place; the standard maund weighed just over eighty-two pounds.*

mir munshi: *head clerk.*

mofussil: *the country stations and districts as opposed to the principal town.*

mohulla: *division or quarter of a town.*

mohurrir: *a clerk.*

muafidar: *a holder of revenue-free land.*

mufti: *one qualified to give a fatwa (q.v.).*

mujtahid: *a religious preceptor or instructor, and in the UP usually applied to the shia (q.v.) ulama.*

mulla: *term often used in British India for a Muslim schoolmaster.*

munsif: *the lowest grade of judge under British government in India.*

mushaira: *a gathering for the purpose of reciting poetry.*

muttafiqa: *unanimous.*

Nadwat-ul-ulama: '*The Congress of Muslim theologians*', *and also the name given to the seminary established at Lucknow, in the 1890s.*

naib: *deputy.*

namaz: *prayers.*

Glossary

nawab: *pl. of naib (q.v.), a style assumed by governors of provinces in later Mughal times and coming under the British to have the general meaning of prince.*

nazra (nazr): *a votive offering or ceremonial present from an inferior to a superior or between persons of equal rank.*

nizam: *governor, ruler, prince.*

pan: *a betel leaf, generally used to wrap up a combination of betel nut, areca nut lime etc. which is politely offered to visitors, and intimates the termination of the visit.*

patti: *a share in a coparcenary estate.*

pattidar: *a coparcenar.*

patwari: *village, or zamindari, record keeper and accountant; the lowest rank in the British revenue administration.*

pesh-Imam: *prayer-leader.*

peshkar: *a subordinate court official.*

peshwa: *leader, guide, high priest; originally the chief minister of the Maratha power.*

pir: *a religious guide.*

pragwal: *a Hindu priest.*

qasida: *an ode in praise of a person, usually the poet's patron, in the form of rhyming couplets.*

qazi: *a judge trained in Islamic law, though often the title was inherited as a name by men with no such training.*

rais: *an Indian of respectable position.*

raj: *a kingdom, rule or sovereignty.*

raja: *king, ruler; head of a Rajput (q.v.) clan.*

Rajput: *a military caste, or clan.*

Rifah-i-Am: *literally 'General Reform'; Rifah-i-Am Club, therefore, is Reform Club.*

sabha: *an assembly, usually of Hindus.*

sadr amin: *subordinate magistrate under East India Company rule.*

Sadr Diwani Adalat: *the chief civil court under East India Company rule.*

sajjada-nashin: *lit. 'sitter on the carpet'; head alim of a muslim school.*

sanad: *a grant, a title deed.*

sanatan dharm: *orthodox religious observance, hence, the organisation to promote and protect orthodox hinduism, the Sanatan Dharm Sabha.*

sati: *a virtuous wife; the faithful wife who burns herself with her husband's corpse, a custom considered by missionaries to be common in the early days of British rule.*

satyagraha: *'truth-force', 'soul-force'; Gandhian passive resistance.*

shaidai: *a religious votary.*

Shaikh-ul-Islam: *the title applied to the mufti of Constantinople, the supreme law-giver of the Ottoman government.*

shams-ul-ulama: *an honorific title, lit. 'sun of the ulama', bestowed by the British on leading ulama (q.v.).*

Glossary

sharia (shariat): *the path to be followed; the divinely revealed law of Islam.*

sherwani: *a long coat worn by Muslims and by Hindus influenced by Urdu culture.*

sheristadar (sarishtadar): *the head Indian officer in a collector's office or court of justice.*

shia: *the followers of Ali, the fourth caliph, who formed a heterodox sect in Islam.*

shuddhi: *'purification', the reconversion to Hinduism of those who have embraced other faiths.*

Subah: *a province of the Mughal empire.*

sufi: *a Muslim mystic.*

sunnet: *a religious ordinance.*

sunni: *'one who follows the trodden path'; an orthodox Muslim.*

swadeshi: *produced in one's own country.*

swaraj: *self-rule.*

tabib: *disciple.*

tafsir: *commentary on Islamic texts.*

tahsildar: *officer in charge of a tahsil, or revenue subdivision of a district; tahsildars were members of the provincial civil service.*

takhullus: *a poet's pen name.*

taluqdar (talukdar): *in the UP a superior zamindar who engaged with the state to collect the revenue from his own and other zamindari estates; after 1858, taluqdars in Oudh were given proprietary rights over the whole area from which they had previously collected revenue.*

taluqdari: *the rights of a taluqdar, collectively.*

tanzim: *consolidation, Muslim efforts to resist the shuddhi (q.v.) movement.*

thagi: *a system of gang robbery and murder.*

Thakur: *landholder, warrior (sub-caste of Kshattriyas).*

ulama (ulema): *pl. of alim (q.v.).*

vakil: *an authorised pleader in a court of justice, though, more generally, it could mean any advocate or representative.*

vedas: *the sacred scriptures of the Hindus.*

Wahabi: *a follower of the puritanical Abdul Wahab, an eighteenth-century Arab reformer.*

waqf: *an irrevocable settlement to safeguard the usufruct of property for charitable purposes.*

zakat: *the alms tax, one of the principal obligations of Islam, reckoned, usually, as a proportion of the Muslim's annual income.*

zamindar (zemindar): *under the British the holder of a right of property in land, who individually or jointly engaged to pay rent to government and had the right to collect rent and to regulate the occupancy of all other tenures on his estate.*

zamindari: *the rights of a zamindar, collectively.*

zenana: *the women's apartments in a Muslim household.*

Sources and bibliography

Only those sources and works cited in the notes to the text and the Appendices are listed below.

PRIVATE PAPERS

India Office Library, London [IOL]
Harcourt Butler Papers, Mss. Eur. F. 116.
Chelmsford Papers,. Mss. Eur. E. 264.
Curzon Papers. Mss. Eur. F. 111.
Dufferin Papers. Microfilm copy.
Elgin Papers. Mss. Eur. F. 84.
Lansdowne Papers. Mss. Eur. D. 558.
Lyall Papers. Mss. Eur. D. 552.
Meston Papers. Mss. Eur. F. 136.
Montagu Papers. Mss. Eur. D. 523.
Morley Papers. Mss. Eur. D. 573.

National Archives of India, New Delhi [NAI]
Gandhi Papers. Microfilm copy.
Gokhale Papers. Microfilm copy.
Sita Ram Papers.

Nehru Memorial Museum and Library, New Delhi [NMM]
Nehru Papers. This collection contains the correspondence of both Motilal and
  Jawaharlal Nehru.
Syed Mahmud Papers.

University Library, Cambridge [CUL]
Hardinge Papers.
Mayo Papers.

Bodleian Library, Oxford
Macdonnell Papers.

Firangi Mahal, Lucknow [FM]
Abdul Bari Papers. This collection contains a large part of the archives of the
  Anjuman-i-Khuddam-i-Kaaba which Abdul Bari transferred from Delhi to
  Lucknow in 1916.

Jamia Millia Islamia, New Delhi [JMI]
Mahomed Ali Papers. This collection also contains part of the archives of the
  Anjuman-i-Khuddam-i-Kaaba, and, in addition, correspondence belonging
  to Dr M. A. Ansari.

The Palace, Mahmudabad, Sitapur district, UP
Mahmudabad Papers. The bulk of this collection relates to Raja Amir Hasan
  Khan although there are a few items that concern the early life of Raja
  Muhammad Ali Muhammad.

440

Bibliography

National Library of Scotland [NLS]

Minto Papers. This collection is, unfortunately, only catalogued temporarily at the moment. I am, however, assured by the National Library that a key will be available to enable scholars to spot my references to the temporary catalogue when the new cataloguing system is in force.

UNPUBLISHED GOVERNMENT RECORDS

The general headings under which government files and proceedings were kept are listed below. Specific references will be found in the text.

India Office Records [IOR]
General Administration Department Proceedings [GAD] and Education Proceedings [Educ.] North-West Provinces and Oudh. Judicial and Public Proceedings.

National Archives of India [NAI]
Records of the Home Department of the Government of India, filed as Home Political [Poll.], Home Public, Home Education, Home Examinations, Home Judicial. Home Department files were divided into A, B, and Deposit [D] categories.

The Uttar Pradesh Secretariat Archives [UPS]
Records of the UP government under the following headings: General Administration Department [GAD], Education, Municipal, Revenue and Agriculture.

Archives of the Commissioner of Lucknow [LCA]
The departments in the Commissioner of Lucknow's archives are marked out not by name but by number. Files have been cited from Department XV, the equivalent of the General Administration Department in the UP secretariat archives.

RECORDS, PUBLISHED AND UNPUBLISHED, OF POLITICAL ORGANISATIONS

A. The British Indian Association, NWP
A Speech by Syud Ahmed Khan on the Institution of the British Indian Association, N.W. Provinces, with the Bye-Laws of the Association (Allygurh, 1867).
Supplement to Bye-Laws of the British Indian Association, N.W.P.: Relative to the Department for encouraging travel to Europe; together with the correspondence of the Association with the Government North Western Provinces on the same subject (Allygurh, 1869).
A Memorial to the British Government soliciting a reduction of the Book Postage with the Governments reply thereto (Allygurh, 1869).
Article on the Public Education of India and correspondence with the British Government concerning the education of the Natives of India through the Vernaculars (Allygurh, 1869).
A Petition to the British Government praying for certain reforms in the Railway arrangements for the convenience of Native Passengers, with the Governments Circular received in reply thereto (Allygurh, 1869).

B. The All-India Muslim League
Pirzada, Syed Sharifuddin (ed.) *Foundations of Pakistan: All-India Muslim League Documents: 1906–1947* (2 vols, Karachi, 1970).

Bibliography

Report of the Inaugural Meeting of the London Branch of the All-India Moslem League with the President's Address Wednesday, May 6th, 1908. The Indian Mahomedans and the Government (London, n.d.).

C. The Indian National Congress

Report of the Fourth Indian National Congress held at Allahabad on the 26th, 27th, 28th and 29th December, 1888 (Calcutta, 1889).

Report of the Proceedings of the Twenty-Seventh Indian National Congress. Held at Bankipur, December 26–28th, 1912 (Bankipur, n.d.).

Report of the Twenty-Eighth Indian National Congress held at Karachi on the 26th, 27th & 28th December 1913 (Karachi, n.d.).

The Indian National Congress 1920–1923 (Allahabad, 1924).

All-India Congress Committee Papers [AICCP] in the Nehru Memorial Museum, New Delhi.

D. Other organisations

The Transactions of the Benares Institute, for the session 1864–65 (Benares, 1865).

Circular from The Mahammedan Anglo-Oriental College Fund Committee (Benares, n.d.).

Records of the Rifah-i-Am Association, Lucknow, Mss. Proceedings Book, 1910–16.

Besant, A. *U.P. Provincial Conference Presidential Address* (Madras, 1915).

'The constitution of the Majlis Muid-ul-Islam', dated Firangi Mahal, Lucknow, 1328 AH (1912). An Urdu leaflet in the private library of Mufti Reza Ansari of Firangi Mahal.

'Presidential address of M. H. Kidwai to the Oudh Khilafat conference at Fyzabad, 1 May 1920'. An Urdu pamphlet in the private library of Mufti Reza Ansari of Firangi Mahal.

Hundred Years of Darululoom Deoband (Department of Tanzeem Abnae Qadeem Darululoom, Deoband, 1967).

INTERVIEWS

Two interviews yielded important information:

29 May 1968. Mufti Reza Ansari, the grandson of Maulana Salamatullah and present head of Firangi Mahal.

On several occasions in June 1968. The Maharajkumar of Mahmudabad, second son of Raja Muhammad Ali Muhammad of Mahmudabad.

NEWSPAPERS

The years given with each newspaper mark the period within which references to it have been made.

Aligarh Institute Gazette (Aligarh), 1913. Maulana Azad Library, Aligarh University.

Amrita Bazar Patrika (Calcutta), 1920. Microfilm, Centre of South Asian Studies, Cambridge.

Bombay Chronicle (Bombay), 1920. Microfilm, Centre of South Asian Studies, Cambridge.

Comrade (Calcutta and Delhi), 1911–14. Jamia Millia Islamia, New Delhi.

Hindu (Madras), 1920. Microfilm, Centre of South Asian Studies, Cambridge.

Independent (Allahabad), 1919–21. Microfilm, Seeley Library, Cambridge.

Indian People (Allahabad), 1903–09. The Leader Press, Allahabad.

New Era (Lucknow), 1917. Jama Millia Islamia, New Delhi.

Leader (Allahabad), 1909–23. The Leader Press, Allahabad.

442

Bibliography

Oudh Punch (Lucknow), 1919–22. The Library, the Palace, Mahmudabad, Sitapur district.
The Times (London), 1909. University Library, Cambridge.
Tribune (Lahore), 1920. Microfilm, Centre of South Asian Studies, Cambridge.
Reports on the Native Newspapers of the NWP, NWP and O, and the UP under the general reference UPNNR, 1869–1923. National Archives of India, New Delhi and the India Office Records, London.

OFFICIAL PUBLICATIONS

Some official publications were published annually or at other intervals of time. When this is so, an abbreviated form of the title is given, the frequency of publication is stated, as well as the period within which references have been made to the publication. All series of this kind are for the UP, NWP & O before 1902, unless otherwise stated.

Administration Reports, NWP. Annual series. 1860/61-1870/71.
Administration Reports. Annual Series. 1887/88–1899/1900.
Agra Civil List, 1 January 1857 (Agra, 1857).
Census Reports and Tables. Decennial series. 1881–1931.
Correspondence on the subject of the education of the Muhammadan Community in British India and their Employment in the Public Service Generally (Calcutta, 1886).
District Gazetteers of the United Provinces of Agra and Oudh (48 vols, Allahabad, 1903–11) [*DG*].
Report by the North-Western Provinces and Oudh Provincial Committee: with evidence taken before the committee and memorials addressed to the Education Commission (Calcutta, 1884) [*ECNWP & O*].
Enquiry into the subject of municipal taxation with special reference to the limitation of the octroi tax (Allahabad, 1909).
Gazettes. Weekly series, 1884–1915.
General Report on Public Instruction in the United Provinces of Agra and Oudh for the quinquennium ending 31st March 1912 (Allahabad, 1913).
Histories of Services. Published quarterly. 1881–1920.
Index Numbers of Indian Prices 1861–1931 (Department of Commercial Intelligence and Statistics India, Delhi, 1933).
Inland Trade Reports. Annual series. 1884/85–1915/16.
Manual of Titles United Provinces of Agra and Oudh (Allahabad, 1917).
Municipal Administration Reports. Annual series. 1884/5-1914/15 [*NWP & OMAR* and *UPMAR*].
Naik, J. P. (ed.), *Selections from the Educational Records of the Government of India* (Delhi, 1963).
Police Administration Reports, NWP. Annual series. 1865–70.
Police Administration Reports. Annual series. 1905.
Proceedings of the Council of His Honour the Lieutenant-Governor, United Provinces Agra and Oudh, assembled for the purpose of making laws and regulations, 1916 (Allahabad, 1917) [*UPLC*].
Proceedings of the Public Services Commission. Vol. II. Proceedings Relating to the North-Western Provinces and Oudh (Calcutta, 1887).
Rajas and Nawabs of the North-Western Provinces (Allahabad, 1877).
Report on the Administration of the Income Tax under Act II of 1886 in the North-Western Provinces and Oudh for the Financial Year ending 31st March, 1889 (Allahabad, 1889).

Bibliography

Report of the Indian Education Commission, Appointed by the Resolution of the Government of India dated 3rd February 1882 (Calcutta, 1883).

Reports of the Director of Public Instruction, NWP. Annual series 1844/45–1870/71 [*RDPI(NWP)*].

Reports of the Director of Public Instruction, Oudh. Annual series. 1870/71–1875/75 [*RDPI(Oudh)*].

Reports of the Director of Public Instruction. Annual series. 1880/81–1920/21. [*RDPI(NWP & O)* and *RDPI(UP)*].

Selections from the Speeches of Sir A. P. MacDonnell, G.C.S.I., Lieutenant-governor. N.-W.P. and Chief Commissioner of Oudh from 1895–1901 (Naini Tal, 1901).

Settlement Reports [*SR*] published in the years stated and for the following districts: *Muzaffarnagar, 1921; Dehra Dun, 1907; Saharanpur, 1891; Meerut' 1940; Bulandshahr, 1919; Aligarh, 1886; Farrukhabad, 1903; Etawah, 1915; Banda, 1909; Hamirpur, 1908; Ballia, 1886; Gorakhpur, 1891; Basti, 1919; Lucknow, 1930; Unao, 1931; Rae Bareli, 1898; Hardoi, 1932; Kheri, 1902; Bara Banki, 1930; Partabgarh, 1896; Sultanpur, 1898; Bahraich, 1939; Gonda, 1944; Fyzabad, 1942.*

PARLIAMENTARY PAPERS [P.P.]

Year	Volume	Command number	Short title
1888	XLVIII	5327	Report of the Public Service Commission, 1886–87 [*PSC 1886–7*].
1900	XXIX	130	Final Report of the Royal Commission on the Administration of Expenditure in India.
1908	XLV	4366	Royal Commission on Decentralisation in India. Volume VII, Evidence taken in the UP[DC].
1910	LXVII	4987	Regulations for giving effect to the Indian Councils Act of 1909.
1914	XXIII	7581	Royal Commission on the Public Services in India. Volume IX, Evidence taken in the UP [*PSC 1913*].
1916	VII	8382	Royal Commission on the Public Services in India. Volume I, Report [*PSC 1913*].
1918	VIII	9109	Report on Indian Constitutional Reforms.
1920	VI	—	First and Second Reports from the Joint Select Committee on the Government of India Act, 1919 (Draft Rules).

Hansard, Third Series (Lords), Vol. CCXLI.
Hansard, Fourth Series (Lords), CXCVII.
Hansard, Fifth Series (Lords), Vol. I.
Hansard, Fifth Series (Commons), Vol. III.
Hansard, Fifth Series (Commons), Vol. IV.
Hansard, Fifth Series (Commons), Vol. LXVIII.
Hansard, Fifth Series (Lords), Vol. XVIII.

Bibliography

PUBLISHED WORKS AND UNPUBLISHED THESES

Ahmad, A. *Studies in Islamic Culture in the Indian Environment* (London, 1964).

Ahmad, A. *Islamic Modernism in India and Pakistan 1857–1964* (London, 1967).

Ahmad, Q. *The Wahabi Movement in India* (Calcutta, 1966).

Ali, A. *Twilight in Delhi* (London, 1966).

Ali, C. M. *The Emergence of Pakistan* (London, 1967).

Ali, D. H. A. *An Illustrated Historical Album of the Rajas and Taluqdars of Oude* (Allahabad, 1880).

Ali, Mrs M. H. *Observations on the Mussulmauns of India*, 2nd edn, W. Crooke (ed.) (London, 1917).

Allami, A. F. *Ain i Akbari*, transl. Col. H. S. Jarrett, Vol. II (Calcutta, 1891).

Ambedkar, B. R. *Pakistan or the Partition of India* (Bombay, 1947).

Andrews, C. F. *Zakaullah of Delhi* (Cambridge, 1929).

Ansari, G. *Muslim Caste in Uttar Pradesh* (Lucknow, 1960).

Anonymous. *The Allahabad High Court: Centenary Volume of the Allahabad High Court, 1868–1968* (Allahabad, 1968).

Anonymous. *Jamiat-ul-Ulema-i-Hind (A Brief History)* (Meerut, 1963).

Anonymous. *Mukhtesat Halat-e-Inc'-qad-e-Jamiat-ul-Ulema-i-Hind* (Delhi, 1920).

Anonymous. *Open Letters to Sir Syed Ahmed Khan, K.C.S.I.* 'By the Son of an Old Follower of His', reprinted from the *Tribune* (Lahore, 1888).

Azad, A. K. *India Wins Freedom: An Autobiographical Narrative* (Bombay, 1959).

Bahadur, L. *The Muslim League: its History, Activities & Achievements* (Agra, 1954).

Baljon, J. S. S. (Jr.) *The Reforms and Religious Ideas of Sir Sayyid Ahmad Khan* (Leiden, 1949).

Bayly, C. A. 'The Development of Political Organisation in the Allahabad Locality, 1880–1925' (Unpublished D.Phil. thesis, 1970, Oxford).

Bayly, C. A. 'Patrons and Politics in Northern India', *Modern Asian Studies*, VII, 3 (1973).

Bhatnagar, S. K. *History of the M.A.O. College Aligarh* (Aligarh, 1969).

Brown, J. M. *Gandhi's Rise to Power: Indian Politics 1915–1922* (Cambridge, 1972).

Buckee, G. F. M. 'An Examination of the Development and Structure of the Legal Profession at Allahabad, 1866–1935' (Unpublished Ph.D. thesis, 1972, London).

Buckland, C. E. *A Dictionary of Indian Biography* (London, 1906).

Butler, S. H. *Oudh Policy: The Policy of Sympathy* (Lucknow, 1906).

Chew, E. C. T. 'Sir Alfred Comyn Lyall: A Study of the Anglo-Indian Official Mind' (Unpublished Ph.D. thesis, 1969, Cambridge).

Clark, T. W. (ed.) *The Novel in India: Its Birth and Development* (London, 1970).

Cohn, B. S. 'The Initial British Impact on India: A Case Study of the Benares Region', *The Journal of Asian Studies*, XIX, 4 (1960).

Constable, A. (ed.) *A Selection from the Illustrations which have appeared in the Oudh Punch from 1877 to 1881* (Lucknow, 1881).

Crooke, W. *Tribes and Castes of the North-Western Provinces and Oudh*, Vols. I–III (Calcutta, 1896).

Currie, Major-General F. *Below the Surface* (London, 1900).

Dar, S. L. and Somaskandan, S. *History of the Banaras Hindu University* (Banaras, 1966).

Bibliography

Das, M. N. *India under Morley and Minto: Politics behind Revolution, Repression and Reforms* (London, 1964).
de Bary, W. T. (ed.) *Sources of Indian Tradition* (New York, 1958).
Desai, A. R. *Social Background of Indian Nationalism* (Bombay, 1948).
Dittmer, K. 'Muslims in the United Provinces', unpublished paper given before the Second European Conference on Modern South Asian Studies, Copenhagen, July 1970; Centre of South Asian Studies, Cambridge.
Dutt, R. P. *India Today*, revised Indian edn (Bombay, 1949).
Farquhar, J. N. *Modern Religious Movements in India*, 1st Indian edn (Delhi, 1967).
Faruqi, Z. *The Deoband School and the Demand for Pakistan* (London, 1963).
Fox, R. G. *From Zamindar to Ballot Box* (Cornell, 1969).
Frykenberg, R. E. (ed.) *Land Control and Social Structure in Indian History* (Wisconsin, 1969).
Frykenberg, R. E. *Guntur District, 1788–1848: a history of local influence and central authority in South India* (Oxford, 1965).
Gallagher, J., Johnson, G. and Seal, A. (eds.) *Locality, Province and Nation: Essays on Indian Politics, 1870 to 1940* (Cambridge, 1973).
Gandhi, M. K. *The Collected Works of Mahatma Gandhi* (Delhi, in process of publication, 1958–) [CWG].
Gandhi, M. K. *An Autobiography: The Story of My Experiments With Truth*, transl. Mahadev Desai, paperback edn (London, 1966).
Garcin de Tassy, J. H. *La Langue et la Littérature Hindoustanies de 1850 à 1869: Discours d'Ouverture du Cours d'Hindoustani*, 2nd edn (Paris, 1874).
Garcin de Tassy, J. H. *Histoire de la Littérature Hindouie et Hindoustanie*, 2nd edn (Paris, 1874).
Garcin de Tassy, J. H. *La Langue et la Littérature Hindoustanies en 1871* (Paris, 1872).
Gibb, H. A. R. and Kramers, J. H. *Shorter Encyclopaedia of Islam* (London, 1961).
Gilbert, M. *Servant of India: A Study of Imperial Rule from 1905 to 1910 as told through the correspondence and diaries of Sir James Dunlop Smith* (London, 1966).
Gopal, M. *Munshi Premchand: A Literary Biography* (London, 1964).
Gopal, R. *Indian Muslims: A Political History (1858–1947)* (Bombay, 1959).
Gopal, S. *British Policy in India, 1858–1905* (Cambridge, 1965).
Gordon, R. A. 'Aspects in the history of the Indian National Congress, with special reference to the Swarajya Party, 1919–1927' (Unpublished D.Phil. thesis, 1970, Oxford).
Gould, H. A. 'Local Government Roots of Contemporary Indian Politics', *The Economic and Political Weekly*, 13 February 1971.
Graham, C. F. I. *The Life and Work of Sir Syed Ahmed Khan, K.C.S.I.* (New and revised edn, London, 1909).
Graham, J. R. 'The Arya Samaj as a Reformation in Hinduism with special reference to caste' (Unpublished Ph.D. thesis, 1942, Yale).
Greenberger, A. J. *The British Image of India: A Study on the Literature of Imperialism 1880–1960* (London, 1969).
Grewal, J. S. *Muslim Rule in India: The Assessments of British Historians* (Oxford, 1970).
Grierson, G. A. *Linguistic Survey of India*, Vol. I. i (Calcutta, 1927), Vol. VI (Calcutta, 1904), Vol. IX, Part I (Calcutta, 1916).
Growse, F. S. *Mathura: A District Memoir* (North-Western Provinces' Government Press, 1874).

Bibliography

Gupta, N. 'Military Security and Urban Development', *Modern Asian Studies*, V, 1 (1971).

Hali, A. H. *Hayat-i-Jawid* (Lahore, 1965).

Hamid, A. *Muslim Separatism in India: A Brief Survey 1858–1947* (Oxford, 1967).

Hampton, H. V. *Biographical Studies in Modern Indian Education* (Oxford, 1947).

Hardy, P. 'The ulama in British India', unpublished seminar paper, 1969, School of Oriental and African Studies, London.

Hardy, P. *The Muslims of British India* (Cambridge, 1972).

Hasan, S. A. *Tarikh-i-Mahmudabad*, Urdu mss. bound in three volumes (Mahmudabad House, Lucknow, n.d.).

Hassan, R. B. M. R. 'The Educational Movement of Sir Syed Ahmed Khan 1858–1898' (Unpublished Ph.D. thesis, 1960, London).

Heimsath, C. N. *Indian Nationalism and Hindu Social Reform* (Princeton, 1964).

Husain, Y. (ed.) *Selected Documents from the Aligarh Archives* (London, 1967).

Hill, J. L. 'Congress and Representative Institutions in the United Provinces, 1886–1901' (Unpublished Ph.D. thesis, 1966, Duke University).

Hunter, W. W. *The Indian Musalmans*, reprinted from the 3rd edn, London, 1876 (Delhi, 1969).

Ikram, S. M. *Modern Muslim India and the Birth of Pakistan (1858–1951)*, 2nd edn (Lahore, 1965).

Iqbal, A. (ed.) *My Life a Fragment: An Autobiographical Sketch of Maulana Mohamed Ali* (Lahore, 1942).

Jain, M. S. *The Aligarh Movement: Its Origin and Development, 1858–1906* (Agra, 1965).

Jones, K. W. 'The Arya Samaj in the Punjab: A Study of Social Reform and Religious Revivalism 1877–1902' (Unpublished Ph.D. thesis, Berkeley, 1966).

Khaliquzzaman, C. *Pathway to Pakistan* (Lahore, 1961).

Khan, H. A. *The Vernacular Controversy: An account and criticism of the Equalisation of Nagri and Urdu as the character for the Court of the North-West Provinces and Oudh, under the Resolution No. 585/III-343C-68 of Sir A. P. MacDonnell, the Lieutenant Governor N.-W.P., and Chief Commissioner, Oudh. Dated 18th April 1900* (Lucknow, 1900).

Khan, P. *The Revelations of an Orderly* (Benares, 1848).

Khan, S. A. *On the Present State of Indian Politics* (Allahabad, 1888).

Krishna, G. 'Religion in Politics', *The Indian Economic and Social History Review*, VIII, 4 (1971).

Lees, W. N. *Indian Musalmans* (London, 1871).

Lelyveld, D. 'Three Aligarh Students: Aftab Ahmad Khan, Ziauddin Ahmad and Muhammad Ali', *Modern Asian Studies*, VIII (1974).

Leonard, K. B. 'The Kayasths of Hyderabad City: their internal history, and their role in politics and society from 1850 to 1900' (Unpublished Ph.D. thesis, Wisconsin, 1969).

Lethbridge, Sir R. *Golden Book of India* (London, 1900).

Lutt, J. *Hindu-Nationalismus in Uttar Prades 1867–1900* (Stuttgart, 1970).

Lutt, J. 'The Hindi-movement and the origin of a cultural nationalism in Uttar Pradesh', unpublished paper given before the Second European Conference on Modern South Asian Studies, Copenhagen, July 1970; Centre of South Asian Studies, Cambridge.

Lyall, Sir A. *Verses Written in India* (London, 1889).

Lyall, Sir A. C. *Asiatic Studies: Religious and Social* (London, 1899).

447

Bibliography

McGregor, R. S. 'Bengal and the Development of Hindi, 1850–1880', *South Asian Review*, v, 2 (1972,) pp. 137–46.

Macpherson, K. 'The Political Development of the Urdu- and Tamil-speaking Muslims of the Madras Presidency 1901 to 1937' (Unpublished M.A. thesis, W. Australia, 1968).

Mahomed Ullah ibn S. Jung. *Leaves from the Life of Al-Haj Afzal-ul-Ulema Nawab Sarbuland Jung, M. Hamee-Ullah Khan, M.A. (Cantab.), Barrister-at-Law, Formerly Chief Justice H.E.H. the Nizam's High Court Hyderabad (Deccan)* (Allahabad, 1926).

Majumdar, R. C. *History of the Freedom Movement in India*, Vol. II (Calcutta, 1963).

Mehta, A., and Patwardhan, A. *The Communal Triangle in India* (Allahabad, 1941).

Morison, T. S. *The History of the M.A.-O. College, Aligarh* (Allahabad, 1903).

Muhammad, S. *Sir Syed Ahmad Khan: A Political Biography* (Meerut, 1969).

Mujeeb, M. *The Indian Muslims* (London, 1967).

Musgrave, P. J. 'Landlords and Lords of the Land: estate management and social control in Uttar Pradesh 1860–1920', *Modern Asian Studies*, vi, 3 (1972).

Natesan, G. A. (ed.) *Eminent Musalmans* (Madras, n.d.).

Nehru, J. *The Discovery of India*, 4th edn (London, 1956).

Nehru, J. *An Autobiography* (London, 1936).

Nesfield, J. C. *A Brief View of the Caste system of the North-Western Provinces and Oudh* (Allahabad, 1885).

Nurullah, S. and Naik, J. P., *A History of Education in India* (Bombay, 1951).

Owen, H. F. 'Negotiating the Lucknow Pact', *The Journal of Asian Studies*, xxxi, 3 (1972).

Pandey, B. N. *The Break-up of British India* (London, 1969).

Philips, C. H. (ed.) *The Evolution of India and Pakistan 1858–1947: Select Documents* (London, 1962).

Qureshi, I. H. *The Muslim Community of the Indo-Pakistan Subcontinent (610–1947)* (The Hague, 1962).

Rahman, M. *From Consultation to Confrontation: a study of the Muslim League in British Indian Politics 1906–1912* (London, 1970).

Reeves, P. D. 'The Landlords' Response to Political Change in the United Provinces of Agra and Oudh, India, 1921–1937' (Unpublished Ph.D. thesis, Australian National University, 1963).

Rizvi, J. D. 'Muslim Politics and Government Policy: Studies in the development of Muslim organisation and its social background in North India and Bengal, 1885–1917' (Unpublished Ph.D. thesis, Cambridge 1969).

Robinson, F. 'Consultation and Control: The United Provinces' government and its allies, 1860–1906'. *Modern Asian Studies*, v, 4 (1971).

Robinson, F. 'Municipal Government and Muslim Separatism in the United Provinces, 1883 to 1916', *Modern Asian Studies*, vii, 3 (1973).

Robinson, F. 'The Politics of U.P. Muslims 1906–1922' (Unpublished Ph.D. thesis, Cambridge, 1970).

Rosselli, J. 'Theory and Practice in North India', *The Indian Economic and Social History Review*, viii, 2 (1971).

Russell, R. and Islam, K. *Ghalib* (London, 1969).

Saeedullah, 'The Life and Works of Muhammad Siddiq Hasan Khan, Nawab of Bhopal (1248/1332 to 1907/1890): (Unpublished M.Litt. thesis, Cambridge, 1970).

Saksena, R. B. *A History of Urdu Literature* (Allahabad, 1927).

Bibliography

Sayeed, K. B. *Pakistan: The Formative Phase 1857–1948*, 2nd edn (London, 1948).

Seal, A. *The Emergence of Indian Nationalism: Competition and Collaboration in the Later Nineteenth Century* (Cambridge, 1968).

Sherring, Rev. M.A. *The Sacred City of the Hindus: An account of Benares in ancient and modern times* (London, 1868).

Singh, S. N. *The Secretary of State for India and his Council (1858–1919)* (Delhi, 1962).

Sivaprasad, *Strictures upon the Strictures of Sayyad Ahmad Khan Bahadur, C.S.I.* (Benares, 1870).

Skrine, F. H. *Life of Sir William Wilson Hunter* (London, 1901).

Smith, W. C. *Modern Islam in India* (London, 1946).

Spate, O. H. K. and Learmouth, A. T. A. *India and Pakistan: A General and Regional Geography*, 3rd edn (London, 1967).

Spear, P. *Twilight of the Mughals: Studies in Late Mughal Delhi* (Cambridge, 1951).

Stokes, E. T. *The English Utilitarians and India* (Oxford, 1959).

Strachey, Sir J. *India*, new and revised edn (London, 1894).

Temple, Sir R. *Men and Events of My Time in India* (London, 1882).

Temple, Sir R. *India in 1880*, 3rd edn (London, 1881).

Temple, Sir R. *James Thomason* (Oxford, 1893).

Tendulkar, D. G. *Mahatma*, vol. I (Government of India Publications Division, New Edition, 1960).

Thacker's Bengal Directory (Calcutta, 1873).

Thacker's Indian Directory for the years 1889, 1899, 1909, 1919, 1929.

Tinker, H. *The Foundations of Local Self-Government in India, Pakistan and Burma* (London, 1968).

Thomas, P. J. *The Growth of Federal Finance in India: Being a Survey of India's Public Finances from 1833 to 1939* (Oxford, 1939).

Tirmizi, S. A. I. *Persian Letters of Ghalib* (Ghalib Academy, New Delhi, 1969).

Trevelyan, G. O. *The Competition Wallah* (London, 1864).

Vakil, C. N. *Financial Developments in Modern India, 1860–1924* (Bombay 1924).

Waley, S. D. *Edwin Montagu* (Bombay, 1964).

Wasti, S. R. *Lord Minto and the Indian Nationalist Movement 1905 to 1910* (Oxford, 1964).

Who's Who in India (Newal Kishore, Lucknow, 1911).

Wolpert, S. A. *Morley and India 1906–1910* (Berkeley and Los Angeles, 1967).

Yule, H. and Burnell, A. C. *Hobson-Jobson*, new edn, W. Crooke (ed.) (London, 1903).

Zafar-ul-Islam, 'Documents on Indo-Muslim Politics (1857–1947): The Aligarh Political Activities (1888–1893)', *Journal of the Pakistan Historical Society*, XII, 1, (1964).

Zakaria, R. *Rise of Muslims in Indian Politics: an Analysis of Developments from 1885 to 1906* (Bombay, 1970).

INDEX

Where there are a number of entries under the same name, they have been listed alphabetically according to the last forename.

451

Index

Index

Balrampur, 85; taluqdari estate 16 n. 3, 188

Banerjee, Jitendralal 320

Banerjee, Surendranath 112, 114, 195 n. 3

Banias 14, 17, 28, 29 and n. 4, 31, 65, 66; landholdings in UP 18–19, 62, 63; and reforms in bureaucracy 46

Banker, Shankerlal 302

Baqr Id 77 and n. 2, 116, 319

Bardoli Resolutions 333–4

Bareilly 11, 17, 32, 36, 53 n. 3, 60 n. 8, 81–2, 82 n. 1, 85, 102, 220

Bareilly school of ulama 265, 267 and n. 1; doctrinal differences with Deoband 269; and with Firangi Mahal 269, 279 and n. 1, 293; see also under Khan, Maulana Ahmad Reza

Bari, Maulana Abdul of Firangi Mahal 3, 213 n. 6, 265, 280 and n. 8, 285 n. 2, 301, 308 n. 4, 350, 351; as a pir 266, 281, 342; and Anjuman-i-Khuddam-i-Kaaba 208–12, 279, 287; and *Al-Nizamiya* 267; and the Bahr-ul-ulum party 270–1; and Madrassa Nizamia 265, 266 n. 1, 270, 274; and Majlis Muid-ul-Islam 277, 284–6; and 'Young Party' 281–3; and Shahabad riots 284; address to Montagu (1917) 284–6; motives 283; and post of Shaikh-ul-Islam 329 and n. 2; and Raja Muhammad Ali Muhammad of Mahmudabad 264; and Mushir Husain Kidwai 266 n. 5, 281, 298; and Mahomed Mian Chotani, 266 n. 5, 308, 316; and Gandhi 297, 298–9, 302, 314, 329, 334; a leader of ulama in politics 281–8, 292–6, 300, 301, 304, 305–6, 309, 314 and n. 2, 325, 327–8, 352; and the Khilafat movement 292–6, 298–9, 301, 302, 304–11, 314–16, 319, 325, 327–30, 334, 338–40; and cow-protection 299, 302, 319, 329 n. 2, 339; biography App. III

Barni, Ziauddin 185 n. 2; biography App. I

Baroda 180–1, 184–5, 186

Bashir, Mahomed of Lucknow 270

Bashir-ud-din, Muhammad 193; biography App. II

Basu, Bhupendranath 254

Bayley, E. C. 103 n. 1

Beames, M. J. 73 n. 3

Beck, Theodore (Principal of Aligarh College) 117, 118, 122 and n. 1, 123, 165, 199

Beg, Mirza Samiullah 196 n. 4, 203, 223, 237 n. 5, 242, 252 n. 7, 261; biography App. I

Benares, city 10, 11, 34, 53 n. 3, 59, 60 n. 8, 62, 69, 77; Maharaja of 74 and n. 3, 110, 120; source of demand for Hindi 74–5; Muslim Committee at 107–8, 128 and n. 2; Congress at (1905) 142

Benares Akhbar (Benares) 72

Benares Institute 73 n. 4, 85, 86 n. 2, 87 n. 2, 116

Bengal 4, 10, 11, 23, 34 n. 2, 42–3, 42 n. 5, 66, 102, 114, 120, 131, 144, 147, 253–5; Muslim education in 102–3; repartition of 203; Muslim League 151 and n. 5; Khilafat Committee 319

Bengalis 115, 116, 119

Besant, Mrs 241, 251, 252, 254, 320

Bharat Bandhu (Aligarh) 75, 116 n. 2

Bharat Dharma Mahamandal 68

Bharat Jiwan (Benares) 75, 116 n. 2

Bhatias 321

Bhatta, Balkrishna 75

Bhimji, Mahomed Ali 120

Bhinga, Raja of 61 n. 3, 76, 83, 120

Bhopal state 126 n. 4; and jobs for UP Muslims 26; *see also under* Khan, Prince Hamidullah

Bhurgri, Mahomed 306

Bihar 74, 78, 102, 140, 203, 241 n. 5, 268; Muslim League 151; Provincial Conference 319

Bijnor 82, 89, 140, 250 n. 5

Bijnori, Abdur Rahman biography App. I

Bilehra, Raja of 25

Bilgrami, Major Syed Hasan 149 n. 3, 150, 155, 163, 176, 217, 218 ns. 4 and 5; biography App. I

Bilgrami, Syed Hosein (Imad-ul-Mulk) 143 and ns. 6 and 7, 148 n. 4, 150, 168 and n. 7, 191; biography App. II

Bombay 59 n. 2, 136, 144, 210, 242–5, 260–1, 279; Muslim League 151; Congress at (1915) 241, 242–5;

453

Index

Bombay (*cont.*)
Khilafat conference at (1920) 290 n. 3, 305–6, 309; Muslim League at (1915) 242–5, (1918) 260–1
Brahmins 17, 28, 29 and n. 4, 65 n. 2, 66 n. 2, 70; landholdings in UP 18–19, 63; and reforms in bureaucracy 46; *see also* Kashmiri Brahmins
Brahmo Samaj 66, 67 and n. 2, 69, 73
British Indian Association of NWP 72 n. 1, 73, 94–8, 117, 346; and government education policy 95–7; and Vernacular University 96–7, 347; divided by language controversy 97–8, and Syed Ahmed Khan 73, 94–8, 117
British Indian Association of Oudh 20 and n. 2, 32 n. 3, 94, 258
Budaun 82, 140, 198, 209
Butler, Sir Spencer Harcourt 42 n. 5, 141, 142, 143 n. 7, 148 and n. 3, 165 and n. 3, 166 and n. 3, 180, 194, 205, 214, 230, 260, 272, 283, 294, 333; and Raja Muhammad Ali Muhammad of Mahmudabad 260; biography App. IV

Calcutta 59 n. 2, 66, 92, 114, 203, 279; Indian Association of 113, 114; Congress at (1920) 313, 317, 319–22, 325, 337; Muslim League at (1912) 227–9; Provincial Khilafat conference at (1920) 306–7
Canterbury, Archbishop of 291, 306
Cawnpore 59 n. 2, 60 and ns. 6 and 8, 62 and n. 1, 82, 242; Mosque agitation 189, 212–16, 224, 230, 238, 278, 281, 350; Mosque Fund 187, 213, 354
Central Provinces (CP) 74, 118, 120, 136
Chak, Prithvi Nath 220 n. 1
Chand, Lala Nihal 49 n. 1, 58 n. 4
Chand, Prem 76 and n. 3
Chandra, Babu Haris 68, 74–6, 74 n. 4
Chelmsford, Lord (Viceroy) 257, 304, 350
Chhatari, Nawab Hafiz Said Khan of 135, 190, 258, 342; estate 20 n. 1; biography App. II

Chinoy, Rahimtulla 311
Chintamani, C. Y. 254; and UP Municipalities Act 1916 250–1
Chirol, Sir Valentine 169
Chotani, Mahomed Mian 294, 295, 303, 310, 311, 321, 324 n. 2, 333; and Abdul Bari 266 n. 5, 308, 316
Choudhury, Nawab Ali 144
Civil and Military Gazette (Lahore) 232
civil disobedience 330–4, 335–6, 352; *see also* non co-operation
Colvin, Sir Auckland 42 n. 5, 50, 90 n. 3, 94 and n. 1, 130; and finance policy 47, 48; and 1883 Municipalities Act 57–8; biography App. IV
Colvin Taluqdars College (Lucknow) 190
communal riots 6, 79 and n. 1, 238, 284 and n. 1, 336, 338–9
Comrade (Calcutta and Delhi) 184–7, 189, 198, 200, 201, 204, 206–7, 213, 216, 217, 272; importance of 202; and *New Era* 259 n. 2
Congress, Indian National 1, 98, 113–14, 241; and Muslims, 4, 5, 115–17, 133, 138, 141, 142–3, 148, 194–6, 203–4, 236–56, 259–61, 289, 312–22, 330–7, 339–42, 343–4, 350, 352; and Muslims as President 237, 341; opposed by Syed Ahmed Khan 117–21; and the 'Young Party' 236–56, 259–61, 289, 314, 322–3, 350, 352; and Muslim League 229, 236–56, 259–61, 350; and ulama 278, 325, 330, 334–8, 339–41, 351–2; and the Khilafat movement 312–15, 317–22, 330–41, 351–2; and non-co-operation 313, 317–22, 326, 328, 351–2; and civil disobedience 331–2, 336; and Civil Disobedience Enquiry Committee 336 and n. 1; and the UP 113–21; British Committee of 171; All-India Committee of 251, 260, 312, 313–14, 317, 331–2, 334–5, 336, 340; UP Committee of 237, 339, 341, and n. 3; and Hindu revivalism 116–17, 195, 347; and reforms 115, 116, 242, 244–56, 260–1, 314, 317–20; sessions: at Allahabad (1888) 115–17, 278, (1892)

454

Index

Index

Index

Index

Husain, Syed Jafar 191; biography App. II

Husain, Maulvi Mahomed 278

Husain, Syed Mahomed 323, 343; biography App. I

Husain, Nawab Mushtaq (Viqar-ul-Mulk) 124, 141, 143, 148 n. 4, 149 n. 3, 150, 162, 190, 194, 200 n. 2, 204, 209 n. 5, 226, 280, 289; and Muslim Political Association 139–40, 140 n. 3; biography App. II

Husain, Nasir (mujtahid) 285 n. 2

Husain, Nasrat 264, 267 n. 5

Husain, Sheikh Shahid 213 n. 6, 223, 237 n. 5, 342; biography App. II

Husain, Maulvi Wilayat 28, 278, 284, 285 n. 2, 301; biography App. III

Husain, Shah Yusuf (mujtahid) 328

Husein, Syed Karamat 135, 148 n. 4, 191, 196, 232–3; biography App. II

Hussain, Mumtaz 301; biography App. I

Hussain, Sajjad 136, 142

Hussain, Syud 3 n. 2, 185 n. 2, 301; biography App. I

Hyderabad state 141, 279; Nizam of 126, 129 n. 1; UP Muslims find jobs in 26, 123, 124, 143 n. 6, 191, 261, 264; UP Kayasths find jobs in 30 n. 2

Ilbert Bill 113, 114

Imad-ul-Mulk, see under Bilgrami, Syed Hosein

Imam, Syed Ali 140, 154–5, 158 and n. 4, 159, 160 and ns. 1 and 3. 163, 201, 236 n. 1; biography App. IV

Imam, Hasan 151

Independent (Allahabad) 303, 316

India Council 168, 172, 258

Indian Daily Telegraph (Lucknow) 136, 251, 271

Indian Majlis of Cambridge 236

Indian National Congress, see under Congress

Indraman, Munshi 68

Iyengar, Kasturiranga 321, 336

Jafri, Kamaluddin Ahmed 225, 236, 301, 323, 341 and n. 3; biography App. I

Jalil, Maulvi Abdul of Benares 279

Jalsi-i-Tahzib: at Lucknow 85, 86–7, 115; at Sitapur 85, 86; at Gonda 85

Jamiat-ul-ulama-i-Hind 304 and n. 3, 326, 327, 331, 334–5, 337, 338, 339, 341, 354

Jan, Abdullah 148 n. 4, 237 n. 5

Jan, Syed Mir biography App. I

Jaunpur city 11, 17, 25, 59, 120, 250 n. 5

Jazirat-ul-Arab 290, 306, 311, 338

Jehangirabad, Raja Tassaduq Rasul Khan of 49 n. 1, 64, 140 n. 9, 190, 192, 213 n. 6, 220, 221, 223, 258, 286, 328, 342; his amendment 249–51; is Rani 266, 271; and Firangi Mahal 270–1; biography App. II

Jenkins, Sir Lawrence 171, 203 n. 2

jihad 293, 294, 356

Jinnah, M. A. 4, 198, 236 n. 1, 243–4, 252, 254, 261, 320

Julahas 24, 27, 213, 245

Kalakankar, Raja of 49 n. 1

Kalwars 63

Karachi city: Congress at (1913) 237, 238; Khilafat conference at (1921) 330, 331; Muslim League at (1907) 149–50

Kashmiri Brahmins 30 n. 1, 40, 85; and Muslims 30–1, 30 n. 2, 252; and Persian literature 31; opposition to Nagri Resolution 136 and n. 3; and UP Municipalities Act 247–51

Kavi Vachan Sudha (Benares) 71, 75, 116 n. 2

Kayasths 17, 28, 40, 54, 85, 86, 115; landholdings in UP 18–19, 63 and n. 3; and Muslims 30–1, 30 ns. 2 and 3, 31 n. 2, 64; and Persian literature 31; and reforms in bureaucracy 46; opposition to Nagri Resolution 31 n. 2, 136 and n. 3

Kempson, M. (Director of Public Instruction) 102 n. 4, 128; support for Hindi 72–3; support for Siva Prasad 72 n. 4, 73; opinion of Muslim learning 72 n. 4; attacks Mayo's education policy 104–5; opposition to Aligarh College 128–9, 128 n. 5

Index

Khair, Maulvi Abul of Ghazipur 268
Khalifa 112, 134, 290, 291, 293, 295,
  311, 351; *see also under* Khilafat
Khalil-ur-Rahman, Maulvi 265
Khaliquzzaman, Chowdry 177, 179,
  183, 207 n. 5, 262, 295, 296, 339,
  343, 344; biography App. I
Khan, Aga 147, 149, 150, 160, 161,
  169, 184, 194, 200 n. 2, 201, 226–7,
  229, 243, 245, 310; biography App.
  IV
Khan, Sahibzada Aftab Ahmad 148
  n. 4, 149 n. 1, 176, 194, 214 n. 1,
  217, 218 n. 5, 223, 226, 258, 280,
  343; biography App. II
Khan, Syed Ahmed 68, 101, 122 n. 1,
  123, 124, 127, 135, 138, 139, 146,
  198, 199, 231, 275, 279, 283, 289,
  346–7; and the Muhammadan
  Anglo-Oriental College, Aligarh 4,
  20, 107–11, 216; and All-India
  Muslim Educational Conference 4,
  119, 124–5, 125, n. 3; and Muslim
  backwardness in education 38–9;
  and the British Indian Association
  of NWP 73, 94–8, 117; and the
  Aligarh Scientific Society 87, 93–5,
  93 n. 1; the man 87–8; background
  88–9; and Wahabis 89, 111; his
  piety 89–90; and Hali 89 and n. 2;
  government view of 89, 96; leader
  of Urdu-speaking elite 87, 90–8;
  concern for Muslim–government
  relations 90, 111–13; criticism of
  government policy 90–1; criticisms
  of government education policy
  91–2, 95–7, 106–8, 110; school at
  Moradabad 91–2; and Ghazipur
  College 92 n. 6, and Ghazipur
  Scientific Society 92–3, 92 n. 6; at
  Calcutta (1863) 92, 93; and 'Public
  Education of India' 95–6; and
  education in Aligarh district 96;
  and vernacular university project
  96–7; begins to work for Muslims
  alone 98 and n. 2, 105–6; visit to
  England 106–7, 106 n. 1, 107 n. 3;
  and Benares Committee 107–8;
  founds *Tahzib-ul-Akhlaq* 109; opposed by ulama 109, 273; and
  pan-Islamism 111–12, 111 n. 3;
  and Jamal al-din al-Afghani 111
  n. 3; reaction to Congress 117–21;
  and legislative councils 91, 117–18;
  and government service 118–19;
  and the United Indian Patriotic
  Association 120–21; and the Muhammadan Anglo-Oriental Defence
  Association 122; his political
  achievement 123–6; importance of
  government support for him 126–
  32; publications: *Asar-i-Sanadid*
  89 and n. 1; *Tabyin al-Kalam* 90
  and n. 1, 124 n. 11; *An Account of
  the Loyal Mahomedans of India* 90;
  The Causes of the Indian Revolt
  90–1, 117; *Strictures on the present
  education system in India* 106; *A
  Series of Essays on the Life of
  Mohammed* 111; review of Hunter's
  Indian Musalmans 111; *On the
  Present State of Indian Politics* 119,
  278
Khan, Hakim Ajmal 3 n. 2, 148 n. 4,
  149 and n. 1, 179, 201, 260, 261–2,
  280, 285, 286 n. 2, 287, 296, 339,
  341, 343, 353; and Khilafat move-
  ment 292, 293, 301, 308 n. 4, 309,
  319, 323, 324, 331, 332, 333–6, 335
  n. 2, 350; biography App. I
Khan, Maulvi Akram 301, 325
Khan, Munshi Asghar Ali 193, 221,
  223, 248; biography App. II
Khan, Hamid Ali 79, 135–6, 140,
  148 n. 4, 234; biography App. II
Khan, Raja Naushad Ali 148 n. 4,
  224 n. 2; biography App. II
Khan, Nawab Sadiq Ali 237 n. 5
Khan, Zafar Ali 124 n. 8, 149 and n. 1,
  201, 315, 323
Khan, Nawab Asadullah 221, 223
Khan, Abdul Hamid 321
Khan, Moulvi Haji Hamidullah,
  Nawab Sarbuland Jung 191; bio-
  graphy App. II
Khan, Prince Hamidullah of Bhopal
  176–7, 188; biography App. I
Khan, Sheikh Yusuf Husain bio-
  graphy App. I
Khan, Nawab Mahomed Ishaq 148
  n. 4, 184, 191, 213 n. 6, 217 n. 6,
  218 n. 5, 237 n. 5, 258; biography
  App. II
Khan, Nawab Ismail 323, 343; bio-
  graphy App. I
Khan, Maulvi Abdul Karim 269 n. 5

Index

Khan, Munshi Abdul Karim (alias Hakim Barham) biography App. II

Khan, Masood-uz-Zaman 342; biography App. II

Khan, Nawab Muhammad Muzammilullah of Bhikampur 148 n. 4, 177 n. 1, 190, 213 n. 6, 257–8, 342; estate 20 n. 1; biography App. II

Khan, Maulana Ahmad Reza of Bareilly 265, 266, 268, 279, 284, 285 n. 2, 293, 325 n. 1; biography App. III

Khan, Raja Salamat 220

Khan, Nawab Salimullah of Dacca 144, 147–9, 147 n. 6, 148 n. 2, 149 n. 1; biography App. IV

Khan, Samiullah 110, 124 and n. 11; biography App. IV

Khan, Wahid Yar 185 n. 2; biography App. I

Khattri, Haji Ahmed 301, 311, 315

Khattris 29, 31, 62, 63, 65 n. 2, 66 n. 2, 115

Khilafat 289, 292, 295, 301, 304, 336, 337, 351, 355; question 290–1, 292, 293, 297, 300, 334

Khilafat Committee: Central 4, 295, 296, 303, 304, 307–8, 309, 310, 311–16, 319, 322, 324, 326, 328, 331, 334–5, 336, 339, 343; Bengal 319, 325; Bombay 294; Delhi 300; UP 310, 323, 325; Lahore, 327; Civil Disobedience Enquiry Committee 336 and n. 1

Khilafat conference, All-India: at Lucknow (1919) 294–5, 296; at Delhi (1919) 300–2, 303, 323, 325; at Amritsar (1919) 303; at Bombay (1920) 290 n. 3, 305–6, 309; at Meerut (1921) 350; at Karachi (1921) 330, 331; at Ahmedabad (1921) 332; at Gaya (1922) 337; Provincial: Madras (1920) 309; Bihar (1920) 309; Bengal (1920) 306–7; UP (1920) 309; Oudh (1920) 312

Khilafat Day: 17 October 1919 295, 296, 300; 19 March 1920 308–9

Khilafat deputation: 1919 294; to Viceroy January 1920 303–4; Mahomed Ali's 306 and n. 1; memorial to Viceroy, June 1920 316

Khilafat Fund 354

Khilafat movement 111 n. 3, 211–13, 261–2, 265, 298, 290–344; and ulama 261–2, 270–1, 279, 292–6, 300–1, 304, 306–7, 309, 314, 322, 324–5, 326–42, 350–3; and UP Muslims 291–5, 300–16, 322–5, 326–44, 350–3; and 'Young Party' 291–2, 300, 301, 315, 316, 322–4, 326, 333–4, 339–40, 342, 343–4, 350–2; and Gandhi 296–7, 298–322, 326–34, 351–2; and Hindus 302–3, 308–9, 312–15, 317–22, 330, 338–9; and Congress 312–15, 317–22, 330–41, 351–2

Khilafat Workers Conference 309, 310, 323

Khilafat Workers League 310, 324

Khojas 244

Khutba 270–1, 270 n. 5, 291

Kidwai, Rafi Ahmed biography App. I

Kidwai, Mushir Husain 196, 203, 208, 209 n. 2, 310, 311, 312, 323, 343; and Abdul Bari 266 n. 5, 281, 298; biography App. I

Kidwai, Ehsanhur Rahman 281

Kidwai, Saidur Rahman 266 n. 5, 281

Kishore, Jugul 64

Kitchlew Saifuddin 315, 320, 323

Koor, Badruddin Abdullah 311

kotwal 30 n. 2, 56 and n. 2, 80, 82

Lal, Pandit Badri 73 n. 4

Lal, Munshi Brij 85

Lal, Babu Kanhya 68

Lal, Munshi Madho 49 n. 1

Lal, Manohar 238 n. 4

Lal, Pandit Sundar 49 n. 1, 52 n. 3

landlords in the UP 15–20; as Muslims 17–20, 176–7, 190; power cut down 33; and government service 26–7; and district boards 49–50; and municipal boards 57–9, 63–4, 65; government policy towards 17, 26–7, 100–1, 130; common interest of 27, 33, 257–8, 342–3

Lansdowne, Lord (Viceroy) 156, 170

Latif, Nawab Abdul 92, 151 n. 5

LaTouche, Sir James John Digges 42 n. 5, 141, 163 n. 3, 168, and n. 7; biography App. IV

Lauh i Mahfuz (Moradabad) 109

Lausanne, Treaty of 333, 336, 337

460

Index

Index

Masud, Syed Ross 129 n. 4, 190, 214 n. 1; biography App. II

Mayo, Lord (Viceroy) 48, 50–1, 100, 107 n. 3, 111; and Wahabis 102–4; gives new direction to Muslim policy 103–5

Meerut 32, 60 n. 8, 82, 220; Quanungo family of 29, 58 n. 3, Khilafat conference at (1921) 330

Mehdi, Hyder 236, 260, 323; biography App. I

Meston, Sir James Scorgie 42 n. 5, 177, 188, 191 n. 2, 192, 201, 255–6; and Cawnpore Mosque 212–15; and 'Old Party' counter-thrust 230–4; and UP Municipalities Act 1916 245, 248–9; on Abdul Bari 283; biography App. IV

Miller, J. O. 127 and n. 6

Minto, Lord (Viceroy): reply to Muslim memorial 146–7, 155 and n. 3, 246; and Council reforms 157–61, 164, 166–8, 172; and Muslims 164, 166–8, 198

Mirza, Aziz 149 n. 3, 191, 195 n. 3, 197–8, 227; biography App. II

Misra, Gokaranath 242

Mitha, Casim 243, 245

Mitter, Charu Chandra 116

Mohani, Hasrat 124 n. 8, 142 and n. 3, 185 n. 2, 280 n. 8, 301, 302, 314, 315, 323, 332 and n. 1; interned 216; biography App. I

Mohiuddin, Maulvi Ghulam of Kasur 209 n. 5, 262

Mohsin-ul-Mulk, see Hasan, Nawab Mehdi Ali

Mohurram 80 and n. 1

Moinuddin, Maulvi 279

Montagu, Edwin Samuel (Secretary of State for India) 257, 291, 328, 350

Montagu–Chelmsford reforms, see reforms

Montagu–Chelmsford Report 240 n. 6, 289–90, 350; and UP Muslims 257–62, 290

Moplahs 336, 338

Moradabad 11, 17, 25, 32, 53 n. 3, 60 n. 8, 82, 140 and n. 3, 220, 221, 250 n. 5; communalism in 80–1, 80 n. 5, 81 n. 5, 249; British Indian Association of 85, 87 n. 2; Syed Ahmed Khan's school at 91–2

Morison, Sir Theodore (Principal of Aligarh College) 111, 137, 139, 165, 168–9, 199, 205 n. 2, 207

Morley, Lord (Secretary of State for India): and Council reforms 142, 143, 154–61, 163 n. 3, 164, 168–71, 172; and Muslims 164, 168–71, 198; and Sir A. P. Macdonnell 172–3, 172 ns. 6 and 8

Morley–Minto reforms, see reforms

Morning Post (Delhi) 232

Mudholkar, R. N. 237

Mughals, Muslim caste 24

Mughal Empire 13, 25, 88–9

Muhammad, Nawab Syed 151, 195 n. 3, 237

Muhammadan Anglo-Oriental College, Aligarh 20, 117, 148 n. 2, 180, 189; and Deoband 279–80; opposed by ulama 109; and Syed Ahmed Khan 4, 20, 107–11, 216; and College Fund Committee 108, 144; and Urdu-speaking elite 107, 110, and UP Muslims 125; and education in English 110–11; financial crises at 123 and n. 4, 130; a centre of Muslim politics 123–6, 143–4, 173, 200; government support for 126–32, 146, 348; and Sir A. P. Macdonnell 130, 133–4, 137, 199; Students Union 142; and Muslim University 146, 199–201; Trustees of 153, 190, 202, 216–17, 239; and 'Young Party' 178–80, 202, 216–17; and 'Old Party' 190–1; Old Boys' Association of 179–80, 179 n. 2, 184, 185, 189, 202, 217 n. 1

Muhammadan Anglo-Oriental Defence Association of Upper India 113 n. 2, 121–3, 126; and Syed Ahmed Khan 122; and Muslim memorial (1896) 123; reorganised as Urdu Defence Association 135

Muhammadan Literary and Scientific Society of Calcutta 92

Muhammadan Political Association of Aligarh 113 n. 2

Muir, Sir William 100, 102 n. 4, 128; *Life of Mahomet* 111

Muir Central College, Allahabad 190

Mujadid, Pir Gulam 330

mujtahids 269, 279, 284; and All-India Shia Conference 277 and n. 6

Index

Index

Nabi, Syed Ali 220, 223, 224 n. 2, 225, 246, 277, 323, 343; biography App. I

Nabiullah, Syed 148 n. 4, 163, 176, 195 n. 3, 201, 213 n. 6, 214 n. 1, 219, 243, 261; biography App. I

Nadvi, Maulana Suleman 275, 295, 306 n. 1

Nadwat-ul-ulama 28, 134, 141, 275–6, 282, 287, 325 n. 1, 327, 328; divisions in 269 and n. 5; dar-ul-ulum of 274, 275; and Shibli's vision 275–6

Nagpur: Congress at (1920) 326; Muslim League at (1910) 195, 200, 201

Nagri Resolution 43–4, 44 n. 2, 76, 135, 138, 141, 142, 182; and Muslims 135–7, 278; and Kayasths 31 n. 2, 136 and n. 3; and Kashmiri Brahmins 136 and n. 3

Nagri script 69–70; 69 n. 2, 71–7, 83, 97, 98, 127, 347; petition to government for (1871) 74 and n. 3, (1898) 76, 134–5; and Congress 115, 116

Naidu, Sarojini 236, 340 n. 3

Nanautavi, Maulana 267 n. 1, 273–4

Nanpara, taluqdari estate 16 n. 3

Nasim, Mahomed 148 n. 4, 188, 213 n. 6; biography App. II

Nath, Pandit Ajudhia 31 and n. 2, 114, 115, 120

Nath, Bishambhar 49 n. 1

Nazarat-ul-Maarif-ul-Qurania 280

Nehru, Jawaharlal 327

Nehru, Motilal 30 n. 2, 180, 236, 254, 313, 314, 321, 322, 336 and n. 1, 339, 340 n. 3; and UP Municipalities Act (1916) 247–51

New Era (Lucknow) 185 n. 2, 259

Nizami, Khwaja Hasan 201, 295

Nomani, Muhammad Hamid 264

Nomani, Muhammad Ishaq 264

Nomani, Muhammad Junaid 264

Nomani, Shibli 28, 124 and n. 8, 179, 261, 264, 266, 269 and n. 5, 279, 305, 347; and the position of the ulama 274–6; biography App. III

non-co-operation 307, 308, 326, 332, 355; and the UP Khilafatists 301, 303, 305–6, 309–16, 322–5, 326, 327, 351–2; and Gandhi 302, 311–

22, 326, 351–2; and ulama 301, 306–7, 309–10, 316, 322, 324–5, 327, 328, 340, 341, 351–3; and Congress 313, 317–22, 326, 328, 351–2; *see also* civil disobedience

Northbrook, Lord (Viceroy) 48, 127 128

Nur ul Afaq (Cawnpore) 109

Nur ul-Anwar (Cawnpore) 109

octroi 50, 55 and ns. 2 and 4, 60

O'Kinealy, J. 103 and n. 1

Old Boy (Benares) 179

'Old Party' 6, 176 n. 2, 179, 190–4, 243, 248, 286, 291, 342–3, 349, 350, 390–418; forerunners of 136, 141, 149–50, 175; background 190; education 190–1; employment 191–2; political approach 192–4; struggle for power with 'Young Party' 216–35, 349–50; counterthrust of 229–35; breaks up 257–8

Oudh 10, 11, 25, 59, 85, 86, 224; landlords in 15–20; *see also* Taluqdars

Oudh Punch (Lucknow) 121, 136

Pahasu, Nawab Muhammad Faiyaz Ali Khan of 49 n. 1, 137, 190, 223, 258; estate 20 n. 1, biography App. II

Pakistan 2, 3, 353, 356

Pal, B. C. 320 and n. 1, 358 n. 2

pan-Islamism 111, 126, 134, 142 n. 3, 151 and n. 5, 179, 189, 196, 267 n. 5, 278, 291; and Turkey 186, 204–5, 207–12; and 'Young Party' 186–7, 206–12

Partabgarh, Raja of 49 n. 1, 64

Pasis 40

Patel, V. F. 336

Pathans 15, 20, 24, 245

Patiala, Maharaja of 110, 129 n. 1

Patna, Congress at (1912) 237

Pattidars 15–16, 62

Percy, Henry Algernon George, Earl Percy 157 and n. 7, 170

Permanent Settlement 23, 104

Persian: language 23, 31, 35, 36, 40, 42, 70, 76–7, 91, 134; script 70, 71, 76, 97, 134, 347; a threat to Hindu supremacy 71–2; schools 91, 101

464

Index

Index

Index

Sulaiman, Maulana Shah Badruddin of Phulwari 268, 279, 328, 329
Sulaiman, Shah Muhammad 183 and n. 1
Sultan of Turkey 25, 112, 126, 134, 270, 271, 282, 290, 291, 295
Sultanniah College Scheme 177–8, 177 n. 2, 188, 219
Sunnis, 25, 134, 244–5, 269; and Shias 25, 220, 227
Swarajists 339–41
Syeds 15, 25; Muslim caste 24

Tahsildars 21 and n. 4, 26, 40, 42, 53 n. 2, 132, 141
Tahzib-ul-Akhalaq (Aligarh) 109, 123
Tajuddin 301
Talibnagar, Nawab Muhammad Abdus Samad Khan of 258; biography App. II
Taluqdars 15, 62; of Oudh 16–17, 16 n. 3, 17 n. 2, 101, 120 and n. 2, 136, 140, 165, 190, 192, 194; Muslim Taluqdars 20; and British Indian Association 17, 20 and n. 2, 32 n. 3, 94, 258
Tauhid (Meerut) 201, 202, 216
Terhawin (Agra) 109
Thana Bhavan, ulama of 325 n. 1
Theosophical Society 67
Thomason, James 35
Tilak, Bal Gangadhar 241, 254, 308, 313, 314
Times, The (London) 103, 155, 156, 169
Tirwa, Raja of 62
traders in the UP 14; as Muslims 14–15; and Municipalities Act (1883) 57–9; and the railway 59–60; and land transfer 60–3; influence in west UP and Doab towns 64–6; and Hindu revivalism 65–6
Turkey 206, 207–12, 240, 300, 301; trade with 207–8; colony in 207–8; Turkish wars and Indian Muslims 126, 204–5, 207, 216, 224, 259, 270–1, 311, 326, 330, 333, 334, 336; Turkish peace terms 311, 313, 314
Tyabji, Badruddin 116 and n. 3

Ulama 4, 6, 136, 202, 262–3; background 263–4; sources of support 264–5; organisation among 265–8; divisions among 268–72, 352, 354; reaction to British rule 272–8; development of connections among 275–7, 278–9; and western-educated Muslims 278–88; oppose Aligarh College 109; position in Muslim society 27–8, 263, 274–6, 328–30; and council reforms 257–8; led by Abdul Bari in politics 281–8, 292–6, 300, 301, 304, 305–6, 314 and n. 2, 325, 327–8, 352; leading role in politics 293–6, 301, 309–10, 319, 322–5, 326–42, 350–1; and 'Young Party' 209–12, 214, 281–6, 292–6, 322, 326, 339, 342, 350–2, 355–6; and Muslim League 261–2, 272, 287–8, 289, 295, 337; and Khilafat movement 261–2, 279, 292–6, 300–1, 304, 306–7, 309, 314, 322, 324–5, 326–42, 350–3; and Congress 278, 325, 330, 334–8, 339–41, 351–2; and non-co-operation 301, 306–7, 309–10, 316, 322, 324–5, 327, 328, 340, 341, 351–3; and civil disobedience 330–2, 335–6
United Indian Patriotic Association 113 n. 2, 120–1, 120 ns. 5 and 7
United Provinces (UP): formation of 10; geography of 8, 10–11; as the North-West provinces and Oudh 3 n. 2; administrative divisions 9; centres of Muslim rule in 11, 17; Hindu holy places in 11; population of 11 and n. 2, 16 n. 1; traders in 14–15; landlords in 15–20; government servants in 20–3, 40, 43–6, 101–2, 114–15, 180–1; government educational policy in 34–9, 102–5; bureaucratic reforms in 22–3, 39–46, 101–2; predilections of lieutenant-governors and governors of 42–3, 42 n. 5; differences between East UP and Oudh and West UP and Doab 59–66; distribution of trade in 59–60; transfer of land in 60–3; capital moves 101; Executive Council for 241–2; and the Congress 113–21; communal tensions in 77–83, 121, 194–6, 338–9; *see also* provincial legislative council, district boards and municipal boards

467

Index

United Provinces' Congress Committee 237, 339, 341 and n. 3

United Provinces' Elementary Education League 237, 238

United Provinces' Muslims: position in the province 10–32; centres of former rule 11, 17, 25; population 11 and n. 2; distribution 12–13; town-dwellers 13; religious differences with Hindus 13–14, 56; as traders 14–15, 14 n. 2; as landlords 17–20, 19 n. 1, 26–7, 28, 62, 63, and n. 3, 176–7, 190; as government servants 22–3, 28, 123–4, 180–1; as lawyers 182–3; divisions among 23–8; ashraf/non-ashraf distinction 23–5; Shia/Sunni division 25; occupational divisions among 25–8; find employment in native states 26, 123, 124, 143 n. 6, 180–1, 191; position of ulama among 27–8; Hindu connections with 29–32, 30 n. 3; Rajput connections with 29–31; Kayasth connections with 30–1, 30 ns. 2 and 3, 31 n. 2, 64; Kashmiri Brahmin connections with 30–1, 30 n. 2, 252; and government educational policy 37–9, 45–6, 90–7, 106–8, 110; and Sir A. P. Macdonnell 43–4, 46, 126, 127 and n. 6, 130–1, 133–7, 171–3; and the Nagri Resolution 44, 135–7, 278; and reforms in the bureaucracy 45–6, 45 n. 5, 101–2; position on East UP and Oudh municipal boards 64 and n. 3; position on West UP and Doab municipal boards 81–3; attitudes to Hindi and Urdu 70; and Hindu revivalism 68–83, 133, 141–2, 346–7; increasing communal activity among 194–201; and government policy 98–105, 126–32, 203–6, 345–6; and council reforms 121, 142–7, 162–3, 257–62, 290–1; and Congress 115–17, 133, 138, 141, 142–3, 148, 194–6, 203–4, 229, 236–56, 259–61, 289, 314, 322–3, 325, 330–41, 343, 350–2; and the Muslim League 4, 5, 149–50, 149 n. 3, 162–3, 173, 225–35, 242–5, 252–6, 343; 'Young Party'/'Old Party' struggle for power 216–35; and Khilafat move-

ment 292–5, 300–16, 322–5, 326–44, 350–3; and non-co-operation 301, 303, 305–6, 309–16, 322–5, 326, 327, 351–2

United Provinces' Muslim Defence Association 257–8

United Provinces' Muslim League 151, 223–5, 246, 257

United Provinces' Provincial Conference: Agra (1909) 239 n. 1; Meerut (1914) 238–9; Gorakhpur (1915) 241; Allahabad (1915) 242; Moradabad (1920) 341

Urdu language 31–2, 42, 75, 97, 141, 195, 198, 347; distinguished from Hindi 69 n. 2; literature stimulated by government 36–7, 70–1; Muslim attitude towards 70; Hindu attitudes towards 71–2, 75–6; and government service 75–6; declining popularity of 76–8; Syed Ahmed Khan's views on 91, 96; and Aligarh Scientific Society 93; United Provinces Conference on 198

Urdu Defence Association 139; formed from the M.A.-O. Defence Association 135; and Nagri Resolution 135–7

Urdu Defence Association of Allahabad 135

Urdu-e-Moalla (Aligarh) 142 and n. 3, 216

Urdu-speaking elite 5, 33, 50, 115, 117, 118, 133, 144, 165, 176, 346–7, 354; defined 31–2; dominance undermined 33–4; threatened by: government education policy 34–9, bureaucratic reform 39–46, growth of elective government 46–66, Hindu revivalism 66–83, 346–7; impact of 1892 council reforms on 49 and n. 1; impact of establishment of district boards on 49–50; impact of introduction of elections in municipal boards on 50, 57–66; impact of demand for Hindi and Nagri on 73–4, 75–6, 97–8, 121; weakened by cow-protection 79–83, 121; response to increasing pressure of British rule 85–98: role of Aligarh Scientific Society in 87, 93–5, Syed Ahmed Khan in 87,

468

Index

22636AUK0000lB/17/P
UKOW04f18501202l4
Milton Keynes UK
Lighting Source UK Ltd.